Contact Languages

Language Contact and Bilingualism 6

Editor
Yaron Matras

De Gruyter Mouton

Contact Languages

A Comprehensive Guide

edited by
Peter Bakker
Yaron Matras

De Gruyter Mouton

ISBN 978-1-5015-1267-4
e-ISBN 978-1-61451-371-1
ISSN 2190-698X

Library of Congress Cataloging-in-Publication Data

A CIP catalog record for this book has been applied for at the Library of Congress.

Bibliographic information published by the Deutsche Nationalbibliothek

The Deutsche Nationalbibliothek lists this publication in the Deutsche Nationalbibliografie; detailed bibliographic data are available in the Internet at http://dnb.dnb.de.

© 2013 Walter de Gruyter, Inc., Boston/Berlin
Cover image: Anette Linnea Rasmus/Fotolia
Printing: Hubert & Co. GmbH & Co. KG, Göttingen
♾ Printed on acid-free paper
Printed in Germany
www.degruyter.com

List of contributors

Peter Bakker
Aarhus University
Denmark
linpb@hum.au.dk

Angela Bartens
University of Helsinki,
University of Turku
Finland
angbar@utu.fi

Margreet Dorleijn
University of Amsterdam
The Netherlands
M.Dorleijn@uva.nl

Lars Johanson
University of Mainz
Germany
johanson@uni-mainz.de

Yaron Matras
University of Manchester
UK
yaron.matras@manchester.ac.uk

April McMahon
Aberystwyth University
UK
April.McMahon@aber.ac.uk

Felicity Meakins
University of Queensland
Australia
f.meakins@uq.edu.au

Jacomine Nortier
Utrecht University
The Netherlands
J.M.Nortier@uu.nl

Mikael Parkvall
Stockholm University
Sweden
parkvall@ling.su.se

Donald Winford
Ohio State University
USA
dwinford@ling.ohio-state.edu

Table of contents

List of contributors v

Abbreviations...viii

Introduction.. 1
Peter Bakker and Yaron Matras

Pidgins 15
Mikael Parkvall and Peter Bakker

Creole languages.. 65
Angela Bartens

Mixed Languages... 159
Felicity Meakins

Multi-ethnolects: Kebabnorsk, Perkerdansk, Verlan, Kanakensprache, Straattaal, etc... 229
Jacomine Nortier and Margreet Dorleijn

Written language intertwining 273
Lars Johanson

Issues in the genetic classification of contact languages 333
April McMahon

Social factors in contact languages 363
Donald Winford

Subject index 417
Languages and geography index.. 422
Author index 433

Abbreviations

ABS	absolutive
ABSOL	absolute
ACC	accusative
ALL	allative
AN	animate
ANT	anterior
ART	article
ATTR	attributive
BEN	benefactive
CAUS	causative
CLASS	classifier
COMP	complementizer
COMPL	completive
CON	connective
COP	copula
DAT	dative
DEF	definite
DEM	demonstrative
DET	determiner
DETRAN	detransitiviser
DIM	diminutive
DU	dual
DYAD	dyad, a pair
EMPH	emphatic
ERG	ergative
F	feminine
FIN	finite
FOC	focus
FUT	future
GEN	genitive
H	high (tone)
HAB	habitual
ID	ideophone
ILL	illative
IMP	imperative
IMPF	imperfective
INAN	inanimate
IND	indicative
INDF	indefinite

INF	infinitive
INST	instrumental
INT	intentional
INTT	intraterminal
IRR	irrealis
L	low (tone)
LOC	locative
M	masculine
MULT	multiplicative (plurality of action)
NEG	negation
NFUT	non-future
N	neuter
NOM	nominative
NOML	nominaliser
OBJ	object
OBV	obviative
PART	participle
PAUC	paucal
PF	perfective
PL	plural
POSS	possessive
POT	potential
PRED	predicative
PRESENT	presentational
PRET	preterite
PROG	progressive
PRS	present
PST	past
PTV	partitive
Q	question marker
REL	relative pronoun
SBJ	subject
SG	singular
SM	subject marker
SRP	subject reprise
SUBORD	subordinator
TOP	topic
TR	transitive
VOC	vocative

Introduction

Peter Bakker and Yaron Matras

1. What are contact languages?

In some sense, all languages are contact languages: Language is the ultimate, uniquely human tool used to establish and to maintain contact between people. But in order to sustain successful oral communication, a common language is needed. In some situations – for example, when people first establish contact with one another – a common means of communication may be lacking at first and needs to be created. In other situations, multiple languages may be available and a new mode of communication drawing on these multiple repertoires may emerge. Contact languages are new languages that have emerged in situations in which the repertoires of languages available to the people in contact did not provide a sufficiently effective tool for communication. Language contact does not always produce contact languages. Codeswitching (or codemixing) is the spontaneous mixture of two or more languages in conversation in multilingual communities. This kind of mixing does not in itself constitute a contact language, but a contact language may arise if switching becomes systematic and regular. Gurindji Kriol and Light Warlpiri are examples of contact languages that appear to have resulted from the conventionalisation of codeswitching patterns in conversation.

Most authors (Thomason 1997, 2001; Winford 2003: 18ff.; Matras 2009) distinguish three types of contact languages: pidgins, creoles and mixed languages (also called intertwined languages or bilingual mixed languages). Others only consider pidgins and creoles to be contact languages. For example, Sebba's book *Contact Languages* (1997) carries the subtitle "Pidgins and Creoles" and does not deal with mixed languages. More extensive documentation of mixed languages and the theoretical discussion surrounding their formation and classification have emerged mainly over the past two decades. Earlier studies tended to ignore or indeed even to dismiss the existence of mixed languages. In recent years more information has become available about pidgins and creoles too, and they are now considered by most authors to constitute very diverse and distinct language types. Mixed languages, too, are not uniform in structure, and thanks to a growing body of documentation we are now aware of the extent of diversity associated with this category of languages. Some mixed languages show a so-called lexicon-grammar split, whereby the language's core lexicon is derived from one source language, whereas its grammatical components derive from another. Other mixed languages show a split within the grammatical structure itself, often one in which nominal grammar derives from one source language and the grammar of verbs from another. The mixed language 'prototype' has therefore been argued to consist primarily of a mixture of components that is not otherwise found in cases of gradual structural borrowing, not even in cases of so-called 'heavy' borrowing (see Matras 2003).

All three types of contact languages – pidgins, creoles, and mixed languages – share certain characteristics: they are new languages, they usually emerged within one or two generations, and they contain major structural components that can be traced back to more than one a single ancestor language. This latter feature has been central to the historical linguistic approach, in which contact languages are identified through the fact that their lexicon and grammatical structures cannot all be traced back primarily to the same source language (Thomason 2001: 158).

In this volume we consider two additional types of contact language. Multi-ethnolects are new varieties that have emerged among a second generation of immigrants, usually in urban environments. Those that are known to us today are relatively recent varieties used by young people. At this point it is difficult to predict whether multi-ethnolects have the potential of developing into new independent languages. Written mixed languages, by contrast, have a documented history of at least 5,500 years – the age of the attested mixture of a form of Akkadian in written documents from Amarna.

2. Types of contact languages

Broadly speaking, any use of a language or variety in a contact situation can be called a contact language. However, as we are interested in the connection between social, cognitive and historical circumstances and the structural properties of languages that result from contact, some types of contact varieties will not be dealt with in this volume.

A *lingua franca*, for example, is a language that is used among different population groups in order to enable communication across language boundaries. The role of English at international conferences may be considered a 'lingua franca'. There are many regional lingua francas, such as Tok Pisin in New Guinea. Some lingua francas unite international groups and associations, as in the use of French at meetings of the Francophonie, the association of francophone states. Akkadian was a lingua franca in Mesopotamia and the ancient Near East, and the technical term *lingua franca* itself derives from the name of a lingua franca based on medieval Romance dialects, which was used around the Mediterranean coastal regions and especially in North Africa. Lingua francas typically show a degree of structural simplification in comparison with their base languages as spoken by native speakers. But such modification does not justify their definition as separate languages or contact languages. It is for that reason that we do not consider lingua francas in this volume.

An *ethnolect* is a variety of a language that is spoken, initially, as a second language by a certain population group, usually an ethnic minority. Certain features of the group's speech, at the initial stage often a foreign accent, are recognised as distinctive and thus come to serve as a marker of ethnicity. Examples are Czech as spoken by the Romani minority in the Czech Republic, Dutch as spoken by Moroccan immigrants and their descendants in the Netherlands, and English as spoken in some Italian communities in New York. If the group shifts entirely to the second (majority) language, then their distinctive variety of that language may become their first language. Here too, the changes in structure are contained and not major, and therefore it does not seem justified to regard the new variety as a separate contact language.

Ethnic groups may also develop special varieties of a local language by using vocabulary from an ancestral language spoken by earlier generations in their community. Examples are the Judeo-German varieties of pre-war rural communities in many regions of Germany, which contained occasional insertions of Hebrew-derived elements (replicated from Hebrew scriptures rather than from a language spoken by the community's immediate ancestors), and the insertion of Romani-derived vocabulary into the speech of English Gypsies. Since admixture in such varieties is limited to a core vocabulary, and since it tends to be used as a stylistic device rather than a means of everyday communication, we do not include such varieties in our present discussion of contact languages.

In multilingual communities, languages are known to become structurally similar to one another through the process called *convergence*. Neighbouring languages belonging to different language families may thus form a linguistic area or *Sprachbund*. The historical changes in structure that languages undergo in convergent or linguistic areas are often considerable, and may result in the emergence of linguistic varieties that are typologically very distinct from related varieties that have not been subjected to similar convergence processes. Examples are Sri Lanka Portuguese and Sri Lanka Malay, originally analytical SVO languages that have developed agglutinative case marking systems through convergence with the contiguous languages Tamil and Sinhala. Other examples include the convergent languages of the Papuan-Austronesian contact zone, such as the Oceanic language Takia and the Papuan language Maisin. Such cases can certainly be considered contact languages, and examples are discussed in this volume in the chapters by Winford and by Meakins.

3. The emergence of contact languages

One of the distinctive characteristics of contact languages is that they are an identifiable product of language contact situations rather than the outcome of gradual language change across generations. This has been described by Thomason and Kaufman (1988) as "broken transmission": a young generation of speakers creates a language that was not transmitted by the parent generation, and the parental language is not carried over in full but only in part into the next generation. In the formation process of contact languages, the founder generation of speakers are innovators who draw on their multilingual repertoire to create a new speech variety. Within one or two generations, this variety undergoes conventionalisation and becomes the principal vehicle of communication at least in certain interaction settings such as interethnic communication, or conversely, in domestic communication in communities of mixed ethnic background.

Invariably, such processes of emergence, propagation and conventionalisation of new languages are connected to processes of identity shift, identity formation, or the emergence of stable and regular intercommunity contacts where no pre-existing language is adopted as a lingua franca. From an historical linguistic perspective, contact languages are thus unique: They allow us to identify a particular point in time in which they evolved as a language; and they lack any direct, single predecessor variety. The precise mechanisms that are involved in the emergence of contact languages have been subject to debate. Firstly, one must distinguish between settings in which the founder generations of the new language have full access to more than one language, and those situations in which communication among members of the founder generation draws on fragmented structures acquired through a very restricted second language acquisition process. The first have been termed "bilingual mixtures" (Thomason 1997). The second are considered to be responsible for the emergence of pidgin and creole languages.

In the case of bilingual settings that give rise to mixed languages, a broad consensus has emerged that conscious, deliberate discourse-strategic choices play a role in the early stages. Such processes are related to emblematic language play. Golovko (2003) documents such emblematic mixing for various contemporary bilingual settings, and Matras (2009: 36–37) documents similar occurrences in child speech in a multilingual household. A connection has been suggested between such discourse-strategic and emblematic mixing patterns and the motivation described by Bakker (1997) to flag bilingual identity in the form of mixed utterances in communities of mixed households. Furthermore, a connection has been postulated between the consolidation of a new ethnic identity in the young generation raised in mixed households, and the conventionalisation of a stable language structure that draws on two (or more) distinct etymological components.

The founder generation of pidgins are thought to draw on the limited lexical resources available to them in an influential speech variety that is contiguous with their own native languages. Here the primary motivation is to facilitate basic communication in a set of very specific interaction contexts. The selection of structures therefore follows communicative needs as well as, arguably, some universals of second language acquisition processes. It must be stressed, though, that the aim in such situations is not the acquisition of the language of the other party, but the creation of a means of mutual communication. Creoles are normally associated with the expansion, among a founder generation, of the pidgin employed by the parent generation. Typically this involves, from the functional perspective, an extension of the variety to all domains of everyday communication, and the subsequent adoption of this variety as the principal or native language in the domestic context. From the structural perspective, the expansion has been discussed in connection with grammaticalisation processes through which lexical items take on more abstract grammatical meanings, adding a stable morpho-syntactic structure to the makeshift, pragmatic arrangement of words in the predecessor pidgin. This process had once been associated primarily with restricted access to a target variety, and thus compared with an idealised situation of structured second-language acquisition. McWhorter (2000) has since suggested that plantation creoles were in fact the outcome of a process through which speakers sought to flag ownership of pre-existing West African pidgins. In this sense, the emergence of creoles might be compared with the conscious, identity-flagging effect that is thought to be responsible for the emergence of mixed languages. In-depth comparative discussions of multi-ethnolects have so far been lacking, but it is conceivable that they serve a similar identity-flagging function, drawing equally on elements of multilingual repertoires mapped onto a single 'privileged' variety.

A further consideration in the creation process leading to contact varieties is the arrested decline of a community language, or what might be considered the "afterlife" of a language (Matras 2010). In such cases, the founder generation are not fully bilingual but have access to a core lexicon and to rather loose and somewhat incoherent impressions of the grammar of the declining parental language. Their emblematic mixing behaviour is therefore different from that of the fully bilingual founders of mixed languages. On the other hand, the founder generation have completed the shift to the surrounding (often majority) language, which provides a coherent and consistent means of everyday communication. The process of mixing that they engage in cannot therefore be compared to the makeshift communication patterns that give rise to pidgins, either.

4. Distinctive structures

There is some discussion as to whether contact languages in general, or specific types of contact languages, display distinctive or diagnostic structural features. Another debate focuses on the effects of language contact and whether contact necessarily leads to simplification (McWhorter 2011) or rather to an increase in structural complexity (Nichols 1992). The latter issue figured centrally in the discussion of pidgins and creoles until the 1990s. Pidgins appear to be less complex than their lexifier languages. It is this process of simplification that makes them identifiable as a distinct language type. This is also regarded as the key to their functionality as makeshift, but limited communication devices. Pidgins usually lack productive inflectional morphology, and their vocabulary is often limited to just a few hundred words. Like pidgins, creoles too tend to lack inflectional morphology and paradigm irregularities, but functionally they are full-fledged languages. McWhorter (2001, 2005) has put forward an explicit claim that creoles are defined through their limited degree of complexity, including the absence of inflection, the absence of tone, and the absence of irregular derivation patterns. Somewhat related observations are offered by Parkvall (2008). Drawing on a large-scale typological database that includes data on several dozen creoles and hundreds of non-creole languages, he has argued that creoles often lack categories, or have fewer grammatical distinctions, than non-creoles, and that they can therefore be argued to be less complex. Nonetheless, the view that creoles are simplified languages remains controversial (cf. Kouwenberg 2010; and some of the papers in Aboh and Smith 2009, e.g. Ansaldo and Nordhoff 2009). Also the claim that creoles constitute a typologically distinct type of language (McWhorter 2005; Bakker et al. 2011) is also challenged (Ansaldo et al. 2007).

Nichols (1992) emphasised the contribution of language contact to an increase in structural complexity. On the basis of a sample of several hundred languages, she distinguished between conservative features and features that tend to change under the influence of neighbouring languages.

The most complex languages in her sample were often found in contact zones. Cliticisation was especially found to correlate with a contact history. This does not necessarily imply that contact languages are more complex than other languages. Most mixed languages combine structures of their donor languages, giving rise to structures that are as complex as their combined components. Bakker (1997) has argued that Michif, a mixed language with Cree verbs and French nouns, combines the most complex parts of the two languages, but that this is accidental and not pre-determined by the process of language intertwining itself. If we consider a mixed language like Media Lengua to be a form of Quechua with Spanish lexical roots, then by implication it shares the same degree of complexity with its grammaticiser language, Quechua. Some Australian mixed languages tend to elaborate certain structures beyond what is found in the source languages. Gurindji Kriol, for instance, developed serial verb constructions that are not found in Kriol. (Meakins 2010) However, its overall complexity is not significantly different from that of its source languages. The same can be said for the result of metatypy or convergence. Slomanson (2008, 2009) points to the significant complexity of Malay in Sri Lanka compared to ancestral Malay, seen for example in the structure of negative constructions. Many of these Sri Lanka Malay constructions were copied from local languages, which tend to show the same overall degree of complexity.

A key focus of attention is the origin of different structural components in contact languages. Some approaches to pidgins and creoles emphasised the continuity of the lexicon from the lexifier language, and explained grammatical formations as a product of universal processes of simplification and language acquisition. Other studies have devoted much attention to the replication of the morpho-syntactic and lexical-semantic blueprint from the assumed, or in some cases even attested substrate or heritage languages, such as West African languages, for Atlantic pidgins and creoles, and Austronesian languages, for Pacific pidgins and creoles) (see for example Holm 1988 or Keesing 1988). In the discussion of mixed languages, the initial impression that the 'prototype' involved a split between the source languages of the lexicon and that of inflectional morphology and morpho-syntax has since been challenged. Instead it has been argued that the diagnostic split is rather more specifically that between the source of core lexicon and especially nominal lexicon, and the source of finite verb inflection (Matras 2003).

5. The contact language debate and state of the art

In very briefly reviewing the history of thinking on contact languages, we disregard of course pre-scientific judgmental depictions of contact languages as corrupted jargons. Possibly the earliest major consideration of the phenomenon of contact languages can be found in connection with the attention given to convergent areas. These were initially regarded as the outcome of large scale language shift by a community of speakers who mapped features of their parental language onto the new language. This kind of radical ethnolect formation continues to be referred to as a linguistic substrate, though the analysis of concrete case studies is often controversial due to the absence of historical data on the underlying process of language shift. The formation of pidgins was attributed at an initial stage to the dynamics of a non-structured language acquisition process and thus to attempts on the part of learners to replicate a target language with just limited success. Since then, the functional dimension of communication has since taken centre stage, and pidginisation is understood as a process through which speakers make use of various components of their linguistic repertoires to conventionalise a mode of communication for very specific interaction settings. Studies of contemporary use of such makeshift communication strategies in the context of immigrant communities have contributed to such understanding of pidginisation (Klein and Perdue 1997).

The study of mixed languages focused in its earlier stages on providing sufficient documentation to demonstrate the viability of such mixtures, whose rather extraordinary and rare structural composition had fuelled much scepticism about their existence as a distinct language type. Although in-depth case studies remain few in number, the distribution of attested cases of mixed languages across multiple continents proves beyond dispute that radical mixtures, not usually encountered either in cases of pidgins and creoles or in gradual contact-induced language change, are indeed a possible outcome in multilingual settings. It is not impossible that mixed languages were once a much more common phenomenon and that many of the world's contemporary languages owe their roots to a process of language intertwining. This sheds new light on the very principles of language-genetic classification and our ability to hypothesise about pre-historic language phyla.

Once the mixed language type had been acknowledged, the discussion moved on to try and account for structural outcomes and for social settings and emergence scenarios. Influential contributions identified mixed languages either as a unique process whose structural outcomes, in the relevant setting, were pre-determined (Bakker 1997); as a combination of common processes that happen to combine to render unusual outcomes (Thomason 1995), or as an interplay of system components that also figures in other language contact phenomena (Myers-Scotton 1998). Since then, the notion of mixed languages as outcomes of conscious or deliberate creations that have their origin in discourse-strategic exploitation of the multilingual repertoire has since been gaining ground (e.g. Matras 2000; Golovko 2003).

The typology of contact languages thus unfolds as a continuum between two poles. At one far end we find settings in which fully bilingual speakers exploit language mixing for conversation-strategic purposes, only to end up conventionalising this mixture as a variety used for particular communicative events. These may include flagging group solidarity, as in Media Lengua, a Spanish-Quechua mixture, or in Ma'á, a Bantu-Cushitic mixed language. In rare cases, the variety may become the default means of domestic communication, as in the case of Michif, the Cree-French mixed language. The opposite pole features speech varieties that arise for purposes of makeshift communication in very basic and specific contexts of interaction. Here, speakers draw as far as possible on shared or otherwise accessible elements of their diverse linguistic repertoires, creating a pidgin. Situated close to the first pole are varieties that flag ethnic distinctness through partial replication of structures from a language to which the founder generation has had some exposure, but which is in the process of being abandoned (as in the case of the Aleut-Russian mixture called Copper Island Aleut, or the English-Gurindji referred to as Gurindji Creole). Adjacent to the opposite end of the continuum are creoles, the all-purpose native languages that are the descendants of makeshift varieties of the pidgin type.

6. The present volume

The chapters in this volume pursue two distinct agendas. Five of the chapters deal with different types of contact languages: Parkvall and Bakker on pidgins, Bartens on creoles, Meakins on mixed languages, Johanson on mixed languages used in writing, and Nortier and Dorleijn on multi-ethnolects. Two papers deal with more general issues: McMahon discusses contact languages from an historical linguistic perspective, more specifically from a viewpoint of genealogical linguistics, language descent and linguistic family tree models. Winford approaches contact languages from a sociolinguistic perspective, identifying specific social contexts in which contact languages emerge.

Pidgins and creoles are often discussed as a single entity or language type, whereby more attention is usually devoted to creoles. Parkvall and Bakker characterise pidgins as contact languages that are different from creoles. They show how pidgins can be placed on a continuum from the use of signs and unsystematic oral communication (jargon), to a conventionalised pidgin. They also discuss a number of structural properties of pidgins. A pidgin community can be as small as two individuals, such as the Swahili-English pidgin developed by two friends, or it can be widespread and even develop into a main vernacular of communication within a local or regional population.

Pidgins serve limited communicative functions. They are often limited to trade situations or to communication in multilingual work places. By contrast, pidgincreoles and creoles can serve a broad range of communicative functions. Bartens provides information about the historical background of creoles and their genesis. Based on her work on a series of English-based and Portuguese-based creoles, she formulates generalisations on the structural properties of creoles. Questions of diachrony, historical and cultural dimensions of creolisation are also discussed. The structural features of creoles often differ considerably from those found in the respective lexifier languages. The lexicon is usually derived from just one source language, with a small quantity of often more peripheral vocabulary from other languages.

Meakins provides an overview of research on mixed languages. She lists and discusses more than twenty case studies that have been argued in the literature to constitute examples of mixed languages, the most comprehensive enumeration of mixed languages to date. Meakins presents a structural typology of mixed languages and discusses various emergence scenarios in detail, giving attention to models of language shift, mixed populations, the emergence of new ethnic identities, on the social-historical side, and to factors such as borrowing, codeswitching, relexification, fusion and more, on the structural side. The chapter highlights the current controversies and analytical issues in the study of mixed languages, such as their degree of functional autonomy and structural independence from the source language, their stability and internal variation. Meakins concludes with a review of the role of codeswitching in the formation process that leads to the emergence of mixed languages.

European urban environments have brought together people from different language backgrounds, and these contact situations provide, to some extent, settings similar to those that are assumed to have given rise to creoles some centuries ago. Some researchers have referred to varieties of European languages spoken by the adult immigrants as pidgins (e.g. Clyne 1968; Forschungsgruppe 1975; see also Fennell 1997). In recent years, language use by the second generation of immigrants in urban centres and suburbs has been studied in several countries. Nortier and Dorleijn provide an overview of the most important studies, comparing them with other language contact phenomena. Multi-ethnolects, as they are called, are spoken among adolescents who use the language of the country creatively as an expression of their distinct identity. Typically, multi-ethnolects are varieties of the languages spoken in cities, with some phonological, morphological and syntactic modifications. In addition, some vocabulary is borrowed from immigrant languages, often including terms for the opposite sex, music, clothing and drugs. Men seem to be more involved in the creation of multi-ethnolects than women. Nortier and Dorleijn's contribution compares Western European multi-ethnolects with the special youth languages used in other parts of the world, most notably in Africa. Although the multi-ethnolects discussed here do not differ radically from their base languages, it has been shown for other contexts that multi-ethnolects may lead to the emergence of distinct languages (see Kießling and Mous 2004).

Johanson's contribution deals with written language intertwining. The term *intertwining* was originally coined (in Bakker and Mous 1994) for a specific type of mixed language, and Johanson adopts it for different types of language mixture in writing. His contribution is the first to provide an overview of the phenomenon. So far, research on language contact has dealt almost exclusively with oral language. The discussion of mixing in written varieties had been limited largely to philological studies on individual languages. Johanson provides examples from diverse regions such as the ancient Middle East, medieval Britain, the Ottoman Empire, and Japan. In addition, he provides a theoretical framework for the classification and typology of these languages.

McMahon's contribution deals with the implications that some types of contact languages have for comparative linguistics. Historical-comparative linguistics, at least in its traditional version, is at odds with contact languages. Many generations of historical linguists have considered contact as a distraction or at best as marginally relevant to their work. This view has, luckily, changed, and historical linguists have, at least since Thomason and Kaufman (1988), developed an interest in language contact and an awareness of the importance of contact-induced language change. McMahon mentions that language contact is not a new phenomenon. While it is possible to determine the more recent pidgin or creole origin of some languages, this is more difficult for languages where little is known about the social history of their speech communities.

McMahon discusses a range of phenomena, from lexical borrowing (including borrowing of basic vocabulary) to problems of reconstruction.

As an alternative to some theoretical models that have difficulty accommodating mixed language on language-genetic trees, McMahon presents a model of phylogenetic networks. This model relies on computer software that is designed to identify not only vertical descent from ancestral languages, but also contact influence. The model has been applied in a range of areas, from English dialectology to Papuan and Austronesian languages in Melanesia and historical relations among English creoles.

Winford's contribution is devoted to the social and societal settings that give rise to contact languages. The chapter provides a concluding overview of types of contact languages, reviewing, in greater detail, some of the issues highlighted in this introduction, such as the distinction between bilingual mixtures (or intertwined languages), converted languages, pidgins and creoles. Winford presents a basic dichotomy among contact languages that are the result of mixing of some kind or other in bilingual contexts, and those that emerge as an outcome of the process of second language acquisition. To the historical emergence scenarios and their distinct structural outcomes he adds a discussion of the societal status of contact languages, reviewing issues such as diglossia, language attitudes, codification and literacy. Special emphasis is placed in this chapter on the motivations for the creation of new speech varieties and we are once again reminded of the extraordinary opportunity that contact languages offer to reconstruct, explore, and indeed sometimes even to witness the actual birth of a new language.

References

Aboh, Enoch O. & Norval Smith (eds.). 2009. *Complex Processes in New Languages*. Amsterdam: John Benjamins.

Ansaldo, Umberto & Sebastian Nordhoff. 2009. Complexity and the age of languages. In Enoch O. Aboh & Norval Smith (eds.), *Complex Processes in New Languages*, 345–363. Amsterdam: John Benjamins.

Ansaldo, Umberto, Stephen Matthews & Lisa Lim (eds.). 2007. *Deconstructing Creole*. Amsterdam/Philadelphia: John Benjamins.

Bakker, Peter. 1997. *A Language of Our Own: The Genesis of Michif, the Mixed Cree-French Language of the Canadian Métis*. New York: Oxford University Press.

Bakker, Peter & Maarten Mous (eds.). 1994. *Mixed Languages: 15 Case Studies in Language Intertwining*. Amsterdam: Uitgave IFOTT.

Clyne, Michael. 1968. Zum Pidgin-Deutsch der Gastarbeiter. *Zeitschrift für Mundartforschung* 35(2). 130–139.

Fennell, Barbara A. 1997. *Language, Literature, and the Negotiation of Identity: Foreign Worker German in the Federal Republic of Germany*. Raleigh: University of North Carolina Press.

Forschungsgruppe Pidgin-Deutsch Spanischer und Italienischer Arbeiter. 1975. *Sprache und Kommunikation Ausländischer Arbeiter: Analysen, Berichte, Materialien.* Kronberg: Scriptor Verlag.
Golovko, Evgeniy V. 2003. Language contact and group identity: The role of 'folk' linguistic engineering. In Yaron Matras & Peter Bakker (eds.), *The Mixed Language Debate: Theoretical and Empirical Advances*, 177–207. Berlin: Mouton de Gruyter.
Holm, John. 1988. *Pidgins and Creoles. Volume I: Theory and Structure.* Cambridge: Cambridge University Press.
Keesing, R. M. 1988. *Melanesian Pidgin and the Oceanic Substrate.* Stanford: Stanford University Press.
Kießling, Roland & Maarten Mous. 2004. Urban youth languages in Africa. *Anthropological Linguistics* 46(3). 303–341.
Klein, Wolfgang & Clive Perdue. 1997. The basic variety. Or: Couldn't natural language be much simpler? *Second Language Research* 13. 301–347.
Kouwenberg, Silvia. 2010. Creole studies and linguistic typology: Part 2. *Journal of Pidgin and Creole Languages* 25(2). 359–380.
McConvell, Patrick & Felicity Meakins. 2005. Gurindji Kriol: A mixed language emerges from code-switching. *Australian Journal of Linguistics* 25(1). 9–30.
Matras, Yaron. 2000. Mixed languages: A functional-communicative approach. *Bilingualism: Language and cognition* 3. 79–99.
Matras, Yaron. 2003. Mixed languages: Re-examining the structural prototype. In Yaron Matras & Peter Bakker (eds.), *The Mixed Language Debate: Theoretical and Empirical Advances*, 151–175. Berlin: Mouton de Gruyter.
Matras, Yaron. 2009. *Language Contact.* Cambridge: Cambridge University Press.
Matras, Yaron. 2010. *Romani in Britain. The Afterlife of a Language.* Edinburgh: Edinburgh University Press.
Matras, Yaron & Peter Bakker (eds.). 2003. *The Mixed Language Debate: Theoretical and Empirical Advances.* Berlin: Mouton de Gruyter.
McWhorter, John H. 2000. *The Missing Spanish Creoles. Recovering the Birth of Plantation Contact Languages.* Berkeley: University of California Press.
McWhorter, John H. 2001. The world's simplest grammars are creole grammars. *Linguistic Typology* 5. 125–166.
McWhorter, John H. 2005. *Defining Creole.* New York: Oxford University Press.
McWhorter, John H. 2011. *Linguistic Simplicity and Complexity: Why Do Languages Undress?* Berlin: Mouton de Gruyter.
Meakins, Felicity. 2010. The development of asymmetrical serial verb constructions in an Australian mixed language. *Linguistic Typology* 14(1). 1–38.
Myers-Scotton, Carol. 1998. A way to dusty death: the Matrix Language Turnover hypothesis. In Leonore A. Grenoble & Lindsay J. Whaley (eds.), *Endangered Languages: Language Loss and Community Response*, 289–316. Cambridge: Cambridge University Press.
Nichols, Johanna. 1992. *Linguistic Diversity in Space and Time.* Chicago: University of Chicago Press.

Parkvall, Mikael. 2008. The simplicity of creoles in a cross-linguistic perspective. In Matti Miestamo, Kaius Sinnemäki & Fred Karlsson (eds.), *Language Complexity. Typology, Contact, Change*, 265–285. Amsterdam: John Benjamins.

Sebba, Mark. 1997. *Contact Languages. Pidgins and Creoles*. New York: St. Martin's Press.

Slomanson, Peter. 2008. The perfect construction and complexity drift in Sri Lankan Malay. *Lingua* 118(10). 1640–1655.

Slomanson, Peter. 2009. Morphological finiteness as increased complexity in negation systems. In Enoch O. Aboh & Norval Smith (eds.), *Complex Processes in New Languages*, 243–264. Amsterdam: John Benjamins Publishers.

Thomason, Sarah Grey. 1995. Language mixture: Ordinary processes, extraordinary results. In Carmen Silva-Corvalán (ed.), *Spanish in Four Continents: Studies in Language Contact and Bilingualism*, 15–33. Washington, DC: Georgetown University Press.

Thomason, Sarah Grey. 2001. *Language Contact: An Introduction*. Edinburgh & Washington, DC: Edinburgh University Press & Georgetown University Press.

Thomason, Sarah Grey (ed.). 1997. *Contact Languages: A Wider Perspective*. Amsterdam: John Benjamins.

Thomason, Sarah Grey & Terrence Kaufman. 1988. *Language Contact, Creolization, and Genetic Linguistics*. Berkeley: University of California Press.

Winford, Donald. 2003. *An Introduction to Contact Linguistics*. Oxford: Blackwell.

Pidgins

Mikael Parkvall and Peter Bakker

1. Introduction

The term 'pidgin' is considered important enough to routinely be mentioned in introductory linguistics classes, and it also frequently figures in titles of books on language contact. A most striking feature of pidgins, then, is that the documentation and systematic study of the language type in no way corresponds to the saliency of the label. While certain individual pidgins have indeed been studied, there exists one single monograph (Heine 1973) devoted to more than one pidgin, and to pidgins alone, and even this work is restricted in scope to only one part of the world (Bantu-speaking Africa). Most textbooks and anthologies on creoles and pidgins devote much more attention to the first, and pay only lip service to the importance of the second.

We believe that pidgins deserve more attention than they have hitherto received, and that the world-wide comparative study of such languages would prove interesting and useful. It has obvious implications for concepts such as 'linguistic complexity' (e.g. Bickerton 1988; Muysken 1988; and more recently McWhorter 2001, 2005; Ansaldo and Matthews 2008 with regard to pidgins and especially creoles; and Kusters 2003; Miestamo et al. 2008; Givón 2009 in general, plus papers in collections like Sampson et al. (eds.) 2009), which in turn are intimately coupled to the understanding of the human language faculty as such. It is also possible to think of potential contributions to applied linguistics: The better we understand naturally occurring and spontaneous simplifications, the better we can design language courses, by starting with features that are easier to learn.

2. Examples

Before embarking on a description of pidgins, we present some examples to give the reader an impression of the category of languages that are discussed. Pidgins usually have a lexical base in one or more other languages (their 'lexifier'), but many of the structural features of those languages have not found their way into the pidgin. We will try to present some examples showing possible equivalents in the source languages as well.

If you want to say 'I want water' in Choctaw, a Muskogean language of the Southeast of the USA, spoken in among others, Mississippi, you would use two words: a noun and an inflected verb (from Drechsel 1997: 300), cf. example (1a); in the pidgin lexically based on Choctaw, called Mobilian, three words are used (1b):

(1) a. *Oka   sa-banna-h*
         water   1SG-want-PRED
     b. *Oka   eno   banna*
         water   1SG   want

The verbal inflections are dropped, and a personal pronoun is used instead.

The traveller Valéry Mayet visited Tunisia, where a Romance-lexicon pidgin called 'sabir' or 'lingua franca' had been spoken for centuries. In Mayet (1887) he quotes several phrases in the pidgin called 'sabir' or 'lingua franca'. Local boys said about a type of snake called *lepha*:

(2) *Lepha   morto   arbi   mesquine*
     snake   dead/die   arab   poor
     'The lepha kills the poor Arabs.'

Here, an uninflected form *morto* derived from a past participle or adjective meaning 'dead' (Italian *morto*, masculine) is used with the meaning 'to kill'. The nouns show no expression of plurality, nor are there any articles. The word *mesquin* is a Mediterranean word meaning 'valueless, poor' (cf. Arabic *miskīn*, Italian *mesquino*). Elsewhere (p. 205) a speaker is quoted as saying *Arbi bono, kifkif Francis* 'I am a good Arab, a friend of the French', literally: 'Arab good, friend French' (in French in the source: *'Je suis un bon arabe, ami des Français'*, though one would have expected '[...] just like a Frenchman'). Sometimes, complex thoughts are brought back to their bare essentials. When someone wants to say something like: 'An Arab wanted to steal my camel but I took my gun and shot him', this event is narrated in just five words *Arbi djemel, moi fusil, besef*, literally 'Arab camel, me gun, much' (French in the source: *'Un Arabe a voulu voler mon chameau; j'ai pris mon fusil et j'ai tiré'*).

In the English-lexifier pidgin of the China coast, the question 'how many children do you have?' is expressed as:

(3) You got how muchee piece children?
    2   have how much   CLASS children
    'How many children have you?'
    (Instructor IV.55; Li, Matthews and Smith 2005)

We notice that the word order is different from English, the distinction between *much* and *many* is not maintained in the pidgin. There is also influence from Cantonese, for instance in the use of *piecee*, a so-called nominal classifier (but as opposed to the situation in Sinitic languages, there is only one universal classifier).

We have presented examples from languages whose lexifiers are of relatively moderate morphological complexity. The final examples are from two pidginised forms of languages with elaborate verbal and significant nominal morphology.

The first is an example of pidginised Eskimo, which means 'I want to go on shipboard'. In the local language this would be *ūm'-ī-ak-pūx-mōx-d'k-tuña*, or in abbreviated form *ūm'-ī-ak-pī-ok'-tuña*, in one word. In the pidgin, this is rendered in four words:

(4) Ōm'-ī-ak-pŭk a-lak'-tok picuktok awoña
    the.ship   he.goes   he.wants 1SG
    'I want to go on shipboard.'
    (Stefánsson 1909: 218)

(Note that the glossing in this case is etymological rather than synchronically valid.) Instead of a lexical stem and three bound morphemes meaning 'movement', 'want' and 'first person', the pidgin uses free morphemes, and these appear to be inflected forms presumably because no uninflected forms or infinitives are available, but the inflection is meaningless: the verbs display third person forms, but the subject is first person.

The final example is from Pidgin Basque, used in the early 1600s in contacts between Basque whalers and local Icelanders (Bakker 1987). First, the pidgin sentence is given, and then the Basque and Icelandic equivalents.

(5) a. Icelandic Pidgin Basque:
    Christ Maria presenta for mi Balia, for mi,
    Christ   Maria give   for me whale   for mi
    presenta for ju   bustana
    give   for you tail

b. Basque:
Kristo eta Maria-k bale-a ema-ten
Christ and Maria-ERG whale-ABS give-PRS
d-i-da-te-n-ean eman-go d-i-zu-t buztan-a
3-to-1-3PL-SUBORD-LOC give-FUT 3-to-2-1SG tail-DEF

c. Icelandic:
Gefe Christur og Maria mier hval, skal
give Christ and Maria 1SG.SBJ whale shall
jeg gefa þier spord-enn
1SG.SBJ give.INF 2SG.OBJ tail-DEF

'If Christ and Maria give me a whale, I will give you the tail.'

This example shows that it is possible to express complex relations between actions in a pidgin, such as counterfactuals, but this is not done by grammatical means, but by mere juxtaposition of the content words in sentences. This example also shows that morphological marking in nouns is dropped, and that nouns are used in their citation form, i.e. with the postposed definite article -*a*.

These examples illustrate the severe reduction in morphological possibilities of the lexifiers, to the point of complete disappearance, as well as the absence or rarity of function words such as conjunctions, articles, prepositions and the like.

3. What is a pidgin?

Several etymologies have been proposed for the word 'pidgin' (Hancock 1979). The correct etymology is believed to be the Chinese Pidgin English word for 'business', derived from English (Baker and Mühlhäusler 1990), as the language was used in trading. In the following sentence, the word is used in this meaning:

(6) *You pidgin number one?*
'Is your business good?'
Pidgin no good just now
'No, the business is not good right now.'
(Shi 1991: 25)

There is no universally accepted definition of the term 'pidgin', and it has indeed (as we shall see) been used in a number of different ways for a wide array of language varieties.

More or less ambitious attempts at defining the term are numerous, and the following examples can be considered fairly typical:

- "[...] a language [...] whose grammar and vocabulary are very much reduced in extent and which is native to neither side." (Hall 1966: xii)
- "[...] a marginal language which arises to fulfil certain restricted communication needs among people who have no common language." (Todd 1974: 1)
- "[...] a language which has been stripped of everything but the bare essentials necessary for communication." (Romaine 1988: 151)
- "[...] a reduced language that results from extended contact between groups of people with no language in common; it evolves when they need some means of verbal communication, perhaps for trade, but no group learns the native language of any other group for social reasons that may include lack of trust or close contact." (Holm 2000: 5)
- "[...] contact vernaculars characterized by highly reduced vocabulary and structure, which are native to no one, and serve as a lingua franca for certain restricted communicative functions such as trade." (Winford 2003: 270)

Attempts at shortening the description include Hammarström (2007), in whose definition a pidgin can simply be defined as a language which fulfils every criterion for being a language, except "full expressive power". In a similar vein, Samarin (2000: 321) sees a pidgin as (i) a language, which (ii) functions as a lingua franca, and which has (iii) a very reduced lexicon. All other characteristics of pidgins would then follow from these traits.

Others have instead tried to include more (or other) details in the description. Baker (1993: 6) defines a pidgin as

> a form of language created by members of two or more linguistic groups in contact as a means of inter-communication, the most basic grammatical rules of which are common to all its habitual users regardless of their own primary language, while at least one and perhaps all of the participating groups recognise that this means of inter-communication is not the primary language of any other.

Baker thus emphasises the uniformity across the various groups involved, while the last phrase serves to distance the phenomenon of pidginisation from that of (targeted) second language acquisition, in which learners may use a variety distinct from the target language.

It is important to distinguish definitions based on social criteria (languages that develop under certain circumstances) from those based on linguistic criteria (languages that have certain structural properties). There may be discrepancies here: there are, for instance, varieties used for interethnic communication that are nobody's mother tongue, but which are not reduced to the most basic grammatical rules. Broken English at international meetings could be an example, but a language used in interethnic communication is not necessarily a pidgin in our use of the word.

Most researchers agree that a pidgin is an interethnic contact language which is created when two or more ethnolinguistic groups lack any other common means of communication, but still have reasons to deal verbally with one another. Some such languages may display only limited simplification, such as Nheengatu/Lingua Geral in Brazil (a second language only for several centuries; now also a first language for some), or Lingala in Africa. These fulfil the social criteria for the existence of a type of language called 'pidgin', and only if those are defined, can one deduct properties of pidgins, without risking circularity.

One can also approach the categorisation of pidgins from a labelling perspective. One possibility could be to accept everything as a pidgin that has been so labelled by one or more authors. However, the terms 'pidgin' or 'pidginisation' have been used for phenomena as diverse as English loans in languages such as German, Italian, Japanese, Russian and Spanish (Ardila 2005; Bergmann 2001; Haller 1987; Hensel 1999; Oshima 2002; Ustinova 2005: 243–4), English as such, due to its role as an international lingua franca (Aldea 1987), various foreign influences in written language (Duszak 2002: 16; Kann 1999), Anglophone schoolchildren's limited French (Hammerly 1987), first or second language immigrant varieties such as broken Swedish among immigrants in Stockholm, Greek as spoken in Australia, and the Spanish of Latin Americans in Sweden (Kotsinas 1996, 2001; Tamis 1990; Borgström 1991), majority influences on linguistic minorities, such as Min-influenced English in Malaysia, English-influenced French in Maine and French-influenced varieties of Alsatian German (Birken-Silverman 1997; Ladin 1982: 77; Crevenant-Werner 1993: 185; Lee 1996; Schweda 1980), the speech of EU bureaucrats in Brussels (Dietze 1976) and even the use of first names by Australian businessmen in their contacts with Japanese colleagues (Marriott 1991).

Among other unorthodox uses of the 'pidgin' label, one could mention Thomas's (2000: 164) assertion that pidginisation is "acquisition of foreign vocabulary in which the original morphology and grammar are maintained", and Schlyter's (2003: 160) inclusion of the intertwined (and natively spoken) Hezhou in the pidgin category.

It is difficult to see any common denominator between these terminological practices, apart from the fact that all varieties mentioned are in some sense the products of language contact. Since virtually every language is in contact with one or several others, and since all written and spoken languages presumably display foreign influences, this would reduce 'pidgin' to simply mean 'language', something that would hardly contribute to our understanding of language in general or of contact phenomena in particular.

Also in studies involving second language, the term 'pidgin' is again often used in ways that it risks losing most of its meaning.

Consider, for instance, the following utterances by Swedish immigrants to the USA, which Karstadt (1996: 27) considers "a stabilized pidgin":

(7) *So, so one of my sisters, dat was she dat died last year, she wrote back.*
And I especially remember vone Christmas, we thought dat my grandmother's house, dat downstairs, was enormously large.
Then he came home like for Christmas denn, and denn that was the first time he saw his boy.

To us, this represents nothing but a version of American English learned as a second language with a (comparatively slight) influence from the first language, mostly in pronunciation.

In other words, we find it untenable to accept every attested usage of pidgin. It would simply drain the term of almost all its meaning.

On the other hand, this leads to an obvious risk of circular reasoning, when we try to empirically explore the linguistic features of pidgins. If we get to define the term ourselves, there is a risk that we choose only the pidgins that fit our preconceptions. We will try to avoid that by taking the social circumstance of genesis and use as the fundamental criteria, and try to generalise over the structural results in order to discover the linguistic properties of pidgins.

It should be borne in mind, though, that the difficulties in sharpening the terminological tools are by no means unique to pidginistics – on the contrary, many of the most basic concepts within linguistics (such as 'language', 'dialect' and 'word') are similarly elusive.

The following properties would seem (cf. the quotes above) to be the most oft-cited components of a definition of pidgins, and we concur that they are indeed essential parts of pidginhood (cf. Matras 2009: 277). A pidgin, then

1. is a language that is conventionalised (and not spontaneous)
2. is used as a lingua franca in a contact situation,
3. is native to no one,
4. fulfils only restricted communicative functions (i.e. is used in a limited number of domains),
5. draws to some extent on one or more of the languages spoken or known by the groups in contact as sources,
6. has some norms of forms and usage and hence some stability,
7. is highly reduced lexically and grammatically compared to its input languages.

The criteria above serve to exclude some speech varieties which we would not consider pidgins. Note that most of these are social criteria, and that only the last one relates to structure.

The 'language' criterion 1 implies that the group of pidgins does not include ad hoc spontaneous communicative solutions made up on the spot, and which are not transmitted to other individuals. It also excludes transient learner varieties such as Gastarbeiterdeutsch and other forms of imperfectly acquired target languages in immigrant communities. Such varieties are never the target of learning. They are individual approximations of German (etc.) as a target. This does not necessarily mean that the processes are irrelevant for pidginisation – the phenomena encountered in untutored second language learning described in Klein and Perdue (1997) are in many ways reminiscent of the processes typically found in pidgins.

The use as a lingua franca (criterion 2) differentiates pidgins from, among other things, certain other limited systems, such as initiation languages (e.g. Papa and Kumenti among the Aluku in Suriname (Hurault 1983: 34–41) or upside-down Warlpiri (Hale 1971)), some cryptolects in which speakers try to prevent intelligibility of their communication by outsiders (e.g. modern Angloromani (Hancock 1986), and 'mother-in-law' registers (Dixon 1980; Haviland 1979)) which are reduced ways of speaking in the presence of certain respected persons. These other limited systems are used within one speech community, by people who also have a full language in common.

Defining pidgins as languages spoken non-natively (criterion 3) serves to set them apart from creoles, which are traditionally considered a separate type (though pidgins may become creoles, and the border is not always clear, cf. sections 4 and 5 below) by contact linguists (though laymen and even general linguists often have difficulties telling the two apart).

A natively spoken language would also more or less by definition not fulfil criterion 4. Arguments given with regard to criterion 2 are also valid here.

Pidgins use materials from other languages as building blocks (criterion 5). No pidgin (except possibly signed ones) makes use exclusively or even partly of invented vocabulary. The vocabulary of pidgins can always be traced back to one, sometimes several, other languages, either spoken natively by the groups in contact, or known by some of the people involved. Some structural traits can also usually be traced to one or several of the languages, for instance certain patterns of word order.

As an elaboration of the above points, we could add that the prototypical pidgin, in our use of the term, should display a certain degree of norms and stability (criterion 6), and function as a target language in the contact situation. Pidgins tend to be mutually incomprehensible with their respective input languages. Their use ought also be reciprocal, so that two speakers address one another in roughly the same language, regardless of their respective mother tongues. This excludes varieties like 'Trader Navaho', which was apparently only used by one of the parties in the contact situation: only the salespersons, not the buyers (Werner 1963).

The social criteria may characterise the situation in which pidgins emerge, and pidgins show a lexical and grammatical reduction of the lexifier (criterion 7).

The presence of these traits has been explicitly pointed out in the case of many attested pidgins, by people who were themselves users of the pidgin and familiar with the first languages of some of the users of the pidgin. For instance, Barrelon (1893: 227) and Nicolas (1900: 21) both make clear that Frenchmen in Vietnam need to learn Tay Boi (Vietnamese French Pidgin), and that they cannot simply improvise a reduction of their own native tongues in order to communicate with the locals. The same point is made with regard to e.g. Chinese English Pidgin by Werner (1863, vol. 1:295), to Fanakalo by Berry (1971: 523), and to Ndyuka-Trio Pidgin by Huttar and Velantie (1996: 103). When a journalist had called Chinese Pidgin English "English baby prattle" and had given some faulty examples, a reader of the American weekly *The Nation* (no. 1596, 62: 98), who was a user of the pidgin, reacted and defended the pidgin as follows:

> [...] to a globe-trotter it may sound so [i.e. like English baby prattle] for a few days, but as soon as he tries to obtain a serious knowledge of it, he should not fail to see that it is a very valuable compromise between Chinese grammar and phonetics and those of European nations. It is not a haphazard, meaningless babble, invented to soothe small children; it has regular rules of construction, and is not left to the individual whim of a globetrotter.

Indeed, some pidgins (although this is an exception) were, or are, even taught by means of printed manuals (e.g. Chinook Jargon on the American Northwest coast, Chinese English Pidgin and Fanakalo in South Africa), in some cases with speakers of the lexifying language as the target audience. Baker and Mühlhäusler (1990: 108) note that there is no evidence whatsoever that Chinese ever strove to learn English as such, and attempts by Europeans to speak Iñupiaq rather than Eskimo Pidgin were even subject to ridicule in Alaska (Stefánsson 1909: 220).

Needless to say, something that needs to be learnt cannot be devoid of norms. Also, if it has to be learnt even by native speakers of the input languages, it cannot be mutually comprehensible with them (or only so to a limited extent). Indeed, the pidgin called Mobilian, for instance, could not be understood by speakers of the Amerindian languages Choctaw or Chickasaw (Holm 1989: 601; Drechsel 1997: 271, 305), despite the fact that its lexicon was overwhelmingly derived from these closely related languages.

The stability across native language groups is also underlined by first-hand observers for many pidgins (e.g. Drechsel 1997: 333 for Mobilian; Foley 1988: 168 and Foley 2006 for Yimas-Arafundi pidgin; Roberts 1995b: 97, 1995a for Pidgin Hawaiian). Again, this confirms that a pidgin is not simply the lexifier filtered through the rules of other languages.

While the varieties that we consider worthy of the epithet 'pidgin' are relatively stable, it could be remarked that a language spoken non-natively is not likely to enjoy the same degree of stability as one that functions as a community language. Ethnolectal and speaker-dependent language-internal variation is thus more significant than in non-pidgins, and even basic word order patterns may vary.

The reduction parameter (criterion 7) is the most troublesome in that there can of course be degrees of reduction, and it seems difficult, if not impossible, to define a certain degree of reduction as a boundary. The problem is similar to the one present when drawing a line between dialects and languages – any such distinctions are bound to contain an element of arbitrariness, including the boundaries, and a complete consensus cannot be expected.

As is the case with the language/dialect distinction (and indeed plenty of other ones both within and outside of linguistics), we cannot avoid the fact that many phenomena represent continua. Few people would be prepared to accept 'night' as the same thing as 'day', with a mere difference in nuances.

The reduction parameter is also the only linguistic parameter, whereas all the others are social ones. It relates to the fact that pidgins make use of a much more limited vocabulary than non-pidgins, and that its structures are always quite simple. Almost all grammatical intricacies of the languages which contributed to pidgin structures are as a rule reduced, or have disappeared in the pidgin.

The reduction displayed by pidgins is related to the fact that they are only used in limited domains (criterion 6). A language thus used needs to be relatively simple in order to be acquired despite a limited exposure, and cannot afford the excessive systemic ballast that vernaculars may (and do) display. In other words, the domain-wise reduction implies that the pidgin not only *must* be simple, but also that it *can afford* to be so.

The obvious problem, though, with the inclusion of this as a defining criterion is the same as in the case of criterion 4, namely that domain extension is a matter of degree, and no clear cut-off point can be a priori defined.

Keeping in mind the problems involved in defining (let alone quantifying) the concept of 'reduction', we are, at the time of writing this, toying with the following minimalistic definition:

> *A pidgin is a language which (a) functions as a* **lingua franca**, *and which (b) is lexically and structurally* **extremely limited** *in its communicative possibilities*

4. The life and death of a pidgin

Pidgins are often thought of as precursors to creole languages, and probably most often mentioned in such a context. It might therefore be tempting to think of the 'pidgin-creole life cycle' as normal:

jargon → pidgin → creole

The jargon stage is characterised by instability, normlessness and extreme variation (see section 4.3 below). It is often presumed to precede the pidgin. It should be emphasised, however, that the vast majority of known pidgins never did (and, for those which are still in use, probably never will) develop into creoles. While it is debated whether or not creoles always (or at least typically) hail from pidgins (see e.g. Baker 2002), it is beyond doubt that most pidgins do not generate creoles.

4.1. Period of use

Some pidgins were (or have been) in use for a long time. The most obvious example is the Romance-lexicon pidgin Lingua Franca, attested in the Mediterranean from medieval times and into the 20th century (Schuchardt

1909), apparently without ever creolising (Operstein 1998). Lingua Geral (a Tupi-based contact language) in Brazil also survived for several centuries.

A more typical example is Tay Boi, the French-lexicon pidgin in Vietnam. It emerged after the French takeover in the early 1860s, and fell into disuse when the United States replaced France as the major imperial power in the area a century later. To the extent that we know anything at all about the history of pidgins, a life span of one hundred years and less is certainly more typical than the long existence of Lingua Franca.

Tay Boi died out because contacts between speakers of French and Vietnamese dwindled, but one thing worth pointing out is that a pidgin can also die because of an *in*crease in contacts. A good example is provided by Russenorsk. It is true that the ultimate coup de grâce to that language was provided by the Bolshevik takeover of Russia in 1917, and the subsequent blocking of Russian ports by the Entente powers. However, the use of Russenorsk was declining even before then, and seemingly because contacts between Russians and Norwegians intensified, which stimulated an increased interest among Norwegians in learning Russian (Broch and Jahr 1984: 78–9; Jahr 1996: 108).

4.2.   The very first contact

There are surprisingly few accounts of the very first contact between two different language groups. Many contact situations where a pidgin was subsequently documented no doubt involved ethnic groups that were in contact with one another long before documentation by Western linguists. But in the case of European overseas expansion, we have at least a number of contacts where there is a more or less specific date for the first encounter. Yet surprisingly many travel accounts mention that Europeans and natives had discussions on various subjects, without there being a single mention on how such communication was achieved. While some European expeditions included people with a knowledge of languages like Latin, Persian, Arabic and Turkish for this particular reason, these could not possibly have been of much use in Australia and the Americas.

One strategy of increasing the availability of interpreters was used by (among others) the Portuguese, who took Africans to Lisbon to teach them Portuguese, so they could act as translators on subsequent journeys (Hair 1966, Naro 1978, Hein 1993). Linguistic diversity on the African coast is great, so the direct knowledge of these interpreters of the local languages must have been minimal. However, African interpreters had such a good reputation that they were sought even for expeditions to North America (Bakker 1995).

In many cases, it is clear that trading contacts took place in complete silence (Hamilton 1903; Burch 2005: 152; see also Bakker 1996a for some examples). But in other cases, it seems like the sources are more silent than the actual trade (or other type of interaction). In the 16th century, European explorers Cartier and Cabeza de Vaca are reported to have successfully communicated with the natives of the New World, without providing any details on exactly how this was done (Axtell 2000: 25–6). Some details on situations of this type, however, are provided in Axtell (2000), Dutton (1987), and Meuwese (2003), but for the most part, we are limited to claims that there was a great use of gestures and mimics (Malcolm 2001: 205; Feister 1973). An overview of the use of gestures in language contact can be found in Hewes (1974).

In a few cases, there is evidence of a chain of interpreters, most famously in the case of the American Lewis and Clark expedition in the early 1800s. When Lewis and Clark encountered speakers of Flathead Salish in 1805, they apparently achieved successful communication through a chain of interpreters where each individual spoke two of the following languages: English, French, Hidatsa (Siouan), Shoshone (Uto-Aztecan) and Flathead (Calloway 1997: 126). The intermediate languages were not pidginised, though – at least not as far as is known.

4.3. The jargon stage

The stage of development between the very first contact and a fully developed pidgin is referred to in the literature as jargon or pre-pidgin. These terms, in other words, refer to intermediate contact varieties at the level of the individual, with some conventions (primarily a lexicon), but not with enough structural norms to qualify as a pidgin.

In a few cases, the entire development from jargon to pidgin and even to creole has been observed. This is true for the English-lexicon varieties of Hawaii, Australia and Melanesia.

As typical examples of jargons, one might mention the so-called Bamboo English used between the American military and Asians in Japan, Korea and Vietnam in the cold war era (Adami 1981; Algeo 1960; Broudy 1970; Goodman 1967; Goral 1976; Horton 1996; Norman 1955; Webster 1960; West 1973). It is somewhat odd that these three Asian locations of war would show similarities, but the geographic diffusion of linguistic items (and sometimes the mechanisms leading to it) is well documented.

For instance, the following sentences produced by Chukchis, and documented by Rosse (1883: 185–7), display pidgin items from locations thousands of kilometres removed:

(8) *Pow Fish,   Bimeby   Pow   wind,   plenty   fish*
    finish fish   then   finish wind plenty   fish
    'There's no fish here right now, but you'll see, when the wind abates, there'll be lots of it'.

(9) *Pick-a-nee-nee   kowkow*
    child   food
    'Please give me some food for my baby.'

Although it is difficult to judge from such a small sample, our impression is that the speaker is not speaking a conventionalised language, but rather enumerating random bits and pieces of lexicon in the hope of being understood: *pow* is from Hawaiian and Hawaiian Pidgin *pau* 'finish', and the last two words are ultimately from Portuguese and probably Chinese and widespread in Pacific pidgin Englishes, as is *bimeby*, from 'by and by'. This also illustrates that certain words and phrases could be used over vast distances, from New Guinea to China to Siberia. Although originally used about a more structured variety (Russenorsk), Fox's (1983: 101) characterisation seems to be in place here – we are dealing with "a strategy [of communication as much] as a language in the normal sense" (cf. discussion of makeshift communication by McWhorter 2011; also Matras 2009: 277).

A nice authentic first-hand account of this is provided by Henri d'Orléans, who, on his trip in Vietnam, was given two native assistants. They spoke no French, but one of them had learnt Latin in a missionary school. Neither the Frenchman nor the Vietnamese boy had practised their Latin in a long time, so

> At first, intercourse was not easy. Our oratorical attempts were hardly brilliant; there were even times when we were not in touch. By degrees, however, we gained fluency, and in a month had completely mastered each other's idiosyncrasies of expression. But what Latin! Horresco referens! Solecisms, barbarisms, neologisms, and all the "isms" invented might be applied to our jargon. Luckily, we had only ourselves for audience. (Orléans 1898: 145)

This, we believe, pretty well illustrates the first stages in contact language development.

It could be added that many varieties which in the literature are reported as pidgins are in fact what we would label jargons. A clear such case is what Bickerton (1984) calls Hawaiian Pidgin English, despite his admitting that it has "no recognizable syntax" (Bickerton 1984: 174). It probably also applies to one of the earliest and therefore most oft-cited definitions of pidgins, Robert Hall's (1966: 116) claim that "[…] a pidgin can grow up in a few days of trading, or in a few hours of contact between an English-speaking tourist and an Italian cicerone". Such an encounter could well lead to a pidgin, but it is doubtful whether such a stability could develop in the span of just a few hours.

4.4. How do pidgins disappear?

Even more than other languages, pidgins may undergo extinction. Pidgins may disappear when there is no need for them anymore, for example (i) because the contact situation in which the pidgin is used, ceases to exist, (ii) because the users of the pidgin learn another language in which they can communicate, or (iii) because the pidgin extends its use and the pidgin becomes an 'expanded pidgin' ('pidgincreole'), or creole (see Bakker 2008 for discussion of terminology). Yaron Matras (p.c.) suggests a possible connection between vitality and the fact that pidgins rarely represent social identities.

The transitions between these three stages are gradual. Once the social context changes to a situation in which a pidgin becomes an official language, a mother tongue or the default language chosen in contact with strangers, they are no longer considered pidgins in our view, as they do not obey the conditions for pidgins discussed in section 3. However, the precise relationship between this expansion to creolisation, nativization and grammaticalisation and other features of 'normal' language development is a disputed issue. For instance, when and how does a pidgin cease being a rudimentary auxiliary language, and when does it start being an expanded pidgin or a creole? Assuming that the development itself is correctly observed and described, how are the various stages in this process best delimited and labelled? These intermediate languages cause a certain confusion, not least by often being called 'pidgin', despite no longer being makeshift solutions. Languages that, in their documented history, started off as pidgins but are now pidgincreoles or creoles include West African Pidgin, Sango, Melanesian Pidgin, Hawaiian Pidgin/Creole English. These (and others) still retain many pidgin characteristics, in the sense of simplifications of the lexifiers, and are used as second languages by many or most of their speakers, but now they find use in all walks of life, as opposed to their predecessors (and, confusingly, namesakes).

4.5. The cline of pidginhood

While not everybody in contact linguistics will agree that the languages known as 'creoles' by definition developed from pidgins, it is undeniable that at least a few of the world's creoles were preceded by pidgins. There is documentation for nativization and some ensuing structural effects for e.g. Kinubi of East Africa (Heine 1982; Wellens 2005; Luffin 2004, 2005) and the nativized Chinook Jargon of Oregon (Zenk 1984, 1988; Grant 1996b; Bakker 2008). Examples of these structural developments include processes of reduplication in Chinook Jargon, the development of systems of definite and indefinite articles based on original demonstratives and the numeral 'one', and the emergence of obligatory expression of aspect and tense. See also Baker (2002) and Parkvall and Goyette (forthcoming) for indirect arguments in favour of a pidgin stage for creoles, even where this was not documented.

A number of languages often called 'pidgins' have expanded their functions to such an extent that they can no longer be considered pidgins. Some have become official languages, some have acquired native speakers and some have become the languages of first choice spoken with strangers (and are thus no longer restricted in their use), for example Tok Pisin in New Guinea, Bislama in Vanuatu, and Sango in Central Africa. Empirical studies by Shnukal and Marchese (1983) and Jourdan (1999) have shown that such developments trigger expansive changes in the structural makeup of pidgins, acquiring properties more typical of creoles than of pidgins.

These are often referred to as expanded pidgins, and as pidgincreoles, a term used in e.g. the works of Peter Bakker (2003b, 2008) (see section 4 for discussion). This applies to the Melanesian English Pidgin varieties (Tok Pisin, Solomons Pijin and Bislama) of the Pacific and to Sango of Central Africa. Other borderline cases between pidgins and creoles are the West African English pidgins, used along most of the coastlines of the officially Anglophone countries in West Africa. Like the cases just mentioned, these varieties are partly nativized, i.e. they have become mother tongues, but there is also ample evidence that they are mainly descended from Krio, the English-lexifier creole of Sierra Leone.

Regardless of the details of one's definition, there are thus bound to be intermediate varieties, with some being 'better' representatives of jargons and others more characteristic of pidgins.

Given the above outline of our use of the term, there are some varieties sometimes called pidgins to which we would hesitate to apply the label. In some cases, the degree of reduction appears to be quite moderate. In others, the language is more than just an auxiliary one, and may have become vernacularised or even nativized. Yet others lack the norms and stability that we would associate with something being a 'language' in the first place.

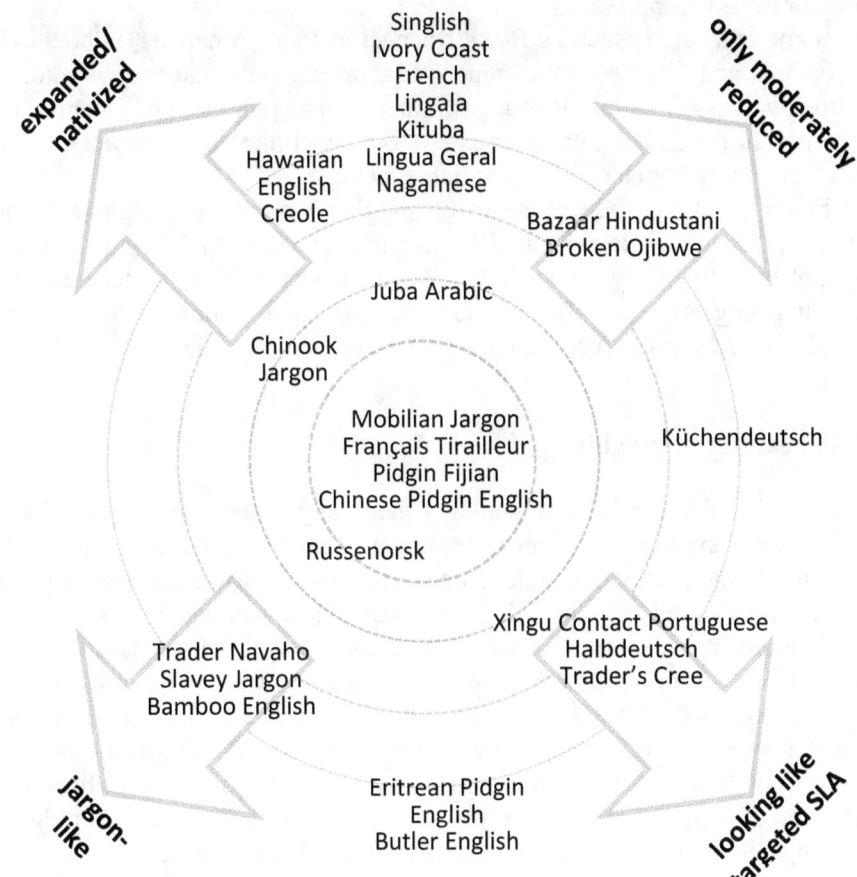

Figure 1. The deviation of a variety of pidgins of 'ultimate pidginhood'. Please note that the graph is impressionistic, and not based on quantifiable data, and should thus be taken with a grain of salt. SLA = second language acquisition.

Cameroonian Fulbe, Éwondo Populaire (Pidgin A70, Alexandre 1963), Ivory Coast Popular French, Kituba, Lingala, Lingua Geral, Nagamese and Singlish (Singapore English) are all varieties which in comparison to more prototypical pidgins display a rather moderate degree of restructuring and reduction (and many of them have been labelled 'semi-pidgins'). The sociolinguistic situation is, or was, such that they were indeed interethnic languages with no native speakers, but they do not display the extreme amount of reduction found in more prototypical pidgins. It needs explanation why that is the case. In some cases, the creators spoke relatively similar languages and therefore there was less need to rid the lexifier of its complexities.

Some languages, such as Bozal Spanish in Latin America, Halbdeutsch in Estonia and Cameroonian French 'Pidgin' are such that they would, in our view, classify as interlanguages rather than as pidgins. They seem – on the basis of the data available to us – not to constitute discrete systems, but rather a motley bunch of highly variable lects.

Finally, pidgins may cease to be pidgins when they merge with the lexifier, through a process called depidginisation. Juba Arabic, for instance, is spoken natively by some, but it has also been subject to far-reaching depidginising influences from its lexifier, colloquial Sudanese Arabic, and is today more similar to colloquial Arabic than it used to be.

5. Features of pidgins

A general problem in pidgin studies is that many of the features associated with these languages is clearly based on intuition rather than empirical research (which is unavoidable, as a nomenclature is needed first to work empirically). One of the clearest examples concerns the suggested profusion of reduplication in pidgin languages. It is possible that the claim is based on the presence of reduplication in creoles (Bakker and Parkvall 2005), combined with the iconic character of some reduplicative strategies, and the presence of some doubled forms or pseudo-reduplications in a number of pidgins. When the claim was subjected to scrutiny, however (Bakker 2003a), it turned out that only one of the dozens of pidgins investigated displayed reduplication as a morphological device.

While it is not uncommon for linguists to refer, as does Winford (2002), to "the well-known characteristics of pidgins", these characteristics are in fact much less known than most linguists might expect, except perhaps when they refer to the absence of certain features commonly found in non-pidgins. Note that many of the impressionistic characterisations of the pidgins quoted above were also formulated in such a way: no verbal inflection, no case marking, few function words, etc.

Empirical research on pidgins, as conducted by a limited number of linguists, is still in its infancy. This article is the first attempt at a new approach, making generalisations on a largish set of documented pidgins. Few pidgins are well described, and materials on individual pidgins are often scarce. We have attempted to take as much as possible into consideration, but additional materials may well prove some of the following claims to be false.

5.1. Lexicon

The pidgin lexicon in most documented cases derives primarily from one single language, with only minor contributions from the other speech varieties involved (this issue will receive further comment below). However, there are also some pidgins where the lexicon is derived from two languages in roughly equal numbers, probably in special social circumstances.

As with any other language, it is not possible to provide a precise measure of the pidgin lexicon size, but it is beyond doubt that the pidgin vocabulary is smaller than that of any of the contributing languages. Where estimates are available, the total number of lexical items claimed for various pidgins are usually below 2000, and in many cases below 1000 or even 500 (Drechsel 1997: 73; Dutton 1983: 94; Grant 1996b: 226; Heine 1973: 221; Holm 1988: 73, 1989: 515; Johnson 1978: 215; Juvonen 2008: 320–321; Kaufman 1971: 276; Manessy 1995: 79; Moag 1979: 66; Mühlhäusler 1997: 137, 2003: 152). In some cases, these numbers are estimated for individual pidgins studied, in other cases, they represent crosslinguistic generalisations.

The lexical reduction can be illustrated by the attested presence of 81 words for 'to cut' in Fijian, as opposed to only two in Fijian Pidgin. Similarly, all baskets are *kako* in the pidgin, while the various types all have their own name in the lexifier (Siegel 1987: 109; Romaine 1988: 34).

The limited vocabulary automatically leads to a broadening of the denotational range of each lexical item, and a staggering amount of polysemy (Drechsel 1997: 334–5; Heine 1973: 49, 1979: 96; Kaufman 1971: 276). For instance, the Chinook Jargon word *tilikam* has been glossed as 'man', 'people', 'person', 'Indians', 'natives', 'relatives', 'kindred', 'non-chiefs', 'same tribe', 'same band', 'friend', and the onomatopoeic *tumtum* has 'heart' as its primary meaning, but can also mean 'mind', 'stomach', 'conscience', 'soul', 'think', 'will', 'opinion' (Johnson 1978: 222, 240–1).

The same phenomenon can also be observed at the grammatical pole of the lexicon, where many pidgins (at least primarily) make do with one single adposition (Faraclas 1990: 128; Hancock 1980: 20; Holm 1988: 73; Mesthrie 2007: 79; Roberts 1995b: 6; Samarin 1967; Stern 2002: 20, 26; Thornell 1997: 84; Vrzić 1999: 97).

Another way of maximally exploiting a limited lexicon is multifunctionality, i.e. the use of one and the same (invariable) word in all part-of-speech categories, such as nouns also used as verbs (Dutton 1983: 95; Juvonen 2008: 330–336; Kaye and Tosco 2001: 93; Mühlhäusler 1997: 137, 159–60; Mühlhäusler et al. 1997: 453; Siegel 2003: 191). A very basic (and common) example is provided the Chinook Jargon item *wawa*, which means both 'language' and 'to speak', 'to tell'.

The processes above can be observed in the Herschel Island Eskimo Pidgin, where the one attested preposition is not even limited to adpositional service, but can also be used as a noun and an adverb (Stefánsson 1909). In the lexifier, it also functions as a noun and preposition or postposition ('in the inside of...').

Some pidgins (e.g. Chinook Jargon, Hiri Motu, Français-Tirailleur and early Tok Pisin) have a tendency or at least the possibility of expressing actions by means of a noun and a 'light verb' meaning 'to do' or 'to make' (Juvonen 2008: 327–328; Mühlhäusler 1997: 160).

Another common strategy, not unexpectedly, is the liberal use of compounds and circumlocutions – sometimes improvised, and sometimes conventionalised. From Chinese English Pidgin, we have *joss pidgin* ('God' + 'business'), meaning 'religion', and from Chinook Jargon come *cikomin lop* 'iron rope' > 'chain', *sasaci mawic* 'bad deer' > 'grizzly', *kaltas ina* 'worthless beaver' > 'muskrat' (Shi 1991: 21; Johnson 1978: 216, 218).

Other examples from a variety of pidgins are "long ears" 'rabbit', "stink tail" 'skunk', "big mouse" 'rat', "cow shirt" 'hide', "big wind" 'storm', "fire place" 'oven', "inside boots" 'sock', "sanity finished" 'mad', "hand boots" 'gloves', "tongue honey" 'skilful orator', "smoke eat thing" 'pipe', "fire burn thing" 'match' and "voice take thing" 'tape recorder' (Hancock 1996: 24–5; Mühlhäusler 1997: 137, 158; van der Voort 1997: 385).

Probably a nonce formation is the KiSetla Swahili Pidgin *kitu kama ndizi only round* 'thing like banana only round' > 'apple' (Vitale 1980: 62), while in Français-Tirailleur, the normal way of saying 'bad' and 'slow' are *pa bon* 'NEG good', *pa vit* 'NEG fast'. Similar uses of the sentence negation to produce antonyms are given for Tok Pisin and Fanakalo by Mühlhäusler (1997: 157).

The presence of such compositional word formation strategies could cast doubt on the common claim that pidgins "lack full expressive power", but we cannot come up with a way of either proving or disproving such a claim. One can expect the spontaneous formation of compounds and circumlocutions in situations of communicative need.

Another expected result of a limited lexicon is that a pidgin discourse typically (although this has been measured only for a few varieties) displays an exceptionally low type/token ratio (Heine 1979: 91–2; Juvonen 2008: 335–336; Robinson 2008). Juvonen's analysis of a Chinook Jargon text yields 381 word forms and 8255 tokens (i.e. a ratio of 1:5), while two comparable English texts yielded a ratio of 1:30–35.

Also expected is the specialisation in certain specific lexical fields. Pidgins are, after all, used in a limited number of domains, and since the Eleman and Koriki Hiri Trade Languages were used in trade involving pottery and sago, it is not surprising that the vocabulary pertaining to these semantic fields were more developed than the lexicon as a whole (Dutton 1983: 95). Pidgins may typically lack vocabulary relating to subjects that are not of interest to the conversation partners, but they may be introduced if needed, or created with circumlocution and compounding.

5.2. Phonology

Concerning phonology, there is less to say. The phoneme inventories of pidgins do not seem to differ quantitatively from those of other languages (Bakker, 2009; cf. Klein 2006a, 2006b for creoles with similar results), and perhaps not qualitatively either. While many sounds perceived by lay people or linguists as 'marked' (e.g. clicks from South African languages and lateral fricatives in languages of the Northwest coast of North America) are often filtered out, it is not clear whether this is due to their universal markedness, or whether it is simply a by-product of the phoneme arsenals of the other input languages. In some pidgins, these marked sounds may survive only in the speech of one of the groups in contact. English speakers of Chinese Pidgin English used cross-linguistically marked interdental consonants, while Chinese speakers replaced them with stops or fricatives (Hall 1944). Similarly, Amerindian speakers of Chinook Jargon tended to use e.g. voiceless laterals, while European speakers mostly replaced them with more familiar phonemes or clusters, and clicks are used by at least some speakers of the Bantu-lexified pidgin Fanakalo in South Africa.

It has often been pointed out (e.g. by Drechsel 1997: 68; Holm 1989: 625; Mühlhäusler 1997: 161; Sebba 1997: 39–40; Shi 1991: 15) that the phonotactic structures of pidgins are simpler than those of other languages (represented by a drift towards a CV syllable template), but again, it is not clear to what extent this is a characteristic of the pidginisation process as such, or an epiphenomenon resulting from a compromise of the creators' pre-existing phonotactical preferences.

Also common in pidgins is that suprasegmental devices such as tone, stress, intonation and segment length carry a small functional load (Heine 1979: 89–90; Holm 1989: 556, 558; Sebba 1997: 39–40). Pidgins tend not to make tonal distinctions, even if the lexifiers do so (Bakker 2008). Not surprisingly, creoles too display no tones, or only very rudimentary use of tone (McWhorter 2005). Even when all the creators of the pidgin were speakers of tone languages, the pidgin often ended up as a language with no phonemic tone, or a severely reduced system, e.g. Sango (Pasch 1997).

Allophony and morphophonemic processes are limited in nature. There is, in other words, a rather small distance between deep and surface phonological representations (Bender 1987: 42; Holm 1989: 572; Kay and Sankoff 1974: 62).

Less expected are the reports claiming a drift towards a bisyllabic word structure. In many cases, not only are long words shortened in comparison to their respective etyma, but monosyllabic ones are also reported to be lengthened to achieve bisyllabicity (Heine 1979: 90; Mühlhäusler 1997: 161; see also Stolz 1986 for a similar observation regarding creoles). This intuitive remark has not been studied empirically. Furthermore, it could be an epiphenomenon of a different syllable structure.

5.3.   Parts of speech

Most pidgins seem to distinguish a number of distinct parts of speech, but such distinctions are somewhat blurred as many stems can be used as both nouns and verbs, and sometimes also other categories (see section 6.1). Apart from nouns and verbs, adjectives and adverbs are also common. This characterisation is of course not limited to pidgins.

In some pidgins, certain parts of speech tend to be indicated in the same way, as if to mark them as belonging to a certain category. For instance, in Icelandic Pidgin French and Tay Boi (Vietnamese Pidgin French) all verbs end in *-er*, even those that have different infinitival endings in the lexifier French. Similarly, Pidgin Hindustani uses the suffix *-wala*, derived from the Hindustani agentive *-wala* (as in *bara-wale gara* 'big house') to mark adjectives. Tok Pisin uses *-fela* as (among others) a marker of adjectives. In Icelandic Pidgin Basque, all nouns and adjectives end in *-a* (Bakker 1994a: 32, Bakker et al. 1991), as do the verbs in Fanakalo (Bold 1958: 54).

Some remarks must be made on minor or functional categories such as adpositions, copulas, personal pronouns and question words.

Pidgins tend to have a limited number of prepositions and postpositions. Some pidgins have what one could classify as 'universal prepositions' in that they have a variety of functions, e.g. Sango *nà*, Pidgin Swahili *ya* or Fanakalo *lapa* (Heine 1979: 94). The Taymir Pidgin Russian postposition *mesto/meste* (< Russian 'place') also functions as a marker of instrumentals, comitatives, datives, goals and comparatives. Fanakalo has several prepositions. In this, pidgins resemble creoles, except that there are more prepositions and postpositions in creoles than in pidgins.

Kyakhta Pidgin Russian has postpositions and one preposition (*za* 'location' from a (rare) form 'for', Herschel Island Eskimo Pidgin has one postposition and no prepositions. Ethiopian Pidgin Italian has four prepositions: *ber* 'for', *kon* 'with', *di* 'of, from', *kome* 'like' (strikingly, no locative preposition is reported). If a pidgin has one preposition, it is often primarily locative with a number of derived functions.

It is sometimes claimed that copulas are absent or rare in specific pidgins, or pidgins in general (Baker 1999: 4, 2001: 38–41, Flanigan 1981: 64, Roberts 1995b: 114, Sebba 1997: 39, Shi 1991: 24). They do occur, however, and in the scarcely documented Saami Pidgin Swedish Borgarmålet, there are even two: *wara*, from the Swedish copula *vara*, and *sit*, from Swedish *sitte(r)* 'to sit'. If we classify Sango as a pidgin, then we have a pidgin which has a copula, despite this not being the case for its lexifier (Pasch 1997: 237):

(10) Ngbandi: *é   á-zi*
 1PL PL-people
 'We are people.'
Sango: *zò   à-yɛkɛ̀   zò*
 person SM-COP person
 'All people are equal.'

Personal pronouns tend to be more limited than the systems in the lexifiers. In no case are there clear gender differences in the pronouns. Case differences also tend to disappear (i.e. the sets like English *I, me, my, mine* tend to be reduced to one form, often *me* (2nd and 3rd person *you, him*) in English pidgins. However, in early attestations of pidgins and creoles, a wider range of forms are found (Baker and Huber 2000). Exceptionally, Ethiopian Pidgin Italian distinguished subject and object forms for first and second person. Politeness differences are neither preserved nor developed in pronouns.

However, some Pacific English pidgins elaborated the pronoun system of the lexifiers and added duals, trials and clusivity distinctions. Forms like *you me two fellow* and *you me three fellow* are first attested in 1897, *me fellow* 'we'/'us' in 1874 and *you and me* 'we'/'us' in 1884 in Melanesian Pidgin English, before the pidgin developed into a pidgincreole. In the closely related Eastern Australian Pidgin English, we also find some comparable complexifications of the pronoun system (Baker and Huber 2000; Baker and Mühlhäusler 1996).

Baker and Huber (2000) suggest that expansions of pronoun systems develop in dialogues, based on the lexifier system, with new forms emerging when needed. These authors survey the historical development of 13 English pidgins and creoles, and they conclude that the influence of English dialects and substrate languages is minimal. Almost all of the languages surveyed filled the gap in English of the separate second person plural forms.

Moving beyond the English pidgins, we find a lot of variation in pronoun inventories. Some pidgins have only singular forms. This may be because of lack of documentation; even for a fairly well documented as Chinese Pidgin English. In this pidgin, all materials constitute dialogues between individual English with another individual Chinese person (Baker and Huber 2000), so lack of plural forms may be due to a lack of data, not a gap in the language. Alternatively, it may reflect the state of affairs, that singular forms are used.

On the other hand, one frequently finds utterances where personal and possessive pronouns are lacking, as in these examples from Eskimo Pidgin and the Lingua Franca:

(11) *kuni   anana   aŋaninni*
     spouse ill   big
     'My spouse is ill.'
     (Stefánsson 1909: 223)

(12) *īmek   picuktu*
     water   want
     'I want a drink.'
     (Stefánsson 1909: 225)

(13) *qué   pensar?*
     what   think
     'What do you think?' (French: 'qu'en pensez-vous?')
     (Anonymous 1830: 94)

(14) *non   star   bouonou*
     NEG   be   well
     'He is not well.' (French: 'Il n'est pas bien.')
     (Anonymous 1830: 94)

When lexifiers have definite and indefinite articles, which is the case for most European languages, they are never used in the pidgins (Taylor 1981: 180; Sebba 1997: 39–40).

Definite and indefinite articles are present in virtually all creole languages, but the forms and function are never derived from articles in the lexifiers. Typically, the definite articles derive from demonstratives and the indefinite articles from the numeral 'one' (Baker 1999: 4, 2001: 38–41).

Articles are rare or absent in pidgins. Fanakalo has nominal markers that are superficially reminiscent of definite articles, but speakers seem to use them for all nouns, not only for nouns that have been mentioned before. Taymir Pidgin Russian has a nominal suffix *-to* derived from a North Russian suffixed definite article, but according to Stern (2005: 309) its function is different, and he prefers to call it a "highlighter". Stern (2009) glosses it as "emphatic", and the suffix is also found on a pronoun and a verb (in his examples 6 and 8).

In short, pidgins tend to display fewer parts of speech, and also fewer members of sets of both lexical and grammatical categories.

5.4. Morphology

The perhaps most salient of all features associated with language restructuring is a development from synthetic to analytic constructions. Such a tendency towards limited morphological complexity is commented upon in most descriptions of pidgins and semi-pidgins, including Eskimo Trade Jargon, Shaba Swahili, Tay Boi, Chinook Jargon, Lingua Franca, Juba Arabic, Chinese Pidgin Russian and Mobilian Jargon (De Rooij 1994; Reinecke 1971: 51; Kaufman 1971: 276; Van der Voort 1994: 145–7; Holm 1989: 572, 601, 608, 625). This took place (seemingly or obviously) within a very short time period.

Some less radically restructured varieties, such as Nagamese Pidgin, Hiri Motu, Fijian Pidgin, Fanakalo, Kituba and Lingala (Roberts and Bresnan 2008; Holm 1989) do retain fair amounts of morphology, but typically less than their lexifiers. For example Naga (northeast India) has five inflectional categories, its lexifier Assamese six, Fanagalo (South Africa) three, its lexifier Zulu five, etc. Lingala, however, has more than its lexifier Bobangi (five and four respectively).

Pidgins also show less allomorphy than non-pidgins (Heine 1979: 91; Boretzky 1983: 21) e.g. Pidgin Hawaiian (Bickerton and Wilson 1987: 65 in Mühlhäusler et al. 1997: 453).

It has often been claimed (e.g. Sebba 1997: 54; Thomason 2001: 168) that pidgins have no or little morphology at all. However, on close scrutiny this appears not to be true. Even though all pidgins show a reduction of morphological marking compared to the lexifier language, or in some cases even a complete absence, it is clear that quite a few pidgins do display productive morphology.

Many pidgins have possibilities of compounding, i.e. the combination of two lexical items to create a new lexical item, as discussed above (section 5.1). This is not at all surprising or controversial – it is a natural way to increase the lexical stock.

Derivational and inflectional morphology is scarcer in pidgins. Bakker (2003b) investigated morphology in some two dozen pidgins, and reported on pidgins marking number, case and gender in nouns, and tense-mood-aspect, valence, number, person and gender in verbs. Compared to the lexifiers, however, the pidgins did in all cases display fewer of the categories and, within the categories, fewer distinctions were available than in the lexifiers. For instance, gender of the lexifier could be dropped but case preserved, or a nine-gender system reduced to two. Fanakalo has reduced the 13 noun classes of Zulu to two, based on the semantically transparent count vs. mass nouns (Polomé 1983: 127).

The most detailed study on pidgin morphology is Roberts and Bresnan (2008), focusing on inflectional morphology. They surveyed 29 pidgins (not all of which we would be happy to label thus), and 14 of them had no inflectional morphology at all, even though all of their lexifiers but one had at least one inflectional category. Of the three pidginised forms of Russian – with five inflectional categories – two ended up with no inflection at all (Russenorsk, Kyakhta Pidgin Russian) and one with two categories (Taymir Pidgin Russian). Assamese and Iñupiaq Eskimo both have six inflectional categories, while pidgins lexically derived from them (Nagamese and Eskimo Pidgin) both preserved four and none, respectively. Thus, some pidgins have up to three or four inflectional categories. Interestingly, two pidgins had developed an inflectional category that was absent in the lexifier. Lingala developed inflectional negation that its lexifier Bobangi does not have, and Nagamese marks gender which its lexifier does not (Roberts and Bresnan 2008: 289). However, not all specialists would consider these languages pidgins, and if they are, they are certainly atypical on several counts. Both Lingala and Nagamese are used in a wide range of contexts, sometimes even as mother tongues. It is also certain that Lingala developed many of its complexities later (Roberts and Bresnan 2008: 271 note 2).

Languages with very little morphology, such as Hawaiian, may also be pidginised. It shows simplification in that the number of exemplars of different parts of speech is reduced: from 55 pronouns to six or nine, case markers from two to zero, definite article from one to zero, etc.

5.5. Constituent order

Whereas virtually all known creole languages display SVO word order (with possibilities of fronting constituents), pidgins display a variety of word orders. The few creoles that have constituent orders other than SVO seem to have developed into other directions due to later developments. This is the case for Philippine Creole Spanish, which has VSO order like the surrounding adstrate languages and Sri Lanka Malay and Sri Lanka Portuguese, which are now SOV, but in the past were SVO languages.

Several authors have expressed the opinion that pidgins have a relatively strict constituent order (e.g. Holm 1989: 590; Drechsel 1997: 334–5), but some pidgins have several orders. Yimas-Arafundi displays free constituent order, but the verb is always sentence-final. Trio-Ndyuka Pidgin has SOV order if the constituents are nominal, but OSV if S is pronominal. Pidgin Ngarluma is predominantly (S)OV (85%), while (S)VO is found in 15% of the material.

There seems to be a drift towards SVO word order even in some pidgins that have a lexifier with a different basic word order (e.g. Pidgin Hawaiian (Bickerton and Wilson 1987: 65), whose lexifier Hawaiian has VSO order. Greenlandic is mostly verb-final, but Greenlandic Pidgin Eskimo is not (van der Voort 1996: 174). Many documented pidginisations have involved languages with this very word order, and since it is the regular one in European languages, whose speakers are not seldom socioeconomically privileged in these situations, it is difficult to say whether this word order is by definition favoured by the pidginisation process itself. Sometimes one can note a diachronic development: Early Pidgin Fijian had VSO word order (whereas the lexifier Fijian has VOS), but later Pidgin Fijian displayed VSO and SVO word order.

With regard to the position of other elements, a number of observations can be made. The order of nouns and their modifiers does not always follow the order of the lexifier. In Icelandic Pidgin Basque, for instance, adjectives precede nouns like in Icelandic, but unlike in Basque, where adjectives follow nouns.

The position of the negative element differs from one pidgin to another. Whereas almost all creoles have a negative marker preceding the TMA elements which in turn precedes the verb, some pidgins have a negative element sentence-initially, or sentence-finally. Mobilian has a negative suffix *-(e)kšo*, inherited from the lexifiers (Holm 1989: 601; Drechsel 1997), and so do Simplified Fula (Bilkiire) and Trio-Ndyuka Pidgin. Broken Oghibbeway (Nichols 1995; see also Bakker 1994b) has dropped its lexifier's negative suffix, but it preserves the preverbal negative particle. In Pidgin Hawaiian, the position of the negative element is not the same as in the lexifier. In Hawaiian, it is placed in the beginning of a sentence, preceding SBJ ASP V, and in the pidgin it is located between the subject and the verb (Roberts 1995: 107–108, 115). Only one of four Hawaiian negators is retained in the pidgin, *aole*, which is the most common one. In Yimas-Alamblak pidgin as well, there was a change in position. In Yimas, negation must be clause-final, but in the pidgin it can appear either clause-finally or clause-initially (Williams 2000: 49, 56). Yimas has two negators, the pidgin only one. The negative element comes from Yimas *kayak* 'there is not'.

The lexifiers may use different constituent orders for different functions, for instance inversion with questions (like English *you will* vs. *will you?*) or different orders for main clauses and subordinate clauses (as in Dutch *hij komt niet* vs. *dat hij niet komt* '(that) he does not come'). Such patterns are never found in pidgins. Chinese Pidgin English for example does not use inversion in questions (Shi 1991: 25).

5.6. Morphosyntax

The grammatical categories of tense, mood and aspect, which figure so prominently in creoles, are rarely obligatory in pidgins. Roberts and Bresnan (2008) found TMA marking in 12 out of 29 pidgins, inherited from the lexifiers, but usually with a reduced number of forms. Most pidgins display invariable verb forms (Manessy 1994: 112; Dench 1998: 52) which do not express tense, mood and aspect. Tense and mood are not obligatory in pidgins, but tense can be expressed with adverbs meaning for instance 'later', 'tomorrow', 'yesterday', 'a long time ago' or 'right now' (Baker 1999: 4, 2001: 38–41; Mühlhäusler 1997: 147). These adverbials are often found in the periphery of the sentences, if expressed at all. Mood can be expressed by particles glossed as 'maybe', 'I don't know', or the like. Aspect is not expressed at all (even though it is quite important in creoles). Modal distinctions are rarely indicated overtly, and the modal interpretation of sentences is usually left to the interlocutor.

In some pidgins, several verbs may be used in one and the same clause, reminiscent of serial verb constructions, for example in Chinese Pidgin English:

(15) *Taipan can sen wum piece cooly come my shop looksee*
 'Your Honour can send a porter to my shop to have a look.'
 (Shi 1991: 28)

5.7. Complex sentences

It is often claimed that pidgins make no use of complex sentences (e.g. Sebba 1997: 39–40). Subordinate clauses are indeed rare, and usually replaced by parataxis/concatenation (Boretzky 1983: 21). In these examples from Eskimo Pidgin, no overt trace can be found for coordination or subordination:

(16) *Kaukau homolûktu kimmik kīlamik ĕlĕkta*
   Eat   plenty   dog quick travel
   'Dogs travel fast when they have plenty to eat.'
   (Stefánsson 1909: 224)

(17) *Tuktu mûkki ila nanakō elekta*
   caribou dead 3SG later travel
   'He killed (some) caribou, then he went away.'
   (Stefánsson 1909: 228)

(18) *Kimmik nagorok pitcûk uŋacĭksu elekta pitcûk awoŋa*
   dog   good   NEG far   travel NEG 1SG
   'When I have poor dogs, I don't like to make long trips.'
   (Stefánsson 1909: 231)

Even coordination is rarer than in most traditional languages (e.g. Pidgin Hawaiian (Mühlhäusler et al. 1997: 453), Papua Pidgin English (Mühlhäusler 1997: 150–1), Chinese Pidgin English (Shi 1991: 28). Heine (1979: 96) claims that pidgins make use of coordination rather than subordination. Reported speech is typically given in direct quotations, and not in complementizer constructions.

5.8. Pragmatics and stylistics

Comments on the pragmatics of pidgin speech are somewhat rare. One feature which receives some comment is an increased reliance on gesturing (Drechsel 1997: 335; Fox 1983: 100; Queffélec 1995: 849; Reinecke 1971: 50; Trumelet 1863: 17).

Also occasionally mentioned is the relative brevity of utterances and a slower speech tempo (Bartens 1996: 104; Drechsel 1997: 334–5), both of which might follow automatically from the fact that pidgins are spoken non-natively. Mühlhäusler (1997: 141–2) admits, however, that the comment on speech tempo is but an assumption, and that there are no data on the subject.

Commonly pointed out is the larger dependence on context created by a lower degree of redundancy and the rampant polysemy (Heine 1979: 92, 96–7, 1991: 36; Shi 1991: 29; Stefánsson 1909: 221–2), but again, it is not clear how this could be quantified.

Pidgins are usually thought to display a narrower range of stylistic variation than other languages, something that is expected from the fact that their use is restricted to certain domains only. This implies a relative shortage of synonyms (Gilman 1985: 11). It also relates to the belief that pidgins are rarely used "to express abstract notions, or for metalinguistic or artistic purposes" (Foley 1988: 164). Romaine (1988: 151) puts it as follows: "There are few, if any, stylistic options. The emphasis is on the communicative or referential rather than the expressive function of language."

While this is no doubt true as a general tendency, it should of course not be taken to mean that pidgins never serve in such roles. For example, Ollonne's (1901: 230) description of his African travels features a first-hand account of a speaker of Français-Tirailleur playing with words. "Having been hit by a pouring rainfall while approaching the village of Baoulo, the pidgin speaker exclaims *Village comme ça, n'y a pas appelé Baoulo, y a appelé Beaucoup l'eau* 'A village like this should not be called Baoulo, but instead "lots of water"'."

While such use is expected to be rarer in pidgins than in natively spoken languages, it certainly does happen occasionally that pidgins are drafted into service even for 'luxury' purposes rather than for the conveying of information alone. For instance, a fair quantity of songs is documented in Chinook Jargon (Boas 1888).

6. Further issues

6.1. The primacy of reduction

While the typological characteristics of the input languages of course play a role in determining the resulting makeup of a pidgin, there is no clear one-to-one relationship between the input and the outcome. This is particularly true when it comes to reduction.

Reduction is of course also part of normal language change, and somewhat more in language contact situations involving adult acquisition. It can be argued that all languages that are learned by large groups of adults undergo reduction in their grammatical systems. Kusters (2003) has shown this with regard to inflectional morphology in North Germanic, Quechua, Arabic and Swahili, and McWhorter (2007) has argued that lingua franca languages like English, Persian and Malay have undergone grammatical reduction not visible in their closest relatives. In pidgins, however, the reduction is much more extreme than in such cases, and even polysynthetic languages may yield isolating pidgins.

Yimas is "highly complex polysynthetic" (Foley 1988: 168), but Yimas-lexicon pidgins are as radically simplified as other pidgins, and the same goes for Chinook Jargon – the lexifier is polysynthetic, but the pidgin arguably is morphologically simpler than any of the contributing languages. This is true for both varieties of Chinook Jargon: the 'real' pidgin as documented e.g. by Boas and in a range of dictionaries, in which morphology was absent, and the variety recorded by Melville Jacobs in the 1930s (Jacobs 1932, 1936) and Zenk in the 1970s in Grand Ronde, which had developed morphology through grammaticalisation of independent pronouns to verbal affixes (Grant 1996b; Zenk 1984, 1988).

In a similar vein, the pronominal system of Arafundi-Enga Pidgin has three persons and two numbers, despite the fact that both the languages involved in its genesis have four pronominal numbers (Williams 1995: 173).

Thus, contrary to popular belief, pidginisation does not necessarily lead to the favouring of the lowest common denominator: pidgin creators also drop plenty of structures found in all of the first languages.

It is in fact doubtful if the complexity of the input languages has any impact at all on the complexity of the resulting pidgin. On the contrary, there is some reason to believe that the 'ideal' pidgin type can emerge regardless of the complexity of the input languages (although, of course, various social factors may inhibit such radical reduction).

One may ask the question: What features are typically dropped from the lexifier languages? Vitale (1980: 60) provides the following table of possible affixes in coastal Swahili and what is left of them in the pidgin KiSetla.

Table 1. Affixes in Pidgin KiSetla and its lexifier Swahili

Affix	Coastal Swahili	KiSetla	Replaced by
Negative	2	1	invariant form
Subject	20	0	personal pronouns
Tense	11	2	present or future
Relative	16	0	two simplex sentences, or avoided
Object	20	0	personal pronouns

None of the verbal suffixes of Swahili (derivations, TMA, modal clitics, number agreement for plural imperatives and a relative marker) are productive in KiSetla, though they may appear occasionally (Vitale 1980: 60).

However, the question itself may be misleading: pidginisation is a creative process that leads to the creation of an interethnic means of communication. In the process, the creators avoid unnecessary features, either occasionally, or systematically. New language norms emerge, and the resulting pidgin typically displays a simple structure. It is convenient to make comparisons between lexifiers and pidgins, and pidgins are indeed simplified vis-à-vis their lexifiers. The comparison may not be fair, however, as our position is that it was never the goal to reproduce the lexifier. People with no common language just needed and wanted to communicate, and make themselves understood, and a trial-and-error process resulted in a new, more or less systematic and normative pattern of communication that we call a pidgin.

Features typically absent from pidgins include the following:

- In the area of morphology: inflection, derivation, reduplication, infixation, suprafixation, allomorphy, any synthetic structures;

- In the nominal realm: gender marking, case marking, number marking, definite and indefinite articles, large sets of demonstratives, adjectival agreement;

- In the verbal realm: person agreement, tense-mood-aspect marking, valence, voice and gender marking;

- In the area of functional categories: definite and indefinite articles, possessive pronouns, moderate or large sets of prepositions, more than one or a few question words, demonstratives, clause connectors;

- In the area of syntax: functional differences between word orders (e.g. questions versus statements);

- In the phonological realm: grammatical tone, distinctive vowel length, certain phonemes not shared by all (or most of the) groups involved;

- In the pragmatic realm: distinctions relating to politeness and biological gender, stylistic variation, verbal art, fast speech.

For almost all of these, exceptions can be signalled (and have been so above). However, the exceptions are typically independent of the type of languages spoken by the creators of the pidgin. The exceptions are most likely the result of social rather than linguistic motivations. This seems true both for the preservation of grammatical categories from the lexifiers and for the creation of new categories.

The reduction during the pidginisation process can be taken to be the main reason that creole languages, despite a range of expansive processes, are relatively less complex compared to older languages (McWhorter 2001; Parkvall 2008).

6.2. The notion of pidgins being mixed

Many uses (cf. section 3 above) of the word 'pidgin' seem to presuppose that a pidgin is a spectacularly mixed language. Among laymen, it is – in our experience – not uncommon to use the label as shorthand for 'mixed language variety', or a language with some obvious elements from other languages, and this occurs even among professional linguists.

Many people seem to adhere to the formula 'languages A and B met, and as a result of that, language C emerged – therefore, language C, must be a combination of A and B', but this is not quite the case.

The concept of mixedness is obviously difficult to quantify, but let us for the sake of the argument use, or at least begin with, the core lexicon.

In the core vocabulary (as defined by the Swadesh list), most pidgins derive 90% or more from one single language, and even among larger samples of words, this proportion is usually above three fourths (Cassidy 1971: 216; Dutton 1983: 96; Foley 1988: 168; Grant 1999: 1–2; Heine 1973: 45, 49; Mühlhäusler 1997: 176; Reinecke 1971: 50; Wurm 1972: 921). These numbers are often not the result of careful counts, but impressionistically true.

To be sure, some pidgins, such as Manchurian Russian Pidgin, Ndyuka-Trio Pidgin, Yimas-Arafundi Pidgin, Ngarluma Pidgin, Hauna Trade Language and Russenorsk are more lexically mixed, with between one half and two thirds of the lexicon derived from one and the same source (Dench 1998: 19; Grant 1999: 1; Holm 1989: 627). The Manambu-Kwoma pidgin (Sepik River) was described as "lexically an amalgam of both languages" (Harrison 1987 quoted in Williams 1983: 361). These pidgins, however, constitute exceptions to the general pattern. Their specificity is routinely interpreted as owing to a relatively symmetric power relationship between the two groups – i.e. that the proportion of lexical material from one specific language reflects the dominant position of the group speaking this language. However, Baker and Huber (1992, 1993) argue that mobility plays a more important role: when (typically European) travellers, traders and sailors deal with different local populations, they may constitute the only link between these 'substrate' languages, thus making the lexifier a more convenient pool to draw on than any of the substrates.

There is some reason to suspect – but further studies will be needed to confirm this – that pidgins are more mixed in the early stages of their development. It is noteworthy that Australian English Pidgin started its career as more mixed than it was in the 19th century (Baker 2001: 34–5; Malcolm 2001: 211), and a rather similar development can be observed with regard to Hawaiian English Pidgin in which many Hawaiian items were used as well, plus words from other languages, but the number of English words has increased through time.

When we broaden our horizons to the non-lexical parts of pidgin languages, things become more complicated, since structure is even more difficult to quantify.

Phonology may be one area where the speakers' language backgrounds reveal themselves even at an early stage of pidgin development. Reinecke (1971) reports that users of Tay Boi basically used their own native phonological systems in pidgin speech, and similar reports are frequent for other pidgins. As for structure, however, it is notable that Baker and Mühlhäusler (1990: 112) claim that there are no syntactic structures in Chinese English Pidgin "of undoubted Cantonese provenance at any stage", while Shi (1991: 3) sees no specifically English features in the same language. On the surface, these two statements might seem contradictory, but in fact, they need not be. One way of looking at things is that the structure of a pidgin is so minimal that there are, as it were, few places for an input language to manifest itself structurally. And if the main languages of the creators have similar word orders, the pidgin can be expected to follow that.

Few would doubt that a given input language (beyond the lexical level) can influence the structure of a pidgin, and that it in fact often does. Many structural features of the input languages are not encountered in the pidgins. Chinese English Pidgin, as just cited, is a case in point. Many structures may at some level of analysis conform to either English or Cantonese (the two major languages involved in its formation), but a minimum of scientific rigor would require that a certain structure can be unequivocally attributed to one or the other language, and for many pidgins, this is not easy to obtain. In fact, there are plenty of cases, where both or all the input languages provided a certain feature, but where the pidgin nevertheless has chosen to ignore it. Both English and Eskimo have some form of verbal agreement, but Eskimo Pidgin doesn't. Both Russian and Norwegian mark tense, number and gender, but the pidgin doesn't. Many more such examples could be adduced.

6.3. How do pidgins spread?

A few pidgins are or were spoken in huge geographical areas, for instance the Lingua Franca in most of the Mediterranean, or Melanesian Pidgin English in the Southwest Pacific. This means that, after an initial contact, a range of individuals agree on the usefulness of the medium of interaction, and use it in contexts and regions not formerly under the influence of the pidgin. In this way, pidgins spread geographically, sometimes at a spectacular rate.

Kaufman (1971), Grant (1996a) and Lang (2008), for instance, studied the spread of Chinook Jargon. In a few decades the language spread from the mouth of the Columbia River as far as to Western Montana and southern Alaska.

A second aspect of spread is the diffusion of certain words, constructions or specific solutions between different pidgins (and creoles). For the English pidgins and creoles, Baker and Huber (2001) tracked more than 300 of those, and they concluded that some of these items were typical for the Atlantic, others for the Pacific and again others appear to be worldwide features. Some of them are lexical, others are functional. Here are some examples:

Table 2. Some Atlantic, Pacific and worldwide features of contact Englishes.

Pacific	World-wide	Atlantic
all as plural marker	*allsame* 'like'	*palaver* 'dispute'
byandby as marker of future	*lili* 'little'	*una/unu* 'second person plural'
chowchow 'eat, food'	*him* '3SG.POSS'	*WH matter* 'why'
	suppose 'if'	

One of the implications of their data is that communicative solutions invented at one place will be tried elsewhere as well, and introduced in other situations in which contact languages developed. The mobility of sailors and labourers, transmitting contact features orally is a precondition for such spread. Alternatively, in some cases the publication of travel accounts with language specimens or even language manuals or vocabularies, printed or in manuscript copies (Shi 1992; Lang 2008), played a role in the maritime spread of such features. Similar reasons could be true for the spread of military expressions used by American soldiers in different East Asian wars: varieties of so-called 'Bamboo English' in Japan (cold war era), Korea and Vietnam show continuities over language borders, apparently through transmission between different 'generations' of soldiers and their officers. Similar histories have to be assumed for widespread words such as *pikinini* for 'child' and *savi* 'to know' in the Atlantic and Pacific (cf. Baker and Huber 2001 for a range of examples).

6.4. What favours the emergence of a pidgin?

Some writers, like Harris (1994: 32), reason that a long tradition of contact between two or more languages should lead to pidginisation. In fact, we believe, the very opposite is true. If two or more peoples have been in touch with one another for an extended period of time, some bi- or multilingualism generally develops among at least parts of the population, thus eliminating the need for a pidgin (cf. section 4.1). In those situations where a pidgin survived for a long period, there were clear and exceptional social reasons. In the case of the Mediterranean Lingua Franca, for example, the Arab slaveholders and traders and the European slaves used the pidgin to uphold a barrier against understanding of their languages by the other group. The creation and use of pidgin in order to keep the native language secret has also been mentioned in the context of Pidgin Hamer, Delaware Jargon (Thomason 1980), Mobilian and Chinese Pidgin English. By using a reduced form of speech, speakers of Hamer (Ethiopia), Delaware (USA), Choctaw-Chickasaw (USA) and Cantonese could conceal their language from the intruders.

On the other hand, a pidgin can of course not come into being if there is no contact at all. So, it seems that there is an optimal degree of contact for a pidgin to emerge – not too little, not too much.

It is not difficult to imagine that mastery of other languages leads to certain advantages in, say, a trading situation, so if there is enough to gain, we would expect traders to have an incentive to make the effort to learn the other party's language. It is when this incentive is not large enough to motivate the effort that pidginisation may occur.

An obvious example is when the contact is somewhat sporadic in nature. In the early days of Russenorsk, for instance, trade was only seasonal, and in the case of Chinese English Pidgin, an individual sailor could only expect to visit Canton one or a few times in his active life, leading to limited exposure to Cantonese, and most certainly also a limited eagerness to acquire it.

But Anglo-Chinese contacts in the Canton area also illustrate another factor which, we believe, is at least as important. Reinecke (1938: 111) talks about the refusal to learn the others' language as a way of holding the others "at arm's length". Learning somebody else's language can be seen as a way of accepting a subordinate position, and when power relations are not obvious (or not viewed similarly by those involved), or if there is an atmosphere of distrust between the parties involved, pidgin creation is favoured. Canton is a prime example of this, as both parties thought of themselves as culturally superior to the other (Baker and Mühlhäusler 1990: 108). Fiji is another – the two major population groups (Fijians and Indians) are roughly equal in size. They inhabit a relatively small country, so one might expect them to be willing and able to learn each other's language – were it not for the strained relations between the two groups. Instead, not only one, but even two pidgins have developed on the islands: one with a predominantly Fijian lexicon, and one with a chiefly Hindustani vocabulary (Siegel 1982, 1987, 1990).

In general, we could say that any relatively sudden (thus not allowing for a gradual adjustment) encounter between groups of people speaking two or (better still) more than two mutually incomprehensible languages, has the potential for giving birth to a pidgin. With an absence of amicable relation or lack of intimate socialisation added to the mix, chances of a pidgin seeing the light of day increases considerably.

Some settings that appear to have been specifically prone to generate pidgins are:

1. Trade. This is probably the most prototypical setting. Long-distance maritime trade (usually in the wake of European exploration and colonisation) may be particularly fruitful (and gave rise to e.g. Chinese English Pidgin, various Eskimo pidgins and Russenorsk), but even trade on a smaller scale with neighbouring ethnicities can yield the same results (e.g. Trio-Ndyuka Pidgin and several indigenous pidgins in New Guinea such as Yimas-Arafundi pidgin and Yimas-Alamblak pidgin).

2. Warfare and policing (where a heterogeneous army or police corps is sent out in a field where yet other languages are spoken). It is in this context that Turku and Juba Arabic Pidgin, Hiri Motu and Français-Tirailleur emerged and/or thrived. These are special cases of the next setting.

3. Multilingual workplaces, where a sudden economic boom draws workers from a large variety of different backgrounds into a limited area. This provided the impetus for at least the spread of Hawaiian Pidgin on plantations and Fanakalo in South African mines (Kaltenbrunner 1996). Also, multilingual work forces on ships provided a context for the development or spread of pidgins. Situations of slavery, as the European slaves held by the Arabs, are a specific case of such work forces. Concentration camps and other types of confinement are also beneficial to pidgin genesis.

Some pidgins, of course (such as Lingua Franca, Mobilian and Chinook Jargon), cannot easily be pigeon-holed into one of these categories, and were used in a wider variety of circumstances.

6.5. How common is pidginisation?

While some treat pidginisation as a trivial by-product of language contact, we hold it to be an exceedingly common phenomenon. With 7,000 or so known languages, all of which are in regular contact with one or more of their neighbours, the number of attested pidgins is remarkably low. Out of thousands or even tens of thousands of potential contact surfaces, the number of attested pidgins is well below 200, even if we include some highly dubious cases. Multilingualism or the use of a (non-pidginised) lingua franca is the norm in interethnic contacts, and pidginisation clearly the exception. The phenomenon of pidginisation is clearly rare.

6.6. Power

It is often assumed that the 'language of power' (which usually implies the language of European colonial powers) automatically becomes the lexifier of a pidgin. This is only partially true, if indeed true at all. Most pidgins in North America were based on the indigenous languages, not on French or English.

Power relations are also mentioned to explain the mixed lexicons of some trade pidgins, when these would have come about in situations where the different groups were on equal footing, as with Russenorsk. While this may be true, the main proof is the existence of a mixed vocabulary, which obviously makes the reasoning circular. Prestige tends to be defined by which language delivers most of the lexicon, and the lexical composition is explained by the power relations.

Fiji is another case in point. On Fiji, both pidginised Fiji and pidginised Hindi have coexisted for a long time, in communication between indigenous Fijians and immigrant Indians. It cannot be possibly that Fiji is more prestigious than Hindi, and Hindi more prestigious than Fijian, but yet, there are pidgins based on both.

While we wouldn't a priori deny that status may matter, it can be argued that the main lexifier is the language with which the most people come in contact. Baker and Huber (2001) point out that more mobile languages have a better chance of spreading their properties than languages that are localised.

6.7. Signed jargons and pidgins

Plains Indian Sign Language was an intertribal contact language used by a range of indigenous groups and Euro-Americans interacting with them. Its use dwindled and ceded to English in the 20th century, although it is still known by some. It has all the properties of a pidgin (cf. Bakker 2012), except that it has no identifiable lexifier (although it is possible that home sign systems or ritual sign systems formed the lexical basis).

Another sign language that received attention in connection with pidginisation and creolisation is Nicaraguan Sign Language. As there were no schools for the deaf in Nicaragua before the Sandinist revolution, deaf people grew up in isolation from one another, and only home sign systems existed. When schools for the deaf were started, the children developed a complete sign language in the course of a few years. This sign language has been compared with a creole, and the initial amalgamation of the home sign systems with a jargon or pidgin, which seems plausible on the basis of the available documentation.

7. Conclusions

Pidgins, as defined here, have been under-researched in contact linguistics. In creolistics, pidgins and creoles have all too often been treated together, as if they share all their structural properties. This view may have been partly motivated by the fact that some pidgins have become creoles in the course of their history, for instance through nativization or through a development away from limited systems of communication (pidgins) to complete natural languages (pidgincreoles, creoles). In this paper we have focused on non-expanded pidgins and their properties. Pidgins are norm-based communication systems that have spontaneously developed in situations where two or more groups developed spoken, and in some rare cases signed, forms of interaction that are effective in the limited domains of use, but they are not fully expressive languages.

In this article we have attempted to survey the current state-of-affairs in pidgin research. Unfortunately the dataset on pidgins is restricted, and of mixed quality. In the past decades some good descriptive and historical studies on pidgins have appeared. Nevertheless, much research on pidgins remains to be done, including descriptive work. Empirical studies on the structural typology of pidgins has been limited thus far, and studies on pragmatic, semantic and social-anthropological aspects of pidgins are virtually non-existent.

References

Adami, Norbert. 1981. Koreanisches Bambus-English. *Bochumer Jahrbuch zur Ostasienforschung* 4. 509–512.
Aldea, Santiago. 1987. Funcion del prestamo en el discurso propagandistico. *Miscelanea* 8. 5–19.
Alexandre, Pierre. 1963. Aperçu sommaire sur le pidgin A 70 du Cameroun. *Cahiers d'Études Africaines* 12. 577–582.
Algeo, John T. 1960. Korean Bamboo English. *American Speech* 35. 117–123.
Anonymous. 1830. *Dictionnaire de la Langue Franque Ou Petit Mauresque, Suivi de Quelques Dialogues Familiers et d'un Vocabulaire des Mots Arabes Les Plus Usuels, a l'Usage des Français en Afrique*. Marseille: Feissat aîné et Demonchy.
Ansaldo, Umberto & Stephen Matthews. 2007. Deconstructing creole: the rationale. In Umberto Ansaldo, Stephen Matthews & Lisa Lim (eds.), *Deconstructing Creole*, 1–18. Amsterdam/Philadelphia: John Benjamins.
Ardila, Alfredo. 2005. Spanglish: An anglicized Spanish dialect. *Hispanic Journal of Behavioral Sciences* 27(1). 60–81.
Axtell, James. 2000. Babel of tongues: communicating with the Indians in Eastern North America. In Edward G. Gray & Norman Fiering (eds.), *The Language Encounter in the Americas*: *A Collection of Essays, 15–60*, 1492–1800. New York/Oxford: Berghahn Books.
Baker, Philip. 1993. Australian influence on Melanesian Pidgin English. *Te Reo* 36. 3–67.
Baker, Philip. 1994. *Creativity in creole genesis*. In Dany Adone & Ingo Plag (eds.), *Creolization and Language Change*, 65–84. Tübingen: Niemeyer.
Baker, Philip. 2002. No creolisation without prior pidginisation. *Te Reo* 44. 31–50.
Baker, Philip & Magnus Huber. 2000. Constructing new pronominal systems from the Atlantic to the Pacific. *Linguistics* 38(5). 833–866.
Baker, Philip & Magnus Huber. 2001. Atlantic, Pacific, and world-wide features in English lexicon contact languages. *English World-Wide* 22. 157–208.
Baker, Philip & Peter Mühlhäusler. 1990. From business to pidgin. *Journal of Asian Pacific Communication* 1. 87–115.
Baker, Philip & Peter Mühlhäusler. 1996. The development and diffusion of pronouns in Pacific Pidgin English. In Stephen A. Wurm, Peter Mühlhäusler & Darrell T. Tryon (eds.), *Atlas of Languages of Intercultural Communication in the Pacific, Asia, and the Americas*, 537–549. Berlin: Mouton de Gruyter.
Bakker, Peter. 1987. A Basque nautical pidgin: a missing link in the history of *fu*. *Journal of Pidgin and Creole Languages* 2(1). 1–30.
Bakker, Peter. 1994a. Pidgins. In Jacques Arends, Pieter Muysken & Norval Smith (eds.), *Pidgins and Creoles. An Introduction*, 25–39. Amsterdam/Philadelphia: John Benjamins.
Bakker, Peter. 1994b. Is John Long's Chippeway (1791) an Ojibwe pidgin? In William Cowan (ed.), *Papers of the 25th Algonquian Conference*, 13–31. Ottawa: Carleton University.

Bakker, Peter. 1995. First African into New Netherland, 1613–1614. *Halve Maen* 68(3). 50–52.
Bakker, Peter. 1996. Language contact and pidginisation in Davis Strait and Hudson Strait (North East Canada). In Ingvild Broch & Ernst Håkon Jahr (eds.), *Language Contact in the Arctic: Northern Pidgins and Contact Languages*, 261–310. Berlin: Mouton de Gruyter.
Bakker, Peter. 2003. Scandinavians and their pidgins and creoles. *Acta Linguistica Hafniensia* 35. 95–114.
Bakker, Peter. 2006. The Sri Lanka Sprachbund: the newcomers Portuguese and Malay. In Yaron Matras, April McMahon & Nigel Vincent (eds.), *Linguistic Areas. Convergence in Historical and Typological Perspective*, 135–159. Houndmills Basingstoke: Palgrave MacMillan.
Bakker, Peter. 2008. Pidgins versus creoles and pidgincreoles. In Silvia Kouwenberg & John Singer (eds.), *The Handbook of Pidgin and Creole Studies*, 130–157. Oxford: Wiley-Blackwell.
Bakker, Peter. 2009. Phonological complexity in pidgins. In Nicholas Faraclas & Thomas Klein (eds.), *Simplicity and Complexity in Creoles and Pidgins*, 7–27. London: Battlebridge.
Bakker, Peter. 2012. Review article about 'Hand Talk: Sign Language among American Indian Nations', Jeffrey E. Davis. Cambridge: Cambridge University Press. *International Journal of American Linguistics* 78(1). 127–132.
Bakker, Peter, Gidor Bilbao, Nicolaas G. H. Deen & José Ignacio Hualde. 1991. *Basque Pidgins in Iceland and Canada*. Donostia/San Sebastian: Gipuzkoako Foru Aldundia/Diputación Foral de Gipuzkoa.
Bakker, Peter & Mikael Parkvall. 2005. Reduplication in pidgins and creoles. In Bernhard Hurch & Veronika Mattes (eds.), *Studies on Reduplication*, 511–531. Berlin: Mouton De Gruyter.
Barrelon, Pierre. 1893. Saïgon. *Le Tour du Monde* 66. 225–256.
Bartens, Angela. 1996. *Der Kreolische Raum. Geschichte und Gegenwart*. Helsinki: Suomalainen Tiedeakatemia.
Bergmann, Bernhard. 2001. Language cultivation and language change. *Sprachdienst* 45(1). 17–18.
Berry, Jack. 1971. Pidgins and creoles in Africa. In Thomas Sebeok (ed.), *Current Trends in Linguistics 7*, 510–536. Berlin: Mouton.
Bickerton, Derek. 1984. The language bioprogram hypothesis. *Behavioral and Brain Sciences* 7. 173–221.
Bickerton, Derek. 1988. Creole languages and the bioprogram. In Frederick J. Newmeyer (ed.), *Linguistics: The Cambridge Survey 2*, 268–284. Cambridge: Cambridge University Press.
Bickerton, Derek & William W. Wilson. 1987. Pidgin Hawaiian. In Glenn G. Gilbert (ed.), *Pidgin and Creole Languages. Essays in Memory of John E. Reinecke*, 61–76. Honolulu: University of Hawaii Press.
Birken-Silverman, Gabriele. 1997. Manifestations of Alsatian-French code-switching: A typological classification. *Linguistische Berichte* 169. 196–210.
Boas, Franz. 1888. Chinook songs. *Journal of American Folklore* 1(3). 220–226.

Bold, John D. 1958. *Dictionary, Grammar and Phrase-Book of Fanagalo (Kitchen Kafir)*. South Africa: Central News Agency Ltd.
Boretzky, Norbert. 1983. *Kreolsprachen, Substrate, und Sprachwandel*. Wiesbaden: Harrassowitz.
Borgström, Maria. 1991. El desarrollo bilingüe de un niño latino-americano en Suecia. *Moderna Språk* 85(2). 187–195.
Broch, Ingvild & Ernst Håkon Jahr. 1984. Russenorsk: a new look at the Russo-Norwegian Pidgin in northern Norway. In P. Sture Ureland & Iain Clarkson (eds.), *Scandinavian Language Contacts*, 21–65. Cambridge: Cambridge University Press.
Broudy, Saul. 1970. Vietnamese Pidgin English. Ms., University of Pennsylvania.
Burch, Ernest. 2005. *Alliance and Conflict: The World System of the Inupiaq Eskimos*. Calgary: University of Calgary Press.
Calloway, Colin. 1997. *New Worlds for All: Indians, Europeans, and the Remaking of Early America*. Baltimore: Johns Hopkins University Press.
Cassidy, Frederic G. 1971. Tracing the pidgin element in Jamaican creole. In Dell H. Hymes (ed.), *Pidginization and Creolization of Languages*, 203–211. Cambridge: Cambridge University Press.
Crevenant-Werner, Danielle. 1993. Französiche Lexeme und Synonyme im Straßburger Sprachraum. Statistische und qualitative Analyse. In Volker Schupp (ed.), *Alemannisch in der Regio,* 165–180. Göppingen: Kümmerle.
De Rooij, Vincent. 1994. Shaba Swahili. In Jacques Arends, Pieter Muysken & Norval Smith (eds.), *Pidgins and Creoles: An Introduction*, 179–190. Amsterdam/Philadelphia: John Benjamins.
Dench, Alan. 1998. Pidgin Ngarluma. An indigenous contact language in North Western Australia. *Journal of Pidgin and Creole Languages* 13(1). 1–63.
Dietze, Gertrud. 1976. Aus der Praxis des Dolmetschens im Rahmen einer Europäischen Behörde. *Die Neueren Sprachen* 75(3–4). 319–326.
Dixon, Robert M. W. 1980. *The Languages of Australia*. Cambridge: Cambridge University Press.
Drechsel, Emanuel J. 1997. *Mobilian Jargon. Linguistic and Sociohistorical Aspects of a Native American Pidgin*. New York: Oxford University Press.
Duszak, Anna. 2002. Us and Others: An introduction. In Anna Duszak (ed.), *Us and Others: Social Identities Across Languages, Discourses and Cultures*, 1–28. Amsterdam/Philadelphia: John Benjamins.
Dutton, Tom. 1983. Birds of a feather: A pair of rare pidgins from the Gulf of Papua. In Ellen Woolford & William Washabaugh (eds.), *The Social Context of Creolization,* 77–105. Ann Arbor: Karoma Press.
Dutton, Tom. 1985. *Police Motu: Iena Sivarai (Its Story)*. Port Moresby: University of Papua New Guinea Press.
Dutton, Tom. 1997. Hiri Motu. In Sarah Grey Thomason (ed.), *Contact Languages: A Wider Perspective*, 9–41. Amsterdam/Philadelphia: Benjamins.
Faraclas, Nicholas G. 1990. From Old Guinea to Papua New Guinea: A comparative study of Nigerian Pidgin and Tok Pisin. In John W. M. Verhaar (ed.), *Melanesian Pidgin and Tok Pisin*, 91–170. Amsterdam/Philadelphia: John Benjamins.

Feister, Lois M. 1973. Linguistic communication between the Dutch and Indians in New Netherland 1609–1664. *Ethnohistory* 20(1). 25–38.
Flanigan, Beverly Olson. 1981. *American Indian English in History and Literature: The Evolution of a Pidgin from Reality to Stereotype*. Indiana University dissertation.
Foley, William A. 1988. Language birth: The processes of pidginization and creolization. In Frederick J. Newmeyer (ed.), *Language: The Sociocultural Context* (Linguistics: The Cambridge Survey 4), 162–183. Cambridge: Cambridge University Press.
Foley, William A. 2006. Universal constraints and local conditions in pidginization: Case studies from New Guinea. *Journal of Pidgin and Creole Languages* 21(1). 1–44.
Fox, James. 1983. Simplified input and negotiation in Russenorsk. In Roger Andersen (ed.), *Pidginization and Creolization as Language Acquisition*, 94–108. Rowley: Newbury House.
Givón, Talmy. 2009. *The Genesis of Syntactic Complexity. Diachrony, Ontogeny, Neurocognition, Evolution*. Amsterdam/Philadelphia: John Benjamins.
Goodman, John Stuart. 1967. The development of a dialect of English-Japanese pidgin. *Anthropological Linguistics* 9(6). 43–55.
Goral, Donald. 1976. Pidginization in Vietnam. *Linguistics of the Tibeto-Burman Area* 2. 233–242.
Grant, Anthony P. 1996a. Chinook Jargon in the Pacific Northwest and beyond. In Stephen A. Wurm & Darrell T. Tryon (eds.), *Atlas of Languages of Intercultural Communication in Asia, the Pacific and the Americas*, 1184–1208. Berlin: Mouton de Gruyter.
Grant, Anthony P. 1996b. The evolution of functional categories in Grand Ronde Chinook Jargon: ethnolinguistic and grammatical considerations. In Philip Baker & Anand Syea (eds.), *Changing Meanings, Changing Functions. Papers Relating to Grammaticalization in Contact Languages*, 225–242. London: University of Westminster.
Hair, Paul Edward Hedley. 1966. The use of African languages in Afro-European contact in Guinea (1440–1560). *Sierra Leone Language Review* 5. 5–26.
Hale, Kenneth L. 1971. A note on a Walbiri tradition of autonymy. In Danny D. Steinberg & Leon A. Jakobovits (eds.), *Semantics: An Interdisciplinary Reader in Philosophy, Linguistics and Psychology*, 472–482. Cambridge: Cambridge University Press.
Hall, Robert A., Jr. 1944. Chinese Pidgin English: grammar and texts. *Journal of the American Oriental Society* 64. 95–113.
Hall, Robert A., Jr. 1966. *Pidgin and Creole Languages*. Ithaca: Cornell University Press.
Haller, Hermann. 1987. Italian speech varieties in the United States and the Italian-American lingua franca. *Italica* 64(3). 393–409.
Hamilton, Philip J. 1903. *The Silent Trade; a Contribution to the Early History of Human Intercourse*. Edinburgh: W. Green.
Hammarström, Harald. 2007. *Handbook of Descriptive Language Knowledge. A Full-Scale Reference Guide for Typologists*. München: LINCOM Europa.

Hammerly, Hector. 1987. The immersion approach: litmus test of second language acquisition through classroom communication. *Modern Language Journal* 71(4). 395–401.
Hancock, Ian F. 1979. On the origins of the term pidgin. In Ian F. Hancock, Edgar Polomé, Morris Goodman & Bernd Heine (eds.), *Readings in Creole Studies*, 81–86. Ghent: Story-Scientia.
Hancock, Ian F. 1980. Lexical expansion in creole languages. In Albert Valdman & Arnold Highfield (eds.), *Theoretical Orientations in Creole Studies*, 63–88. New York: Academic Press.
Hancock, Ian F. 1986. The cryptolectal speech of the American roads: Traveler Cant and American Angloromani. *American Speech* 61(3). 206–220.
Hancock, Ian F. 1996. The special case of Arctic pidgins. In Ingvild Broch & Ernst Håkon Jahr (eds.), *Language Contact in the Arctic. Northern Pidgins and Contact Languages*, 15–32. Berlin: Mouton de Gruyter.
Harris, Barbara. 1994. Chinook Jargon: Arguments for a pre-contact origin. *Pacific Coast Philology* 29(1). 28–36.
Harrison, Simon. 1987. Cultural efflorescence & political evolution on the Sepik River. *American Ethnologist* 14. 491–507.
Haviland, John. 1979. Guugu Yimidhirr brother-in-law language. *Language in Society* 8. 365–393.
Hein, Jeanne. 1973. *Pidgin-Sprachen im Bantu-Bereich*. Berlin: Reimer.
Hein, Jeanne. 1979. Some linguistic characteristics of African-based pidgins. In Ian F. Hancock, Edgar Polomé, Morris Goodman & Bernd Heine (eds.), *Readings in Creole Studies*, 89–98. Ghent: Story Scientia.
Hein, Jeanne. 1982. *The Nubi Language of Kibera: An Arabic Creole: Grammatical Sketch and Vocabulary*. Berlin: D. Reimer.
Hein, Jeanne. 1993. Portuguese communication with Africans on the sea route to India. *Terrae Incognitae* 25. 41–51.
Hensel, Horst. 1999. Verteidigung der Muttersprache – eine neue Aufgabe für den Deutschunterricht. *Pädagogik* 51(5). 57–58.
Hewes, Gordon W. 1974. Gesture language in language contact. *Sign Language Studies* 4(1). 1–34.
Holm, John. 1988–1989. *Pidgins and Creoles*. 2 volumes. Cambridge: Cambridge University Press.
Holm, John. 2000. *Introduction to Pidgins and Creoles*. Cambridge: Cambridge University Press.
Horton, Michael. 1996. Deros: A year in Vietnam. http://jerry.pcisys.net/~drmforge/chap7.htm (downloaded 15 May 2001).
Hosokawa, Komei. 1987. Malay talk on boat: an account of Broome pearling lugger pidgin. In Donald C. Laycock & Werner Winter (eds.), *A World of Language: Papers Presented to Professor S. A. Wurm on His 65th birthday* (Pacific Linguistics A-100), 287–296. Canberra: Australian National University.
Hurault, Jean. 1983. Elements de vocabulaire de la langue Boni (Aluku Tongo). (*Special issue of Amsterdam Creole Studies VI*. Publication No. 39.) Institute for General Linguistics, University of Amsterdam.

Huttar, George & Frank J. Velantie. 1997. Ndyuka-Trio Pidgin. In Sarah Grey Thomason (ed.), *Contact Languages: A Wider Perspective,* 99–124. Amsterdam/Philadelphia: Benjamins.
Jacobs, Melville. 1932. Notes on the structure of Chinook Jargon. *Language* 8. 27–50.
Jahr, Ernst Håkon. 1996. On the pidgin status of Russenorsk. In Ernst Håkon Jahr & Ingvild Broch (eds.), *Language Contact in the Arctic. Northern Pidgins and Contact Languages,* 107–122. Berlin: Mouton de Gruyter.
Jacobs, Melville. 1936. Texts in Chinook Jargon. *University of Washington Publications in Anthropology* 7(1). 1–27.
Johnson, Samuel V. 1978. Chinook Jargon: A computer-assisted analysis of variation in an American Indian pidgin. Lawrence, KS: University of Kansas Dissertation.
Jourdan, Christine. 1991. Pidgins and creoles: the blurring of categories. *Annual review of Anthropology* 20. 187–209.
Juvonen, Päivi. 2008. Complexity and simplicity in minimal lexica. The lexicon of Chinook Jargon. In Matti Miestamo, Kaius Sinnemäki & Fred Karlsson (eds.), *Language Complexity. Typology, Contact, Change* (Studies in Language Companion Series 94), 321–340. Amsterdam/Philadelphia: John Benjamins.
Kaltenbrunner, Stefan. 1996. *Fanakalo. Dokumentation einer Pidginsprache.* Vienna/Wien: Institute für Afrikanistik und Ägyptologie der Universität Wien.
Kann, Hans-Joachim. 1999. New Germanisms in time. *Sprachdienst* 43(3). 104–108.
Karstadt, Angela. 1996. Relative markers in Swedish-American English: Evidence for a contact language phenomenon? *American Speech* 71. 27–48.
Kaufman, Terrence. 1971. A report on Chinook Jargon. In Dell H. Hymes (ed.), *Pidginization and Creolization of Languages,* 175–178. Cambridge: Cambridge University Press.
Kay, Paul & Gillian Sankoff. 1974. A language-universals approach to pidgins and creoles. In David De Camp & Ian Hancock (eds.), *Pidgins and Creoles,* 61–72. Georgetown: Georgetown University Press.
Kaye, Alan S. & Mauro Tosco. 2001. *Pidgin and Creole Languages: A Basic Introduction.* München: LINCOM Europa.
Klein, Thomas. 2006a. Creole phonology typology: phoneme inventory size, vowel quality distinctions and stop consonant series. In Parth Bhatt & Ingo Plag (eds.), *The Structure of Creole Words: Segmental, Syllabic and Morphological Aspects,* 3–21. Tübingen: Niemeyer.
Klein, Thomas. 2006b. Segmental typology of African Creole languages. In Frank Olaoba Arasanyin & Michael Pemberton (eds.), *Selected Proceedings of the 36th Annual Conference on African Linguistics,* 42–50. Somerville, MA: Cascadilla.
Klein, Wolfgang & Clive Perdue. 1997. The Basic Variety. Or: Couldn't natural language be much simpler? *Second Language Research* 13. 301–347.
Kotsinas, Ulla-Brit. 1996. Aspect marking and grammaticalization in Russenorsk compared with immigrant Swedish. In Ernst Håkon Jahr & Ingvild Broch

(eds.), *Language Contact in the Arctic: Northern pidgins and contact languages,* 123–154. Berlin: Mouton de Gruyter.

Kotsinas, Ulla-Brit. 2001. Pidginization, creolization and creoloids in Stockholm, Sweden. In Norval Smith & Tonjes Veenstra (eds.), *Creolization and Contact,* 125–155. Amsterdam/Philadelphia: John Benjamins.

Kusters, Wouter. 2003. *Linguistic Complexity: The Influence of Social Change on Verbal Inflection.* Leiden: University of Leiden Center for Linguistics.

Ladin, Wolfgang. 1982. *Der Elsässische Dialekt – Museumsreif?* Strasbourg: SALDE.

Lang, George. 2008. *Making Wawa. The Genesis of Chinook Jargon.* Vancouver: University of British Columbia Press.

Lee, Charlie. 1996. English in Malaysia – background. *Exeter Working Papers in English Language Studies* 1. 29–39.

Li, Michelle, Stephen Matthews & Geoff Smith. 2005. Pidgin English texts from the Chinese English instructor. In Geoff Smith & Stephen Matthews (eds.), *Chinese Pidgin English: Texts and Contexts* (Special Issue of the Hong Kong Journal of Applied Linguistics), 79–167. Hong Kong: Center for Applied Linguistics, University of Hong Kong.

Luffin, Xavier. 2004. *Kinubi Texts.* München: LINCOM Europa.

Luffin, Xavier. 2005. *Un Créole Arabe: Le Kinubi de Mombasa, Kenya.* München: LINCOM Europa.

Malcolm, Ian. 2001. Aboriginal English: Adopted code of a surviving culture. In David Blair (ed.), *English in Australia,* 201–222. Amsterdam/Philadelphia: John Benjamins.

Manessy, Gabriel. 1994. *Le Français en Afrique Noire: Mythe, Stratégies, Pratiques.* Paris: L'Harmattan.

Manessy, Gabriel. 1995. *Créoles, Pidgins, Variétés Véhiculaires. Procès et Genèse.* Paris: CNRS.

Marriott, Helen. 1991. Native-speaker behavior in Australian-Japanese business communication. *International Journal of the Sociology of Language* 92. 87–117.

Matras, Yaron. 2009. *Language Contact.* Cambridge: Cambridge University Press.

Mayet, Valéry. 1887. *Voyage Dans le Sud de la Tunisie.* Paris: Challamel aîné.

McWhorter, John H. 2001. The world's simplest grammars are creole grammars. *Linguistic Typology* 5(2/3). 125–166.

McWhorter, John H. 2005. *Defining Creole.* New York: Oxford University Press.

McWhorter, John H. 2007. *Language Interrupted. Signs of Non-Native Acquisition in Standard Language Grammars.* Oxford: Oxford University Press.

Mesthrie, Rajend. 2007. Differentiating pidgin from early interlanguage – a comparison of pidgin Nguni (Fanakalo) and interlanguage varieties of Xhosa and Zulu. *Southern African Linguistics and Applied Language Studies* 25(1). 75–89.

Meuwese, Marcus. 2003. *'For the Peace and Well-being of the Country': Intercultural Mediators and Dutch-Indian Relations in New Netherland and Dutch Brazil, 1600–1664.* Notre Dame, IN: University of Notre Dame dissertation.

Miestamo, Matti, Kaius Sinnemäki & Fred Karlsson (eds.). 2008. *Language Complexity. Typology, Contact, Change* (Studies in Language Companion Series 94). Amsterdam/Philadelphia: John Benjamins.
Moag, Rodney. 1979. The systems perspective: the genesis of language. In Kenneth C. Hill (ed.), *The Genesis of Language*, 62–88. Ann Arbor: Karom Publishers.
Mühlhäusler, Peter. 1997. *Pidgin and Creole Linguistics. Expanded and Revised Edition*. London: University of Westminster Press.
Mühlhäusler, Peter. 2003. Sociohistorical and grammatical aspects of Tok Pisin. In Peter Mühlhäusler, Thomas Dutton & Suzanne Romaine (eds.), *Tok Pisin Texts. From the Beginning to the Present*, 1–34. Amsterdam/Philadelphia: John Benjamins.
Naro, Anthony J. 1978. A study on the origins of pidginization. *Language* 54(2). 314–349.
Nichols, John D. 1995. The Ojibwe verb in 'Broken Oghibbeway'. *Amsterdam Creole Studies* 12. 1–18.
Nicolas, Pierre. 1900. *Notes Sur la Vie Française en Cochinchine*. Paris: Flammarion.
Norman, Arthur M. Z. 1954. Linguistic aspects of the mores of U.S. occupation and security forces in Japan. *American Speech* 29. 301–302.
Norman, Arthur M. Z. 1955. Bamboo English. The Japanese influence upon American speech in Japan. *American Speech* 30. 44–48.
Ollonne, Henri-Marie-Gustave d'. 1901. La mission Hostains-d'Ollonne. *Le Tour du Monde* 7. 193–288.
Operstein, Natalie. 1998. Was Lingua Franca ever creolized? *Journal of Pidgin and Creole Languages* 13. 377–80.
Operstein, Natalie. 2007. On the status and transmission of Lingua Franca. In Wolfgang Hock & Michael Meier-Brügger (eds.), *Dar Sloves'ny. Festschrift für Christoph Koch zum 65. Geburtstag*, 235–250. München: Otto Sagner Verlag.
Oshima, Kimie. 2002. *Gairaigo Usage in Japan: From Cultural Controversy to a New Analytical Framework*. Tokyo: International Christian University dissertation.
Parkvall, Mikael. 2008. The simplicity of creoles in a cross-linguistic perspective. In Matti Miestamo, Kaius Sinnemäki & Fred Karlsson (eds.), *Language Complexity. Typology, Contact, Change*, 265–285. Amsterdam/Philadelphia: John Benjamins.
Parkvall, Mikael & Stéphane Goyette. forthcoming. *Principia Creolica*.
Pasch, Helma. 1997. Sango. In Sarah Grey Thomason (ed.), *Contact languages: A wider perspective*, 209–270. Amsterdam/Philadelphia: Benjamins.
Polomé, Edgar. 1983. Creolization and language change. In Ellen Woolford & William Washabaugh (eds.), *The social context of creolization*, 126–136. Ann Arbor: Karoma Press.
Queffélec, Ambroise. 1995. Le français en Afrique noire. In Gérald Antoine & Robert Martin (eds.), *Histoire de la langue française*, 823–860. Paris: CNRS.

Reinecke, John E. 1937. *Marginal Languages: A Sociological Survey of the Creole Languages and Trade Jargons*. New Haven, CT: Yale University dissertation.
Reinecke, John E. 1971. Tây Bôy: Notes on the Pidgin French of Vietnam. In Dell H. Hymes (ed.), *Pidginization and Creolization of Languages*, 47–56. Cambridge: Cambridge University Press.
Roberts, Julian. 1995a. Pidgin Hawaiian: a sociohistorical study. *Journal of Pidgin and Creole Languages* 10(1). 1–56.
Roberts, Julian. 1995b. A structural sketch of Pidgin Hawaiian. *Amsterdam Creole Studies* 12. 97–126.
Roberts, Sarah J. & Joan Bresnan. 2008. Retained inflectional morphology in pidgins: A typological study. *Linguistic Typology* 12. 269–302
Robinson, Stuart. 2008. Why pidgin and creole linguistics needs the statistician: Vocabulary size in a Tok Pisin corpus. *Journal of Pidgin and Creole Languages* 23(1). 141–146.
Romaine, Suzanne. 1988. *Pidgin and Creole Languages*. London: Longman.
Rosse, Irving C. 1883. The first landing on Wrangel Island: with some remarks on the northern inhabitants. *Journal of the American Geographical Society of New York* 15. 163-214.
Samarin, William J. 1967. *A Grammar of Sango*. The Hague: Mouton.
Samarin, William J. 2000. The status of Sango in fact and fiction. On the one-hundredth anniversary of its conception. In John H. McWhorter (ed.), *Language Change and Language Contact in Pidgins and Creoles*, 301–333. Amsterdam/ Philadelphia: John Benjamins.
Sampson, Geoffrey, David Gil & Peter Trudgill (eds.). 2009. *Language Complexity as an Evolving Variable* (Studies in the Evolution of Language 13). Oxford: Oxford University Press.
Schlyter, Birgit. 2003. Sociolinguistic changes in transformed Central Asian societies. In Jacques Maurais (ed.), *Languages in a Globalising World*, 157–187. West Nyack: Cambridge University Press.
Schuchardt, Hugo. 1909. Die Lingua Franca. *Zeitschrift für Romanische Philologie* 33. 441–461. (Translated as: The Lingua Franca. In Glenn G. Gilbert (ed.), *Pidgin and Creole Languages. Selected Essay by Hugo Schuchardt*, 65–88. Cambridge: Cambridge University Press. Also in Thomas L. Markey (ed.), *The Ethnography of Variation. Selected Writings on Pidgins & Creoles*, 26–47. Ann Arbor: Karoma.)
Schweda, Nancy Lee. 1980. Bilingual education and code-switching in Maine. *The Linguistic Reporter* 23(1). 12–13.
Sebba, Mark. 1997. *Contact Languages. Pidgins and Creoles*. New York: St. Martin's Press.
Shi, Dingxu. 1991. Chinese Pidgin English: its origin and linguistic features. *Journal of Chinese Linguistics* 19(1). 1–41.
Shi, Dingxu. 1992a. Learning Pidgin English through Chinese characters. In Francis Byrne & John Holm (eds.), *Atlantic Meets Pacific: A Global View of Pidginization and Creolization*, 459–465. Amsterdam/Philadelphia: John Benjamins.

Shi, Dingxu. 1992b. On the etymology of pidgin. *Journal of Pidgin and Creole Languages* 7. 343–347.
Shnukal, Anna & Lynell Marchese. 1983. Creolization of Nigerian Pidgin English: a progress report. *English World-Wide* 4. 17–26.
Siegel, Jeff. 1982. Plantation Pidgin Fijian. *Oceanic Linguistics* 21(1/2). 1–72.
Siegel, Jeff. 1987. *Language Contact in a Plantation Environment. A Sociolinguistic History of Fiji*. Cambridge: Cambridge University Press.
Siegel, Jeff. 1990. Pidgin Hindustani in Fiji. In Jeremy H. C. Davidson (ed.), *Pacific Island Languages: Studies in Honor of G. B. Milner,* 173–197. London: School of Oriental & African Studies, University of London.
Siegel, Jeff. 2003. Substrate influence in creoles and the role of transfer in second language acquisition. *Studies in Second Language Acquisition* 25(2). 185–209.
Stefánsson, Vilhjalmur. 1909. The Eskimo trade jargon of Herschel Island. *American Anthropologist (New Series)* 11. 217–232.
Stern, Dieter. 2002. Russische Pidgins. *Die Welt der Slaven* 47. 1–30.
Stern, Dieter. 2005. Taimyr Pidgin Russian. *Russian Linguistics* 29. 289 – 318.
Stern, Dieter. 2009. The Taimyr Pidgin Russian morphology enigma. *International Journal of Bilingualism* 13(3). 378–395.
Stolz, Thomas. 1986. *Gibt es das Kreolische Sprachwandelsmodell?* Frankfurt: Peter Lang.
Tamis, Anastasios M. 1990. Language change, language maintenance and ethnic identity: the case of Greek in Australia. *Journal of Multilingual and Multicultural Development* 11(6). 481–500.
Taylor, Allan R. 1981. Indian lingua francas. In Charles A. Ferguson & Shirley B. Heath (eds.), *Language in the U.S.A.,* 175–195. Cambridge: Cambridge University Press.
Thomas, Helen. 2000. *Romanticism and the Slave Narratives: Transatlantic Testimonies*. Cambridge: Cambridge University Press.
Thomason, Sarah Grey. 1980. On interpreting 'The Indian Interpreter'. *Language in Society* 9. 167–193.
Thornell, Christina. 1997. *The Sango language and its lexicon* [Sêndâ-yângâ tî Sängö] (Travaux de l'Institut de Linguistique de Lund, 32). Lund: Lund University Press.
Todd, Loreto. 1974. *Pidgins and Creoles*. London: Routledge.
Trumelet, Corneille. 1863. *Les Français Dans le Désert: Journal d'une Expédition aux Limites du S'ah'ra Algérien*. Paris: Garnier Frères.
Ustinova, Irina. 2005. English in Russia. *World Englishes* 24(2). 239–251.
Vitale, Anthony J. 1980. KiSetla: Linguistic and sociolinguistic aspects of a pidgin Swahili of Kenya. *Anthropological Linguistics* 22. 47–65.
Van der Voort, Hein. 1994. Eskimo Pidgin. In Jacques Arends, Pieter C. Muysken & Norval Smith (eds.), *Pidgins and Creoles: An Introduction,* 137–151. Amsterdam/ Philadelphia: John Benjamins.
Van der Voort, Hein. 1996. Eskimo Pidgin in West Greenland. In Ingvild Broch & Ernst Håkon Jahr (eds.), *Language Contact in the Arctic: Northern Pidgins and Contact Languages,* 157–258. Berlin: Mouton de Gruyter.

Van der Voort, Hein. 1997. New light on Eskimo pidgins. In Arthur K. Spears & Donald Winford (eds.), *The Structure and Status of Pidgins and Creoles*, 373–394. Amsterdam/Philadelphia: John Benjamins.

Vrzić, Zvjezdana. 1999. *Negotiating Features in Pidgin/Creole Genesis: Universals and Contact Influence in Chinook Jargon Syntax*. New York: New York University dissertation.

Webster, Grant. 1960. Korean Bamboo English once more. *American Speech* 35. 261–265.

Wellens, Ineke. 2005. *The Nubi Language of Uganada: An Arabic Creole in Africa*. Leiden: Brill.

Werner, Oswald. 1963. *A Typological Comparison of Four Trader Navaho Speakers*. Indiana University dissertation.

Werner, Reinhold. 1863. *Die Preußische Expedition nach China, Japan und Siam in den Jahren 1860, 1861 und 1862*. Leipzig: F. A. Brockhaus.

West, Fred. 1973. GI-ese and instant replay. *American Speech* 48(3–4). 290–293.

Williams, Jeffrey P. 1993. Documenting the Papuan-based pidgins of insular New Guinea. In Francis Byrne & John Holm (eds.), *Atlantic Meets Pacific: A Global View of Pidginization and Creolization*, 355–367. Amsterdam/Philadelphia: John Benjamins.

Williams, Jeffrey P. 1995. A note on the pronominal system of Arafundi-Enga pidgin. *Journal of Pidgin and Creole Languages* 10(1). 171–175.

Williams, Jeffrey P. 2000. Yima-Alamblak Tanim Tok: an indigenous trade pidgin of New Guinea. *Journal of Pidgin and Creole Languages* 15(1). 37–62.

Winford, Donald. 2002. Creole formation and second language acquisition. Paper presented at the conference of the Society for Caribbean Linguistics, St. Augustine, 14–17 August 2002.

Winford, Donald. 2003. *An Introduction to Contact Linguistics*. Malden: Blackwell.

Wurm, Stephen A. 1972. Police Motu. In Peter Ryan (ed.), *Encyclopaedia of Papua and New Guinea*, 921–22. Carlton: Melbourne University Press.

Zenk, Henry. 1984. *Chinook Jargon and Native Cultural Persistence in the Grand Ronde Indian Community, 1856–1907: A Special Case of Creolization*. Eugene, OR: University of Oregon dissertation.

Zenk, Henry. 1988. Chinook Jargon in the speech economy of Grand Ronde Reservation, Oregon: an ethnography of speaking approach to an historical case of creolization in process. *International Journal of the Sociology of Language* 71. 107–124.

Creole languages

Angela Bartens

0. Short definition

A creole language is a language that has arisen from a language contact situation where speakers of a multitude of languages had to acquire a *Means of Interethnic Communication* (MIC, Baker 1990). It is a language that is capable of fulfilling all the linguistic functions of the relevant speech community. Frequently, but not always, these speakers were socially subjugated by a small elite. Creoles usually have one lexifier language, i.e. they derive the bulk of their lexicon from one language, whereas the other levels of the language structure are a result of complex processes that creolists are still trying to understand and describe in full.

1. Introduction: socio-historical settings and some basic terminological issues

The first European nation to embark on the enterprise we now know as the 'Voyages of Discovery' were the Portuguese. A crucial role came to be played by Prince Henry the Navigator (1394–1460), the driving force behind the extension of Portuguese expansion onto the African continent (the conquest of Ceuta in 1415 and subsequent exploratory expeditions down the African coast). The Spanish were to follow soon, but due to the Treaties of Tordesillas and Zaragoza (signed in 1494 and 1529, respectively), most of Asia and, more importantly, Africa, could only be claimed by Portugal. The absence of Spanish colonies in Africa (present-day Equatorial Guinea was obtained in exchange for land in the south of Brazil as late as 1777/1778), resulted in Spanish dependency on other European nations for the supply of African slaves. It has been argued that this fact is intrinsically related to the scarcity of Spanish-lexified creoles (see McWhorter 1995, 2000; but note that the quest for such language varieties is not yet over, cf. Lipski 2008). From the 17th century onwards, the French, British, and Dutch, to a limited extent also other nations for example the Danish, participated in the conquest of non-European territories.

During the final decades of the 20th century a fairly wide-spread consensus existed among creolists that basically only varieties arising from the colonial expansion of the European nation-states from the 15th century onwards were to be considered creole languages (cf. Smith 1995: 331–332). The respective European lexifier languages are English, French, Portuguese, Spanish and Dutch. Varieties lexified by languages other than the aforementioned European languages were included in the group only as long as there was sufficient socio-historical evidence that the new variety had emerged from a specific kind of language contact situation.

The most typical setting for creole emergence was (and still is) considered to be the plantation economy in which a politically and economically superior but numerically small group of people settled. These territories are typically islands that were previously uninhabited or had been rendered so through conquest. The invaders subjugated a numerical majority of people coming from a multitude of ethno-linguistic backgrounds, who had no common language and therefore had to create a Means of Interethnic Communication (MIC, Baker 1990). These plantation economies were created in the Atlantic region with the help of slave labour from the 15th century onwards. When the slave trade was abolished in the first half of the 19th century, plantation owners resorted to contract labourers. The British especially expanded their radius of action to the Southwestern Pacific. One term used for these plantation creoles is 'exogenous creoles', as neither the socially dominant nor the subjugated group was indigenous to the region (Chaudenson 1974).

Creoles also formed in enclaves where the Europeans built trade forts along their trade routes on the coasts of Africa and Asia. In these contexts, the Europeans came into contact with the indigenous population groups. These found themselves in a more egalitarian position with the newcomers, especially as far as trade was concerned. Nevertheless, a MIC was still needed between the Europeans and the often quite diverse indigenous groups as well as with populations whom the Europeans brought in from previously settled forts and colonies. The Portuguese, for instance, organised quite important population displacements around their forts bordering the Indian Ocean and in South East Asia (Boxer 1969). As a result of more intense contact with the speakers of the lexifier language, these fort creoles or 'endogenous' creoles were and still are structurally often less divergent from the lexifier language than so-called plantation creoles. This has been the case for the now largely extinct Portuguese creoles of the Indian subcontinent. Guinea Bissau Kriyôl, on the other hand, is clearly structurally further removed from Portuguese than any variety of the Cape Verdean Creole cluster to which it is historically related (cf. Rougé 2001: 84, 2005: 9), which is a result of the prolonged contact with local indigenous languages and the much lesser presence of Portuguese (cf. Bartens 1995: 28, 54, 58).

In addition to plantation and fort creoles, Bickerton (1981) introduced a third category of creoles, the Maroon creoles. This concept applies first and foremost to certain regions of the Americas that were difficult to access: the Guyanas, especially present-day Suriname, the mountainous region of Jamaica, etc. Maroons (< Spanish *cimarrón* 'wild') were slaves who had run away from plantations and formed settlements based on common ethnic origin, or on having escaped from the same plantations. Initially, the leaders of Maroon communities were African-born. But from approximately 1700 onwards, they also included former slaves born in the Americas. This has been taken as proof for the immersion of African and European-based cultural norms. Probably the most famous Maroon state, Palmares, existed for almost the entire 17th century in Northeastern Brazil. In Suriname, several maroon creoles are spoken, such as Ndyuka and Saramaccan. Outside Suriname a Maroon creole is spoken to this day in Palenque de San Basilio, Colombia, and by emigrant communities elsewhere in Colombia and in Venezuela, especially Caracas (cf. Courlander 1976; Price (ed.) 1979; Palmié 1993; Bartens 1996a: 55–61).

For a long time the language of the politically superior group and/or the group that contributed the bulk of the lexicon was called 'superstrate language'. We consider the term 'lexifier language' preferable because it reflects the role of this language more clearly. In most cases, a creole has one lexifier language, for example English or French. Jamaican Creole English, for example, is an English-lexifier creole, while Haitian is a French-lexifier creole. The other languages involved in the language contact setting are called 'substrate' or 'adstrate languages' depending on whether or not they continue to be spoken alongside the creole language. Creoles usually have one lexifier but several sub-/adstrate languages.

As so often, the exception confirms the rule and counter-examples do exist: The lexicon of Saramaccan, a Maroon creole spoken in Suriname, is derived from both English and Portuguese. However, Portuguese is clearly dominant in present-day Saramaccan (Bakker et al. 1995: 165, 168; Good 2009), with the exception being the verbal domain (Bakker 2009). The situation appears to have been the reverse in the late 18th century, which may point toward subsequent relexification (Perl 1993: 97–98; Smith 1987). Papiamentu, the creole of the Dutch Caribbean islands Aruba, Bonaire and Curaçao, has been claimed to be a Spanish-lexifier creole (Munteanu 1991), although there are strong arguments to view it as both Spanish- and Portuguese-lexified (cf. Jacobs 2012). As far as substrate languages are concerned, the non-Dutch component of Berbice Dutch, another creole spoken in Suriname, is clearly dominated by the Eastern Ijo language cluster (Kouwenberg 1993). Schwegler (e.g. 1996b) claims that the non-Spanish element of Palenquero, spoken 60 km southeast of

Cartagena de las Indias in Colombia, is KiKongo. In the case of Palenquero, however, the apparent KiKongo bias may be due to the fact that the KiKongo varieties now spoken in the Democratic Republic of the Congo (e.g. Laman 1936), are better described and more frequently consulted than descriptions of KiKongo varieties spoken in northern Angola (e.g. Bentley 1887) or the related Bantu languages Kimbundu (Philip Baker p.c.). The exceptional Eastern Ijo bias in Berbice Dutch may have been discovered by accident (Smith et al. 1987). Still, as Robertson (2011) points out, salient Ijo-derived suffixes such as *-apu* forming nominal plurals, *-are* for durative and habitual imperfectives and *-e* for the perfective aspect were morphophonologically reduced or even replaced (as in the case of imperfective *doz*) before the language became extinct. This suggests that other creoles may have undergone similar reduction and replacement processes before proper documentation became available. It is possible that interesting cases of substrate influence were never discovered and that Berbice Dutch is not as exceptional as it is presented in the literature.

As a result of the context they are spoken in, the substrate languages of exogenous creoles have usually ceased to coexist with the creoles at some point in history. Nonetheless, in some contexts the numerically and/or culturally more prominent substrate languages appear to have lived on as adstrate languages in the new setting for quite a long time. According to Alleyne (1986: 307–311), Twi survived in Jamaica until the early 20th century. Warner-Lewis (1996: 36) claims that (varieties of) KiKongo and Yoruba were maintained in Trinidad until the second half of the 20th century. There is little doubt that the introduction of indentured labourers after Emancipation in 1883 helped keep up collective language skills. At the same time, the retention of African languages in the New World has been cited as a reason for the non-formation of creole languages in parts of the Americas (see Noll 1999: 165 for Brazil).

Endogenous creoles, on the other hand, tend to coexist with their adstrate languages, although population movements may turn some of them into substrate languages as the corresponding population group moves out of the area and new adstrates are added as a result of immigration. This can be exemplified by the previously mentioned case of Guinea Bissau Kriyôl and closely related Casamance Portuguese Creole of Senegal. When the Portuguese first arrived in the region in the 1440s, the most important current adstrate languages, Mandinka and Wolof, were already spoken there. Only Temne, used as a vehicular language at the time (especially in the kola nut trade) is no longer spoken in the region and is now limited to Sierra Leone (Rougé 1994).

Some creolists have argued that a creole can only be identified where a socio-historical setting of extreme social inequality can be documented. After all, 19th century contract labourers in the Pacific region were not much better off than slaves in the Atlantic area from the 15th to the 19th centuries. This notion has been questioned only fairly recently. McWhorter (1998, 2005, 2011) has proposed a specific configuration of linguistic features (see section 2.2), the co-occurrence of which would warrant identifying a language as a creole without knowing anything about its socio-history. This again would allow us to identify more creoles that are not lexified by European languages, alongside the 'established' creoles. (For a recent discussion of non-Indo-European pidgins and creoles, see Versteegh 2008.) Holm (1989), for instance, discusses only 24 varieties that were lexified by other languages, as opposed to 64 English-, Portuguese-, Spanish-, Dutch- and French-lexified ones. Among the former the majority are pidgins and jargons, while among the latter the majority are creoles. McWhorter's approach has drawn much criticism (e.g. Mufwene 1999, 2009; DeGraff 2001, 2005; Ansaldo and Matthews 2007). One point of criticism relates to the fact that he lumps creoles with non-creoles (Bakker et al. 2011: 7; see also Hagège 2001: 170). It is of course possible that a language might be discovered some day that will show the feature configuration discussed by McWhorter for creoles, but which has arisen in situations that are distinct from the ones that have given rise to the majority of recognised creoles (cf. Gil 2001). In the meantime, a growing body of studies supports the idea that creoles do indeed constitute a distinct typological class (most recently Bakker et al. 2011).

Another long-standing controversy exists in Creole Studies, namely the idea that creoles arise from pidgins as a result of nativization. This is also known as the life-cycle model, introduced by Hall (1962: 151) and taken up by Bickerton (1981, 1984), among others. Pidgins, in turn, could have arisen from jargons (see Bakker 2008; and Parkvall and Bakker in this volume for definitions). Creolists working on French-lexifier creoles have often claimed that pidgins do not constitute a pre-requisite for creolisation (Alleyne 1971; Chaudenson 1978, 2001; Mufwene 2001), though the arguments remain unconvincing. However, the category of so-called 'extended' or 'expanded' pidgins, called "pidgincreoles" by Bakker (2008), has challenged the life-cycle model. These languages are referred to as pidgins since none or very few of their speakers acquired them as a first language. Yet compared to 'ordinary' pidgins they show considerable structural expansion. It is therefore no longer justified to argue that a pidgin can only evolve into a creole when spoken by a population that has acquired it as its first language. Instead, the crucial feature of a creole language is that it can fill all the communicative and stylistic functions that are needed in a speech community (cf. Bartens 1996a: 137; Bakker 2008: 137). Nigerian Pidgin English and (Papua New Guinean) Tok Pisin (see also Romaine 1988: 68–69) are examples of 'pidgincreoles' (despite their misleading names). It is also worth mentioning that Baker (2002) attempts to identify pidgin features in a number of creoles.

2. Creole Studies

2.1. Different approaches to creole genesis

Originally, the term 'creole' was used to refer to persons, animals and plants originating from elsewhere but born and raised in or autochthonous of a colony. For instance, Holm (1988: 15) mentions a 1590 attestation of *criollo* for Spanish descendants born in the West Indies. This meaning prevails in Spanish, where for example in historiographical discourse the *criollos* are Spaniards born in the American colonies. Haitians speak until this day of *riz créole* 'creole rice' and *cochons créoles* 'creole pigs'. The extension of the term to designate languages is a later development.

The first mention of a creole language (without calling it a creole) is possibly found in a travelogue written by the Portuguese André Álvares de Almada in 1594. It refers to present-day Guinea Bissau, though the quote is subject to interpretation:

> [...] os negros de esta aldeia, por serem muito entendidos e práticos na nossa língua [...] Entre estes negros andam muitos que sabem falar a nossa língua portuguesa [...]
>
> [the Africans of this village who knew and used our language [...] There are many among these Africans who know how to speak our language] (Almada ([1594] 1946: 48, 59) cited in Do Couto 1994: 34–35; my translation)

It is not quite clear what kind of Portuguese the Africans mentioned in the text were speaking. Pinto Bull (1989: 71) was the first to suggest that the reference was to a Portuguese-lexifier pidgin or even creole.

The term 'creole' is explicitly used to refer to a language in two travelogues written in the years 1684 and 1685. The Portuguese Francisco de Lemos Coelho (1684) mentions the "creoulo de Cacheu" in current Guinea Bissau (Couto 1994: 35) and the Frenchman M. J. De La Courbe (1685) writes:

> Il y a parmi eux [les Malinké] de certains nègres et mulastres qui se disent Portugais parce qu'ils sont issus de Portugais qui y ont habité autrefois; ces gens-là, outre la langue du pays, parlent encore un certain jargon qui n'a

que très peu de ressemblance à la langue portugaise et qu'on nomme créole comme dans la Mediterranée la langue franque.

[Among them [the Malinké] there are certain Negroes and Mulattoes who claim to be Portuguese because they are descendants of Portuguese who lived there before; alongside the tongue of the country, these people speak a certain jargon which has very little resemblance with the Portuguese tongue and which is called creole like the Lingua Franca in the Mediterranean.] (Tarallo and Alkmin 1987: 98; my translation)

In all three cases, reference is most likely made to a predecessor of the Portuguese-based creoles now spoken in Guinea Bissau and the province Casamance in Senegal, or, more accurately, their predecessors.

In all likelihood, De La Courbe was alluding to the functional similarity of the Mediterranean Lingua Franca and the creole he observed. The following passage from Father Sandoval's description of the slave populations of Cartagena de las Indias, Colombia, *De instauranda Aethiopium salute* (written in 1617–1619 but published in 1657), has been interpreted as proof of (or at least as hinting at) the possibility of a monogenetic model of creole genesis, namely the transplantation of the Portuguese-lexifier creole of São Tomé to Cartagena (Granda 1970: 6–10), although this passage, too, is ambiguous:

[...] y los que llamamos criollos y naturales de San Thomé, con la comunicación que con tan bárbaras naciones han tenido el tiempo que han residido en San Thomé, las entienden casi todas con un lenguaje muy corrupto y revesado de la portuguesa que llaman lengua de San Thomé, al modo que ahora nosotros entendemos y hablamos con todo género de negros y naciones con nuestra lengua española corrupta, como comúnmente la hablan todos los negros.

[and we call them Creoles and natives of São Tomé, as a result of their interaction with such barbarous nations during their stay on São Tomé, almost all of them understand it by means of a kind of corrupted language which is distorted Portuguese and they call it "language of São Tomé", just as we now understand and communicate with all kinds of negroes and other nations with a corruption of our Spanish language in the way as it is commonly spoken by all negroes.] (Granda 1970: 6; my translation)

In 1640, the Frenchman Jacques Bouton recorded some examples of a jargon containing words of French, Spanish, English, and Dutch origin that was used by Caribs on Martinique. This jargon seems to have caught his attention precisely because of the mixture of languages. The French priest Pelleprat wrote in 1659 that the African slaves on the island spoke a variety of French corrupted by their owners in order to facilitate communication (Holm 1987: 16).

Quite often it took a speaker of a language that was different from the lexifier language to realise that the language in question constituted an autonomous speech variety. For instance, the German traveller Georg Meister noticed that the people of Batavia spoke a Portuguese-lexifier creole ("Indianisch-Portugiesisch", as he called it). He published a short dialogue in the language in his 1692 travelogue *Der Orientalisch-Indianische Kunst-und Lustgärtner* (recently edited and translated by Maurer (2011: 343–348), who calls it a "pidgin"). The 'transcription' of the dialogue, which reportedly took place between a Dutch and a Swedish soldier, reflects the notion which would have been prevalent among Europeans for a much longer time, namely that creoles were a gibberish put together from different sources, in this case including Latin, French and Dutch (Schuchardt 1890: 14–15).

The first descriptive works on creole languages were produced in the 18th and early 19th centuries. Most of these works were composed by Protestant missionaries of Moravian and other origin. In 1731, Count Nikolaus von Zinzendorf had granted land to the Moravian Brethren in 1722, when he met Andres, a slave from St. Thomas, at the coronation ceremony of the Danish King Christian VI. Zinzendorf was deeply moved by the slave's request to send missionaries to his community. The German missionaries who were sent there tried to communicate in Dutch with the slaves who spoke the Dutch-lexifier creole Negerhollands (now extinct), but to little avail. The missionaries learned the creole language, developed a writing system and started teaching the slaves to read and write in their language. This launched the Moravian tradition of descriptive work on creole languages, a characteristic of which was the early recognition of creoles as autonomous language systems.

Other orders followed suit. The Danish Lutheran missionary Joachim Melchior Magens published the first Negerhollands grammar in 1770, frequently considered the first grammar of a creole language in print (Holm 1988: 17–18). In 1777 the Moravian missionary Christian Oldendorp published a history of the Virgin Island mission, which "contains a dozen pages on the creole" (Holm 1988: 18). The original (much longer) manuscript was published in 2000 (Oldendorp 2000). In fact, the printed book was a profoundly modified and abridged version of the original manuscript, produced by Johann Jakob Bossart, which was published in 1777. Christian Georg Andreas Oldendorp's critique and reclamations went unheeded (Baldauf 2000: 9, 13). Oldendorp's original description of Negerhollands, though never published as a separate volume like Magens (1770; see also Dyhr 2001), probably dates from the same period or even prior to Magens' grammar (Oldendorp 2000: 681).

The Moravians also described the Suriname creoles Sranan and Saramaccan. C. L. Schumann produced a 55-page dictionary of Saramaccan in 1778 (Kramp 1983) and a 135-page dictionary of Sranan in 1783 (Holm 1988: 20). Another Moravian, Johannes Andreas Riemer, stayed in Suriname in 1779–1780 and compiled a manuscript of another Saramaccan dictionary, possibly influenced in part by the Schumann dictionary edited in Arends and Perl (1995). They also published three early Sranan texts: Herlein (1718), Nepveu (1770) and Van Dyk (c. 1765), as well as three Saramaccan letters written in 1790–1791. Van Dyk's manual for "Bastert Engels" is discussed in Schuchardt (1914: xxii) as well. The 1780s also saw the publication of the first Malayo-Portuguese grammar and dictionary and the first text in Haitian Creole (Holm 1988: 20).

In the 19th century, the number of publications on creole languages increased. Ducœurjoly (1802) is a guide to Haiti including sample conversations and a dictionary part. The Wesleyan Mission Press started publishing texts in Sri Lanka (then Ceylon) Creole Portuguese in 1818. A first Papiamentu catechism was published in 1925, the entire New Testament in Sranan in 1829, followed by descriptions of various other French-lexifier creoles (Goux 1842 on Lesser Antillean; Thomas 1869 on Trinidad Creole French; Saint-Quentin 1872 on Guyanais; Baissac 1880 on Mauritian; and Mercier 1880 and Fortier 1885 on Louisianais). Further a grammar and two dictionaries of Sranan were printed (Anonymous 1854; Focke 1855; and Wullschlägel 1856, respectively) as well as the first descriptions of Guinean Kriyôl (Bertrand-Bocandé 1849) and Jamaican Creole English (Russell 1868; Holm 1988: 20–24).

It seems warranted to say that creole languages became the subject of scientific enquiry only during the second half of the 1800s. Addison Van Name's *Contributions to Creole Grammar* (1869–1870) draws on earlier descriptions and work with informants and constitutes the first comparative study. One of the pioneers of comparative Creole Studies, the German-Austrian philologist Hugo Schuchardt, published approximately 700 pages on creole languages, most of them during the 1890s. It has been claimed about his writings that he presented all the theoretical tendencies manifest in 20th-century creolistics in an embryonic form (Gilbert 1980). In other words, he did not represent any single theoretical position. The Portuguese philologist Adolfo Coelho, a contemporary of Hugo Schuchardt, supported the view that creoles were the outcome of universals of (imperfect) L2 acquisition.

During the first half of the 20th century, creole languages became a recognised object of inquiry for such linguists as the Dutchmen J. van Ginneken and Dirk Christian Hesseling and the Haitian Suzanne Sylvain.

Hesseling (1923: 59) took up Schuchardt's idea of semi-creolisation ("Halbkreolisch", Schuchardt 1889: 480), though he was mainly concerned with Afrikaans, which he argued had stopped halfway in the process of becoming a creole. Reinecke (1937: 559) first used the term "semi-creole" when discussing Afrikaans, and this was calqued by Silva Neto (1950a: 12, 1950b: 166) as *semi-crioulo* when referring to relusitanised varieties of Indo-Portuguese and the varieties of Portuguese that may have been spoken by non-Portuguese during the early settlement of Brazil. In the 1980s and 1990s, Holm reintroduced the term 'semi-creolisation' into Creole Studies (e.g. 1992) but subsequently abandoned it as socio-politically inadequate (2004: xii-xiii). In addition, the term 'semi-creole' can be criticised for having been used for languages with quite diverse distances to their respective lexifier languages (cf. Bartens 1998).

Whereas Van Ginneken and Hesseling favoured universalist explanations in terms of imperfect L2 acquisition, Sylvain, a trained Africanist, was a defender of the central role of sub- and adstrate languages in the first instance. She is remembered for her 1936 definition of Haitian Creole French as "un français coulé dans le moule de la syntaxe africaine, [...] une langue éwé à vocabulaire français [a form of French cast in the mould of African syntax, [...], an Ewe language with French vocabulary]" (Sylvain 1936: 178). Holm (1988: 37–38) nevertheless reports a personal communication by Robert A. Hall Jr., according to which this was not Sylvain's own opinion but an addendum requested by her mentor. In 1928, Rudolph (Rodolfo) Lenz published a grammar of Papiamentu (Lenz 1928) that is still useful to modern-day scholars.

The aforementioned John E. Reinecke has been called the "Father of modern Creole Studies" (Holm 1987: 38) because of his (at the time) comprehensive 1937 dissertation on 'marginal languages', i.e. jargons, pidgins, and creoles. Others see the pertinent milestone in a conference organised in 1959 in Mona, Jamaica, as a result of which creolistics emancipated itself from emergent (North American) sociolinguistics (cf. Bartens 1996a: 69). At first, there was a strong theoretical polarisation between advocates of the so-called monogenesis and polygenesis hypotheses. The monogenesis theory argued that all creoles can be traced back to an Afro-Portuguese Pidgin and possibly even to the Mediterranean Lingua Franca, which were subsequently relexified to form present-day creoles. In its strong version it stated that all creoles can be traced back to a Portuguese pidgin. Taylor (1963) and Whinnom (1956) were the most vigorous defenders of the theory. More recent evidence, both intra- and extra-linguistic, has rendered this scenario untenable. Whinnom's strongest argument in favour of the monogenesis hypothesis was the alleged transplantation of a Portuguese creole from the Moluccas to the Manila Bay area (Philippines) at the beginning of the 17th century. Even though this scenario is – at least to a certain extent – possible according to historical records, the transplanted creole appears to have constituted at best a minor ingredient in the formation of the Philippine Spanish-lexifier creoles (Lipski 1986, 1988). Subsequently, monogenesis within a certain group of creoles has been proposed, especially in the case of English-lexifier Atlantic creoles (Hancock 1986; McWhorter 1997), but also for the Atlantic French- and Dutch-lexifier creoles (Goodman 1964, 1987).

Advocates of the polygenesis hypothesis drew on different types of universals in order to explain creole genesis: universals of L2 acquisition, L1 simplification (i.e. 'Foreigner Talk'), and cognitive universals of L1 acquisition. Derek Bickerton (1974 and subsequent) has been a key contributor in this area. His models inspired a vibrant discussion, as scholars took issue with his 'Language Bioprogram Hypothesis' and the arguments that related to semantic transparency and tendencies inherent to the lexifier languages or substrate influence, including 'relexification' from the substrate languages into creoles. Claire Lefebvre (e.g. 1986) has been an advocate of the relexification hypothesis, although in her most recent work it is no longer as manifest. Siegel (2008: 210) reminds us of the light that L2 research can shed on pidgin and creole genesis, and Veenstra (2008: 234–235) emphasises the roles of L1 and L2 acquisition as well as substrate influence in creole genesis. The field has continued to expand and while it may still have been possible to present a rather concise overview in the early 1990s, it is no longer now.

At present, mono-causal explanatory models like the ones introduced above no longer find any advocates (Kouwenberg and Singler 2008: 5–6; Winford 2008: 43). Instead, the focus has shifted to the question of whether it could be possible to identify a creole on the basis of linguistic features alone after all, or whether socio-historical information is a necessary and crucial part of the definition. As stated above, McWhorter (1998 and subsequent), Bakker et al. (2011), and others argue in favour of the first, while others, e.g. Holm (2004: xiv), strongly defend the second. Seuren and Wekker (1986), among others, have also put forward arguments in favour of the hypothesis that creoles are indeed structurally distinguishable from non-creoles. Over the past decade or so, this theoretical discussion has been linked to more global issues. Thus DeGraff (2001, 2005, etc.) argues that the idea that creoles (as 'young' languages) are structurally less complex than 'old' languages amounts to a claim that creole speakers are different from, and possibly inferior to, speakers of 'normal' languages.

An older discussion concerns the speed of the creolisation process, i.e. whether creole languages typically crystallise rapidly, within, say, 25 years, roughly corresponding to a generation (especially during earlier centuries), or whether the development occurs more gradually. The latter position has been supported especially by those who have studied creoles documented in earlier centuries, such as the Suriname creoles, e.g. the late Jacques Arends (cf. Arends 1989, 1993). On the other hand, scholars studying French-lexifier creoles have considered creolisation to be a fairly rapid process where no intermediate pidgin stage is required (see section 1 above). Pidginisation was an essential element of Bickerton's hypothesis.

A third, still unresolved issue regards the related concepts of a 'creole continuum' and 'decreolisation'. The creole continuum is a model developed from the 1960s onwards by such scholars as Bailey (1966, 1971), DeCamp (1971), and Bickerton (1973, 1975). The creole continuum model seeks to account for variation in creole speech production by attributing linguistic features to different sectors of a scale that stretches from the basilect, the variety furthest away from the lexifier language, via the intermediate stage of mesolect, to the acrolect, which is the variety closest to the lexifier language. An assumption inherent in this model is that the basilect represents the original creole, whereas all further developments constitute 'decreolisation' towards the acrolect. However, scholars like Chaudenson (1992) have proposed that the inverse development may have been prevalent, i.e. that 'basilectalisation' rather than decreolisation has occurred in several cases. Chaudenson argues that French became more creole-like with each generation of non-native learners.

Many creoles coexist in a more or less stable diglossic relationship with their lexifier languages. This situation could theoretically lead to structural adjustment towards the lexifier languages as for instance schooling in creole becomes more accessible. However, even in the cases where contact with the lexifier language has not been interrupted, decreolisation cannot be postulated without the support of textual evidence. As a matter of fact, there is evidence from a number of creoles documented at earlier stages of their diachrony that the overall language structure may have changed very little over time (e.g. Wood 1972 on Papiamentu). A more plausible explanation for the apparent phenomenon of decreolisation is that variation has existed in creole speech communities throughout their history, but that the numerical proportions of different speaker groups have changed over time, thus leading to the impression that decreolisation has taken place (Bartens 1996a: 140). The Jamaican Creole continuum is a good example (D'Costa and Lalla 1989: 5–6). This does not mean that there are no instances of genuine decreolisation. Indeed, in certain contexts, prolonged contact with the lexifier language almost inevitably leads to decreolisation. This appears to be the case of Nicaraguan Creole English as described by

Holm (1978), as opposed to the present-day variety documented in Bartens (in preparation).

As remarked above, variation is an inherent characteristic of creole languages. While different groups of speakers employ different varieties, variation also occurs in the speech of a single speaker. Now it might be argued that this speaker is adjusting her speech production to particular contexts and situations. However, this is not always the case: Speakers may employ variants belonging to different sectors of the hypothetical creole continuum even within a single sentence without there being for instance phonotactic or morphosyntactic requirements to choose one or the other variant. In such cases it is impossible to argue that variation would be indicative of any kind of language change (Bartens 2008).

Language change obviously occurs in creoles just as in any other living language. However this change is not always linear, but rather cyclical. In fact, cycles of recreolisation account for cases where a creole is transplanted from one territory to another. Considering that the ethno-social make-up of the population usually varies from one contact situation to another, in this case between the speech communities involved before and after transplantation, we may speak not only of diffusion but of a model or mechanism of componential diffusion in which the components consist of the specific socio-historical input (both linguistic and populational) in a given context (cf. Bartens 1996a: 133–145, 2000b, 2005; also Hancock 1986; Holm 1986). This model accounts for such situations as the diverse varieties of Cape Verdean Creole Portuguese, the Spanish-lexifier creoles of the Philippines or the relationship between Jamaican and e.g. San Andrés Creole English. In the last case, San Andrés Creole English is a second generation creole vis-à-vis Jamaican, which is the first generation creole or parent language. The genetic relationships between the English-based creoles of the Western Caribbean have become obscured as a result of the frequent back and forth migrations in the area. Bocas del Toro Creole English, essentially created by immigrants from San Andrés to Panama, could therefore be considered a third generation creole.

Finally, creolists traditionally have considered how in slavery contexts the subjugated majority would aim at learning the politically dominant minority's languages and that this would also have been possible to a certain extent in early colonial settings. These were called "société d'habitation" ('dwelling' or 'cohabitation societies') by the French creolist Robert Chaudenson (Chaudenson 1979, 1992). The term captures settings where the numerical gap between the two groups was still relatively small. When the corresponding societies moved on to the next stage, the "société de plantation" (plantation societies), the increase in the need for labour would have rendered even the acquisition of an approximation of the coloniser's language impossible. This, in turn, would have led to the formation of 'genuine' creoles (Chaudenson 1992). During the "société d'habitation" phase of the English and French colonies, which lasted approximately until the mid-17th century in the Caribbean, the linguistic input of the European contract workers and, to a lesser degree, the Filibusters and Buccaneers, must have contributed to the emerging varieties (cf. Fleischmann 1983, 1986). But even this scenario seems questionable. Based on what we know about resistance and cultural reinterpretation in creole societies, it seems more likely that slaves and contract labourers in plantation societies first aimed at creating a 'Means of Interethnic Communication' (MIC; Baker, e.g. 1998: 346) when no common language was available. Communication with each other was at least as important as acquiring a perfect copy of the oppressor's language. As noted above, African languages continued to coexist and to function as such MICs for much longer than creolists initially assumed.

2.2. The *raison d'être* of the field and recent debates

In his (2002) article entitled "Cutting off the branch", Mikael Parkvall discusses the view still widely held by creolists that creoles are essentially the result of imperfect L2-acquisition and that they do not differ from other languages in any way other than with regard to the circumstances of their genesis. If true, this leads to a state of affairs where the field has no justification for its existence. In this way, he argues, mainstream creolists are cutting off the very branch they are sitting on. Following McWhorter's thesis (McWhorter 1998 and subsequent), he states that "creolistics has a place among the various subfields of linguistics *if it studies phenomena that are more profitably studied within creolistics than simply as part of general linguistics or any of its other subdisciplines*" (Parkvall 2002: 361; italics in the original). As a result, creolistics would no longer be able to inform general linguistic theory with regard to language creation and linguistic universals, a view still widely held in the early 1990s (e.g. Muysken 1988: 288–289).

Even if creoles are seen as no different from other languages, their specific features still require an explanation. Mufwene (2001) has taken up the notion of a feature pool, later discussed by Aboh and Ansaldo (2007). It is a mechanism akin to koineization, a term traditionally used when talking about the levelling of features among varieties of the same language (cf. Tuten 2003). The specific ecology of the language contact situation determines which features are selected from a pool of available linguistic features. According to Mufwene (2006: 464), it is irrelevant whether the idiolects in contact are native or xenolectal. Many internal and external ecological factors are not yet fully understood. They all bear on the competition and selection of certain variants in creole genesis, which would resemble the intervention of an "invisible hand" in Keller's terms (1994). Although Mufwene considers creoles as continuations of their lexifiers (note also the postulation of a koineization process), he does not deny the influence of substrate languages (Mufwene 2001: 12, 28; see also Mufwene 1986). This framework, adopted by other scholars as well, essentially refutes the notions of simplicity and complexity that are inherent to McWhorter's approach, while nevertheless admitting that in case of doubt complexity is the more useful notion for describing the 'hybrid phenotypes' of creoles (e.g. Aboh and Smith 2007: 19; Aboh 2007: 323, 340). Plag (2011) and McWhorter (2012) have criticised the feature pool approach.

The framework outlined by McWhorter (1998 and subsequent, latest version 2011) for identifying a creole consists of the following prototypical configuration:

– a lack of inflectional morphology (other than at most two or three inflectional affixes),

– a lack of tone on monosyllabic words, and

– a lack of semantically opaque/non-compositional derivation

This prototype has been subject to critique (see, inter alia, the multiple commentaries to McWhorter 2001). Gil (2001) argues that, according to this metric, Riau Indonesian should be a creole, yet extra-linguistic evidence suggests that it is not. On a much more modest scale, Bartens (2009a) has argued that Iberoromance-lexifier creoles do possess opaque derivational morphology, albeit to different degrees, which of course refers to only one of the criteria stipulated by McWhorter.

At the same time, there is a growing body of research that gives empirical support to the idea that creoles are indeed less complex or simpler than other languages (Parkvall 2008). This does by no means imply that creoles lack complexity altogether. Even more importantly, these findings apply to creoles as a group and do not exclude the fact that some non-creoles may be even less complex than creoles (Bakker et al. 2011: 8). In addition, irrespective of the complexity issue, creoles are similar to each other in the sense that they have a specific typological profile which cannot be explained either by a specific lexifier language, the type of creole (plantation, fort, maroon), the geographical area or the assumed age of the creole. The same most likely also applies to the substrate languages involved. Creoles like Krio, Ndyuka and Jamaican on the one hand, and

Cape Verdean and Guinea Bissau Creole Portuguese on the other, constitute an exception as they derive at least in part from a common ancestor (cf. Bakker et al. 2011: 10, 25, 28, 30).

Interestingly, Huber et al. (2011) working with the *Atlas of Pidgin and Creole Language Structures* (APiCS) data have found that the pidgins and creoles in the sample appear to cluster according to lexifier language. Bakker et al. (2011), however, have attributed only limited importance to the lexifier language. What is more, in phylogenetic network modelling, creoles clearly cluster together and not with languages which Bakker et al. (2011: 31–32) call "morphologically challenged". The reason for the relative lack of complexity – or "frills" or "ornaments" as McWhorter (2005: 99, 139) labels the features of many non-creoles – is the fact that initially an MIC was created that was subsequently expanded to meet all the communicative needs of the speech community (cf. Baker 2001). Expansion could take place through grammaticalisation (Bakker et al. 2011: 36) – whether language-internal or substrate-influenced and thus more obvious (Bruyn 2008) – or else through reanalysis (i.e. a restructuring process where no proper grammaticalisation has to be postulated, for instance the recruiting of the French past participle *été* as an anterior marker; cf. Detges 2000).

Studies of creole typology often draw on data from comparative studies such as Hancock (1987) and Holm and Patrick (eds., 2007). A major breakthrough in our knowledge of creole typology can be expected from the up-coming publication of the *Atlas of Pidgin and Creole Language Structures* (APiCS) coordinated through the Max Planck-Institute for Evolutionary Anthropology in Leipzig (Michaelis et al. to appear).

In the meantime, refuters of creole exceptionalism (cf. also Winford 2008: 43) find it difficult to keep defending their position; cf. "Creoles are a class of languages distinguished from others by a high degree of language hybridity" (Aboh 2011). As a matter of fact, no one has claimed that speaking a creole language implies less cognitive processing, a postulate attributed to the defenders of creole exceptionalism; cf. "Until now, there is no study showing that if you speak a creole language, you engage in less cognitive processing" (Aboh 2011).

2.3. A brief note on cultural creolisation

Current Anglophone creolistics largely concentrates on language description and the formulation and testing of models of creole genesis. Recent years have also seen an upsurge of interest in applied issues such as education and language revitalisation (see, for instance, Siegel 1999, 2005,

2006a, 2006b; and Migge, Léglise and Bartens (eds.) 2010). Cultural aspects continue to be treated in other fields such as Anthropology, Folkloristics, Religious Studies, Musicology, and History. See, in this case, the seminal work by Abrahams (1984), Bascom (1992), Courlander (1976), Dawthorne (1981), Herskovits (1966), Herskovits and Herskovits (1936, 1958), Jackson (1990), Wilson (1973), and many others. Again, over the past few years, this situation has changed to some extent, particularly when the object of study is the language-culture interface, e.g. specific types of discourse. For instance, Faraclas et al. (2005) compare ritualised insults in Nigerian Pidgin English and African American Vernacular English. Figueroa (2005) revisits the phenomenon of "suck-teeth" (a gesture and accompanying sound widely used in Africa and the diaspora) previously discussed by Rickford and Rickford (1981) and Figueroa and Patrick (2002). Farquharson (2005) examines homophobic speech acts by which Jamaican Dancehall deejays construct a positive (heterosexual and masculine) face for themselves while threatening and even violating both the positive and the negative face of homosexual listeners.

Price (2007: 29–32) recalls that although the concept of 'creolisation' was originally taken over by anthropologists from linguistics (and has more recently been appropriated by other fields, see below), creolists studying languages should be aware of the findings of historians and anthropologists if an accurate picture of linguistic creolisation is to be achieved. For instance, Saramacca society must have formed by the mid-18th century to resemble present society much more than any African society (Price and Price 1999: 277–308), a fact that doubtlessly had bearings on the crystallisation of the language. Just like linguistic creolisation, cultural creolisation processes (Palmié 2006) are unique, depending on the specific circumstances, and are not unidirectional (Price 2007: 23; Berlin 1998: 3, 5). Contrary to the stance of so-called African-centred scholars, current research on cultural creolisation emphasises to an increasing degree that cultural and historical creolisation processes have been extremely complex, akin to a repeated miracle. The formation of New World African identities such as 'Yoruba' or 'Nago' (term used for the Yoruba in colonial Brazil) are first and foremost discursive formations (Matory 2005: 56–57; Trouillot 2002: 191). The re-creation of African identities is also discussed for example by Schwegler (1996a, 1998, 2011) and Álvarez López (2004; see below).

Research published in the Portuguese- and Spanish-speaking academic world still seems to be seeking its own particular note. However with regard to cultural aspects (other than linguistic, considering, as we do, that language is a central component of culture), the discussion is very similar to that of the Anglophone academic context as outlined above (but see e.g.

Granda 1977: 282ff. on the hybrid character of the folklore of the Colombian province of Chocó where features of Medieval Romance literature appear to predominate).

In French-language and particularly French academia, on the other hand, the rupture between scholars studying linguistic and other aspects of creole societies that are former French colonies has been much less pronounced. See, for instance, d'Ans (1987) for a global view of Haitian society and culture, and Benoist (1972) for the same for the French Antilles, Price-Mars (1973) on Antillean Folklore, Métraux (1958) and Pluchon (1987) on the Haitian Benin-derived but syncretic (with Catholicism) religion Voodoo. Bougerol (1983), writing on traditional medicine in Guadeloupe, shows that the roots of Guadeloupean traditional medicine (which may appear alien to most Westerners) lie more in Europe than in West Africa. Lafontaine (1982) described French Antillean musical traditions and Laplante (1972) discussed the cosmovision of the predominantly White inhabitants of Marie-Galante (a sister island of Guadeloupe), to name but a few studies. Our argument in favour of the integration of results of such fairly specialised studies into French-language creolistics is bolstered by the considerations offered by Chaudenson (1992: 290, 2001). According to him, creolisation affects certain domains more strongly than others: Folklore is most susceptible to incorporating foreign influence, music constitutes first and foremost an expression of common identity, medicine and cuisine are shaped by external circumstances and language use is dictated by the dominance of a specific group (cf. however the MIC postulated by Baker 1990). The observation that creolisation does not affect all facets of the cultural system to an equal degree finds its replica in the formulation of Nunes (1994), according to whom different levels of a creole language system do not manifest the same degree of basi-, meso- or acrolectality (given that creoles tend to be defined as being globally more or less basi- or acrolectal for these terms; see section 2).

Nowadays, research on cultural creolisation is no longer restricted to (formerly) creole-speaking communities, a fact that has also been criticised (e.g. Sheller 2003: 188–196). Cohen (2007) conceives of cultural creolisation as a way of contemplating cultural globalisation and cross-fertilisation in as distinct societies as Brazil, South Africa, and the USA. Cox (2004) applies the concept to (post-)colonial Argentina.

Following Price (2007: 18), who argues for the usefulness of the concept of 'creolisation' to the understanding of the formation of Afro-American cultures, Bolland (2006: 1) states that creole cultures were 'discovered' at the height of the ideological decolonisation of the Caribbean during the 1970s, "when the analysis of the origins of a common culture in a creole community became part of the process of nation-building". According to the author, the concept of cultural creolisation retains its importance "because it avoids both the view that enslaved Africans were stripped of their cultures and acculturated into a European culture, and also the view that evidence of the African heritage in the Caribbean lies only in 'retentions' or 'survivals'" (Bolland 2006: 1; cf. also Burton 1997: 6). He also signals the problems and conflicts involved in extending the concept to groups of other ethnic origin and/or located in other geographic regions (Bolland 2006: 9–10). In the long run, the concept of 'creolisation' may prove more useful than Herskovits' (1966) "acculturation", Ortiz' (1940) "transculturation" or Bastide's (1967) "cultural interpenetration" (Price 2007: 18).

3. Prototypical features of creole languages

In this section, I discuss a number of prototypical features of creole languages. By prototypical I mean that the features are considered to be characteristic of creoles, since their occurrence in this group of languages is very frequent. However, no single feature nor a particular combination of features need to occur in order to make a language a creole. In this way, I understand the terms 'prototype' and 'prototypical' in a less restrictive manner than McWhorter (1998 and subsequent). The discussion is divided into phonetics/phonology, morphology, syntax, lexicosemantics, and pragmatics. I give examples from different lexifier creole languages. There is, however, a certain bias in favour of creoles spoken in the Atlantic region.

3.1. Phonetics and phonology

3.1.1. Syllable structure

Creole languages tend to follow the universal tendency towards the crosslinguistically most frequent syllable structure CV, which is also the most typical syllable structure found in African languages (cf. Maddieson 2011; Clements 2000: 140), and in fact in the languages of the world. For instance Portuguese-lexifier Sãotomense has [ʃipiˈtali] 'hospital' < Portuguese *hospital* (Ferraz 1978: 44). Non-adherence to this tendency often reflects a lower degree of creolisation or adstrate influence, cf. Maquista (Macao Creole Portuguese) *isquevê* 'to write' < Portuguese *escrever* and *lichim* 'slippery, smooth' < Malay *licin* (Fernandes and Baxter 2004: 92, 100). On the other hand, aforementioned Sãotomense which is usually taken to be quite basilectal, permits consonant clusters where the second element is the liquid /l/ arising from metathesis of the original Portuguese lexemes, as in [ˈklupa] 'blame' < Portuguese *culpa*, [vlɛˈgoɲa] 'shame' < Portuguese *vergonha*, and a few cases of word-initial /ʃtl/ as in [ʃtlɛˈka] 'to surround' < Portuguese *cercar*, at times presenting a variant with /ʃkl/ (Ferraz 1978: 46–47). Word-initial /ʃtl/ is also found in Portuguese items incorporated into Kishikongo, e.g. /ʃtliˈʒyõ/ 'surgeon' < Portuguese *cirurgão* (Bartens 1996b: 75). The additional change /r/ > /l/ occurring in *vergonha* > [vlɛˈgoɲa] will be discussed below.

In Principense, one of the basilectal Gulf of Guinea creoles, the Portuguese definite article has been agglutinated to some nouns in clear violation of the CV syllable structure. In most cases, we are dealing with the masculine definite article *o* but there are also instances of the feminine article *a*: *ugalu* 'rooster' < Portuguese *o galo*, *ugatu* 'cat' < Portuguese *o gato*, *apa* 'spade, shovel' < Portuguese *a pá* (and even *i*; see below). In a few cases there appears to be a mismatch between the gender of the Portuguese article and the resulting Principense form: *ubuka* 'mouth', cf. Portuguese *a boca*, *arê* 'king', Portuguese *o rei* (cf. Maurer 2009: 213, 239), which cannot be explained in terms of the changes of gender certain nouns underwent during the history of the Portuguese language (cf. Gouveia 1993). Recent work by Hagemeijer (2009) suggests that different chronological layers need to be distinguished in the formation of the Gulf of Guinea creoles. The Portuguese gender distinction would have played a role only in the oldest stratum. The relevant mechanism was adapting nouns to the pattern of Edoid languages where all nouns start with a vowel, a remnant of a former noun class system. Subsequently, vowel harmony processes (see section 3.1.2) became predominant, leading to such forms as Principense *ixize* 'ashes' < Portuguese *cinza* 'ash'. Among the Gulf of Guinea creoles, Principense and to a lesser degree Annobonese have retained many nouns with vowel agglutination, whereas Sãotomense and especially Angolar, which subsequently underwent strong influence from Bantu languages, retained very few.

French-lexifier creoles feature the (partial) agglutination of the definite and partitive articles, e.g. Haitian *lékol* 'school' < French *l'école*, *diri* 'rice' < French *du riz* 'some rice', *zòrèy* 'ear' < French *les oreilles* 'the ears'. This phenomenon is even more widespread in the French-lexifier creoles of the Indian Ocean. For instance, considering only count nouns featuring an initial syllable entirely derived from a French article, Baker (1984) identified 112 cases in Haitian but 471 in Mauritian, 337 in Rodrigues and 444 in Seychelles Creole French. The latter three, spoken in the Indian Ocean, have undergone influence from Bantu languages, which is why the author suggested Bantu class prefixes might have played a role in the recruitment of the forms. A very important motive for these cases of morpheme boundary shift is nevertheless also constituted by the facts that in spoken French, these specific items almost canonically occur with articles, and that the resulting forms begin with a CV-syllable. Forms like *zongles* '(finger)nails' < French *les ongles* /lezõŋgl/ can equally be observed in both L1- and L2-acquisition of French (cf. Tremblay and Demuth 2007; Carroll 2004).

Similar shifts of morpheme boundaries also occur, albeit to a lesser degree, in creoles lexified by other languages, cf. Papiamentu *sanka* 'buttocks' < Spanish *las ancas*, Portuguese *as ancas*, Sãotomé Creole Portuguese *zonda* 'wave' < Portuguese *as ondas* 'waves' (Maurer 1986: 8), or Sranan *didibri* 'devil' < English *the devil* (Holm 1988: 97).

The fact that there is a tendency towards CV syllables and, consequently, CVCV morpheme structure (Romaine 1988: 63), is by no means absolute. Plag and Schramm (2006) demonstrate that even in the earliest documented varieties of certain English-lexifier creoles, CV was not the only possible syllable structure. Klein (2011) also studied creole syllabification, and found creoles unremarkable compared to non-creoles on this count.

3.1.2. Phonological systems

As far as creole phonological systems are concerned, they differ to varying degrees from those of their lexifier languages. Furthermore, as Smith (2008: 103) notes, the vowel systems of creoles tend to resemble those of their lexifier languages more than their consonant systems do.

In general terms, cross-linguistically more marked sounds of both lexifier and substrate languages tend to be eliminated from a creole's phonological system as a result of creolisation. More marked phonemes present in adstrate languages are more likely to be conserved as a result of the ongoing language contact situation: For example, unlike in Spanish and Portuguese, /ŋ/ has phonemic status in Ternate Spanish Creole Chabacano ([ŋa] 'emphatic particle'; Sippola 2011: 50) and possibly in Guinea Bissau Creole Portuguese ([ˈluŋa] 'moon' < Portuguese *lua*; Kihm 1994: 15–16; Couto 1994: 69). In Guinea Bissau Creole Portuguese word-initial /ŋ/ is restricted to borrowings from adstrate languages, e.g. the Mandinka loan [ŋoroto] 'scythe' (Kihm 1994: 16). The phonological system of Ternate Chabacano also features the glottal stop /ʔ/ typical of Philippine languages such as Tagalog, cf. [ʔaˈsa] 'to roast' < Spanish *asar* vs. [kaˈsa] 'to marry' < Spanish *casar* (Sippola 2011: 46).

For marked phonemes of the lexifier languages, let us consider the French rounded front vowels /y, ø, œ/: only very acrolectal varieties of French-lexifier creoles conserve them. Other creoles deround them to [i, e, ɛ] as in Haitian *dife* [diˈfe] 'fire' < French *du feu* [dy fø] 'part fire', *kè* [ˈkɛ] 'heart' < French *cœur* [ˈkœr] is the general outcome. Likewise, French /ə/ is replaced by /e/ or /i/ (e.g. Mühlhäusler 1986; Brousseau 2011). Philippine languages in general lack the relatively more marked sound /f/, and all Chabacano varieties replace Spanish /f/ with /p/, e.g. *puelza* 'strength' < Spanish *fuerza*.

English-lexifier creoles have replaced /θ/ and /ð/ with /t/ (occasionally /f/) and /d/, respectively. San Andrés Creole English features *ting* 'thing', *dis* 'this'. In the Suriname creoles, /t/ is selected for /θ/ in initial, /f/ in non-initial position, e.g. *tifi* 'tooth' < English *teeth* (Smith 2008: 105). On the other hand, in Angolar Creole Portuguese, both /θ/ and /ð/ have phonemic status although they occur in complementary distribution with /s, z/ where the latter are used before /i/, the former before all other vowels, at least excluding recent borrowings from Portuguese and São Tomé Creole Portuguese where /s, z/ are frequent (Maurer 1995: 30, 37). According to Lorenzino (1998: 76), the interdental fricatives are increasingly being replaced with both alveolar and palatal sibilants by younger but also older speakers of Angolar. The same author discusses proposals of substratal origin, all of which seem unlikely (Lorenzino 1998: 76), a scenario also hinted at by Bartens (1998b: 183).

The cross-linguistically marked sounds /x/ and /ɣ/ have been lost in Dutch-lexifier creoles, e.g. Saramaccan /dáka/, Berbice Dutch /daka/ < Dutch *dag* /dax/, and Sranan /éigi/ < Dutch /ɛiɣə/ (Smith 2008: 105–106).

A plausible context for the preservation of marked phonemes of the substrate languages are loanwords, but at times they also occur in words of lexifier origin. The occurrence of such phonemes usually correlates with the more basilectal character of a creole. In the case of the Atlantic creoles, these cross-linguistically marked phonemes are first and foremost the implosive stops /ɓ, ɗ/, the labiovelar doubly articulated stops /k͡p, g͡b/ and the prenasalised stops (or sequences), above all /mb, nd/.

The implosive stops /ɓ, ɗ/ occur at least in São Tomé, Angolar and Principe Creole Portuguese and the Surinamese (mainly) English-lexifier creoles Ndyuka and Saramacca (Ferraz 1978: 21; Maurer 1995: 28, 2009: 9; Smith 2008: 107). In the first four varieties there are no voiced plosive counterparts /b, d/ in the phonological system (cf. Smith 2008: 107). Maurer (2009: 9) nevertheless reports /b/ to occur as a variant of the labiovelar stop /g͡b/ in the speech of some speakers of Principense, e.g. *igbê – ibê* 'body'. Likewise /k͡p/ has the variant /p/ which does form part of the phonological system, e.g. *ukpaka – upaka* 'skin' (probably from Edo *ègbé*,

Emai *égbè* 'skin' and Edo *íkpàkpá* 'skin, peel, bark', Emai *úkpàkpà* 'scale of fish', respectively (Maurer 2009: 220, 239). In Angolar /ɗ/ and /r/ appear to be in free variation, as in *ɗa – ra* 'to give' (< Portuguese *dar*), which leads Maurer (1995: 29, 37) to conclude that only /ɓ/ has phonemic status. In Sãotomense, the degree of implosion is variable (Ferraz 1978: 21). In Saramaccan, where the existence of implosives was discovered only recently (Haabo 2002), two strata of English-derived lexicon can be identified according to Smith and Haabo (2007), thus calling for a re-evaluation of the proportion of the original English-derived lexicon with initial implosive labial stops vis-à-vis Portuguese and a later stratum of borrowings from Sranan with initial plain voiced stops, cf. *ɓaáka* 'black' < English *black* vs. *bégi* 'to beg, pray' < English *beg* (Smith and Haabo 2007: 104).

The labiovelar doubly articulated stops /k͡p, g͡b/ occur at least in Saramaccan and Ndyuka (Smith 2008: 107), and the Gulf of Guinea creoles Angolar and Principense (Maurer 1995: 28, 2009: 9). In Saramaccan, /k͡p, g͡b/ occur in West African lexical retentions such as *agbán* 'earthenware pot' < Fon *agbăn* 'dish, pot', *dɛkpɛ* 'dagger' < Fon *dɛnkpɛ* 'cutlass' and in items from disparate sources originally containing /kw, gw/ with some allophonic variation between the two realisations. The realisations [k͡p, g͡b] are typical of Upriver, [kw, gw] of Downriver Saramaccan, e.g. *kpéfa – kwéfa* 'baby's bonnet' < Portuguese *coifa* 'coif', *kpéi – kwéi* 'to square off the end of a log' < English *square* (Smith 2008: 107–108). Maurer (2009: 10) observes that the labiovelar doubly articulated stops are not very frequent in Principense: /g͡b/ occurs in 24, /k͡p/ in 11 lexical items, cf. *ugbami* 'chin' and *ukpami* 'fish dryer (frame)'. As far as the first item is concerned, Maurer (2009: 239) identifies cognates for it in Etsako (*ɛkpàmĩ*), Edo (*àgbɑ̀mḛ́*), and Emai (*àgbɑ̀*).

Prenasalised stops are less restricted to basilectal creoles. The most frequently occurring phonemes are /mb, nd/ but larger inventories can also be found. Angolar Creole Portuguese features the series /mp, mb, nd, ndʒ, nk, ng, nf/ (Maurer 1995: 28, 37). At present there is nevertheless variation between prenasalised and simple stops in Angolar, e.g. *mbézi – mézi* 'month' < Portuguese *mês*, which suggests that prenasalised consonants constitute a weak point in the phonological system of Angolar and that a linguistic change might be underway (Maurer 1995: 34). Indeed, a similar scenario has been proposed for those areas of Spanish-speaking America for which the hypothesis of a previous pan-Hispanic creole has been formulated (e.g. Granda 1976: 5–6): the nasal element of prenasalised stops would have been lost even in lexical items of African origin, supposedly due to the perceived stigmatised character of those phonemes (Granda 1988: 101, 201), cf. *gombo* 'okra' < Kimbundu, KiKongo *kiŋgombo* (e.g.

Parkvall 2012: s.v.). Interestingly, Lipski (2012: 77) finds no synchronic evidence for prenasalised consonants in Afro-Bolivian Spanish but observes that they exist in literary texts containing imitations of pidginised Afro-Hispanic language from colonial Bolivia.

The fact that prenasalised stops, at least in the minimal inventory /mb, nd/, are not restricted to relatively basilectal creoles correlates with the fact that they widely occur in lexifier-origin vocabulary. For instance, Cape Verdean Creole Portuguese, often considered an acrolectal creole, features prenasalised stops in Portuguese-derived items such as *nbarka* ['mbarka] 'to embark' < Portuguese *embarcar*, *nzami* 'exam' < Portuguese *exame* (note that the latter must be of fairly recent origin). Palenquero has *ngalá* [ŋga'la] 'to seize hold of' < Spanish *agarrar* 'to seize hold of, grab', *mbosa* 'bag' < Spanish *bolsa*, *ndo* 'two' < Spanish *dos*. As the first linguistic documentation of Palenquero occurs in Bickerton and Escalante (1970), it is impossible to determine the time depth of the phenomenon but it may constitute part of the general re-Africanisation tendency in the community over the last few decades (cf. Schwegler 1998: 276) and observed in other Afro-American communities, e.g. Álvarez López (2004) on an Afro-Brazilian community. At times one can question whether we are dealing with prenasalised stops or sequences consisting of a nasal and a stop, cf. Smith (2008: 109), Maurer (1995: 33–34), Bartens (1996b: 78).

The instability of apical consonants, especially /r/ and /l/, is a result of the convergence of universal tendencies and the phonemic inventories of sub-/ adstrate languages. As a result, the neutralisation of the opposition /r/ – /l/ results more frequently in lambdacism than in rhotacism but we may find both processes in the same language, e.g. Angolar *mari* 'bad' < Portuguese *mal* and *alê* 'king' < Portuguese *o rei* (Maurer 2009: 257). At times, other apical sounds are involved as well, cf. Palenquero *ría* 'day' < Spanish *día*, *kumina* 'food' < Spanish *comida*, *pelo* 'dog' < Spanish *perro*.

In French- and Portuguese-lexifier creoles which have been influenced by African languages, nasalisation of vowels has both superstratal (regressive nasalisation only) and substratal (both progressive and regressive) origin, whereas the nasalisation of Atlantic English-, Spanish- and Dutch-lexifier creoles has to be attributed to the substrate (Bartens 1996a: 111–112). In Haitian Creole French, nasal assimilation goes beyond the word boundary, as in *jũ* in the following example:

(1) *bɛt la te afɔ̃m jũ mũn* Haitian Creole French
 animal ART.DEF ANT form ART.INDF person
 'The animal had the shape of a human being.'
 (Tinelli 1981: 145)

Vowel harmony is a long-distance assimilatory phonological process. Smith (1975) and McWhorter and Good (2012) show that some of the Surinam creoles display ATR (Advanced Tongue Root) harmony. In creole languages generally, vowel harmony affects typically but not exclusively the selection of epenthetic and paragogic vowels. Meanwhile, no complete vowel harmony systems have been copied into the emerging creoles from African languages possessing them (e.g. Ewe, Fante, KiKongo). Vowel copying in epenthetic and paragogic vowels has been attributed to substratal influence (e.g. Holm 1988: 124–125). Paragogic vowels are more frequent in the creoles of the Atlantic than the Pacific region and have therefore been attributed to African substrate languages, whereas the insertion of epenthetic vowels can be satisfactorily explained by universal phonological tendencies (Singh and Muysken 1995). Some examples of vowel harmony from Annobonese are: affecting an epenthetic vowel: /ˈxabala/ 'goat' < Portuguese *cabra*; a paragogic vowel: /ˈsukulu/ 'sugar' < Portuguese *açúcar*; progressive /ʃiˈzolo/ 'scissors' < Portuguese *tesoura*; regressive /seˈbe/ 'to know' < Portuguese *saber*. Note that it is not necessarily the vowel of the stressed syllable which is copied, as in the case of epenthetic /ˈutulu/ 'other' < Portuguese *outro* [ˈoutru], [ˈoːtru] (Ferraz 1976: 39–40).

Palatalisation of consonants tends to occur cross-linguistically before close front vowels or palatal glides. In Sãotomense there is a near complementary distribution where /tʃ, ʤ, ʃ, ʒ/ occur before the close front vowels /i, ɪ/ and the glide /j/, and /t, d, s, z/ before all other vowels, e.g. /vɛˈdɛ/ 'truth' < Portuguese *verdade* vs. /ˈtaji/ 'afternoon' < Port *tarde*. Similar distributional patterns are found in several distinct KiKongo varieties (Ferraz 1978: 22–23, 51–52). Caribbean French-lexifier creoles frequently palatalise /t, d/ before /j/ and /k, g/ before the close/mid front vowels /e, ɛ, y, œ/ and the diphthong /ɥi/, all resulting in /tʃ, ʤ/. This process has been linked to dialectal variation between varieties of Twi on the one hand, which have /tj, dj/ or /kj, gj/, and parallels in 17th and dialectal varieties of French on the other (Holm 1988: 131–133; Hull 1968). The puzzling thing is that /k, g/ followed by /i/ do not palatalise (Smith 2008: 122–124). Caribbean English-lexifier creoles present some lexical items with /c, ɟ/ partly reflecting British usages subsequently replaced by /k, g/ or /tʃ, ʤ/ (cf. Cassidy and LePage 1980: lviii, 238; Alleyne 1980: 58), cf. San Andrés Creole English *gyal* [ɟaɫ] 'girl', *kyan* [cæn] 'can'.

To conclude this section, Tables 1 and 2 below summarise the phonological system of San Andrés Creole English, the variety we are most familiar with, even if it does not contain such cross-linguistically marked sounds as implosives, or doubly articulated or prenasalised stops.

Table 1. The vowel system of San Andrés Creole English

	front	central	back
close	i, iː, ĩ		u, uː
close-mid	e		o
open-mid	ɛ̃		
open		a, aː, ã	

Table 2. The consonant system of San Andrés Creole English

		bilabial	labio-dental	dental/alveolar	palato-alveolar	palatal	velar	labio-velar	glottal
plosive	vl	p		t		c	k		
	vd	b		d		ɟ	g		
nasal		m		n			ŋ		
trill				r					
fricative	vl		f	s	ʃ				h
	vd		v	z					
affricate	vl				tʃ				
	vd				dʒ				
approx.				l		j		w	

3.1.3. Suprasegmental phonology

Creoles, like all languages of the world, can be divided into stress-accent, pitch-accent and tone languages. Stress accent languages mark one syllable of all words except clitics as prominent through longer duration, or greater amplitude or changes in pitch. Pitch-accent languages feature restricted tone systems that make use of high tones to mark one syllable of the word as prominent (Smith 2008: 112–113).

European lexifier languages are stress languages, whereas African languages rely on pitch, as either tone or pitch-accent languages. During creolisation, the European language's primary stress accents would be reinterpreted as high tones and the creole word's stress accents would move to other syllables. A typical example of such a pitch-accent language is Papiamentu. Bisyllabic verbs of Iberoromance origin have the tone sequence LH and form their participles by means of stress shift from the penultimate to the last syllable. Nouns can be derived from these verbs by reversing the tone sequence to HL whereas stress remains on the first syllable, e.g. *máta* 'to kill' (HL), *matá* 'killed' (LH), *kaská* 'to peel' (LH), *káska* 'peel' (HL). *Pápa* 'porridge' (HL) and *papá* (LH) 'father' form an example of a lexical opposition (Kouwenberg and Murray 1994: 12, 15). In Papiamentu, only approximately 250 lexical items are distinguished by tonal oppositions, thus not warranting its characterisation as a tone language (Joubert 1991; Smith 2008: 115). Tone plays no role in the grammar of Papiamentu.

For San Andrés Creole English, only a small number of rising tone – falling tone oppositions have so far been identified, which can be grammatical, lexical, or pragmatic, e.g. *kyan* 'can' (rising – falling) vs. *kyaan* 'cannot' (falling – rising), *huol* 'whole' (rising – falling) vs. *huol* 'to hold' (falling – rising), *no* 'no' (falling), vs. *noh* 'no (emphatic)' (rising).

Stress accent languages are no rarity among creoles: Berbice Dutch, otherwise strongly influenced by tone language Eastern Ijo, is such a language (Kouwenberg 1993). Only the Gulf of Guinea creoles Angolar and Principense appear to be genuine tone languages (Maurer 1995, 2009). As Annobonese appears to reflect a proto-Gulf of Guinea Creole together with Principense (cf. Hagemeijer 2009), it is not to be excluded that Annobonese is a tone language as well. Granda (1992) suggests that Annobonese is a tone language. The example in (2) from Post (1995: 194) shows that "[s]yllables with long vowels are not obligatorily stressed, but they are always pronounced with a high rise tone while the following syllable, stressed or not, is pronounced with a high tone" (Post 1995: 194):

(2) [páːtu] LH-H 'plate'
 [páːtu] LH-H 'plate'
 [pátu] H-H 'bird'

 [déːntʃi] LH-H 'in front of'
 [déntʃi] H-H 'tooth'

 [keːsé] LH-H 'to grow up'
 [kesé] HH (sic.; H-H) 'to forget'

3.2. Morphology

It is often claimed that creole languages do not possess morphology. For instance, two of the structural features on the basis of which McWhorter (1998 and subsequent) claims that creole languages can be identified as such without knowing anything about their sociohistory deal with morphology: (i) no or very little inflectional morphology; (ii) only transparent and compositional derivational morphology.

Farquharson (2007) points out several morphological phenomena in creoles. A growing body of research makes it clear that the previously fairly frequently formulated postulate that creoles do not possess morphology has to be refuted, although there is a tendency towards simplification in the morphological domain, especially as regards inflectional morphology (pidgins tend to possess more inflectional morphology than creoles; Bakker 2003, 2008: 142). According to Crowley (2008: 77), this simplification can be understood in terms of the avoidance of redundancy and sequences of inflectional and derivational morphemes, regularisation (including the reduction of allomorphic variation and suppletion), and transparency (including the avoidance of discontinuous morphology and portmanteau morphemes). Other authors prefer to speak of analyticity which is not to be equalled with simplicity. Siegel et al. (in press) demonstrate, however, that at least Tok Pisin and Hawaii Creole English are not more analytical but less synthetic than non-creole languages, i.e. there is a higher rate of analyticity to syntheticity.

Inflectional morphology is more likely to be retained in acrolectal creoles. The Barlovento varieties of the Cape Verdean language cluster feature Portuguese conjugational morphemes and even subjunctive forms, although the latter appear to be fossilised. Likewise, the Indo-Portuguese creoles conserve a multitude of Portuguese conjugated verb forms (cf. Clements 1996: 111–112; Cardoso 2009: 109–112). Angolar Creole Portuguese of São Tomé Island, on the other hand, expresses only the indefinite article and the adjectivally used past participle by means of inflectional morphology, according to the metrics of Arends et al. (2006: 225–226). Inflectional morphology is also more likely to be retained when the sub-/adstrate languages involved in creole genesis are typologically relatively uniform as in the case of the Pacific region English-lexifier creoles (Keesing 1988; Crowley 2008: 80). In certain cases, substratal inflectional morphology is also retained, as in the case of Palenque Creole Spanish KiKongo-derived *ma-* used as a plural marker of nouns, e.g.

(3) ma   nimá   ta   aí   Palenque Creole Spanish
    PL   animal   be   there
    'The animals are there.'
    (Schwegler 2011: 239)

A similar scenario applies to derivational morphology. Creoles which are more acrolectal and have remained in contact with the lexifier language show a larger inventory of derivational morphemes than more basilectal creoles which have had little contact with their lexifiers. Studying six Portuguese- and Spanish-lexifier creoles, Bartens (2009a) found that the inventory of Angolar Creole Portuguese consists of three productive suffixes. Arends et al. (2006) consider *-du/-ru* an inflectional suffix since they do not take into account its use for emphasising adjectives and *môtxi* 'a lot, much'. The lists cited for Cape Verdean Creole Portuguese (Santiago variety) and Papiamentu consist of a multitude of derivational affixes. On closer inspection, however, it becomes clear that only part of the derivational affixes of Cape Verdean and Papiamentu are productive: Prevailing contact with the lexifier languages has left the possibility open that derived constructions formed in them, were borrowed as unanalysed lexical units. Guinea Bissau and 19th-century Sri Lanka Creole Portuguese, on the other hand, have (had) less contact with the lexifier and more productive use is (was) made of derivational morphology. In the case of Sri Lanka Creole Portuguese, contact with English and the preservation of Portuguese dialectal forms led to allomorphy. Prolonged language contact with the indigenous languages of present-day Guinea Bissau resulted in the incorporation of the Manding causative suffix *-ndi* as *-ndV/-ntV*, with the Portuguese suffix *-antar* nevertheless probably having played a converging role (cf. *ciganta* 'to make arrive' < *ciga* 'arrive' < Portuguese *chegar*). Finally, Chabacano (Zamboanga and Cotabato varieties) has eight derivational prefixes all of which are of Philippine, mainly Ilongo, origin, whereas ten out of the twelve suffixes are of Spanish origin. Some of the latter are of questionable productivity (see also Steinkrüger 2003: 257). In general terms, the derivational morphology of Chabacano testifies to the hybrid character of the language, which has emerged as a result of centuries of language contact. In the creoles surveyed, the productive derivational morphology is mostly used in a transparent manner. Counterexamples do occur, although at least Guinea Bissau Creole Portuguese *mamesiñu* 'stepmother', *papesiñu* 'stepfather' (lit. 'small mother/father') are probably calques from adstrate languages. Just as Guinea Bissau Creole Portuguese has borrowed a causative affix from Manding as a result of prolonged language contact, Papiamentu features the not very productive Dutch-origin suffix *-shi* (< Dutch *-tie* '-tion') as in *redashi* 'rumour' < *reda* 'to spread a rumour'.

So far, only lexifier languages, substratal and adstratal (whether a prestige language like Dutch in the case of Papiamentu or an indigenous language like Ilongo or Mandinka) have been discussed. Veenstra (2006) argues for discontinuity in creole genesis where a given structure, in this case the Saramaccan polyfunctional derivational suffix *-ma*, does not directly arise from the languages involved in the contact situation but rather as a result of "a breakdown of grammatical cohesiveness" and "innovations within the child population" (2006: 218).

Obviously, creole morphology also arises as a result of grammaticalisation. It can be argued that, at least for some creoles, the TMA (tense-mood-aspect) particle systems, which most saliently set creoles apart from their lexifier languages, constitute a most illustrative example. TMA markers are usually grammaticalised from lexifier language auxiliaries or adverbs occurring in verbal periphrases. For example the Haitian progressive marker *ap* is derived from the French verbal periphrasis *être après à/de* + infinitive which survives in Quebecois French (Gougenheim 1971), but is otherwise unknown in modern French:

(4) *m   ap   manje*   Haitian Creole French
    1   PROG eat
    'I am eating.'
    (DeGraff 2007: 104)

Nevertheless, as signalled in section 2.2, grammaticalisation can also be apparent, or rather a question of reanalysis than of grammaticalisation proper, as in the case of the French creole anterior marker *t(e)* derived from the French past participle *été*, cf.

(5) *Bouki te   konn   repons   lan*   Haitian Creole French
    Bouki ANT   know   answer   ART.DEF
    'Bouki knew the answer.'
    (DeGraff 2007: 103)

In some creoles, e.g. Sranan (Smith 1987: 225) and Ternate Chabacano (Eeva Sippola p.c.), it is a matter of definition and/or convention whether such TMA markers should be considered inflections or particles.

In the nominal domain, where European lexifier languages use inflectional morphology to mark number and, in the case of Romance lexifiers, also gender, creoles resort to analytical structures actually pertaining to the level of syntax. A typical pluralisation strategy which mostly has sub-/adstratal parallels is the use of the 3rd person plural pronouns, e.g. Tok Pisin (an English-lexifier creole spoken in Papua New Guinea):

(6) *Ol   mangi   (i)   kam   na   ol   (i)*   Tok Pisin
    PL   child   (SRP)   come   and   3PL   (SRP)
    kros   pait
    be.angry   hit
    'The children came and they fought.'
    (Faraclas 2007: 367)

or Principense:

(7) *ina mosu me*   Principense
    PL   boy   1SG.POSS
    'my sons'
    (Maurer 2009: 31)

Note that Tok Pisin and Principense are different from many other creoles in that the pronominal plural marker is preposed, unlike most creoles, which have postposed plural markers.

Animacy and definiteness are factors which usually increase the likelihood of overt plural marking. Other determiners such as numerals may take the plural marker's place but may also co-occur with it, cf. Principense:

(8) *ine dôsu mosu*   Principense
    PL   two   boy
    'the two men'
    (Maurer 2009: 32)

This same plural marker also forms the associative plural. The reading then is 'X and his/her family/friends etc.', cf. San Andrés Creole English:

(9) *Alma-dem*   San Andrés Creole English
    Alma-PL
    'Alma and her family'

and Principense:

(10) *ine Pedu vika*   Principense
    PL   Pedu   come
    'Pedu and his family/his friends came.'
    (Maurer 2009: 33)

The Asian Portuguese-based creoles resort to reduplication as a means of forming nominal plurals (see example (24) below).

Instead of marking (morphological) gender, creoles mark an animate referent's sex if this is relevant for the interpretation of the message. As a result, gender marking is less frequent than plural marking. The predominant strategy is to either pre- or postpose the lexical items meaning 'man', 'woman', e.g. Principense:

(11) *minu omi* Principense
    child man
    'son'
    (Maurer 2009: 30)

(12) *minu mye* Principense
    child woman
    'daughter'
    (Maurer 2009: 30)

All creoles also contain lexicalised pairs of nouns indicating the two genders, e.g. Kabuverdianu:

(13) *baka* 'cow', *toro* 'bull' Kabuverdianu

and San Andrés Creole English:

(14) *kou* 'cow', *bul* 'bull' San Andrés Creole English

(15) *gyal* 'girl', *bwai* 'boy' San Andrés Creole English

Just like derivational forms, compounds can be borrowed as unanalysed lexical units from the lexifier or another language. In addition, they can be calqued, as is the case with the following compounds, which are widespread both in the Atlantic creoles and their African substrate languages:

(16) *ai-waata* San Andrés Creole English
    eye-water
    'tears'

(17) *doa-mout* San Andrés Creole English
    door-mouth
    'entrance'

(18) *swiit-mout* San Andrés Creole English
    sweet-mouth
    'to flatter'

However, compounding generally constitutes a highly productive morphological strategy of lexicon building in creoles, e.g.:

(19) *maunten   paia*   Tok Pisin
     mountain   fire
     'volcano'
     (Crowley 2008: 86)

(20) *nil-fis*   Bislama
     nail-fish
     'porcupine fish'
     (Crowley 2008: 86)

Substrate patterns such as the order of the head and the modifier tend to be retained in pidgins and creoles (Brousseau 1989).

Reduplication, understood as "the combination of the formal change involving iteration with a certain semantic and/or categorical change [which] can be stated as a word formation rule" (Kouwenberg 2003: 1), is at times considered the least marked of all morphological processes (Haiman 1980). Typical meanings achieved by reduplication are 1. intensification; 2. aspectual; 3. pluralisation; 4. augmentation and accumulation; 5. distribution; 6. indeterminacy; 7. attenuation; and 8. other/miscellaneous (derivational). Following Kouwenberg and La Charité (2003), functions 1–3 can be regarded as inflectional, functions 4–8 as derivational. Beside 'inflectional' and 'derivational', it is also possible to use the terms 'iconic' and 'non-iconic'. Non-iconic reduplication is mostly language-specific and can be considered semantically complex and marked, thus a good candidate for the transfer hypothesis. Haiman's (1980) claim of reduplication being the least marked of phonological processes therefore does not take into account non-iconic reduplication or the patterns of partial reduplication, which are sometimes very idiosyncratic.

In a study of ten Portuguese- and/or Spanish-lexifier creoles, Bartens (2004) found essentially the same distribution of the functions as outlined in Kouwenberg and La Charité (2003). Aspectual functions were divided into a. iterative/ frequentative/ habitual and b. durative/ continuative/ progressive. Function 7, attenuation, also termed "X-like reduplication" by Kouwenberg and La Charité (2003), included such functions as "dispersive", "diminutive", and "approximation" (cf. Kouwenberg and La Charité 2003: 14). Finally note that function 1 is typical of adjectives and adverbs, 2 of verbs, 3 and 4 of nouns, and 5 of numerals. The results of the study are summarised in Table 3. Note that 2a stands for "iterative/ frequentative/ habitual", 2b for "durative/ continuative/ progressive".

Table 3. Functions of reduplication in Portuguese and/or Spanish-lexifier creoles (+ = presence, - = absence, (+) = marginal presence of the function in question)

	1	2a	2b	3	4	5	6	7	8
Cape Verdean Creole Portuguese, Santiago variety	+	+	-	-	-	+	-	-	+
Guinea Bissau Creole Portuguese	+	+	+	-	(+)	+	-	-	+
São Tomé Creole Portuguese	+	+	+	+	+	+	+	(+)	+
Angolar Creole Portuguese	+	+	+	-	+	+	-	-	+
Principense Creole Portuguese	+	-	(+)	-	+	+	-	-	(+)
Indo-Portuguese	+	(+)	+	+	-	+	-	-	+
Malayo-Portuguese and Papia Kristang (Creole Portuguese)	+	+	+	+	+	+	+	+	+
Macaista Creole Portuguese	+	+	+	+	-	+	+	-	+
Chabacano	+	+	+	+	-	+	+	+	+
Papiamentu	+	+	-	-	+	+	-	-	+

Examples of the languages and functions are given below:

(21) intensification (function 1) Guinea Bissau Creole Portuguese
pikininu-pikininu
small-small
'very small'
(Kihm 1994: 25)

(22) iterative/frequentative/habitual (f. 2a) Guinea Bissau Creole Portuguese
fura-fura
pierce-pierce
'lacerate'
(Couto 1994: 83–84)

(23) durative/continuative/progressive (f. 2b)   Angolar Creole Portuguese
    foga-foga-foga
    dance-dance-dance
    'to keep dancing'
    (Maurer 1995: 154)

(24) pluralisation (function 3)   Macaista Creole Portuguese
    kaza-kaza
    house-house
    'houses'
    (Alan Baxter, p.c.)

(25) augmentation and accumulation (f. 4)   Angolar Creole Portuguese
    tê   anu-anu
    have year-year
    'to have many years'
    (Ladhams et al. 2003: 167)

(26) distribution (function 5)   Principense Creole Portuguese
    wétu   wétu
    eight   eight
    'eight each'
    (Günther 1973: 64)

(27) indetermination (function 6)   Zamboanga Chabacano
    kyen-kyén
    who-who
    'whosoever'
    (Forman 1972 142)

(28) attenuation (function 7)   Papia Kristang Creole Portuguese
    chua   pichi   pichi
    rain   small   small
    'drizzle'
    (Alan Baxter, p.c.)

(29) other/miscellaneous (function 8)   Cape Verdean Creole Portuguese
    bóka-bóka
    mouth-mouth
    'in secret'
    (Baptista 2002: 180–181)

These functions are by no means exclusive of Portuguese and Spanish-lexifier creoles (cf. Kouwenberg (ed.) 2003). Although Farquharson (2011) refutes the influence of Akan languages in Jamaican Creole English aspectual reduplication, one of the oft-cited Kwa languages, Gã, possibly itself the outcome of intense language contact (a brief period of pidginisation followed by rapid creolisation according to Kropp Dakubu 2011), expresses at least plurality, iterativity and distribution alongside diverse derivational functions by means of reduplication (Kropp Dakubu 2002: 42–44).

3.3. Syntax

3.3.1. The verb phrase

3.3.1.1. Verbs

In most cases, the unmarked verb form of creole languages is derived from the infinitive of the lexifier language. An exception to this rule are Portuguese- and Spanish-lexifier creoles, in which the third person singular form of the indicative of high frequency verbs has been recruited as the basic verb form. This could be a result of the third person singular forms frequently combining with infinitives (Lipski 1988: 31), or, being morphologically as complex as the infinitive and occurring more frequently in natural speech than the infinitive, a general characteristic of L2 acquisition of Spanish (Lipski 2002: 127–128).

In several French-lexifier creoles (Réunionnais, Mauritian, Seychellois, Haitian, Louisianais), a long form derived from the past participle as well as the infinitive and other French verbal forms (e.g. the imperative), alternates with a short form derived from the third person singular. Attempts have been made to attribute the alternation to phonotactic, syntactic, semantic and aspecto-temporal factors as well as to different sociolects (cf. Baker and Corne 1982; Syea 2009; Alleyne 1996: 49–56; Bartens 1998a: 387).

The distinction between verbs and adjectives is problematic, if one follows the model of European grammar. Creole predicative adjectives do not take an overt copula (leading to the Euro-centric notion of zero copulas) but use TMA-markers instead (see section 3.3.1.2 below). Unmarked verbs tend to refer to the moment in focus. For stative verbs this preferred reading corresponds to the present tense in languages like English, whereas for dynamic verbs it corresponds to the past tense (cf. Holm 1988: 150). The unmarked verb form is used as an imperative but it may require the use of a personal pronoun when directed at the second person plural:

(30) *Kom   ya!*   San Andrés Creole English
    Come   here
    'Come here!' (one addressee)
    (Bartens 2003: 115)

(31) *Unu kom   ya!*   San Andrés Creole English
    2PL come   here
    'Come here!' (more than one addressee)
    (Bartens 2003: 115)

Some Portuguese-lexifier creoles (e.g. Cape Verdean and the Indo-Portuguese varieties) have retained some Portuguese verbal inflections. Papiamentu and Angolar also have separate past participle forms.

3.3.1.2.   The TMA-system

TMA-systems, i.e. systems of mostly preposed (vis-à-vis the verb) particles marking tense, mood, and aspect, have been singled out as the linguistic structure that most clearly distinguishes creoles from their lexifier languages while covering the same conceptual areas (cf. Bickerton 1981: 90). The categories most frequently marked are:

1. anterior/past tense
2. progressive aspect
3. habitual aspect
4. completive aspect
5. irrealis mode (including the future)

   and combinations thereof.

3.3.1.2.1. Anterior/past

Prototypical creoles mark anterior tense. Taking into account the division into dynamic verbs and stative predicates, the anterior of the former would correspond to the English pluperfect, the anterior of the latter to the English simple past. See, for instance:

(32) *Kòkòti   te   konnét   li*   Dominican Creole French
    Kòkòti   ANT   know   3SG
    'Kòkòti knew her.'
    (Chapuis 2007: 85)

(33) *Kòkòti   te   li   liv-la   avan*   Dominican Creole French
     Kòkòti ANT read book-DET before
     mwen   genyen   i
     1SG   buy   3SG
     'Kòkòti had read the book before I bought it.'
     (Chapuis 2007: 85)

However, there are also creoles that appear to be moving towards a tense marking system where the marker is not a marker of relative past, i.e. anterior, tense but one of absolute past. This appears to be the case of Nicaraguan Creole English:

(34) *Shi   ded   wen   shi*   Nicaraguan Creole English
     3SG.F   die   when 3SG.F.SBJ
     did   hav   35   yierz.
     PST have   35   year-PL
     'She died when she was 35 years old.'

(35) *Wan   taim   wa   rat   mi*   Nicaraguan Creole English
     one   time ART.INDF   rat   PST
     fain   wa   big   piis   a   kiek.
     find   ART.INDF big   piece   of cake
     'Once a rat found a big piece of cake.'
     (FOREIBCA 2005a: 4)

3.3.1.2.2. Progressive aspect

Whereas progressive aspect is usually marked by means of a preverbal marker, some more acrolectal English-lexifier creoles use a reflex of the English gerund, *-in*, for marking progressives:

(36) *Dehn   de   du   evri-ting   fi*   San Andrés Creole English
     3PL   PROG do   everything COMP
     get   Turkl   souba.
     get   Turtle   sober
     'They are doing their best to get Turtle sober.'

(37) *Iivn   in   di   Inglish   klaas,*   Nicaraguan Creole English
     even   in ART.DEF English class
     dei   taak-in   Kriol.
     3PL.SBJ talk-PROG   Creole
     'Even in the English class, they are talking Creole.'

Many creoles also permit the formation of an anterior progressive:

(38) *Pòlet te ka dansé.*   Dominican Creole French
Paulette ANT PROG dance
'Paulette was dancing.'
(Chapuis 2007: 86)

3.3.1.2.3. Habitual aspect

Many creoles feature a distinct habitual marker, some use the progressive marker, and others do not mark habitual aspect overtly at all. For instance, Dominican Creole French does not possess a marker that expresses habitual aspect and resorts to the progressive or zero marking for such meaning:

(39) *Jan ka vini lékòl an lé.* Dominican Creole French
Jean PROG/HAB come school on time
'Jean comes to school on time.'
(Chapuis 2007: 87)

(40) *Tou tan i (te) vwè kéchòy*   Dominican Creole French
every time 3SG (ANT) want something
bon, i (te ka) genyen i.
nice 3SG (ANT PROG/HAB) buy 3SG
'Whenever he saw something nice, he would buy it.'
(Chapuis 2007: 87)

San Andrés Creole English uses distinct forms for the contemporaneous and anterior habitual aspect:

(41) *Wi stodi mek da ero.*   San Andrés Creole English
1PL HAB.PRS make DEM error
'We always make that mistake.'
(Bartens 2003: 87)

(42) *Ai yuuztu go chorch bee fut,*   San Andrés Creole English
1SG HAB.PST go church bare foot
widout shuuz.
without shoe
'I would go to church barefoot, without shoes.'
(Bartens 2003: 88)

3.3.1.2.4. Completive aspect

If a separate marker of completive aspect exists, it may or may not be combined with the anterior marker. This is the case of Nicaraguan and San Andrés Creole English, respectively:

(43) Iin   a   tach   hous   Nicaraguan Creole English
     in   ART.INDF   thatched   house
     di   sik   uman   di   don   instaal [...]
     ART.DEF sick   woman   PST   COMPL   install
     'The sick woman had been installed in a thatched house [...]'
     (FOREIBCA 2005b: 9)

(44) Wen   ihn   don   iit,   him   San Andrés Creole English
     when 3SG.SBJ   COMPL   eat   3SG.SBJ
     kyan   go   out   an   plie.
     can   go   out   and   play
     'When he will have eaten/has finished eating, he may go out and play.'
     (Bartens 2003: 88)

This latter example from San Andrés Creole English is also an example of the subject pronouns alternation rule to be discussed in section 3.3.2.3 below.

At times, the completive aspect marker is postverbal. In both Sãotomense and Angolar Creole Portuguese, the completive marker *kaba* either precedes the verb or is sentence-final:

(45) n   kaba   taba/   n   Sãotomense/Angolar Creole Portuguese
     1SG COMPL   work/ 1SG
     taba   kaba
     work COMPL
     'I finished working.'
     (Lorenzino 2007: 7)

3.3.1.2.5. Irrealis mood

Irrealis mood includes the expression of futurity. Thus, a combination of the future marker with the anterior marker often expresses conditionals and future-in-the-past. However, this combination is not allowed in the Portuguese-lexifier creoles of the Gulf of Guinea (cf. Bartens 1995: 92). In Haitian, the progressive marker *ap* is used to express futurity with stative predicates whereas dynamic verbs take *a(va)*. In conditional clauses, *ap* expresses greater likelihood than *a(va)*:

(46) *Bouki ap konn leson an.*   Haitian Creole French
    Bouki FUT know lesson DEF
    'Bouki will know the lesson.'
    (DeGraff 2007: 104)

(47) *Si Bondye vle, m ap monte*   Haitian Creole French
    if God want 1SG FUT go.up
    nan syèl.
    in heaven
    'God willing, I'm going to go to heaven.'
    (DeGraff 2007: 107)

(48) *Si Bondye vle, m a(va) monte*   Haitian Creole French
    if God want 1SG IRR go.up
    nan syèl.
    in heaven
    'God willing, I might/will go to heaven.'
    (DeGraff 2007: 107)

In Principense, one of the Gulf of Guinea creoles, *ka* expresses future, future-in-the-past as well as both present and past counterfactuals, alongside other meanings, e.g.:

(49) *Xi n ka tê tempu, n*   Principense Creole Portuguese
    if 1SG IRR have time 1SG
    ke lala.
    IRR.go there
    'If I had the time, I would go there. / If I had had the time, I would have gone there.'
    (Maurer 2009: 79)

3.3.1.3. Serial verbs

Serial verb constructions, often attributed to ad-/substratal influence especially in the creoles of the Atlantic region, consist of two or more verbs. These verbs have the same subject and take only one internal argument but are not connected by means of a linking element. TMA-marking and negation occur only on one element, usually the first one. The ensuing sequence constitutes a prosodic unit and its semantic meaning is complex, i.e. not merely the sum of its components (cf. Muysken and Veenstra 1995: 290; Byrne 1987, 1988; Bartens 1996a: 117). Widespread serial verb constructions involve the directional verbs 'go' and 'come' as well as 'give' for forming benefactive, 'take' for instrumental and 'pass' for comparative constructions:

(50) *Taawan   waka   go   a   opu*   Ndyuka Creole English
     other-one walk   go   LOC upward
     se,   taawan   waka   go   a   bilo.
     side, other-one walk   go   LOC   downward
     'Some walked upriver, others went downriver.'
     (Huttar 2007: 229)

(51) *Ne   a   boi   kon   doo.*   Ndyuka Creole English
     then DEF boy   come   arrive
     'Then the boy arrived.'
     (Huttar 2007: 229)

(52) *seni wan   boskopu   gi   tigri*   Sranan
     send ART.INDF message   give tiger
     'Send a message to Tiger/ Send Tiger a message.'
     (Muysken and Veenstra 1995: 296)

(53) *no   teki   baskita   tyari   watra*   Sranan
     NEG   take   basket   carry   water
     'Don't carry water with a basket.'
     (Muysken and Veenstra 1995: 295)

(54) *Olu sabi   swim   pas   mi.*   Krio
     Olu know   swim   pass   1SG
     'Olu can swim better than I can.'
     (Yillah and Corcoran 2007: 189)

Many Atlantic English-lexifier creoles feature an element *se* 'that', which is (nearly) homophonous with the verb meaning 'to say' and which introduces subordinate clauses after verbs of speaking, perception and judgment. It has been conceived of as a serial verb, not least because of the existence of *sɛ* 'to say; that' in Twi. In Twi, however, *sɛ* also introduces purpose clauses (Bartens 2011a: 217–218). The grammaticalisation of 'say' to 'that' is an areal feature of West African languages (Güldemann 2005). Cf. example (55):

(55) Ai   doun waa   dem   nou   se   Nicaraguan Creole English
     1SG   NEG   want 3PL   know COMP
     Ai   tiif di   ring.
     1SG   steal ART.DEF   ring
     'I don't want them to know I stole the ring.'

3.3.1.4. Copulas

Postulating a category of stative predicates instead of insisting on a division into stative verbs and adjectives (cf. section 3.3.1.1) has the advantage that no zero copulas have to be postulated for creole languages. Cf.

(56) Kòkòti malad.   Dominican Creole French
     Kòkòti sick
     'Kòkòti is sick.'
     (Chapuis 2007: 85)

Most descriptions of creole languages discuss copulas, even if they are not overtly realised in the language in question. In part, this appears to be a carry-over from studies describing the creole continuum, where overt copulas were found to surface at later stages of the postulated decreolisation process (cf. Bickerton 1975; Rickford 1988; Bartens 1996a: 116).

To be sure, zero copulas are considered equative copulas when the conjoined element is not an NP, a structure where at least Atlantic creoles mostly require a copula or linking element. This function could also be called identification. Other 'copula' functions are the locational, existential and highlighting ones. Negerhollands and Sranan both have five distinct overt copulas (de Kleine 2007: 265–266; Arends 1989).

(57) Am   a   e:n   difman.   equative with NPs *a*, Negerhollands
     3SG   COP   ART.INDF   thief
     'He is a thief.'
     (Stolz 1986: 153)

(58) Wama ju   bi   hi?   locative *bi*, Negerhollands
     why   2SG   COP   here
     'Why are you here?'
     (Stolz 1986: 153)

(59) Mi   mi   kwa:t.   equative with adjectives *mi*, Negerhollands
     1SG   COP   angry
     'I am angry.'
     (Stolz 1986: 153)

(60) A   mi   ka: mata   am.   highlighter *mi*, Negerhollands
     HL   1SG   COMP   kill   3SG
     'It is I who killed him.'
     (Stolz 1986: 153)

(61) Di   ha   e:n   jun.   existential *ha*, Negerhollands
     3SG   have ART.INDF boy
     'There is a boy.'
     (de Josselin de Jong 1926: 11, cited in de Kleine 2007: 266)

Existentials, whether to be considered copular constructions or not, are prototypically expressed by means of the verb meaning 'to have', e.g. San Andrés Creole English:

(62) *San Andrés gat plenti biich.*   San Andrés Creole English
     San Andrés have plenty beach
     'San Andrés has many beaches.'
     (Bartens 2003: 46)

An alternative way of expressing existentials in the same language is:

(63) *Tu moch   hous   iina   Nort   End.*   San Andrés Creole English
     too much house   in   North End
     'There are too many houses in North End.'
     (Bartens 2003: 46)

3.3.1.5. Passive voice

Prototypical creoles do not feature a morphological passive. Instead, dynamic verbs are used statively. Consider:

(64) *Ihn   brok   di   pliet.*   San Andrés Creole English
     3SG   break   ART.DEF   plate
     'He/she broke the plate.'
     (Bartens 2003: 75)

(65) Di   pliet   brok.   San Andrés Creole English
    ART.DEF   plate   break
    'The plate is broken.'
    (Bartens 2003: 75)

Other options are constructions with the 3rd person plural pronoun and *get*-passives:

(66) Dem   kil   im.   San Andrés Creole English
    3PL   kill   3SG
    'They killed him.' [or 'He was killed.']
    (Bartens 2003: 75)

(67) Yo   kraze   machin   lan.   Haitian Creole French
    3SG   demolish   car   DEF
    'They have demolished the car.' [or 'The car was demolished.']
    (DeGraff 2007: 112)

(68) Ihn   get   biit   op.   San Andrés Creole English
    3SG   get   beat   up
    'He/she got beaten up.'
    (Bartens 2003: 93)

(69) U   liku   pu   gay   sote.   Seychellois Creole French
    2SG   neck   IRR   get   jump
    'Your head will get cut off.'
    (Corne 1977: 162)

Papiamentu, on the other hand, which possesses a past participle (see above), has developed three different passive constructions: the construction in example (70), modelled on Dutch, first entered the language in mid-19th century and is now used in spoken language as well, whereas the constructions shown in examples (71) and (72), calqued from Spanish, arose a hundred years later and are essentially restricted to the written register (Sanchez 2006):

(70) E   pòtrèt   aki   a   wordo   saká   dor   Papiamentu
    ART.DEF   picture   DEM   PFV   COP   take   by
    die   mucha   hòmber [...]
    ART.DEF   child   male
    'This picture was taken by the boy [...]'
    (Kouwenberg and Murray 1994: 37)

(71) Na   mei   e   projekto a   ser   Papiamentu
     LOC   May   ART.DEF   project   PFV   COP
     entregá   pa   X.
     hand-in   by   X
     'In May, the project was handed in by X.'
     (Kouwenberg and Murray 1994: 37)

(72) Ela   keda   medio   paralisá.   Papiamentu
     3SG   remain   half   paralyzed
     'It left her half paralyzed.'
     (Kouwenberg and Murray 1994: 44)

3.3.1.6. Negation

Most creoles feature a single verbal negator which is usually preposed to all TMA markers and therefore also to the basic verb form. Other creoles feature a second negative element at the end of the utterance in scope, placing one negational element before and the other after the basic verb form:

(73) Pòlèt   pa   té   ké   alé   a   Dominican Creole French
     Paulette   NEG   ANT   IRR   gone   to
     makèt-la.
     market-DET
     'Paulette would not have gone to the market.'
     (Chapuis 2007: 91)

(74) e   na   ka   mɛ   ombo   wa   Angolar Creole Portuguese
     3SG   NEG   HAB   eat   goat   NEG
     'He doesn't eat goat.'
     (Lorenzino 2007: 13)

(75) pechiri   tua   tia   mangaθo   wa   Angolar Creole Portuguese
     pest   take   country   really   NEG
     'The pest spread [sic.] through the country.'
     (Lorenzino 2007: 13)

Negative concord is often mentioned as a characteristic of creoles vis-à-vis their lexifiers. This is true of French and the Germanic languages but not for instance of Portuguese or Spanish. Here are some creole examples:

(76) *Nan katye   sa-a   pèsonn*   Haitian Creole French
     in   neighbourhood DEM-SG   nobody
     pa   di   pèsonn   anyen.
     NEG say   nobody   nothing
     'In this neighbourhood, nobody says anything to anybody.'
     (DeGraff 2007: 111)

(77) *A   no   waahn   go   nowe.*   San Andrés Creole English
     1SG NEG want   go   nowhere
     'I don't want to go anywhere.'
     (Bartens 2003: 101)

(78) *Nit   en   kopu   am   na   kan   kri.*   Negerhollands
     NEG ART.INDF   cent   3SG   NEG   can   get
     'He cannot even get a cent.'
     (Stolz 1986: 139)

(79) *ningẽ   nu   ja-ve.*   Korlai Creole Portuguese
     no.one NEG   PST-come
     'No one came.'
     (Clements 1996: 174)

3.3.1.7. Adverbs

Creole adverbs tend to have the same form as the corresponding adjectives/stative predicates:

(80) *Di   man   lisn   gud.*   San Andrés Creole English
     ART.DEF   man   listen   good
     'The man listened carefully.'
     (Bartens 2003: 74)

(81) *Pwe   xiga   fo   xivisu   kansadu.* Principe Creole Portuguese
     father arrive come.from   work   tired
     'His father arrived tired from work.'
     (Maurer 2009: 47)

At times a distinct form, usually modelled on the lexifier language, is used:

(82) *hapi, hapli*   San Andrés Creole English
     'happy, happily'

(83) *kontinuo, kontinuamente* Papiamentu
    'continuous, continuously'
    (Kouwenberg and Murray 1994: 29)

3.3.2. The noun phrase

3.3.2.1. Nouns

Many creoles use bare nouns to refer to a whole category, cf.:

(84) *Aligieta   gou   ap   tu   footiin   fiit.*   Nicaraguan Creole English
    alligator   go   up   to   fourteen   feet
    'Alligators measure up to fourteen feet.'[1]

(85) *Wosiyòl* [sic.] *manje   kowosòl.*   Haitian Creole French
    nightingale   eat   soursop
    'Nightingales eat soursops.'
    (DeGraff 2007: 117)

Nominal plurals are formed, especially in Atlantic creoles, by postposing the 3rd person plural pronoun. The same construction frequently also serves to express the associative plural, a construction clearly calqued on West African substrate languages.

(86) *di   bwai   dem*   San Andrés Creole English
    ART.DEF   boy   3PL
    'the boys'
    (Bartens 2003: 31)

(87) *Mis   Aurora   dem*   Providence Creole English
    Miss Aurora   3PL
    'Miss Aurora and her folks/family/friends'
    (Bartens 2003: 31)

On the other hand, e.g. Principe Creole Portuguese preposes *ine* (in older texts *ina*):

(88) *Ine   manse   vika.*   Principe Creole Portuguese
    3PL   man   arrive
    'The men arrived.'
    (Maurer 2009: 31)

(89) *Ine   Pedu   vika.* Principe Creole Portuguese
     3PL   Pedu   arrive
     'Pedu and his family/friends came.'
     (Maurer 2009: 33)

The sex of a referent is typically expressed only when it is not obvious from the context and needs to be specified. This may occur by means of postposing the words meaning 'man', 'woman':

(90) *ugatu omi,   ugatu   mye* Principe Creole Portuguese
     cat   man,   cat   woman
     'male cat, female cat'
     (Maurer 2009: 30)

There are, however, always also at least some lexicalised pairs, e.g.:

(91) *ugalu,   ginhan* Principe Creole Portuguese
     'rooster, hen'
     (Maurer 2009: 30)

In the creoles lexified by Romance languages, which mark gender morphologically on some nouns, the masculine has been recruited into the creoles as the default form although exceptions do occur as well, e.g. the indefinite article *ũa* of São Tomé Creole Portuguese.

Nominal possession is expressed in three distinct ways: juxtaposition, the insertion of a preposition, and the insertion of a possessive. In the first and third construction, the possessor comes first.

(92) *di   kui   bik* Negerhollands
     ART.DEF   cow   stomach
     'the cow's stomach'
     (Stolz 1986: 126)

(93) *di   na:m   fan di   dri   fan sinu* Negerhollands
     ART.DEF   name   of   ART.DEF   three of   them
     'the name of the three of them'
     (Stolz 1986: 126)

(94) *di   me:nsi   si   coach* Negerhollands
     ART.DEF   girl   POSS   coach
     'the girl's coach'
     (Stolz 1986: 126)

3.3.2.2. Articles

Definite articles of the lexifier language are frequently lost in creolisation and subsequently recreated from demonstratives, e.g.:

(95) *Patriyòt la kouri.*   Haitian Creole French
      patriot ART.DEF run
      'The patriot ran away.'
      (DeGraff 2009: 117)

Compare French: *le patriot* 'the patriot', *ce patriot* 'this/that patriot', *ce patriot-là* 'that patriot'.

Few creoles conserve superstratal articles, e.g.:

(96) *Y el vieja ya*   Cavite Chabacano Spanish Creole
      and ART.DEF old.person PFV
      viví peliz [...]
      live happy
      'And the old lady lived happily [...]'
      (Whinnom 1956: 52)

Creoles often have an indefinite article typically derived from the numeral meaning 'one' in the lexifier:

(97) *wan buk*   San Andrés Creole English
      ART.INDF book
      'a book'
      (Bartens 2003: 36)

3.3.2.3. Pronouns

Creole languages tend to make fewer case distinctions with personal pronouns than their lexifier languages. Table 4 presents the personal pronouns of San Andrés Creole English. The 1SG subject pronoun variant *a* (and even more so *ai* which indeed occurs in spontaneous San Andresan speech) has to be considered a borrowing from English.[2] In the domain of possessive pronouns, some speakers use the adpositional *fi* + personal pronoun construction only for independent possessives. In adnominal contexts, they use bare personal pronouns. Others, probably the majority, use the *fi* + pronoun construction in adnominal contexts as well.

Table 4. Person pronouns of San Andrés Creole English

	Subject	Object	(Adnominal) Possessives	Reflexive pronouns
1SG	mi, a	mi	fi mi	miself
2SG	yu	yu	fi yu	yuself
3SG	ihn, (h)im	(h)im	fi ihn/him	(h)imself
3SG.n	ich	ich	fi ih	ihself
1PL	wi	wi	fi wi	wiself
2PL	unu	unu	fi unu	unuself
3PL	dehn, dem	dem	fi dem	demself

During my fieldwork on San Andrés I came across what I have since called the "Subject Pronoun Alternation Rule" (Bartens 2003: 43). This 'rule' implies that one variant of the 3SG subject pronoun in the first clause of a complex sentence requires the use of another variant in the second, irrespective of which is the main clause:

(98) *So nou Beda Daag de paas* San Andrés Creole English
    so now brother dog PROG pass
    an wen him gaan, ihn sii di kow tombl
    and when 3SG go.PST 3SG see ART.DEF cow tumble
    dong ded so him kot uopn di kow beli.
    down dead so 3SG cut open ART.DEF cow stomach
    'So now Brother Dog was passing and when he went by, he saw the cow tumble down dead so he cut open the cow's belly.'
    (Bartens 2003: 47)

When pronouns are conjoined with full NPs both San Andrés and Nicaraguan Creole English prefer the order pronoun-NP, whereas the reverse order has to be considered an English-derived construction (cf. examples (99) and (100) below and Bartens forthcoming a, b, and c):

(99) *Mi an Mary gaan huom.* Nicaraguan Creole English
    1SG.SBJ and Mary go.PST home
    'I and Mary went home.'

(100) *Mary an Ai gaan huom.* Nicaraguan Creole English
    Mary and 1SG.SBJ go.PST home
    'Mary and I went home.'

Reflexive pronouns are at times constructed with body part terms such as 'head' or 'body':

(101) *N   odja   nha   kabesa*   Cape Verdean Creole Portuguese
     1SG   see   1SG.POSS   head
     na   spedju.
     in   mirror
     'I looked at myself in the mirror.'
     (Baptista et al. 2007: 78)

(102) *Tin   ora   mi   mester   tapa   mi   kurpa*   Papiamentu
      have   hour   1SG   must   cover   1SG.POSS   body
      pa   sangura   no   pika-mi.
      for   mosquito   NEG   bite-1SG
      'Sometimes I have to cover myself for mosquitoes not to bite me.'
      (Kouwenberg and Murray 1994: 41)

Note, however, that some creoles feature the Portuguese-derived construction, for instance Papiamentu:

(103) *Te   ainda   mi   no   por   konsiderá*   Papiamentu
      until   yet   1SG   NEG   can   consider
      mi   mes   komo   landadó.
      1SG   REFL   as   swimmer
      'Up to now I cannot consider myself a swimmer.'
      (Kouwenberg and Murray 1994: 41)

Reciprocal pronouns are formed periphrastically, e.g.

(104) *Nhós   kré   kumpanheru   tcheu.*   Cape Verdean Creole Portuguese
      2PL   love   companion   much
      'You love each other a lot.'
      (Quint 2000: 180)

San Andrés and Providence Creole English make use of the English constructions 'one another' and 'each other':

(105) *Dehn   help   wan   anada.*   San Andrés Creole English
      3PL   help   one   another
      'They help each other.'
      (Bartens 2003: 50)

(106) *Hia in Pravidens evribady*   Providence Creole English
here in Providence every-body
andastan iich ada.
understand each other
'Here in Providence everybody understands each other.'
(Bartens 2003: 50)

Creoles differ as to whether they make use of relative pronouns or particles. Basilectal Nicaraguan Creole English features a relative particle *we(h)*, meso- and acrolectal registers English-derived pronouns such as *wat* and *huu*:

(107) *Iin di praimari skuul we*   Nicaraguan Creole English
in ART.DEF primary school REL
Ai wook [...]
1SG work
'In the primary school where I work [...]'

(108) *So di wat wi taak*   Nicaraguan Creole English
so DEM REL 1PL.SBJ talk
iz Kriol?
COP.PRS Creole
'So is this (language) which we talk Creole?'

(109) *Dem iz huu woz*   Nicaraguan Creole English
3PL.SBJ COP.PRS REL COP.PST
marginat-ed.
marginate-PTCP
'It is/was them who were marginalised.'

In addition, the existence of relativisers is disputed for instance in Haitian Creole French: DeGraff (2007: 110) argues that the element *ki* in the following example is a complementizer, not a relative pronoun:

(110) *Moun ki pa travay p ap*   Haitian Creole French
people COMP NEG work NEG FUT
touche.
get.paid
'Those who don't work won't get paid.'
(DeGraff 2007: 110)

Bimorphemic interrogative pronouns consisting of a question particle and a noun typically occur in the creoles of the Atlantic region but also elsewhere (Muysken and Smith 1990). Their formation has been attributed to the tendency towards semantic transparency (cf. Bartens 1996a: 124). Creoles lexified by Portuguese and Spanish present 'mixed' systems, i.e. both bimorphemic and lexifier-derived opaque interrogatives (Bartens 1996c). Compare the following examples for both bimorphemic and opaque interrogatives from Principe Creole Portuguese:

(111) *Ki minda urôsô txi pwê na*   Principe Creole Portuguese
what quantity rice 2SG put LOC
teempi?
cooking-pot
'How much rice did you put into the cooking-pot?'
(Maurer 2009: 45)

(112) *Kantu bana ki txi kume a?*   Principe Creole Portuguese
how.many banana REL 2SG eat Q
'How many bananas did you eat?'
(Maurer 2009: 45)

Cross-linguistically, demonstrative pronouns tend to be derived from adverbs and subsequently they may grammaticalise into definite articles (cf. Heine and Kuteva 2002: 330). For instance in San Andrés Creole English, adnominal demonstratives are preposed to the item they modify and cannot co-occur with a definite article. In addition, there is a two-way contrast between *dis* 'this' vs. *da(t)* 'that'. Both the proximal and distal demonstratives can be emphasised: *dis-ya, dat-de*. These emphatic demonstratives can be used discontinuously. However, the prenominal variants are preferred and while the discontinuous variant *dat...de* sounds natural according to native speakers, the discontinuous variant *dis...ya* does not:

(113) *dis hous*   San Andrés Creole English
DEM house
'this house'

(114) *dat hous*   San Andrés Creole English
DEM house
'that house'

(115) *dis-ya hous*   San Andrés Creole English
DEM-EMPH house
'this very house'

(116) *dat-de   hous*   San Andrés Creole English
     DEM-EMPH   house
     'that very house'

Indefinite pronouns have frequently been retained from the lexifier languages (cf. Bartens 1996c: 249). In addition, they tend to be based on generic nouns:

(117) kada   Cape Verdean Creole Portuguese
      every
      'every'
      (Quint 2000: 187)

(118) *No   sábi   yo   náda!*   Chabacano de Ternate
      NEG   know   1SG   any.thing
      'I didn't know anything.'
      (Sippola 2011: 132)

(119) *Mek   Ai   tel   yu   somting   now.*   San Andrés Creole English
      make 1SG tell 2SG some.thing now
      'Let me tell you something now.'

3.3.2.4. Adjectives

As suggested in sections 3.3.1.1 and 3.3.1.7, the category of adjectives overlaps with stative verbs. As a result, some Atlantic creoles feature predicate clefting where the predicate, which can be either an adjective or a verb, is fronted to the highlighter position and followed by the original sentence:

(120) *Da   kliin   ihn   wehn   de   kliin*   San Andrés Creole English
      FOC   clean   3SG   ANT   PROG clean
      an   no   de   kuk.
      and   NEG PROG cook
      'She was cleaning and not cooking.'

Some of these creoles also use the serial verb construction with 'pass' for verbal and adjectival predicates (Holm 2007: ix). Cf. example (54) above and (121):

(121) *A   dagu   ya   bigi   moo/   pasa   dem   taawan.*   Ndyuka
      DEF   dog   here big   more   pass   DEF   other-one
      'This dog is bigger than the other ones.'
      (Huttar 2007: 227)

Note, however, that the construction with *moo* (followed by optional *e(n)ke* 'as, like') is more common in Ndyuka than the serial verb construction with *pasa* (cf. Huttar 2007: 227).

Considering the previous discussion, a division into verbs and adjectives would seem rather artificial at first sight. Indeed, this specific area of grammar is covered by the term 'property items/concepts' coined by Thompson (2004) and Dixon (1977). This term is appropriate to describe the situation in the Suriname creoles where property items occur as either verbal heads or adjectival complements. Only the latter construction is allowed if the item belongs to the small set of 'true adjectives', e.g. Saramaccan *bunu/bumbuu* 'good; well', or is an ideophone, e.g. Ndyuka *pii* 'quiet' (Winford 1997; Huttar 2007: 226; van den Berg forthcoming):

(122) *Efu   den   sikin   de   bunbun   da   a   bun!*   Ndyuka
      If   3PL.POSS   body   COP   good   then   it   good
      'If their bodies are in a good/healthy state, then it is OK.'
      (Migge 2000: 220)

3.3.2.5.   Quantifiers

Nominal plural formation, which can be considered a form of quantification, have been discussed in section 3.3.2.1 above. Definite quantifiers or numerals are divided into ordinal and cardinal numbers in the lexifier languages. Creoles usually only conserve ordinals and sometimes the term for 'the last' from the first lexifier language. Cf.:

(123) *um, dós, trés, kuátu, sinku/xinku, séx, séti, oitu,*   Cape Verdean Creole
      nóvi, dés
      'one, two, three, four, five, six, seven, eight, nine, ten'
      (Quint 2000: 193)

(124) *purmeru, sugundu, tirseru, kuártu*   Cape Verdean Creole
      'first, second, third, fourth'
      (Quint 2000: 193)

(125) *fos, sekant, tord, fort, fif*   San Andrés Creole English
      'first, second, third, fourth, fifth'
      (Bartens 2003: 64)

Haitian Creole features both numerals and cardinals derived from French, for example:

(126) *katrevendiznef, katrevendisnevyèm*   Haitian Creole
    'ninety-nine, ninety-ninth'
    (Savain 1995: 50–51)

Papiamentu forms cardinal numbers with *di* + ordinal number (in the case of 'the first', *di* is optional):

(127) *un, dos, tres, kuatër, sinku, ...*   Papiamentu
    'one, two, three, four, five, ...'
    (Maurer 1988: 39)

(128) *(di) promé, di dos, di tres, ...*   Papiamentu
    'first, second, third, ...'
    (Maurer 1988: 40)

This might reflect the influence of Bantu languages. The influence of Bantu languages has also been made responsible for the expression of numerals in the Gulf of Guinea creoles in general (cf. Bartens 1996a: 122). For instance Angolar Creole Portuguese features only one genuine ordinal:

(129) *pumbê(lu)*   Angolar Creole Portuguese
    'first'
    (Maurer 1995: 48)

As for the cardinals, hundreds and thousands are joined by *ki* 'and, with', tens and smaller numbers with *ne* which appears to be derived from Kimbundu *ni* 'and, with', e.g.

(130) *ũa thentu ki ũa*   Angolar Creole Portuguese
    'one hundred and one'
    (Maurer 1995: 48)

(131) *kwin ne rôthu*   Angolar Creole Portuguese
    'twelve'
    (Maurer 1995: 47)

Indefinite or non-numeral quantifiers include concepts such as 'many, few, several' (with count nouns) and 'much, little, enough' (with non-count nouns). They tend to be derived from the lexifier language:

(132) *plenti, fyue, moch, likl, nof*   San Andrés Creole English
    'many, few, much, little, enough'
    (Bartens 2003: 65)

(133) *sevral*   Providence Creole English
    'several'
    (Bartens 2003: 65)

Alongside Spanish-derived non-numeral quantifiers Ternate Chabacano also features at least the Tagalog-derived quantifier *báwat* 'every':

(134) *El   báwat   kása   tyéni   tasé*   Ternate Chabacano
    ART.DEF   every   house   have.to   IPFV.make
    handá   máski   un   pukitín
    preparations   even.if   ART.INDF   little
    'Every house has food which is being prepared, even if it be a little.'
    (cf. Sippola 2011: 117)

3.3.3. Relational elements

3.3.3.1. Prepositions

The scarcity of prepositions retained from the lexifier languages has been cited as a reason for (i) the use of serial verbs (cf. section 3.3.1.3) and (ii) for the formation of complex prepositions derived from nouns, such as:

(135) *bak a*   Belize Creole English
    'behind'
    (Crosbie et al. 2007: 39)

(136) *fronta*   San Andrés Creole English
    'in front of'
    (Bartens 2003: 103)

(137) *batamsaid*   Jamaican Creole English
    'under'

A phenomenon amply discussed in the literature is the occurrence of an all-round preposition *na* (and certain variants such as San Andrés Creole English *iina*) employed to express both location at and movement towards a position (e.g. Holm 1988: 90; McWhorter 2005: 77). It occurs in most Portuguese-lexifier but also in many Atlantic English-lexifier creoles and Spanish-lexified Chabacano. *Na* is homophonous with the Portuguese contraction of the locative preposition *em* with the feminine definite article *a* (and not the expected masculine counterpart *o*; cf. section 3.3.2.1). Its use in non-Iberian contact languages leads such authors as Whinnom (1956: 28) and Naro (1978) to propose its spread as due to the use of nautical Portuguese as a lingua franca during the first centuries of the colonial expansion of the European nation states. Subsequently McWhorter included *na* in his list of features which would support his Cormantin scenario of a common ancestor of all Atlantic English-lexifier creoles and the role played by Igbo speakers in the formation of this Proto-Creole (McWhorter 2000: 142), a second diffusionist approach to the phenomenon. The origin of the item in Igbo had been proposed decades earlier by Taylor (1971).

All the aforementioned proposals have centred around a single origin. As far as Chabacano is concerned, Lipski (1986: 7) cautions that "the formal similarity with standard and creole Portuguese may be fortuitous" and suggests that *na* may have arisen in multiple foci of evolution as a result of local language contacts. This may very well be the case for other languages featuring *na* as well (cf. Bartens 2010). This hypothesis is supported by the fact that for example in the Philippino-Spanish Creoles of Ternate and Zamboanga, *na* also expresses motion from a place:

(138) *Está   na   kasa.*   Zamboanga Chabacano
   be   LOC   house
   'He is at home.'
   (Lipski and Santoro 2007: 395)

(139) *Ya   andá   na   pwéblo?*   Zamboanga Chabacano
   PST   go   to   market
   'Did you go to the market?'
   (Lipski and Santoro 2007: 396)

(140) *Ya   káy   yo   na   pwénte.*   Zamboanga Chabacano
   PST   fall   1SG.SBJ   from   bridge
   'I fell from the bridge.'
   (Forman 1972: 196)

(141) *Kyére   lé   salé   na   ágwa.*   Zamboanga Chabacano
   want   3SG.SBJ   come.out   of   water
   'He wants to get out of the water.'
   (Forman 1972: 197)

Haitian Creole French prepositions display a similarly wide range of semantic functions (cf. DeGraff 2007: 122).

When comparing creoles to their lexifier languages, another striking feature is that verbs of motion with concepts of location (e.g. place names) do not require a preposition:

(142) *Timoun yo al Mache Pòspyewo.*   Haitian Creole French
  child DEF.PL go market Post-Pierrot
  'The children have gone to the Post-Pierrot market.'
  (DeGraff 2007: 122)

(143) *M ba minga i na mata*   Angolar Creole Portuguese
  1SG.SBJ go sea and NEG kill
  kikie fo.
  fish NEG
  'I went to the sea and didn't kill any fish.'
  (Lorenzino 2007: 21)

(144) *A gwain Pravidens tumara.*   San Andrés Creole English
  1SG.SBJ FUT Providence tomorrow
  'I am going to Providence tomorrow.'
  (Bartens 2003: 105)

Whereas 'coming from a place' tends to require a preposition, the situation in the Western Caribbean English-lexifier creoles is interesting in the sense that *faan/fram* is used not only for spatial but also temporal relations:

(145) *Ai neva went bak*   Nicaraguan Creole English
  1SG.SUBJ NEG.PST go.PST back
  dier agen fram fuo yier-z.
  there again from four year-PL
  'I have not gone back there since I was four years old.'

This may reflect substrate influence, e.g. from the Akan languages (Bartens 2011b).

3.3.3.2. Conjunctions

There are creoles which use the same item to coordinate both clauses and clause parts, first and foremost NPs:

(146) *An dehn uopn di doa* San Andrés Creole English
and 3PL open ART.DEF door
an ihn gaan iin.
and 3SG.SBJ go.ANT in
'And they opened the door and he went inside.'

(147) *Beda Naansi an Beda Taiga* San Andrés Creole English
Brother Anansi and Brother Tiger
'Brother Anansi and Brother Tiger'

Some creoles employ a distinct conjunction, especially when one of the conjunct NPs is a personal pronoun. In addition, the conjoining item is often the same as the comitative 'with'. This is the case of Sotavento Cape Verdean Creole Portuguese which uses optional *y* 'and' to join sentences and *ku* 'and, with' to join sentence parts (Baptista, Mello and Suzuki 2007: 78):

(148) *El kai (y) el* Sotavento Cape Verdean Creole Portuguese
3SG fall (and) 3SG
parti un brasu.
break ART.INDF arm
'He fell and broke an arm.'
(Veiga 1982: 161)

(149) *di-mi ku di-bo* Sotavento Cape Verdean Creole Portuguese
of-1SG with of-2SG
'mine and yours'
(Veiga 1982: 160)

Nicaraguan Creole English *wi(d)* 'with' was used in the language described by Holm (1978) not only as a preposition used for comitatives and instrumentals but also for joining NPs, as in:

(150) *Di kaptin wi evibadi* Nicaraguan Creole English
ART.DEF captain with every.body
waz der.
COP.PST DEM.LOC
'The captain and everybody was there.'
(Holm 1978: 291)

However, no traces of this construction could be found during my fieldwork conducted in 2006–2009.

Creoles also feature adversative coordinating conjunctions, e.g.

(151) *Maji ê pinxipi fô, ê pinseza,*   Principe Creole Portuguese
but 3SG prince NEG 3SG princess
maji modi ki ê sa fêê a ka kuda pinxipi.
but way REL 3SG HAB do ART.INDF HAB think prince
'But she is not a prince, she is a princess, but from the way she behaves, one could believe she is a prince.'
(Maurer 2009: 160)

as well as disjunctive coordinating conjunctions:

(152) *kárni di pwérku o di báka*   Ternate Chabacano
meat of pork or of cow
'pork or beef'
(Sippola 2011: 274)

(153) *N daka ô n daka fa?*   Principe Creole Portuguese
1SG bring or 1SG bring NEG
'Did I bring her back, yes or no?'
(Maurer 2009: 160)

(154) *N fala fa ni m pidi fa.*   Principe Creole Portuguese
1SG speak NEG nor 1SG ask NEG
'I didn't speak nor did I ask for anything.'
(Maurer 2009: 160)

It has frequently been claimed (e.g. Bickerton 1988) that creoles rarely use subordinated structures. This is not quite true (cf. Bartens 1996a: 125), and as a result, subordinating conjunctions do exist in creoles. I shall discuss subordinated clauses in section 3.3.5 below.

3.3.4. Exclamatives and/or vocatives

A number of creoles, for example Seychellois Creole French, Principense Creole Portuguese, and San Andrés Creole English, feature postposed vocative markers, which in many cases might also be classified as exclamatives or emphatic particles.

(155) *Dafne-o!*   Seychellois Creole French
Daphne-EMPH
'Daphne! Hey, Daphne!'
(Corne 1977: 59)

(156) *Sun   me   ê!*   Principe Creole Portuguese
     Sir   1SG.POSS   VOC
     'Sir!'
     (Maurer 2009: 169)

(157) *Ma-yo!*   San Andrés Creole English
      mother-VOC
      'Hey, old lady!'

(158) *Alma-oi!*   San Andrés Creole English
      Alma-VOC
      'Hey, Alma!'

They are clear carry-overs from the African substrate languages. For example Twi has a postposed vocative (and also exclamative) particle *e*; the Fante dialect also has a variant *(u)o* (Christaller 1875: 37; Welmers 1946: 43):

(159) *Kwasi-e!*   Akuapem Twi
      Kwasi-VOC
      'Hey, Kwasi!'
      (Christaller 1875: 37)

3.3.5. Word order and sentence structure

Creole languages, especially those of the Atlantic region, manifest a preference for the basic word order SVO. This applies not only to declarative but also to interrogative and imperative sentences. Yes/no-questions are distinguished by means of a rising intonation (cf. Winford 2008: 21). In the aforementioned creoles of the Atlantic region, this configuration is bolstered by the converging influence of most sub-/adstrate languages (excluding, for instance, Eastern Ijo, whose basic word order is SOV).

The situation is somewhat different in the case of creoles spoken outside the Atlantic-Pacific area: Nagamese maintains the SOV word order of Assamese even in questions which are nevertheless distinguished from statements by adding the question marker *-(na)ki*:

(160) *Muy   bat   khay.*   Nagamese
      1SG   rice   eat
      'I eat rice.'
      (Bhattacharjya 2007: 253)

(161) *Apuni modu kha-bo naki?*   Nagamese
      2SG   wine   eat-IRR   Q
      'Would you like to drink?'
      (Bhattacharjya 2007: 253)

Likewise, the basic word order of Ternate Chabacano is VSO, in accordance with Austronesian languages including Tagalog (Dryer 2008; Schachter and Otanes 1972: 60). Nevertheless, this basic word order varies according to factors such as definiteness and the nominal vs. pronominal character of the nominal constituents involved:

(162) *Ta-dáli éli regálu kon su*   Ternate Chabacano
      IPFV-give   3SG.OBJ   present   OBJ   3SG.POSS
      kapitbáhay.
      neighbour
      'S/he gives presents to her/his neighbours.'
      (Sippola 2011: 183)

(163) *Ya-komprá éli kóchi, kon kel*   Ternate Chabacano
      PFV-buy   3SG   car   OBJ   DEF
      mi íha.
      1SG.POSS   daughter
      'He bought a car for my daughter.'
      (Sippola 2011: 183)

(164) *Ta-dáli lótro konmíngu págo.*   Ternate Chabacano
      IPFV-give   3PL.OBJ   1SG.OBJ   payment
      'They are paying me.'
      (Sippola 2011: 183)

Sri Lanka Creole Portuguese presumably changed basic word order from SVO to SOV under the pressure of the adstrate languages Sinhalese and Tamil between the late 19th and the second half of the 20th century. However, Ian Smith (p.c.) believes that we are actually dealing with a distortion produced by the standardisation efforts of the Wesleyan missionaries during the early 19th century for the purpose of creating a literary variety, and not with a genuine case of adstrate influence.

Descriptions of creole languages tend to feature a (sub)chapter on focusing and cleft constructions, usually attributed to the importance of pragmatic issues in the language use of creole communities where oral tradition clearly predominates (cf. Bartens 2003: 133–134). Some examples are:

(165) *Da   kom   mi   de   kom.*   Sranan Creole English
     FOC   come 1SG   PROG come
     'I'm coming'
     (Cassidy 1964: 273)

(166) *Ya   Pedu   la   na   ufi-kumi.*   Principe Creole Portuguese
     PRESENT³ Pedu   there LOC   thread-road
     'Look, Pedu is on the road.'
     (Maurer 2009: 171)

(167) *da   ensa   dektɛ   ju   kujar*   Berbice Creole Dutch
     be   3PL.FOC   take.PF   2SG   canoe
     '(It) is them that stole your canoe.'
     (Kouwenberg 1993: 425)[4]

As suggested in section 3.3.3, subordinated structures are thought to be relatively infrequent in creoles and parataxis is thought to be the predominant pattern. Below I will illustrate the use of subordinated clauses primarily with examples from San Andrés Creole English.

San Andrés Creole English features a complementizer *fi*, homophonous with and most likely historically related to, prepositional and modal *fi* (cf. Winford 1985):

(168) *Mi   tel   im   fi   stap.*   San Andrés Creole English
     1SG.SBJ   tell   3SG.OBJ   COMP   stop
     'I told him/her to stop.'
     (Bartens 2003: 127)

Saramaccan *fu* and Papiamentu *pa* share the properties of San Andrés Creole English *fi*, but in addition allow for tensed complement clauses (cf. Lefebvre and Loranger 2006; Lefebvre and Therrien 2007), e.g.:

(169) *A   ke   fu   a   bi   sa   baja.*   Saramaccan
     3SG   wish   COMP   3SG   ANT   IRR   dance
     'She wished she could dance./She wanted to be able to dance.'
     (Wijnen and Alleyne 1987: 48 cited in Lefebvre and Loanger 2006: 293)

(170) *Hose   ke   pa   Ramon   a   bai   (kaba).*   Papiamentu
     Hose   want   COMP   Ramon   PERF   go   (already)
     'Hose wishes that Ramon were gone.'
     (Maurer 1988: 178)

Subordinated clauses following verbs of speaking or knowing are introduced by a complementizer derived from, or homophonous with, a verb meaning 'to say, to speak, to talk', here *se*:

(171) *Ai   tel   im   se   A*   San Andrés Creole English
     1SG.SBJ tell 3SG.OBJ COMP 1SG.SBJ
     gwain   kom   bak   dis   maaning.
     FUT   come   back DEM   morning
     'I told him I would come back this morning.'

(172) *An   di   daata   nuo   se*   San Andrés Creole English
     and ART.DEF daughter knew   COMP
     da   neva   ihn   muma.
     FOC   NEG.PST   3SG.POSS   mother
     'And the daughter knew that it wasn't her mother.'

An exception is the (near-)homophonous verb *se(i)* 'to say' which is not usually followed by the complementizer *se* in San Andrés Creole:

(173) *Naansi se   yu   da   ihn*   San Andrés Creole English
     Anansi say 2SG.SBJ   FOC   3SG.POSS
     faada   bes   raiding   haas.
     father   best   riding   horse
     'Anansi says that you are his father's best riding horse.'

(174) *Taiga   se   se   him   neva*   San Andrés Creole English
     Tiger   say   COMP   3SG   NEG.PST
     de   kech   no   fish.
     PROG   catch   NEG   fish
     'Tiger said he wasn't catching any fish.'

The relatively rare occurrences of the sequence *se se* in San Andrés Creole English may be due to speakers' linguistic insecurity as to the status of *se* – complementizer or serial verb (see section 3.3.1.3). Note that in Akan where *sɛ* is both a serial verb and a complementizer, this sequence is strictly disallowed (Christaller 1875: 156).

Same-subject complement clauses of *waahn* 'want' do not require an overt complementizer:

(175) *An   den   dehn   waahn   kil*   San Andrés Creole English
      and   then   3PL.SBJ want   kill
      Beda   Naansi.
      Brother   Anansi
      'And then they wanted to kill Brother Anansi.'

Frequent subordinators introducing adverbial clauses in San Andrés Creole English are for instance *afta* 'after', *bikaaz(n)* 'because', *fram/faahn* 'since', *if* 'if', *wen/wentaim* 'when', etc.:

(176) *Fram   A   smaal,   A   no*   San Andrés Creole English
      from   1SG.SBJ small   1SG.SBJ NEG
      laik   ih.
      like   3SG.N.OBJ
      'Since I was small, I have not liked it.'
      (Bartens 2003: 129)

Reflexive clauses were discussed in section 3.3.2.3 above.

3.3.6. Lexicosemantics

The great majority of the lexicon of creole languages is derived from their lexifier language. Cases where the non-lexifier element accounts for more than a few percent of the total lexicon (counting types, not tokens) are relatively rare: Tok Pisin is often referred to as having a staggering 20% non-English vocabulary (e.g. Bartens 1996: 128), Principe Creole Portuguese another 20% non-Portuguese vocabulary (Maurer 2009: 211), Angolar Creole Portuguese between 10% and 20% non-Portuguese vocabulary (Lorenzino 1998: 100), Seychelles Creole French 10.7% non-French lexicon (Michaelis and Rosalie 2009: 224), and all Chabacano varieties together 8% non-Spanish vocabulary (Quilis and Casado-Fresnillo 2008: 475–476). If Saramaccan is not considered to have two distinct lexifier languages but rather as a case of partial relexification (cf. section 1), then the non-English element would amount to 38.3% (Good 2009b; Tadmor 2009: 56).

As any other language, creoles continue to adopt loanwords from other languages in addition to adstrate languages, regional or global prestige languages such as English. Although Dutch is not one of Papiamentu's lexifier languages, the amount of Dutch vocabulary is considerable in some areas of the lexicon, e.g. vocabulary referring to the administration, the judicial system, industry and commerce, technology, etc. (e.g. Kowallik and Kramer 1994). At the same time, numerous borrowings derive from English, e.g. *T-shirt* 'T-shirt', *buts* 'boots'. Detecting calques from other languages is far more challenging, especially when we are dealing with potential calques from substrate languages we have little information on (cf. Parkvall and Baker 2012).

In the lexica of San Andrés and Providence Creole English, both examples of creoles with many non-lexifier lexical items, the overwhelming majority of the lexicon derives from English. (Percentages are unavailable as no comprehensive lexical database has been compiled.) There are a number of English archaisms such as *koropshon* 'pus' (< *corruption*) and *lah* 'custom' (< *law*) (cf. Holm 1983: 19; Bartens 2009b: 306). Some English-derived items survive as regionalisms in Great Britain, e.g. *bak* 'to carry on back' (Southeast), *drawndid* 'drown' (North, Midlands *drownd*), *hahgish* 'irritable' (Midlands *hoggish*), *kliyn* 'clear (land)' (Midlands *clean*; Holm 1983: 22; Bartens 2009b: 306). For obvious reasons, loans from the Nicaraguan indigenous language Miskito, which has played an important role in the formation of closely related Nicaraguan Creole, are less common than in San Andrés and Providence Creole English. Nevertheless, the following lexical items are commonly used on the islands as well: *briybriy* 'a shrub species', *ishili* 'a lizard species', *pyampyam* 'a bird species', *rahti* 'a crab species', *shangkwa* 'a turtle species', *wawa* 'foolish', and *wowla* 'boa constrictor' (cf. Holm 1983: 14; Bartens 2009b: 306).

Due to the intense contact with Spanish especially during the 20th century, Spanish loanwords and loan meanings are very common, cf. *bwelta* 'a stroll, an errand', *chiklet* 'gum tree, chewing gum', *desowdorant* 'deodorant', *egzamen* 'exam', *elado* 'ice cream', *gwardía* 'police', *histari* 'story', *kalij/koléjio* 'high school', *komadri* 'close female', *kompadri* 'close male', *kompanyero* 'companion', *madriyna* 'godmother', *mansana* '1.7 acres', *masa* 'dough', *merengge* 'a dance', *more[y]no* 'creole, black, dark-skinned', *now tu* 'know how to' (cf. Spanish *saber* 'know to'), *nuwmatik* 'care tire', *padriyno* 'godfather', *papiyto* 'dear (used towards men and little boys)', *pasear* 'go on outing', *peg op* 'adhere' (cf. Spanish *pegar* 'to glue'), *pik* 'bite (of fish)', *potrero* 'pasture', *puwro* 'cigar', *puwta* 'whore', *sambrero/sombrero* 'hat', *teremowto* 'earthquake', *tragiyto* 'a drink', *vakuwna* 'vaccination', *yuwka* 'cassava' (Holm 1983: 13; Bartens 2009b: 305–306). Some lexical items which now appear to be loans from Spanish were once current in Standard English but have since become obsolete or archaic, e.g. *moles* (Standard English *molest* 'annoy', last attested in 1726), *sawpowrt* (Standard English *support* 'endure', last attested in 1805), *bread* (Standard English *bread* 'loaf of bread', last attested in 1643), and *dayrekshon* (Standard English *direction* 'address', last attested in 1886; cf. Holm 1983: 12; Bartens 2009b: 306).

Creole-internal neologisms manifest themselves in semantic shift (e.g. *jenereyshon* 'ancestors', *piyz* 'beans'), change of valency (e.g. *raip* 'to ripen'), compounding (e.g. *kil awt* 'exterminate'), and reanalysis of morpheme boundaries (e.g. *kangks* 'conch'; cf. Holm 1983: 22–23; Bartens 2009b: 307).

San Andrés, Providence, and Nicaraguan Creole English share most of their African-derived lexical items with the other Creole Englishes of the Western Caribbean with the exception of Jamaican, which features approximately 300 Africanisms for which etymologies have been relatively well established (Farquharson 2008). Bartens and Farquharson (2012) present a list of 119 African-retained lexical items that are largely shared by San Andrés, Providence, Nicaraguan, Belize, and Limón, as well as Bahamian Creole English, and for which fairly robust etymologies could be identified. The occurrence of the items is presented in Table 5.

Table 5. Number and percentage of secure Africanisms in Jamaican and the Western Caribbean Creole Englishes (Bartens and Farquharson 2012: 186)

Creole	Total no. of Africanisms	No. shared with Jamaican	Africanisms shared by two or more of these languages	Percentage of 107
Jamaican CE	306 (93%)		96	90%
Nicaraguan CE	79 (24%)	66 (84%)	76	71%
Providence CE	59 (18%)	50 (85%)	59	55%
San Andrés CE	48 (15%)	44 (92%)	48	45%
Belize CE	46 (14%)	40 (85%)	43	40%
Bahamian CE	37 (11%)	32 (86%)	32	30%
Limón CE	21 (6%)	20 (95%)	20	19%
	N = 329	N = 96	N = 107	

As far as semantic domains are concerned, the domain with the highest number of items was 'Flora' (18%), followed by 'Food and Drink' (13%) in second place, and 'Beliefs and Customs' and 'Unpleasantness' both with 10% in third place. The high number of terms referring to flora is due to the fact that the words entered these varieties at a time when the communities were largely agrarian. African words were applied not only to local species which bore some resemblance to those the slaves had known in Africa, but also to food crops introduced from Africa (e.g. yams; Bartens and Farquharson 2012: 189). On the other hand, especially where the domain 'Beliefs and Customs' but also to some extent 'Unpleasantness' is concerned, the fairly high percentages reflect the tendency first formulated by Alleyne (1971: 176) for Caribbean creoles to retain substratal lexical items for what could be conceived of as the private life sphere. Almost half of the items (46%) were of Kwa language origin, followed by Bantu (25%), Benuic (19%) and Mande (9%) etyma. Loans included such items as (cf. Bartens and Farquharson 2012: 180, 182, 183):

(177) *bubu* < Gbe (Eʋe) *bubuí* 'bogey man', KiKongo *mbùubu* 'something frightening; terror': San Andrés, Providence *bubu, babu* 'ghost' (Bartens 2003: 159); Nicaraguan Creole English *búubuu* 'anything that jumps out to frighten you, such as a ghost or a tiger' (Holm 1978: 213); Belize Creole English *bubu* '1. ghost or anything that frightens; 2. dry nasal mucus' (Crosbie et al. 2007: 68); Bahamian Creole English *booboo, booboo-man* '1. a frightening spirit; 2. nickname for a large, ugly person' (Holm and Shilling 1982: 24).

(178) *gungu* as in *gungu piz* < KiKongo (Vili) *ngungu* 'peas' (Laman 1964: 695: 'pois'): San Andrés, Providence *gungú piiz* 'a species of peas'; Nicaraguan Creole English: *gúnggo piiz, gungu biinz* 'a species of beans'.

(179) *kuntang* < Akan *kũntũŋ* 'to bend or subdue under one's rule, to rule, govern, sway' (Christaller 1933: 272): San Andrés, Providence *kuntang* '(command used in children's game)' (archaic; Edwards 1974: 12–13), '(gesture of crossing index and middle fingers)' (Bartens 2003: 147); Nicaraguan Creole English *kuntang* '(command used in children's game)'.

Some widely used calques occurring at least in San Andrés and Providence Creole English and amply discussed in the pertinent literature are for example *big yai* '(to be) covetous, greedy' (lit. 'big eye'), *noos huol* 'nostril' (lit. 'nose hole'), *bad mout* 'to curse' (lit. 'bad mouth'), *bobi mout* 'nipple' (lit. 'breast mouth'), *doamout* 'entrance' (lit. 'door mouth'), and *swiit mout* 'to flatter' (lit. 'sweet mouth'; see Bartens 2003: 150–152, 163–166 for parallel structures from potential substrate languages and references). 'Big eye' and 'sweet mouth' for instance can also be found in Haitian Creole French and Popular Brazilian Portuguese, at times suggested to have undergone some degree of creolisation in the past: *olho grande* and *adoçar a boca* as well as *gwo ye* and *bouch dous*, respectively (Holm 1994: 55, 58).

I shall end this chapter with a discussion of ideophones. Ideophones occur in many languages of the world (e.g. South East Asian languages or Japanese). In creole languages, they are typical of the Atlantic region where the substrate languages are African and possess ideophones to varying degrees. A preliminary definition of ideophones in Atlantic creole languages is offered by Bartens (2000a: 25):

> Ideophones constitute a word class of the sublinguistic[5] level which may enter the slots N, Adj, V, Adv of the syntactic level. They can be characterized in terms of the prototype definition consisting of phonological, morphonological, syntactical, semantic, and pragmatic characteristics.

A more comprehensive characterisation is presented in Bartens (2000a: 41–43) and includes, *inter alia*, mention of sounds and sound combinations otherwise not found in the language in question as well as differences in the frequency of certain phonemes which form part of the regular phonological system. Ideophones tend to be invariant; however, there is one morphonological process so characteristic of them that it can often be used to identify ideophones: reduplication/reiteration (cf. section 3.2).

We also find a division into phonomimes and phenomimes as far as exemplifying/quotative ideophones are concerned, as well as ideophones with their own signifié[6]. Intensifying ideophones, with a subclass of attenuating ideophones, are subject to strict syntactic collocational restrictions. The semantics of ideophones are usually highly elusive and, above all, context-sensitive which means that they may serve to concretise the meaning of the modified item in a specific context. There are certain semantic fields where the occurrence of ideophones is highly likely, e.g. colour terms are often modified by intensifying ideophones.

Ideophones are often accompanied by both paralinguistic features and corporeal gestures and can be replaced by either of them altogether. They are more or less restricted to affirmative declarative sentences and occur therefore above all in certain oral genres such as storytelling. As a symbol of a local and mostly rural identity, ideophones are lost during koineization and pidginisation, particularly during urbanisation. In Bartens (2000a) and (2006) I argue that African ideophones have been retained in the Atlantic creoles even in contexts where they no longer coexist with their substrate languages (cf. Kihm 1994: 76), albeit in reduced numbers, and that possible (often multiple) etyma can be proposed. The following are examples of an intensifying ideophone, an exemplifying phonomime, an exemplifying phenomime and an ideophone that has its own signifié, respectively:[7]

(180) *dos* cep   Guinea Bissau Creole Portuguese
     sweet ID
     'very sweet'
     (Kihm 1994: 76)

(181) *jolé gúdugúdu* Annobón Creole Portuguese
　　　run　ID
　　　'to run heavily'
　　　(Barrena 1957: 29)

(182) E　　labanta　prikiti. Cape Verdean Creole Portuguese
　　　3SG　get.up　　ID
　　　'He got up in a flash.'
　　　(Bartens 2000a: 83)

(183) *Diri　fè　　tchouloulout　sispann.* Haitian Creole French
　　　rice　make　ID　　　　　　stop
　　　'Rice makes the diarrhoea stop.'
　　　(Bartens 2000a: 106)

4. Concluding remarks

Writing an overview of creole languages for a volume on contact languages turned out to be a far more challenging task than I ever anticipated. The reason is straightforward: if we take, for example, the 1959 Mona conference as the starting point of modern Creolistics as suggested in section 2.1, the only conclusion we can draw is that half-a-century of scholarly research has produced an impressive body of work (of course choosing this cut-off point instead of, say, Reinecke's 1937 dissertation, is by no means intended to downplay the importance of all the previous work which creolists need to be familiar with). What is more, the pace of publication seems to increase by the year, as more and more linguistics students are attracted to this fascinating field. In the early 1990s at least I believed it was not only necessary but also possible to keep up to date with the field as a whole instead of reading, for instance, only publications dealing with French-lexifier creoles (cf. for example the naive pretension in Bartens 1996). It seems to me that this is no longer possible – bearing in mind, of course, that there are no or very few jobs which allow a scholar to work exclusively on creole languages. This relates to the *raison d'être* of the field (see section 2.2) as far as academic organisational structure is concerned.

In this chapter, I have aimed to argue that creoles manifest a specific typological configuration which sets them apart from other languages. Consequently, it seems not only possible but also necessary to study them as a group, comparing them both with each other and with other languages.

The bulk of this chapter consists of a presentation of prototypical (in terms of McWhorter 1998) features occurring in creole languages. Some of the features considered to be prototypical of creoles here are the same as those listed by e.g. Bickerton (1981): no comprehensive description of a creole would go without an often substantial part discussing its TMA system. The expression of [±specificity] and/or [±definiteness] in nouns is another issue which continues to be discussed (see also 3.3.2.1 above). More features have been added and the APiCS project mentioned in section 2.2 constitutes the culmination of creolists' efforts to identify more precisely those linguistic features which will enable us to gain a better understanding of what is prototypical of creoles, or, put more succinctly, what creole languages are.

In order to maintain the argument that Creolistics should exist as a field of inquiry in its own right, it is crucial for creolists to keep refining the creole prototype. However, I believe it would be (at least) as desirable for creolists to pay (even) more attention to issues of variation and language change, language use and policy, as well as the intricate relationships between language and (the rest of) culture in the future. Whereas language endangerment started to receive a considerable amount of attention once the link between the fading of linguistic diversity and biodiversity was discovered (e.g. Gorenflo et al. 2012), the fact that many creole languages are more or less highly endangered has gone virtually unnoticed. This is most probably due to the historical stigmatisation of creole languages by speakers and non-speakers alike, as well as the fact that creole communities are often not considered the indigenous inhabitants of a given territory. Nevertheless, since creole languages are capable of fulfilling all the linguistic functions of the relevant speech community as outlined above and therefore serve as primary if not first languages in their respective speech communities, the loss of a creole has as devastating a result for the community as does the loss of any other language.

Notes

1. This example was recorded as part of the Finnish Academy Project n° 111544 "Right to Language and Mother Tongue Education" in 2006.
2. Speakers of San Andrés Creole English tend to spell *A* (and *Ai*) with a capital letter in adherence to English orthographic conventions.
3. Maurer (2009: 170–171) calls *ya* a presentational element.
4. Original glosses and translations maintained.
5. Or paralinguistic.
6. The justification of the class of "ideophones with their own signifié" has been subsequently questioned (e.g. G. Tucker Childs p.c.) but originally this idea arose from the observation that although ideophones tend to be invariant, they profess derivational relationships to other word classes which can be

bidirectional, both cross-linguistically and at the language-specific level (Bartens 2000a: 42).
7. For etymology proposals and their references, please see Bartens (2000a: 52, 67–68, 83, 106).

Acknowledgements

I gratefully acknowledge the support of the Academy of Finland, without which my work on San Andrés, Providence, and Nicaraguan Creole English would not have been possible: in 2001–2002 through an individual grant for research on San Andrés and Providence Creole English (grant n° 73187), in 2006–2008 through a research project on language and language use in Nicaragua and Guatemala (grant n° 111544), and in 2008 through the position of a senior research fellow (grant n° 119750). I would also like to thank the Kone Foundation for post-doctoral grants awarded me in 2006 and 2009.

References

Aboh, Enoch O. 2007. Competition and selection: that's all! In Enoch O. Aboh & Norval Smith (eds.), *Complex Processes in New Languages* (Creole Language Library 35), 317–344. Amsterdam/Philadelphia: John Benjamins.
Aboh, Enoch O. 2011. Creoles are not distinct languages! Plenary paper presented at the Society for Pidgin and Creole Linguistics meeting in Accra, 2–6 August 2011.
Aboh, Enoch O. & Umberto Ansaldo. 2007. The role of typology in language creation: a typological take. In Umberto Ansaldo, Stephen Matthews & Lisa Lim (eds.), *Deconstructing Creole,* 39–66. Amsterdam/Philadelphia: John Benjamins.
Aboh, Enoch O. & Norval Smith. 2007. Simplicity, simplification, complexity and complexification: Where have all the interfaces gone? In Enoch O. Aboh & Norval Smith (eds.), *Complex Processes in New Languages* (Creole Language Library 35), 1–25. Amsterdam/Philadelphia: John Benjamins.
Abrahams, Roger D. 1984. Folk-tales and event-centered analysis: Anansi stories on St. Vincent. In Geneviève Calame-Griaule, Veronika Görög-Karady & Michèle Chiche (eds.), *Le Conte, Pourquoi? Comment?,* 485–509. Paris: Éditions du CNRS.
Alleyne, Mervyn C. 1971. Acculturation and the cultural matrix of creolisation. In Dell H. Hymes (ed.), *Pidginization and Creolization of Languages,* 169–86. Cambridge: Cambridge University Press.
Alleyne, Mervyn C. 1980. *Comparative Afro-American.* Ann Arbor, MI: Karoma.

Alleyne, Mervyn C. 1986. Substratum influences – guilty until proven innocent. In Pieter Muysken & Norval Smith (eds.), *Substrata Versus Universals in Creole Genesis,* 301–315. Amsterdam/Philadelphia: John Benjamins.
Alleyne, Mervyn C. 1996. *Syntaxe Historique Créole.* Paris: Karthala/P. U. C.
Álvarez López, Laura. 2004. *A Língua de Camões com Iemanjá: Forma e Funções da Linguagem do Candomblé* [The language of Camões and Iemanjá: Form and function of the Candomblé language]. Stockholm: University of Stockholm dissertation.
http://urn.kb.se/resolve?urn=urn:nbn:se:su:diva-54 (accessed 24 September 2011).
Anonymous. 1854. *Kurzgefasste Neger-Englische Grammatik.* Bautzen: Ernst Moritz Monse.
Ansaldo, Umberto & Stephen Matthews. 2007. Deconstructing creole: the rationale. In Umberto Ansaldo, Stephen Matthews & Lisa Lim (eds.), *Deconstructing Creole,* 1–18. Amsterdam/Philadelphia: John Benjamins.
Arends, Jacques. 1989. *Syntactic Developments in Sranan.* Nijmegen: Katholieke Universiteit Nijmegen dissertation.
Arends, Jacques. 1993. Towards a gradualist model of creolisation. In Francis Byrne & John Holm (eds.), *Atlantic Meets Pacific: A Global View of Pidginization and Creolisation,* 371–380. Amsterdam/Philadelphia: John Benjamins.
Arends, Jacques & Matthias Perl. 1995. *Early Suriname Creole Texts. A Collection of 18th-century Sranan and Saramaccan Documents* (Bibliotheca Ibero-Americana 49). Frankfurt: Vervuert.
Arends, Jacques, Josje Verhagen, Eva van Lier, Suzanne Dikker & Hugo Cardoso. 2006. On the presence versus absence of morphological marking in four Romance-based creoles. In Parth Bhatt & Ingo Plag (eds.), *The Structure of Creole Words. Segmental, Syllabic and Morphological Aspects* (Linguistische Arbeiten 505), 223–241. Tübingen: Niemeyer.
Bailey, Beryl Loftman. 1966. *Jamaican Creole Syntax. A Transformational Approach.* Cambridge: Cambridge University Press.
Bailey, Beryl Loftman. 1971. Jamaica Creole: Can dialect boundaries be defined? In Dell H. Hymes (ed.), *Pidginization and Creolization of Languages,* 341–348. Cambridge: Cambridge University Press.
Baissac, Charles. 1880. *Etude sur le Patois Créole Mauricien.* Nancy: Imprimerie Berger-Levrault.
Baker, Philip. 1984. The significance of agglutinated French articles in the creole languages of the Indian Ocean and elsewhere. In Mark Sebba & Loreto Todd (eds.), *Papers from the York Creole Conference, September 24–27 1983* (York Papers in Linguistics 11), 19–29. University of York: Department of Linguistics.
Baker, Philip. 1990. Off target? *Journal of Pidgin and Creole Languages* 5(1). 107–119.
Baker, Philip. 1998. Investigating the origin and diffusion of shared features among the Atlantic English Creoles. In Philip Baker & Adrienne Bruyn (eds.),

St Kitts and the Atlantic Creoles. The Texts of Samuel Augustus Mathew in Perspective (Westminster Creolistics Series 4), 315–364. London: Battlebridge.

Baker, Philip. 2001. No creolization without prior pidginization? *Te Reo* 44. 31–50.

Baker, Philip & Chris Corne. 1982. *Isle de France Creole: Affinities and Origins*. Ann Arbor, MI: Karoma.

Bakker, Peter. 2003. The absence of reduplication in pidgins. In Silvia Kouwenberg (ed.), *Twice As Meaningful. Reduplication in Pidgins, Creoles and Other Contact Languages* (Westminster Creolistics Series 8), 37–46. London: Battlebridge.

Bakker, Peter. 2008. Pidgins versus creoles and pidgincreoles. In Silvia Kouwenberg & John Victor Singler (eds.), *The Handbook of Pidgin and Creole Studies*, 130–157. Malden, MA: Wiley-Blackwell.

Bakker, Peter. 2009. The Saramaccan lexicon: Verbs. In Rachel Selbach, Hugo C. Cardoso & Margot van den Berg (eds.), *Gradual Creolization. Studies Celebrating Jacques Arends*, 155–172. Amsterdam/Philadelphia: John Benjamins.

Bakker, Peter, Aymeric Daval-Markussen, Mikael Parkvall & Ingo Plag. 2011. Creoles are typologically distinct from non-creoles. *Journal of Pidgin and Creole Languages* 26(1). 5–42.

Bakker, Peter, Norval Smith & Tonjes Veenstra. 1995. Saramaccan. In Jacques Arends, Pieter Muysken & Norval Smith (eds.), *Pidgins and Creoles: An Introduction* (Creole Language Library 15), 165–178. Amsterdam/Philadelphia: John Benjamins.

Baldauf, Ingeborg. 2000. Die Entstehung der Oldendorpmanuskripte und -dokumente – eine Einführung zur Textedition. In Christian Georg Andreas Oldendorp (ed.), *Historie der Caribischen Inseln Sanct Thomas, Sanct Crux und Sanct Jan. Kommentierte Edition des Originalmanuskriptes. Erster Teil* (Abhandlungen und Berichte des Staatlichen Museums für Völkerkunde Dresden 51), 9–13. Berlin: Verlag für Wissenschaft und Bildung.

Baptista, Marlyse. 2002. *The Syntax of Cape Verdean Creole: The Sotavento Varieties* (Linguistik Aktuell/Linguistics Today 54). Amsterdam: John Benjamins.

Baptista, Marlyse, Heliana Mello & Miki Suzuki. 2007. CV/GB: Kabuverdianu, or Cape Verdean, and Kriyol, or Guinea Bissau (Creole Portuguese). In John Holm & Peter L. Patrick (eds.), *Comparative Creole Syntax. Parallel Outlines of 18 Creole Grammars* (Westminster Creolistics Series 7), 53–82. London: Battlebridge.

Barrena, P. Natalio. 1957. *Gramática Annobonesa*. Madrid: Instituto de Estudios Africanos. Consejo Superior de Investigaciones Científicas.

Bartens, Angela. 1995. *Die Iberoromanisch-Basierten Kreolsprachen: Ansätze der Linguistischen Beschreibung*. Frankfurt/Main: Peter Lang.

Bartens, Angela. 1996a. *Der Kreolische Raum: Geschichte und Gegenwart*. Helsinki: Finnische Akademie der Wissenschaften.

Bartens, Angela. 1996b. Phonologische Merkmale atlantischer Iberokreols. *Lusorama* 29. 73–88.

Bartens, Angela. 1996c. Interrogativa und verwandte Wortarten in den iberoromanisch-basierten Kreolsprachen. In Annette Endruschat & Eberhard Gärtner (eds.), *Untersuchungen zur Portugiesischen Sprache* (Beihefte zu Lusorama. 1. Reihe. 7. Band), 243–262. Frankfurt/Main: TFM/Domus Editoria Europaea.
Bartens, Angela. 1998a. Existe-t-il un système verbal semi-créole? *Neuphilologische Mitteilungen* 94(4). 379–399.
Bartens, Angela. 1998b. Review of 'L'angolar. Un créole afro-portugais parlé a São Tomé', by Philippe Maurer, 1995, Hamburg: Buske. *Journal of Pidgin and Creole Languages* 13(1). 180–187.
Bartens, Angela. 2000a. *Ideophones and Sound Symbolism in Atlantic Creoles.* Helsinki: The Finnish Academy of Science and Letters.
Bartens, Angela. 2000b. Notes on componential diffusion in the genesis of the Kabuverdianu cluster. In John H. McWhorter (ed.), *Language Change and Language Contact in Pidgins and Creoles* (Creole Language Library 21), 35–61. Amsterdam/Philadelphia: John Benjamins.
Bartens, Angela. 2003. *A Contrastive Grammar. Islander – Caribbean Standard English – Spanish.* Helsinki: The Finnish Academy of Science and Letters.
Bartens, Angela. 2004. A comparative study of reduplication in Portuguese- and Spanish-based creoles. In Mauro Fernández, Manuel Fernández-Ferreira & Nancy Vázquez Veiga (eds.), *Actas del III Encuentro de ACBLPE,* 239–253. Madrid: Iberoamericana and Frankfurt: Vervuert.
Bartens, Angela. 2005. Les créoles portugais de l'Asie: entre superstrat et adstrats. *Études Créoles* 28(1). 115–146.
Bartens, Angela. 2006. The ideophones of African Portuguese-based creoles revisited. Paper presented at the ACBLPE meeting, Coimbra, 28–30 June 2006.
Bartens, Angela. 2008. ¿Explicar la variación morfológica y morfosintáctica en los criollos es siempre posible? *Actas del XXV Congreso Nacional de Lingüística, Literatura y Semiótica.* Medellín: Universidad de Antioquia, Universidad EAFIT and Universidad de Medellín. (CD-ROM)
Bartens, Angela. 2009a. Observações sobre o uso dos afixos derivacionais em alguns crioulos de base lexical portuguesa e espanhola [Observations on the use of derivational affixes in some Portuguese- and Spanish-lexifier creoles]. *Lingüística* 4(1). 59–83.
Bartens, Angela. 2009b. A comparison of the English-based creoles of Nicaragua and San Andrés and Old Providence. *Neuphilologische Mitteilungen* 110. 299–318.
Bartens, Angela. 2010. All roads lead to Rome – observations with regard to the semantic expansion of the preposition *em/en* expressing directionality. Paper presented at the conference Crioulos Ibero-Asiáticos: Perspectivas Comparativas, Macao, 28 October 2010.
Bartens, Angela. 2011a. Substrate features in Nicaraguan, Providence and San Andrés Creole Englishes: A comparison with Twi. In Claire Lefebvre (ed.), *Creoles, Their Substrates, and Language Typology,* 201–224. Amsterdam/Philadelphia: John Benjamins.

Bartens, Angela. 2011b. Akan substrate influence on three Western Caribbean Creoles revisited. Paper presented at the 2011 Summer Conference of the Society for Pidgin and Creole Linguistics: Traces of Contact. Accra, Ghana, 2–6 August 2011.

Bartens, Angela. forthcoming a. San Andrés Creole English. In Susanne Michaelis, Philippe Maurer, Magnus Huber & Martin Haspelmath (eds.), *Atlas of Pidgin and Creole Language Structures*. Oxford: Oxford University Press.

Bartens, Angela. forthcoming b. Nicaraguan Creole English. In Susanne Michaelis, Philippe Maurer, Magnus Huber & Martin Haspelmath (eds.). *Atlas of Pidgin and Creole Language Structures*. Oxford: Oxford University Press.

Bartens, Angela. forthcoming c. San Andres-Providence Creole English. In Bernd Kortmann & Kerstin Lunkenheimer (eds.), *The Mouton World Atlas of Variation in English,* Berlin: Mouton de Guyter.

Bartens, Angela. in preparation. Una gramática contrastiva del kriol nicaragüense y del inglés.

Bartens, Angela & Joseph T. Farquharson. 2012. African words in the English-lexifier creoles of San Andrés, Providence, and Nicaragua and other Western Caribbean varieties. In Angela Bartens & Philip Baker (eds.), *Black through White. African Words and Calques in Creoles and Transplanted European Languages,* 169–196. London: Battlebridge.

Bascom, William. 1992. *African Folktales in the New World*. Bloomington: Indiana University Press.

Bastide, Roger. 1967. *Les Amériques Noires*. Paris: Payot.

Benoist, Jean (ed.). 1972. *L'Archipel Inachevé. Culture et Société aux Antilles Françaises*. Montréal: Les Presses de l'Université de Montréal.

Bentley, William. 1887. *Dictionary and Grammar of the Kongo Language*. London: Missionary Society.

Berlin, Ira. 1998. *Many Thousand Gone: The First Two Centuries of Slavery in North America*. Cambridge, MA: The Belknap Press/Harvard University Press.

Bhattacharjya, Dwijen. 2007. Nagamese (restructured Assamese). In John Holm & Peter L. Patrick (eds.), *Comparative Creole Syntax. Parallel Outlines of 18 Creole Grammars* (Westminster Creolistics Series 7)*,* 237–254. London: Battlebridge.

Bickerton, Derek. 1973. The nature of a creole continuum. *Language* 49(3). 640–669.

Bickerton, Derek. 1974. Creolisation, linguistic universals, natural semantax and the brain. *University of Hawaii Working Papers in Linguistics* 6. 3, 124–141. (Also in Rita Day (ed.), *Issues in English Creoles. Papers from the 1975 Hawaii Conference (Varieties of English Around the World, G2),* 1–18. Amsterdam: John Benjamins, 1980.)

Bickerton, Derek. 1975. *Dynamics of a Creole System*. Cambridge: Cambridge University Press.

Bickerton, Derek. 1981. *Roots of Language*. Ann Arbor, MI: Karoma.

Bickerton, Derek. 1984. The language bioprogram hypothesis. *The Brain and Behavioral Sciences* 7. 173–221.

Bickerton, Derek. 1988. Creole languages and the bioprogram. In Frederik J. Newmeyer (ed.), *Linguistics: The Cambridge Survey. Volume II. Linguistic Theory: Extensions and Implications,* 268–284. Cambridge: Cambridge University Press.
Bickerton, Derek & Aquiles Escalante. 1970. Palenquero: a Spanish-based creole of northern Colombia. *Lingua* 24. 254–267.
Bolland, O. Nigel. 2006. Reconsidering creolisation and creole societies. *Shibboleths: Journal of Comparative Theory* 1(1). 1–14.
Bougerol, Christiane. 1983. *La Médecine Populaire à la Guadeloupe*. Paris: Karthala.
Boxer, Charles R. 1969. *The Portuguese Seaborne Empire*. London: Hutchinson.
Brousseau, Anne-Marie. 1989. De "n'u-flo" à "po-bouche": hypothèse sur l'origine des composés en haïtien. *Revue Canadienne de Linguistique* 34. 285–312.
Brousseau, Anne-Marie. 2011. One substrate, two creoles: The development of segmental inventories in St. Lucian and Haitian. In Claire Lefebvre (ed.), *Creoles, Their Substrates, and Language Typology* (Typological Studies in Language 95), 105–125. Amsterdam/Philadelphia: John Benjamins.
Bruyn, Adrienne. 2008. Grammaticalization in pidgins and creoles. In Silvia Kouwenberg & John Victor Singler (eds.), *The Handbook of Pidgin and Creole Studies,* 385–410. Malden, MA: Blackwell.
Burton, Richard D. E. 1997. *Afro-Creole: Power, Opposition, and Play in the Caribbean*. Ithaca, NY: Cornell University Press.
Byrne, Francis. 1988. Review of 'The syntax of serial verbs', by Mark Sebba. *Journal of Pidgin and Creole Languages* 3(1). 146–152.
Byrne, Francis (ed.). 1987. *Grammatical Relations in a Radical Creole. Verb Complementation in Saramaccan*. (Creole Language Library 3). Amsterdam/ Philadelphia: John Benjamins.
Cardoso, Hugo. 2009. *The Indo-Portuguese Language of Diu*. Utrecht: LOT.
Carroll, Susanne E. 2004. Segmentation: Learning how to 'hear words' in the L2 speech stream. *Transactions of the Philological Society* 102(2). 227–254.
Cassidy, Frederic G. 1964. Toward the recovery of early English-African Pidgin. In *Symposium on multilingualism (Brazzaville),* 267–277. London: Conseil Scientifique pour l'Afrique/Commission de Coopération Technique en Afrique.
Cassidy, Frederic G. & Robert B. LePage. 1980. *Dictionary of Jamaican English*. Cambridge: Cambridge University Press.
Chapuis, Daniel. 2007. Dominican (Creole French), or Kwéyòl. In John Holm & Peter L. Patrick (eds.), *Comparative Creole Syntax. Parallel Outlines of 18 Creole Grammars* (Westminster Creolistics Series 7), 83–100. London: Battlebridge.
Chaudenson, Robert. 1974. *Le Lexique du Parler Créole de la Réunion,* 2 vols. Paris, Champion.
Chaudenson, Robert. 1979. *Les Créoles Français*. Paris: Fernand Nathan.
Chaudenson, Robert. 1992. *Des Iles, des Hommes, des Langues: Essais sur la Créolisation Linguistique et Culturelle*. Paris: L'Harmattan.
Chaudenson, Robert. 2001. *Creolisation of Language and Culture*. London: Routledge.

Christaller, Rev. J. G. 1875. *A Grammar of the Asante and Fante Language Called Tshi [Chwee, Twi] Based on the Akuapem Dialect with References to the Other (Akan and Fante) Dialects*. Basel: Basel Evang. Missionary Society.

Christaller, Rev. J. G. 1933. *Dictionary of the Asante and Fante Language Called Tshi (Twi)*, 2nd edn. Basel: Basel Evangelical Missionary Society.

Clements, George N. 2000. Phonology. In Bernd Heine & Derek Nurse (eds.), *African Languages. An Introduction,* 123–160. Cambridge: Cambridge University Press.

Clements, J. Clancy. 1996. *The Genesis of a Language: The Formation and Development of Korlai Portuguese* (Creole Language Library 16). Amsterdam/ Philadelphia: John Benjamins.

Cohen, Robin. 2007. Creolisation and cultural globalization: the soft sounds of fugitive power. *Globalizations* 4(3). 369–384.

Corne, Chris. 1977. *Seychelles Creole Grammar: Elements for Indian Ocean Proto-Creole Reconstruction*. Tübingen: Narr.

Courlander, Harold. 1976. *A Treasure of Afro-American Folklore*. New York: Crown.

Couto, Hildo Honório do. 1994. *O Crioulo Português da Guiné-Bissau* [The Creole Portuguese of Guinea Bissau] (Kreolische Bibiothek 14). Hamburg: Buske.

Cox, David. 2004. *From Intransigence to Integration: English-Speaking communities and the Emergence of the National Self in Post-Colonial Argentina*. Helsinki: University of Helsinki, Renvall Institute MA thesis.

Crosbie, Paul (ed.). 2007. *Kriol-Inglish Dikshineri* [English-Kriol dictionary]. Belmopan: Belize Kriol Project.

Crowley, Terry. 2008. Pidgin and creole morphology. In Silvia Kouwenberg & John Victor Singler (eds.), *The Handbook of Pidgin and Creole Studies,* 74–97. Malden, MA: Wiley-Blackwell.

d'Ans, Marcel-André. 1987. *Haïti. Paysage et Société*. Paris: Karthala.

Dawthorne, Oscar R. 1981. *Dark Ancestor. The Literature of the Black Man in the Caribbean*. Baton Rouge: Louisiana State University Press.

D'Costa, Jean & Barbara Lalla (eds.). 1989. *Voices in Exile. Jamaican Texts of the 18th and 19th Centuries*. Tuscaloosa, AL: The University of Alabama Press.

DeCamp, David. 1971. Toward a generative analysis of a post-creole speech continuum. In Dell H. Hymes (ed.), *Pidginization and Creolization of Languages,* 349–370. Cambridge: Cambridge University Press.

DeGraff, Michel. 2001. On the origin of creoles: A Cartesian critique of 'neo'- Darwinian linguistics. *Linguistic Typology* 5(2/3). 213–310.

DeGraff, Michel. 2005. Linguists' most dangerous myth: The fallacy of creole exceptionalism. *Language in Society* 34. 533–591.

DeGraff, Michel. 2007. Kreyòl Ayisiyen, or Haitian Creole ('Creole French'). In John Holm & Peter L. Patrick (eds.), *Comparative Creole Syntax. Parallel Outlines of 18 Creole Grammars* (Westminster Creolistics Series 7), 101–126. London: Battlebridge.

de Kleine, Christa. 2007. Negerhollands. In John Holm & Peter L. Patrick (eds.), *Comparative Creole Syntax. Parallel Outlines of 18 Creole Grammars* (Westminster Creolistics Series 7), 255–272. London: Battlebridge.
Detges, Ulrich. 2000. Two types of restructuring in French creoles: A cognitive approach to the genesis of tense markers. In Ingrid Neumann-Holzschuh & Edgar Schneider (eds.), *Degrees of Restructuring in Creole Languages* (Creole Language Library 22), 135–162. Amsterdam/Philadelphia: John Benjamins.
Dixon, Robert M. W. 1977. Where have all the adjectives gone? *Studies in Language* 1. 19–80.
Ducœurjoly, S. J. 1802. *Manuel des Habitants de Saint-Domingue*. Paris: Chez Lenoir.
Dryer, Matthew S. 2008. Order of subject and verb. In Martin Haspelmath, Matthew S. Dryer, David Gil & Bernard Comrie (eds.), *The World Atlas of Language Structures Online*, Chapter 82. München: Max Planck Digital Library.
http://wals.info/feature/82 (accessed 20 Aug 2012).
Dyhr, Sebastian Adorján. 2001. *'Grammatik over det Creolske Sprog' af Joachim Melchior Magens i en Lingvistisk og Historisk Kontekst* ['Grammar of the creole language' by Joachim Melchior Magens in a linguistic and historical perspective]. Aarhus: Aarhus University MA thesis.
Edwards, Jay. 1974. African influences on the English of San Andrés Island, Colombia. In David Decamp & Ian F. Hancock (eds.), *Pidgins and Creoles: Current Trends and Prospects*, 1–26. Washington, DC: Georgetown University Press.
Faraclas, Nicholas. 2007. Tok Pisin (Creole English). In John Holm & Peter L. Patrick (eds.), *Comparative Creole Syntax. Parallel Outlines of 18 Creole Grammars* (Westminster Creolistics Series 7), 355–372. London: Battlebridge.
Faraclas, Nicholas, Lourdes Gonzalez, Migdalia Medina & Wendell Villanueva Reyes. 2005. Ritualized insults and the African diaspora: Sounding in African American Vernacular English and wording in Nigerian Pidgin. In Susanne Mühleisen & Bettina Migge (eds.), *Politeness and Face in Caribbean Creoles* (Varieties of English Around the World G34), 45–72. Amsterdam/Philadelphia: John Benjamins.
Farquharson, Joseph T. 2005. *Faiya-bon*: The socio-pragmatics of homophobia in Jamaican (Dancehall) culture. In Susanne Mühleisen & Bettina Migge (eds.), *Politeness and Face in Caribbean Creoles* (Varieties of English Around the World G34), 101–118. Amsterdam/Philadelphia: John Benjamins.
Farquharson, Joseph T. 2007. Creole morphology revisited. In Umberto Ansaldo, Stephen Mathews & Lisa Lim (eds.), *Deconstructing Creole*, 21–37. Amsterdam/Philadelphia: John Benjamins.
Farquharson, Joseph T. 2008. *The African Lexis in Jamaican: Its Linguistic and Sociohistorical Significance*. Mona: University of the West Indies dissertation.
Farquharson, Joseph T. 2011. Aspectual reduplication in Jamaican and Akan. Paper presented at the SPCL meeting in Accra, 2–6 August 2011.

Fernandes, Miguel Senna & Alan Norman Baxter. 2004. *Maquista Chapado. Vocabulary and Expressions in Macao's Portuguese Creole*. Macao: Instituto Cultural da R. A. E. de Macau.

Ferraz, Luiz. 1976. The substratum of Annobonese Creole. *International Journal of the Sociology of Language* 7. 83–93.

Ferraz, Luiz. 1978. The creole of São Tomé. *African Studies* 37(1). 3–66 and 37(2). 235–288.

Figueroa, Esther. 2005. Rude sounds: kiss teeth and negotiation of the public sphere. In Susanne Mühleisen & Bettina Migge (eds.), *Politeness and Face in Caribbean Creoles* (Varieties of English Around the World G34), 73–99. Amsterdam/ Philadelphia: John Benjamins.

Figueroa, Esther & Peter L. Patrick. 2002. Kiss-teeth. *American Speech* 77. 383–397.

Fleischmann, Ulrich. 1983. Communication et langues de communication pendant l'esclavage aux Antilles. *Études Créoles* IV (2). 29–46.

Fleischmann, Ulrich. 1986. *Das Französisch-Kreolische in der Karibik. Zur Funktion von Sprache im Sozialen und Geographischen Raum*. Tübingen: Narr.

Focke, Hendrik C. 1855. *Neger-Engelsch Woordenboek* [Negro-English dictionary]. Leiden: Van den Heuvell.

FOREIBCA. 2005a. *Kuos Riijan Stuoriz I* [Coast region stories I]. Bluufiilz: IPILC/URACCAN/MECD.

FOREIBCA. 2005b. *Kuos Riijan Stuoriz II* [Coast region stories II]. Bluufiilz: IPILC/URACCAN/MECD.

Forman, Michael L. 1972. *Zamboangueño Texts with Grammatical Analysis*. Ithaca, NY: Cornell University dissertation.

Fortier, Alcée. 1885. The French language in Louisiana and the Negro French dialect. *Transactions of the Modern Language Association of America* 1. 96–111.

Gil, David. 2001. Creoles, complexity and Riau Indonesian. *Linguistic Typology* 5(2/3). 325–371.

Gilbert, Glenn G. 1980. Introduction. In Glenn G. Gilbert (ed.), *Pidgin and Creole Languages. Selected Essays By Hugo Schuchardt*, 1–13. London: Cambridge University Press.

Good, Jeff. 2009a. A twice-mixed creole? Tracing the history of a prosodic split in the Saramaccan lexicon. *Studies in Language* 33. 459–498.

Good, Jeff. 2009b. Loanwords in Saramaccan, an English-based creole of Suriname. In Martin Haspelmath & Uri Tadmor (eds.), *Loanwords in the World's Languages: A Comparative Handbook*, 918–943. Berlin: Walter de Gruyter.

Goodman, Morris F. 1964. *A comparative study of Creole French Dialects*. London: Mouton & Co.

Goodman, Morris F. 1987. The Portuguese element in American creoles. In Glenn G. Gilbert (ed.), *Pidgin and Creole Languages: Essays in Memory of John E. Reinecke*, 361–405. Honolulu: University of Hawaii Press.

Gorenflo, Larry J., Suzanne Romaine, Russell A. Mittermeier & Kristen Walker-Painemilla. 2012. Co-occurrence of linguistic and biological diversity in

biodiversity hotspots and high biodiversity wilderness areas. *Proceedings of the National Academy of Sciences of the United States of America* 109(21). 8032–8037.
Gougenheim, Georges. 1971. *Étude sur les Périphrases Verbales de la Langue Française.* Paris: Nizet.
Gouveia, Maria Carmen de Castro Duarte de Frias e. 1993. *Um Aspecto de Morfologia Historica: O Género Gramatical dos Substantivos e Adjectivos em Português. Trabalho de Síntese Apresentado à Faculdade de Letras da Universidade de Coimbra no Âmbito das Provas de Aptidão Pedagógica e de Capacidade Científica* [An issue in historical morphology: the grammatical gender of substantives and adjectives in Portuguese. Synthetic study presented to the Faculty of Arts of the University of Coimbra as part of the Educational Aptitude and Scientific Capacity Tests]. Coïmbra: Faculdade de Letras, Universidade de Coïmbra.
Goux, Abbé. 1842. *Catéchisme en Langue Créole, Précédé d'un Essai de Grammaire sur l'Idiome Usité dans les Colonies Françaises.* Paris: Imprimerie H. Vrayet de Surcy.
Graham, Ross. 2010. Honduras/Bay Islands English. In Daniel Schreier, Peter Trudgill, Edgar W. Schneider & Jeffrey P. Williams (eds.), *The Lesser-Known Varieties of English: An Introduction,* 92–135. Cambridge: Cambridge University Press.
Granda, Germán de. 1970. Un temprano testimonio sobre las lenguas 'criollas' en África y América. *Thesaurus* XXV: 1–11.
Granda, Germán de. 1976. Algunos rasgos morfosintácticos de posible origen criollo en el habla de áreas hispanoamericanas de población negra. *Anuario de Letras* 14. 5–22.
Granda, Germán de. 1977. *Estudios sobre un Área Dialectal Hispanoamericana de Población Negra. Las Tierras Bajas Occidentales de Colombia.* Bogotá: Instituto Caro y Cuervo.
Granda, Germán de. 1988. *Lingüística e Historia: Temas Afro-Hispánicos.* Valladolid: Universidad de Valladolid, Secretariado de Publicaciones.
Granda, Germán de. 1992. Retenciones africanas en el nivel fonético de criollo palenquero (Colombia). In Dieter Kremer (ed.), *Actes du XVIII Congrès International de Linguistique et de Philologie Romanes,* 542–552. Tübingen: Niemeyer.
Güldemann, Tom. 2005. The alleged grammaticalization of quotative-complementizers in Atlantic creoles: A West African substrate perspective. Paper presented at the conference Creole Language Structure between Substrates and Superstrates, Leipzig, 3–5 June 2005.
Günther, Wilfried. 1973. *Das portugiesische Kreolisch der Ilha do Príncipe.* Marburg an d. Lahn: H.-J. Greschat (Auslfg.: Universitäts-Bibliothek).
Haabo, Vincent. 2002. Fonologie van het Saramaccaans [Phonology of Saramaccan]. Ms., University of Leiden.
Hagège, Claude. 2001. Creoles and the notion of simplicity in human languages. *Linguistic Typology* 5(2/3). 167–387.

Hagemeijer, Tjerk. 2009. Initial vowel agglutination in the Gulf of Guinea creoles. In Enoch O. Aboh & Norval Smith (eds.), *Complex Processes in New Languages* (Creole Language Library 35), 29–50. Amsterdam/Philadelphia: John Benjamins.
Haiman, John. 1980. The iconicity of grammar. *Language* 56(3). 515–540.
Hall, Robert A., Jr. 1962. The life cycle of pidgin languages. *Lingua* 11. 151–156.
Hancock, Ian F. 1986. The domestic hypothesis, diffusion and componentiality. In Pieter Muysken & Norval Smith (eds.), *Substrata Versus Universals in Creole Genesis,* 71–102. Amsterdam/Philadelphia: John Benjamins.
Hancock, Ian F. 1987. A preliminary classification of the anglophone Atlantic creoles with syntactic data from thirty-three representative dialects. In Glenn G. Gilbert (ed.), *Pidgin and Creole Languages: Essays in Memory of John E. Reinecke,* 264–333. Honolulu: University of Hawaii Press.
Heine, Bernd & Tania Kuteva. 2002. *World Lexicon of Grammaticalization.* Cambridge: Cambridge University Press.
Herskovits, Melville J. 1966. *The New World Negro* (edited by Frances S. Herskovits). Bloomington, IN: Indiana University Press.
Herskovits, Melville J. & Frances S. Herskovits. 1936. *Suriname Folk-Lore.* New York, NY: Columbia University Press.
Herskovits, Melville J. & Frances S. Herskovits. 1958. *Dahomean Narrative. A Cross-Cultural Analysis.* Wyoming: Northwestern University Press.
Hesseling, Dirk Christian. 1923. *Het Afrikaans. Bijdrage tot de Geschiedenis der Nederlandse Taal in Zuid-Afrika* [Afrikaans. Contribution to the history of the Dutch language in South Africa]. Leiden: E. J. Brill.
Holm, John. 1978. *The Creole English of Nicaragua's Miskito Coast: Its Sociolinguistic History and a Comparative Study of its Lexicon and Syntax.* London: University of London dissertation.
Holm, John. 1983. Nicaragua's Miskito Coast Creole English. In John Holm (ed.), *Central American English* (Varieties of English around the world T2), 95–130. Heidelberg: Julius Groos.
Holm, John. 1986. Substrate diffusion. In Pieter Muysken & Norval Smith (eds.), *Substrata Versus Universals in Creole Genesis,* 259–278. Amsterdam/ Philadelphia: John Benjamins.
Holm, John. 1987. Creole influence on popular Brazilian Portuguese. In Glenn G. Gilbert (ed.), *Pidgin and Creole Languages: Essays in Memory of John E. Reinecke,* 405–430. Honolulu: University of Hawaii Press.
Holm, John. 1988. *Pidgins and Creoles. Volume I: Theory and Structure.* Cambridge: Cambridge University Press.
Holm, John. 1989. *Pidgins and Creoles. Volume II: Reference Survey.* Cambridge: Cambridge University Press.
Holm, John. 1992. Popular Brazilian Portuguese: a semi-creole. In Ernesto Andrade, Dulce Pereira & Maria Antónia Mota (eds.), *Crioulos de Base Portuguesa* [Portuguese-based creoles], 37–66. Braga: Associação Portuguesa de Linguistíca.
Holm, John. 1994. A semi-criulização do português vernáculo do Brasil: evidência de contacto nas expressões idiomáticas [The semi-creolisation of Brazilian

Vernacular Portuguese: evidence of contact in idiomatic expressions]. *Papia* 3(2). 51–61.
Holm, John. 2004. *Languages in Contact. The Partial Restructuring of Vernaculars.* Cambridge: Cambridge University Press.
Holm, John. 2007. Introduction. In John Holm & Peter L. Patrick (eds.), *Comparative Creole Syntax. Parallel Outlines of 18 Creole Grammars* (Westminster Creolistics Series 7), v-xi. London: Battlebridge.
Holm, John & Alison W. Shilling. 1982. *Dictionary of Bahamian English.* Cold Spring: Lexik House.
Holm, John & Peter L. Patrick (eds.). 2007. *Comparative Creole Syntax. Parallel Outlines of 18 Creole Grammars* (Westminster Creolistics Series 7.) London: Battlebridge.
Huber, Magnus, Martin Haspelmath, Susanne Michaelis & Philippe Maurer. 2011. Substrate traces, superstrate traces and universals in Atlantic pidgins and creoles. Findings based on the Atlas of Pidgin and Creole Language Structures with a special focus on Africa. Paper presented at the 2011 Summer Conference of the Society for Pidgin and Creole Linguistics: Traces of Contact. Accra, Ghana, 2–6 August 2011.
Hull, Alexander. 1968. The origins of New World French phonology. *Word* 24. 255–269.
Huttar, Mary L. 2007. Ndyuka (Creole English). In John Holm & Peter L. Patrick (eds.), *Comparative Creole Syntax. Parallel Outlines of 18 Creole Grammars* (Westminster Creolistics Series 7), 217–236. London: Battlebridge.
Jackson, Kenneth David. 1990. *Sing without Shame: Oral Traditions in Indo-Portuguese Creole Verse.* Amsterdam/Philadelphia: John Benjamins and Macau: Instituto Cultural de Macau.
Jacobs, Bart. 2012. *Origins of a Creole. The History of Papiamentu and Its African Ties* (Language Contact and Bilingualism 3.) Berlin: Mouton de Gruyter.
Joubert, Sidney M. 1991. *Dikshionario (Handwoordenboaek) Papiamentu-Hulandes* [Papiamentu-Dutch dictionary]. Willemstad, Curaçao: Cromotip.
Keesing, Roger M. 1988. *Melanesian Pidgin and the Oceanic Substrate.* Stanford, CA: Stanford University Press.
Keller, Rudi. 1994. *On Language Change: The Invisible Hand in Language.* London: Routledge.
Kihm, Alain. 1994. *Kriyol Syntax. The Portuguese-based Creole Language of Guinea-Bissau* (Creole Language Library 14.) Amsterdam/Philadelphia: John Benjamins.
Klein, Thomas. 2011. Typology of creole phonology: Phoneme inventories and syllable templates. *Journal of Pidgin and Creole Languages* 26(1). 155–193.
Kouwenberg, Silvia. 1993. *A Grammar of Berbice Dutch.* Berlin: Mouton de Gruyter.
Kouwenberg, Silvia. 2003. Introduction. In Silvia Kouwenberg (ed.), *Twice as Meaningful. Reduplication in Pidgins, Creoles and Other Contact Languages* (Westminster Creolistics Series 8), 1–6. London: Battlebridge.
Kouwenberg, Silvia. 2012. The Ijo-derived lexicon of Berbice Dutch Creole: an a-typical case of African lexical influence. In Angela Bartens & Philip Baker

(eds.), *Black through White. African Words and Calques in Creoles and Transplanted European Languages,* 135–144. London: Battlebridge.

Kouwenberg, Silvia (ed.). 2003. *Twice as Meaningful. Reduplication in Pidgins, Creoles and Other Contact Languages* (Westminster Creolistics Series 8.) London: Battlebridge.

Kouwenberg, Silvia & Darlene La Charité. 2003. The meanings of 'more of the same'. Iconicity in reduplication and the evidence for substrate transfer in the genesis of Caribbean Creole languages. In Silvia Kouwenberg (ed.), *Twice as Meaningful. Reduplication in Pidgins, Creoles and Other Contact Languages* (Westminster Creolistics Series 8), 7–18. London: Battlebridge.

Kouwenberg, Silvia & Eric Murray. 1994. *Papiamentu* (Languages of the World Materials 83). München: LINCOM Europa.

Kouwenberg, Silvia & John Victor Singler. 2008. Introduction. In Silvia Kouwenberg & John Victor Singler (eds.), *The Handbook of Pidgin and Creole Studies,* 1–16. Malden, MA: Blackwell.

Kowallik, Sabine & Johannes Kramer. 1994. Influencias del neerlandés en el papiamentu. In Jens Lüdtke & Matthias Perl (eds.), *Lengua y Cultura en el Caribe Hispánico. Actas de una Sección de Hispanistas Alemanes Celebrado en Augsburgo marzo de 1993 4–7,* 205–218. Tübingen: Niemeyer.

Kramp, André A. 1983. *Early Creole Lexicography: A Study of C. L. Schumann's Manuscript Dictionary of Sranan.* Leiden: University of Leiden dissertation.

Kropp Dakubu, Mary Esther. 2002. *Ga Phonology* (Language Monograph No. 6). Legon: Institute of African Studies, University of Ghana.

Kropp Dakubu, Mary Esther. 2011. The birth of languages in Ghana: contact the onlie begetter? Plenary paper presented at the 2011 Summer Conference of the Society for Pidgin and Creole Linguistics: Traces of Contact. Accra, Ghana, 2–6 August 2011.

Ladhams, John, Tjerk Hagemeijer, Philippe Maurer & Marike Post. 2003. Reduplication in the Gulf of Guinea creole languages. In Silvia Kouwenberg (ed.), *Twice as Meaningful. Reduplication in Pidgins, Creoles and Other Contact Languages* (Westminster Creolistics Series 8), 165–176. London: Battlebridge.

Lafontaine, Marie-Céline. 1982. Musique et société aux Antilles. *Présence Africaine* 121/122. 72–108.

Laman, Karl E. 1936. *Dictionnaire Kikongo-Français, Avec une Etude Phonétique Décrivant les Dialectes les Plus Importants de la Langue Dite Kikongo.* Brussels: Librairie Falk.

Laplante, André. 1972. L'univers marie-galantais. Quelques notes sur la cosmologie des Marie-Galantais de la région des Bas. In Jean Benoist (ed.), *L'Archipel Inachevé. Culture et Société aux Antilles françaises,* 205–232. Montréal: Les Presses de l'Université de Montréal.

Lefebvre, Claire. 1986. Relexification in creole genesis revisited: The case of Haitian Creole. In Pieter Muysken & Norval Smith (eds.), *Substrata Versus Universals in Creole Genesis,* 279–300. Amsterdam/Philadelphia: John Benjamins.

Lefebvre, Claire & Virginie Loranger. 2006. On the properties of Saramaccan *fu*: synchronic and diachronic perspectives. *Journal of Pidgin and Creole Languages* 21(2). 275–337.
Lefebvre, Claire & Isabelle Therrien. 2007. On the properties of Papiamentu *pa*: synchronic and diachronic perspectives. In Magnus Huber & Viveka Velupillai (eds.), *Synchronic and Diachronic Perspective on Contact Languages*, 215–255. Amsterdam/Philadelphia: John Benjamins.
Lenz, Rodolfo. 1928. *El Papiamento: Lengua Criolla de Curazao (La Gramática Más Sencilla)*. Santiago, Chile: Balcells and Cia.
Lipski, John M. 1986. The Portuguese element in Philippine Creole Spanish: a critical assessment. *Philippine Journal of Linguistics* 17. 1–17.
Lipski, John M. 1988. Philippine Creole Spanish: assessing the Portuguese element. *Zeitschrift für Romanische Philologie* 104. 25–45.
Lipski, John M. 2002. Partial Spanish: Strategies of pidginization and simplification (from Lingua Franca to 'Gringo Lingo'). In Caroline L. Wiltshire & Joaquim Camps (eds.), *Romance Phonology and Variation*, 117–143. Amsterdam/ Philadelphia: John Benjamins.
Lipski, John M. 2008. *Afro-Bolivian Spanish* (Lengua y Sociedad en el Mundo Hispánico 20). Madrid/Frankfurt: Iberoamericana/Vervuert.
Lipski, John M. 2012. Africanisms in Afro-Bolivian Spanish. In Angela Bartens & Philip Baker (eds.), *Black through White. African Words and Calques in Creoles and Transplanted European Languages* (Westminster Creolistics Series 11), 73–80. London: Battlebridge.
Lipski, John M. & Maurizio Santoro. 2007. Zamboangueño Creole Spanish. In John Holm & Peter L. Patrick (eds.), *Comparative Creole Syntax. Parallel Outlines of 18 Creole Grammars* (Westminster Creolistics Series 7), 373–398. London: Battlebridge.
Lorenzino, Gerardo A. 1998. *The Angolar Creole Portuguese of São Tomé: Its Grammar and Sociolinguistic History* (LINCOM Studies in Pidgin and Creole Linguistics 11). München: LINCOM Europa.
Lorenzino, Gerardo A. 2007. Angolar (Creole Portuguese), or Lunga Ngola. In John Holm & Peter L. Patrick (eds.), *Comparative Creole Syntax. Parallel Outlines of 18 Creole Grammars* (Westminster Creolistics Series 7), 1–24. London: Battlebridge.
Maddieson, Ian. 2011. Syllable structure. In Matthew S. Dryer & Martin Haspelmath (eds.), *The World Atlas of Language Structures Online,* Chapter 12. München: Max Planck Digital Library.
http://wals.info/chapter/12 (accessed 13 June 2011).
Matory, J. Lorand. 2005. *Black Atlantic Religion: Tradition, Transnationalism and Matriarchy in the Afro-Brazilian Candomblé*. Princeton: Princeton University Press.
Maurer, Philippe. 1986. Le papiamento de Curaçao: un cas de créolisation atypique? Paper presented at the 5ᵉ Colloque International d'Études Créoles, La Réunion, 7–13 April 1986.

Maurer, Philippe. 1988. *Les Modifications Temporelles et Modales du Verbe dans le Papiamento de Curaçao (Antilles Néerlandaises)* (Kreolische Bibiothek 9). Hamburg: Buske.
Maurer, Philippe. 1995. *L'Angolar. Un Créole Afro-Portugais Parlé à São Tomé* (Kreolische Bibiothek 16). Hamburg: Buske.
Maurer, Philippe. 2009. *Principense. Grammar, Texts and Vocabulary of the Afro-Portuguese Creole of the Island of Principe, Gulf of Guinea*. London: Battlebridge.
McWhorter, John H. 1995. The scarcity of Spanish-based creoles explained. *Language in Society* 24. 213–244.
McWhorter, John H. 1997. It happened at Cormantin: Locating the origin of the Atlantic English-based creoles. *Journal of Pidgin and Creole Languages* 12(1). 59–102.
McWhorter, John H. 1998. Identifying the creole prototype. Vindicating a typological class. *Language* 74(4). 788–818.
McWhorter, John H. 2000. *The Missing Spanish Creoles: Recovering the Birth of Plantation Contact Languages*. Berkeley: University of California Press.
McWhorter, John H. 2001. The world's simplest grammars are creole grammars. *Linguistic Typology* 5(2/3). 125–166.
McWhorter, John H. 2005. *Defining Creole*. Oxford: Oxford University Press.
McWhorter, John H. 2011. *Linguistic Simplicity and Complexity. Why Do Languages Undress?* (Language Contact and Bilingualism 1). Berlin: De Gruyter Mouton.
McWhorter, John H. 2012. Case closed? Testing the feature pool hypothesis. *Journal of Pidgin and Creole Languages* 27(1). 171–182.
McWhorter, John H. & Jeff Good. 2012. *A Grammar of Saramaccan Creole*. Berlin: Mouton De Gruyter.
Mercier, Alfred. 1880. Etude sur la langue créole en Louisiane. *Comptes-rendus de l'Athenée Louisianais* 5. 378–383.
Meister, Georg. 1692. *Der Orientalisch-Indianische Kunst-und Lustgärtner*. Dresden: Meister/Riedel.
Métraux, Alfred. 1958. *Le Vaudou Haïtien*. Paris: Gallimard.
Michaelis, Susanne, Philippe Maurer, Martin Haspelmath & Magnus Huber (eds.). to appear. *The Atlas of Pidgin and Creole Language Structures*. Oxford: Oxford University Press.
Michaelis, Susanne & Marcel Rosalie. 2009. Loanwords in Seychelles Creole. In Martin Haspelmath & Uri Tadmor (eds.), *Loanwords in the World's Languages: A Comparative Handbook,* 215–229. Berlin: Walter de Gruyter.
Migge, Bettina. 2000. The origin of property items in the Surinamese Plantation Creole. In John H. McWhorter (ed.), *Language Change and Language Contact in Pidgins and Creoles,* 201–234. Amsterdam/Philadelphia: John Benjamins.
Migge, Bettina, Isabelle Léglise & Angela Bartens (eds.). 2010. *Creoles in Education: An Appraisal of Current Programs and Projects* (Creole Language Library 36). Amsterdam/Philadelphia: John Benjamins.

Mufwene, Salikoko. 1986. The universalist and substrate hypotheses complement one another. In Pieter Muysken & Norval Smith (eds.), *Substrata Versus Universals in Creole Genesis*, 129–162. Amsterdam/Philadelphia: Benjamins.

Mufwene, Salikoko. 1999. Accountability in descriptions of creoles. In John Rickford & Suzanne Romaine (eds.), *Creole genesis, Attitudes and Discourse*, 157–185. Amsterdam/Philadelphia: John Benjamins.

Mufwene, Salikoko. 2001. *The Ecology of Language Evolution*. Cambridge: Cambridge University Press.

Mufwene, Salikoko. 2006. Multilingualism in linguistic history: Creolization and indigenization. In Tej K. Bhatia & William C. Ritchie (eds.), *The Handbook of Bilingualism*, 460–488. Malden, MA: Blackwell.

Mufwene, Salikoko. 2008. *Language Evolution: Contact, Competition and Change*. New York/London: Continuum International Publishing Group.

Mufwene, Salikoko. 2009. The evolution of language: Hints from creoles and pidgins. In James Minnet & William Wang (eds.), *Language Evolution and the Brain*, 1–33. Hong Kong: University of Hong Kong Press.

Mühlhäusler, Peter. 1986. 'Bonnet blanc' and 'blanc bonnet': Adjective-noun order, substratum and language universals. In Pieter Muysken & Norval Smith (eds.), *Substrata Versus Universals in Creole Genesis*, 41–56. Amsterdam: John Benjamins.

Munteanu, Dan. 1991. *El Papiamento, Origen, Evolución y Estructura* (Bochum-Essener Beiträge zur Sprachwandeltheorie XV). Bochum: Brockmeyer.

Muysken, Pieter. 1988. Are creoles a special type of language? In Frederik J. Newmeyer (ed.), *Linguistics: The Cambridge Survey. Volume II: Linguistic Theory: Extensions and Implications*, 285–301. Cambridge: Cambridge University Press.

Muysken, Pieter & Norval Smith. 1990. Question words in pidgin and creole languages. *Linguistics* 28. 889–903.

Muysken, Pieter & Tonjes Veenstra. 1995. Serial verbs. In Jacques Arends, Pieter Muysken & Norval Smith (eds.), *Pidgins and Creoles: An Introduction* (Creole Language Library 15), 289–301. Amsterdam/Philadelphia: John Benjamins.

Naro, Anthony. 1978. A study on the origins of pidginization. *Language* 54. 314–347.

Noll, Volker. 1999. *Das Brasilianische Portuguesisch: Herausbildung und Kontraste*. Heidelberg: Winter.

Nunes, Mário Pinharanda. 1994. Conçepção de tempo e espaço no kristang e no malaio [The concepts of time and space in Kristang and Malay]. *Papia* 3(2). 116–126.

Oldendorp, Christian Georg Andreas. 2000. *Historie der Caribischen Inseln Sanct Thomas, Sanct Crux und Sanct Jan. Kommentierte Edition des Originalmanuskriptes. Erster Teil.* (Abhandlungen und Berichte des Staatlichen Museums für Völkerkunde Dresden 51). Berlin: Verlag für Wissenschaft und Bildung. (Originally written in 1769; abridged version published in 1777.)

Orléans, Henri d'. 1898. *Du Tonkin aux Indes: Janvier 1895 – Janvier 1896.* Calmann: Levy.

Ortiz Fernández, Fernando. 1940. *Contrapunteo Cubano del Tabaco y el Azúcar*. La Habana: Jesús Montero.

Palmié, Stephan. 1993. African States in the New World? Remarks on the tradition of transatlantic resistance. In Thomas Bremer & Ulrich Fleischmann (eds.), *Alternative Cultures in the Caribbean. First International Conference of the Society of Caribbean research, Berlin 1988*, 55–67. Frankfurt: Vervuert.

Palmié, Stephan. 2006. Creolisation and its discontents. *Annual Review of Anthropology* 35. 433–456.

Parkvall, Mikael. 2002. Cutting off the branch. In Glenn G. Gilbert (ed.), *Pidgin and Creole Linguistics in the Twenty-First Century* (Studies in Ethnolinguistics 9), 355–367. New York: Peter Lang.

Parkvall, Mikael. 2008. The simplicity of creoles in a cross-linguistic perspective. In Matti Miestamo, Kaius Sinnemäki & Fred Karlsson (eds.), *Language Complexity. Typology, Contact, Change*, 265–285. Amsterdam/Philadelphia: John Benjamins.

Parkvall, Mikael. 2012. *Afrolex. Africal Lexical Influences in Creoles and Transplanted European Languages*. London: Battlebridge.

Parkvall, Mikael & Philip Baker. 2012. Idiomatic calques and semantic borrowing. In Angela Bartens & Philip Baker (eds.), *Black Through White. African Words and Calques in Creoles and Transplanted European Languages*, 231–248. London: Battlebridge.

Perl, Matthias. 1993. Studien zur Lexikentwicklung des Saramakkischen. In Matthias Perl, Axel Schönberger & Petra Thiele (eds.), *Portuguesisch-Basierte Kreolsprachen. Akten des 2. Gemeinsamen Kolloquiums der Deutschsprachigen Lusitaniostik und Katalanistik (Berlin, 10. -12. September 1992), Lusitanistischer Teil, Band 6*, 71–102. Frankfurt/Main: Teo Ferrer de Mesquita: Domus Editoria Europaea.

Pinto Bull, Benjamin. 1989. *O Crioulo da Guiné-Bissau: Filosofia e Sabedoria* [The creole of Guinea Bissau: philosophy and wisdom]. Lisboa/Guiné-Bissau: ICALP/INEP.

Plag, Ingo. 2011. Creolisation and admixture: Typology, feature pools, and second language acquisition. *Journal of Pidgin and Creole Languages* 26. 89–110.

Plag, Ingo & Mareile Schramm. 2006. Early creole syllable structure: A cross-linguistic survey of the earliest attested varieties of Saramaccan, Sranan, St. Kitts and Jamaican. In Parth Bhatt & Ingo Plag (eds.), *The Structure of Creole Words. Segmental, Syllabic and Morphological Aspects* (Linguistische Arbeiten 505), 131–150. Tübingen: Niemeyer.

Pluchon, Pierre. 1987. *Vaudou, Sorciers, Empoisonneurs. De Saint-Domingue à Haïti*. Paris: Karthala.

Post, Marike. 1995. Fa d'Ambu. In Jacques Arends, Pieter Muysken & Norval Smith (eds.), *Pidgins and Creoles: An Introduction* (Creole Language Library 15), 191–204. Amsterdam/Philadelphia: John Benjamins.

Price, Richard. 2007. Some anthropological musings on creolisation. *Journal of Pidgin and Creole Languages* 22(1). 17–36.

Price, Richard (ed.). 1979. *Maroon Societies: Rebel Slave Communities in the Americas*. Baltimore: The Johns Hopkins University Press.

Price, Richard & Sally Price. 1999. *Maroon Arts: Cultural Vitality in the African Diaspora*. Boston: Beacon Press.
Price-Mars, Jean. 1973. *Ainsi Parla l'Oncle*. (Nouvelle Édition. Présentation de Robert Cornevin.) Ottawa: LEMÉAC.
Quilis, Antonio & Celia Casado-Fresnillo. 2008. *La Lengua Española en Filipinas. Historia. Situación Actual. El Chabacano. Antología de Textos* (Anejos de la Revista de Filología Española). Madrid: CSIC.
Quint, Nicolas. 2000. *Grammaire de la Langue Cap-Verdienne. Étude Déscriptive et Compréhensive du Créole Afro-Portugais des Iles du Cap-Vert*. Paris: L'Harmattan.
Reinecke, John E. 1937. *Marginal Languages: A Sociological Survey of the Creole Languages and Trade Jargons*. New Haven, CT: Yale University dissertation.
Rickford, John R. 1988. *Dimensions of a Creole Continuum*. Stanford: Stanford University Press.
Rickford, John R. & Angela E. Rickford. 1976. Cut-eye and suck-teeth: African words and gestures in New World guise. *Journal of American Folklore* 89. 294–309.
Robertson, Ian E. 2011. Morphological simplification of the substrate in Creole formation. Paper presented at the SPCL meeting in Accra, 2–6 August 2011.
Romaine, Suzanne. 1988. *Pidgin and Creole Languages*. London: Longman.
Rougé, Jean-Louis. 1994. A propos de la formation des créoles du Cap Vert et de Guinée. *Papia* 3(2). 137–149.
Rougé, Jean-Louis. 2001. D'où viennent les verbes? In Ernesto Andrade, Dulce Pereira & Maria Antónia Mota (eds.), *Crioulos de Base Portuguesa* [Portuguese-based creoles], 81–95. Braga: Associação Portuguesa de Linguistíca
Rougé, Jean-Louis. 2005. L'influence manding sur la formation des créoles du Cap-Vert et de Guinée-Bissau et Casamance. In Jürgen Lang, John Holm, Jean-Louis Rougé & Maria João Soares (eds.), *Cabo Verde: Origens da Sua Sociedade e do Seu Crioulo* [Cape Verde: the origins of the society and the creole], 63–74. Tübingen: Gunter Narr.
Russell, Thomas. 1868. *The Etymology of Jamaica Grammar*. Kingston, Jamaica: Decordova, MacDougall & Co.
Saint-Quentin, Alfred de. 1872. *Introduction à l'Histoire de Cayenne, Suivi d'un Recueil de Contes, Fables et Chansons en Créole avec Traduction en Regard*. Antibes: J. Marchand.
Sanchez, Tara. 2006. Layers of borrowing in a multilingual society: transfer and calquing as changes from above in Papiamentu passive constructions. Paper presented at the Penn Linguistics Colloquium 39, 24–26 February 2006.
Savain, Roger E. 1995. *La Langue Haïtienne en Dix Étapes. Dis Pa nan Lang Ayisyen-an*. Rochester, VT: Schenkman Books.
Schachter, Paul & Fe Otanes. 1972. *Tagalog Reference Grammar*. Los Angeles: University of California Press.
Schuchardt, Hugo. 1889. Beiträge zur Kenntnis des Kreolischen Romanisch V. *Zeitschrift für Romanische Philologie* 13. 476–516.

Schuchardt, Hugo. 1890. Kreolische Studien IX. Über das Malaioportugiesische von Batavia und Tugu. *Sitzungsberichte der Kaiserlichen Akademie der Wissenschaften zu Wien* 122(9). 1–256.
Schuchardt, Hugo. 1914. *Die Sprache der Saramakkaneger in Surinam.* Amsterdam: Johannes Müller.
Schwegler, Armin. 1996a. *'Chi ma nkongo': Lengua y Rito Ancestrales en El Palenque de San Basilia (Colombia).* Frankfurt/Madrid: Vervuert.
Schwegler, Armin. 1996b. Lenguas criollas en hispano-América y la contactos y transferencias lingüísticas en hispanoamérica. *Signo y Seña* 6. 295–346.
Schwegler, Armin. 1998. Palenquero. In Matthias Perl & Armin Schwegler (eds.), *América Negra: Panorámica Actual de los Estudios Lingüísticos sobre Variedades Criollas y Afrohispanas,* 220–291. Frankfurt: Vervuert.
Schwegler, Armin. 2011. Palenque(ro): The search for its African substrate. In Claire Lefebvre (ed.), *Creoles, Their Substrates and Language Typology* (Typological Studies in Language 95), 225–249. Amsterdam/Philadelphia: John Benjamins.
Seuren, Pieter A. M. & Herman Wekker. 1986. Semantic transparency as a factor in creole genesis. In Pieter Muysken & Norval Smith (eds.), *Substrata Versus Universals in Creole Genesis,* 57–70. Amsterdam/Philadelphia: Benjamins.
Sheller, Mimi. 2003. *Consuming the Caribbean: From Arawaks to Zombies.* London: Routledge.
Siegel, Jeff. 1999. Creoles and minority dialects in education: An overview. *Journal of Multilingual and Multicultural Development* 20(6). 508–531.
Siegel, Jeff. 2005. Literacy in pidgin and creole languages. *Current Issues in Language Planning* 6(2). 143–163.
Siegel, Jeff. 2006a. Keeping creoles and dialects out of the classroom: Is it justified? In Shondel J. Nero (ed.), *Dialects, Englishes, Creoles, and Education,* 39–67. Mahwah, NJ: Lawrence Erlbaum.
Siegel, Jeff. 2006b. Language ideologies and the education of speakers of marginalized language varieties: Adopting a critical awareness approach. *Linguistics and Education* 17. 157–174.
Siegel, Jeff. 2008. Pidgins/creoles, and second language acquisition. In Silvia Kouwenberg & John Victor Singler (eds.), *The Handbook of Pidgin and Creole Studies,* 189–218. Malden, MA: Blackwell.
Siegel, Jeff, Benedikt Szmrecsanyi & Bernd Kortmann. in press. Measuring analyticity and syntheticity in creoles. *Journal of Pidgin and Creole Languages.*
Silva Neto, Serafim da. 1950a. Falares Crioulos. *Brasilia* 5. 1–28.
Silva Neto, Serafim da. 1950b. *Introdução ao Estudo da Língua Portuguêsa no Brasil* [Introduction to the study of the Portuguese language in Brazil]. Rio de Janeiro: Departamento de Imprensa Nacional.
Singh, Rajendra & Pieter Muysken. 1995. Wanted: A debate on pidgin/creole phonology. *Journal of Pidgin and Creole Languages* 10(1). 157–169.
Sippola, Eeva. 2011. *Una Gramática Descriptiva del Chabacano de Ternate.* Helsinki: University of Helsinki dissertation.

Smith, Norval. 1975. Vowel harmony in two languages of Surinam. *Spektator* 4. 315–320.
Smith, Norval. 1987. *The Genesis of the Creole Languages of Surinam.* Amsterdam: University of Amsterdam dissertation.
Smith, Norval. 1995. An annotated list of creoles, pidgins, and mixed languages. In Jacques Arends, Pieter Muysken & Norval Smith (eds.), *Pidgins and Creoles: An Introduction* (Creole Language Library 15), 331–374. Amsterdam/Philadelphia: John Benjamins.
Smith, Norval. 2008. Creole phonology. In Silvia Kouwenberg & John Victor Singler (eds.), *The Handbook of Pidgin and Creole Studies,* 98–128. Malden, MA: Blackwell.
Smith, Norval & Vincent Haabo. 2007. The Saramaccan implosives: Tools for linguistic archaeology? *Journal of Pidgin and Creole Languages* 22(1). 101–122.
Smith, Norval, Ian E. Robertson & Kay Williamson. 1987. The Ijo element in Berbice Dutch. *Language in Society* 16. 49–90.
Steinkrüger, Patrick. 2003. Morphological processes of word formation in Chabacano (Philippine Spanish Creole). In Ingo Plag (ed.), *Phonology and Morphology in Creole Languages,* 253–268. Tübingen: Niemeyer.
Stolz, Thomas. 1986. *Gibt es das Kreolische Sprachwandelmodel? Vergleichende Grammatik des Negerholländischen.* Frankfurt: Peter Lang.
Syea, Anand. 2009. The short and long form of verbs in Mauritian Creole: Functionalism versus formalism. *Theoretical Linguistics* 18(1). 61–97.
Sylvain, Suzanne. 1936. *Le Créole Haïtien: Morphologie et Syntaxe.* Port-au-Prince/Wetteren: Meester.
Tadmor, Uri. 2009. Loanwords in the world's languages: Findings and results. In Martin Haspelmath & Uri Tadmor (eds.), *Loanwords in the World's Languages: A Comparative Handbook,* 55–75. Berlin: Walter de Gruyter.
Tarallo, Fernando & Tania Alkmin. 1987. *Falares Crioulos. Línguas em Contato* [Creole languages. Languages in contact]. São Paulo: Ática.
Taylor, Douglas. 1963. The origin of West Indian creole languages: Evidence from grammatical categories. *American Anthropologist* 65. 800–814.
Taylor, Douglas. 1971. Grammatical and lexical affinities of creoles. In Dell H. Hymes (ed.), *Pidginization and Creolization of Languages,* 293–296. Cambridge: Cambridge University Press.
Thompson, Sandra A. 2004. Property concepts. In Geert Booij, Christian Lehmann, Joachim Mugdan, Stavros Skopeteas & Wolfgang Kesselheim (eds.), *Morphology,* 1111–1117. Berlin: Walter de Gruyter.
Tinelli, Henri. 1981. *Creole Phonology.* The Hague: Mouton.
Tremblay, Annie & Katherine Demuth. 2007. Prosodic licensing of determiners in children's early French. In Alyona Belikova, Luisa Meroni & Mari Umeda (eds.), *Proceedings of the 2nd Conference on Generative Approaches to Language Acquisition North America (GALANA),* 426–436. Somerville, MA: Cascadilla Proceedings Project.

Trouillot, Michel-Rolph. 2002. Culture on the edges: Caribbean creolisation in the historical context. In Brian Keith Axel (ed.), *From the Margins: Historical Anthropology and its Futures,* 189–210. Durham, NC: Duke University Press.

Tuten, Donald N. 2003. *Koineization in Medieval Spanish* (Contributions to the Sociology of Language 88). Berlin: Mouton de Gruyter.

van den Berg, Margot. forthcoming. Multilingual language use and creole formation: The case of property items in Early Sranan. *Ghana Journal of Linguistics.*

Veenstra, Tonjes. 2006. Head ordering in syntactic compounding: Acquisition processes and Creole genesis. In Parth Bhatt & Ingo Plag (eds.), *The Structure of Creole Words. Segmental, Syllabic and Morphological Aspects* (Linguistische Arbeiten 505), 201–221. Tübingen: Niemeyer.

Veenstra, Tonjes. 2008. Creole genesis: The impact of the language bioprogram hypothesis. In Silvia Kouwenberg & John Victor Singler (eds.), *The Handbook of Pidgin and Creole Studies,* 219–241. Malden, MA: Blackwell.

Veiga, Manuel. 1982. *Diskrison Strutural di Lingua Kabuverdianu* [Structural description of the Cape Verdian language]. Lisbon/Praia: Instituto Caboverdiano do Livro.

Versteegh, Kees. 2008. Non-Indo-European pidgins and creoles. In Silvia Kouwenberg & John Victor Singler (eds.), *The Handbook of Pidgin and Creole Studies,* 158–186. Malden, MA: Blackwell.

Warner-Lewis, Maureen. 1996. *Trinidad Yoruba: From Mother Tongue To Memory.* Tuscaloosa, AL: The University of Alabama Press.

Welmers, William Everett. 1946. *A Descriptive Grammar of Fanti* (Language Supplement: Language dissertations 39). Baltimore: Linguistic Society of America.

Whinnom, Keith. 1956. *Spanish Contact Vernaculars in the Philippine Islands.* Hong Kong: Hong Kong University Press.

Wilson, Peter. 1973. *Crab Antics. The Social Anthropology of English-Speaking Negro Societies of the Caribbean.* New Haven, CT: Yale University Press.

Winford, Donald. 1985. The syntax of *fi* complements in Caribbean English Creole. *Language* 61(3). 588–624.

Winford, Donald. 1997. Property items and predication in Sranan. *Journal of Pidgin and Creole Languages* 12(2). 237–301.

Winford, Donald. 2008. Atlantic Creole syntax. In Silvia Kouwenberg & John Victor Singler (eds.), *The Handbook of Pidgin and Creole Studies,* 19–47. Malden, MA: Blackwell.

Wood, Richard E. 1972. New light on the origins of Papiamentu: an eighteenth-century letter. *Neophilologus* 56. 18–30.

Wullschlägel, H. R. 1856. *Deutsch-Negerenglisches Wörterbuch.* Löbau: J. A. Duroldt.

Yillah, Sorie M. & Chris Corcoran. 2007. Krio (Creole English), or Sierra Leonean. In John Holm & Peter L. Patrick (eds.), *Comparative Creole Syntax. Parallel Outlines of 18 Creole Grammars* (Westminster Creolistics Series 7), 175–198. London: Battlebridge.

Mixed Languages[1]

Felicity Meakins

1. Introduction

Mixed languages[2] are the result of the fusion of two identifiable source languages, normally in situations of community bilingualism. As recently as the 1990s, the existence of these languages had often been denied or labelled as cases of codeswitching, adstrate influence or borrowing (see e.g. Greenberg 1999). Nonetheless they were brought to the attention of contact linguistics by Thomason and Kaufman (1988) as a legitimate form of contact language. Bakker and Mous' (1994) and Thomason's (1997) edited volumes drew together substantial amounts of data from various languages which have been identified as 'mixed', and Bakker's (1997) *A Language of Our Own* provided the first detailed account of a mixed language, Michif. These descriptions of mixed languages have allowed cross-linguistic comparisons of the socio-historical origins of these languages and their typological make-up. They have also stimulated debates such as whether a definable subclass of contact languages called 'mixed languages' actually exists and whether mixed languages are the result of other contact phenomena such as codeswitching, or whether special contact processes are required. These discussions formed the basis of a volume edited by Matras and Bakker, *The Mixed Language Debate* (2003).

One of the issues with this earlier work was the dearth of data on mixed languages. Many of the languages studied were spoken by few speakers and scanty information about their socio-historical context and development was available. More recently a number of large-scale projects have focused specifically on mixed languages, aiming to provide a rich documentation of actively-spoken mixed languages. For example Sri Lankan Malay, Gurindji Kriol[3,4] and Angloromani[5] have been sampled across various social contexts and have been placed within their socio-historical context. As a result, grammatical sketches, ethnographic descriptions of the language ecologies and information about the socio-historical origins of these languages have become available[6]. Additionally, corpora of sound-linked annotated transcripts are now accessible. More specific aspects of mixed languages have been the focus of other projects. For example, the central question of the Aboriginal Child Language project[7] in Australia has been the relationship between language acquisition and shift in highly fluid multilingual contexts. The documentation of new

Australian varieties, such as the mixed languages Light Warlpiri and Gurindji Kriol, has formed a large part of this project.

These documentation projects provide the field of contact linguistics with a more solid foundation for the discussion of these mixed varieties. This chapter utilises these new contributions to provide an overview of the debates and more recent developments and issues arising in the study of mixed languages. I discuss the classification and origins of mixed languages in relation to their socio-historical context (section 3.1) and typological features (section 3.2), as well as some more recent issues including how to ascertain whether mixed languages are autonomous language systems (section 4.1), the description and role of variation in mixed language systems (section 4.2), whether two phonological systems can be present in the one language (section 4.3) and whether codeswitching can lead to mixed language genesis (section 4.4). I use data from well-known cases of mixed languages such as Angloromani (section 2.1), Ma'á (section 2.2), Media Lengua (section 2.4), Mednyj Aleut (section 2.6) and Michif (section 2.7), Gurindji Kriol and Light Warlpiri (section 2.8), and other mixed varieties such as Bilingual Navajo (section 2.3), Old Helsinki Slang (section 2.5) and Sri Lankan Malay (section 2.9).

2. Examples of mixed languages

Table 1 lists mixed varieties which have been labelled as mixed languages. The status of a number of these languages is questionable. Indeed often following closely in pursuit of every claim for the existence of a mixed language lies a counter-claim about its non-existence. For example, the mixed status of Sri Lanka Malay has been challenged by Smith and Paauw (2006) who suggest it is a creole (section 2.9). Other identified cases are more doubtful, such as Barranquenho (Clements 2009; Clements, Amaral, and Luís 2008). Barranquenho is Portuguese with some Spanish influence such as clitic placement. Due to its close proximity to the Portuguese/Spanish border, it is not clear how the restructuring found in this variety would differ from that found along a dialect chain. Given some of these arguments over language classification, this table is meant as an overview of the literature rather than a definitive statement on the status of these languages.

Table 1. Some languages which have been identified as mixed languages

Language	Country	Speakers	Mix	Selected sources
Angloromani	England	Romani	Grammar: English Lexicon: English and Romani	(Smart and Crofton 1875; Hancock 1970, 1976; Kenrick 1979; Boretzky and Igla 1994; Bakker 1998, 2002; Thomason 2001; Matras and Bakker 2003; Matras et al. 2007; Matras 2010)
Barranquenho	Border of Spain and Portugal	Barranquenho	Grammar and lexicon: Portuguese with some Spanish influence	(Clements, Amaral, and Luís 2008; Clements 2009)
Callahuaya	Bolivia	Callahuaya Travelling Healers	Lexicon: Puquina Grammar: Quechua	(Muysken 1994a, 1997a)
Chindo	Indonesia	Peranakan Chinese	Lexicon: Malay Grammar: Javanese	(Dreyfuss and Oka 1979; Matras and Bakker 2003)
Gurindji Kriol	Australia	Gurindji	VP: Kriol[8] NP: Gurindji Lexicon: Gurindji and Kriol	(Dalton et al. 1995; Charola 2002; Jones, Meakins and Buchan 2011; Jones, Meakins and Muawiyath 2012; McConvell and Meakins 2005; McConvell 2008; Meakins 2008a, 2008b, 2009, 2011a, 2011b, 2001c, 2012; Meakins and O'Shannessy 2005, 2010, 2012; O'Shannessy and Meakins 2012)

Table 1. Some languages which have been identified as mixed languages (cont.)

Language	Country	Speakers	Mix	Selected sources
Jenisch	Germany	Jenisch traders	Grammar: German Lexicon: Rotwelsch[9], Hebrew, Romani, Romance	(Matras 2000, 2003, 2009)
Lekoudesch	Germany	Jewish cattle traders	Grammar: Judeo-German Lexicon: some Hebrew	(Matras 2000, 2003, 2009)
Light Warlpiri	Australia	Warlpiri	VP: Kriol NP: Warlpiri Lexicon: Warlpiri and Kriol	(Meakins and O'Shannessy 2005, 2010, 2012; O'Shannessy 2005, 2006, 2008, 2009, 2011a, 2011b, 2012; O'Shannessy and Meakins 2012)
Ma'á	Tanzania	Mbugu	Grammar: Bantu Core Lexicon: Cushitic	(Brenzinger 1987; Mous 1994, 2000, 2003a, 2003b; Thomason and Kaufman 1988; Thomason 1983, 1997a; Myers-Scotton 2003)
Media Lengua	Ecuador	Quechua	Lexicon: 90% Spanish Grammar: Quechua	(Muysken 1981, 1988, 1994b, 1997b; Myers-Scotton 2003; Gómez Rendón 2008; Shappeck 2011)

Table 1. Some languages which have been identified as mixed languages (cont.)

Language	Country	Speakers	Mix	Selected sources
Mednyj Aleut	Bering Strait, Russia	Aleut	VP (finite): Russian NP: Aleut Lexicon: 90% Aleut	(Golovko 1994, 1996; Golovko and Vakhtin 1990; Sekerina 1994; Thomason 1997b; Myers-Scotton 2003)
Michif	Canada	Métis	VP: Cree NP: French Lexicon: Cree verbs, French nouns	(Bakker 1994, 1997; Bakker and Papen 1997; Papen 1987a, 1987b, 2003; Rosen 2000; Myers-Scotton 2003)
(Bilingual) Navajo	United States	Navajo	Grammar: Navajo Lexicon: Navajo and English	(Schaengold 2003, 2004)
New Tiwi	Australia	Tiwi	VP: Tiwi NP: Aboriginal English/Kriol	(Lee 1987; McConvell 2002)
Old Helsinki Slang	Finland	Finnish and Swedish gangs	Grammar: Finnish Lexicon: 80% Swedish	(Paunonen 2006; Jarva 2008; de Smit 2010)
Shelta	Ireland	Irish Travellers	Grammar: English Lexicon: distorted Irish and unknown	(Grant 1994; McCann, Síochain, and Ruane 1994)

Table 1. Some languages which have been identified as mixed languages (cont.)

Language	Country	Speakers	Mix	Selected sources
Sri Lanka Malay	Sri Lanka	Malay	Forms: Contact variety of Malay Grammar: Tamil and Sinhala	(Aboh and Ansaldo 2007; Ansaldo 2008; 2011a, 2011b; Smith, Paauw, and Hussainmiya 2004; Smith and Paauw 2006; Bakker 2003; Slomanson 2006, 2007; Nordhoff 2009)
Sri Lanka Portuguese	Sri Lanka	Portuguese	Forms: Contact variety of Portuguese Grammar: Tamil and Sinhala	(Smith 1977, 1979a, 1979b, 1984, 2001; Bakker 2003)
Wutun	China/Tibet	Tibetan	Lexicon: Northwest Mandarin, Amdo Tibetan, Mongolian Grammar: Amdo Tibetan	(Chen 1986; Lee-Smith and Wurm 1996; Janhunen et al. 2008)

The languages which are discussed in this paper have been chosen partly because they are representative of the typological composition and socio-historical background of the languages described as 'mixed', and partly because they are the best documented examples of mixed languages. Some of these languages such as Media Lengua (section 2.4), Ma'á (section 2.2), Michif (section 2.7) and Mednyj Aleut (section 2.6) have been discussed extensively in the literature and require little introduction. Other languages have been identified more recently, for example Gurindji Kriol and Light Warlpiri (section 2.8). Mixed languages such as Angloromani (section 2.1) and Sri Lanka Malay (section 2.9) have been present in the literature on mixed languages; however more information about their origins and structure is now available as a result of recent documentation projects. These languages will be presented in order of degree of mixing from the languages which exhibit predominantly lexical mixing such as Angloromani, Ma'á, Bilingual Navajo, Media Lengua and Old Helsinki Slang, to languages which source significant amounts of structural resources from two languages, such as Mednyj Aleut, Michif, Gurindji Kriol and Light Warlpiri. This continuum of mixing is discussed in section 2.10, with the sections that follow an exploration of the socio-historical and linguistic origins of these outcomes of language contact.

2.1.   Angloromani

Most mixed languages exhibit a split between the lexicon and grammar. Bakker (2003: 125) calls these G(rammar)-L(exicon) mixed languages and lists 25 in a typological survey. The first example of a G-L mixed language presented here is Angloromani. Angloromani is spoken by some Romanies in Britain. They continue to be a travelling population, many of whom live in caravans. Romanies who now live in permanent accommodation generally do not speak this mixed language (Matras 2010). Matras et al. (2007) consider Angloromani to be endangered. Currently it is not the language of conversation but rather it is restricted to individual utterances. These utterances can be characterised as the use of a restricted set of Romani-derived lexicon, which Matras et al. (2007) call a 'lexical reservoir', within an English grammatical frame. This lexical reservoir exists largely in parallel with an English lexicon and is drawn on in situations where speakers want to mark a sense of solidarity or group cohesion. In this respect, Matras et al. (2007) find that the use of these utterances is prompted by the presence of outsiders or the emotive content of the speech act. An example of the coupling of Romani-derived lexicon with English grammar is given in (1). This sentence contains Romani words inserted into an English frame, for example nouns *mush* (man), a verb *rocker* (talk) and a function word *maw* (NEG). The Romani-derived words are given in bold.

(1)   ***Maw*** be ***rocker****ing in front of the **mush** and **rakli**!*
       'Don't be talking in front of the man and [the] girl!'
       (Matras et al. 2007: 170)

Although the grammatical frame of Angloromani is predominantly English, some structural differences can be observed. For instance, Angloromani also contains some remnants of Romani morphology such as a genitive *-engra* suffix which attaches to lexical roots to create a related word *masengra* (from *mas* 'meat') (Matras et al. 2007).

Matras et al. (2007) also observe that Angloromani speakers do not always use the definite article, aspect and existential auxiliaries and co-referential pronouns in places where they would be expected in English.

They argue that these features are not specifically Romani but they indicate that Angloromani has slightly different grammatical rules to English.

The status of Angloromani as a mixed language is somewhat controversial. It was originally described as a dialect of English which contained large amounts of Romani vocabulary (Smart and Crofton 1875). Hancock (1970, 1976) then raised the possibility of it being classified as a pidgin or creole language. Kenrick (1979) suggested it was an English ethnolect. It was only later that it was described as a mixed language (Bakker 1998; Thomason 2001)[10]. Matras et al. (2007) argue that these various descriptions of Angloromani have been largely a product of the interests of linguistic research at the time. For example, Hancock's suggestion of labelling Angloromani as a creole language came about at a time when this was the dominant framework for discussing contact languages. Similarly the classification of Angloromani as a mixed language occurred when mixed languages became a serious object of study with Thomason and Kaufman's (1988) seminal work. Matras et al.'s (2007) description of Angloromani as making use of a lexical reservoir is the most recent characterisation of this language. See Matras (2010) for more details.

Equally contentious is the origin of Angloromani. Thomason and Kaufman (1988: 103–104) suggest that Angloromani is the result of the wholesale adoption of the English grammatical system coupled with the maintenance of lexical material from Romani. However the case for massive grammatical borrowing is not clear-cut, and counter claims which favour relexification of the dominant language using the ancestral language are made for Angloromani. For example Boretzky and Igla (1994: 61) suggest that Angloromani came about after the Romani had already shifted to English. Under this model, the mixed language is the result of a U-turn, that is an attempt by the Romanies to reclaim their heritage language through the use of Romani vocabulary.

Angloromani is not the only mixed language to make use of Romani. Other varieties on mainland Europe include languages which mix Romani with Portuguese, Spanish, Catalan, Basque, French, Low German, Norwegian, Swedish, and Turkish.

2.2. Ma'á

Another mixed language that makes use of a reservoir of lexical material from the ancestral language, is Ma'á. This mixed language is spoken by Mbugu communities in the Usambara mountains in Tanzania. Like Angloromani, Ma'á is spoken alongside one of its source languages, Mbugu (Bantu). The Mbugu were originally a Cushitic-speaking group from Lackipya in Kenya. In order to escape persecution from the Maasai, they moved to the Usambara mountains via the Pare mountains (Mous 2003a). The mixed language, Ma'á is considered to be the result of resisting assimilation with the neighbouring Pare. In this respect it represents the stubborn persistence of an ethnic group (Mous 1994: 175–76). Ma'á combines a Bantu grammar, similar to Pare, with a lexicon composed of Southern Cushitic and Bantu words and some Maasai words. In the following example, the non-Bantu elements are in bold.

(2)   hé-ló   mw-**agirú**   é-sé-we   kimwéri   **dilaó**   w-a
      16-have   1-elder   1-call-PST.PF   Kimweri   king   1-CON
      'There was an elder called Kimweri.'
      (Mous 2003a: 9)

Thomason (1997a: 481–83) believes that Ma'á is the product of massive grammatical borrowing from Pare, including inflectional categories, for example noun classes. However this view differs sharply from Brenzinger (1987), Sasse (1992) and particularly Mous (1994, 2000, 2003a, 2003b) who believe that Ma'á is a conscious and deliberate result of an attempt to undo a shift to Pare, where speakers tried to relearn their ancestral language. Mous (2003a, 2003b) suggests this happened through a paralexification process where a Bantu lexicon, and a combined Cushitic and Maasai lexicon exist in parallel. Mbugu draws from the Bantu lexicon, whereas speakers use Cushitic and Maasai words in Ma'á. In this sense, he considers Ma'á to be a register of Mbugu (1994: 96–97, 2003a), not entirely unlike, but probably more extreme than, the cases of lexical manipulation found in urban youth languages, slang and taboo codes (Mous 2003b: 217). This notion of paralexification is also similar to the lexical reservoir described for Angloromani.

2.3.   Bilingual Navajo

Both Ma'á and Angloromani can be characterised as deriving their grammar from the introduced language, Bantu and English respectively, and lexical items from the ancestral language, Cushitic and Romani, respectively. Bilingual Navajo demonstrates the reverse, combining the grammar of Navajo, the ancestral language, with some English nouns, adjectives and verbs (Schaengold 2003, 2004).

Bilingual Navajo was developed by Navajo children when they were placed in boarding schools in the early to mid-20th century. They were often placed in these schools against their will and were punished for speaking

Navajo. As a result, some children ceased to use Navajo, though many more spoke it in secret, using English words where they had not had a chance to learn the Navajo equivalents. This mixed code became an in-group language for many Navajo-English bilinguals who graduated from the boarding school system and moved back to their Navajo communities. Eventually this mixed code stabilised into the mixed language spoken today (Schaengold 2004: 8).

Nowadays few Navajo children learn Navajo as their first language, although they hear it spoken among adults. Indeed most Navajos over 60 years of age are monolingual in Navajo. All children learn English through the school system and require English to function outside of the Navajo Nation. Thus the language ecology of the Navajo Nation now consists of Navajo, Navajo English, and Bilingual Navajo. In addition, bilingual speakers may change from one code to another in accordance with the situation and interlocutor. Depending on the age of a Bilingual Navajo speaker, s/he may be also fluent in either Standard Navajo or English or both. Younger speakers show greater capacity in English and older speakers tend to have full control of Standard Navajo. The situation described for Navajo people and their languages is also the case for Gurindji and Warlpiri people in northern Australia as discussed in section 2.8.

Bilingual Navajo is characterised by English noun, adjective and verb insertions in a Navajo morpho-syntactic frame. English insertions are nativised to Navajo phonotactic rules. Although Navajo nouns are relatively uninflected with only some directional and possessive suffixes, English nouns are fully integrated morphologically. English nouns may also be inflected with Navaho discourse and interrogative clitics. Adverbs are created from English nouns with the use of the Navaho suffix -*go* (Schaengold 2004: 58–60). English verbs are also found but they require the use of a conjugated Navajo verb *áshlééh* 'to prepare/make' as an auxiliary (see also section 4.1.2). The following example demonstrates the use of an English noun *face* and a verb *clean* in Bilingual Navajo. Navajo elements are in bold.

(3) **bi**-*face*   *clean* **doo** **bee**   **áshlééh**   **da**
    3POSS-face   clean   not   3INST   1SG.make   not
    'I didn't wash his face.'
    (Schaengold 2004: 53)

Navajo word order is also maintained in Bilingual Navajo. Constituents are ordered according to topic and comment rather than by ordering grammatical roles such as subject and object, although the default SOV order is found in sentences with two arguments. More generally, information about grammatical roles is provided by the polysynthetic verbs, therefore a strict word order is not required by the syntax (Schaengold 2004: 44).

2.4. Media Lengua

Another mixed language which retains the grammar of the ancestry language is Media Lengua. This mixed language is spoken in Central Ecuador by a Quechuan group known as the Obreros (Muysken 1997b: 374). The morpho-syntactic frame of Media Lengua is essentially Quechua (the ancestral language) and therefore agglutinating with around 90% of its stems replaced by Spanish forms (the introduced language). Muysken (1997b: 399) also claims that Spanish does contribute some structural features which are not found in Quechua, for example the structure of embedded WH-questions. Other features of the grammar seem to have developed independently. The following example demonstrates the pattern of Spanish stems with Quechuan suffixes (in bold).

(4) *Unu   fabur-**ta**   pidi-**nga-bu**   bini-**xu-ni**.*
 one   favour-ACC   ask-NOM-BEN   come-PROG-1
 'I come to ask a favour.'
 (Muysken 1997b: 365)

Muysken suggests that the structure of Media Lengua is the result of a relexification process where Quechuan stems were replaced with Spanish forms on the basis of semantic equivalence. This process began around 1967. Around this time many young Quechuan men started working in the construction industry in a nearby provincial town and learning Spanish. This was the group who created Media Lengua. Muysken (1997b: 376) claims that the genesis of this mixed language occurred "because acculturated Indians could not completely identify with the traditional Quechua culture or the urban Spanish culture".

Currently it is not clear whether it is still being spoken (Shappeck 2011). Even at the time Muysken was observing the use of Media Lengua, the language ability of Media Lengua speakers varied. Older speakers of Media Lengua continued to speak Quechua and no Spanish whereas younger speakers speak a variety of urban Spanish fluently and rarely speak Quechua without some mixing (Muysken 1997b: 374). This community profile is not unlike that of Bilingual Navaho (and Gurindji Kriol and Light Warlpiri, cf. section 2.8). The current situation would suggest that Media

Lengua represents a language shift situation where Spanish has become increasingly dominant, with the mixed language representing a stage in this shift.

2.5. Old Helsinki Slang

Mixes consisting of the grammar from one language and the lexicon from another may also be the result of a compromise between two different groups wishing to mark a new identity. Old Helsinki Slang is one such example. This mixed language was spoken in Helsinki between 1890 and 1950 by *saki* gangs which consisted of both Finnish and Swedish speaking boys and young men (de Smit 2010; Jarva 2008; Paunonen 2006). This mixed language has a similar structure to Media Lengua where Swedish stems are inserted into a Finnish morpho-syntactic frame. According to Paunonen (2006: 51) approximately 80% of stems in Old Helsinki Slang are of Swedish origin, although, as Jarva (2008: 66) suggests, this figure is mostly likely the upper limit and a lot of variation probably existed between the use of Swedish and Finnish vocabulary making it more like the lexical reservoir described for Angloromani (section 2.1) or the process of paralexification which is used by Ma'á speakers (section 2.2). Jarva (2008: 68) admits, however, that 80% of verbs, adjectives and nouns in a 200-word Swadesh list are of non-Finnish origin. Nonetheless function words and closed class lexical items in Old Helsinki Slang are derived from Finnish, for example conjunctions, adpositions, pronouns and numerals (Jarva 2008: 67). An example of Old Helsinki Slang is given below. Finnish elements are represented in bold.

(5) *föra*-**kaa**   **nyt**   **toi**   *Väiski*   *bastu*-**un**   **ja**
    take-IMP.2PL   now   that   Väiski   sauna-ILL   and
    tvetta-**kaa**   **se**-**n**   *klabbi*-**t**
    wash-IMP.2PL   he-GEN   foot-PL
    'Take Väiski to the sauna and wash his feet.'
    (Jarva 2008: 53)

Old Helsinki Slang originated in Helsinki at the end of the 19th century as a result the migration of Finnish to Helsinki and the increased bilingualism among Swedish speakers. Helsinki was established in a Swedish-speaking area of Finland. At the time Swedish had a high status and was spoken by the upper-class in Finland. Swedish was also the language of most teachers, university staff, government officials and priests, and Finnish-speaking migrants to Helsinki would often switch to

Swedish. This situation changed after the 1870s with increasing numbers of Finnish immigrants to Helsinki and the increasing use of Finnish by the upper-classes. Increasingly Swedish speakers became bilingual in Finnish, though Finnish speakers generally remained monolingual (Jarva 2008: 54–55). Old Helsinki Slang was born in the working class areas in the northern quarters of Helsinki. Two thirds of the population were Finnish speakers, however Swedish was still considered more prestigious. It was common for boys and young men to spend most of their time on the streets due to the lack of compulsory education and over-crowding in apartments. Many of these boys formed gangs called *saki* which consisted of both Finnish and Swedish speakers. The language mixture which emerged from these gangs was probably the result of a communicative compromise between these different groups of speakers and a way of marking a new in-group identity.

Although Old Helsinki Slang can be characterised as Swedish stems alternating with Finnish suffixes, this mixed language also contains innovative forms. For example, the variety of Finnish used in Old Helsinki Slang differs from both Standard Finnish and Finnish dialects spoken at the time. Verbs (of both Swedish and Finnish origin) are conjugated according to a mix of the first and fourth conjugational classes of a Finnish dialect spoken near Helsinki (Jarva 2008: 73). Additionally many words of both Swedish and Finnish origin are augmented by slang suffixes such as *-ari, -is* and *-tsi*. These suffixes are unique to Old Helsinki Slang, differing from the epenthetic vowels required to borrow Swedish words into standard Finnish (Jarva 2008: 70).

2.6.   Mednyj Aleut

Although most mixed languages such as Angloromani, Ma'á, Bilingual Navajo, Media Lengua and Old Helsinki Slang exhibit a split between the lexicon and grammar, other languages are more structurally mixed as the following sketches of Mednyj Aleut, Michif, Gurindji Kriol and Light Warlpiri demonstrate. In these languages, both of the source languages contribute to the structure of the resultant mix creating a composite morpho-syntactic frame. I begin with Mednyj Aleut.

Mednyj Aleut was spoken on Mednyj Island in the Bering Strait until recently. The island was first settled by Russian fur seal hunters in the early 19th century, and Aleutians were brought to the island soon after. Marriages between Russian men and Aleutian women resulted, and the subsequent population were called "creoles" (Golovko and Vakhtin 1990; Sekerina 1994). Thomason (1997b: 462 onwards) suggests that it was the creoles who created Mednyj Aleut. She assumes that they were bilingual in both languages but their half-way position in society led them to mark themselves out as a separate group. Nonetheless Golovko (1994: 117) claims that they considered themselves Aleut, and regarded their language as a variety of Aleut. The use of Mednyj Aleut declined in the 1940s when the Russians introduced Russian education (Thomason 1997b). At the last report, only 10–12 Mednyj Aleut speakers remained (Golovko 1994: 113).

The lexicon of Mednyj Aleut is 90% Aleut. The structure consists of many Aleut nominal inflections, including two case distinctions, absolutive and relative. Aleut also provides various derivational suffixes such as agent, instrumental, location, detransitive, inchoative markers and so on. Mednyj Aleut derives much of its finite verbal inflectional morphology from Russian, including portmanteau morphemes which express tense, number, person markers; and a negative verb prefix derived from the Russian negative particle *ne* (Golovko and Vakhtin 1990; Sekerina 1994; Thomason 1997b). Some of this structure is demonstrated in (6). All Aleut elements are in bold.

(6) *segodnja* **ta:ŋa-x̂** *bud-ut* **su-la-x̂či-t'**
    today spirits-SG FUT-3PL take-MULT-CAUS-INF
    'Today they will sell spirits.'
    (Golovko 1996: 67)

This structural outcome does not provide clear clues about the genesis of Mednyj Aleut. Although it is the result of mixed marriages, whether Aleut elements were transferred to Russian or vice versa remains a point of contention. Different linguistic environments at the point of formation have also been proposed. Golovko (1994) suggests that it is the result of creative word play, whereas Thomason (1997b) proposes the less consciously manipulative route of codeswitching.

2.7. Michif

Michif is also the result of mixed marriages, in this case between Plains Cree-speaking women and French Canadian fur traders. Its genesis probably occurred in the early 1800s when the fur trade was strong. Nowadays it is spoken in Métis communities in the prairie provinces of Canada and the northern parts of the United States. Michif is spoken by the elderly descendants of the fur traders and Cree women. It is an endangered language with fewer than 1000 speakers, mostly elderly, and no children acquiring it as a first language (Bakker 1994, 1997).

Like Mednyj Aleut, Michif shows a great degree of structural mixing. It combines the verbal system of Cree with the nominal system of French, and is classified as a V(erb)-N(oun) mixed language under Bakker's (2003: 122) typology. Bakker observes that the systems from both languages are absorbed in their entirety without simplification. In terms of word classes, Michif is composed of 83–94% French nouns and 88–99% of Cree verbs depending on the speaker. Question words, post-positions, demonstratives and person pronouns are mostly Cree; and prepositions and numerals are almost exclusively French. This NP/VP language divide is also reflected in the grammar – verbal inflections are derived from Cree and the nominal system is dominated by French, as demonstrated in the presence of French plural marking in the article and adjectival agreement. The NP-VP split is clearly demonstrated in (7). Cree elements in bold.

(7) **êkwa** pâstin-am sa bouche **ôhi** le loup
    and   open-he.it his.F mouth this.OBV the.M wolf
    ê-wî-otin-át
    COM-want-take-he.him
    'And when the wolf came to him, he opened his mouth.'
    (Bakker 1997: 5)

Some Cree influence in the NP can also be observed. For instance, the Cree obviative marker is used with French nouns and the locative suffix is calqued (Bakker 1997: 89). However the use of Cree nominal morphology is only found in conjunction with the very few Cree nouns. For example, Michif speakers use both the French preposition and Cree locative suffix, yet this suffix is only found on the very few Cree stems present (Bakker 1997: 110). This lack of mixing between stems and morphology contrasts with Gurindji Kriol and Light Warlpiri where stems and suffixes are commonly derived from different languages within the same word (see section 2.8).

As with all mixed languages, the origins of Michif are a matter of speculation based on its resultant structure. Bakker claims that Michif is the result of language intertwining, a process particular to mixed languages (see section 3.2.1.1). McConvell (2002 cf. Bakker 1997; 2008) suggests that the typology of Cree (head-marking) contributed to the maintenance of Cree verbal morphology (see also section 3.2.2.3). The conventionalisation of French-Cree codeswitching has also been offered as an explanation for its formation (e.g. Drapeau 1991), though Bakker (2003: 128 onwards) gives arguments against this claim.

2.8. Gurindji Kriol and Light Warlpiri

Two more recently identified V(erb)-N(oun) mixed languages come from Australia – Gurindji Kriol and Light Warlpiri. Gurindji Kriol[11] is spoken by Gurindji people in northern Australia. Its source languages are apparent from the name of the language – Gurindji, a Pama-Nyungan language, and Kriol, an English-lexified creole language. Gurindji Kriol originated from contact between non-indigenous settlers and Gurindji people. From 1855 onwards, the traditional lands of the Gurindji and neighbouring groups were seized by colonists who were searching for good cattle pastures. After initial attempts to cull the original inhabitants, cattle stations were set up and the remaining Gurindji people were brought to work on the stations in slave-like conditions with other Aboriginal groups (Meakins 2008b). The cattle station owners communicated with the Aboriginal workers in a cattle station pidgin which later developed into a creole now referred to as Kriol. The Gurindji added this language to their communicative repertoire and it is likely that codeswitching and a certain amount of levelling between Gurindji and the neighbouring dialects provided fertile ground for the formation of this mixed language (McConvell and Meakins 2005; Meakins 2011c).

The fact that a mixed language formed amongst Gurindji people is significant given that many Aboriginal groups in northern Australia have shifted almost completely to Kriol. In this respect Gurindji Kriol represents an attempt to maintain an ancestral language under severe cultural incursion and functional pressure from Kriol (Meakins 2008b). Gurindji Kriol continues to be spoken alongside Gurindji and Kriol. It is the first language of all Gurindji people under the age of 35 years. Older Gurindji people speak Gurindji amongst themselves albeit often mixed with Kriol in codeswitching. All Gurindji people speak Kriol to varying extents when they visit Kriol-speaking areas to the north, though they do not speak Kriol among themselves. English is the language of the school, media and other services in Kalkaringi but plays little role in people's home lives (Meakins 2008a).

Structurally, Kriol contributes much of the verbal grammar including tense and mood auxiliaries, and transitive, aspect and derivational morphemes. Gurindji supplies most of the nominal structure including case and derivational morphology. In this respect the structure of Gurindji Kriol is quite similar to the V-N split seen in Michif. However, in Gurindji Kriol nouns and verbs also come from both source languages, which contrasts with Michif where the nominal structure and nouns are derived from one language and the verbal structure and verbs are derived from the other. For example, although the case morphology is derived from Gurindji, it is used productively with Kriol nouns, as shown in (8). Gurindji elements are in bold. Note that Gurindji verbs are also in evidence in Gurindji Kriol, although Kriol provides the TMA markers.

(8) dat **karu-ngku** i=m luk hol-**ta walyak**.
 the child-ERG 3SG=PRS look hole-LOC inside
 'The child looks inside the hole.'
 (Meakins 2011)

Both languages also contribute small amounts of grammar to the systems they do not dominate in Gurindji Kriol. For example, the Gurindji continuative suffix is found in the VP, and Kriol determiners are common in the NP. Kriol also provides Gurindji Kriol with an SVO word order, though the word order is more flexible than Kriol with information structure determining word order to some extent which reflects word order patterns in Gurindji. Complex clauses are constructed using both Gurindji and Kriol strategies, for example coordinating and relative clauses use Kriol conjunctions and relative pronouns, and subordinate clauses are formed using Gurindji-derived case and factive marking. In terms of the lexicon, Gurindji Kriol derives its lexicon relatively evenly from both languages (Charola 2002; Meakins, 2008a, 2009, 2011c; Dalton et al. 1995).

Although it is easy to identify which language the lexemes and morphemes are derived from, this approach is actually quite deceptive. Gurindji Kriol is not merely the result of a simple replication of features from these languages. Although Gurindji Kriol bears some resemblance to both of its source languages, it uses the forms from these languages to function within a unique language system. For example Gurindji Kriol has adopted ergative marking from Gurindji; however, where ergative marking is obligatory in Gurindji, it is optional in Gurindji Kriol. The ergative marker has become optional with the adoption of word order from Kriol as the main means of marking arguments. As a result, the function of the ergative marker has shifted to marking the prominence and agentivity of a discourse entity (Meakins 2009, 2011a; Meakins and O'Shannessy 2010; O'Shannessy and Meakins 2012). Ergative marking is just one example of the types of changes which language features have undergone in the process of mixed language genesis. The need to describe the structure of mixed languages beyond the mixing of forms is the topic of section 5.

Light Warlpiri is spoken just 100 km from Gurindji Kriol. Structurally it is very similar to Gurindji Kriol in exhibiting a split in the language dominance of the nominal and verbal system. For example, the nominal structure comes from the heritage language, Warlpiri, and Aboriginal

English/Kriol provides the verb structure (O'Shannessy 2005), and is also classified as a V-N mixed language in this respect. Light Warlpiri is also quite mixed lexically; however a crucial difference between Gurindji Kriol and Light Warlpiri is that verbs are almost always derived from Aboriginal English/Kriol in Light Warlpiri. This differs from Gurindji Kriol where many Gurindji Kriol verbs are Gurindji in origin (Meakins and O'Shannessy 2012). In the example below, Warlpiri elements are in bold.

(9) en   **karnta-pawu**   i-m   kam   geit-**kirra**.
     and   girl-DIM   3SG.SBJ-NFUT   come   gate-ALL
     'And the girl came to the gate.'
     (O'Shannessy 2006: 32)

Although Light Warlpiri is structurally similar to Gurindji Kriol, it has a different social function. O'Shannessy (2006) suggests that Light Warlpiri is an expression of the identity of a particular Warlpiri community rather than an attempt to maintain an ancestry language. Unlike Gurindji Kriol speakers, Light Warlpiri speakers also speak their heritage language, Warlpiri. Warlpiri also continues to be acquired by children, though their main language of use is Light Warlpiri. Adults and children alike codeswitch between these languages and O'Shannessy (2008, 2012) suggests that it is likely that Light Warlpiri also found its origins in such linguistic practices.

The close proximity of Gurindji Kriol and Light Warlpiri begs the question of whether other such mixed languages exist or have existed in Australia. Indeed a youth variety of Tiwi (spoken in the north on an island off Darwin) has been described (Lee 1987). Additionally Disbray (2008, 2009) and Disbray and Simpson (2005) have described a creolised variety of English spoken 500 km away called Wumpurrarni[12] English. This variety includes some inflectional morphology (possessive and allative case suffixes) from the local Aboriginal language, Warumungu. What is interesting about Wumpurrarni English is that older speakers speak something which is akin in structure to Gurindji Kriol and Light Warlpiri. For instance, their variety includes more Warumungu structural elements, and more rarely ergative case marking, as shown in (10) on the corrected nominal. Warumungu elements are shown in bold. This similarity in structure suggests that a mixed language may have been spoken in this area with the Warumungu structural features gradually eroded by Kriol functional equivalents such as prepositions.

(10) **nyili**   bin   pok-im   **jina**,   no   masbi   **wintirrij**-ja.
     prickle PST pierce-TR foot, no must.be stick-**ERG**
     'A prickle pierced (his) foot, no maybe a stick.'[13]

2.9.   Sri Lanka Malay

The final mixed language to be discussed is Sri Lanka Malay. This language is quite different from other mixed languages. Not only is most of the lexicon derived from Malay, but all of the morphology and function words also find their forms in Malay though the underlying structure is Tamil. In this respect it contrasts with Media Lengua, for example, because the forms of the grammatical elements are still Quechuan though the lexicon is mostly Spanish-derived. The composition of Sri Lanka Malay makes it difficult to classify as either an Austronesian (lexicon) or Dravidian language (grammar).

Sri Lanka Malay is spoken in a number of communities in Sri Lanka by the Malay minority who make up less than 1% of the population of Sri Lanka. Lexically Sri Lanka Malay consists almost entirely of words from a Malay-based trade language called Vehicular or Bazaar Malay (Austronesian) (Smith, Paauw, and Hussainmiya 2004: 200). However its grammar is derived from Tamil (Dravidian) and perhaps Sinhala[14] (Indo-Aryan) with the result that it became unintelligible to other Malay speakers. Sri Lanka Malay seems to be the result of Vehicular Malay developing from an isolating language to an agglutinating language under the influence of Tamil. It has also developed SOV word order, postpositions, and pre-nominal determiners and adjectives due to this contact (Ansaldo 2008, 2011a, 2011b; Hussainmiya 1987; Nordhoff 2009). This structure is demonstrated in (11).

(11) *Sir*   anak-pada-yang   ruuma-nang   e-luppa.
     teacher   child-PL-ACC   house-DAT   PST-send
     'The teacher sent the children to school.'
     (Ansaldo 2008: 27)

Sri Lanka Malay is an endangered language, now restricted to home use and generally not being spoken by younger generations, with Sinhala/English bilingualism becoming dominant (Smith and Paauw 2006: 160; Ansaldo 2008; Nordhoff 2009). Traditionally the Malay community have had close ties with the Tamil-speaking Moor community who are also Muslims, like the Malays. The Sri Lanka Malays are descendants of immigrants who were brought to Sri Lanka at different times by Dutch

(1656 onwards) and British colonists (1796 onwards). Although they are called Malays, they came from a number of places including Banda, Balu, Java, with only a Malay trade language in common.

There are different views on how Sri Lanka Malay developed. The first is that it is a pidgin which was creolised by the children of mixed marriages between Malay men who spoke a Vehicular Malay and Tamil-speaking Moor women. Smith and Paauw (2006) suggest that the mothers must have tried to make Malay the language of the home, and the children nativised the Malay pidgin in a process of creolisation. Perhaps an added factor here is that the women learnt Vehicular Malay or the Malay language of their husbands but their version of Malay showed first language interference from Tamil which was the inter-language that the children nativised. Smith and Paauw (2006) propose that this whole process occurred before Malay was reintroduced by the British in the schools between 1802 to 1873, therefore creating a diglossic situation. During this period Sri Lanka Malay had extended contact with the Malay language (Smith, Paauw, and Hussainmiya 2004).

Bakker (2003: 116) and more recently Ansaldo (2011b) propose another interpretation of the resultant structure of Sri Lanka Malay. He interprets the structural outcome of Sri Lanka Malay as a subcategory of mixed language which he calls a converted language (see section 3.2). By a converted language, Bakker is drawing similarities to a process Ross (1996, 2001) calls metatypy. Metatypy refers to the maintenance of the surface forms of one language, that is its lexical and morphological material, which are restructured according to the grammar of another language. Bakker suggests that this convergence of Vehicular Malay and Tamil occurred much later than suggested by Smith. Both Smith and Paauw (2006) and Ansaldo (2008) dispute this claim on historical and linguistic grounds which will not be discussed here.

The third theory about the origins of Sri Lanka Malay is proposed by Ansaldo (2008). Ansaldo supports Bakker's genesis hypothesis; however he believes that it took place over a longer time span. Ansaldo challenges the claim that pervasive intermarriage occurred between Malay immigrant soldiers and Moor women, noting that the Malay soldiers generally brought their wives and children to Sri Lanka, at least during the British colonial phase. This observation has ramifications for a genesis scenario. Tamil and Sinhala would have been present but external to the Malay community and therefore not languages of acquisition. This picture does not support an abrupt nativization hypothesis but rather change that took place over an extended period of contact. Under Ansaldo's hypothesis, the Malays were more segregated as a community than suggested by Smith and Paauw, which suggests they must have been highly multilingual in order for such a pervasive restructuring to have taken place. The origins of Sri Lanka Malay are discussed further in Nordhoff (2012).

2.10. Degrees and types of mixing

The languages sketched out in the previous sections demonstrate the degree of typological variation which exists in the category of contact languages labelled 'mixed languages' (see also Matras 2000). One obvious way in which these mixed languages vary is in their degree of grammatical mixing. For most mixed languages, the grammar is predominantly derived from only one of the source languages, for example Angloromani, Ma'á, Bilingual Navaho, Media Lengua and Old Helsinki Slang. In other languages both source languages contribute significant amounts of grammar, for example Michif, Mednyj Aleut, Light Warlpiri and Gurindji Kriol. This degree of grammatical mixing is represented on the continuum in Figure 1.

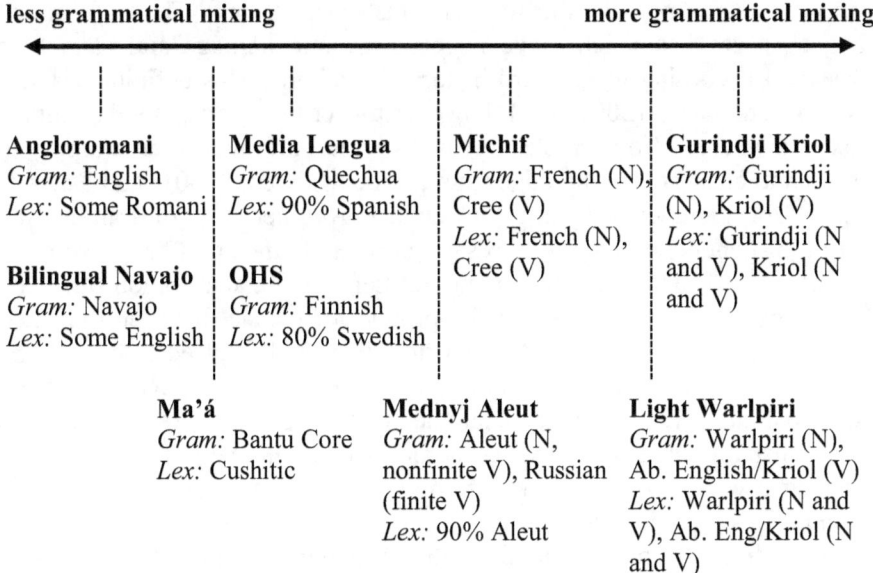

Figure 1. A continuum of grammatical mixing in mixed languages.

Most of these mixed languages can be categorised as either G-L mixed languages or V-N mixed languages (see Bakker 2003 for an overview of ML types). Interestingly these types cannot be predicted from the sociohistorical background of the languages and their speakers. For example, although Michif and Gurindji Kriol are both V-N mixed languages, Michif is the result of mixed marriages and Gurindji Kriol is the result of language shift by a single cultural group. Similarly, although Angloromani and Media Lengua exhibit a grammar-lexicon split, the grammar of Media Lengua is provided by the ancestral language whereas the grammar of Angloromani comes from the new language. Thus, although the structures of some mixed languages look similar from a synchronic typological perspective, they originate from very different social circumstances. The following sections discuss the socio-historical origins of these mixed languages and the linguistic practices of the speaker communities at the time of genesis. The difficulty of matching social and structural typologies becomes clear in these sections.

3. The origins and features of mixed languages

A number of general definitions have been used to identify mixed languages. The earliest definition was that of *genetic ambiguity*. Thomason and Kaufman (1988) argue that mixed languages can be identified on the basis of their non-classification in historical terms. That is, mixed languages are deemed to have no clear genetic heritage and cannot be classified according to standard historical methods. This definition is still used by Thomason (2001: 198); however this criterion does not distinguish mixed languages from creole languages which are also often claimed to have an unclear genetic heritage (though see Mufwene (2001) and DeGraff (2005) for arguments against this claim). Another way of framing the notion of genetic ambiguity is to say that mixed languages have two clear parents. This criterion relates to another general characterisation of mixed languages – they are said to be the product of contact between only two languages (Bakker 1994: 27; McWhorter 2005: 253). Indeed it seems to be the case that most identified mixed languages have two clear and often equal parents, in contrast, for example, with pidgin and creole languages which usually have one lexifier parent and a number of other source languages which contribute to varying extents to the grammar, including spontaneous grammaticalisations.

Apart from this more general definition, two main approaches have been taken to describe the origins and features of mixed languages – socio-historical approaches (section 3.1) and structural approaches (section 3.2). This divide is typical of the kind found for other contact languages such as creole languages. Examples of approaches which combine socio-historical and typological features can be found, see for example Matras and Bakker (2003) who posit six types of mixed languages based on the mixed language speakers' knowledge of the source languages, the level of functionality of the mixed language, the typology of its structure, and various social factors.

In general the next sections will demonstrate that the category of contact language contains a diverse range of structural mixes which derive from varied socio-historical backgrounds.

3.1. Socio-historical origins and features of mixed languages

Most generally mixed languages contrast with creole languages in that their genesis was a product of expressive rather than communicative needs (Golovko 2003: 191; Muysken 1997b: 375). This social definition argues that pidgin and creole languages are born out of the need for communication between people of a number of language groups, whereas mixed languages are created in situations where a common language already exists and communication is not at issue. Thus the mixed language serves as an expression of an altered identity, be it new, or differing significantly from an older identity. For example Light Warlpiri is spoken by Warlpiri people who had no need for a new language to communicate with. Warlpiri was already fulfilling this function, and is indeed still spoken. Thus Light Warlpiri marks an identity shift for younger Warlpiri people from a particular community, Lajamanu, who simultaneously express their continuing Warlpiri heritage coupled with their Lajamanu identity in the mixed language (O'Shannessy 2008).

More specifically, discussions about the sociolinguistic and historical features of mixed languages have fallen into three categories: the *direction of language shift* which contributed to the formation of a mixed language (section 3.1.1), whether speakers of mixed languages constitute a *separate ethnic group* (section 3.1.2) and whether the mixed language is used as *the native language of the group* (section 3.1.3).

3.1.1. The direction of language shift

A number of theories of mixed language genesis are based on the direction of language shift between the ancestry language and the introduced language. Many of these theories are set within borrowing or codeswitching theories (see section 3.2.1). Most of this work focuses on the grammatical interaction of the source languages. Other work takes a broader approach looking at the socio-linguistic conditions which influence the direction of the language shift (Croft 2000, 2003; Matras 2000). Croft (2000: 214–221; 2003: 52–60) proposes a social typology of mixed languages which is based on the change in dominance between languages during the process of mixed language genesis. His approach relies on the relationship between the ancestry language and the introduced language, and the direction of shift between the two languages. He suggests this process may take one of three forms: *mixed marriages*, *semi-shift*, and *death by borrowing*. Mixed languages which are the result of mixed marriages represent the identification with a new society and subsequent fusion of two languages. Semi-shift occurs when speakers of an ancestry language move part-way towards the introduced language but do not complete the shift. Finally death by borrowing involves languages which borrow to such an extent that they replace much of their basic vocabulary, and in more intense cases, grammatical elements. Croft's categories represent two directions of shift – firstly a shift from the ancestral language to the introduced language which occurs in degrees (lexicon then grammar) and secondly the convergence of two languages. Another possibility is the deliberate 'undoing' of a shift towards an introduced language where a group attempts to reclaim its ancestral language. Boretzky and Igla (1994) call such a shift a "U-Turn". These three directions of shift are summarised in Figure 2.

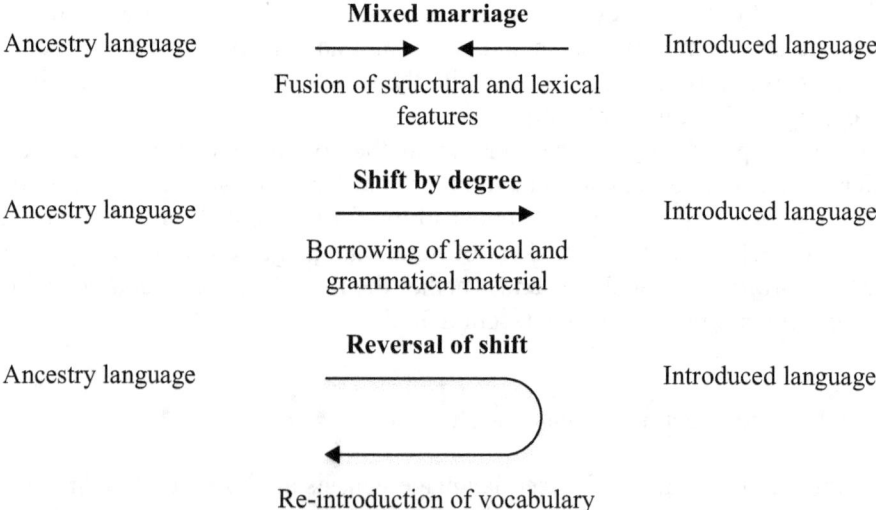

Figure 2. Direction of shift in mixed language genesis.

The first category of language shift involves mixed marriages between men from one society and women from another (Bakker 1997). The children of these mixed marriages are said to form their own distinct cultural identity, with the mixed language as an enactment of this identity. The relative dominance of the languages in this situation is less clear, and it is likely that they converge and fuse (see also section 3.2.2). In this respect they do not represent a clear shift in either direction. Michif is the classic example of this type of mixed language genesis. As was shown in section 2.7, this Canadian mixed language and its speakers are the product of marriage between French Canadian fur traders and Amerindian women. Mednyj Aleut also seems to fit into this category. It is said to have emerged from mixed marriages between Aleut women and Russian seal fur traders in the early 1800s.

The second category consists of mixed languages which undergo a shift by degree from the ancestral language to the introduced language. A change in the dominance of languages occurs when speakers shift towards the introduced language. This process does not go to completion, and what remains is the mixed language. Thus the mixed language can have varying amounts of material from the introduced language from borrowed nouns right up to morphology. This shift stops part-way because the speakers may not have full access to the introduced language, or because the remaining part of the ancestral language may be a marker of social identity. Media Lengua is an example of a mixed language which resulted from a partial shift. The relexification of Quechua with Spanish was a consequence of Quechuan men becoming more fluent in Spanish. Similarly Bilingual Navajo and Old Helsinki Slang fit well in this category. Gurindji Kriol and Light Warlpiri are examples of languages which have progressed further along the scale, incorporating large amounts of structural material from Kriol/Aboriginal English as they shifted away from their ancestral languages, Gurindji and Warlpiri respectively.

Croft (2003) considers Ma'á and Angloromani cases of languages at the extreme end of this scale of shift. He suggests that they are the mirror-opposite of languages such as Media Lengua, resulting from the extreme absorption of another language's grammatical structure into the ancestral language. In the case of Ma'á, the relevant grammatical system is Bantu (section 2.2), and English for Angloromani (section 2.1). Croft (2003: 53) suggests that these languages were created within societies under great social pressure. Whilst they attempted to avoid cultural assimilation, they gradually adopted more and more of the introduced language as it became more dominant, leaving only vocabulary from the ancestral language. This view of the formation of Ma'á and Para-Romani varieties follows Thomason's (2001) proposal, however, it is not without controversy. As was discussed in section 2.2, Mous (2003a) suggests that Ma'á represents an attempt to undo the shift to Mbugu by maintaining basic Cushitic vocabulary. In this respect, Mous' view of Ma'á fits better with the third category, the reversal of a language shift.

The third category of language shift includes mixed languages which formed as the result of a reversal of shift. In this category are mixed languages which are the product of a group shifting almost completely to an introduced language and attempting to reverse this shift by re-introducing material from the ancestral language. In this scenario, the ancestral language is still available, perhaps still spoken by older generations. Generally only lexical material is found from the ancestral language in the mix. Mixed languages such as Angloromani or Ma'á which utilise lexical reservoirs from the ancestral language could be regarded as examples of such a linguistic U-turn.

3.1.2. Mixed language speakers as a separate ethnic group

Another sociolinguistic feature, which has been discussed in relation to mixed languages, is whether speakers constitute a separate ethnicity group or a continuation of an older identity (Bakker and Mous 1994: 2). Creoles are considered to be markers of a separate or more encompassing group of people. For example, although speakers of the English-based Australian creole language, Kriol, still identify with the smaller substrate languages such as Marra, a larger identity of Aboriginality is marked through the use of Kriol. This identity contrasts again with the group of non-Indigenous Australians which is associated with English. Unlike creole languages, a single coherent story of ethnic identity associated with the genesis and use of mixed languages does not emerge from the data available. Two main processes seem to be apparent. As Thomason (2003: 25) suggests, the new language is either associated with a new ethnic identity, or it is seen as a means of continuing an ancestral group membership.

First, some mixed languages are spoken by new ethnic groups which are generally derived from mixed marriages. For example, Michif speakers call themselves Métis which reflects the mixed identity of their group (Matras and Bakker 2003: 2; Bakker 1994: 14). At the time Mednyj Aleut was spoken, the speakers also formed a separate group, although they considered themselves Aleut (Golovko 1994: 117). The Sri Lankan Malay s also constitute a separate ethnic group. Although this language combines a contact variety of Malay with Tamil and Sinhala, the speakers do not identify directly with any of these groups. This is probably because they come from a variety of Austronesian speaking backgrounds and were originally immigrants to Sri Lanka and remain a minority group. However whether this mixed language is the result of mixed marriages is controversial as discussed in section 2.9. One mixed language which is marks a new identity without the background of mixed marriage is Old

Helsinki Slang. In this case, the new identity was formed between mixed Swedish and Finnish-speaking gangs.

Mixed languages are also spoken by people who *do not* constitute a separate ethnic identity. Speakers of Media Lengua are not separate from Quechua people, although they are a sub-group who identify to a certain extent with urban Hispanic society. There are also a number of in-group mixed languages labelled secret languages. Angloromani is spoken by people who simultaneously mark their Romani heritage and maintain their separation from mainstream English society. There are suggestions in earlier literature that Romanies would relexify English more densely with Romani vocabulary to prevent non-Romani people from understanding their conversations (Boretzky and Igla 1994). Speakers of Bilingual Navajo are also not deemed separate from Navajo people in general. This mixed language represents an attempt to maintain Navajo under the continuing colonial pressure of English. Similarly speakers of Gurindji Kriol also do not belong to a separate ethnic group. This mixed language is spoken by Gurindji people whose parents and grandparents were predominantly speakers of Gurindji until at least the late 1940s. Gurindji Kriol speakers continue to identify as Gurindji and also call their mixed language, Gurindji, despite the Kriol content (Meakins 2012: 109). The strong maintenance of Gurindji lexicon and noun phrase structure in this mixed language marks the Gurindji as separate from other Kriol speakers, and indeed the encroaching and assimilative non-Indigenous world (Meakins 2008b).

3.1.3. Mixed languages used as native languages

Related to the association of mixed languages with a new or continuing identity is their use as native languages by speaker communities. There are a couple of ways that 'native-ness' may be defined. A mixed language may be independent from its input languages, that is, speakers have no knowledge of the input languages. Alternatively a mixed language may be the main language of use within a community of speakers, where the source languages are still spoken. In this respect it may also be the first language of the community (see also section 4.1.1).

First, independence can be defined by speaker use. In these cases speakers do not use or understand the input languages and therefore the mixed language is spoken in isolation from these languages. This criterion is used to distinguish creole languages from pidgins. Whilst pidgins are usually associated with a particular domain such as trade and therefore are not a first language for speakers, creole languages are usually the first language of a community and tend to exist in a greater degree of isolation from their source languages, though this is not the case for many of the Pacific creoles. In fact Michif is the only mixed language which is spoken today largely independent of its source languages. Most Métis no longer speak either of the contributing languages, French or Cree. English is spoken and has now become the principal language in the communities (Matras and Bakker 2003: 3), with only older people using Michif, Amerindian languages and/or French.

The majority of mixed languages are the native language of a community, however they are spoken alongside one or more of their source languages. Smith (2000) calls these languages *symbiotic* mixed languages. For example Mednyj Aleut was spoken concurrently with a number of Aleut dialects and Russian, though it is not clear whether Mednyj Aleut speakers always had control of one or more of its input languages (Golovko 1994: 114). According to Muysken (1994b: 210), Media Lengua is learnt either as a first or second language. Middle-aged speakers of this mixed language also may have access to both input languages. Younger speakers tend to speak Spanish better and older speakers, Quechua. All Bilingual Navajo speakers also have either Navajo or English or both in their linguistic repertoire. In the case of Angloromani, English which provides the grammatical base, is the main language for speakers of this mixed language. Similarly, Gurindji Kriol and Light Warlpiri are the first languages of their speaker communities, although Gurindji, Warlpiri and Kriol are still used to varying extents, as will be discussed in more detail in section 4.1.1.

3.2.   Structural origins and features of mixed languages

As section 3.1 shows, mixed languages are a product of the social circumstances of their speakers. There is a general consensus that severe social upheaval is a major factor which contributes to the formation of mixed languages, whether the speaker community is marking a new identity or maintaining an old one. What distinguishes mixed languages from other contact varieties is that they emerge as expressions of identity rather than as a result of a communicative need. There is much less agreement on the kinds of grammatical processes which are required for a relatively stable language to emerge. Generally theories of genesis are divided over whether mixed languages are the extraordinary results of ordinary contact processes (cf. Thomason 1995), or whether special processes are required. Ordinary contact processes include borrowing (section 3.2.1.1) or codeswitching (section 3.2.1.2) whereas Bakker's

(1997) language intertwining theory (section 3.2.2.1) and Muysken's relexification theory (section 3.2.1.3) are examples of special processes.

Theories of mixed language formation take on two main forms – (i) unidirectional approaches (section 3.2.1), for example borrowing (Matras 2003; Thomason 2001), codeswitching (Auer 1999; Myers-Scotton 2002, 2003), relexification (Muysken 1981), paralexification (Mous 2003a), or Matras et al.'s (2008) language repertoire approach; and (ii) fusion approaches (section 3.2.2), such as Bakker's language intertwining theory, language competition approaches (Ansaldo 2008; Meakins 2011c) (section 3.2.2.2) and McConvell's (2002, 2008) centre of gravity hypothesis (section 3.2.2.3). In general, these diachronic accounts of mixed language genesis are based on synchronic descriptions of the languages (although see Matras 2010 for an account of the genesis of Angloromani based on an evaluation of historical sources). Further, the diversity of genesis theories is largely the result of extending an explanation for the formation of one mixed language to other varieties. In this respect, no one theory provides a unified account of mixed language genesis which accounts for all languages which have been identified as mixed.

Finally, with the exception of Myers-Scotton and the language competition and relexification approaches, one shortcoming of most of these theories is their reliance on form (i.e. the phonological shape of a lexeme or morpheme) as the basis of mixing. Often mixing is more intricate involving different layers of the lexeme or morpheme, such as combining the forms from one source language that have a function from another language (see section 5).

3.2.1. Unidirectional approaches to mixed language genesis

Unidirectional approaches to mixed language genesis assume a one-way shift from a source language to a target language. They consist of borrowing or switching scenarios where lexical and morphological material is replicated from the source language into the target language. Mixed languages are considered to be a half-way house for this language shift, no longer classifiable as a variety of one language or the other. Note that the separation of borrowing and codeswitching approaches (particularly in relation to insertional codeswitching) in the literature is somewhat artificial and largely the product of a separation between historical linguistics, which is focussed on language-level change, and contact linguistics, which tends to have the bilingual individual in mind.

3.2.1.1. Borrowing approaches

Thomason and Kaufman (1988) and Thomason (2001) base a theory of mixed language genesis on their model of borrowing. This model combines language features with social factors, proposing that features can be borrowed regardless of the typological distance between the affected languages (Thomason and Kaufman 1988: 53). Social factors play a fundamental and determinate role in the linguistic outcome of language contact and, given the right level of social disruption, substantial structural borrowing including that of inflectional morphology is possible (Thomason and Kaufman 1988: 37). Under Thomason and Kaufman's (1988: 47) model, two social features are necessary for extensive borrowing – time and a level of bilingualism. Extensive and prolonged community bilingualism is considered a necessary condition for borrowing structural elements of a language, such as inflectional morphology. The end result is a borrowing scale (Table 2) which is reminiscent of Whitney's (1881), Haugen's (1950), Moravcsik's (1978) and Appel and Muysken's (1987) earlier scales. See also Matras and Sakel (2007), Matras (2009) and Aikhenvald and Dixon (2007).

Table 2. Thomason and Kaufman's borrowing scale (based on Thomason and Kaufman 1988: 74–75; Thomason 2001)

Degree of contact	Borrowing type	Features borrowed
1. Casual contact	lexical	non-basic vocabulary before basic
2. Slightly more intense contact	lexical	functional vocabulary e.g. conjunctions and adverbs
	syntactic	only new functions borrowed
3. More intense contact	lexical	pre/postpositions, derivational affixes, inflectional affixes (attached to stem), pronouns, low numerals
	syntactic	change in word order, borrowing postpositions in a prepositional language
4. Strong cultural pressure	syntactic	extensive word order change, inflectional affixes (e.g. case)
5. Very strong cultural pressure	syntactic	typological disruption, changes in word structure (e.g. adding prefixes in suffixing language), change from flexional to agglutinative morphology

Language shift may stabilise somewhere along this scale of borrowing. For example mixed language formation may halt at the least disruptive end of the scale and exhibit only lexical borrowings. Bakker (2003: 109) identifies this pattern as a class of mixed language: *L-G languages* (although he does not consider this to be an 'ordinary' process). They comprise by far the largest category, and are characterised by a clear division between the lexicon and the grammar where these systems are dominated by a different source language. Examples include Angloromani (English grammar, Romani words), Ma'á (Bantu grammar, Cushitic core vocabulary), Bilingual Navajo (Navajo grammar, English vocabulary), Media Lengua (Quechua grammar, Spanish lexicon) and Old Helsinki Slang (Finnish grammar, Swedish lexicon). Note that this category includes mixed languages where the language contributing the grammar is the ancestral language, for example Media Lengua and Bilingual Navajo, and languages where the introduced language provides the grammar, for example Angloromani and Ma'á.

At the other end of the scale are fossilised mixes which contain inflectional morphology from both languages. At this stage other borrowings such as lexical and more minor structural borrowings are assumed. A number of mixed languages exhibit this grammar mixture, including Michif, Mednyj Aleut, Gurindji Kriol and Light Warlpiri. For example, inflectional morphology from both French and Cree is present in Michif. Verbal inflections are derived from Cree and in the NP, Michif preserves both French plural marking and adjectival agreement and some case-marking from Cree. For instance, the Cree obviative suffix marks French nouns in Michif, albeit in a somewhat reduced distribution (Bakker 1997: 89). Another language, which has also retained inflectional morphology from both source languages, is Mednyj Aleut. The structure of Mednyj Aleut includes both Aleut nominal inflections such as two case distinctions (absolutive and relative) and Russian finite verbal inflectional morphology, including portmanteau morphemes which express tense, number and person (Thomason 1997b: 457–59). Finally, Gurindji Kriol and Light Warlpiri combine Kriol/Aboriginal English, the language of the verbal inflectional categories (tense and mood markers), with Gurindji and Warlpiri nominal inflections, both syntactic case suffixes (ergative, dative, possessive) and semantic case suffixes (locative, allative, ablative) (Meakins 2009, 2011a, 2011b; Meakins and O'Shannessy 2005, 2010; O'Shannessy 2011).

The situation described for these four languages is exceptional given the fragility of inflectional morphology in other language contact situations. For example, inflectional morphology is rarely borrowed (Thomason and Kaufman 1988; Heath 1978; Weinreich [1953] 1974; Aikhenvald and

Dixon 2007; Gardani 2008; Matras 2007; Meakins 2011a), is mostly derived from the more dominant language in codeswitching (Myers-Scotton 2002; Muysken 2000), is rarely found in pidgin and creole languages (Plag 2003a, 2003b; McWhorter 1998), and is one of the first systems to be reduced or lost in situations of language obsolescence (Maher 1991; Sasse 1992). In this respect, the disappearance or maintenance of inflectional morphology is indicative of the relative strength of the interacting languages. The loss of inflectional morphology is one of the first signs of language death, thereby demonstrating the weakening of the morpho-syntactic frame of the language. In the cases of borrowing and codeswitching one language is more dominant, as defined by the presence of inflectional morphology. On the other hand, the maintenance of inflectional morphology from both languages in mixed languages would suggest a relatively equal weighting given to both languages, with neither language definitively stronger. Inflectional morphology in this level of language contact neither disappears nor is selected for by only one language. Therefore no one language can be identified as the grammar language, but rather the morpho-syntactic frame represents a composite of the languages.

Indeed Matras (2003: 158) suggests that a particular feature of mixed languages is the seemingly unconstrained borrowing of grammatical elements, which in the past have been labelled as 'loan proof'. Included in the list of loan proof items is inflectional morphology. Matras (2003: 171) goes on to suggest that this violation of borrowing tendencies is what characterises a mixed language. He includes in his assessment of the presence of these rarely attested borrowings, not only inflectional morphology such as case affixes, but also in-/ definite articles, bound pronouns and TMA markers, possessive markers, sentential negation, personal pronouns, demonstratives, existentials (copula), place deictics, the basic interrogatives *what* and *who*, numerals under 5, and adpositions which express basic local relations (*in, at, out of*) (2003: 158–159).

3.2.1.2. Codeswitching approaches

Related to borrowing theories is the idea that mixed languages are derived from codeswitching. Auer (1998, 1999) and Myers-Scotton (1993, 2003) suggest that mixed languages are the result of the gradual fossilisation of codeswitching. The empirical evidence for codeswitching origins is discussed in section 4.4. A distinction which is relevant is Muysken's (2000) typological differentiation of *insertional* and *alternational* codeswitching. Generally speaking, these two types of codeswitching can be distinguished by the level of involvement of the grammars of the interacting languages. Alternational codeswitching involves the alternation of structures from different languages. On the other hand, the grammar of one language is more dominant in insertional codeswitching, with elements from another language inserting into the more dominant language's structure (Muysken 2000: 3).

The first account of the transition from codeswitching to a mixed language comes from Auer (1999: 309–10; 1998). He presents a model of the fossilisation of codeswitching (Stage 1) into a mixed language (Stage 3) via language mixing (Stage 2). A 'cline' from pragmatics to grammar can be observed between these three stages of mixing, where codeswitching loses its pragmatic function over time and the shape of the mixing is increasingly determined by grammatical constraints (1998: 16). These three forms of bilingual speech are differentiated by the type of mixing, and their degree of variation and social markedness. First *codeswitching* is the most variable and socially-marked form. By "socially marked", Auer (1999: 310) is referring to the social weight carried by each language and the associated social meaning of switching between languages. Typologically, codeswitching at this stage can be alternational and/or insertional (1999: 313–314). Stage 2 *language mixing* also exhibits patterns of codeswitching, but the social meaning associated with the switches is lost. Instead syntactic factors in the form of structural constraints play a role in the language switches. Both alternational and insertional codeswitching may be present in the language mixing stage. However Auer (1999: 315) believes that these patterns converge making it difficult to distinguish them. Finally *mixed languages* differ from language mixing in a number of ways. Auer suggests that they lose any hint of alternational codeswitching, looking entirely like insertional structures. They contain much less syntactic variation than language mixing; functionally equivalent structures from both languages may develop more specialised uses in the mixed language; and mixed language speakers do not need to be speakers of either of the contributing languages (1999: 321).

Myers-Scotton (2002, 2003) provides the second major approach which theorises the move from *insertional* codeswitching to a mixed language. She frames this transition within her Matrix Language Frame (MLF) model. She labels this transition the Matrix Language Turnover Hypothesis. The relevant concepts in this hypothesis are the Matrix Language (ML), which is the language which provides the grammatical frame for switching or mixing, and the Embedded Language (EL), which is the weaker language which contributes mostly lexical material to the mix. The Matrix Language Turnover Hypothesis is concerned with the change in dominance of the participating languages. Myers-Scotton proposes that mixed languages arise when there is a turnover under way which does not go to completion. That is, the source languages do not entirely change in dominance but stabilise someway through this process resulting in a language which is a combination of the source languages.

Like Auer, Myers-Scotton also proposes three steps from insertional codeswitching to composite codeswitching (convergence) to the mixed language itself. The first step in the Matrix Language Turnover is *classic* codeswitching which is basically insertional codeswitching, with alternational codeswitching incorporated in the form of EL Islands. The more dominant language takes the role of the Matrix Language, with the less dominant language inserting or embedding morphemes within this grammatical frame (2002: 110). More lengthy switches to the less dominant language create EL Islands. The second stage, *composite* codeswitching, occurs when the participating languages begin to converge, such that one of the participating languages loses its undisputed role as the Matrix Language. In this respect, the weaker or embedded language gains strength. The Matrix Language splits and recombines to form a composite structure consisting of abstract material from both languages. The convergence of the EL and the ML represents a change in the morpho-syntactic frame. This convergence precedes the third mixed language stage. Myers-Scotton suggests that mixed languages "represent turnovers that do not go to completion, but 'stop along the way'" (2002: 249). Mixed languages may stop at different places along the scale, which explains why they surface in different forms and with the split in different places.

Myers-Scotton calls this process the Matrix Language Turnover hypothesis. The outcome is a language which contains structural material such as inflectional morphology from the weaker language, that is the language which was the embedded language in the codeswitching (2003: 92). This analysis is similar to Thomason and Kaufman's and Matras' view of mixed language genesis which is based on borrowing models. Indeed, as section 3.2.1.1 shows, mixed languages with structural material from the weaker language do exist. Michif, Mednyj Aleut, Gurindji Kriol and Light Warlpiri all exhibit inflectional morphology from both of their source languages. Like the borrowing approaches, the gradual conventionalisation of codeswitching is unidirectional where material from one language is subsumed into another language. Although some problems exist for both Auer and Myers-Scotton's models, such as the need to lose alternational structures (see section 4.4.2), empirical evidence for codeswitching preceding mixed language genesis exists (section 4.4.1), though it must be noted that empirical evidence for each of the three stages that Auer and Myers-Scotton propose is not available.

3.2.1.3. Relexification

The process of relexification is more familiar as an account of the origin of creole languages (see e.g. Lefebvre 1998, 2004), nonetheless relexification has also been offered as an explanation for the formation of one mixed language, Media Lengua (Muysken 1981, 1994b, 1997b). Relexification differs from borrowing in that it is only the phonological form which is borrowed from another language rather than the whole structure of the lexical and morphological item. This form is then mapped onto the recipient language's own structure. For example, while the form of a verb may be borrowed, it is mapped onto the predicate argument structure of the recipient language.

In the case of Media Lengua, Muysken (1981) argues Spanish forms have been borrowed into Quechua but in the process have adopted the structure and meaning of the equivalent Quechuan forms. For example Muysken (1981: 57) observes that Spanish pronominal forms have been mapped onto Quechuan pronominal paradigm. In the case of third person singular pronouns, Quechua does not distinguish masculine/feminine in the third person whereas Spanish does. Media Lengua also does not make this distinction but uses the form *el* as a general third person pronoun which is a phonological compromise between the Spanish *él* 'he' and *ella* 'she'.

3.2.1.4. Paralexification and language repertoires

The final set of unidirectional theories are Mous' (2003b) *paralexification* and Matras et al.'s (2008) notion of *language repertoires*. These two theories give explanations for the development of Ma'á and Angloromani, respectively. They provide an understanding of mixed languages which have tried to undo a complete shift to a regionally dominant language. These theories also bear some resemblance to the borrowing and codeswitching models of mixed language genesis. However, as will be shown, the major difference is in choice – the presence of alternative means, usually lexical, of expressing a notion. Both of these models challenge the notion of a mixed language as a closed system, rather posturing a fluidity of language choice reliant on social context.

First, paralexification involves the existence of two lexicons in parallel. One language involved in the mix exists in its entirety with its grammar and lexicon intact. The other language merely provides a substantial reservoir of lexical material for inserting into the more dominant language's grammatical frame. Lexical insertion may be a strategy for maintaining a waning ancestry language. For example, as discussed in section 2.2, Mous (2003a: 89) believes that Ma'á is a deliberate attempt to undo a shift to Pare (Bantu), which occurred through a paralexification process. In this situation the Bantu lexicon, and a Cushitic and Maasai lexicon exist in parallel. People speak both Mbugu, which draws from the Bantu lexicon, and Ma'á, which replaces many Bantu words with Cushitic and Maasai equivalents.

Matras et al. (2008) characterise mixed languages such as Ma'á in a similar way. They consider these mixed varieties as more fluid and less contained entities which do not have clearly definable boundaries. Matras et al. suggest that secret languages such as Angloromani which consist largely of lexical insertions with little grammatical alterations are not separate languages but involve lexical reservoirs which may be drawn on to express particular social functions. The broadest social function this kind of mixed language might have is marking a sense of solidarity to express speech acts such as warnings. In this respect, Matras paints a speaker of mixed language (and indeed any bilingual speaker) as someone who uses their language resources consciously and creatively.

Indeed secret languages are not the main language of communication for the community. Rather, they are a marked form of speech used in restricted functional domains. Other mixed languages exhibit less optionality. These tend to be the mixed languages which are the unmarked language of communication for a speech community and are used in a broad range of functional domains. For example, Gurindji Kriol is the language of general interaction for younger Gurindji people. Switches to lesser-used Gurindji or Kriol elements are marked and perform particular social functions. For example some variation is present in the lexicon. 28% of the lexicon contains semantically equivalent forms from Gurindji and Kriol where language choice expresses social meaning (Meakins 2011c: 19–20). This is similar to Ma'á's parallel lexicon or Angloromani's lexical reservoir. In the case of Gurindji Kriol, the choice often depends on whether the speaker is talking to an older or younger person. In general, however, most of the structure and lexicon of Gurindji Kriol and other mixed languages such as Michif[15] and Light Warlpiri are quite invariable and cannot be said to find their origins in the social markedness of linguistic choice.

3.2.2. Fusion approaches to mixed language genesis

Fusion approaches differ from unidirectional approaches in the direction of shift. Unidirectional approaches are one-way, describing language shift which progresses from the ancestral language to an introduced language or from the introduced language back to the ancestral language. It both cases the shift stops along the way to form the mixed language. On the other hand, fusion approaches consider mixed languages to be the result of two languages merging. Bakker's (1997) *language intertwining* approach was the first of these theories. More recently *language competition* models based on Croft (2000) and Mufwene's (2001) language evolution theories have been proposed (Aboh and Ansaldo 2007; Meakins 2011c).

3.2.2.1. Language intertwining

Bakker's (1997) theory of language intertwining was one of the first explanations for the formation of mixed languages. It proposes a process specific to mixed language genesis rather than relying on other language contact processes such as borrowing or codeswitching. Bakker (1997: 210) takes *combination* rather than *replacement* to be the central process. In this respect no language is shifting to another, rather a new language is created in the intertwining of structures and vocabulary. Specifically, intertwining involves mixing aspects of the two languages based on two morphological distinctions: lexical/grammatical, free/bound. Generally the free lexical morphemes come from one language and the bound grammatical morphemes from the other. Free grammatical morphemes can come from either language. The grammatical system comes from the language speakers are most familiar with, or the language that the speakers wish the mixed language to 'sound' like (1997: 211). The last specification is needed to account for mixed languages such as Angloromani. Bakker (1997: 206) suggests that in fact the English grammatical system was adopted so that Angloromani would sound more like English, and English speakers would not notice when Romanies were speaking their mixed language around them.

Bakker's theory, along with adjustments for Michif, provides an explanation for how L(exicon)-G(rammar) mixed languages, which constitute most mixed languages, are created. Language competition approaches look beyond this mix, as is shown in the next section. What is also missing in Bakker's theory is an idea of how the speakers used the two source languages at the point of creation of the mixed language, that is their linguistic practices. Codeswitching is one way that both languages are used with more or less emphasis. The role of codeswitching in mixed language genesis is discussed in section 4.4.

3.2.2.2. Language competition and evolution

A more recent fusional approach to mixed language genesis utilises concepts from evolutionary theory to provide an explanation for the formation of these languages. This approach sits within general theories of language change which use concepts of variation and competition to account for both internally and externally-motivated language change (Mufwene 2001; Croft 2000; Labov 1994). Explanations for the formation of mixed languages can be positioned within these approaches. What is relevant here is not the direction of language shift but the competition between features in the source languages. Note that the importance of variation for the origin of mixed languages will be discussed further in section 4.2.

Croft's model of language change is based on the evolutionary view that repeated copies of objects change their properties over time (imperfect replication). Croft (2003: 41) utilises this view to suggest that languages evolve through the replication and selection of particular linguistic structures in normal language use. In biological evolution the basic unit of replication is the gene. Replication involves copying genes in a process of reproduction. Replicated genes can be identical (normal replication) or altered (altered replication) which may occur via mutation or recombination from parents in sexual reproduction (Croft 2000: 23). Croft suggests that this process can also be applied to language, where features of language structure, called *linguemes* are taken as the basic unit of replication.

> Replication also occurs in the production of utterances. Every time I produce an utterance, I replicate linguistic structures from prior utterances that I have been exposed to and have internalised in some way. These linguistic structures, named *linguemes* are of (at least) three types familiar to historical linguists: sounds, words/morphemes and constructions. In any utterance, I replicate a large number of linguemes, and these linguemes may be replicated from a multiplicity of prior utterances. (Croft 2003: 42)

Replication may follow similar patterns to biological evolution in that the replicated structure may be more or less identical to that of the original structure (normal replication). In this situation a speaker is conforming to the linguistic conventions of the speech community. On the other hand, the structure may change in replication (altered replication), which is where linguistic innovation finds its origins. Linguistic innovation can only occur where more than one lingueme or variant is available to mark a particular function. This variation is an essential part of language evolution. Mufwene (2001) calls this a feature pool, that is the set of variables available to speakers from within a language system or as a result of external pressures. It is here that the process of competition, replication and change takes place. External pressures occur when more than one language is a part of the pool. Language mixing results when links are made between linguemes or variants between two languages. In these situations speakers identify forms in one language as performing the same function as a form in another language. Once this identification is made, "the way is open to interference", that is the replication of a lingueme from one language into another (Croft 2003: 46). Forms may also be transferred when there are no equivalents in the recipient language, for example when the speakers want to express a new concept which is not encoded in their language. The linguemes or pieces of linguistic structure are either replicated in a way that does not differ from their source, or they undergo altered replication to form unique structures. In general, a high level of bilingualism and fluidity between the languages is a precondition of the language ecology for language competition to occur (Mufwene 2001). Pervasive codeswitching as the unmarked linguistic practice is the most obvious way to produce such an intense level of language contact (Meakins 2011c).

This model of language change can be applied to mixed languages. Rather than providing an explanation for the overall shape of the mixed language (e.g. grammar-lexicon mix or N-V mix), this model can be used to demonstrate how subsets of the language's structure eventuated. For example, Meakins (2011a: 75–77) describes the competition between Kriol-derived locative preposition and the Gurindji-derived allative case marker in Gurindji Kriol. These forms are used to mark inanimate goals in their respective languages. In the process of mixed language genesis they came into contact and competition. The end result was the use of the Gurindji-derived locative case suffix to mark goals where it is not used in this function in Gurindji. This functional shift occurred as a result of the form from Gurindji being mapped onto a Kriol pattern (locations and goals are not distinguished in Kriol).

Competition between linguemes has had other results in the formation of mixed languages. For example, in Sri Lanka Malay, Malay-derived TMA markers have shifted their alignment from a Malay mood and aspect system to a tense system based on Tamil categories (Bakker 2000a, 2000b; Smith and Paauw 2006). The TMA markers have retained the form of Vehicular Malay whilst mapping onto the Tamil tense system. For example the progressive marker has become a present tense marker (Smith and Paauw 2006: 161). More examples of this type of change as the result of contact between functionally equivalent elements is discussed in section 4.1.2 and section 5. In these examples, descriptions of mixing go beyond the level of form to looking at other features of the morpheme or lexeme including its semantics, function and distribution.

3.2.2.3. Centre of gravity hypothesis

Another final fusion theory is McConvell's (2002, 2008) *centre of gravity* hypothesis which relies on the distinction between head and dependent marking languages (cf. Nichols 1986). This hypothesis differs from most other theories of mixed language genesis because McConvell is mostly concerned with the more intricate mixes which involve NP-VP splits rather than grammar-lexicon mixes. McConvell suggests that the typology of the ancestry language may have something to do with the nature of the split, and the way in which this ancestry language shifts to an introduced language via an intermediary period of codeswitching and perhaps more structural language mixing. McConvell observes that head-marking and dependent-marking languages have different centres of gravity. The typology of the ancestry language affects the path of the 'turnover' to the new language by producing different results in the intermediate language stages. He suggests that head-marking languages have a tendency to retain the verbal grammar after the nominal grammar has 'turned over' to the introduced language. For example, Michif has retained the Cree verbal grammar whilst adopting French nominal grammar. Conversely dependent-marking languages keep the nominal structure of the ancestry language whilst turning over to the VP structure of the new language (McConvell 2002: 345). McConvell suggests this is the case with Gurindji Kriol. The turnover to Kriol has frozen midway maintaining the nominal grammar of Gurindji.

Although McConvell's model is heavily based on typology, it focuses on the typology of the ancestry language. McConvell does not discuss the typology of the introduced language which may be relevant the resultant structural mix. By comparison, the language competition approach presented in section 3.2.2.2 takes into consideration the typology of both languages. It is also incorrect to assume that Cree was the ancestry language in the case of Michif, because Michif is the result of mixed marriages between Cree-speaking women and French-speaking men (Bakker 1997: 208). In this respect neither language can be assumed to be the ancestry or introduced language. McConvell's analysis works better for Gurindji Kriol, where the original language of the population was clearly Gurindji. Thus it is more reasonable to suggest that Gurindji was the ancestry language and speakers stopped midway in a shift towards Kriol. However the typological analysis of the ancestry language, Gurindji, is problematic given that it is neither strongly head- nor dependent-marking. Gurindji contains both case-marked nouns and cross-referencing pronominal clitics which, though not always marked directly on the verb, are a part of the verb complex.

4. Current issues for the study of mixed languages

4.1. Are mixed languages really autonomous language systems?

One of the criticisms which is often levelled at descriptions of mixed languages is the autonomy of the language variety presented (Bakker 2003; Meakins 2012). The term 'autonomous language system' refers to the ability of the language to function as a stand-alone linguistic entity with only minimal continuing input from its source languages. Following Saussure ([1916] 1983: 86), the parts of a language must be "synchronically interdependent". Thus changes in the source languages do not feed into the mixed language and vice versa. Whether such a level of autonomy is possible for a mixed language is indeed questionable given that most are spoken alongside one or both of their source languages (section 3.1.3). Further there is often a close synchronic and diachronic relationship between other mixing practices and mixed languages. For example, the composition of mixing in many cases resembles patterns which may also be found in codeswitching. Indeed Bakker (2003: 129) observes that the majority of mixed languages, which exhibit grammar-lexical mixed structures such as that found in Media Lengua, reflect the patterns found in insertional codeswitching. Historically, codeswitching also most likely preceded the formation of many mixed languages, and synchronically the mixed language and codeswitching may continue to co-exist within the same speaker population. This connection has been demonstrated for at least one mixed language, Gurindji Kriol (McConvell and Meakins 2005; Meakins 2011c) and has been proposed for many other cases (Myers-Scotton 2003; O'Shannessy 2012) (see section 4.4). These kinds of similarities cast some doubt on the 'language-ness' of these mixed languages. Yet, despite the symbiotic nature of these types of language mixing, they can also be distinguished from each other.

The purpose of this section is not to be drawn into debates about what is a 'language' but to demonstrate that mixed languages have as much right to the pre-theoretical label 'language' as other linguistic objects which have been called languages. A number of criteria have been used to support the claim of language autonomy in mixed languages: (i) the stability of the language section 4.1.1, (ii) the independent development of the source or mixed language section 4.1.2, and (iii) the presence of structural features from both languages in a clause section 4.1.3. A detailed discussion of the application of these criteria to Gurindji Kriol can be found in Meakins (2012).

4.1.1. Language stability

The term 'stable' is used in conjunction with mixed languages by a number of writers (see e.g. Thomason 2003). The notion of 'stability' is meant in a relative sense, i.e. just how established and predictable patterns are in a mixed system in relation to so-called normal languages. Actually defining and measuring stability is highly problematic. Part of the problem relates to the degree of variation found in the language, an issue which will be discussed more fully in section 4.2. The other issue is that stability is not something which is generally in question for normal languages. It is acknowledged that variation exists and is meaningful and quantifiable, and that language change occurs. However there are no benchmarks or measures of stability to gauge a mixed language against. This section offers some social and grammatical indicators which may be used to judge the stability of a mixed language: (i) whether the mixed language is spoken outside of its source language context, (ii) the degree of consistency between speakers, and (iii) whether it is being acquired as an L1.

First, the clearest demonstration of language stability occurs when a mixed language is *spoken outside of the bilingual context in which it arose*, that is speakers are no longer fluent in the source languages (Thomason 2003: 24). Michif is one such example. Although Michif is derived from French and Cree, most of its speakers are not fluent in either language. Indeed nowadays most Michif speakers are elderly and the main language of Michif communities has become English (Bakker 1997). Similarly Mednyj Aleut was spoken long after the Russians had withdrawn from Copper Island and speakers of Mednyj Aleut were no longer fluent in Aleut or Russian (Golovko 1994). In other situations, mixed language speakers may not be fluent in the source languages but they may have a good passive knowledge of one or both of them. This situation may occur where the mixed language is an attempt to maintain an ancestral language which is endangered. For example, Gurindji Kriol speakers have a limited command of Gurindji; however they hear Gurindji being spoken by older people and have little difficulty understanding them. Indeed Gurindji Kriol speakers are still often addressed in Gurindji by their parents and it is common to hear conversations where the older person speaks in Gurindji and the younger person replies in Gurindji Kriol (Meakins 2008a: 296). In these situations, the case for language autonomy becomes quite blurred because, though speakers are not fluent in the source languages, there is still potential for influence or input from the source languages making the language less stable.

Cases of mixed languages which exist in total isolation from their source languages are actually quite rare. Most mixed languages are spoken alongside their source languages, and most mixed language speakers are fluent in one or both of the source languages. Smith (2000) calls these *symbiotic* mixed languages, as discussed in section 3.1.3. Language stability is harder to achieve in such situations because of the continued link with the language's origins, and as a result, the claim of an autonomous language system is more difficult to establish in these situations. Mixed languages can resemble codeswitching or perhaps a sociolect or variety of one of the source languages. For example, Ma'á (Inner Mbugu) speakers are also fluent in (Outer) Mbugu and even codeswitch between these languages (Mous 2003a: 86 onwards). Similarly Light Warlpiri speakers are fluent Warlpiri speakers and are in constant contact with other Warlpiri speakers from neighbouring communities who are not speakers of Light Warlpiri. Moreover they have a reasonable command of Kriol and Aboriginal English from their contact with other Aboriginal people. Light Warlpiri speakers also codeswitch between the mixed language and Warlpiri and a contact variety of English (O'Shannessy 2006). Being able to demonstrate that Ma'á or Light Warlpiri operates as a closed linguistic system which is only minimally influenced by its continued contact with the source languages is difficult in such a language ecology.

These three situations – complete separation from the source languages, contact but non-fluency in the sources, and ongoing bilingualism – illustrate three points along a scale of mixed language autonomy, both in the ecological and structural sense. Generally speaking, increased distance from the source languages promotes stability in the mixed system. At the extreme end of the scale where speakers are not only in contact with the source languages but are fluent in one or both, other indicators for stability must be sought.

Another measure of stability in a mixed language is the *degree of consistency* both between and within speakers in their use of lexicon and grammar. This notion relates closely to variation which is discussed in section 4.2. For example the choice of lexical items and syntactic constructions is very consistent across speakers in Gurindji Kriol. As a result, Gurindji Kriol speakers use virtually identical constructions to express the same event. This point can be demonstrated looking at a small subset of data consisting of 18 tokens of the sentence 'the dog bit the man on the hand' from 18 different speakers (Meakins 2012). Of these 18 sentences, the Gurindji word *warlaku* (the dog), *marluka* (old man) and *wartan* (hand) is used in all 18 sentences, with the Kriol *baitim* 'bite' used in 89% of sentences in variation with the Gurindji equivalent *katurl*. Syntactically all pronouns present are Kriol-derived free forms, and similarly any verbal inflection found is of Kriol origin. The Gurindji-derived ergative marker -*ngku* is used in 61% of the sentences[16], and the locative marker -*ta* is found 83.5% of the time, with the Kriol preposition *la* used in the remaining sentences (Meakins 2012: 116).

(12) det **warlaku-ngku** i   bin bait-im **marluka wartan-ta**.
 the dog-ERG 3SG.SBJ PST bite-TR old.man hand-LOC

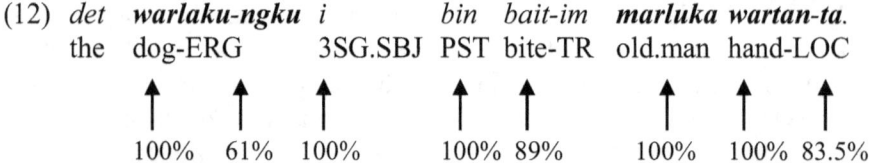

The level of uniformity in lexical and syntactic choices shown by Gurindji Kriol speakers supports its status as a language independent of its sources. For example, though speakers regularly hear Gurindji verbal morphology from older speakers, they consistently use Kriol tense and aspect markers, e.g. *bin* (past) in (12). This degree of consistency and stability in Gurindji Kriol developed as particular lexical choices and structures in the language became dominant and impervious to further outside influence and change. Unfortunately consistency is difficult to demonstrate for all mixed languages because a large corpus is required to characterise variation and consistency within the mixed language. Moreover the corpus needs to include examples of equivalent sentences by different and same speakers. Mixed languages, such as Michif, which have elderly speaker populations or Angloromani which is not the main everyday language of the speech community do not lend themselves well to this type of study.

A final indicator of language stability is whether or not children are learning the language as a first language. Many mixed languages such as Mednyj Aleut are now highly endangered with only elderly speakers and no child learners. The process of language acquisition is a matter of speculation in these cases. Other mixed languages such as Light Warlpiri, Gurindji Kriol and Bilingual Navajo have child language learners and more observations about the context and process of acquisition can be made. For example, O'Shannessy (2006) recorded five Warlpiri children over three years. The recordings were made in naturalistic situations where the children interacted with their caregivers who included parents, grandparents and older children. O'Shannessy found that children are spoken to in both Warlpiri and Light Warlpiri, and the language ecology that children grow up in also includes mixing between these languages and Aboriginal English/Kriol. She observed that, though there is quite a lot of overlap between the Warlpiri and Light Warlpiri, children acquire the languages separately. They begin speaking Light Warlpiri first but from the age of around five, they include Warlpiri in their linguistic repertoire though they remain almost exclusively Light Warlpiri speakers. Observations of children acquiring a mixed language such as Light Warlpiri as a separate code support the case for language stability. Clearly a separate linguistic entity is being identified and singled out for specific attention by children.

These three factors – independence from source languages, speaker consistency and language acquisition – contribute to the stability of a mixed language. Although it is difficult to compare stability across contact and non-contact languages, it is clear that there is a correlation between stability and language autonomy.

4.1.2. Independent development of the mixed language and source languages

Language autonomy may also be demonstrated by the independent development of the mixed language and its sources. In this scenario a change in the source languages does not necessarily imply a change in the mixed language and vice versa. Bakker (2003: 126) gives examples of cases where changes in the source languages are not reflected in the mixed language. Here I examine independent developments which have occurred in mixed languages, firstly where unique forms have been created in the mixed language system and secondly where forms from the source languages have developed new functions in the mixed language.

First, mixed language developments are not always reflected in the source languages. In the case of Light Warlpiri, O'Shannessy (2005: 39) identifies a unique auxiliary paradigm in Light Warlpiri which consists of a pronominal proclitic and a tense-aspect element.

Table 3. Light Warlpiri auxiliary paradigm (adapted from O'Shannessy 2006: 39)

Auxiliary form	1SG.SBJ	1PL.SBJ	2SG.SBJ	2PL.SBJ	3SG.SBJ	3PL.SBJ
Non-future	a=m	wi=m	yu=m	–	i=m	de=m
Future	a=rra	wi=rra	yu=rra	**yumob=rra**	i=rra	de=rra

This system is based on Kriol morphemes but has a Warlpiri flavour to the structure since Warlpiri also has a single auxiliary structure which combines these elements, although in the reverse order. Although part of this paradigm is present in Kriol, it is not a complete paradigm. The bolded elements in Table 3 show the gaps in the Kriol paradigm. In these gaps, Kriol uses full forms rather than clitics – *bin* rather than =*m* and *garra* rather than =*rra*. Thus the Kriol forms have developed further in Light

Warlpiri, and there is no evidence that this development is feeding back into Kriol. Further it is not the case that this system is replacing the auxiliary system in Warlpiri. O'Shannessy (2005: 52) also observes speakers do not use this auxiliary when codeswitching between Warlpiri and Kriol. She presents this auxiliary system as a diagnostic for Light Warlpiri utterances in mixed conversations. Thus Light Warlpiri has a unique system which has developed independently of its source languages which suggests that Light Warlpiri operates as an autonomous language.

Another example of the development of a unique system comes from Sri Lanka Malay. Smith, Paauw and Hussainmiya (2004: 2004) observe that Malay-derived prepositions have become post-positional case-markers under the influence of Tamil. What is particularly interesting is that syncretism occurs between dative and accusative marking (only distinguished by optionality – accusative marking is optional where dative marking is not)[17]. This syncretism is not observed in any of its source languages. Tamil and Sinhala distinguish these categories with separate markers and Vehicular Malay marks the dative but not the accusative with a preposition. Further, although the forms of the case suffixes come from Vehicular Malay, the origin of the accusative/dative case suffix *-n(y)a(ng)* is obscure, perhaps *punya* 'to have, of'. Thus in both distribution and form, the accusative/dative marker is a unique form in Sri Lanka Malay and there is no evidence that this marker has fed back into its source languages.

Forms in a mixed language may also develop different functions from the source language it is derived from. For example, in Bilingual Navajo some constituents function in unique ways which contrast from their language source. In particular, the verb *áshlééh* 'to prepare/make' is used as a light verb in Bilingual Navajo in order to integrate English verbs into the Navajo morpho-syntactic frame, see example (13). This verb is not used in this manner in Navajo, as shown in (14), moreover it is not used in this manner by English-Navajo codeswitchers who do not speak the mixed language.

(13) *bi-'éé'*   ***change***   ***íí-lééh***
3POSS-clothes   change   1DU-make
'The two of us are changing her clothes.'
(Schaengold 2004: 68)

(14) *bi-'éé'*   *lahgo*   *át'éhí*   *bii*   *ndeezhteeh*
3POSS-clothes   different   one   3.into   1DU.move.animate
'The two of us are changing her clothes.'
(Schaengold 2004: 68)

These examples demonstrate one of the ways in which elements from Bilingual Navajo's source languages operate in different ways in the mixed language. Through these differences, Bilingual Navajo can be shown to be an autonomous language rather than a spontaneous or ad-hoc mixture of two separate language systems. The development of Navajo elements in the mixed language has not extended to Navajo itself. Moreover the use of Navajo constituents in codeswitching generally does not differ radically from monolingual clauses. Navajo systems, which have been altered in the mixed language, continue to be used unchanged in the source languages, which demonstrates that these developments are a feature of the mixed language.

The distribution of forms may also change in the mixed language where they remain unchanged in the source languages. For example, as was discussed above, Sri Lanka Malay case markers consist of a Vehicular Malay-derived phonological form which has become postposed under the influence of Tamil case-marking. Sri Lanka Malay now contains the same case-marking categories as Tamil. Nonetheless some distributional differences occur. For example, the Sri Lanka Malay locative marker -*ka* is derived from the Vehicular Malay dative preposition. It is used to mark both locations and goals in Sri Lanka Malay where Tamil (and Sinhala) uses dative to mark goal and locative to mark location (Smith, Paauw and Hussainmiya 2004: 206), although see Aboh and Ansaldo (2007: 59) for a different analysis). Although the case markers generally function as they do in Tamil, this is one example where the form has been extended to new functions. Although Sri Lanka Malay is still in contact with Tamil, this change in distribution is not reflected in Tamil. This is evidence that Sri Lanka Malay is operating as an autonomous language.

4.1.3. Presence of structural elements from both languages

Another argument for treating a mixed language as a coherent linguistic entity is the presence of structural features from both languages. As was discussed in section 3.2.1.1, this is considered to be one of the features of mixed languages because it defies trends seen in other language contact scenarios such as borrowing or creole languages where generally one language dominates the morpho-syntactic frame of the mix. Such patterns are a defining feature of N(oun)-V(erb) splits such as Michif, Mednyj Aleut and Gurindji Kriol rather than L(exicon)-(G)rammar mixes such as Angloromani and Media Lengua.

The structure of *Michif* is shared by French and Cree, as was introduced in section 2.7. French and Cree share the load between the verb and noun systems. In this respect Cree provides the verbal morpho-syntactic frame, as seen in tense marking and cross-referencing pronouns, and the French, the NP frame. In terms of the NP, Michif preserves French determiners, plural marking and adjectival agreement in Michif. Another language which distributes the structural load over both source languages is *Mednyj Aleut*. Again this split largely follows an N-V split with Aleut nominal structure including the Aleut case frame and other suffixes such as agent, instrumental and location markers. On the other hand Mednyj Aleut derives much of its finite verbal inflectional morphology from Russian, such as person and tense marking (Thomason 1997b: 457–59).

Both source languages also contribute to the structure of *Gurindji Kriol* and *Light Warlpiri* (Meakins 2012). Again the different source languages dominate different parts of the grammar. In the nominal structure, inflectional morphology of Gurindji and Warlpiri origin is clearly demonstrated in case marking. Gurindji/Warlpiri-derived ergative, dative, locative, allative and ablative case markers are all present in the mixed language. Kriol is responsible for the verbal frame. In both Gurindji Kriol and Light Warlpiri, Kriol contributes two verbal suffixes, the continuative and transitive markers. Kriol-derived tense, aspect and mood markers are also present for example *bin* (past), *garra* (potential), *yusta* (habitual). Additionally, TMA clitics, such as =*m* (non-future) and =*rra* (potential) from Kriol, are also present (Meakins and O'Shannessy 2012). These are based on reduced forms of Kriol tense and aspect auxiliary forms. Finally Kriol-derived clitic pronouns cross-reference optional nominals. Thus, like Michif and Mednyj Aleut, the grammatical frame of Gurindji Kriol and Light Warlpiri represents a composite structure, with both source languages contributing significant structural elements to the mix. The rarity of this kind of composite structure in other language contact varieties (see section 3.2.1.1) speaks to the uniqueness of this phenomenon. It suggests that these languages are not merely cases of codeswitching or borrowing but language systems in their own right.

4.2.   Characterising variation in mixed languages

Related to the issue of autonomy and stability is variation. The presence of variation in mixed languages is seldom discussed and sometimes even downplayed in order to avoid questions of autonomy (Matras and Bakker 2003: 7–8; Mous 2003a: 7; but see Bakker 1997: 159; Smith and Paauw 2006: 165, for observations of variation in Michif, Angloromani, Ma'á and Sri Lanka Malay, respectively). Nonetheless variation plays an important role in the formation of mixed languages and continues to affect their evolution, as was introduced in section 3.2.2.2. Variation is, at once, one of the key ingredients of language change and one of the results of this change, and in this respect it is indicative of perpetual change. There are a number of sources of this variation including continuing external input from the source languages, as well as internal variation from shared forms which are unique to the mixed language (see also section 4.1.2) and idiolectal varieties. This variation is part of an autonomous language system, which can be mapped using variationist methodology. This section considers the external and internal sources of variation in relation to mixed languages, and demonstrates how variation may be characterised in a mixed language.

External variants exist due to the symbiotic nature of many mixed languages, in that they continue to be spoken alongside one or more of their source languages (see section 4.1.1). Although they may not actively speak the languages themselves, speakers still have access to the source language lexicon and grammar, and these may continue to affect the structures used in the mixed language. For example Bakker (1997: 159) admits that in Michif, though many speakers have no knowledge of the source languages, French or Cree, knowledge of these languages creates some variation among speakers. Specifically, he observes that speakers who know French tend to use more French elements, particularly function words. Bakker (1997: 160) also observes that speakers vary in their use of French or Cree elements in Michif depending on their interlocutor.

The other source of variation is language *internal* where a language may contain a choice of structures or vocabulary which can mark a particular function. Language internal variation may be quite complex, involving forms from the source languages which both appear in the mixed language, as well as unique forms which have formed within the mixed language system (see section 4.1.2), and finally idiolectal variation. It is often the situation that more variants exist than are contributed by the source languages. These new variants represent amalgams of the source languages. For example in Gurindji Kriol speakers use the Gurindji-derived locative case marker *-ta* 87% of the time to mark static location. However, younger speakers occasionally use Kriol-derived *langa* preposition (9.5%) or a double-marked construction (3.5%) which contains both the case marker and preposition. The double-marked constructions are specific to Gurindji Kriol and represent a compromise strategy (Meakins 2011c: 180).

The presence of variation does not undermine the notion of an autonomous language system. Variation has long been recognised as a normal and integral part of all language systems. Indeed the program of variationists from Labov (1972) onwards has been to challenge the assumption of linguistic uniformity which is a characteristic of formal grammatical theory. Variation within a language system is not necessarily, and indeed very rarely, random, but is meaningfully distributed. Variationists argue that the use of particular variants in language can be predicted by the presence or absence of other linguistic and sociolinguistic factors. This theoretical underpinning is based on Weinreich, Labov and Herzog's (1968: 100) notion of "ordered heterogeneity". Labov (1969) claims that speakers make choices when they use language and these choices are systematic and can be predicted through statistical modelling. In this respect, the grammar of a language can be characterised as probabilistic, rather than categorical. Thus the data can be described using a set of variable rules which constitute the grammar of a language. As Labov (1969: 759) concludes "we are dealing with a set of quantitative relations which are the form of the grammar itself". Poplack (1993: 253) also observes that treating the patterns of variation as the grammar of a language bases the endeavour of grammatical description in empiricism, rather than unobservable underlying structures and rules.

Within the context of mixed languages, variationist methodology offers a way of characterising the use of functionally equivalent forms, such as the Gurindji locative case marker or Kriol preposition as discussed above for Gurindji Kriol. The presence of variation is not indicative of instability or a lack of language autonomy, but can be treated as meaningful within a contained linguistic and social system. The presence of variation does not undermine the notion of a coherent mixed system because it is motivated by other factors or variables with the system. Variables may be non-linguistic and linguistic. For example, some variationist studies measure the effect of *social* factors such as age, gender and socio-economic classes, and stylistic factors such as the formality of a communicative context on the choice of one linguistic variant over another (see Meyerhoff 2011 for a good overview). Other studies have broadened the pool of factors to include *linguistic* factors. For example, in an early study of the constraints on the use of passive vs. active sentences in English, Weiner and Labov (1983) found that the choice of syntactic structure carried neither stylistic nor social significance but the choice was constrained almost entirely by syntactic factors[18]. In some cases, both linguistic and social factors may play a role in the realisation of one variant over another. For example age is a factor in Gurindji Kriol. The younger the speakers, the more likely they will use a Kriol preposition or a double-marked construction. Linguistic context also plays a role. Again the preposition is more likely to be used if the following NP includes a determiner (Meakins 2011c: 181–186).

The use of a variable in relation to other variables is measured using statistical modelling, most commonly regression models which measure the likelihood of a linguistic variable such as a phoneme, morpheme or syntactic structure occurring with respect to other social and linguistic variables, of the type described above. Regression models can be applied to mixed languages to see whether a variable can be characterised as a part of the mixed language system, or whether it is external to the system. Another example from Gurindji Kriol: the Gurindji-derived ergative marker is only used optionally, which contrasts with the categorical use of the ergative marker in Gurindji. This optionality seems to be the result of the ergative marker coming into contact with the equivalent Kriol system of argument marking – word order. One interpretation of this variation may be that continuing interplay between Gurindji and Kriol argument marking systems has made this Gurindji Kriol system unstable. However Meakins (2009) shows that the variable application of the ergative marker acts in a coherent manner. In a study of the motivations for the appearance of the ergative marker, Meakins (2009: 71 onwards) tests the use of the ergative marker against ten variables: two sociolinguistic variables – age of speaker and the formality of context; a lexical variable – the language of the stem; a number of grammatical and semantic variables relating to the degree of transitivity of the clause: potentiality, actualisation of the event indicated by the verb, agent[19] animacy, object animacy, and whether the object is overt; and finally two variables which relate to the clause structure: the position of the agent in relation to the verb, and the presence of a co-referential pronoun. She finds that the ergative marker is more likely to appear if the agent is inanimate, found post-verbally and in conjunction with a co-referential pronoun. The use of the ergative marker decreases when the verb is marked with continuous aspect and the event denoted by the verb has not come to completion (Meakins 2009: 79). Meakins interprets these results as an indication that the main function of the ergative marker in Gurindji Kriol is discourse related, specifically its presence highlights the agentivity of a subject nominal (see also Meakins and O'Shannessy 2010). Similar analyses exist for languages with optional ergative marking (see McGregor 2010 for an overview). Studies of this kind demonstrate that variation in a mixed language system is not a sign of the fragility of the language, but rather is a part of a systematic grammar. Moreover variation can be quantified in such a way that its meaning can be deciphered.

4.3. Can two phonological systems exist in the one language?

The fusion of lexical and morphological material from different languages begs the question of what happens at the phonological level. Do the words and affixes maintain their original phonological forms thereby producing a stratified system or are they integrated into one phonological system? The debate about phonological stratification in mixed languages has centred around the phonology of Michif, though more recently van Gijn (2009) has compared the phonological systems of four mixed languages (and see also Jones, Meakins and Buchan (2011) and Jones, Meakins and Muawiyath (2012) for a discussion of Gurindji Kriol phonology).

Papen (1987) and Bakker and Papen (1997) claim that two separate phonological systems function in Michif, with separate phoneme inventories for both the French and Cree components and separate sets of phonological rules and processes. Implicit in this claim is that each lexical item in Michif must be marked for its language of origin (Bakker and Papen 1997: 312). However Rosen (2000: 6) suggests that this assumption presents 'learnability' problems as there are insufficient phonological cues for learners to determine whether a lexical item is from either French or Cree. She suggests that any differences in the French and Cree components are historical artefacts and are no longer functional in Michif. For example, Rosen (2000: 16) follows Bakker (1997) that the French rule of liaison is no longer productive in the French component of Michif. Liaison applies to the (former) final consonant of a determiner or adjective. In certain syntactic environments in French, it is pronounced as the onset of the following noun. Instead Rosen claims that all vowel-initial words in Michif have been reanalysed as /n/, /l/ or /z/ initial. Indeed this claim was originally presented by Bakker and Papen (1997: 309). Papen (2003) revisits this problem finding synchronic evidence for a stratified phonology. He notes that most of the Michif dictionary entries of French vowel initial words include the liaison consonant. Nonetheless Papen suggests that "the only valid argument in favour of considering liaison to no longer be functional in Michif would be to show that the 'wrong' (e.g. unexpected) consonant occurs [...] or that there is no consonant at all" (2003: 5). Papen finds that only 10% of cases contain unexpected liaison consonants, which he posits as evidence for the continuing existence of the liaison rule. However it seems reasonable to suggest correct use of the liaison consonants does not rule out the possibility that these now consonant-initial words are now lexicalised as the result of the liaison process which occurred historically. And indeed Papen does not present any arguments which would suggest that Michif speakers analyse these words as vowel initial.

Although it can be argued that Michif has a stratified phonology, this generalisation does not necessarily hold for all mixed languages. Van Gijn (2009) suggests that the typology of the mixed language determines whether one language is subsumed into another's phonology, or whether two phonological systems are maintained. He compares Michif with Media Lengua. Media Lengua differs greatly from Michif in terms of typology, being a grammar-lexicon mixed language rather than exhibiting an N-V split. Van Gijn (2009: 96) notes that, unlike Michif, Media Lengua has only one phonological system, that of Quechua, which may be the product of the level of mixing at the prosodic word level.

> In Media Lengua, almost all words have both Spanish (stems) and Quechua (affixes) elements, in Michif, on the other hand, there are more unmixed words: verbs are generally Cree (both stems and affixes), noun phrases, or at least nouns, are to a large extent unmixed French. In other words, Michif has larger unmixed domains [...] where French or Cree words can apply. (van Gijn 2009: 109)

He suggests that the mixed nature of Media Lengua words makes it difficult to maintain two phonological systems, whereas language mixing in Michif occurs at a higher point in the prosodic hierarchy making a stratified phonology more viable.

4.4.   Can codeswitching lead to the formation of a mixed language?

A further issue for mixed languages is the characterisation of the language practices of speakers at the time of genesis. This section looks specifically at codeswitching and its role in the formation of mixed languages. The extent to which codeswitching is a factor in the formation and resulting structure of mixed languages is debated extensively. Bakker (2003: 129) is the strongest critic of codeswitching approaches suggesting that they play no role in the genesis of intertwined languages, and that typological resemblances between mixed languages and codeswitching are the product of selective comparison on the part of researchers. However, McConvell and Meakins (2005) and Meakins (2011c) present empirical evidence demonstrating that codeswitching contributed to the formation of at least one mixed language, Gurindji Kriol (section 4.4.1). Recent work supports the contribution of codeswitching to mixed languages (Gardner-Chloros 2000; Auer 1999; Backus 2003; Myers-Scotton 1993). Within this literature, there are two main approaches. The first considers the different structures of mixed languages and compares them directly to different types of codeswitching, such as insertional and alternational codeswitching (Backus 2003) (section 4.4.2). The second approach is more explanatory, proposing a transitory stage between codeswitching and a mixed language. This approach utilises structural constraint theories of codeswitching to better understand the resultant character of mixed languages (Auer 1999; Myers-Scotton 2003). This approach was discussed in section 3.2.1.2.

4.4.1. Empirical evidence for the link between codeswitching and mixed languages

One of the main disclaimers in the debate about a link between codeswitching and mixed languages concerns the lack of empirical evidence to support a claim for the link between codeswitching and the formation of mixed languages. While Bakker states that "we have no documentation of a transitory phase between the supposed code-switching behaviour preceding the genesis of the mixed language" (2003: 129), Auer suggests that claims about the transition from codeswitching to mixed languages are "plausible guesses rather than empirically based" (1999: 324). Myers-Scotton (2002: 249) believes that the next step in her Matrix Language Turnover theory (see section 3.2.1.2) which outlines the progress from codeswitching to a mixed language is to demonstrate the process using actual data. Finally, Backus says that all of these claims "call for evidence which, to the best of my knowledge, has not been brought forward" (2000: 104), and later he suggests that it is doubtful whether this sort of evidence would ever be available (2003: 241).

Indeed many of the mixed languages which have been documented are generally 100 or more years old. Evidence, then, is a matter for the historical record in these cases, and few of these languages have a significant body of written work associated with them. Nonetheless empirical evidence for codeswitching preceding a mixed language now exists for one mixed language, Gurindji Kriol. McConvell and Meakins (2005) and Meakins (2011c: 109–153) show that codeswitching not only preceded the formation of Gurindji Kriol, but that a number of structures found in the mixed language correspond with the pattern of Gurindji-Kriol codeswitching.

McConvell (1988) suggests that multilingualism was a traditional social practice of the Gurindji before Kriol was added to this repertoire after colonisation (see section 2.8). By the mid-1970s, it appeared that inter-sentential and intra-sentential codeswitching between Gurindji and Kriol/English was a very common style of communication (McConvell 1985: 96). McConvell and Meakins (2005) and Meakins (2011c) demonstrate that resonances of the mixed language, Gurindji Kriol, can be found in the patterns of codeswitching from this time.

In a study of a conversation between six Gurindji stockmen who were butchering a cow in a bush paddock near Kalkaringi, they find that 73% of the mixed utterances used a Kriol verbal structure as became the norm for Gurindji Kriol two decades later. It appears that during this period the Kriol verbal structure was already becoming dominant. Indeed now Kriol forms the basis of the VP structure of Gurindji Kriol with Gurindji verb morphology never found. Despite the predominance of Kriol in the VP of the codeswitched utterances, Gurindji morphology, including case and derivational morphemes, was also present in the structure of the noun phrases in codeswitched utterances. Codeswitched utterances from the 1970s bear a strong resemblance to the mixed language spoken today. Compare (15) with (16). Gurindji elements are in bold.

(15) **kaa-rni-mpal** said orait yutubala kat-im
east-UP-ACROSS side alright 2DU cut-TRN
ngaji-rlang-kulu.
father-DYAD-ERG
'You two, father and son, cut it across the east (side of the cow).'
(1970s Gurindji-Kriol codeswitching; Meakins 2011c: 112)

(16) an skul-**ta=ma** jei bin hab-im sport
and school-LOC=TOP 3PL.SBJ PST have-TR sport
karu-walija-ngku.
child-PAUC-ERG
'And the kids had sport at school.'
(2006 GK mixed language; Meakins 2011c: 112)

Through these general observations of Gurindji-Kriol codeswitching in the 1970s, McConvell and Meakins (2005) and Meakins (2011c) provide the missing empirical link for arguments about the transition between codeswitching and mixed languages for at least this mixed language. A more recent study by O'Shannessy (2012) of Light Warlpiri provides similar evidence. Of course this evidence does not exclude the possibility that other mixed languages have derived from different bilingual practices at their point of genesis.

4.4.2. Typological similarities between codeswitching and mixed languages

A number of studies have examined the typological similarities between codeswitching and the structure of mixed languages (Bakker 2003; Backus 2003; Mous 2003a). Muysken's (2000) distinction between *insertional* and *alternational* codeswitching is relevant for this work (see section 3.2.1.2). Insertional codeswitching is generally considered to have the greatest influence on mixed language genesis in these comparisons, because the mixed languages studied generally do not resemble a fossilised form of alternational codeswitching, whereas they look remarkably like insertional codeswitching. For example, Michif has been compared with various synchronic descriptions of insertional codeswitching between pairs of English or French, and an Algonquian language, for example, Plains Cree-English codeswitching (Bakker 1997: 181–182) and Montagnais-French (Drapeau 1991, cited in Bakker 1997: 184–86). Insertional codeswitching can be characterised by a nested ABA pattern (Muysken 2000: 63). This means that the segments on either side of the inserted constituent are grammatically related and are derived from the same language. Bakker finds this to be a common pattern of switching in all of these cases which involve noun phrase and prepositional phrase insertions from French or English. This insertion pattern reflects the NP-VP split found in Michif, where French dominates the NP structure. Bakker presents a number of objections to the link between this type of codeswitching and Michif[20]. Nonetheless he suggests that insertional codeswitching and mixed languages in general do show striking typological similarities.

A similar comparison can be made between Gurindji-Kriol codeswitching and Gurindji Kriol, the mixed language. This comparison is more diachronic because the language varieties are linked historically and the speakers are socially connected, i.e. the speakers of the mixed language are the children and grandchildren of the codeswitchers from the 1970s. Many aspects of the structure of Gurindji Kriol bear a striking resemblance to insertional patterns which are also found in the codeswitching from the 1970s (Meakins 2011c: 131ff.). For example, in both cases Gurindji insertions of single content words such as direct objects, intransitive subjects and verbs occur often in both the codeswitching and the mixed language. Nonetheless alternational patterns are also present in both forms of language mixing. Alternational switches can be characterised by *peripherality* (Muysken 2000; Treffers-Daller 1994). Peripherality refers to how marginal the switched elements are to the argument structure of the clause and also to the structural position of switches. Constituents which are adjuncts or are switched on the physical edge of a clause are prototypical cases of alternational codeswitching. This is a common pattern in Gurindji-Kriol codeswitching (Meakins 2011c: 133–134). This feature often goes hand-in-hand with the relationship of the switched element to the predicate argument structure of the matrix clause. Constituents which are peripheral to the argument structure of the clause often occur at clause boundaries in this data. These kinds of switches are also found in the mixed language (Meakins 2011c: 139–40). Common alternational switches which are found in both forms of mixing include Gurindji locational adjuncts switched on the right and left periphery of the clause.

The continued presence of alternational patterns in Gurindji Kriol is interesting given that, as discussed above, most comparisons between mixed languages and codeswitching find the insertional pattern to be dominant. This observation is probably just a sampling issue in that most identified mixed languages are of the grammar-lexicon kind. In these cases, one language is stronger providing the grammatical frame while the other language contributes only lexicon. This mixing pattern has strongly supported the idea that mixed languages are the result of insertional codeswitching. Nonetheless Backus (2003) raises another issue with the notion that alternational codeswitching can contribute to the structure of mixed languages – the *predictability* of switches. The key to forming a mixed language lies in the ability of codeswitching patterns to conventionalise. Conventionalising requires switching between languages to be predictable, thereby narrowing the degree of structural variation (see section 3.2.1.2). Alternational codeswitching is considered to be a socially-marked form of language mixing which is unconstrained by the structures of the interacting languages, and is therefore unlikely to grammaticalise into a stable autonomous language. On the other hand, insertional codeswitching is assumed to be more rule-governed and predictable, properties which lend themselves to grammaticalisation. Backus suggests that one of the characteristics of alternational codeswitching is that it is impossible to predict when a speaker will use language A or language B. In this respect, alternational codeswitching "entails unbridled variation" (2003: 240). Backus suggests that the unpredictability of alternational codeswitching is the result of discourse functions which he believes are marked by this type of switching. These functions include alignments with another culture and topic changes which he observes in Turkish-Dutch mixed lects (2003: 248). Backus concludes that it is simply not in the nature of alternational codeswitching to conventionalise because this would mean losing its inherent communicative function. The choice of language, rather than the lexical item itself, is always a communicative choice.

5. Conclusion: Beyond characterising mixed languages as mixed forms

There are a variety of languages which have been classified as mixed languages. Lexically they range from languages which derive an extraordinary amount of vocabulary from one language and their grammar from another (Media Lengua, Old Helsinki Slang) to languages which selectively replace lexical items according to specific communicative contexts (Angloromani, Ma'á). Mixed languages also differ according to structure. In some mixed languages the structure is clearly derived from one language (Media Lengua, Angloromani, Ma'á, Bilingual Navajo, Old Helsinki Slang). In other cases, the two source languages contribute relatively equal amounts of structure to the mix in a way that contrasts dramatically with other language contact scenarios (Michif, Mednyj Aleut, Gurindji Kriol, Light Warlpiri). Yet other examples have restructured one language on the basis of another such that, on the surface, the language 'looks' like one of its sources, however it has mapped these forms onto the other language's grammar (Sri Lanka Malay).

Despite these differences, what is common to all of these languages is that they have emerged in situations of bilingualism where a common language is already present. In this respect, they do not serve a communicative function, but rather they are markers of an in-group identity, whether it be a new identity created through mixed marriages (Michif) or the maintenance of an old identity which is under threat (Angloromani, Gurindji Kriol, Light Warlpiri, Ma'á, Bilingual Navajo). Despite this common socio-historical cradle, little more can be predicted. It appears from the variation in structural outcomes that different contact situations can result in similar mixed languages, and different mixed languages may arise from similar contact situations.

One theme which emerged strongly from a discussion of these languages has been the inadequacy of *form* as a basic descriptor in the structure of a mixed language. What is meant by 'form' is the phonological shape of a morpheme or lexeme, that is – what is said. Many mixed languages are described in this manner, for example, as mixes of the stems from one language and the affixes from other, or as splits between nouns and verbs and their accompanying morphology. Yet these descriptions do not adequately characterise mixed languages. Sri Lanka Malay, of a different type, demonstrates this problem most clearly. This language consists almost entirely of the lexical and morphological material from a contact variety of Malay. Yet Sri Lanka Malay is unintelligible to a speaker of any Malay variety. Whilst the forms are Malay-derived, their syntactic position, distribution and function are based on Tamil and Sinhala. Mixing occurs below the level of the form. Gurindji Kriol also demonstrates this kind of mixing. For example, as has been shown, although this mixed language maintains Gurindji-derived case-marking, these suffixes have shifted in their function and distribution under the influence of Kriol-derived prepositions and word order. One needs to look below the surface of this language because the mixing occurs within the lexical entry. It is here that the features of the lexeme or morpheme including its semantics, word class, syntactic distribution, pragmatic force and function may be split between the source languages. In this respect the surface form masks the true extent of language fusion or mixing.

Although some of these types of observations were made in earlier descriptions of mixed languages, analyses such as these have emerged from the more recent large scale documentation of some mixed languages (for example, Sri Lanka Malay, Gurindji Kriol, Light Warlpiri). Indeed other studies of language contact and contact varieties have utilised this notion of layering in the lexical entry as a basis for explaining language change, for instance studies of first language interference in second language learning, descriptions of processes such as calquing and convergence, composite codeswitching (Myers-Scotton 2003) and the Relexification Hypothesis in creole studies (Lefebvre 1998). It is likely that this approach to describing language mixing will influence analyses of mixed languages in further studies.

In general, mixed languages provide a unique opportunity to study the often observable birth, life and death of languages both in terms of their socio-historical context and structural changes. These debates continually benefit from the identification of new mixed languages, some of which reinforce current views, while others challenge us with a new range of structural outcomes that result from the intense interaction between the grammars of two languages.

Notes

1. Thanks to Peter Bakker, Yaron Matras and Eva Schultze-Berndt for comments on an earlier draft of this chapter and more generally for conversations in and around the topic of these very strange and fascinating languages.
2. Also called "split languages" by Myers-Scotton, "bilingual mixed languages" by Thomason, and "fused lects" by Auer. For consistency I use the term 'mixed language' which is the most widely-used term.
3. The Volkswagen Foundation in Germany funds endangered language documentation projects, see www.mpi.nl/dobes. Two relevant projects are the Sri Lankan Malay project (CI Umberto Ansaldo, Universiteit van Amsterdam) and the Jaminjungan/Ngumpin project which includes work on Gurindji Kriol (CI Eva Schultze-Berndt, Patrick McConvell and Felicity Meakins, University of Manchester).
4. The Endangered Languages Documentation Program (Hans Rausing Foundation, UK, see http://www.hrelp.org/) funded the documentation of Gurindji Kriol (CI Felicity Meakins, University of Manchester), see: http://www.hrelp.org/grants/projects/index.php?projid=159
5. The Romani project is based at the University of Manchester (CI Yaron Matras), see http://romani.humanities.manchester.ac.uk
6. Angloromani material is held in an archive at the University of Manchester. Sri Lanka Malay and Gurindji Kriol recordings and transcripts are digitally available through the DOBES archive at the Max Planck Institute in Nijmegen (The Netherlands) and the ELDP archive at SOAS (London). Light Warlpiri

material is also held at the Max Planck Institute in Nijmegen (The Netherlands).
7. The ACLA project is headed by Gillian Wigglesworth, Jane Simpson and Patrick McConvell at the University of Melbourne, see http://acla.languages-linguistics.unimelb.edu.au/
8. Kriol is an English-based creole language spoken across northern Australia. The name 'Gurindji Kriol ' is somewhat deceptive as it seems to suggest that Gurindji Kriol is a variety of this creole, however it is a clear and balanced bilingual mix of Gurindji and Kriol.
9. Rotwelsch is camouflaged German and not an independent language.
10. For a historical overview of the various treatments of Angloromani, see Matras et al. (2008).
11. For a discussion of the origin of the name Gurindji Kriol, see Meakins (2012).
12. The word *wumpurrarni* means 'black' in the local Aboriginal language Warumungu.
13. This example comes from Samantha Disbray's corpus of Wumpurrarni English. The speaker is aged in her late 30s.
14. Smith and Paauw (2006: 160) suggest that the Sri Lanka Malays were bilingual in Tamil and Malay with knowledge of Sinhala less widespread. Ansaldo (2008) argues for a stronger Sinhala influence though he notes that it is often difficult to separate the Tamil and Sinhala influence because much structural convergence has already taken place between the languages.
15. There is some variation present in Michif but it is community dependent.
16. Which is consistent with the pattern of optional ergativity seen in Gurindji Kriol, see section 4.2.
17. Although Aboh and Ansaldo (2007: 58) observe that these case forms are distinguished in the Kirinda variety of Sri Lanka Malay.
18. Questions about the legitimacy of the comparison of active and passive sentences given the dubious equivalence of their semantics have been raised in reference to this study and others (see for example Lavandera 1996).
19. Where agent is taken to mean the subject of a transitive clause.
20. Thomason (2003) provides some good counter-arguments to Bakker's objections about a causal link between French-Cree codeswitching and Michif.

References

Aikhenvald, Alexandra Y. & Robert M. W. Dixon. 2007. *Grammars in Contact: A Cross-Linguistic Typology*. Oxford: Oxford University Press.

Aboh, Enoch & Umberto Ansaldo. 2007. The role of typology in language creation. In Umberto Ansaldo, Stephen Matthews & Lisa Lim (eds.), *Deconstructing Creole,* 39–66. Amsterdam: John Benjamins.

Ansaldo, Umberto. 2008. Sri Lanka Malay revisited: Genesis and classification. In David Harrison, David Rood & Adrienne Dwyer (eds.), *Lessons from Documented Endangered Languages*. 13–42. Amsterdam: Benjamins.

Ansaldo, Umberto. 2011a. Sri Lanka Malay and its Lankan adstrates. In Claire Lefebvre (ed.), *Creoles, Their Substrates, and Language Typology*. 367–382. Amsterdam: Benjamins.
Ansaldo, Umberto. 2011b. Metatypy in Sri Lanka Malay. In Ghanshyam Sharma & Rajenda Singh (eds.), *Annual Review of South Asian Languages and Linguistics*, 3–16. Berlin: Walter de Gruyter.
Appel, René & Pieter Muysken. 1987. *Language Contact and Bilingualism*. London: Edward Arnold.
Auer, Peter. 1998. Introduction: Bilingual conversation revisited. In Peter Auer (ed.), *Code-switching in Conversation: Language, Interaction and Identity*, 1–24. London: Routledge.
Auer, Peter. 1999. From codeswitching via language mixing to fused lects: Toward a dynamic typology of bilingual speech. *Journal of Bilingualism* 3(4). 309–332.
Auer, Peter. 2000. Insertional codeswitching in an immigrant language: 'just' borrowing or lexical re-orientation. *Bilingualism: Language and Cognition* 3(2). 103–105.
Auer, Peter. 2003. Can a mixed language be conventionalized alternational codeswitching? In Yaron Matras & Peter Bakker (eds.), *The Mixed Language Debate: Theoretical and Empirical Advances*, 237–270. Berlin: Mouton de Gruyter.
Bakker, Peter. 1994. Michif, the Cree-French mixed language of the Metis buffalo hunters in Canada. In Peter Bakker & Maarten Mous (eds.), *Mixed Languages: 15 Case Studies in Language Intertwining*, 13–33. Amsterdam: Uitgave IFOTT.
Bakker, Peter. 1997. *A Language of Our Own: The Genesis of Michif, the Mixed Cree-French Language of the Canadian Métis*. New York: Oxford University Press.
Bakker, Peter. 1998. Para-Romani language versus secret languages: Differences in origin, structure and use. In Yaron Matras (ed.), *The Romani Element in Non-Standard Speech*, 69–96. Wiesbaden: Harrassowitz.
Bakker, Peter. 2000a. Convergence intertwining: An alternative way towards the genesis of mixed languages. In Dicky Gilbers, John Nerbonne & Jos Schaeken (eds.), *Languages in Contact*, 29–35. Amsterdam: Rodopi.
Bakker, Peter. 2000b. Rapid language change: Creolization, intertwining, convergence. In Colin Renfrew, April McMahon & Larry Trask (eds.), *Time Depth in Historical Linguistics*, 585–620. Cambridge: McDonald Institute for Archaeological Research.
Bakker, Peter. 2002. An early vocabulary of British Romani (1616): A linguistic analysis. *Romani Studies Fifth Series* 12(2). 75–101.
Bakker, Peter. 2003. Mixed languages as autonomous systems. In Yaron Matras & Peter Bakker (eds.), *The Mixed Language Debate: Theoretical and Empirical Advances*, 107–50. Berlin: Mouton de Gruyter.
Bakker, Peter & Maarten Mous. 1994. Introduction. In Peter Bakker & Maarten Mous (eds.), *Mixed Languages: 15 Case Studies in Language Intertwining*, 1–11. Amsterdam: Uitgave IFOTT.

Bakker, Peter & Robert A. Papen. 1997. Michif: A mixed language based on Cree and French. In Sarah Grey Thomason (ed.), *Contact Languages: A Wider Perspective*, 295–363. Amsterdam: John Benjamins.

Bakker, Peter & Maarten Mous (eds.). 1994. *Mixed Languages: 15 Case Studies in Language Intertwining*. Amsterdam: Uitgave IFOTT.

Bertrand-Bocandé, Emmanuel. 1849. Notes sur la Guinée portugaise ou Sénégambie méridionale. *Bulletin de la Société de Géographie* 12. 57–93.

Bickerton, Derek. 1981. *Roots of Language*. Ann Arbor: Karoma.

Boretzky, Norbert & Birgit Igla. 1994. Romani mixed dialects. In Peter Bakker & Maarten Mous (eds.), *Mixed Languages: 15 Case Studies in Language Intertwining*, 35–68. Amsterdam: Uitgave IFOTT.

Brenzinger, Mathias. 1987. *Die Sprachliche und Kulturelle Stellung der Mbugu (Ma'a)*. Cologne: University of Cologne MA thesis.

Charola, Erika. 2002. *The Verb Phrase Structure of Gurindji Kriol*. Melbourne: Melbourne University Honours dissertation.

Chen, Naixiong. 1986. Guanyu Wutun Hua (An outline of the Wutun linguistic structure). *Journal of Asian and African Studies* 31. 33–52.

Clements, J. Clancy. 2009. *Linguistic Legacy of Spanish and Portuguese*. Cambridge: Cambridge University Press.

Clements, J. Clancy, Patrícia Amaral & Ana Luís. 2008. Cultural identity and the structure of a mixed language: The case of Barranquenho. *Proceedings of the Annual Meeting of the Berkeley Linguistics Society* 34S.

Croft, William. 2000. *Explaining Language Change: An Evolutionary Approach*. Harlow, England: Longman.

Croft, William. 2003. Mixed languages and acts of identity: An evolutionary approach. In Yaron Matras & Peter Bakker (eds.), *The Mixed Language Debate: Theoretical and Empirical Advances*, 41–72. Berlin: Mouton de Gruyter.

Dalton, Lorraine, Sandra Edwards, Rosaleen Farquarson, Sarah Oscar & Patrick McConvell. 1995. Gurindji children's language and language maintenance. *International Journal of the Sociology of Language* 113. 83–98.

de Smit, Merlijn. 2010. Modelling mixed languages: Some remarks on the case of Old Helsinki Slang. *Journal of Language Contact* 3. 1–19.

DeGraff, Michel. 2005. Linguists' most dangerous myth: The fallacy of creole exceptionalism. *Language in Society* 34. 533–91.

Disbray, Samantha. 2008. *More Than One Way to Catch a Frog: Children's Discourse in a Language Contact Setting*. Melbourne: University of Melbourne dissertation.

Disbray, Samantha & Jane Simpson. 2005. The expression of possessive in Wumpurrarni English, Tennant Creek. *Monash University Linguistics Papers* 4(2). 65–85.

Drapeau, Lynn. 1991. Michif replicated: The emergence of a mixed language in northern Quebec. Paper presented at 10th International Conference on Historical Linguistics, Amsterdam, August 12–16, 1991.

Dreyfuss, Gail R. & Djoehana Oka. 1979. Chinese Indonesian: A new kind of language hybrid? *Papers in Pidgin and Creole Linguistics (Pacific Linguistics)* A-57, 247–274.
Gardani, Francesco. 2008. *Borrowing of Inflectional Morphemes in Language Contact*. Frankfurt: Peter Lang.
Gardner-Chloros, Penelope. 2000. The tortoise and the hare: Distinguishing processes and end-products in language contact. *Bilingualism: Language and Cognition* 3(2). 112–114.
Givón, Talmy. 1979. *On Understanding Grammar*. New York: Academic Press.
Golovko, Evgeniy V. 1994. Mednyj Aleut or Copper Island Aleut: An Aleut-Russian mixed language. In Peter Bakker & Maarten Mous (eds.), *Mixed Languages: 15 Case Studies in Language Intertwining*, 113–121. Amsterdam: Uitgave IFOTT.
Golovko, Evgeniy V. 1996. A case of nongenetic development in the Arctic area: The contribution of Aleut and Russian to the formation of Copper Island Aleut. In Ernst Håkon Jahr & Ingvild Broch (eds.), *Language Contact in the Arctic. Northern Pidgins and Contact Languages*, 63–77. Berlin: Mouton de Gruyter.
Golovko, Evgeniy V. 2003. Language contact and group identity: The role of 'folk' linguistic engineering. In Yaron Matras & Peter Bakker (eds.), *The Mixed Language Debate: Theoretical and Empirical Advances*, 177–208. Berlin: Mouton de Gruyter.
Golovko, Evgeniy V. & Nikolai Vakhtin. 1990. Aleut in contact: The CIA enigma. *Acta Linguistica Hafniensia* 72. 97–125.
Gómez Rendón, Jorge. 2008. *Typological and Social Constraints on Language Contact. Amerindian Languages in Contact with Spanish*. Utrecht: LOT Dissertation Series.
Grant, Anthony. 1994. Shelta: The secret language of Irish travellers viewed as a mixed language. In Peter Bakker & Maarten Mous (eds.), *Mixed Languages: 15 Case Studies in Language Intertwining*, 123–150. Amsterdam: Uitgave IFOTT.
Greenberg, Joseph. 1999. Are there mixed languages? In A. A Visagin, R. Vroon & M. L. Gasparov (eds.), *Essays in Poetics, Literary History and Linguistics Presented to Viacheslav Vsevolodovich Ivanov on the Occasion of his 70th Birthday*, 626–33. Moscow: OGI.
Hancock, Ian F. 1970. Is Anglo-Romanes a creole? *Journal of the Gypsy Lore Society* 49. 41–44.
Hancock, Ian F. 1976. The pidginization of Angloromani. In George N. Cave (ed.), *New Directions in Creole Studies*, 1–23. Georgetown: University of Guyana.
Haugen, Einar. 1950. The analysis of linguistic borrowing. *Language* 26. 210–231.
Heath, Jeffrey. 1978. *Linguistic Diffusion in Arnhem Land*. Canberra: AIAS.
Heine, Bernd, Ulrike Claudi & Friederieke Hünnemeyer. 1991. *Grammaticalization: A Conceptual Framework*. Chicago: University of Chicago Press.
Heine, Bernd & Mechthild Reh. 1984. *Grammaticalisation and Reanalysis in African Languages*. Hamburg: Helmut Buske.
Hopper, Paul & Elizabeth Traugott. 1993. *Grammaticalization*. Cambridge: Cambridge University Press.

Hussainmiya, Bachamiya Abdul. 1987. Melayu Bahasa: Some preliminary observations on the Malay creole of Sri Lanka. In Bachamiya Abdul Hussainmiya (ed.), *Lost Cousins: The Malays of Sri Lanka*, 153–172. Malaysia: Universiti Kebangsaan.

Janhunen, Juha, Marja Peltomaa, Erika Sandman & Xiawu Dongzhou. 2008. *Wutun*. München: LINCOM Europa.

Jarva, Vesa. 2008. Old Helsinki Slang and language mixing. *Journal of Language Contact* 1. 52–80.

Jones, Caroline, Felicity Meakins and Heather Buchan. 2011. Citation-speech vowels in Gurindji Kriol and local Australian English. *Australian Journal of Linguistics* 31(3). 305–327

Jones, Caroline, Felicity Meakins and Shujau Muawiyath. 2012. Learning vowel categories from maternal speech in Gurindji Kriol. *Language Learning* 62(4). 997–1260

Kenrick, Donald. 1979. Romani English. *International Journal of the Sociology of Language* 19. 111–120.

Labov, William. 1969. Contraction, deletion, and inherent variability of the English copula. *Language* 45(4). 715–762.

Labov, William. 1972. *Sociolinguistic Patterns*. Philadelphia: University of Pennsylvania Press.

Labov, William. 1994. *Principles of Linguistic Change. Volumes 1 and 2*. Oxford: Blackwell.

Lavandera, Beatriz. 1996. Where does the sociolinguistic variable stop? In Rajendra Singh (ed.), *Towards a Critical Sociolinguistics*, 17–30. Amsterdam: John Benjamins.

Lee, Jennifer. 1987. *Tiwi Today: A Study of Language Change in a Contact Situation*. Canberra: Pacific Linguistics.

Lee-Smith, Mei W. & Stephen A. Wurm. 1996. The Wutun language. In Stephen A. Wurm, Peter Mühlhäusler & Darrell T. Tryon (eds.), *Atlas of Languages of Intercultural Communication in the Pacific, Asia and the Americas Vol. 2*, 883–897. Berlin: Mouton.

Lefebvre, Claire. 1998. *Creole Genesis and the Acquisition of Grammar: The Case of Haitian Creole*. Cambridge: Cambridge University Press.

Lefebvre, Claire. 2004. *Issues in the Study of Pidgin and Creole Languages*. Amsterdam: John Benjamins.

Maher, Julianne. 1991. A crosslinguistic study of language contact and language attrition. In Herbert W. Seliger & Robert M. Vago (eds.), *First Language Attrition*, 67–84. Cambridge: Cambridge University Press.

Matras, Yaron. 2000. Mixed languages: A functional-communicative approach. *Bilingualism: Language and Cognition* 3(2). 79–99.

Matras, Yaron. 2003. Mixed languages: Re-examining the structural prototype. In Yaron Matras & Peter Bakker (eds.), *The Mixed Language Debate: Theoretical and Empirical Advances*, 151–176. Berlin: Mouton de Gruyter.

Matras, Yaron. 2007. The borrowability of structural categories. In Yaron Matras & Jeanette Sakel (eds.), *Grammatical Borrowing in Cross-Linguistic Perspective*, 31–73. Berlin: Mouton de Gruyter.

Matras, Yaron. 2009. *Language Contact*. Cambridge: Cambridge University Press.
Matras, Yaron. 2010. *Romani in Britain. The Afterlife of a Language*. Edinburgh: Edinburgh University Press.
Matras, Yaron & Peter Bakker. 2003. The study of mixed languages. In Yaron Matras & Peter Bakker (eds.), *The Mixed Language Debate: Theoretical and Empirical Advances,* 1–20. Berlin: Mouton de Gruyter.
Matras, Yaron, Hazel Gardner, Charlotte Jones & Veronica Schulmann. 2007. Angloromani: A different kind of language? *Anthropological Linguistics* 49(2). 142–184.
Matras, Yaron & Jeanette Sakel. 2007. *Grammatical Borrowing in Cross-Linguistic Perspective*. Berlin: Mouton de Gruyter.
Matras, Yaron & Peter Bakker (eds.). 2003. *The Mixed Language Debate: Theoretical and Empirical Advances*. Berlin: Mouton de Gruyter.
McCann, Mary, Séamas Síochain & Joseph Ruane (eds.). 1994. *Irish Travellers: Culture and Ethnicity*. Belfast: Institute of Irish Studies, The Queen's University of Belfast and the Anthropological Association of Ireland.
McConvell, Patrick. 1985. Domains and codeswitching among bilingual Aborigines. In Michael Clyne (ed.), *Australia, Meeting Place of Languages,* 95–125. Canberra: Pacific Linguistics.
McConvell, Patrick. 1988. Mix-im-up: Aboriginal codeswitching old and new. In Monica Heller (ed.), *Codeswitching: Anthropological and Sociolinguistic Perspectives,* Berlin: Mouton de Gruyter.
McConvell, Patrick. 2002. Mix-im-up speech and emergent mixed languages in indigenous Australia. *Texas Linguistic Forum (Proceedings from the 9th Annual Symposium about Language and Society)* 44(2). 328–349.
McConvell, Patrick. 2008. Mixed languages as outcomes of code-switching: Recent examples from Australia and their implications. *Journal of Language Contact* 2. 187–212.
McConvell, Patrick & Felicity Meakins. 2005. Gurindji Kriol: A mixed language emerges from code-switching. *Australian Journal of Linguistics* 25(1). 9–30.
McWhorter, John H. 1998. Identifying the creole prototype: Vindicating a typological claim. *Language* 74. 788–818.
McWhorter, John H. 2005. *Defining Creole*. Oxford: Oxford University Press.
Meakins, Felicity. 2008a. Unravelling languages: Multilingualism and language contact in Kalkaringi. In Jane Simpson & Gillian Wigglesworth (eds.), *Children's Language and Multilingualism: Indigenous Language Use at Home and School,* 247–264. New York: Continuum.
Meakins, Felicity. 2008b. Land, language and identity: The socio-political origins of Gurindji Kriol. In Miriam Meyerhoff & Naomi Nagy (eds.), *Social Lives in Language,* 69–94. Amsterdam: John Benjamins.
Meakins, Felicity. 2009. The case of the shifty ergative marker: A pragmatic shift in the ergative marker in one Australian mixed language. In Johanna Barðdal & Shobhana Chelliah (eds.), *The Role of Semantics and Pragmatics in the Development of Case,* 59–91. Amsterdam: John Benjamins.

Meakins, Felicity. 2010. The development of asymmetrical serial verb constructions in an Australian mixed language. *Linguistic Typology* 14(1). 1–38.
Meakins, Felicity. 2011a. Borrowing contextual inflection: Evidence from northern Australia. *Morphology* 21(1). 57–87.
Meakins, Felicity. 2011b. Spaced out: Inter-generational changes in the expression of spatial relations by Gurindji people. *Australian Journal of Linguistics* 31(1). 33–78.
Meakins, Felicity. 2011c. *Case Marking in Contact: The Development and Function of Case Morphology in Gurindji Kriol*. Amsterdam: John Benjamins.
Meakins, Felicity. 2012. Which mix? – code-switching or a mixed language – Gurindji Kriol. *Journal of Pidgin and Creole Languages* 27(1). 105–140.
Meakins, Felicity & Carmel O'Shannessy. 2005. Possessing variation: Age and inalienability related variables in the possessive constructions of two Australian mixed languages. *Monash University Linguistics Papers* 4(2). 43–63.
Meakins, Felicity & Carmel O'Shannessy. 2010. Ordering arguments about: Word order and discourse motivations in the development and use of the ergative marker in two Australian mixed languages. *Lingua* 120(7). 1693–1713.
Meakins, Felicity & Carmel O'Shannessy. 2012. Typological constraints on verb integration in two Australian mixed languages. *Journal of Language Contact* 5(2). 216–246.
Meyerhoff, Miriam. 2011. *Introducing Sociolinguistics*. London: Routledge.
Moravcsik, Edith. 1978. Universals of language contact. In Joseph Greenberg (ed.), *Universals of Human Language. Vol. 1: Method and Theory*, 95–122. Stanford CA: Stanford University Press.
Mous, Maarten. 1994. Ma'á or Mbugu. In Peter Bakker & Maarten Mous (eds.), *Mixed Languages: 15 Case Studies in Language Intertwining*, 175–200. Amsterdam: Uitgave IFOTT.
Mous, Maarten. 2000. Selective replacement is extreme lexical reorientation. *Bilingualism: Language and Cognition* 3(2). 115–116.
Mous, Maarten. 2003a. *The Making of a Mixed Language: The Case of Ma'á/Mbugu*. Amsterdam: John Benjamins.
Mous, Maarten. 2003b. The linguistic properties of lexical manipulation and its relevance or Ma'á. In Yaron Matras & Peter Bakker (eds.), *The Mixed Language Debate: Theoretical and Empirical Advances*, 209–236. Berlin: Mouton de Gruyter.
Mufwene, Saliko. 1996. The Founder Principle in creole genesis. *Diachronica* 13. 83–134.
Mufwene, Saliko. 2001. *The Ecology of Language Evolution*. Cambridge: Cambridge University Press.
Muysken, Pieter. 1981. Halfway between Quechua and Spanish: The case for relexification. In Arnold Highfield & Albert Valdman (eds.), *Historicity and Variation in Creole Studies*, 52–78. Ann Arbor: Karoma.
Muysken, Pieter. 1988. Media Lengua and Linguistic Theory. *Canadian Journal of Linguistics* 33(4). 409–22.

Muysken, Pieter. 1994a. Callahuaya. In Peter Bakker & Maarten Mous (eds.), *Mixed Languages: 15 Case Studies in Language Intertwining*, 207–211. Amsterdam: Uitgave IFOTT.

Muysken, Pieter. 1994b. Media Lengua. In Peter Bakker & Maarten Mous (eds.), *Mixed Languages: 15 Case Studies in Language Intertwining*, 201–205. Amsterdam: Uitgave IFOTT.

Muysken, Pieter. 1997a. Callahuaya. In Sarah Grey Thomason (ed.), *Contact Languages: A Wider Perspective*, 427–447. Amsterdam: John Benjamins.

Muysken, Pieter. 1997b. Media Lengua. In Sarah Grey Thomason (ed.), *Contact Languages: A Wider Perspective*, 365–426. Amsterdam: John Benjamins.

Muysken, Pieter. 2000. *Bilingual Speech: A Typology of Code-Mixing*. Cambridge: Cambridge University Press.

Myers-Scotton, Carol. 1993. *Duelling Languages: Grammatical Structure in Codeswitching*. Oxford: Clarendon Press.

Myers-Scotton, Carol. 2002. *Contact Linguistics: Bilingual Encounters and Grammatical Outcomes*. Oxford: Oxford University Press.

Myers-Scotton, Carol. 2003. What lies beneath: Split (mixed) languages as contact phenomena. In Yaron Matras & Peter Bakker (eds.), *The Mixed Language Debate: Theoretical and Empirical Advances*, 73–106. Berlin: Mouton de Gruyter.

Nichols, Johanna. 1986. Head-marking and dependent-marking grammar. *Language* 62(1). 56–119.

Nordhoff, Sebastian. 2009. *A Grammar of Upcountry Sri Lanka Malay*. Utrecht: LOT Dissertation Series.

Nordhoff, Sebastian (ed.). 2012. *The Genesis of Sri Lanka Malay. A Case of Extreme Language Contact*. Leiden: Brill.

O'Shannessy, Carmel. 2005. Light Warlpiri: A new language. *Australian Journal of Linguistics* 25(1). 31–57.

O'Shannessy, Carmel. 2006. *Language Contact and Children's Bilingual Language Acquisition: Learning a Mixed Language and Warlpiri in Northern Australia*. Sydney: University of Sydney dissertation.

O'Shannessy, Carmel. 2008. Children's production of their heritage language and a new mixed language. In Jane Simpson & Gillian Wigglesworth (eds.), *Children's Language and Multilingualism: Indigenous Language Use at Home and School*, 261–282. New York: Continuum.

O'Shannessy, Carmel. 2009. Language variation and change in a north Australian indigenous community. In Dennis Preston & James Stanford (eds.), *Variationist Approaches to Indigenous Minority Languages*, 419–439. Amsterdam: John Benjamins.

O'Shannessy, Carmel. 2011a. Competition between word order and case-marking in interpreting grammatical relations: A case study in multilingual acquisition. *Journal of Child Language* 38(4). 763–792

O'Shannessy, Carmel. 2011b. Young children's social meaning making in a new mixed language. In Ute Eikelkamp (ed.), *Growing up in central Australia: New anthropological studies of Aboriginal Childhood and Adolescence*, 131–154. New York: Berghahn Books.

O'Shannessy, Carmel. 2012. The role of code-switched input to children in the origin of a new mixed language. *Linguistics* 50(2). 305–340.
O'Shannessy, Carmel & Felicity Meakins. 2012. Comprehension of competing argument marking systems in two Australian mixed languages. *Bilingualism: Language and Cognition* 15(2). 378–396.
Papen, Robert A. 1987a. Can two distinct grammars coexist in a single language? The case of Metif. In A. M. Kinloch (ed.), *Proceedings of the 10th Annual Conference of the APLA,* 144–157. Fredericton: University of New Brunswick.
Papen, Robert A. 1987b. Linguistic variation in the French component of Metif grammar. In William Cowan (ed.), *Papers of the 18th Algonquian Conference,* 247–259. Ottawa: Carleton University.
Papen, Robert A. 2003. Michif: One phonology or two. *University of British Columbia Working Papers in Linguistics* 12. 47–58.
Paunonen, Heikki. 2006. Vähemmistökielestä varioivaksi valtakieleksi [From a minority language to a varying majority language]. In Kaisu Juusela & Kateriina Nisula (eds.), *Helsinki Kieliyhteisönä* [Helsinki as a speech community], 142–61. Helsinki: Helsingin yliopiston suomen kielen ja kirjallisuuden laitos.
Plag, Ingo. 2003a. *Phonology and Morphology of Creole Languages.* Tübingen: Max Niemeyer Verlag.
Plag, Ingo. 2003b. *Yearbook of Morphology 2002.* Alphen aan den Rijn, Netherlands: Kluwer.
Poplack, Shana. 1993. Variation theory and language contact. In Dennis Preston (ed.), *American Dialect Research,* 251–283. Amsterdam: John Benjamins.
Rosen, Nicole. 2000. *Non-stratification in Michif.* Toronto: University of Toronto dissertation.
Rosen, Nicole. 2003. Demonstrative position in Michif. *Canadian Journal of Linguistics* 48(1/2). 39–69.
Ross, Malcolm. 1996. Contact-induced change and the comparative method: Cases from Papua New Guinea. In Mark Durie & Malcolm Ross (eds.), *The Comparative Method Reviewed: Regularity and Irregularity in Language Change,* 180–217. New York: Oxford University Press.
Ross, Malcolm. 2001. Contact-induced change in Oceanic languages in north-west Melanesia. In Alexandra Y. Aikhenvald & Robert M. W. Dixon (eds.), *Areal Diffusion and Genetic Inheritance: Problems in Comparative Linguistics,* 134–166. Oxford: Oxford University Press.
Sasse, Hans Jürgen. 1992. Theory of language death. In M. Brenzinger (ed.), *Language Death: Factual and Theoretical Explorations with Special References to East Africa,* 7–30. Berlin: Mouton de Gruyter.
Saussure, Ferdinand de. 1983 [1916]. *Course in General Linguistics.* Translated by *Roy Harris.* London: Duckworth.
Schaengold, Charlotte. 2003. The emergence of bilingual Navajo: English and Navajo languages in contact regardless of everyone's best intentions. In Brian Joseph, Johanna DeStefano, Neil G. Jacobs & Ilse Lehiste (eds.), *When Languages Collide,* 235–54. Columbus, OH: Ohio State University Press.

Schaengold, Charlotte. 2004. *Bilingual Navajo: Mixed Codes, Bilingualism and Language Maintenance*. Columbus, OH: Ohio State University dissertation. http://etd.ohiolink.edu/view.cgi?osu1092425886 (accessed 8 January 2013).
Sebba, Mark. 1998. A congruence approach to the syntax of code-switching. *International Journal of Bilingualism* 2. 1–20.
Sekerina, Irina A. 1994. Copper Island Aleut: A mixed language. *The Languages of the World* 8.1. 14–31.
Shappeck, Thomas. 2011. *Qichua-Spanish Language Contact in Salcedo, Ecuador: Revisiting Media Lengua Syncretic Language Practices*. Urbana, IL: University of Illinois dissertation.
Slomanson, Peter. 2006. Sri Lankan Malay morphosyntax: Lankan or Malay. In Ana Deumert & Stephanie Durrleman (eds.), *Structure and Variation in Language Contact*, 135–158. Amsterdam: John Benjamins.
Slomanson, Peter. 2007. On the areal character of Sri Lanka Negation. Paper presented at the Society for Pidgin and Creole Linguistics Conference, Amsterdam, 18–20 June 2007.
Smart, Bath C. & Henry T. Crofton. 1875. *The Dialect of the English Gypsies*. London: Asher.
Smith, Ian R. 1977. Sri Lanka Creole Portuguese Phonology. *International Journal of Dravidian Linguistics* 7. 248–406.
Smith, Ian R. 1979a. Convergence in South Asia: A creole example. *Lingua* 48. 193–222.
Smith, Ian R. 1979b. Substrata versus universals in the formation of Sri Lanka Portuguese. In Peter Mühlhäusler (ed.), *Papers in Pidgin and Creole Linguistics 2*, 183–200. Canberra: Pacific Linguistics.
Smith, Ian R. 1984. The development of morphosyntax in Sri Lanka Creole Portuguese. In Mark Sebba & Loreto Todd (eds.), *Papers from The Creole Conference, York University*, 291–301. York University: York University.
Smith, Ian R. 2001. Creolization and convergence in morphosyntax: Sri Lanka Portuguese and Sourashtra nominal marking typology. In Peri Bhaskararao & Karumuri Venkata Subbarao (eds.), *The Yearbook of South Asian Languages and Linguistics, 2001: Tokyo Symposium on South Asian Languages: Contact, Convergence and Typology*, 391–409. New Delhi: Sage.
Smith, Ian R. & Scott Paauw. 2006. Sri Lanka Malay: Creole or convert. In Ana Deumert & Stephanie Durrleman (eds.), *Structure and Variation in Language Contact*, 159–182. Amsterdam: John Benjamins.
Smith, Ian, Scott Paauw & Bachamiya Abdul Hussainmiya. 2004. Sri Lankan Malay: The state of the art. In Rajendra Singh (ed.), *Yearbook of South Asian Languages 2004*, 197–215. Berlin: Mouton de Gruyter.
Smith, Norval. 2000. Symbiotic mixed languages: A question of terminology. *Bilingualism: Language and Cognition* 3(2). 122–123.
Thomason, Sarah Grey. 1983. Genetic relationship and the case of Ma'a (Mbugu). *Studies in African Linguistics* 14(2). 210–211.
Thomason, Sarah Grey. 1995. Language mixture: ordinary processes, extraordinary results. In Carmen Silva-Corvalan (ed.), *Spanish in Four Continents: Studies in*

Language Contact and Bilingualism, 15–35. Washington: Georgetown University Press.
Thomason, Sarah Grey. 1997a. Ma'a (Mbugu). In Sarah Grey Thomason (ed.), *Contact Languages: A Wider Perspective,* 467–487. Amsterdam: John Benjamins.
Thomason, Sarah Grey. 1997b. Mednyj Aleut. In Sarah Grey Thomason (ed.), *Contact Languages: A Wider Perspective,* 449–468. Amsterdam: John Benjamins.
Thomason, Sarah Grey. 2001. *Language Contact: An Introduction.* Edinburgh and Washington, DC: Edinburgh University Press and Georgetown University Press.
Thomason, Sarah Grey. 2003. Social factors and linguistic processes in the emergence of stable mixed languages. In Yaron Matras & Peter Bakker (eds.), *The Mixed Language Debate: Theoretical and Empirical Advances,* 21–40. Berlin: Mouton de Gruyter.
Thomason, Sarah Grey & Terrence Kaufman. 1988. *Language Contact, Creolization, and Genetic Linguistics.* Berkeley: University of California Press.
Traugott, Elizabeth & Ekkehard König. 1991. The semantics-pragmatics of grammaticalisation revisited. In Elizabeth Traugott & Bernd Heine (eds.), *Approaches to Grammaticalisation,* Amsterdam: John Benjamins.
Thomason, Sarah Grey (ed.). 1997. *Contact Languages: A Wider Perspective.* Amsterdam: John Benjamins.
Treffers-Daller, Jeanine. 1994. *Mixing Two Languages: French-Dutch Contact in a Comparative Perspective.* Berlin: Mouton de Gruyter.
van Gijn, Rik. 2009. The phonology of mixed languages. *Journal of Pidgin and Creole Languages* 24(1). 93–119.
Weiner, Judith & William Labov. 1983. Constraints on the agentless passive. *Journal of Linguistics* 19. 29–58.
Weinreich, Uriel. 1974 [1953]. *Languages in Contact: Findings and Problems.* The Hague: Mouton.
Weinreich, Uriel, William Labov & Marvin Herzog. 1968. Empirical foundations for a theory of language change. In Winfred Lehmann & Yakov Malkeil (eds.), *Directions for Historical Linguistics,* 95–188. Austin, TX: University of Texas Press.
Whitney, William Dwight. 1881. On mixture in language. *Transactions of the American Philosophical Association* 12. 5–26.

Multi-ethnolects: Kebabnorsk, Perkerdansk, Verlan, Kanakensprache, Straattaal, etc.

Jacomine Nortier and Margreet Dorleijn

1. Introduction

In large urban areas all over Europe where many relatively recent immigrant communities of various ethnic and linguistic origin have settled, highly specific slang-like linguistic styles emerge among multi-ethnic adolescent groups. In these styles, elements from immigrant languages are combined with the dominant language of the society. For example, in the Netherlands, one can encounter utterances such as in the following example from Dorleijn and Nortier (2008b) (regular type for Dutch, italics for Turkish, bold for Moroccan Arabic):

(1) wreed *olmazmi* **ah sahbi?**
    great would.be.NEG.Q VOC friend.my
    'Wouldn't that be great my friend?'

The use of elements of the three languages in (1) does not imply that the speaker is necessarily of Dutch, Turkish or Moroccan origin. He/she may be so, but may as well be of Afghan, Iranian, Iraqi or any other origin. Similar speech styles can be found all over Europe and beyond.

In this chapter we want to discuss the position of multi-ethnolects among contact languages. We will argue that it is a type of contact language. We define the term multi-ethnolect for the moment as follows:

A linguistic style or variety (cf. the discussion below) that is part of linguistic practices of speakers of more than two different ethnic and (by consequence) linguistic backgrounds, and contains an unusually high number of features from more than one language, but has one clear base-language, generally the dominant language of the society where the multi-ethnolect is in use.

Below, we will refine this definition after having discussed some notions we believe to be relevant with respect to multi-ethnolects.

The term 'contact languages' implies a certain degree of stability of the varieties that would fall under this category, but multi-ethnolects are in fact more often than not quite ephemeral phenomena. They are, at most, pre-stages or initial stages of stabilised contact languages. And this is precisely why we would like to argue that they deserve a place in a study on contact languages (along, in fact, with other synchronic manifestations of language contact). The synchronic study of linguistic contact will undoubtedly offer insights about how language contact actually 'works' in daily interaction. It may shed light on the mechanisms and processes of propagation, spread, and conventionalisation of linguistic features, through which more stable contact varieties and contact languages emerge or have emerged. If for no other reason, it deserves to be discussed in a volume on contact languages.

In this chapter we will set out with a discussion of a few notions and terms we consider relevant for the concept of multi-ethnolect (in section 2); in the process, we will discuss several research perspectives and methods and the different questions those perspectives seek to answer. We will argue that in order to come to a full understanding of multi-ethnolects, it may be rewarding to study them from diverse perspectives, with more language-structure-oriented, variationist, quantitative survey approaches at the one end, and detailed, ethnographic, micro-level conversation analysis-oriented approaches at the other. These two types of approaches may prove complementary in a fruitful way, especially if they are based on the study of the same datasets and/or the same groups of respondents.

In section 3, we present a selection of important earlier and current research on multi-ethnolects. In section 5, we will position multi-ethnolects within a typology of contact languages. We will end with a brief conclusion in section 6.

2. Concepts, terminology, definitions

In this section, we will discuss certain notions we consider relevant with respect to multi-ethnolects. First of all, we want to contrast the term multi-ethnolect with the more familiar term ethnolect. Then we will discuss the (macro-) sociological circumstances that seem to encourage the emergence of multi-ethnolects. After that we will address the issue whether one should speak of varieties or rather of styles in the case of multi-ethnolects. This will be followed by a brief discussion of the mechanisms that may be at work in the emergence or creation of multi-ethnolects, linguistic features that characterise multi-ethnolects and the diverse functions that multi-ethnolects are often observed to perform. At the end of this section we will discuss a few research gaps. We need a more refined definition of multi-ethnolects, present some questions that in our view are in urgent need of research, a few methods that may turn out to be fruitful when investigating multi-ethnolects and some alternative terms that have been proposed for the term multi-ethnolect.

2.1. Multi-ethnolects vs. ethnolects

Multi-ethnolects enjoy increasing attention in sociolinguistic research. Over the last decades several multi-ethnolects have been attested and discussed in the literature (see section 3 below). In the previous sentence the term multi-ethnolect is, for reasons of brevity, presented as if it described a clear-cut phenomenon, but the reader should bear in mind that this is not the case.

One is tempted to ascribe this recent attention to the fact that multi-ethnolects have emerged only recently, in the wake of migration waves toward Western urban areas; that they are, in fact, a logical product of late modernity but, as one can infer from, for example, studies by Kießling and Mous (2004), multi-ethnolects certainly exist outside the Western world as well. Moreover, multi-ethnolects are not a new phenomenon, but more a phenomenon of all times, that was only waiting for linguists to give it a name. For example, Walt Wolfram reported already in 1974 on Puerto Rican-American groups where, as Fought (2006: 450) formulates it, "[…] adolescents in particular have been found to use certain features of African American Vernacular English (AAVE) in their English". Wolfram's (1974) study reports on Puerto Rican-speakers in New York using AAVE habitual *be*. This would probably have fitted well under the label of multi-ethnolect. Wolfram attributed this to frequent contacts of these Puerto-Ricans with AAVE-speakers, which, of course, makes sense, cf. the discussion below.

The term multi-ethnolect should not be confused with the term ethnolect, although there is a reference to the common and overlapping notion of ethnicity in both terms. Where multi-ethnolects may have been attested, labelled and classified as a consequence of research approaches prevailing today, the term ethnolect pertains to studies of a more variationist type. In the sociolinguistic tradition, ethnicity has always been considered an important social variable, along with regional background, gender, class, which as such can be expressed in the language use of individuals.

Research on this topic takes as a starting point that some (isolated or clusters of) linguistic variables are indexical for the ethnic background of speakers, whereas, by contrast, one of the characterising features of multi-ethnolects is that speakers use features that are taken from another ethnic/linguistic resource than their own. The focus of research on ethnolects is largely oriented on language structure, driven by questions such as: To what extent do elements related to ethnicity contribute to the emergence of a stable linguistic variety? Or: How do ethnolects contribute to language change? Yet other questions could be: To what extent and in which way do ethnic elements contribute to the emergence of a contact variety of a given language and/or a mixed language? To what degree and how can the occurrence of an ethnic variety be explained by the process of second language acquisition? Definitions of ethnolects like the following typically reflect matters such as: "[An ethnolect is] a variety of a language that results when speakers of different ethnolinguistic backgrounds attempt to speak the dominant language (e.g. 'Chicano English')" (Danesi 1985: 118). Another type of definition with more diachronic connotations is developed by Wölck and Carlock (1981: 17), specifically for ethnolects of English: "[…] the English of the descendants of immigrant families long after their original language is lost […] a linguistic variety of a majority language whose special structure has developed through a history of community bilingualism."

Questions and definitions like the above take as a starting point that an ethnolect is a variety spoken by L2-speakers in which their L1 is reflected. Research of this type often implies that the ethnic features in such a variety are beyond the control and monitoring of the speakers, in other words, that ethnolects reflect what one is, rather than what one does. Examples of such studies are Labov (1972) and Wolfram (1974).

During the past few decades, however, the orientation in studies of language variation and language contact has shifted towards different types of questions and research methods that can be conceived as complementary to the above-mentioned research. This other type of research is mostly qualitative in orientation and it makes use of ethnographic fieldwork methods. Therefore, recent studies are more focused on the social meaning and/or the interactive function of certain 'ethnic linguistic variables'. In this type of research, questions of the following type are asked: What communicative intentions are served by ethnic elements? Why are these elements used, and in which (situational or conversational) contexts? What communicative effects are obtained by which linguistic means? Which linguistic means are used in which way to construct/present an identity? Rampton's work on linguistic practices ("crossing", as it is coined by him) among young people in multi-ethnic peer groups, is a ground-breaking example of such research (cf. Rampton 1995), though the topic has received some attention earlier as well (see section 3 below). As will be inferred from the overview of the literature below, this type of research on multi-ethnolects is mainly concentrated in North-Western Europe and the United States.

2.2. Macro-social, political and macro-sociolinguistic circumstances

As we will show in section 3 below, multi-ethnolects are typically used by speakers of diverse ethnic backgrounds, including the dominant, mainstream background. Multi-ethnolects appear to be typically urban phenomena that emerge in particular among adolescents in the context of migration in cities. We already remarked in the introduction that multi-ethnolects are mainly attested in big cities in Western Europe, but this should certainly not be taken as an indication that multi-ethnolects occur only there. One expects them to emerge anywhere in the world in large urban multi-ethnic areas (e.g. Kießling and Mous 2004; see also further below.) This is not surprising: below it will be illustrated that users of multi-ethnolects are to a high degree involved in the process of constructing and presenting a social identity, and such actions are of course unavoidable consequences of living in the highly dynamic circumstances that multi-ethnic neighbourhoods in large urban areas are. In such circumstances adolescents are left as it were in a strange place without a map, and are invited on a quest through a landscape with all kinds of linguistic and cultural possibilities and challenges but no clear directions, no obvious dominant tendencies, no fixed social positions, and therefore an appeal is made to their own creativity in designing their identity.

That multi-ethnolects are mainly observed in circumstances such as the ones above does not mean that they only occur there. But these circumstances seem at least to facilitate the emergence of ethnolects. However, if we stick to the definition of multi-ethnolects given in the introduction, we should include centenarians in rural environments as well, as long as they are of diverse ethnic background and speak a variety in which elements from more than two languages can be found. There is, for example, a brief report on a specific variety of Arabic, called Mahallemi, which is spoken by (elderly) people of diverse ethnic backgrounds originating from the Kurdish area of South-Eastern Turkey, and contains elements of Kurdish, Turkish and (Aramaic) Turoyo (Leezenberg and Dorleijn 1998). This variety still needs to be investigated further, but at first sight it seems to share characteristics with other multi-ethnolects. As we will discuss further below, the function rather than the formal aspects should form the crucial part of a definition of multi-ethnolects. People with heterogeneous ethnic backgrounds find themselves together and are in need of a new group-identity. Under such circumstances a multi-ethnolect is likely to emerge.

Apart from social developments like mass migration, urbanisation, etc., the need for a new group identity may arise because of concrete political developments or even incidents. An example is the city of Utrecht in the

Netherlands, where the multidisciplinary research program TCULT was carried out in a multi-cultural neighbourhood between 1998 and 2002. In those days, there was no indication of the existence of the specific multi-ethnolect MFD, 'Moroccan Flavoured Dutch', as it was labelled by Nortier and Dorleijn (2008). However, a few years later, this MFD multi-ethnolect, spoken by adolescents of a Moroccan, Turkish, Dutch and other ethnic backgrounds had emerged (Dorleijn and Nortier 2006; Nortier and Dorleijn 2008). In this multi-ethnolect, especially Moroccan (Berber and Arabic) elements were added to the base language (Dutch). This happened mainly, but not exclusively, on the level of pronunciation.

Respondents indicated that the growing anti-Muslim attitude in Dutch public opinion following the assassination of the Dutch politician Pim Fortuyn in 2002 and the 9/11 attacks a year earlier, caused Muslims of diverse ethnic backgrounds to flock together. Thus, they would form a group with one migrant identity, instead of separate ethnic groups along national lines (i.e., Moroccans, Turks, etc.). In the Netherlands, the term 'allochtones' is used for migrants and their descendants, where no distinction is made between separate ethnic groups. Adolescents of for example South-Asian origin would not belong to this group, although these are, strictly speaking, allochtones as well. The assumption that Muslim or immigrant identity plays an important role in this matter is based mostly on anecdotal information. A young woman with a Turkish background (aged 18) told us that she sometimes feels more 'allochtonous' (i.e. 'an immigrant', 'a foreigner') than Turkish, and an Afghan (aged 17) said that he felt insulted when he heard nasty things about Moroccans in the Netherlands, since "I am a foreigner, too!". The way we interpret this, both informants expressed solidarity with other ethnic minority groups.

For the actual structural and formal manifestation of a multi-ethnolect, sociolinguistic tendencies like language maintenance and shift, degree of multilingualism, etc., in the ethnic groups that contribute to the multi-ethnolect, seem to be important factors as well. For example, one of the multi-ethnolects attested in the Netherlands (Nortier and Dorleijn 2008; Dorleijn and Nortier 2008) draws in particular on Moroccan resources, rather than e.g. Turkish, even though both communities in the Netherlands are comparable in terms of size and cultural background. The sociolinguistic situation of the two communities differs considerably, e.g. in the role the mother tongue plays in each of the communities and the prestige attributed to it, making the Moroccan elements more prone to appropriation by members of other groups, as will be explained below.

Apart from Dutch, which is the dominant language among second and third generation speakers, two languages are spoken in the Dutch-Moroccan community: Colloquial Moroccan Arabic and Berber, which are not mutually intelligible. Although the two languages differ considerably, there are similarities on the level of pronunciation and prosody. An estimated 70% of the Moroccans living in the Netherlands are Berber speaking. Although most Berber speaking Moroccans are more or less familiar with Moroccan Arabic, this does not imply that every Berber speaks Moroccan Arabic fluently. Therefore, Dutch is often the unmarked mode within the community. Another reason for the preference of Dutch is the low status the Moroccan oral languages have. Classical Arabic (or *fusha*) is a language with high status, used in formal situations and only learned through explicit education but most Moroccans in the Netherlands are unable to use this high status language. In daily communication it plays a minor role.

In the close-knit Turkish community in the Netherlands, on the other hand, Turkish is still very vital (cf. Eversteijn 2002, 2011). The unmarked mode among Dutch-Turkish bilinguals is the bilingual codeswitching mode, which is considered an in-group mode by its speakers and by (Dutch) outsiders; the latter often complain that they feel excluded in all-Turkish company, "because they speak Turkish all the time" (cf. Nortier and Dorleijn 2008). Moreover, by using Turkish, one shows one's Turkish identity and pride in being so. A final reason why (phonetic) elements from Moroccan languages are easily taken over by other groups is the fact that the Moroccan community is more open to outsiders than the Turkish community, and therefore, their way of speaking Dutch is more easily recognised and more admissible than the way Turks use Dutch. It is not surprising, then, that Moroccan elements play a more conspicuous role than Turkish elements in this Dutch multi-ethnolect, as may be inferred from the following conversation (Nortier and Dorleijn 2008: 133–134). M is a Moroccan girl (aged 16), I is the Dutch interviewer and T is a Turkish girl (aged 16):

(2) M: *[...] ik zou niet met een Turks eh groepje kunnen eh praten, [...] die praten ook alleen maar Turks, daar zou ik niet zo gauw bij willen zitten*
'[...] I wouldn't be able to talk with a Turkish group [...] they speak only Turkish, I wouldn't want to sit with them.'

I: *Want ze praten Turks dus dat is echt een belemmering voor jou*
'Since they talk Turkish, so that is a real hindrance for you.'

T: *Ja bij Marokkaans is dat niet zo, die praten gewoon echt Nederlands, daar kan je gewoon bij staan of zitten of wat dan ook. [...] ik heb echt nooit Marokkaanse meisjes gezien die Marokkaans praten, die lopen alleen maar Nederlands te praten*

'Yes, that's not the case with Moroccans, they really speak Dutch, you can easily sit or stand with them or whatever […] I've never seen Moroccan girls who speak Moroccan, they go round speaking only Dutch.'

In some multi-ethnolects, elements from one (of several) contributing languages are predominant, as is the case with Moroccan elements in the above-mentioned Dutch multi-ethnolect. Similarly, Turkish is predominant in German multi-ethnolects (e.g. Dirim and Auer 2004). This may partly be due to the fact that speakers of such a language constitute a majority within the multi-ethnolect speaking group, but this is not necessarily the only factor. It is also likely that the speakers of the language that predominantly provides ethnic elements have a certain covert prestige compared to other ethnic groups. For example, in the Netherlands, respondents repeatedly have stated that "Moroccans are tough and Turks are dull" (own fieldnotes). One is tempted to assume that also intrinsic salient features of the pertinent languages may play a role. Again in the Netherlands, respondents have also repeatedly declared that the Moroccan accent is more 'fun' than other accents (Nortier and Dorleijn 2008: 136–137); M is a Moroccan girl (16), D is the Dutch interviewer, A is an Afghan (17) and T is a Turkish girl (16):

(3) M: *Het is algemeen bekend dat Marokkanen een beetje leuk, ja, een beetje leuk accent hebben.*
'It is generally known that Moroccans have a, yeah, a kind of funny accent.'

D: *Is dat omdat er meer Marokkanen zijn dan Turken?*
'Is that because there are more Moroccans than Turks?'

A: *Nee.*
'No.'

D: *Is dat zo? In Utrecht misschien wel.*
'Is that so? In Utrecht maybe there are?'

T: *Nee volgens mij niet, er zijn meer Turken!*
'No, I think there are more Turks!'

D: *Maken ze meer lawaai? Offe*
'Do they make more noise? Or uh'

T: *Ja, Marokkanen zijn meer aanwezig*
'Yes, Moroccans manifest themselves much more.'

M: *Nee, maar 't accent valt gewoon heel erg op. Ik gga naar šgool, ik denk van hallo! Dat merk je gewoon heel sterk.*
'No, but the accent is striking. 'I am going to school' [said with multi-ethnolect-pronunciation], then I think hello! That is something you just notice very strongly.'

An example of the saliency of a Moroccan accent is the popular Dutch/Surinamese stand-up comedian Jörgen Raymann. In his TV show *Raymann is laat* ('Raymann is late') he plays with foreign accents in Dutch, not only Surinamese (his own background) but also Moroccan (as the Moroccan butcher Achmed[1]). He is popular among a broad audience which is not only Dutch but Surinamese and Moroccan as well, among others. Also Moroccan comedians like Salaheddine and Najib Amhali[2], who are both able to speak Dutch without a noticeable Moroccan accent, use this accent in an exaggerated way in their shows. In a hilarious scene, Salaheddine even teaches his Dutch audience how to speak with a Moroccan accent.[3] It is of course likely that saliency of linguistic features *does* play a role. The question in which way, exactly, these linguistic factors interact with social and sociolinguistic factors is an empirical question that is still waiting for a straightforward answer.

2.3. Variety, style, stylistic practice

Although this is not the place to discuss all intricacies that are associated with the concept of style versus the term variety, we must devote a few words to these terms, as they appear to be relevant for the definition of multi-ethnolect.

Quist (2008: 44) rightly remarks: "A 'lect' term like 'multiethnolect', implies a (more or less focused) set of linguistic features that separates it from a standard language or other 'lects'." However, the term multi-ethnolect as it is used in this chapter (and by Quist) is not something fixed or clear-cut. Although some obvious features can be pointed at, and although a lay audience would immediately be able to identify a multi-ethnolect as such, it is yet too early to speak of fixed, standardised varieties. A certain degree of conventionalisation is inevitable, though. After all, time (and of course the right social circumstances) are needed for a multi-ethnolect to develop into such a focused variety, and this type of ethnolect has the tendency to be ephemeral.

Another argument not to consider multi-ethnolects as independent varieties of standard languages is the fact that they are only used in particular circumstances and/or with particular interlocutors, as transpires from most of the work on this topic. They can be put on and taken off like a glove (Dorleijn and Nortier 2008). Therefore the term 'multi-ethnic style' would have been more appropriate in this respect. 'Style' or 'linguistic style' is a complicated topic in which several dimensions play a role (cf. Rickford and Eckert 2001; Auer 2007; Coupland 2007; Keim 2008; Quist 2008). What concerns us here is that linguistic style can be mobilised by speakers in the appropriate situation, and can be associated with specific situations and/or interlocutors, and/or specific interaction types. Style, a "clustering of linguistic resources and an association of that clustering with social meaning" (as defined in Eckert 2001), implies some agentivity by the speaker, something one *does*, rather than something one *is*. As has been reported by numerous researchers on the topic, metalinguistic awareness among speakers of multi-ethnolects is high (see for example Svendsen and Røyneland 2008): the use of multi-ethnolects is a deliberate choice.

2.4. Mechanisms of interference

Thomason (2001, 2004) has proposed seven mechanisms of interference that have been at work in contact varieties. With multi-ethnolects, we are dealing with linguistic contact in action, so it is an ideal locus to see which of these interference mechanisms do play a role, and how. The first and second of Thomason's mechanisms are codeswitching and code alternation, the difference being that codeswitching may take place in the same conversation with the same speaker, while in code alternation, speakers use "one of their languages in one set of environments and the other language in a completely different set of environments" (Thomason 2001: 136). These two mechanisms do not seem to play an important role in the formation of multi-ethnolects. Of course, in multi-ethnolects single words (typically tags, discourse particles and formulaic expressions) from several languages may be inserted by speakers from diverse linguistic backgrounds. Typical is the use of *wallah* 'I swear' (literally: 'to Allah'; originally Arabic but also used by speakers of other languages such as Turkish, for whom Islam plays a role), cf. the example below, taken from Quist (2008: 47):

(4) A: *Jeg så Sabrina i dag*
'I saw Sabrina today'

M: *Wallah?*

A: *Ude foran bussen*
'next to the bus'

M: *Wallah?*

A: *Wallah*

However, this does not fit in the definition of codeswitching and code alternation, as not all users of a multi- ethnolect are bilingual, and the two mechanisms are mainly used by and among bilinguals.

The third mechanism that Thomason proposes is passive familiarity: adopting features from a language one understands but never speaks. Thomason notes that "[…] Perhaps the most common type of situation in which passive familiarity is a significant mechanism of structural interference is in a shift situation when some features are adopted by original target-language speakers from the version of the target language (i.e. the TL2) spoken by members of the shifting group" (2001: 141–142). This seems to be the case with the users of multi-ethnolects as well. But what Thomason implies is that this mechanism would operate below the level of consciousness of the speakers and without the intention of social meaning. Multi-ethnolect users, however, though using words from languages they never speak as such, do this deliberately, and there is social meaning attached to it as well. Thomason (2001: 145) mentions the use of AAVE-elements in the prison slang of White inmates in the State Correctional Institution of Pittsburgh as an example. The situation there is comparable to what is going on in multi-ethnolects, where linguistic features that don't 'belong' to the speakers are adopted in the act of crossing. However, this example differs widely from the other examples she gives for this mechanism, so this sort of phenomenon could be classified as stylisation rather than as passive familiarity, since the latter does not seem to imply something like deliberate action of the speaker.

The fourth mechanism (negotiation) is not relevant here in the sense Thomason uses it, that is as strategies employed by the speakers in order to attain a better understanding of each other, also known as convergent strategies. According to Thomason, this is typically a mechanism to make communication more effective, to meet communicative needs. However, as will be shown below, one of the functions of multi-ethnolects is to express social meaning, not to facilitate the expression of referential meaning.

The fifth mechanism Thomason proposes is second-language acquisition strategies. For multi-ethnolect speakers in general this is not a central mechanism. However, interlanguage features often do play a role in the creation of multi-ethnolects. In many ethnolects it is observed that typical interlanguage features become stylised, exaggerated and stereotyped to form an integral part of a multi-ethnolect (cf. Cornips 2008; and below). For the same obvious reasons, the role of Thomason's sixth mechanism, bilingual first-language acquisition, can be ignored here, too.

The seventh mechanism, however, "deliberate decision", is an important mechanism in the creation of multi-ethnolects. In fact, most linguistic characteristics seem to be based on this mechanism. "Sometimes a group of people will deliberately change their language in order to differentiate it more sharply from those of neighbour communities" (Thomason 2001: 150). In the case of multi-ethnolects, this mechanism is applied by the groups under consideration, in order to differentiate themselves from the mainstream society.

Several ways in which languages can deliberately be manipulated have been attested in the literature. Mous (2003: 222–223) lists a range of strategies that are used in lexical manipulation, which is often encountered, as Mous suggests, in certain registers within a language: respect, taboo, secret languages, etc.; in short, wherever "[...] people are conscious about which form of the paralexis they are using [...] decisions as to which form to use are probably always conscious and functional" (Mous 2003: 218). Among the strategies Mous lists, borrowing and word-inversion seem to be important strategies in multi-ethnolects. Word inversion is a much-encountered strategy in ludlings and secret languages, but is also attested in multi-ethnolects like Verlan, Bahasa Gaul and Bahasa Prokem (see discussions and references in section 3 below). The borrowing of words is a very common strategy in multi-ethnolects. This is particularly true for words that structure a conversation (discourse particles, tags) or the whole communicative situation (greetings, formulaic expressions) as well as 'taboo' words. Interestingly, also the deliberate insertion of function words is attested. One respondent told us that it is common to insert the Arabic numeral and indefinite article *wahed* 'one' instead of Dutch *een*, because, as he told us in a metalinguistic interview, inserting content words is easy and no fun, inserting function words is more of a challenge (unpublished fieldnotes of the authors)[4].

There are also reports of the manipulation of grammatical elements (mostly stereotyped L2 'mistakes') in a number of Western European ethnolects (cf. Nortier and Dorleijn 2008). The following is a fragment from the metalinguistic interview mentioned above; R is the respondent and I is the interviewer.

(5) R: *Dat is het slechte Nederlands*
 'That is the bad kind of Dutch.'

 I: *En heeft dat ook een naam?*
 'Does it have a name?'

R: *Ja, niet echt, maar 't is in principe dan eh lidwoorden die gebruik je dan expres verkeerd.*
'Yes, not really, but in principle you uhm just use the articles deliberately in the wrong way.'

I: *Ja, ja, die gebruik je dan exprès verkeerd, net als –*
'Right! So you use them in the wrong way deliberately? Just like –'

R: *Ja dus*
'Yes, like'

I: *Die meisje*
'That girl [*dat meisje* in standard Dutch – neuter demonstrative pronoun].'

R: *Die huis zeg ik dan. Terwijl ik weet ik bedoel ik weet heus wel dat het dat huis is, maar 't staat zo dom als ik dat op straat zeg, als ik zeg*
'I would say that house [*dat huis* in standard Dutch]. At the same time I know, I mean, I am very well aware of the fact that it should actually be *dat huis*, but it would make a stupid impression if I would say...' [*dat* is neuter demonstrative pronoun]

I: *Ja*
'Yes'

R: *Als ik zeg dat huis*
'If I say *dat huis*'

I: *Jaja*
'Yes, yes'

R: *'t Is gewoon die huis* [*die* is common gender demonstrative pronoun]. *Maar als ik met jullie spreek dan wordt 't gewoon dat huis.*
'It is just *die huis*. But when I speak with you [the authors – both Dutch and middle-aged] it is just *dat huis*.'

Other important deliberate strategies are concerned with pronunciation, intonation and prosody. Metalinguistic awareness about these features is very high among the users of multi-ethnolects where these play a role, cf. the following (Norwegian) metalinguistic data taken from Svendsen and Røyneland (2008: 72):

(6) *hissig (.) jeg veit ikke på tonefall og lik som trykket på orda det virker mye mer hissig* (Thomas)
'Aggressive (.) I don't know in intonation and like the stress on the words it sounds a lot more aggressive.'

(7) *tonefall fra arabisk og ting og tang* (Anders)
'intonation from Arabic and stuff'

(8) *det blir litt sånn annet tonefall* (Maia)
'It's kind of a different intonation.'

(9) *du får veldig mye sats da (.) i ordene (1.0) her nede så får du stort sett sats i alle ordene [...] det blir mye mer trykket ned da* (Ummar)
'You get a lot of force/stress (.) in the words (1.0) down here you get force/stress in all the words [...] it's more squeezed down.'

The last part of example (3) above, repeated as (10) here, is an illustration of the saliency of a Moroccan accent in Dutch, of which the (Moroccan background) speaker is well aware:

(10) *Nee, maar 't accent valt gewoon heel erg op. Ik gga naar šgool, ik denk van hallo! Dat merk je gewoon heel sterk.*
'No, but the accent is striking. 'I am going to school' [said with multi-ethnolect-pronunciation] Then I think hello! That is something you just notice very strongly.'

To summarise, linguistic features of multi-ethnolects consist of exaggerated and consciously stereotyped interlanguage features (grammatical structures, pronunciation, prosodic features), of insertions of formulaic expressions, greetings, discourse particles, all kinds of interjections, sometimes (taboo) content words and even occasionally function words from diverse linguistic sources that are not necessarily one's own ('crossing', cf. section 2.1). In some multi-ethnolects also word reversion is attested. These characteristics are (mainly) the result of conscious agentivity by multi-ethnolect users, and they always carry social meaning.

2.5. Functions of multi-ethnolects

The main characteristic of multi-ethnolects is that their function is confined to in-group communication. It is a style, actively brought about by the speakers. It is used to index social identities rather than to express the 'collective' identity (ethnicity, gender, class, etc.). The use of a multi-ethnolect is a continuous act of identity, a way of seeking a position within the in-group and towards consolidating in-group solidarity versus the out-group. Interestingly, in the literature it is reported that the kind of social identity that users of multi-ethnolects wish to convey is fairly universally a tough, 'gang-like', 'street' identity. It is generally associated with other non-linguistic stylisation, like clothing, musical preference, etc. On the level of in-group interaction, multi-ethnolects are often observed to perform the specific function of playfully joking around. It has been noticed in earlier research that on the intra-conversational level multi-ethnolect use may be topic-related (Nortier 2001; Cornips and Reizevoort 2006; Cornips and De Rooij 2003). The task of the researcher, then, is not so much oriented toward description of the linguistic structural properties themselves of the multi-ethnolects, but to describe and find universals in the way these are mobilised to symbolically express these identities.

2.6. Multi-ethnolects redefined

In the light of the discussion above, we may expand the definition of multi-ethnolect now, to include not only linguistic and macro-sociolinguistic aspects, but also the aspects that are perhaps the most crucial: the way it is created and the functions it has.

> *A multi-ethnolect is a linguistic style that is part of linguistic practices of speakers of more than two different ethnic and (by consequence) linguistic backgrounds, and contains features from more than one language, but has one clear lexical and grammatical base language, generally the dominant language of the society where the multi-ethnolect is in use. It is largely the result of the conscious agentivity of its users, and it has the function to index social identities.*

We will now turn to a selection of studies on multi-ethnolects.

3. Research on multi-ethnolects: a selection

Over the past few decades an increasing number of studies on multi-ethnolects has been published. Some work on multi-ethnolects will be presented below to illustrate the development of this relatively young field. Of course we don't pretend to be giving a complete list; the overview is far from exhaustive.

Although there are huge differences between the studies, they have a lot in common as well. In the first place they concentrate mostly on young people in urban areas, which as discussed above, is a typical situation in which multi-ethnolects emerge. The studies presented below all stress the young people's basic need to express and often even construct identity through the use of non-native linguistic elements. They also stress that language is just one way to express identity and in order to fully understand the role language plays, it is necessary to adopt a holistic view in which not only language but all aspects of communication are included, such as body language, clothing or music style. Everybody has a repertoire of identities, not just one. Among friends and peers, the identity is different from the one at school, at work, or at home among family members.

In all studies mentioned, elements from the language or variety spoken by immigrant groups, often stigmatised and with strong covert prestige, are appropriated and used by young speakers of other varieties, including mainstream and high prestige varieties. Judging from studies that have appeared on the topic, the conclusion could be drawn that multi-ethnolects emerge only in the Western world (cf. also the discussion above). However, the emergence and use of multi-ethnolects is a global phenomenon. In the following, we will pay relatively more attention to the few non-Western European studies we are aware of. However, there is an increasing interest in the field and more studies may have appeared by the time the present book is published.

Although we have more or less clearly defined what a multi-ethnolect is, we will not strictly adhere to this definition in our (rather arbitrary) choice from the literature. Some of the varieties studied may be ethnolects rather than multi-ethnolects (cf. the discussion in section 2). The reason why we include them here is that they all are concerned with questions of identity in ethnically mixed peer groups, where members adopt elements from each other's languages which in their turn are used to express this identity. Finally, it should be noted that the works mentioned may be using a term other than 'multi-ethnolect'.

3.1. United Kingdom

In his book from 1986, Hewitt describes the relationships and interracial friendships between Black and White adolescents in the Southwest of London. He focuses on the sociolinguistic impact of London Jamaican Creole on both Black and White adolescent speakers. The use of Creole in English is not standardised; there is no 'average number' of Creole elements in English (cf. also Sebba 1997). This is typical for all multi-ethnolects discussed below.

As mentioned previously, Rampton introduced the term 'crossing' in his (1995) book. It is one of the most influential publications in the field of multi-ethnolects. Crossing refers to language sharing and exchange in order to overcome race stratification, thus constructing a new dimension of mixed youth, class and neighbourhood or group community. The phenomenon is illustrated by describing communication and friendship between Panjabi, Afro-Caribbean and English speaking youth. Example (11), a fragment from a 1987 interview (Rampton 1995: 41), illustrates this. Mohan and Jagdish are Indian males aged 15, talking about interactions with Black peers. '*Raas klaat*' is a term of abuse in Creole [simplified transcription].

(11) Mohan: *we sometimes we just say you're a 'raas klaat' and all this*
Jagdish: *yeh yeh stuff like that... they even know some Panjabi words as well*

In more recent work, Kerswill, Khan and Torgersen (2008) demonstrate that London is the source of innovation in British English speech. Linguistic innovation was found among young inner-city non-Anglo speakers specifically and among inner-city speakers with dense multi-ethnic friendship networks generally. They thoroughly studied phonetic and phonological aspects. Their conclusion is that the continued use of certain characteristic features into adulthood is the key to understanding the influence of multicultural speech on British speech more generally (Kerswill, Khan and Torgersen 2008).

3.2. Belgium

Stefania Marzo is currently conducting a study on Citétaal 'City language', which is used by young people in the former ghettoised mining areas in Belgium. It is characterised by typical ethnolectal features such as morphological overgeneralisation and borrowing. Like in the Dutch, German and Scandinavian forms of multi-ethnolects (see below), common gender is overused, at the cost of neuter. Quite consistently /s/ is pronounced [ʃ]: <stijl> /stɛjl/ sounds like [ʃtɛjl] 'style'.

Since the first and largest group of guest workers who migrated to the Belgian mining areas were Italians, there is still a relatively great Italian influence in this *smeltkroestaal* 'melting pot language', which is mainly used in the old Flemish-speaking mining areas in the eastern part of the country. The influence is recognisable on the intonational and lexical levels in particular. An example is the verb *scasseren* 'to irritate, to tell lies', which is based on Italian *scassare* 'destroy' and used as in the following fragment (Ramaekers 1998):

(12) A: *Ik ga trouwen*
'I am going to marry'

B: *Scasseer niet!*
'Don't tell lies!'

This variety is used by young people, both with immigrant and non-immigrant background. According to the people who use it, Citétaal is not used in order to be tough and cool but just for fun and to create a sense of togetherness (Marzo 2005, 2008).

Further to the west, a multi-ethnolectal youth variety has been studied in Antwerp, also a Flemish-speaking area. Jaspers (2008) reports on young immigrants of Moroccan descent who are aware of the stereotypical image of the Moroccan who has a poor command of Dutch, as in the following example (Jaspers 2008: 98–99).

(13) Jamal: *[...] da's nie Marokkaans, die spreekt gewoon Vlaams maar met fouten d'r in*
'[...] that's not Moroccan, he just speaks Flemish but with mistakes in it.'

Imran: *wij spreken zo nie*
'We don't talk like that.'

Jamal: *(die spreekt) me fouten wij helemaal nie*
'(He speaks) with mistakes we not at all'

Imran: *toen wij in 't lagere school zaten okee t-toen, toen misschien toen spraken wij toen spreken wij misschien zo van die rare, raar accent en dan onthouden die da [...]*
'When we were in primary school okay t-then, then maybe then we spoke then we spoke perhaps like a strange, strange accent and then uh they remember that [...]'

They play with this belief and use the 'poor' accent in front of native speakers of Dutch but at the same they also use versions of the local Antwerp dialect to establish their identity.

In his article, Jaspers (2008) also gives a critical discussion of the term ethnolect.

3.3. United States

Just like Jaspers, Eckert (2008) criticises the use of the term ethnolect. She discusses the role of ethnicity in the construction of a peer-based social order among pre-adolescents in California. She shows that the Chicano pattern does not simply index ethnicity, but also the place in the peer-based social order, regardless of ethnicity.

On the East coast, multi-ethnolects are found as well. We mention here the work by Cutler (1999), who described the use of AAVE by a White boy in New York, who grew up in a White neighbourhood and had White friends. Black culture was supposed to represent a forbidden narrative and a symbol of rebellion.

In 2008, Cutler focused on immigrants from Eastern European countries in New York City, who feel strongly affiliated with hip-hop culture. This is expressed through stylisation and use of characteristics from hip-hop culture, which sets them apart from their compatriots, who wish to identify with the White mainstream language and culture. In the following example from Cutler (2008: 15), an 18-year-old Bulgarian who emigrated to the US at age eight uses characteristics of African American English:

(14) *She is PISSIN' me off! All the shit she's sayin'. I [aː] feel like smackin' 'em. I'm like "Ø you stupid? Do you hear what you're (r-Ø) saying"? (..) She Ø mad racist! (...)*

In (14), typical AAVE features are monophthongal [a] instead of /aɪ/; /r/-lessness, Ø-copula and the use of *mad* as an intensifier.

3.4. Sweden

Ulla-Britt Kotsinas described Rinkeby-Svenska in Sweden (Kotsinas 1988, 1992, 1998). This variety was observed in Rinkeby, a suburb of Stockholm, with a predominantly immigrant population. It is characterised by the use of a deviant grammar and pronunciation of Swedish and by the use of elements from minority languages. Originally it was used by immigrant youth, though it is spreading now; Kotsinas observed the phenomenon in Swedish used by second-generation speakers, born in Sweden.

From the early eighties onwards, she has published about the use of elements from minority languages in majority varieties. Besides lexical elements, she also discusses the restricting and expanding characteristics on the grammatical level of Rinkeby-Svenska. The most striking characteristic on the phonological level is prosody, "[…] which is often described as 'choppy' or 'uneven' by the speakers themselves. Exactly what it is that gives this impression cannot easily be analyzed. One explanation may be the non-occurrence or smaller frequency of certain reductions and assimilations common in native spoken Swedish, another may be slight changes of vowel length" (Kotsinas 1998: 136).

As in other languages with a grammatical gender distinction, e.g. Dutch, Norwegian or Danish, the common gender is often overgeneralised and also used for neuter words: *en bord* is used instead of *ett bord* 'a table'. Also "[v]ery frequent is the replacement of the inverted word order by a SV order in sentences with a topicalized short temporal or locative adverbial, e.g. *igår jag var sjuk* 'yesterday I was ill' (correct in English but not in Swedish)" (Kotsinas 1998: 137). These are examples of simplification, but there are also expanding processes such as the incorporation of new words that find their origins in immigrant languages. Examples are *chok* (*çok*) 'very, much', *güsel* (*güzel*) 'nice' from Turkish, or *tjora* 'steal' from Romani.

Research on Rinkeby-Svenska, begun by Kotsinas, has expanded to other geographical areas such as Göteborg and Malmö, and nowadays Swedish multi-ethnolects are studied often in close cooperation with researchers from the other Scandinavian countries (Fraurud 2004; Fraurud and Bijvoet 2004; Bodén 2004).

3.5. Denmark

Pia Quist published work on multi-ethnolectal Copenhagen. In Quist (2008), she presents two perspectives: one is a variety approach, and the other one is a stylistic approach where the multi-ethnolect is seen as part of a range of stylistic repertoires in a local community of practice. Examples to illustrate the variety approach resemble the Swedish Rinkeby-Svenska examples above, e.g. the SV order is used in sentences that require inversion in Danish (Quist 2008: 47):

(15) *når man er i puberteten man tænker mere*
'When one is in puberty one thinks more' (instead of standard Danish *tænker man* 'thinks one')

According to Quist, only a holistic view in which a variationist and stylistic analysis are combined can help us to understand the multi-ethnolect.

The multi-ethnolect she describes is not to be seen as a secret code. The use of it is not restricted to speakers of Danish as a second language only; native Danish adolescents also use it.

Jørgensen published on multilingual youth groups (2001) and 'polylingualism' among urban youth in Denmark (Jørgensen 2008). Polylingualism is defined as follows (Jørgensen 2008: 143): "Language users employ whatever linguistic features are at their disposal to achieve their communicative aims as best as they can, regardless of how well they know the involved languages; this entails that the languages users may know – and use – the fact that some of the features are perceived by some speakers as not belonging together."

Quist and Møller (2003) present an overview of the study of youth language in Denmark.

3.6. Norway

Svendsen and Røyneland (2008) describe characteristics of the multi-ethnolect used in Oslo, Norway, by migrants and indigenous Norwegians. They draw parallels with comparable phenomena in the other Scandinavian countries. Like Kotsinas (1998), they (and their informants) observe characteristics on the level of prosody, as quoted in example (16) below (Svendsen and Røyneland 2008: 72):

(16) *eller så høres det ut som de går rundt og er forbanna konstant [...] blir så hardt [...] [tonen, trykket] helt feil*
'Or it sounds like they are constantly angry [...] it's so harsh [...] [tone, stress] all wrong'.

Like in the other Scandinavian languages, deviant syntactic patterns that are characteristic in interlanguages are also observed in language use by native speakers (Svendsen and Røyneland 2008: 75):

(17) *hvis en av oss vinner vi deler halvparten*
'If one of us wins we split half.' (standard Norwegian *deler vi*).

Aarsæther (2010) observes that the majority of the multi-ethnolect-speaking adolescents in his study carried out in Oslo consider the use of multi-ethnic youth language an optional linguistic practice. He observes that there seems to be a link between ethnicity and the use of multi-ethnic youth language, but its use is not restricted to adolescents with an immigrant background. It is also used by adolescents with a Norwegian background (especially by girls who wish to create a contrast to the 'posh'

West End of the city), to construct an identity as a young 'Eastender' in Oslo.

3.7. Germany

Several publications have been written on the emergence of multi-ethnolects in German cities. In all cases, Turkish plays a crucial role. We mention here the work by Dirim and Auer (2004), who describe young people in Hamburg who learn and use Turkish together with German. These young people do not necessarily have a Turkish background.

Keim (2008) writes about 'power girls' in Mannheim, young female immigrants with a Turkish background who revolted against both traditional Turkish and German norms. Beside a preference for certain clothes and behaviour, specific communication patterns are part of the 'power girl' identity. Both Turkish and German play an essential role, which makes this more a codemixed variety than a multi-ethnolect.

Deppermann (2007) discusses Türkendeutsch or Kanaksprak, which is developed and used by second and third generation immigrants, predominantly male. What they have in common with Keim's 'power girls' is that they rebel against German mainstream society and the values it represents, and at the same time refuse to continue their parents' life style as well. However, the variety they use is German in the first instance (i.e. German is the main lexifier language). Originally, *Kanake* refers to the indigenous population of Polynesia, but in modern German the meaning has a negative connotation ('nitwit'). Nowadays, *Kanake* is a pejorative term, used for people with foreign, southern looks. The difference to Turkish/German 'power girls' is that Kanaksprak is not only used by speakers of Turkish origin, but also by Germans, Romanies, Moroccans, Egyptians, etc. Characteristics of Kanaksprak are found on all linguistic levels: phonetically, e.g., sometimes the umlaut is omitted as in *grunst* instead of *grünst* ('gets green'); <ch> (/x/) is coronalised and becomes [ʃ]: *ich* is pronounced [iʃ] <isch> (as in many non-standard varieties of German). Word order patterns are different in Kanaksprak as in the following example:

(18) *hab isch gekauft neue BMW*
 'I bought a new BMW.' (Standard German: *ich habe einen neuen BMW gekauft*)

According to Androutsopoulos (1998), adverbials *voll* 'full', *echt* 'real'. *Scheiß* 'shit' etc. belong to German youth slang. They are also used in Kanaksprak. They use highly ritualised opening/greeting formulae such as *was geht – was geht* 'what's up?'. (Examples from Deppermann 2007: 329). Freidank (2001) is a parody on Kanaksprak.

3.8.   The Netherlands

In the Netherlands, the first serious article about an urban youth variety was Appel (1999), where he showed that young people from several ethnic backgrounds use Straattaal 'street language'. The variety is characterised by the use of lexical elements from minority languages, and its use is restricted to informal communication settings. There seems to be a strong preference for words from Surinamese (Sranan) in this Amsterdam variety. Appel (1999) presents some frequently used Straattaal words with their translation, in a somewhat simplified version in Table 1.

Table 1.   Some words in Straattaal, and their origin.

Straattaal word	Origin
duku	money (Surinamese)
lusu	gone (Surinamese)
chick(ie)	girl (English)
osso	house (Surinamese)
afoe	(last) part (Surinamese)
faja	fire (N), now meaning 'very, dirty' (Adv, Adj) (Surinamese)
fittie	fight (Surinamese)
kill	guy (Surinamese)
fatoe	joke (Surinamese)
tata	Dutch person (Surinamese)

These are all common day-to-day words. They often have multiple meanings, such as *afoe* 'a part', 'a half', 'a cigarette that has been smoked partly', 'the last part of a cigarette', or 'a puff'.

In 2001, Nortier published a book on two varieties: Murks and Straattaal, the former being an accent used mainly by mono-ethnic Dutch-speaking groups, who jokingly imitate immigrant peers; the latter, characterised by non-native lexical elements, is used predominantly in multi-ethnic peer groups (Nortier 2001).

Nortier and Dorleijn (2008) found that in order to express identity, the use of a Moroccan accent is spreading among young people with not only Moroccan but also Dutch, Turkish, Greek and many more ethnic backgrounds. The authors showed that the accent is used whenever the speakers find it suitable to express a certain identity and that it can be stressed or exaggerated if necessary. A quote from Nortier and Dorleijn (2008: 138) underlines this statement:

(19) *Nederlandse taal klinkt gewoon niet, dat Marokkaans accent zorgt ervoor dat het "rap-achtig" wordt net als in de Bronx NY*
'Dutch just doesn't sound good, that Moroccan accent makes it sound more "rap-like" just like in the Bronx NY.'

The overgeneralisation of common gender is characteristic of multi-ethnolects in the Netherlands. Leonie Cornips (2008) asks the question whether this loss of grammatical gender distinction is the consequence of incomplete second language acquisition only, or an active act of identity. Cornips and de Rooij (2003) have published about a variety of Straattaal, which is used among young people with a Surinamese background. In Cornips and de Rooij (2003), specific attention is paid to the overgeneralisation of the common gender. In Cornips and Reizevoort (2006), interviews with some speakers of Straattaal are analysed, regarding, inter alia, the use of Straattaal, as in example (20):

(20) *[...] Hij gaat dus geen Straattaal praten met zijn moeder snap je? Maar [...] als een vriend van hem vraagt **eej hoe was scoro vandaag**? Hoe was het op school ja? Dan zegt ie **nooooh scoro was weri man** [...]*
'[...] So he is not going to talk Straattaal with his mother you see? But [...] if a friend of his asks *eej hoe was scoro vandaag*? How was school today yeah? Then he says *nooooh scoro was weri man* ['school was tough man'] [...]'

Ariën van Wijngaarden and Hanke van Buren are currently carrying out a project in which the use of Dutch by Turkish and Moroccan teenagers is investigated (van Wijngaarden 2008). The study aims to explore the roots of ethnolects, which result from the interaction between second language acquisition, multilingual language use, and in-group/out-group dynamics in urban settings. One of the research questions is whether there is any evidence of spread of ethnic varieties to peers outside of the ethnic group? If so, do 'uniquely' ethnolectal traits spread to peers outside the ethnic networks merely because of their 'covert prestige' or rather because they represent less marked options?

An example of the type of phenomenon studied are the pronominal adverbs. In standard Dutch, pronouns preceded by a preposition normally refer to an animate object, as in (21) and (22). To refer to inanimate objects, the neuter pronoun (e.g. *het*) is replaced by an R-word like *er*, as in (24).

The resulting combination (e.g. *ervan*) is traditionally called *pronominal adverb*:

(21) *Jan houdt van hem.* [masc, + animate]
'Jan loves him.'

(22) *Jan houdt van haar.* [fem, + animate]
'Jan loves her.'

(23) **Jan houdt van het.* [neut, – animate]
'Jan likes it.'

(24) *Jan houdt ervan.*
'Jan likes it.'

Although *ervan* in (24) is written as one word, pronominal adverbs are frequently split up, as in (25):

(25) *Jan houdt er niet van.*
'Jan doesn't like it.'

In the corpus, several instances of non-standard-like use of pronouns in prepositional phrases have been found. These include (i) the omission of *er*, (ii) inanimate pronouns preceded by prepositions, and (iii) deviations from standard Dutch with respect to splitting up pronominal adverbs. In the project, the possible 'roots' of these phenomena will be examined, including (but not necessarily limited to) substrates, second language acquisition and surrounding local non-standard varieties of Dutch.

In the Netherlands, Straattaal has gained the status of 'interesting curiosity' for some non-users. People who are aware of the existence of Straattaal have the image that they know what is going on in the big world. This attitude has led to a stream of word lists, TV programs, quizzes, etc. about Straattaal. There is even a TV commercial in which two grey-haired grandmothers are talking over a cup of coffee. They use Straattaal which is wholly unexpected for grandmothers, just like the topic of their conversation (driving too fast on a motor cycle)[5]. Every year Dutch television has a writing contest, the so-called Nationaal Dictee ('national dictation'), and a few years ago there was an alternative version in Straattaal. Recently, a list with signs in Dutch Sign Language for Straattaal words has been published on the Internet.[6]

3.9. France

With respect to Verlan in the suburbs of the major French cities, we refer to work by Doran (2000, 2004, 2010), who describes the use and structure of this variety of French in which characteristically words are used backwards, among other things. The word Verlan itself is an inversion of *l'envers*, 'backward'. Lexical elements are borrowed from Argot, Romani and other minority languages spoken in France. Other publications on Verlan include Lefkowitz (1989, 1991) and Sherzer (1976).

Verlan emerged among immigrant youth, but it is spreading rapidly through a broader group of young people all over the country. It has the characteristic of a secret language and its social status is low. Below is a poem in Verlan[7], with an explanation of the Verlan forms and a rough translation into English:

Table 2. A song in Verlan.

Verlan		English translation
J'neco ap La Marseillaise	*J'neco ap = je ne connais pas* *La Marseillaise =* French national anthem	I don't know La Marseillaise
Mais c'est ici que je mange mes fraises		But I belong here
Au deblé, j'suis céfran	*deblé = bled* *céfran = français*	Back home I am French
Et j'suis robeu en cefran	*robeu = beur* (Verlan for *arabe*) *cefran =* France	And here I am an Arab
Kéblo entre ici et là-bas	*kéblo = bloqué*	Blocked between here and there
Des fois j'ai envie de me séca	*séca = casser (ici j'ai envie de partir)*	Sometimes I feel like leaving
Mais c'est près d'Paris qu'j'ai grandi		But I grew up near Paris
Et l'Algérie j'l'ai tchav' quand j'étais p'tit	*tchav'* = left (Romani)	And I left Algeria when I was small
Alors où j'me vétrou?	*vétrou = trouve*	So where do I find myself?
J'me sens perdu, c'est chelou	*chelou = louche*	I feel lost, it is bizarre
Fierté d'être un djez à Paris	*un djez = un Algérien*	Proud of being an Algerian
Tous les soirs, c'est Allah que je prie.		Every night I pray to Allah.'

3.10. Africa

African cities are melting pots of cultures and ethnicities where a large variety of new urban varieties and multi-ethnolects have seen (and will see) the light. Here, we mention three studies: Slabbert (1994), Goyvaerts (1988), and Abdulaziz and Osinde (1997).

Slabbert (1994) describes the situation in Johannesburg where Tsotsitaal is spoken. This variety is originally used by Afrikaans-speaking Tswana. Tsotsitaal was used as a secret language by thieves and street gangs. Nowadays it is disappearing in favour of Isicamto, which in its turn is associated with a gang with a Zulu background. It has traces from Zulu, English, and a range of other languages. Isicamto started out as an urban youth language but is spreading now to other groups as well. In example (26), Afrikaans, English and Zulu are recognisable:

(26) *If u-roof-a i-bank ya-se-lokishi-ni u-ya-tabalaza?*
    'If you rob a bank in the townships, is that fighting for survival?'

The word *roof* has roots in Afrikaans (Dutch); from English we find *bank* and *lokishi* (from *location*), and *tabalaza* has its origins in Zulu (*zabalaza* 'struggle').

Goyvaerts (1988) wrote about the use of Indoubil in the major cities in Zaire. Indoubil emerged in the sixties in Kinshasa as a mix of Lingala, French and other European languages. In the beginning it was associated with criminal practices and drugs, later it developed into a more general youth variety. Musicians, traders and migrants helped to spread it to other parts of the country, where Swahili became the base language, instead of Lingala. Indoubil was only used among socially equal people, never in front of strangers, elderly people or superiors. It was used in places where many ethnic groups gather, the more heterogeneous the better the chances for Indoubil to be used. Indoubil was used to bridge ethnic gaps. Nowadays, Indoubil is being replaced by a newer version called Lingala ya Bayankee. Its function is comparable to the function of Indoubil. In the following example from Indoubil, elements from French and English can be traced[8]:

(27) mi-na-sikia   ni-ko   kao.   ni-go   o-mar   ku-sumba
     1SG-PRS-feel   1SG-LOC   KO   1SG-go to-market INF-buy
     finite   na   ni-go   ku-lakse   mu   ba-kotelete ya
     cigarettes and 1SG-go   INF-walk.around   LOC   PL-side   of
     kartum
     Khartoum
     'I'm feeling tired. I'm on my way to the market to buy some cigarettes and then I'm going to walk around for a while in the outskirts of town.'
     (Goyvaerts 1988: 238)

Kao is derived from French *K.O.*; *nigo* from English *I go*; *omar* from *au marché* 'at the market'; *kulakse* 'walk in a relaxed way' from French *se relaxer*; *bakotelete* from French *côtelette, côte*, 'side', 'outskirt'; and *Kartum* 'Khartoum' is the name for Bukavu in Indoubil.

Abdulaziz and Osinde (1997) describe the situation in Kenya. In the eastern part of the country, Sheng is used among young people, a mix of Swahili, English and some other local languages. Sheng started out in Nairobi about 30 years ago, and the first speakers were teenagers whose behaviour was so deviant that they were not accepted by mainstream society. It was a typical secret in-group language, not intelligible to outsiders. Nowadays it has spread to other school youth in the east as a means to distinguish themselves. English and some French are recognisable in example (28):

(28) *See you akina pass for mwa morrows in your wheels [...]*
     'Come for me tomorrow in your car [...].'

Mwa is related to French *moi* 'me, my'; *morrows* is from English 'tomorrow' and *wheels* is a pars pro toto for 'car'.

Engsh is the youth variety of the posh areas in Nairobi. The name Engsh is derived from Sheng by inversion. The main basis is English, besides other languages such as Swahili and other local languages. Engsh is associated with young well-to-do European immigrants, rich South-Africans and Asians, who wear fashionable clothes, go to discos, and can afford to smoke and drink. The speakers of Sheng are from lower social classes and they find Engsh speakers rather unattractive imitators. Both varieties are in a constant state of change. (Examples from African multi-ethnolects, Maarten Mous, p.c.).

3.11. Indonesia

Nancy Smith-Hefner (2007) described the use of Bahasa (language) Gaul in Jakarta, Indonesia. Originally, Gaul belonged to marginals and delinquents, but nowadays Gaul is more positively associated with social and economic upward mobility and an internationally oriented youth culture. Being Gaul goes hand in hand with the use of certain (often English) words. Someone who doesn't use those words cannot be considered Gaul. Gaul is not only used in in-group situations but also with adults or other people who are not assumed to share the same youth values. According to the author (Smith-Hefner 2007: 191),

> [...] Gaul style is fast, fluent and self-confident. It is achieved through prosody, intonation and gesture as well as pragmatics. *Kacihaan deh lho* 'too bad/what a pity' is said with a lispy, singsong falling/rising intonation and accompanied by an S-like movement traced in the air with the indexfinger moving downwards. The response, *biarin* 'leave it/whatever', is accompanied by a similar gesture, but moving upward. *So what gitu lho* 'who cares' and *Please deh, want to know* 'come on tell me', are also pronounced with a characteristically playful prosody, often accompanied by a shrug or laughter.

A variety spoken in Jakarta in the past is Bahasa Prokem (Chambert-Loir 1984). Contrary to Gaul, Prokem was an argot (a thieves' slang) and used to have strong negative connotations. It consisted of a few hundred words, the grammar and the rest of the vocabulary were Jakarta Indonesian. These words were not new words but duplicates of already existing words. One of the characteristics was that existing words were played with, they were inverted or *-ok-* was infixed in the middle of existing words. Thus *burung* 'bird' became *rubung* and the word *prokem* derives from *preman*, which in its turn derives from Dutch *vrijman* 'free man'. According to the author, Prokem was not a youth language in itself but served as one of its many sources.

3.12. Hong Kong

Jones (2008) explores the construction of social meaning among skateboarders in Hong Kong as an example of the ways global and local discourses interact in contemporary youth cultures. There are three aspects of Hong Kong skateboarders' discourse. The first is the interaction between global and local flows of discourse, not just in the language skaters use, but also in multimodal forms of the construction of meaning like music, fashion, skateboard stickers, and of course, the physical performance of skating itself. The second is the way various social groups interact around skateboarding in Hong Kong, where a diversity of individuals come together in order to produce a fertile environment for language crossing. Finally, it focuses on the way skateboarders in Hong Kong interact with their physical environment, the compositional and representational mode of skateboarding in which participants strategically appropriate aspects of time and space from their urban surroundings and impose their own socio-spatial rhythms upon them, a process of using time and space to both 're-write' the city and to compose their own socio-cultural identities within it.

4. Discussion

4.1. Spread

In some of the studies mentioned above, a variety that started out as a youth language has spread to other social and age groups as well. Isicamto in Johannesburg is an example, and Verlan in France is also spreading outside the suburbs where it was spoken originally. As far as we know, these varieties have not developed into native languages. They still fulfil a role in certain domains and circumstances, and they are not acquired as a first language by children. Multi-ethnolects do not necessarily spread outside the group where they were established, and varieties such as Verlan and Isicamto seem to be rather exceptional in that sense. Towards the end of this chapter we will return to the question of whether there are more differences or similarities between multi-ethnolects, or multi-ethnolects on the one hand, and other contact languages and varieties such as pidgins, creoles, mixed languages, mixed codes and interlanguages on the other.

4.2. Quantitative vs. qualitative approaches

Most older studies discussed here have used ethnographic and qualitative methods; large quantitative studies are exceptional. However, the interest in the field is increasing, and therefore the money available for larger projects, too. There are some larger quantitative studies currently being carried out, such as the one in Amsterdam/Nijmegen (Netherlands) and in several cities in the Scandinavian countries.

The studies by Kerswill, Khan and Torgersen (2008) in the UK and the Roots of Ethnolects project that is currently being carried out by Ariën van Wijngaarden and Hanke van Buren in the Netherlands (van Wijngaarden 2008), are typical exponents of the variationist tradition. In their work, structural analyses are more foregrounded than in work by other researchers. Of course, this does not mean that they close their eyes to identity matters, which in turn are central to other studies. They use quantitative methods to collect and analyse their data.

The Developmental Processes in Urban Linguistic Contexts (UPUS) project being carried out in Oslo[9] is both quantitative and qualitative in nature. In their study, the Norwegian researchers pay attention to both the (objective) distribution of linguistic features and the interpretation of (subjective) interviews about style and social categories in a broader sense than merely linguistic features.

One of the characteristics of multi-ethnolects is that they are subject to rapid change. What is fashionable this year or this month, may be outdated the next. If the aim of a study is to describe the situation, it may have changed before the data are analysed. There is a danger in quantitative studies in that respect: they are time-consuming. But if the aim is to find underlying linguistic mechanisms leading to the emergence of new varieties, the situation might be different.

We have noticed another danger which we, however, do not necessarily associate with a quantitative approach: By establishing exactly what a certain multi-ethnolect is, researchers actively create a standard that would not always have occurred in the natural situation. An example is Murks, in the Netherlands. A small group of (White) teenagers in the city of Utrecht used a non-native accent in informal in-group situations. Some of them called it Murks. For most of them, however, it did not have a name. After the publication of Nortier (2001) the label Murks spread and started to get used by people using the variety themselves. And even in 2009, Nortier was approached by the impresario of two well-known rappers, who said that the rappers would not use any Murks (which, they thought erroneously, was suggested by the author). Murks has acquired a sort of emblematic status, which it never had in the time that it was described for the first time.

Although most studies on multi-ethnolects are qualitative and focused on identity matters, we want to ask the question here whether research on multi-ethnolects should be based on qualitative in-depth ethnographic studies exclusively, or whether a combination with a more quantitative approach would give more insight. In the studies cited above, some linguistic features are quantified, but other relevant aspects would also benefit from a more quantitative approach. For example, how widespread is the use of multi-ethnolects? How many members of a certain age group within a certain geographic area use the multi-ethnolect, how many are aware of its mere existence? What is the relation between attitude and actual use of a multi-ethnolect in quantitative terms? What is the relation between membership of a certain subculture and the use of a multi-ethnolect? For example, in a study on the mixing of languages and cultures in Utrecht, carried out between 1998 and 2002 (Bennis et al. 2002) it was found that heavy metal fans are less inclined to use a multi-ethnolect than rappers and hip-hoppers. We do not know whether this is true for all members of these subgroups and how significant such memberships are in relation to the variety used.

4.3. Other questions

Some other questions that could be asked we have already dealt with in the studies mentioned above. These questions have to do with gender (Are the users of multi-ethnolects boys or girls? What is the distribution?), with social class and educational background. Such questions can be answered by conducting in-depth interviews but a more survey-like method may throw a new light on the phenomenon.

A recurrent question in the studies above has to do with standardisation. For the outside world, multi-ethnolects are ways of speaking that belong to 'the other'. A multi-ethnolect is often thought of as a separate language that can be learned: You speak it or you don't speak it. But in fact, the majority of multi-ethnolects should be considered as a colour or a flavour on top of a well-established base language. There is no such thing as a separate grammar, or a lexicon. Where does a multi-ethnolect begin? Is the use of a single word in a longer conversational setting enough to identify someone as a speaker of a multi-ethnolect? Do multi-ethnolectal words or features need to be used in every sentence? In the article about Bahasa Gaul (Smith-Hefner 2007), it was mentioned that for a speaker to be identified as a speaker of Gaul, a certain number of Gaul elements have to be used and recognised. How many features of a specific multi-ethnolect style cluster must speech contain in order to qualify as 'multi-ethnolect'?

The studies presented above are all concerned with oral language use. Multi-ethnolects in written form are not uncommon either (cf. Androutsopoulos 2006, among others). Dorleijn and Nortier (2009) have reported on written (multi-) ethnolects in Moroccan-Dutch and Turkish-Dutch bilingual Internet forum sites, as well.

4.4. Are multi-ethnolects urban phenomena?

The studies on multi-ethnolects are all carried out in urban contexts. In section 2 above we discussed why it is less obvious to find multi-ethnolects in rural areas (though they may be not entirely absent). Urbanisation is a global tendency. In cities worldwide people live close to each other, old physical ethnic boundaries may vanish and new boundaries emerge, along lines other than ethnicity, e.g., social class. Therefore, members of different ethnic groups may get in touch with each other, leading to all kinds of mixing, of which language is one. Therefore, the presence of members with different ethnic backgrounds, and the fact that they need to share the same physical space, distinguishes urban from rural areas, which are therefore more favourable for the development of multi-ethnolects.

There are places outside the cities where new ethnolects might develop, such as the Dutch centres where asylum seekers and refugees live before they are issued a residence permit or are sent back to their country of origin. In these centres, up to a few hundred people stay for anything from a few months to several years. We are not aware of any study where the emergence of typical asylum seekers varieties of Dutch or other varieties is described. Moreover, we are not sure whether such varieties could emerge at all, since proficiency in Dutch is low and the length of stay is too short for a new variety to develop. After their stay in such centres, people usually don't remain in the area but move to other parts of the country, depending on available work and housing.

Steurtjestaal takes an exceptional position. It arose in a place that superficially has a lot in common with the asylum seekers' centres in the Netherlands. This mixed language arose in an orphanage on the island of Java, Indonesia which was founded by "Pa" van der Steur in 1885. The orphans were called *Steurtjes* 'little Steurs', hence the name Steurtjestaal 'Steurtjes language'. They would stay in the orphanage for several years, five hundred children at a time. Steurtjestaal developed within a few years after the founding of the orphanage. According to van Rheeden (1998), who investigated Steurtjestaal, newly arrived orphans from all over Indonesia had to learn Steurtjestaal as soon as possible in order to be accepted as group members. The orphans typically had indigenous mothers who were abandoned by their partners, Dutch militaries.

Although both the orphanage and the Dutch asylum seekers' centres are places where people from a diversity of backgrounds live together for some time, this does not necessarily mean that a new language will emerge. The refugees don't have as much in common as the orphans in the orphanage, who shared a common background (Indonesian mothers, Dutch fathers) and language, with all orphans speaking some form of Malay, besides other languages.

5. The social and linguistic positioning of multi-ethnolects – a taxonomy of contact varieties

Finally, we want to address the question whether it is justified, from both a linguistic and a sociolinguistic perspective, to position multi-ethnolects among other forms of contact languages and varieties. In some respects, there are similarities with other, longer-established contact phenomena such as creoles and pidgins. In other respects, multi-ethnolects don't fit in. We will discuss this in more detail now. We want to stress that this discussion is a first attempt to include multi-ethnolects in a range of contact varieties and we hope that this will – at best – generate more discussion. In what follows, we will restrict ourselves to pidgins and creoles, mixed languages, interlanguages and codemixed varieties, since they seem at first glance to have the most in common with multi-ethnolects.

Multi-ethnolects do not emerge out of any form of communicative need, and in that sense they differ from pidgins and creoles. In the same vein, multi-ethnolects differ from interlanguages that are used by people who cannot otherwise make themselves understood. The members of ethnic groups who use a multi-ethnolect do not need it for their daily communication. After all, most multi-ethnolects are forms of a base language. This characteristic however they share with mixed languages such as Media Lengua, since both emerge from a desire of group members to express an identity to distinguish themselves from others. Code mixing or codeswitching (we won't go into the difference here) takes a middle position. It is not used out of communicative need. Sometimes bilinguals switch codes in order to distinguish themselves from other speakers. In those cases, codeswitching is marked. In unmarked cases, codeswitching or mixing is part of the normal communication patterns of a speech community (Myers-Scotton 1993).

Some contact languages are typically in-group phenomena and others are used between groups. Pidgins and interlanguages are used between members of different groups who are not otherwise able to communicate. Of course, this is strongly related to the reason why they emerged at all. If they developed out of a need to communicate with other groups, they will be used between groups. If they were born out of a need to establish identity, and the wish to be distinguished from others, the emerging variety is used within the group, 'against' outsiders. Mixed languages, multi-ethnolects and codemixed varieties are typically in-group phenomena.

Most types of contact languages are difficult to discuss in terms of standardisation. Compared to long-established official languages such as English or Portuguese, they allow a high degree of variation. Relative to each other, however, there are interesting differences. The term conventionalisation, rather than standardisation, is appropriate here, since there may be no standard but still some consensus about what belongs to a variety and what does not. Compared to pidgins, creoles are much more conventionalised, where conventionalisation should be seen as a continuum rather than an absolute presence or absence of conventionalisation (cf. chapters by Parkvall and Bakker, and Bartens in this volume). Although both mixed languages and codemixed varieties are based on (usually) two languages, the former are strongly conventionalised and the latter are not. The same is true for interlanguages, where the extent to which the interlanguage features belong to one or the other language may differ from speaker to speaker not only synchronically, but diachronically as well. In that sense, multi-ethnolects have more in common with codemixed varieties than with mixed languages or interlanguages.

Of all contact languages mentioned here, only creoles and mixed languages are known to be native languages, although there are exceptions to this rule. Multi-ethnolects are based on, or are even forms of, established languages that are first languages, though not necessarily for all speakers. In the African context, however, there are multi-ethnolects that have become native languages (e.g. Sheng) and we could ask ourselves whether they should still be called multi-ethnolects or perhaps considered other varieties, e.g. mixed languages. Bakker and Matras (2003) have described mixed languages that resemble the multi-ethnolects we have presented above. Instead of distinct categories, it would perhaps be better to assume a continuum where it is possible to distinguish prototypical mixed languages, multi-ethnolects, etc., as Bakker and Matras (2003) suggested in the introductory chapter of their book. It is exactly the status of this type of criteria we want to question here. Someone in the Netherlands, for example, may have learned Berber as a first language, acquired Dutch as a second language, and in addition uses a multi-ethnolect based on Dutch. Interlanguages are never first languages, per definition. In code mixing, usually one of the two languages involved is the native language.

The question whether multi-ethnolects can be distinguished from other contact languages on the basis of the number of languages they are based on, cannot be answered with a simple yes or no. Creoles and pidgins do not necessarily have a fixed number of base languages, that is languages they are directly derived from. The situation is clearer for mixed languages, although exceptions do occur: the most prototypical mixed languages are mainly built on two 'parent' languages, where one typically provides more lexical and the other more grammatical material. Codemixed varieties and interlanguages are based on two languages, although again exceptions are possible here, too. Multi-ethnolects as we know them from Western Europe and North America have one strong base language and an unspecified number of other languages that provide some lexical elements, some phonological and sometimes some grammatical features.

Another dimension on which multi-ethnolects can be related to other contact phenomena is the function of the varieties. Most pidgins are functionally restricted, and so are multi-ethnolects. They are only used in specific situations, under specific circumstances. In formal situations or e.g. in teacher-pupil communication, multi-ethnolects cannot be used, since they are typical low-status in-group varieties. Communication between teachers and pupils are instances of more formal between-group encounters. Other contact varieties such as mixed languages are also in-group varieties but they can be acquired as first languages. People who use mixed languages can be in touch with each other under all circumstances, theoretically – at home, at work, during leisure time – thus using their language for all possible functions. Multi-ethnolects only exist when peers are together, and not when individuals are at home with their families, or in class, for example. Codemixing may be used without any functional restriction, depending on the type of codeswitching (marked versus unmarked) and the degree of conventionalisation (and of course the obvious restriction of the interlocutor's needing to be familiar with the mixed code and/or the languages that contribute to it). Interlanguages are used without restrictions, other than the level of proficiency. For the users of interlanguages there is no other possible means of communication, which brings us to one of the earlier mentioned core differences between contact varieties. For some of them it can be stated that they are the only available means of communication. It seems that the most important dichotomy in contact varieties is exactly along this line of communicative vs. social need.

The similarities and differences between some contact varieties as they are discussed here are summarised in Table 3 below. Along some lines, multi-ethnolects share characteristics with pidgins, in other respects they have more in common with mixed languages, codemixed varieties or interlanguages. Surprisingly, codemixed varieties and multi-ethnolects share the most characteristics. There are more possible characteristics or parameters than we chose to use in Table 3. The discussion so far seems to justify the positioning of multi-ethnolects as contact varieties.

Table 3.   A comparison between six contact varieties.

	Pidgin	Creole	Mixed language	**Multi-ethnolect**	Code-mixing	Inter-language
Emerged from communicative need	yes	yes	no	**no**	no	yes
Emerged from need to distinguish from others	no	no	yes	**yes**	yes/no	no
Used for communication within or between groups	between	within	within	**within**	within	between
Conventionalised or standardised	yes/no	yes	yes	**no**	no	no
Native language (L1)	no	yes	yes	**no**	no	no
One single base language	no (several)	no (several)	no (two)	**yes**	no (two)	no?
Functionally restricted	yes	no	no	**yes**	no	no
Domain restricted	yes	no	no	**yes**	yes	no
Number of characteristics shared with multi-ethnolects	3 (4)	1	3	N/A	5 (6)	2

6.   Conclusion

Multi-ethnolects share a number of characteristics with some contact varieties, but differ most conspicuously from some others in that they are not yet a conventionalised variety and mostly ephemeral. As can be inferred from the literature discussed above, though, some multi-ethnolects are quite longstanding and even spreading outside the original group, such as some African varieties and French suburban Verlan. Others may vanish along with changing social circumstances, e.g. changing migration patterns, etc. As we observed above, one characteristic of a multi-ethnolect is that it contains linguistic elements from migrant languages from socially stigmatised communities (and is often a stigmatised linguistic style itself). As the pertinent groups merge with society and enter the process of social mobility, the multi-ethnolect will probably die out. This was the case with the use of a Surinamese ethnolect, which was highly stigmatised (and therefore had strong covert prestige) in the Netherlands in the 1970s. Multi-ethnolects constitute, however, a locus where language contact can be, as it were, 'caught red-handed', and may therefore shed light on which social, communicative, interactional patterns and processes are at work in the creation of contact varieties.

Notes

1. http://www.youtube.com/watch?v=dwjEAQBKzkI (accessed March 2011).
2. http://www.youtube.com/watch?v=gq9q2SMnKGQ (accessed March 2011).
3. http://www.youtube.com/watch?v=IpPb4Uj3v5c (at 3 minutes in) (accessed March 2011).
4. This informant was a member of the Moroccan community in Rotterdam, spent a lot of time outside with his friends and at the same time held an academic degree in Arabic. This combination allowed him to reflect on linguistic matters that he might not have been aware of without his academic background.
5. http://www.youtube.com/watch?v=Qp5R7Dx6krU (accessed April 2009).
6. https://veiligbetalen.gebarencentrum.nl/abowoordenboekflv2.asp (accessed Nov 2010).
7. http://www.didaweb.net/mediatori/articolo.php?id_vol=1354 (accessed Feb 2009).
8. The glossing to this example was added here following personal communication with the author Didier Goyvaerts.
9. http://www.hf.uio.no/iln/forskning/prosjekter/upus/ (accessed Jan 2013).

References

Aarsæther, Finn. 2010. The use of multiethnic youth language in Oslo. In Pia Quist & Bente Ailin Svendsen (eds.), *Multilingual Urban Scandinavia. New Linguistic Practices*, 111–126. Clevedon: Multilingual Matters.

Abdulaziz, Mohamed H. & Ken Osinde. 1997. Sheng and Engsh: Development of mixed codes among the urban youth in Kenya. *International Journal of the Sociology of Language* 125. 43–63.

Androutsopoulos, Jannis K. 1998. *Deutsche Jugendsprache*. Frankfurt am Main: Lang.

Androutsopoulos, Jannis K. 2006. Multilingualism, diaspora and the Internet: Codes and identities on German-based diaspora websites. *Journal of Sociolinguistics* 10(4). 520–547.

Appel, René. 1999. Straattaal. De mengtaal van jongeren in Amsterdam [Street language. The mixed language of young people in Amsterdam]. *Toegepaste Taalwetenschap in Artikelen* 62(2). 39–57.
Auer, Peter. 2007. Introduction. In Peter Auer (ed.), *Style and Social Identities. Alternative Approaches to Linguistic Heterogeneity*, 9–21. Berlin: Mouton de Gruyter.
Backus, Ad. 1996. *Two In One. Bilingual Speech of Turkish Immigrants in the Netherlands*. Tilburg: Tilburg University Press.
Bakker, Peter & Yaron Matras (eds.). 2003. *The Mixed Language Debate*. Berlin: Mouton de Gruyter.
Bennis, Hans, Guus Extra, Pieter Muysken & Jacomine Nortier (eds.). 2002. *Een Buurt in Beweging* [A dynamic neighbourhood]. Amsterdam: Aksant.
Bodén, Petra. 2004. A New Variety of Swedish? In Steve Cassidy, Felicity Cox, Robert Mannell & Sallyanne Palethorpe (eds.), *Proceedings of the 10th Australian International Conference on Speech Science and Technology*, 475–480. Sydney: Macquarie University.
Carlock, Elizabeth & Wolfgang Wölck. 1981. A method for isolating diagnostic linguistic variables: The Buffalo ethnolects experiment. In David Sankoff & Henrietta Cedergren (eds.), *Variation Omnibus*, 17–24. Edmonton: Linguistic Research.
Chambert-Loir, Henri. 1984. Those who speak Prokem. *Indonesia* 37. 105–118.
Cornips, Leonie. 2008. Loosing grammatical gender in Dutch: the result of bilingual acquisition and/or an act of identity? *International Journal of Bilingualism* 12(1–2). 105–124.
Cornips, Leonie & Birgit Reizevoort. 2006. Taal en identiteiten: de dynamische aspecten van een urbane jongerenvariëteit [Languages and identities: the dynamic aspects of an urban youth variety]. In Tom Koole, Jacomine Nortier & Bert Tahitu (eds.), *Artikelen van de Vijfde Sociolinguïstische Conferentie* [Papers of the Fifth Sociolinguistic Conference], 88–99. Delft: Eburon.
Cornips, Leonie & Vincent de Rooij. 2003. Kijk, Levi's is een goeie merk, maar toch hadden ze hem gedist van je schoenen doen em niet [Look, Levi's is ok but they had teased him like your shoes are no good]. In Jan Stroop (ed.), *Het Nederlands van Nu en Straks. Waar Gaat het Nederlands Naar Toe?* [Dutch now and later. What is Dutch going to be in the future?], 131–142. Amsterdam: Prometheus.
Coupland, Nick. 2007. *Style: Language Variation and Identity*. Cambridge: Cambridge University Press.
Cutler, Cecilia. 2003 [1999]. Yorkville crossing. In Roxy Harris & Ben Rampton (eds.), *The Language, Ethnicity and Race Reader*, 314–327. London: Routledge. (Originally in *Journal of Sociolinguistics* (1999) 3. 428–452.)
Cutler, Cecilia. 2008. Brooklyn style: Hip-hop markers and racial affiliation among European immigrants in New York City. *International Journal of Bilingualism* 12(1–2). 7–24.
Danesi, Marcel. 1985. A glossary of lectal terms for the description of language variation. *Language Problems and Language Planning* 89(2). 115–124.

Deppermann, Arnulf. 2007. Playing with the voice of the other: Stylized Kanaksprak in conversation among German adolescents. In Peter Auer (ed.), *Style and Social Identities. Alternative Approaches to Linguistic Heterogeneity*, 325–360. Berlin: Walter de Gruyter.

Dirim, İnci & Peter Auer. 2004. *Türkisch Sprechen Nicht Nur die Türken: Über die Unscharfe Beziehung Zwischen Sprache und Ethnie in Deutschland*. Berlin: Walter de Gruyter.

Doran, Meredith. 2000. Speaking Verlan: performing hybrid identity in suburbian Paris. Paper presented at the American Association of Applied Linguistics Conference, Vancouver, 11–14 March 2000.

Doran, Meredith. 2004. Negotiating between *Bourge* and *Racaille*: 'Verlan' as youth identity practice in suburban Paris. In Aneta Pavlenko & Adrian Blackledge (eds.), *Negotiation of Identities in Multilingual Contexts*, 93–124. Clevedon: Multilingual Matters.

Doran, Meredith. 2010. The value of Verlan: understanding street language in the French suburbs. Paper presented at the Sociolinguistics Symposium 18, Southampton, 3–5 September 2010.

Dorleijn, Margreet & Jacomine Nortier. 2006. Het Marokkaanse accent in het Nederlands: marker of indicator? [A Moroccan accent in Dutch: marker or indicator?]. In Tom Koole, Jacomine Nortier and Bert Tahitu (eds.), *Artikelen van de Vijfde Sociolinguïstische Conferentie* [Papers of the Fifth Sociolinguistic Conference], 138–148. Delft: Eburon.

Dorleijn, Margreet & Jacomine Nortier. 2008. The hand and the glove. Code and style as bilingual options among young people of Turkish and Moroccan descent in the Netherlands. In Jens Normann Jørgensen & Vally Lytra (eds.), *Multilingualism and Identities Across Contexts* (Copenhagen Studies on Bilingualism 45), 109–128. Copenhagen: University of Copenhagen, Faculty of Humanities.

Dorleijn, Margreet & Jacomine Nortier. 2009a. Van de hand en de handschoen: Code en stijl als tweetalige opties voor jongeren met een Turkse en Marokkaanse achtergrond [The hand and the glove. Code and style as bilingual options among young people of Turkish and Moroccan descent in the Netherlands]. In Ad Backus, Merel Keijzer, Ineke Vedder & Bert Weltens (eds.), *Artikelen van de Zesde Anéla-conferentie* [Papers of the Sixth Sociolinguistic Conference], 83–92. Delft: Eburon.

Dorleijn, Margreet & Jacomine Nortier. 2009b. Codeswitching on the internet. In Barbara E. Bullock & Almeida Jacqueline Toribio (eds.), *The Cambridge Handbook of Linguistic Code-switching*, 127–141. Cambridge: Cambridge University Press.

Eckert, Penelope. 2008. Where do ethnolects stop? *International Journal of Bilingualism* 12(1–2). 25–42.

Eversteijn, Nadia. 2002. 'We praten Turks over de zaktelefoon'. Processen van in- en uitsluiting door taalkeuze en code-wisseling onder Turkse jongeren ['We speak Turkish in our mobile phones'. Processes of in- and exclusion by language choice and code-switching among young Turks]. In, Hans Bennis, Guus Extra, Pieter Muysken & Jacomine Nortier (eds.), *Een Buurt in*

Beweging. Talen en Culturen in het Utrechtse Lombok en Transvaal [A dynamic neighbourhood. Languages and cultures in Utrecht's Lombok and Transvaal], 169–182. Amsterdam: Aksant.

Eversteijn, Nadia. 2011. 'All At Once'. Language Choice and Codeswitching by Turkish-Dutch Teenagers. Tilburg: Tilburg University dissertation.

Fought, Carmen. 2006. Ethnicity. In J. K. Chambers, Peter Trudgill & Natalie Schilling-Estes (eds.), The Handbook of Language Variation and Change, 444–472. Malden, MA: Blackwell.

Fraurud, Kari. 2004. Några sociolingvistiska förutsättningar för språklig variation och mångfald i Rinkeby [Some sociolinguistic conditions for linguistic variation and diversity in Rinkeby]. In Björn Melander (ed.), Svenskans Beskrivning [The description of Swedish], 25–47. Uppsala: Hallgren & Fallgren.

Fraurud, Kari & Ellen Bijvoet. 2004. Multietniska ungdomsspråk och andra varieteter av svenska flerspråkiga miljöer [Multiethnic youth languages and other varieties of Swedish in multilingual circles]. In Kenneth Hyltenstam & Inger Lindberg (eds.), Svenska som Andraspråk [Swedish as a second language], 389–419. Lund: Studentlitteratur.

Freidank, Michael. 2001. Kanakisch-Deutsch. Dem krassesten Sprakbuch übernhaupt. Frankfurt am Main: Eichborn.

Goyvaerts, Didier. 1988. Indoubil: A Swahili Hybrid in Bukavu. Language in Society 17. 231–242.

Hewitt, Roger. 1986. White Talk, Black Talk. Cambridge: Cambridge University Press.

Jaspers, Jürgen. 2008. Problematizing ethnolects: Naming linguistic practices in an Antwerp secondary school. International Journal of Bilingualism 12(1–2). 85–104.

Jones, Rodney Hale. 2008. Rewriting the city: Discourses of Hong Kong skateboarders. Paper presented at the Sociolinguistics Symposium 17, Amsterdam, April 3–5, 2008.

Jørgensen, Jens Normann. 2008. Polylingual languaging around and among children and adolescents. International Journal of Multilingualism 5(3). 161–176.

Jørgensen, Jens Normann (ed.). 2001. Multilingual Behavior in Youth Groups (Copenhagen Studies in Bilingualism, The Køge Series, Vol. K11). Copenhagen: Danish University of Education.

Keim, Imken. 2008. Linguistic variation, style of communication, and social identity: case study of a migrant youth group in Mannheim, Germany. In Jens Normann Jørgensen & Vally Lytra (eds.), Multilingualism and Identities Across Contexts (Copenhagen Studies on Bilingualism 45), 178–226. Copenhagen: University of Copenhagen, Faculty of Humanities.

Kerswill, Paul, Arfaan Khan & Eivind Torgersen. 2008. Multicultural London English and linguistic innovation. Paper presented at the Sociolinguistics Symposium 17, Amsterdam, April 3–5, 2008.

Kießling, Roland & Maarten Mous. 2004. Urban youth languages in Africa. Anthropological Linguistics 46(3). 303–341.

Kotsinas, Ulla-Britt. 1988. Immigrant children's Swedish – a new variety? *Journal of Multilingual and Multicultural Development* 9(1–2). 129–140.
Kotsinas, Ulla-Britt. 1992. Immigrant adolescents. Swedish in multicultural areas. In Cecilia Palmgren, Karin Lövgren & Göran Bolin (eds.), *Ethnicity in Youth Culture* (Youth Culture at Stockholm University), 43–62. Stockholm: University of Stockholm.
Kotsinas, Ulla-Britt. 1998. Language contact in Rinkeby, an immigrant suburb. In Jannis Androutsopoulos & Anno Scholz (eds.), *Jugendsprache, Langue des Jeunes, Youth Language*, 125–148. Frankfurt am Main: Peter Lang.
Labov, William. 1972. *Language in the Inner City: Studies in the Black English Vernacular*. Philadelphia: University of Pennsylvania Press.
Leezenberg, Michiel & Margreet Dorleijn. 1998. Is Mahallemi een mengtaal? [Is Mahallemi a mixed language?]. In Adrienne Bruyn & Jacques Arends (eds.), *Mengelwerk voor Muysken* [Mixed work for Muysken] (Publikaties van het Instituut voor Taalwetenschap 72), 143–148. Amsterdam: Instituut voor Algemene Taalwetenschap.
Lefkowitz, Natalie. 1989. Verlan: Talking backwards in French. *The French Review* 63. 312–322.
Lefkowitz, Natalie. 1991. *Talking Backwards, Looking Forwards: The French Language Game Verlan*. Tübingen: Günter Narr Verlag.
Marzo, Stefania. 2005. Between two languages: the linguistic repertoire of Italian immigrants in Flanders. In James Cohen, Kara T. McAlister, Kellie Rolstad & Jeff MacSwan (eds.), *Proceedings of the 4th International Symposium on Bilingualism (ISB4)*, 1545–1559. Somerville, MA: Cascadilla Press.
Marzo, Stefania. 2008. Social practice in language variation: the spread of linguistic elements in ethnolects. Paper presented at the Sociolinguistics Symposium 17, Amsterdam, 3–5 April 2008.
Mous, Maarten. 2003. The linguistic properties of lexical manipulation and its relevance for Ma'á. In Yaron Matras & Peter Bakker (eds.), *The Mixed Language Debate: Theoretical and Empirical Advances*, 209–236. Berlin: Mouton de Gruyter.
Myers-Scotton, Carol. 1993. *Social Motivations of Code-Switching*. Oxford: Clarendon Press.
Nortier, Jacomine. 2001. *Murks en Straattaal* [Murks and Street Language]. Amsterdam: Prometheus.
Nortier, Jacomine & Margreet Dorleijn. 2008. A Moroccan accent in Dutch: A sociocultural style restricted to the Moroccan community? *International Journal of Bilingualism* 12(1–2). 125–142.
Quist, Pia. 2008. Sociolinguistic approaches to multiethnolect: Language variety and stylistic practice. *International Journal of Bilingualism* 12(1–2). 43–62.
Quist, Pia & Janus Møller. 2003. Research on youth language in Denmark. *International Journal of the Sociology of Language* 159. 45–55.
Ramaekers, Ward. 1998. Mi, maak me geen eiers! Het algemeen cités [My, don't fix me eggs! The general cité language]. *Onze Taal* 4. 95–96.
Rampton, Ben. 1995. *Crossing*. London/New York: Longman.

Rheeden, Hadewych van. 1998. The role of functional categories in language contact and change. Paper presented at the annual meeting of the Deutsche Gesellschaft für Sprachwissenschaft, Halle, 4–6 March 1998.

Rickford, John R. & Penelope Eckert. 2001. Introduction. In Penelope Eckert & John R. Rickford (eds.), *Style and Sociolinguistic Variation*, 1–18. Cambridge: Cambridge University Press.

Sebba, Mark. 1997. *Contact Languages. Pidgins and Creoles*. Houndmills: MacMillan.

Sherzer, Joel. 1976. Play languages: implications for (socio) linguistics. In Barbara Kirshenblatt-Gimblett (ed.), *Speech Play*, 19–35. Philadelphia: University of Pennsylvania Press.

Slabbert, Sarah. 1994. A re-evaluation of Tsotsitaal. *South African Journal for Linguistics* 12(1). 31–41.

Smith-Hefner, Nancy. 2007. Youth language, Gaul sociability, and the new Indonesian middle class. *Journal of Linguistic Anthropology* 17(2). 184–203.

Svendsen, Bente Ailin & Unn Røyneland. 2008. Multiethnolectical facts and functions in Oslo, Norway. *International Journal of Bilingualism* 12(1–2). 63–84.

Thomason, Sarah Grey. 2001. *Language Contact: An Introduction*. Edinburgh: Edinburgh University Press.

Wijngaarden, Ariën van. 2008. Ethnic variation: Morpho-syntactic aspects of Moroccan Dutch and Turkish Dutch. Paper presented at the Sociolinguistics Symposium 17, Amsterdam, 3–5 April 2008.

Wolfram, Walt. 1974. *Sociolinguistic Aspects of Assimilation: Puerto Rican English in New York City*. Arlington, VA: Center for Applied Linguistics.

Written language intertwining

Lars Johanson

1. Analysis and classification

The present contribution is a first general overview over phenomena that might be tentatively characterised as 'written language intertwining'. It deals with a number of examples from the world of written letters, in particular from older literate societies, cases that have not been systematically compared, analysed, and classified before.

The phenomena are rather different and thus do not constitute a uniform class. Their definitions have mostly lacked precision and clear demarcations of the relevant types. In general, they have been rather neglected in the linguistic literature. Their study is theoretically and empirically much more controversial than the study of spoken varieties as dealt with in the literature on so-called mixed spoken languages, e.g. in Bakker and Mous (1994) or in Matras and Bakker (eds., 2003), and the discussions about them have been characterised by even more confusion.

In what follows, we shall ask how the phenomena involved are realised and how they interrelate from a contact-linguistic standpoint. They represent several forms of unusual language interaction, for which the vague term *intertwining* seems most appropriate. We will not deal with more or less 'mixed' spoken languages that also happen to be written, e.g. Maltese, or with written texts that are representations of oral texts in which two languages alternate, e.g. the Latin-German codeswitching in Martin Luther's table-talks, but rather with ways of writing in which the genre requires some kind of intertwining. The property referred to as 'intertwining' thus mostly characterises texts rather than languages.

Since written or literary languages are often engineered in partly 'artificial' ways, e.g. through measures of language policy, they may be expected to display contact-linguistic features different from those observed in more natural languages. Many interesting questions will be left open here, e.g. the influence of the types of script system on the different kinds of intertwining.

What do the phenomena have in common? They arise in bilingual settings as a result of marked language contact. They are of dual nature, displaying elements from two different historical sources, elements derivative of two linguistic codes. 'Code' is used here as a neutral term for languages, dialects, and other kinds of language varieties. None represent mixing in the sense of a random or untidy collection of dissimilar elements or an indiscriminate confusion that would make it in principle impossible to distinguish the individual elements.

The relative prestige of the interacting codes is an important ingredient. The phenomena concern the relation between higher-ranking and lower-ranking codes. The former are dominant, more prestigious, the latter are dominated, less prestigious. The sociolinguistic rating grades HIGH 'high(er)' and LOW 'low(er)' will be used to indicate them. Higher-ranking codes are culturally dominant mainstream codes, superior in authority, influence, and/or status. They are cultured, ceremonial, cultic, administrative, scientific, literary varieties, official standards, hegemonial, colonial languages, lingua francas, sometimes international superstandards such as Latin, Arabic or today's English. Lower-ranking codes are often vernaculars, nonstandard varieties, local dialects, more limited native varieties of a country or a region, sometimes nonstandard varieties of global languages. Higher-ranking codes are not linguistically superior to the corresponding lower-ranking ones, and they are not always politically superior to them. Their common feature is their higher cultural prestige in specific historical situations.

The phenomena to be dealt with are of five types:

Type A: Users of a lower-ranking code take over copies of elements from a higher-ranking code.

Type B: Users of a lower-ranking code carry over copies of elements from this code into their variety of a higher-ranking code.

Type C: Elements of a higher-ranking code alternate in texts with elements of a lower-ranking code.

Type D: A lower-ranking code is used to explicate texts in a higher-ranking code.

Type E: Elements of a higher-ranking code are used in texts to represent a lower-ranking code.

The five types may be exemplified with the roles of Latin, once the dominant written language in Western Europe, and so-called vernaculars (Italian, German, etc.) used in the early history of European literature.

A. Copies from Latin are taken over in a written vernacular.
B. Copies from a vernacular are carried over to a variety of Latin.
C. Latin and vernacular elements alternate in texts.
D. Vernacular elements are used to explicate texts in Latin.
E. Latin elements are used to represent vernacular elements.

1.1. General observations

The realisation of the types dealt with here is subject to considerable variation. The intertwining usually concerns matters of linguistic 'purity' as opposed to kinds of 'hybridity'. The higher-ranking codes are often conservative, in some cases not genuinely living native varieties any more. They tend to be idealised, used as symbols of authority, power, wisdom, education, learning, etc., fulfilling formal and ceremonial functions. Efforts to keep them 'pure' are often undermined by phenomena of intertwining. Scribal traditions and their degrees of strictness are important factors for their development. Scribal traditionalism may produce more or less 'artificial' results. An extreme form of this is *alloglottography*, the use of a written language different from the language of utterance, particularly observable in old cuneiform traditions (section 6).

Writers and readers involved may have very different degrees of competence in the codes concerned.

Some types are connected with the spread of religions and other cultural movements. Some may appear as markers of cultural separateness. Lower-ranking codes may be used to secure wide accessibility of a message, e.g. of religious and political teachings. A well-known example is the use of European vernaculars, formerly under Latin hegemony, for the successful spread of religious writings in the course of the Protestant Reformation movement. Gautama Buddha preferred to teach in local languages. Sultān Veled, the son of Jelāleddīn Rūmī (section 4.1), used 'rough' Anatolian Turkish instead of Persian to spread the Sufi wisdom of his father in less literate circles (Johanson 1993).

Some types have specific functions in different domains: literature, religion, administration, trade, etc. They often acquire particular stylistic functions, dictated by conventions of certain genres.

A more prestigious code may serve as a kind of tutor or mentor to a less prestigious code. This is observed in most variations of the types dealt with here.

1.2. Types A and B

What is the position of Types A and B in terms of contact-induced change? They represent code copying in the sense that copies of elements of a model code X are inserted into a basic code Y, which therewith becomes more X-like. The copying may proceed in two directions:

Type A. Take-over influence (adoption). Users of a lower-ranking basic code take over copies of linguistic elements from a higher-ranking model code.

Type B. Carry-over influence (imposition). Users of a lower-ranking model code carry over copies of linguistic elements from this code to their own variety of a higher-ranking basic code.

In both types, features emerge that are not originally present in either of the two interacting codes. It is in principle possible to identify two 'sources', X and Y, but the resulting basic code does not consist of a simple combination of X-derived and Y-derived elements. Among the known written languages displaying this kind of intertwining, none seem to have arisen through fusion of two distinct languages from which they have taken their elements, equally or almost equally. One of the codes is the basic code, which copies elements from the other code, the model code. The intertwined codes are not of mixed breed: each has a single parent in the genealogical sense (cf. Dixon 1997: 11–12). If family metaphors are needed, it would be preferable to speak of relatives by marriage, i.e. step-parents. This does not mean that we are, in practice, always able to determine the lines of descent of a pair of intertwined codes.

In both Type A and Type B, a code may exhibit an excessive number of copies from the other code. Not even excessive copying, however, causes languages to break away from their families and to enter new genealogical affiliations. For example, though High Ottoman (section 2.3) displays an inordinately large admixture of conventionalised lexical copies from Arabic-Persian, it is still a Turkish variety and a member of the Turkic family. The lexicon is not a reliable diagnostic instrument for the genealogical classification. General assumptions to the effect that the basic vocabulary is resistant to copying are far from trustworthy. Even large parts of basic vocabularies may be copied. According to a classification based on the lexicon, Ottoman sentences full of lexical elements of Arabic-Persian origin would have to be defined as non-Turkic.

This would mean a situation where the normal transmission of the language as a totality of interrelated structures has ceased to operate. More reliable instruments are morphosyntactic subsystems, e.g. features of inflectional morphology, which are less prone to replacement through copying. Thus, for instance, the so-called 'Amarna Akkadian' is likely to be a West Semitic rather than an East Semitic variety (section 2.1).

1.2.1. Type A: Subtypes Aa and Ab

In Type A, take-over copying, copies from a higher-ranking code are inserted into texts of a lower-ranking code. The latter provides the morphosyntactic frame for the insertion. All known human languages show this behaviour.

Some written codes of this kind are characterised by excessive copying. In exceptional cases they may have arisen like certain spoken languages such as Michif, which can historically be regarded as a Cree structure into which copies of French noun phrases have been inserted. Even relexification is possible, with large parts of the lexicon of a lower-ranking code being replaced by that of a higher-ranking code, though without any drastic changes to the grammar. If excessive copying is enough to define a language as mixed, written English with its heavy amount of lexical copies from Romance would be a good case in point (Jespersen 1922: 210). It rather represents normal contact-induced phenomena with numerous lexical copies incorporated and more or less adapted to the basic code. This subtype of A, which will be labelled Aa, does not seem to deserve to be characterised as 'intertwined', 'mixed', or 'hybrid', even if it involves excessive copying.

Yiddish, a rich literary language written with Hebrew script, was formerly described as a mixed language. Baumgarten (2005: 14–15) mentions assumptions whose echoes were still detectable up to the 19th and 20th centuries. Zunz (1832: 438–442) characterised Yiddish as a hybrid and composite dialect. Today, nobody in the field of Yiddish linguistics would assign the language to a type displaying extreme intertwining. On the linguistic features of written Yiddish see Birnbaum (1979), Katz (1987) and Jacobs (2005).

Certain high-copying languages, however, seem to deviate from this pattern by a tendency to keep the copies separate from the native elements of the basic code. Elements copied from the higher-ranking code are less adapted 'foreign elements' (as opposed to 'loan elements'), comparable to unadapted Latin elements in older European languages, e.g. German *von den pronominibus* 'of the pronouns', with a Latin case ending (Jespersen 1922: 213), or unadapted Hebrew elements in Yiddish, e.g. *ganovim* 'thieves', with a Hebrew plural ending. The copies are thus consciously treated as a foreign layer, a distinct segregated component separated from the indigenous material, as if they still belonged to a foreign code. Such cases of compartmentalisation make it reasonable to reckon with mixed systems. This subtype of A will be referred to as Ab. It will be exemplified below with Akkadian influence on West Semitic (section 2.1), Arabic influence on written New Persian (2.2), and New Persian influence on the Turkic written languages Ottoman (2.3) and Chaghatay (2.4).

1.2.2. Type B

In the case of Type B, carry-over copying, copies from a lower-ranking code are inserted into texts in some variety of a higher-ranking code. The latter provides the morphosyntactic frame for the insertion. A bi- or multilingual group with a relatively low-ranking primary code may, for example, choose another code in their linguistic repertoire, a prestige code, as their medium of written expression.

The product deviates more or less from the standard or mainstream variety of the higher-ranking code. In the literature, the attribute 'deviant' often has pejorative or negative overtones, as if the varieties in question were corrupt or depraved. This is by no means intended here. The deviations from the mainstream variety may be a result of imperfect learning, i.e. the authors may fail to learn the more prestigious code. Imperfect literacy is often of considerable importance for the development of a cultural community. Writers may also, however, be competent users of the higher-ranking code but deliberately deviate from the mainstream version for cultural and stylistic reasons. In both cases, the resultant variety is hardly 'freewheeling', without concern for rules, as is sometimes claimed. It simply does not obey the orthodox rules of the corresponding mainstream variety. In both cases, the differences may be conventionalised and remain as substratum influence.

Type B will be exemplified below with Prākrit carry-over influence on non-canonical written versions of Sanskrit (section 3.1), Indic influence on deviant Chinese (3.2), Japanese influence on deviant Chinese (3.3), Mongolian influence on deviant Chinese (3.4), and Manchu influence on deviant Chinese (3.5).

1.3. Type C

Groups participating in language contacts may be bi- or multiliterate, i.e. literate in more than one of the languages involved. The types of literacy created in such settings display specific phenomena of interaction.

The literature offers many examples of bi- and multiliterate texts. Linguistic and cultural contacts in the ancient world brought forth numerous written products of this kind, documented in monuments of various kinds. Two or more texts conveying the same meaning may appear at the same location, e.g. on the Rosetta Stone with parallel texts in Egyptian – in hieroglyphic and Demotic script – and classical Greek, or in the trilingual Bīsitūn inscription with cuneiform texts in Old Persian, Elamite and Babylonian (section 6.3). Other inscriptions may combine different texts, e.g. a funerary inscription in one language and an epigram in another language. Numerous inscriptions of these kinds are known throughout the ancient world (Adams et al. 2002). For example, ostraca, pieces broken off from earthenware vessels, in Roman Egypt would contain scattered words of the higher-ranking language Greek (Fewster 2002). There are, of course, innumerable cases of simple quotations, e.g. spoken Aramaic phrases quoted in the Greek text of the New Testament.

The phenomenon that will interest us here is, however, the alternate use of two codes in one text, typical of biliterate writers. It does not represent code copying, the insertion of copies from one code into a structure of another code. It rather corresponds to code switching in spoken registers, the succession of two languages in the course of a single speech event. Unlike spontaneous speech, however, it tends to be conscious, deliberate, and planned.

Biliterate competence may supply enlarged repertoires for expressing differentiated meaning. Careful writers can take advantage of these possibilities, at least in specific genres. They address a biliterate readership that understands the function of the alternations and appreciates their stylistic value. Complex cultural, social, political, and historical factors may underlie the conscious use of two codes. Each of them may have distinct symbolic or emblematic functions. Elements of a higher-ranking code may be used as markers of prestige in texts that are largely written in a lower-ranking code. Reversely, elements of a lower-ranking code may occur in texts that are largely composed in a higher-ranking code. Writers choosing this option are often native speakers of the lower-ranking code. The choice may mark their identity and sometimes express a certain distance or even resistance to a hegemonial language. Characteristics associated with the culture connected with a lower-ranking code may lead authors to switch to it in order to describe persons or events mentioned in the text. Historically, alternation has often been a sign of incipient literacy, heralding the birth of new literary languages. Authors may initially have failed to master the lower-ranking code, or they may have hesitated to use it because it still lacked literary acceptance.

Japanese literary works offer interesting examples of LOW alternating with HIGH in texts. A good part of the Old Japanese corpus alternates between the use of Chinese and Japanese, although not within a single poem, but rather within one work. Martine Robbeets remarks (p.c.) that the Kojiki, a history dating back to 712, consists of a preface written in

Chinese, a main text written in *hentai kanbun* (see section 3.3) and 112 phonographically written songs in Japanese. The Nihon Shoki (720) is written in Chinese, but contains 128 songs written phonographically in Japanese. These phenomena support the observation that the alternate use of two codes in one text tends to be a sign of incipient literacy.

Type C will be exemplified below with bilingual poems, often referred to as 'macaronic' (section 4.1), bilingual Hebrew-Romance texts (4.2), Manchu-Chinese mixed poetry (4.3), and mixed text-types in medieval British commercial writing (4.4).

1.4. Type D

A lower-ranking code may be used to explicate texts in a higher-ranking code. The results are not hybrid languages, but hybrid written styles. There are various subtypes of strategies of this kind. What may seem to be a mixed language may thus in reality be a text in a foreign higher-ranking code with added information in a lower-ranking code, aimed at helping to read and understand the text. It is a didactic technique, a reading aid intended to resolve linguistic comprehension difficulties.

One subtype encompasses special translation techniques for elucidating the original texts. A case in point is a heavily Graecised variety of Syriac found in translations of Greek biblical, theological and philosophical texts of the 6th–8th centuries. It has been called an "extraordinary hybrid variety of Syriac for use in translating Greek texts", and characterised as "perhaps the most extreme example of the interference of one language in another to be found in the ancient world" (Taylor 2002: 328). It was a deliberately chosen translation strategy for evoking the original text lying behind the translations, motivated by the need to produce authoritative Syriac texts that reflected the Greek originals accurately (Taylor 2002: 330). It is not a 'hybrid' reflecting the Syriac language of the time. Fluent bilingual writers would hardly have admitted, in normal texts, this kind of influence of the higher-ranking secondary code on the lower-ranking primary code.

Hybrid written styles of Type D will be exemplified below with Japanese annotation techniques for reading and deciphering Chinese texts (section 5.1), Burmese reading aids for written Pali (5.2), Sinhalese reading aids for Pali texts (5.3), and Karaim word-by-word translations as a resource for literal exegesis of Hebrew texts (5.4).

1.5. Type E

A higher-ranking code may be used to represent an utterance in a lower-ranking code. There may be wide gaps between the graphic representation in the written higher-ranking code and the way the messages conveyed are read aloud.

The use of the conservative graphic system of a higher-ranking code may conceal much of the actual phonic substance of the corresponding forms in a lower-ranking code. This was, for example, the case with Ottoman Turkish, Chaghatay, and many other Islamic languages written in Arabic script.

There are, however, also far more complex and intriguing forms of gaps between the graphic representation and the corresponding spoken message. A text in one code may be dealt with as if it represented another code. One specific form is so-called alloglottography, whereby a text in one code is read out in another code. A given message formulated in a lower-ranking code must be recovered from a document composed in a higher-ranking code. The principles for this representation are reminiscent of the modern practice of reading 'that is' for *i.e.* (Latin *id est*), 'namely' for *scil.* (Latin *scilicet* < *scire licet*), 'for example' for *e.g.* (Latin *exempli gratia* 'for the sake of an example'), 'namely' for *viz.* (Latin *videlicet*), etc.

Type E will be exemplified below with Semitic and other codes represented in cuneiform writing (sections 6.1, 6.2), Old Persian represented in Elamite writing (6.3), Middle Iranian represented in Aramaic writing (6.4), and Japanese represented in Chinese writing (6.5).

2. Type A: LOW takes over copies from HIGH

Copies from a higher-ranking code are taken over in a lower-ranking code.

2.1. Akkadian take-over influence on West Semitic

Akkadian and cuneiform were employed for administration and correspondence far beyond the limits of Mesopotamia. The native languages of the scribes sometimes influenced their usage, giving rise to features untypical of mainstream Akkadian. These deviant varieties were not necessarily the result of imperfect learning, products of scribes who failed to learn Akkadian sufficiently, but could also be deliberately chosen distinct varieties in their own right.

In spite of its designation, so-called 'Amarna Akkadian ', often referred to as a mixed Kanaanite-Akkadian language, is not likely to be a variety of this kind. It is documented in a diplomatic correspondence from the middle of the 14th century BCE, in the so-called 'Amarna letters' sent to the Egyptian Pharaoh by vassal kings and provincial governors in Syria and Palestine. The letters are part of a collection of clay tablets found in Tell el-Amarna in Egypt and first edited by Jørgen A. Knudtzon (1907–1915). They are mostly written in Akkadian cuneiform, the writing system of ancient Mesopotamia (section 4.1). Linguistic studies on Amarna Akkadian include Böhl (1909), Moran (1950), Rainey (1973, 1975), Izre'el (1978, 1991, 2005), Kossmann (1989, 1994), and Gianto (1990).

The documents written in Palestine and Syria, the regions where the Kanaanite languages Hebrew and Phoenician were spoken later, do not represent a deviant variety of Akkadian into which scribes carried over copies from their West Semitic native code. They represent the ancestor of Kanaanite, which belongs to the Northwestern subgroup of the West Semitic branch, and are thus composed in the oldest attested form of West Semitic. Akkadian represents the East Semitic branch, which differs considerably from West Semitic in many respects.

Most texts represent a variety dealt with by Kossmann (1989). Its orthography is a peculiar variant of the Akkadian spelling systems. It combines Akkadian lexical items with West Semitic inflectional morphemes. West Semitic features include affixes, apophony patterns, clause and sentence syntax, e.g. word order (SVO instead of Akkadian SOV). It is doubtful whether this variety was ever a spoken language; it may have been used exclusively by scribes.

'Amarna Akkadian' of this kind is probably not a 'West-Semitised' East Semitic variety (Kossmann 1989). The basic code was West Semitic, into which lexical copies from the higher-ranking Akkadian code were inserted. Though the cuneiform system conceals most of the phonic substance, the lexical copies were obviously treated as a segregated component, which makes this variety a candidate for Subtype Ab. With respect to the treatment of the lexical material, there are similarities to Type E, in which a higher-ranking code is used to represent a lower-ranking code.

2.2. Arabic take-over influence on New Persian

Many Iranian languages have been deeply influenced by Semitic. The first one to be massively affected by Arabic was New Persian. Arabic was the first language of Islam, the original medium by which the new religion was established over a huge geographic area. It replaced Middle Persian as the administrative language of the Iranian-speaking world in the 8th century CE. New Persian, however, started its career simultaneously. The Islamic conquest of Persia (633–656), which led to the end of the Sassanid Empire, marks the beginning of its upswing.

The Middle Iranian non-Islamic language Soghdian had long been used as a lingua franca along the Silk Road between China and Transoxiana. New Persian eventually took over this function in the north-eastern part of the Iranian-speaking area, a region of mixed ethnic composition. It started as a koiné along the trade routes in the western part of Central Asia, a region with speakers of Iranian varieties such as Middle Persian, Parthian, Soghdian, Khwarezmian, Baktrian, and Khotanese, other Indo-European varieties such as Tokharian, and a number of Turkic varieties. It developed into a transregional lingua franca of the eastern parts of the Islamic world, a medium of interethnic communication that replaced both Middle Persian and Soghdian.

New Persian is the first Islamicised language in history, i.e. it became the second language of Islam, after Arabic. It was made fit for this function by taking over an extreme amount of lexical copies from Arabic. New Persian was established as a written language by the 9th century. Within one century it developed into a consolidated written standard language fulfilling a variety of functions. This was the result of specific religious, political and cultural circumstances. A written standard of composite character took over the role of a Muslim medium of interethnic communication. An Islamic cultural network employing New Persian as its medium spread geographically from the 11th century on. The language gained increasing acceptance, both as a primary code of large groups and as a secondary code of native speakers of other languages. It was used for administrative purposes, and it became the official and cultural language of numerous Islamic dynasties.

New Persian did not continue its existence as a marginal language in the shade of Arabic. It evolved into a new prestigious standard language under the hegemony of Islam. It did not reach its position as a literary and standard language in opposition to Arabic, but as a functionally complementary tool. There was a division of tasks between written Arabic and written New Persian. Certain domains, theology, philosophy, and related sciences, were originally reserved for Arabic. Persian literature – narrative prose, epics, and poetry – enjoyed high prestige and a popularity that supported the spread of the language. The works of Firdousī, Nizāmī, and others became models for literatures far beyond the New Persian area. Other important Islamic literary languages were established according to this pattern of Islamicisation, in particular Ottoman Turkish, Chaghatay, and Urdu, which emerged, as it were, as cultural 'daughter languages' of

New Persian. For Ottoman Turkish and Chaghatay see sections 2.2 and 2.3. On New Persian as an Islamic and Arabic-influenced language see Utas (2004) and Fragner (2006).

Certain linguistic properties made New Persian suited for this career. It was based on Sasanian Middle Persian, albeit simplified and refashioned, comprising elements from other varieties of the region. Its morphology was reduced compared to Middle Persian. The nominal inflection system was scanty, and the verbal system had a simple structure.

Written New Persian was profoundly influenced by Arabic. The use of the Arabic script had a high symbolic value, clearly identifying the language as Islamic. The language was unlimitedly open for copies of Arabic lexical elements and thus totally reshaped. By the 12th century, almost half of the vocabulary was Arabic-derived. The semantics of native Iranian words was influenced. Numerous calques were created, e.g. *namāz* 'ritual worship', *rūza* 'fast(ing)', or the names of the times of prayer. Arabic grammar became the model for scholarly attempts to analyse New Persian. The main interest of the native grammarians was poetics and lexicography on Arabic patterns, a continuation of the old *frahang* (New Persian *farhang*) tradition (section 6.4). The Arabic metrical system was applied to Persian poetry (Johanson and Utas 1994; Johanson 1994). Domestic lexicography focused on words used in poetry, e.g. on inventories of possible rhyme words, a legacy from Arabic philology (Utas 2004).

Though New Persian copied excessively from Arabic, it is not a hybrid in the sense of a mixed breed, a fusion of two source languages that cannot be classified as belonging to either of the language families. The excesses did not lead it to break away from its family and to enter a new glossogenetic process. It remained an Iranian language, a genealogical descendant of Indo-European, not of Semitic. Arabic is not a 'parent', but rather, as it were, a 'step parent'. To continue the old outworn biological metaphors, the connection is thus not 'by blood', but rather 'by marriage'. With another metaphor, Arabic could be said to act as a kind of tutor or mentor to New Persian. It was a strong lexifier, from which a substantial part of the lexicon was copied, replacing much of the Iranian-derived vocabulary.

On the other hand, written New Persian is a mixed system in the sense of compartmentalisation (section 1.2.1). Its large Arabic-derived element is a relatively segregated component, treated as a layer separated from the indigenous component, the distinctive feature being a low degree of adaptation to the native system. This fact makes it a representative of Subtype Ab and a close structural counterpart of High Ottoman Turkish (section 2.3), even if the segregation may be less strict than in the latter.

2.3. New Persian take-over influence on High Ottoman

Speakers of Iranian and Turkic have been in a more than millennium-long continuous cultural interaction (Johanson and Bulut 2006). Turkic-speaking groups began to adopt Iranian linguistic habits early on. New Persian was the medium through which Turks of Central Asia were acquainted with Islam and urban forms of Islamic culture. Persian elements, including originally Arabic elements, were copied early in direct contact situations. Thus numerous loans penetrated Oghuz Turkic, the predecessor of Turkish, Azeri and Turkmen. The term 'Arabic-Persian' will be used here for Persian elements copied directly, but also for Arabic lexical elements that entered Turkic via Persian. The Turkic Islamic literary languages that emerged in the late Middle Ages were immediately subject to strong Persian impact and thoroughly influenced by the prestigious Arabic-Persian vocabulary.

The first Oghuz varieties in Anatolia are known as Early Anatolian Turkish (Mansuroğlu 1954). One variety, Ottoman Turkish, became the official language of the Ottoman empire and thus gained wide transregional validity. Its functions were expanded, and its resources were complemented by numerous elements of Arabic-Persian origin (Johanson 1989). Ottoman was the only recognised literary medium of the new state. It developed – as Middle Ottoman, from the 16th century onwards, thereafter as Late Ottoman – into the leading Turkic language, which produced an abundantly rich literature comprising a variety of forms and styles.

Ottoman as a whole was not, as is sometimes claimed, an 'artificial' Arabic-Persian hybrid language written by and for an, without connection to the language of the illiterate layers of the society. It displays a considerable diversity, from elaborated registers comprehensible only to a learned, to simple, unsophisticated registers closer to the spoken language.

Three registers of Ottoman were commonly distinguished by indigenous scholars: a high *faṣīḥ türkče* 'correct or eloquent Turkish', an intermediate *orta türkče* 'middle Turkish', and a low *ḳaba türkče* 'rough, vulgar Turkish'. The less formal middle register was based on educated Istanbul speech. In the course of the centuries, it was modified by speakers of different origin, incorporating elements from various sides. It was a spoken register that was only occasionally written. It is poorly documented, since the preserved written sources mostly represent the high register.

What interests us here is this written high register, High Ottoman, which was not a standard language usable for everyday communication. It was thoroughly immersed in the prestigious tradition of Islamic high culture, accessible to persons with a solid knowledge of New Persian. The mass of users of Ottoman would only master a small portion of its vocabulary, in more or less adapted forms. High Ottoman was used for florid, ornate written styles, providing a remarkable wealth of expressive resources and stylistic refinement. From the latter part of the 15th century on, refined registers emerged, tailored for official correspondence and literature and overloaded with Arabic-Persian elements, e.g. the highly elaborated literary style known as *inšā* ('composition').

Ottoman-Turkish poetry was essentially modelled on Persian poetry in style, diction, and meter, only slightly adapted to the requirements of the native language. It was extremely absorptive as regards Arabic-Persian lexical elements, but the claim that Ottoman poetry, as a whole, looks like an immense corpus of *mulamma'* or 'macaronic' poems (section 4.1) is clearly erroneous.

The cultivation of High Ottoman in order to strengthen its efficacy played an important role in the empire, but Ottoman as a whole was never codified systematically. Dictionaries and grammars were produced by foreigners. Ottoman grammarians largely ignored the native component, but endeavoured to determine and cultivate the Arabic-Persian component, setting up rules for its vocabulary, spelling, pronunciation, and grammar. Only after the introduction of a new education system in the 19th century did the study of the Turkic element become more important.

The strength of written Ottoman increased with the power of the Ottoman empire, which culminated in the 17th century. Owing to the overwhelming mass of copied words and expressions, a deep discrepancy emerged between the high register and other registers. High Ottoman almost seemed to have lost its 'Turkic character'. The abundance of Arabic-Persian lexical elements led to strong puristic efforts in the 20th century to create a so-called 'Pure Turkish'. The language reform drastically reduced and weakened the status of the Arabic-Persian loans in modern Turkish (Lewis 1999).

What are the linguistic features of High Ottoman? Even texts overloaded with lexical copies can be clearly defined as Turkic on the basis of a native layer of lexical elements including bound morphology. Inflectional and derivational markers, most pronouns, quantifiers, and postpositions are of Turkic origin. In particular, the finite and infinite inflectional markers of the complex Turkic verb morphology are maintained. They are typical of the Turkic agglutinative system, in which each formative in principle encodes a single category.

The lexicon contains numerous items whose structure can be analysed within the Arabic grammar. Many are connected with each other by associative bonds and even by certain phonological-morphological correspondences, e.g. *kita:b* 'book', *ka:tib* 'clerk, scribe', *mektub* 'letter', *mekteb* 'school', which represent the semantic field of 'writing' on the basis of the root *K-T-B*. Correlations of this kind do not, however, allow us to establish regular correspondences with the basic Turkic-derived elements, i.e. to classify Ottoman as genealogically belonging to the Semitic family. In spite of massive copying, the basic code has clearly remained Turkic. As in the case of New Persian, strong and intensive contacts have not led the language to break away from its family. High Ottoman is not a fusion of source languages that leaves the question about its genealogy open (Johanson 2002a, 2002b).

An example of Ottoman prose from Evliya Çelebi's *Seyahatname* ('Book of Travels'):

(1) *Xuda: 'a:lim-dir   bu   kadar   seya:hāt-de   an-lar gibi*
    God   wise-COP   this   much   travel-LOC   they   like
    ǰeng-a:ver   feta:-lar   ve   dil-a:ver   ser   veriǰi   server-ler
    pugnacious   youth-PL   and   brave   head   giving   chief-PL
    gör-me-di-m.
    see-NEG-PRET-1SG
    'Heaven is my witness that in all my travels I have never seen such courageous youths and pugnacious warriors as these.'
    (Translation by Dankoff 1990: 213)

Of Arabic origin: *'a:lim* 'wise, knowing', *fetā* 'youth, lad', *kadar* 'amount, as much as', *seya:hāt* 'journey, travel', *ve* 'and'. Of Persian origin: *dil-a:ver* 'brave, courageous', *ǰeng-a:ver* 'warrior', *ser* 'head', *Xuda:* 'God'. Of Turkic origin: *an-lar* 'they', *bu* 'this', *gibi* 'like', *ver-* 'to give', *-(y)iǰi* '-er' (agent noun).

The following Ottoman sentence only contains Arabic lexemes:

(2) *Bir   müs̱elles̱-in mesa:ḥa:-i   saṭhi:ye-si,*
    a   triangle-GEN   superficies-POSS.3SG
    ka:ide-si-nin   irtifa:'-ï-na
    base-POSS.3SG-GEN   height-POSS.3SG-DAT
    ḥa:ṣïl-ï żarb-i-nin   nïṣf-ï-na   müsa:vi:-dir.
    product-POSS.3SG-GEN   half-POSS.3SG-DAT   equal-COP
    'The area of a triangle is equal to the length of the base multiplied by half the height.'

The lexemes *mesa:ḥa:-i saṭhi:ye* and *ḥa:ṣïl-ï żarb* are so-called *iżāfet* nominal constructions copied from Persian. They consist of *mesa:ḥa:* 'measure', *saṭhi:ye* 'superficial', *ḥa:ṣïl* 'result', *żarb* 'multiplication', respectively, with a connecting vowel element *-i /-ï* in between. The word *saṭhi:ye* 'superficial' bears an Arabic feminine suffix.

In its modern Turkish neologistic version, the sentence has the following form:

(3) *Bir üçgen-in yüzölçüm-ü taban-ı-nın*
 a triangle-GEN superficies-POSS.3SG base-POSS.3SG-GEN
 yükseklğ-in-e çarpım-ı-nın
 height-POSS.3SG-DAT product-POSS.3SG-GEN
 yarı-sı-na eşit-tir.
 half-POSS.3SG-DAT equal-COP

Historically, High Ottoman is a Turkic language into which thousands of copies of foreign words, even many representing the core vocabulary, were taken over. Did these loans just enrich its vocabulary, or did they create some kind of mixed system? If this extraordinary hypertrophy is enough to classify the language as 'mixed', this would be equally valid for English with its abundance of lexical loans from Romance. This is the implication of Otto Jespersen's comparison between English and what he simply referred to as 'Turkish' (1922: 210).

A reason why it might be justified to postulate a special mixed or dual system for written High Ottoman is the special status of the Arabic-Persian loans, which constitute a stratum consciously separated from the indigenous part of the vocabulary. They are only slightly adapted to the native system and thus show peculiarities alien to Turkish word structure, e.g. unusual phonological representations. The two components of the lexicon are strictly segregated, similar to the treatment of Arabic loans in New Persian. This compartmentalisation, which has much in common with the use of a foreign language, is far from typical of high-copying languages in general, e.g. of English, whose lexical elements of Romance origin show high degrees of adaptation.

The duality observed in High Ottoman makes the language a representative of Subtype Ab and a close structural counterpart of New Persian (section 2.1). It is the result of a scholarly tradition. Ottoman was one of the principal languages of the Islamic cultural sphere, strongly influenced by the prestige language New Persian, and itself the prestigious language of an educated elite. It flourished at the court, in the administration, the clergy, the theological schools, the dervish orders, etc. Its architects and their followers endeavoured to maintain the purity, the original form, of the copied elements. These scholars had a thorough knowledge of Arabic and Persian, a result of Ottoman education, in which reading was based on Arabic-Persian materials and texts were pronounced according to traditional rules. These conventions prevented any significant influence of the vernacular on written High Ottoman.

On the basis of these facts, Julius (Gyula) Németh (1953) defined High Ottoman as a "Mischsprache". With reference to Stalin's linguistic doctrines, he characterised the dual system as morbid or unhealthy ("krankhaft"). Under extraordinary social conditions, he argued, features of the language of the higher layers may overgrow. Certain literary products of the learned classes bear witness to a dual linguistic consciousness in which the foreign part is decisive and the native part is unimportant. Modern Turkey had finally overcome this dilemma through its language reforms. The foreign words had to a high degree been removed, and the foreign grammatical elements had been almost totally eliminated. Németh predicted that Turkish would face a new and healthy development owing to the fact that its grammar and its basic vocabulary had essentially remained Turkish.

Which were the specific features of the Arabic-Persian-derived elements in High Ottoman? The language had two separate phonological systems that did not influence each other essentially. Violation of sound harmony rules was an important distinctive phenomenon of Arabic-Persian-derived elements. Foreign initial consonants, *f-*, *h-*, *l-*, *m-*, *n-*, *p-*, *r-*, *š-*, *z-*, avoided in the vernacular, were permitted. Long vowels and glottal stops were pronounced as such. The Arabic-Persian loans defied certain historical sound changes that were observed in native words. The script played a conserving role. The Arabic-Persian elements were written essentially in the same way during the entire history of Ottoman, whereas native words were often subject to graphic changes and vacillations.

Though the grammar was essentially Turkic, it also contained some deviant morphosyntactic features, e.g. copies of Arabic-Persian function words and syntactic patterns, some of which led to considerable sentence complexity. Compounds reflecting Persian noun phrase structure, formed according to the so-called *iżāfet* construction – with a marker connecting adjectival and possessive attributes with their heads – were highly productive in the written language, whereas in spoken Ottoman they only occurred in formulaic expressions. Compound verbs formed according to Persian patterns – based on copied lexical elements with a Turkish auxiliary meaning 'to do' as the second component – were employed in immense numbers. In the more elevated styles, periphrastic verbs of this kind almost totally replaced native Turkish verbs. In nonfinite uses, the Turkish auxiliary could even be omitted.

Other phenomena included Arabic so-called broken plurals, e.g. *meka:tib* 'schools' (cf. *mekteb* 'school'), plural markers such as Arabic *-a:t*, *-i:n*, Persian *-a:n*, even the Arabic dual marker *-eyn*. Gender distinctions, alien to Turkic, were expressed by feminine endings, e.g. *mu'allime* 'female teacher' (cf. *mu'allim* 'teacher'). Adjective attributes could agree in gender with their head in the Arabic way. There were calques such as *gün-be-gün* 'from day to day' (cf. Persian *ru:z-be-ru:z*), with the copied Persian preposition *be*.

Ottoman also displayed numerous cases of innovation with respect to the Arabic-Persian-derived material, e.g. formation of pseudo-Arabic words unknown in Arabic, 'barbarisms' and generally known 'erroneous' expressions, so-called *γalata:t-i mešhu:re*. Arabic morphological markers could be added to non-Arabic stems; for example, a noun *ḳira:li:yet* 'kingdom' was formed from the Slavic loanword *ḳira:l* 'king'. Turkish words occasionally occurred with Arabic plural markers to form pseudo-Arabic words, e.g. *geliš-a:t* 'circumstances, promise of development' (cf. *geliš* 'arrival'). In the last stage of the Ottoman era, many pseudo-Arabic neologisms were coined, mostly designating phenomena of the modern world, e.g. political, scientific and technological terms.

Yaron Matras (p.c.) draws my attention to the fact that there are genres of Yiddish (usually limited to religious teaching) that resemble, to some extent, certain genres of Ottoman Turkish in that they incorporate freely not just words but entire phrases from written Hebrew. They are cases of intertwining in the sense that they involve the integration of an entire subsystem into the language. An exceptional example of strong Hebrew influence on a specific Yiddish scribal language is mentioned in Jacobs (2005: 295–296).

2.4. New Persian take-over influence on Chaghatay

Chaghatay, another candidate for Subtype Aa, was the transregional Turkic literary language of Central Asia and other eastern parts of the Turkic-speaking world from the 15th to the early 20th century. Since its path of development was similar to that of Ottoman, it will not be dealt with in detail here. The Chaghatay vocabulary was overloaded with lexemes of Arabic-Persian origin, whereas elements such as pronouns, simple verb stems, etc. were of Turkic origin, e.g.:

(4) *Ger saŋa   müškil   ėr-ür   bu iš,   ėr-ür   a:sa:n   maŋa*
    if   you.DAT difficult be-INTT this work be-INTT easy   I.DAT
    'If this work is difficult for you, it is easy for me.'
    (Eckmann 1966: 212)

Of Persian origin: *a:sa:n* 'easy', *(e)ger* 'if'. Of Arabic origin: *müškil* 'difficult'. Of Turkic origin: *iš* 'work', *bu* 'this', *saŋa* 'to you' (*sėn* 'thou' + dative), *maŋa* 'to me' (*mėn* 'I' + dative), *ėr-* 'to be' in the simple intraterminal ('present') form *ėr-ür*. Note that the first occurrence of *ėr-* in this sentence is not a conditional form *ėr-se*, which would be expected in normal Turkic syntax.

The designation Chaghatay has its origin in the name of Chinggis Khan's second son, who inherited most Central Asian parts of the Mongol empire in 1227. After the conquests of Timur Lenk (Tamerlan), who came to power in 1405, Chaghatay spread as a literary language over the entire Turkic-speaking parts of Central Asia.

Chaghatay, often called Turki, was a Uyghur-Karluk (Southeast) Turkic language with some Kipchak (Northwest) Turkic and Oghuz (Southwest) Turkic elements. Chaghatay continued the traditions from the Karakhanid and Khorezmian literary languages of the East Middle Turkic period. It was the precursor of the modern literary languages Uzbek and Uyghur. However, since the old Uzbeks originally spoke a Kipchak Turkic language, it is therefore incorrect to refer to Chaghatay as 'Old Uzbek' (Russian *starouzbekskij jazyk*), which was its official designation in the Soviet Union. Chaghatay texts were written in a vast territory in Islamic Eurasia by speakers of different varieties of Turkic. Its centres of literary activity shifted in time and space: Kashgar, Surkhandarya, Khwarezm, Samarkand, Herat, Ferghana, Northern India, etc. A great deal of variation is found in Chaghatay texts. Owing to the complex mingling of Turkic-speaking populations and the shifting geographical centres, it is impossible to establish a specific dialectal basis for Chaghatay. On its linguistic features see Eckmann (1966) and Bodrogligeti (2001).

Classical Chaghatay is the high literary language of the 15th–16th centuries, cultivated in Samarkand, Herat and other centres of the Timurid realm. Some of the greatest works of Islamic literature, texts belonging to the canon of high style prose and poetry, were written in this language. 'Alī Šėr Nevā'ī (1441–1501) developed it to a magnificent medium of literary expression, an unrivalled model for subsequent generations of writers. A famous piece of work is the autobiography *Bāburnāme* ('Book of Babur'), written by Ẓahīru'd-dīn Muḥāmmed Bābur (1483–1530), the Timurid ruler and first Moghul emperor.

Chaghatay was an Islamic language, written in Arabic script and developing under the impact of the Islamic civilisation and the increasing orientation towards urban culture. It was originally a lower-ranking written code, characterised by an abundance of Arabic-Persian lexical loans and a complex syntax copied from Persian. The Mongolian influence, however, was restricted to loans from the domains of warfare and administration. The Persian impact was a result of widespread bilingualism. Throughout its entire life cycle, literary Chaghatay coexisted with literary Persian, most of its authors being bilingual in Turkic and Persian. Much of Chaghatay literature consists of translations from Persian. Interestingly enough, the leading Chaghatay poet ʿAlī Šēr Nevāʾī argued, in his famous treatise *Muḥākamat al-luγatayn* ('Judgment of the two languages', 1499), that "Türkī" was superior, or at least not inferior, to Persian (Devereux 1966).

It should be clear from this short sketch that Chaghatay was a highly developed and, at the same time, flexible written language. It reached the level of a high-ranking code, uniting a widespread literate population. Later Chaghatay became the dominant written language of Central Asia, eventually conquering an immense area of validity and developing regional varieties. It remained the literary language of all non-Oghuz Muslim Turks until a century ago. A pre-modern period of development, from the 16th century onwards, led to increasing influence of the dialects of the local spoken languages and thus to a number of regional varieties – in Western Turkistan, Eastern Turkistan (Ḳašγar tili), the Volga region, the Crimea, Turkmenistan, etc. This was a preparatory stage preceding the formation of a number of modern written Turkic languages. In Soviet Central Asia, Chaghatay disappeared from use in the 1920s and was replaced by the modern Uzbek standard language.

3. Type B: LOW carries over copies to HIGH

Copies from a lower-ranking code are carried over into a (deviant) variety of higher-ranking code.

3.1. Prākrit carry-over influence on deviant Sanskrit

So-called 'Buddhist Hybrid Sanskrit' is sometimes claimed to be a hybrid form combining elements from Sanskrit and local Middle Indic Prākrit languages, and thus referred to as 'mixed Sanskrit'. It is rather the product of copies of Prākrit linguistic features carried over to non-canonical written versions of Sanskrit. Some authors claim that it would rather merit the designation 'Buddhist Hybrid Prākrit'. For a first attempt to describe its grammar and vocabulary see Edgerton (1953).

Prākrit vernaculars were early used for Buddhist writing in various regions of India and eventually codified. Texts in local languages contributed to the accessibility of Buddhist teaching. What is called 'Buddhist Hybrid Sanskrit' appeared after Sanskrit, owing to Pāṇini's efforts (5th century BCE), had begun to become the dominant literary language throughout India. Buddhist scriptures in local Prākrit languages were now translated into versions of the higher-ranking language Sanskrit to grant them greater authority. This led to the emergence of written varieties used almost exclusively for religious texts. Regional variation played an important role. The texts of the northern Buddhist scriptures were mostly composed in such varieties. With the spread of Buddhism outside India, further innovative features were added. 'Buddhist Hybrid Sanskrit' is well-known as the language of the collection *Mahāvastu* ('The great story') dealing with the legendary life of the Buddha and produced by the Mahāsāṃghika school of early Buddhism.

'Buddhist Hybrid Sanskrit' varieties do not represent mainstream Sanskrit. Texts of this tradition have often been mistaken for normal Sanskrit texts, and it has been doubted that the varieties in question are distinct enough from Sanskrit to constitute a separate category. However, the translated texts deviate significantly from the rules of mainstream Sanskrit, displaying innovations copied from local Prākrit varieties in certain domains. They exhibit a specific vocabulary, certain simplified grammatical forms and expressions that are not used by non-Buddhist writers. The deviations are not errors resulting from incomplete knowledge of Pāṇini's system. The varieties in question were written varieties in their own right, not simply Prākrit varieties under heavy Sanskrit impact. 'Buddhist Hybrid Sanskrit' was designed as a specific new 'religiolect', a simplified version of Sanskrit that differed from other varieties. Its creators carried over linguistic habits typical of their local vernaculars into their deviant version of the prestige language Sanskrit.

'Buddhist Hybrid English' (Griffiths 1981) is an analogous, but inadequate, designation suggested for modern translation texts that coin new English phrases and employ English words in semantically anomalous ways (e.g. own-being for Sanskrit *svabhāva*) in order to render Buddhist originals in a faithful way.

3.2. Indic carry-over influence on deviant written Chinese

'Buddhist Chinese' was a 'religiolect' created for the dissemination of Buddhist ideas in East Asia (Meisig 2008a). It came into existence during processes of translating Buddhist texts from Sanskrit and Prākrit into Chinese. The translations were interspersed with copied elements, e.g. Indic lexemes and features of Indic word order, to the effect that contemporaneous Chinese readers perceived it as a kind of secret language. 'Buddhist Chinese' is still largely unintelligible to educated Chinese and probably even to most Sinologists.

3.3. Japanese carry-over influence on deviant written Chinese

So-called Sino-Japanese varieties, which have been characterised as 'mixed', offer several different phenomena of interest to our topic. For a general introduction to the problems see Frellesvig (2010), especially Chapter 9, 'The signification of Japanese' (pp. 258–294), which also contains highly interesting examples. I am much indebted to Martine Robbeets and Tooru Hayasi for providing valuable additional information including examples of various relevant phenomena.

The study of Chinese in Japan began in the 5th century, motivated by the great prestige of the Chinese culture and the lack of a native writing system for Japanese. In Heian times (794–1192) and beyond, classical Chinese was a prestige language for officials and scholars, much like Latin in the West.

The term *kanbun* 'Chinese writing' refers to various text types produced from the late Heian period until after World War II. Originally, it referred to Classical Chinese texts that were used in Japan, written in Chinese characters and read in Chinese wording. So-called *jun kanbun* 'pure Chinese writing' or *seisoku kanbun* 'correct Chinese writing' meant a well-formed Chinese text of a normal Chinese structure.

The impact of Tang China on early Japanese society was massive. Japanese was heavily influenced by Chinese, particularly in the Early Middle Japanese period (800–1200). The strong dominance of Chinese led to Type A (take-over) copying of Chinese lexical elements into early forms of literary Japanese. Numerous loans entered through the *ondoku* 'sound reading' practice, a Japanese phonological interpretation of the original sound values of Chinese characters. The direct Chinese influence on spoken Japanese was highly limited, since utterly few native speakers of Chinese lived in Japan. In the course of its development, Japanese came to copy not only loanwords, but also grammatical structures from Chinese and 'variant Chinese' (see below). Vocabulary and other elements from Chinese were copied into various forms of literary Japanese.

Chinese was the first written language employed by the Japanese. Type B copying came into existence when Japanese speakers started carrying over copies of elements of their own lower-ranking code into their deviant variety of the higher-ranking written Chinese code. This caused substratum influence in phonology, word order, etc. Their Chinese became increasingly interspersed with copies from Japanese. Among the codes used in the literate society of the Heian period, written Japanese enjoyed much less prestige than this kind of 'variant Chinese'. This fact reflects the close ties to China and the wish to emulate the advanced culture transmitted by means of the Chinese language. As in similar cases, it is doubtful whether these styles of written Japanese really originated in imperfect attempts to write Chinese. The term *kanbun ondoku* 'pronunciation reading' refers to the reading of Chinese texts in Chinese, learned as a foreign language, without translation into Japanese (Frellesvig 2010: 258–294).

With respect to the vocalisation of Chinese, Martine Robbeets (p.c.) also supposes Korean carry-over influences of this kind. The initial contact with Chinese, in the 5th–6th centuries, is thought to have been indirect and mediated by visiting scholars from the Korean peninsula, who transmitted readings based on southern Chinese varieties. Later, in the 7th–8th centuries, other readings were introduced through extensive direct contact with Tang China, before becoming a fossilised norm in the 9th–10th centuries. The deviation of *ondoku* readings was a matter of substratum influence from Japanese or Korean, but also a result of diachronic factors.

So-called *hentai kanbun* 'deviant Chinese writing', sometimes translated as 'variant Chinese' (Minegishi 1986, Rabinovitch 1996), means Chinese texts displaying carry-over influence from Japanese. It was widely used throughout the pre-modern period. Of the above-mentioned literary works of the 8th century, Kojiki, the oldest chronicle, is written in *hentai kanbun*, whereas the second oldest chronicle, Nihon-Shoki, is mainly written in *seisoku kanbun*. According to Rabinovitch (1996: 99), some two-thirds of all extant pre-modern Japanese texts are written in some form of *hentai kanbun*. It did not disappear from use until the early decades of the 20th century. The texts include government records and communiqués, biographies, temple histories, and a range of literary materials. It was the preferred choice for official materials, used in court records, government documents, formal correspondence, private journals and memoirs kept by emperors, the civil nobility, military leaders, and scholars. It was also employed in literary or quasi-literary genres, e.g. historical narratives.

'Variant Chinese' began as an attempt to use standard Chinese as a written language. Early writers may not have been conscious of the extent to which their Chinese texts deviated from the norms. This 'hybrid' form eventually emerged as a distinct literary Japanese style that reached maturity around the late 12th–13th centuries. *Hentai kanbun* became the preferred language for most official materials.

The so-called *kiroku-tai* 'documentary form', a variant of *hentai kanbun*, emerged in the Heian period and enjoyed a prestige similar to that of mainstream Chinese. It became increasingly more Japanese-like in vocabulary and syntax and was thus not intelligible to readers without a knowledge of Japanese. Some styles display minor deviations from mainstream Chinese grammar and vocabulary, whereas others show a higher degree of deviation. Late Heian *kiroku-tai* is characterised by features that native Chinese speakers would consider ungrammatical. The degree of deviation increased from the 11th century on, the copies from Japanese becoming more conspicuous.

The distinctive linguistic characteristics of *hentai kanbun* texts were present to varying degrees in grammar, vocabulary, and orthography. They included copies of Japanese words and phrases including colloquialisms. Almost any Japanese lexical item could be copied. The texts contained Chinese-like neologisms created in Japan and many words whose meanings diverged from mainstream Chinese usage. They exhibited copies of Japanese syntactic patterns and orthographical features unknown in China, e.g. Japanese syllabic letters (*kana*) embedded within *kanji* texts.

Rabinovitch (1996: 121–126) cites examples of characteristic features. A common phenomenon is said to be reversal of verb and object, i.e. OV order occurring instead of VO. Another phenomenon is misplacement of "auxiliary verb suffixes". The auxiliaries in question are, however, obviously particles rather than suffixes, e.g. honorific elements such as Japanese -*raru*. The use of Japanese vocabulary is said to be virtually unrestricted. Rabinovitch (1996: 125) also mentions the use of rebus-like orthographies (*ateji*) based on purely phonetic coincidences between words, e.g. *mutsukashi* 'difficult', a combination of *mutsu* 'six' and *kashi* 'to lend', which are homophonous but semantically unrelated. Tooru Hayasi (p.c.) mentions cases of *detarame* 'nonsense' (written with the characters for *de* 'going out', *tara* 'codfish', and *me* 'eye'), which consist of completely nonsensical sequences of meanings. On the rebus-like insertion of pictures and letter symbols, based on phonetic values of homophonous word, see also section 6.5 below. Minegishi (1986) is the first monograph describing typical *hentai kanbun* features. On word order principles see Aldridge (2000).

Hentai kanbun is thus of dual nature, showing elements derivative of both Chinese and Japanese. As Rabinovitch (1996: 106) remarks, it came to possess anomalous and distinctive features not originally present in either of the two languages. But if it is described as a Japanised variety of Chinese, it cannot at the same time be a specific code possessing two 'parent languages'. The 'naturalised' styles cannot be seen as "heavily Sinicized styles of written Japanese" (Rabinovitch 1996: 101), and the numerous Chinese lexical elements cannot be considered a "vast number of Chinese loans" (Rabinovitch 1996: 103).

It is interesting to note that Japanese -derived elements used in 'variant Chinese' were eventually copied back ("crossed back") into literary Japanese, sometimes in modified form (Rabinovitch 1996: 112).

3.4. Mongolian carry-over influence on deviant written Chinese

During the Mongol (Yüan) rule in China (partially from 1215, entirely 1279–1368), a written variety emerged that has been called Hybrid Chinese or Mongolized Chinese (Zograf 1989; de Rachewiltz 1996). This deviant Chinese variety developed as a result of heavy carry-over influence from Mongolian. It was used in what has been called 'Yüan officialese', a formal style characteristic of official documents issued by government and local administration bureaus. The documents were verbatim translations of Mongolian texts, closely corresponding to the originals. The translators carried over copies from Mongolian into their own vernacular-oriented variety of Chinese. Characteristic features include copies of Mongolian vocabulary, morphology, and syntax, as well as calques of Mongolian chancellery formulae.

Mongolian influence is also found in translations of Chinese classics into a similar vernacular-based written language. Popular plays of the Yüan and even the Ming period contain lexical and grammatical Mongolisms, rendered in Chinese phonetic transcription. Mongolian words frequently occur in mixed Chinese-Mongolian scenes, which mirror the spoken language.

Examples: *(h)ala* 'kill!', *anda* 'sworn friend', *ba:tur* 'hero, brave', *darasun* 'wine', *ma'u* 'bad', *miqan* 'meat', *morin* 'horse', *numu(n)* 'bow', *qulaqai* 'thief', *sadun* 'relative', *sauqa* 'gift', *sayin* 'good', *tana* 'large pearl, jewel', *teri'ün* 'head, chief', *ula'ači* 'groom', *ügei* 'not, nothing' (Waley 1957).

The grammatical peculiarities of this 'hybrid Chinese' are also found in the translation of Chinese classics into the vernacular. Texts by Kuan Yün-Shih (1286–1324) thus exhibit an "unmistakably hybrid Chinese-Mongol flavour" (de Rachewiltz 1996: 906). There is, for instance, an element that corresponds to the Mongolian copula *bui, buyu* 'is, are, etc.' and serves as an affirmative final particle. Both this text type and 'Yüan officialese' display syntactic copies such as the use of Mongolian *ke'en* or *ke'ejü* 'saying' to indicate quotations.

3.5. Manchu carry-over influence on deviant written Chinese

So-called *zidi shu* texts, sometimes referred to as 'mixed Chinese-Manchu texts', document how Manchu speakers in China carried over copies from their primary code to their own variety of Chinese. The Manchus conquered China in 1644 and established the Qing dynasty, which lasted until 1911. Manchu became the first language at the imperial court. For two centuries it was the main language of government and served as a lingua franca. Literary works of the Qing period were, however, written in Chinese. By the middle of the 19th century, numerous Manchus had shifted to Chinese as their first language and lost fluency in their native language. Nonetheless, imperial documents were produced in both Manchu and Chinese until the end of the Qing dynasty.

Manchu is a Tungusic language of Northeast China with utterly few native speakers left today. It is very close to the Shibe language, spoken near the Ili valley in Xinjiang by descendants of a group that was moved there in 1764. Written Manchu exhibited a high degree of regularity and simplicity, thus differing considerably from the spoken languages of the Tungusic family. It possessed a large amount of Chinese and Mongolian lexical loans and also some non-native phonological features copied from Chinese. On written Manchu see Haenisch (1961) and Gorelova (2002).

The *zidi shu* texts represent a special genre that emerged under the Qing dynasty: lyrical texts or songs composed in an unusual linguistic style. They belong to a type of performance art called *quyi* and were initiated by the *baqi* 'the Eight Banners' (Manchu *gûsa*), the basic administrative framework of the Manchu military organisation. The texts are highly important for the study of contacts between Chinese and Manchu. They are indicative of the linguistic situation in Northern China in the Qing period, probably mirroring the typical language of the numerous Manchu bannermen who lived in and around Beijing. It is, however, unknown whether the texts represent a common form of songs of their period and what kind of audience they were performed for (Wadley 1991: 5).

Hidehiro Okada (1992) dealt with *zidi shu* texts as products of Chinese-Manchu language contacts and published facsimiles of two of them. *Katuri jetere zidi shu* and *Cha guan zidi shu* were edited by Stephen A. Wadley (1991). Wadley also undertook to analyse the language of the texts in a framework of contact-induced change, drawing attention to the existence of numerous copies of Manchu lexical items as well as influences in phonology and, especially, in the domain of syntax, e.g. occasional SOV constituent order. His conclusion is that these features are results of imperfect learning during a process of language shift to Chinese, i.e. errors made by members of the shifting group. The texts may document one developmental stage on the road to the extinction of the Manchu language. The texts may certainly mirror the shift of a group of Manchu speakers to Chinese, but they do not prove that the authors had failed to learn standard Chinese. It is equally conceivable that they had developed their own variety of Chinese, to which they carried over copies from their primary Manchu code.

Interestingly enough, this deviant variety seems to have exerted considerable influence on Chinese as spoken in the Beijing region. The features appear to have been imitated by original speakers of Chinese and spread to other varieties. This contradicts the widespread assumption that Chinese is essentially resistant to outside influence. The overwhelming cultural dominance of the Chinese civilisation in pre-20th-century Asia has been thought to preclude the possibility of any external influence on Chinese. Thus, Li and Thompson (1974: 206) supposed that any change observed in Chinese word order must have originated "internally". This view of Chinese as a closed system has been challenged recently. The study of areal linguistic features, especially in northern China, may provide valuable new information on the development of Chinese. The late Hashimoto Mantarō, who took a particular interest in *zidi shu* texts, advocated this in a number of contributions (Wadley 1996).

4. Type C: LOW alternates with HIGH

Type C covers cases in which segments of a given text are composed in two different languages. The text contains elements of a lower-ranking code that alternate with elements of a higher-ranking code. Such products of textual mixture have sometimes been characterised as written in mixed languages. Some examples will be given below.

Alternation is typical of bilingual cultures, especially of diglossic situations. The linguistic situation holding in the bilingual community is reflected in a specific choice of languages. The functions of the languages are mostly distinguished, each being used in particular situations or for particular purposes. In the literature, bilingual writing of this kind often has specific artistic functions. It may be used for humorous, travestying purposes, or, in more serious texts, as an aesthetic device, e.g. for lyrical effects in bilingual poems.

4.1. Mixed poems

Type C is represented by medieval poetic texts showing alternation between Latin and a European vernacular. European bilingual poetry goes back at least to the Middle Ages, to a period when Latin was still the language of intellectuals, though it began to lose ground to the vernaculars. Numerous medieval European poems are written in a mixture of Latin and a vernacular. The *Carmina Burana*, collected around 1230, contain poems in which Latin alternates with Medieval German or French. The text of the

Christmas carol *In dulci jubilo*, written by Heinrich Seuse (c. 1300–1366), alternates Latin with German, e.g. *In dulci jubilo, nun singet und seid froh* 'In sweet rejoicing, now sing and be glad'. On mixed sermons in medieval England see Wenzel (1994).

Genuine macaronic texts are of a somewhat different nature (Bernardi Perini 2001). The word *macaronicus* emerged in the late 14th century from dialectal Italian *maccarone* 'macaroni', a kind of pasta eaten by peasants. The oldest example is thought to be Tifi Odasi's comical poem *Macaronea* of the 15th century (Paoli 1959; Paccagnella 1979). Macaronic texts are the product of a scholarly exercise, composed to ridicule the broken Latin written in certain learned circles. The texts often contain vernacular words or 'Latinised' Italian words provided with Latin endings. For instance, when Tibi Odasi writes *facit tremare pilastros* 'makes the pillars tremble', he uses *tremare* instead of Latin *tremere*, a syntactic calque on the model of vulgar *far tremare*, and a masculine plural *pilastros*, instead of a neutral plural that would be expected if *pilastro* were 'Latinised' as *pilastrum*.

Francesco Colonna's *Hypnerotomachia Poliphili* (1499) used Italian syntax and morphology, but a vocabulary made up of Latin and Greek elements. Humorous texts of this kind became highly popular in the 16th and 17th centuries.

The *muwaššaha* of Muslim Spain were mostly written in Arabic and contained a coda with archaic Spanish elements. For example, the poet would express, in the higher-ranking language Arabic, his love to a slave girl, whereupon the girl replied in the lower-ranking language of the people (Forster 1970: 12).

In the traditional Oriental world, mixed poems of this kind were known as *mulamMa'át*, sometimes called 'patch-work poems' or 'pied verse' (Browne 1906: 66). For example, they were common under the Muslim rule in medieval India. Poems were written alternatingly in two languages, with Hindi verses followed by Persian verses or vice versa. A master of this style was the Sufi poet Amīr Khusrow Dehlawī (1253–1325 CE). Many other examples could be added. In early Armeno-Turkic literature, for instance, Armenian poems were intercalated by Turkic verses (Berberian 1964: 813–814).

The kind of intertwining we are concerned with here is thus code alternation in written texts. It is not a matter of inserting elements of one code into a text written in another code. Neither of the codes can be considered the basic code of the whole text. One of them is basic in certain portions, the other one in other portions. There may be a more or less regular alternation from stanza to stanza, from line to line, or from half-line to half-line.

A text of this kind addresses an audience that is sufficiently bilingual to understand and appreciate it. Even if the whole poem is of popular nature, it presupposes knowledge of more than one of the languages involved. Its complex functions make it less translatable than monolingual texts. It must be rendered in as many codes as it was composed in, and the specific functions of these codes must be somehow reproduced. In certain situations, polyphonic texts of this kind may express a wish for seclusion. A specific mixture may thus be used to exclude monolingual groups as addressees. Foreign elements in poetry, however, do not always presuppose a polyglot audience. In particular cases of stylistic use, the understanding of the foreign elements may not be essential or not even intended (Elwert 1972).

In European medieval literature as well as in traditional Oriental literature, the language choice was basically determined by the genre and not by the author's nationality. Language alternation varied from literature to literature, and, within the same culture, from period to period, according to the tolerance of the audience, the literary genre, the taste of the period, and the stylistic intentions of the author (Elwert 1969, 1972). The technique can be reduced to a few basic types, but each type is rather variable.

Alternation may originate in very different motives and serve various aesthetic effects. The use of foreign elements in poetry is essentially a stylistic problem with a broad diversity of motivations. The question of how the two codes used are interrelated is intricate, especially since too little is known in general about the organisation of languages coexisting in the same mind. As a rule, it is not possible to switch freely between the languages. They serve different purposes, with unique functions that cannot be fulfilled by the other component. One language may characterise a milieu, supplying local colour or demonstrating artistic virtuosity. Certain kinds of intercalations may serve humorous purposes. Bilingual poems are often produced when a language of a high emotional value is used together with a culturally dominant one, a higher-ranking code. The use of a much liked language that is otherwise not employed for literary purposes may convey a pleasant flavour to a poem.

Biliteracy as poetic technique is attested in many literary genres in the Middle Ages. For Latin in German poems see Grünewald (1908), Henrici (1913); for Latin in French poems see Müller (1919). The higher-ranking code is in general an established literary medium and can as such serve, as it were, as a kind of tutor or mentor to the lower-ranking code. It is easier to write in a language that offers rich stylistic facilities than to transfer these facilities into an 'unpractised' language.

Up to the Romantics, European poets often wrote Latin with greater ease than their mother tongue. They preferred Latin, since it offered them familiar models of poetic diction, a prefabricated system of expressions and formulae, patterns of wording and versification. Poets would form their style in the less elaborated language and learned to master its stylistic resources by reformulating what they had already formulated in the dominant literary language. European poets would translate their own Latin poems as an exercise to develop their diction in the vernacular. European Renaissance poets often wrote in their mother tongue as if it were Latin, profiting from an established style ready for use. Reformulation of formulae acquired in a second language (*imitatio*) was, however, not always an easy task. Many authors writing brilliant Latin poems were relatively helpless when trying to master their vernacular (Forster 1970: 33).

Bilingual poems can help activate a literarily non-active popular language, even if the poems are not written with this aim. The mixed structure allows the poet to exercise the literarily non-elaborated language in the framework of a poem in the elaborated language. The poem is not only a model, but it constitutes the structural framework itself.

The situation was similar in the Orient. ʿAlī Šėr Nevāʾī, the first major Turkic poet to use his Turkic vernacular, testifies, in his above-mentioned treatise *Muḥākamat al-luγatayn* ('Judgment of the two languages'; 1499), that it is easier for the beginner to write in Persian: The novice gets annoyed with the difficulties connected with composing poetry in Turkic and inclines to the 'easier' language, in this case Persian. When poets of Khorasan and Transoxiana first tried to write Turkic poems in the Arabic-Persian *ʿarūḍ* meter, they probably started with Turkic-Persian *mulammaʿ* verses (Köprülü 1964: 253). Also in the Azeri area with its Persian dominance, poets early began to write *mulammaʿ*'s in Persian and the Turkic vernacular (Caferoğlu 1964).

The situation found here is thus often the beginning of the use of a lower-ranking code for literary purposes. It may be a preliminary stage of literature written in the dominated language, a first sign of the emergence of a new literary medium. Periods of bi- or multilingualism have been decisive for the emergence of many literary languages. Mixed verses may mark the multilingual starting-point of a literary development. The bilingual texts are exponents of a certain stage in the typical 'Ausbau' process of new language varieties on their way to performing more qualified communicative tasks (Kloss 1952). The language is, typically, first practised for humorous or folkloristic purposes, then adopted by lyric writers, and finally used by prose narrators.

The mixed poetry of Amīr Khusrow Dehlawī played a major role for the emergence of Urdu as a written language. Written Persian played a substantial role for the beginnings of a Turkic high literature. It offered a developed vocabulary, poetic models, pre-existing styles, a ready-made diction. The Anatolian Seljuk court culture, including the literary education, was basically Persian. Turkish, which was considered 'rough', did not yet serve as a literary medium, a poetic tool which poets could have used immediately and adequately for their purposes. The Anatolian cultural centre Konya was the multilingual environment in which the great poet Jelāleddīn Rūmī (1207–1273) created his Sufic chefs d'œuvre in a highly elaborated Persian style.

In addition, he also wrote a few simple Turkic verses, mostly Persian-Turkic *mulamma'āt*, playful mixtures of segments in two languages. The Turkic component, which contains an everyday vocabulary, stands for modest, intimate elements of everyday life, referring to the private life of the poet. I have suggested that these poems are closely connected with the birth of Turkish poetry (Johanson 1993). They are less likely to fulfil, as has been claimed, subversive functions. In Rūmī's *mulamma*'s, the texts sometimes show a very close integration of the two languages: a sentence may consist of phrases from both. In one poem, almost every half-line ends in a Turkish sequence, e.g. *zān-i šakar labānat* 'from those sweet lips of yours' (Persian) *bir öpkinen diler men* (Turkish) 'I want a little kiss'. In some other cases, the Turkish element just consists of direct quotations.

4.2. Bilingual Hebrew-Romance texts

Hebrew-Romance varieties based on Romance dialects were, in the Middle Ages, spoken by Jewish communities in Spain, Catalonia, Provence, etc., where they acquired a certain recognition as languages in their own right. Bilingual Hebrew-Romance texts written in Hebrew script were produced in many diaspora communities. Regional Romance varieties were, to various degrees, used to compose texts serving liturgical purposes or employed at other ceremonies and celebrations: hymns, prayers, elegies, songs, poems, etc. Though they represent various categories of bilingual poetic practice, their common feature is alternation of verses in the two languages, sometimes with the Romance and Hebrew verses rhyming with each other.

Some texts are the works of known Jewish poets in Provence, Spain, and Italy. Interesting examples of bilingual texts are found in Lazar (1971), an edition of four songs (*épthalamia*) that are documented in 15th century manuscripts and were probably composed in the 14th century. It contains three Provençal-Catalan songs and a fourth one, which was composed in Spain, but probably copied in Italy, since it reflects the Aragon dialect mixed with Italianisms. For the use of Hebrew in French poems see Blondheim (1926a, 1926b).

4.3. Manchu-Chinese mixed poetry

Manchu-Chinese mixed poems known as *manju nikan yangsanggai acamjiha ucun* represent a similar type, and should not be confused with the deviant Chinese texts referred to as *zidi shu* and mentioned above (section 3.4). This genre is regarded as artistic poetry at a high level, reminiscent of T'ang poetry and composed according to very rigid principles of the simultaneous use of the two languages (Stary 1985: 203).

4.4. Mixed text types in medieval British writing

Medieval England was characterised by multiliteracy. The three languages Middle English, Anglo-Norman, and Medieval Latin interacted systematically in certain text types of late medieval British writing (Schendl 1996, 1997). Many legal texts were trilingual, but the three languages occurred in discrete monolingual passages. There are comparable later cases, e.g. the relatively long-lived convention in the Channel Islands of Guernsey and Jersey, where formal and ceremonial functions, e.g. legal proceedings, required the use of Standard French, for which an English translation had to be supplied (Price 2000: 191).

What interests us here is, however, the occurrence of non-monolingual text types. One case in point is the role of Latin-English texts as a medium of administration. A relevant text type used for professional purposes is that of trade: mixed-language business writing, found in large numbers of documents. Here we are confronted with instances of mixed texts, and not with mixed languages.

The business writing system used from the time of the Norman conquest until the rise of standard English has been discussed by Laura C. Wright in numerous contributions (e.g. 1995, 1998, 2001a, 2001b, 2002a, 2002b, 2005). Her investigations focus on the language of merchants, particularly of London merchants trading with merchants from abroad.

Medieval business writing in London was not monolingual. Traders and accounts-keepers did not write in their own Middle English dialect, but in a mixture of Middle English and Medieval Latin or Anglo-Norman. The languages were not randomly distributed, but incorporated into the texts in an orderly way. Scribes obviously maintained control over which components belonged to which language. In monolingual Middle English and monolingual Latin text types, the different languages were kept separate, but different principles were applied to bilingual texts. Business writing displayed an orderly mix of Medieval Latin and Middle English. Uniformity was not an ideal strived for in this text type, a useful type that facilitated trading with merchants who spoke and read languages other than English. It even functioned in cases where the English-speaking readers had only a very small grasp of Latin. A text could be read, at least partially, as Medieval Latin or as Middle English. Traders could extract from the texts whatever they needed to know. Two examples of mixed-language business writing in Medieval Latin and English; accounts-keeping for the financial year 1460–1461 (Wright 2001b, 2002a):

(5) a. *Reman j vile and j Serra*
 'There remains 1 file and 1 saw.'
 b. *It P j noua serra empt*
 'And for 1 new saw bought.'
 c. *It P j vyle P acuacoe de ley Tide sawes empt and reman xijd*
 'And for 1 file for sharpening of the tidesaws bought and remaining, 12d.'

It was the usual practice in this text type to translate a simplex element such as *saw* into Medieval Latin, *serra*, but to write the word in English if it occurred as part of a compound, *tidesaw*. The scribe knew how to write the word in monolingual Medieval Latin, but used both languages because that was the custom of the text type.

The mixed-language business text type was used all over Britain. Unlike monolingual Middle English texts, which varied greatly from region to region, it was, in its fundamental structure, comparatively stable geographically. Still it is characterised by a range of options. It used a highly developed, sophisticated writing system with variable spelling and heavy use of the medieval abbreviation and suspension system, which enabled writers to exploit overlaps between the languages. Non-standardised spellings and shapes of single lexemes served pragmatic purposes, often suggesting the French or Latin equivalents of the English forms, which was of advantage to traders from different language backgrounds.

In this text type, Middle English was variably used for content words, i.e. nouns, adjectives, and verb stems. Medieval Latin was compulsorily used for function words and variably used for other parts of speech. Both Germanic and Romance word-order and gender agreement rules were applied. As for calques, Middle English patterns were mostly followed for compounds, and Medieval Latin or Anglo-Norman patterns for simplex forms.

The medieval mixed-language text type was in use until the end of the 15th century. It vanished concurrently with processes of standardisation owing to changing trade and business patterns. The styles of written English that eventually emerged were decreasingly tolerant of the variation found in this business text type.

5. Type D: LOW explicates HIGH

In Type D, a lower-ranking code is used to explicate texts in a higher-ranking code.

5.1. Japanese reading aids for Chinese texts

Japanese supplies interesting examples of Type D, explication of HIGH texts by means of LOW elements. *Kunten* is a cover term for annotation techniques aiming at reading and deciphering Chinese texts. It provided a variety of reading aids added to allow texts to be read in Japanese. It rearranged the sentences according to Japanese syntax, provided Japanese glosses for lexemes, and added necessary grammatical elements. The reading aids were Japanese syllabograms, dots, and other reading marks. According to Numamoto (2008), the earliest *kunten* texts were produced in the early Heian period, i.e. in the late 8th century. The systems developed under the strong influence of the development of contemporary philological studies by Chinese scholars. Similar annotation techniques for deciphering Chinese texts are found in Korea.

The Japanese reading aids included inserted *katakana* glosses indicating Japanese readings of lexical stems, *kaeriten* word order marks for reverse reading of characters, syllabic *hiragana* signs for Japanese grammatical morphemes, and *okoten* dots for Japanese inflections. They were typical of so-called *kanbun-kundoku* reading.

The text type called *kanbun-kundoku* offered a system for translating Chinese texts into Japanese and an aid to read the translations. It involved verbalising texts in Japanese, using Japanese pronunciation (*ondoku*) and morphosyntax. The text type represented a style of a special kind. The texts were composed in order to be read out in Japanese. They used an annotation system with glosses and reading marks inserted by the author or later annotators, reading aids that facilitated the understanding of the text. Various signs, dots, numbers, and other symbols indicated word order, inflections, particles, and other essential elements. At the first stage of development, only word order differences were indicated, but the system evolved gradually, growing more complex and systematised. Old texts with *kundoku* reading marks provide valuable phonological, lexicological, and other information, thus also contributing to the interpretation of Classical Chinese literature. Different *kundoku* systems were used by scholars, priests, and officials. It became a common practice to read Chinese texts in this kind of Japanese translation. The *kundoku* practice came to function as a form of written Japanese in its own right, eventually evolving as a distinct literary style.

Though *kundoku* is the translation of Chinese texts into Japanese, it exhibits features that are not found in ordinary Japanese. Tooru Hayasi (p.c.) remarks that many lexemes, especially adverbs, are exclusively used in *kundoku*, e.g. *iwanya* in:

(6) *Eigo   wa   yoku   yom-e-nai,   iwanya   kak-u*
    English TOPIC   well   read-POT-NEG,   much.less   write-
    PART
    koto   ya
    fact   FIN.PART
    'He does not read English well, much less than he writes it'.

The word *iwanya* is a contracted form of *iw-aku ni wa* (say-NOML DAT TOPIC, literally 'in addition to saying') and used as a relator meaning 'much more, to say nothing of'. The construction is a combinational copy under the influence of a literal translation of Chinese. The expression is entirely made up of native Japanese elements, but mirrors the function of 曰 *yue* 'say', used in Classical Chinese to introduce reported speech. The very un-Japanese but typically Chinese word order VO, is a syntactic combinational copy from Chinese. Moreover, verbs in *kundoku* may be used both as transitives and intransitives, as in Classic Chinese, whereas most verbs used in ordinary Japanese function either as transitives or intransitives.

The specific *kunten* ways of rendering texts were, as Roy Andrew Miller puts it, "a kind of lazy schoolboy's trot to a classical text" (1967: 31). The long-term effect of practising the method was that Chinese and Japanese were virtually treated as if they were the same language. Writers were often not really aware of which language they were using: "If a Chinese text when read and studied sounded just like a Japanese text, it was indeed and for all practical purposes a Japanese text. And if you wrote Chinese and read Japanese, why not go one step further and write Chinese even when the intention from the beginning was to read [...] Japanese" (1967: 131).

Bjarke Frellesvig (2010), who offers a good description of early writing in Old Japanese sources, makes interesting remarks on the tradition to read Chinese as though it were Japanese.

The developing use of *kanbun* 'Chinese writing' can be demonstrated with a set of examples suggested by Martine Robbeets (p.c.). At the first stage, it is used to be read in Chinese wording, e.g.

(7) Chǔ rén yǒu yù   dùn   yǔ   máo
    Chu man be   sell shield and   spear.NOML
    'Among the Chu men there is one who is selling shields and spears'.

At the next stage, it is a method to read Chinese in Japanese translation, e.g. *So jin yū juku jun yo mu sha* 'Among the Chu men there is one who is selling shields and spears'. The sentence is read with the word order *So jin jun mu yo juku sha yū*. The texts make use of small signs to indicate the word order in Japanese. At the *kundoku* stage, *kanbun* is used for reading Japanese texts written with Chinese characters, e.g.

(8) So   hito ni   tate   to   hoko   o   hisa-gu
    Chu man   DAT shield and spear ACC sell-ATTR
    mono   ari
    NOML   be.IND
    'Among the Chu men there is one who is selling shields and spears'.

Japanese script signs are inserted to designate function elements, e.g. に *ni* 'dative', と *to* 'conjunction', を *o* 'accusative', ぐ *gu* 'attributive form', *mono* 'nominaliser', り *-ri* 'finite indicative'.

Tooru Hayasi (p.c.) provides, as an example of *kanbun*, a famous poem written by the Japanese poet-philosopher-historian Rai Sanyoo (1781–1832). The first line reads:

(9) **ben-sei**   **shuku-shuku** yoru   kawa   (o)   wata(ru)
    whip-sound   silently   night river ACC   cross.INF
    '(Our cavalry) are crossing the river in the night, making a slightest noise of whips'.

Bold letters show readings according to Chinese pronunciation, and non-bold letters show readings according to Japanese pronunciation. Letters given in brackets are not written, but added when the poem is read out.

The so-called 'mixed styles' of medieval and later written Japanese were products of the long-standing multilingualism of Japanese. The coexistence of written Chinese, *hentai kanbun*, and *kanbun-kundoku* led to complex dynamic interplays that influenced the development of mainstream literary Japanese. Elements of Japanese and Chinese origin were recurrently copied between the varieties.

5.2. Burmese reading aids for Pali texts

An interesting similar method, which has erroneously been referred to as a mixed language, is the so-called 'Nissaya Burmese', known from the 15th century onwards. Up to this period, the Sino-Tibetan language Burmese is only known from stone inscriptions. The earliest record is found in the quadrilingual *Myazedi* inscription (1112 CE), in which one and the same story is told in the four languages Pali, Pyu, Mon, and Burmese.

Pali, an Indo-European, Middle Indic language, unrelated to Burmese, later came to exert a substantial impact on the Burmese history of writing, namely as the language of Theravāda Buddhism. The decisive source was the Pali canon of Buddhism. When Theravāda Buddhism was adopted as the state religion, numerous Pali texts were brought from Ceylon. In spite of translations, Pali remained the main literary medium for centuries. It was one of the various Prākrit languages associated with different religious communities and standing in a specific opposition to Sanskrit, the classical high language of ancient India. Its functions are comparable to 'Buddhist Hybrid Sanskrit' discussed above (section 3.1).

The oldest and most widely known version of the *Tripitaka* ('The three baskets'), the canon of the holy scriptures of Buddhism, is the Pali canon (*tipitāka*) of the Theravāda school. On Pali and its tradition in Burma see von Hinüber (1982, 1983), Okell (1965, 1967), and Pruitt (1994).

Pali became the high-ranking prestige language of books and learning in Burma. It was held in high esteem and exerted a strong influence on Burmese. A number of loanwords from Pali had entered Burmese already at the time of the earliest records. With the introduction of Theravāda Buddhism, some early Sanskrit loanwords were replaced by Pali equivalents.

The study of Pali texts flourished in Burma. The Buddhist scriptures were first rendered in Pali with Burmese interlinear translations. This led to the so-called *nissaya* form, in which each Pali word or phrase was followed by its Burmese translation including grammatical markers corresponding to the Pali markers. This procedure is similar to the interlinear glossing practised in modern linguistic literature. *Nissaya* texts have been known since at least the mid-15th century, before the emergence of corresponding texts in Burmese. They represent a strong system with widespread acceptance up to modern times. The same grammatical conventions have been preserved for more than four centuries.

This technique was intended to give readers the meaning of the Pali text and to enable them to interpret its grammar. Pali inflections and syntax were represented in an accurate way. The word-by-word arrangement simulated a close structural correspondence with Pali. Burmese is largely monosyllabic, expressing grammatical relations by means of postposed particles. The technique took advantage of the fact that the position of the particles at the end of words made them similar to suffixes. Certain particles were conventionally used to represent number, case, tense, mood, etc. For the student, texts of this kind "could be a kind of grammar or manual as well as a dictionary" (Okell 1965: 187). By scanning the lines and learning the meaning of Pali words or phrases, the student could also grasp unfamiliar syntactic constructions, e.g. relative clauses, which were rendered according to Pali word order.

Texts of this kind thus served as reading aids, as tools for didactic purposes. They were texts in a foreign higher-ranking code with added information aimed at helping to read and understand it. A code of one type was systematically interpreted and reflected in terms of a code of a different type. It would be wrong to claim that Burmese was adapted to represent the structure of Pali, that it was analysed in terms of Pali structure, or that Pali was relexified in the sense that its lexicon was replaced with Burmese lexical items. The texts were not composed in a mixed language, but represent a different kind of intertwining: a method for reading a higher-ranking code according to the familiar structure of a lower-ranking code. The parallels with the Japanese *hentai kanbun* 'deviant Chinese writing' (cf. section 3.3) are obvious. The technique is also reminiscent of Persian and Turkic interlinear Koran translations. Interestingly enough, the design of the texts was later modified. Burmese words could be omitted in cases where the Pali words were intelligible. Grammatical markers could also be omitted. Texts could be composed directly in the *nissaya* style without citing a Pali original. The result was written Burmese structured according to *nissaya* conventions. For several centuries, *nissaya* conventions dominated non-*nissaya* Burmese prose, which largely consisted of translations and adaptations of Pali texts. They constituted the basic structure of the written registers, making the texts look as though they were composed in a Pali frame. Burmese sentences were shaped in the same way as their Pali analogues.

Okell (1965) presents the 'Nissaya Burmese' as an example of a language of one type that is deliberately and systematically adapted to the structure of a language of another type. His careful analysis of some texts (Okell 1965: 195–226) is too detailed to be dealt with in the present survey.

It may be mentioned that Pali passive constructions are turned into active constructions, since no satisfactory passive construction can be produced in Burmese. Relative clauses receive no special treatment as a whole; each word is rendered just as it stands in the Pali clause. Pali numeral adjectives need special treatment because counting in Burmese entails the use of classifiers. Pronouns are declined in the same way as nouns.

Up to the 20th century, writers modelled their prose on Pali patterns. Burmese grammars were virtually modified Pali grammars in Burmese dress. Owing to stylistic habits, comparable to bookish scribal traditionalism in the treatment of texts in antique languages, plain Burmese prose styles conserved certain *nissaya*-like properties. Some features of Pali grammar were even copied into spoken Burmese. Two separate sets of rules may be necessary to describe the contemporary situation: one set for the more indigenous component, and one set for the Pali-derived component. This segregation would be reminiscent of the compartmentalisation observed in written High Ottoman (section 2.3).

5.3.   Sinhalese reading aids for Pali texts

Buddhist texts originating from the Indic Sanskrit tradition and translated into Pali were also studied and developed by Sinhalese Buddhists. Their way of dealing with Pali texts played a similar role as in the Burmese example. On the Sinhalese Buddhist literature see Bechert (2005); cf. Meisig (2008b). The cultural languages used by the Sinhalese have been literary Sinhala (also called Elu in its more ancient variant) and Pali. The development of literary Sinhala is characterised by lexical copying from Sanskrit and Neo-Sanskrit and, to a high degree, by Pali influence. Literary Sinhala differs considerably from colloquial Sinhala.

5.4.   Karaim reading aids for Hebrew texts

A similar language of translation is found in what the Turkic-speaking Karaims called *peshaṭ*, a piece of literal exegesis that pursued the 'plain sense' of Old Testament texts, a word-by-word translation of Hebrew originals. This was the way Karaim scholars, educated in Biblical Hebrew, translated texts into their Kipchak Turkic vernacular. The oldest known translation in Halich Karaim is from the 16th century and the oldest one in Trakai Karaim is from the 18th century. The translations were meant to make the Hebrew original understandable and also to show its linguistic structure. This way of translating became a kind of biblical exegesis. In order to mirror the original structure of the text, the translators copied various linguistic features of the Hebrew original. The resulting texts bear evidence of strong adherence to the Hebrew origin and are characterised by non-Turkic syntactic features.

Shapira (2003: 667) remarks that a special archaic 'language of translation' was produced. The translation of the biblical original was learned by heart, and most teachers used to prepare their own translations for their students. Such translations were by definition exegetical in nature. It was common for the interpreter to read aloud the translation during the service. The result was the emergence of a tradition of fixed blocks of translation-bits which could even be linguistically adapted to other Turkic idioms such as Crimean Tatar or even vernacular Ottoman Turkish. New translations/commentaries emerged in which "the translator/exegete felt free to render difficult passages, verses or words in his own way".

As far as the liturgy of the Lithuanian Karaims is concerned, Karina Firkavičiūtė confirms that the community was expected to understand the Hebrew texts. "When using original (Hebrew) language prayer-books and the Old Testament during services, the priest and other educated members of the community would translate the text simultaneously in their heads and sing the prayer in their native Karaim language. The translation was more or less literal, but did not distort the meaning" (Firkavičiūtė 2003: 858).

The syntax of the texts shows, like the Hebrew original, the word order noun + genitive, i.e. the possessor follows the head noun, e.g. *alyïš-ï Tenri-nin* (blessing-POSS.3SG God-GEN) 'God's blessing' instead of *Tenri-nin alyïš-ï*. The order noun + adjective is the same as in the Hebrew original, contrary to the normal Turkic word order. The demonstrative pronoun *ol* 'she/he/it' functions, against the general rule in Turkic languages, as an article that corresponds systematically to the Hebrew definite article *ha*. The enclitic *da* 'and', which is postposed in other Turkic languages, is preposed on the model of Hebrew *wa-*.

The following example shows a part of an original Hebrew sentence from the book of Genesis and its Halich Karaim *peshaṭ* translation (Olach 2010):

(10) a. Hebrew original:
 wəšēm *hannāhār*
 and.name.M.SG.CONSTRUCT the.ART.river.M.SG.ABSOL
 haššəlîšî
 the.ART.third.M.SG.ABSOL

b. Halich Karaim translation:
da	at-i	ol	ezen-nin	ol	icinci
and	name-POSS.3SG	that	river-GEN	that	third

   'And the name of the third river…'

It is a matter of controversy to what extent the Karaim language, in particular spoken Karaim, has been influenced by biblical Hebrew through these literal translations. The habit to translate Biblical texts word by word in a 'slavish' way is sometimes thought to have been most important reason for the syntactic changes in Karaim. The language would have developed under strong continuous influence of the sacral language Hebrew, and the *peshaṭ* translation tradition would have caused far-reaching changes. Dan Shapira argues that the learned language of translation "was unnatural, copying Hebrew modes and syntax, but enjoyed a high status" (2003: 668).

Turcologists have acknowledged the influence of Hebrew on the language of the translations, without ascribing the non-Turkic properties of Karaim solely to copying from Hebrew. Typological changes in Karaim have also been induced by the long-lasting influence of Slavic and Baltic languages known to the Karaims, e.g. Polish, Russian, White Russian, Ruthenian, and more recently Lithuanian. The Slavic influence is strongest in the colloquial language and manifests itself in a large number of loanwords and idiomatic expressions translated literally from Slavic (Kowalski 1929: xxxviii–xxxix). Hebrew has not necessarily played a decisive role in the formation of Karaim (Musaev1964: 32).

Éva Á. Csató (2011) argues that the word order properties of Karaim developed under the influence of the non-Turkic contact languages of the area. Karaim biblical translations show peculiarities which can be explained as a result of the one-to-one mapping of the structure of the Hebrew original. However, the word order properties of the spoken language cannot be traced back solely to the influence of those translations. They are results of changes induced by contact with the non-Turkic languages of the area in which the Karaim speakers live. Several typological properties have been acquired through intensive copying from non-Turkic languages: the basic VO order, the noun + genitive order, and the use of relative clauses introduced by a relativiser. The typological coincidence between areal features and certain properties of biblical Hebrew reinforced each other. But Karaim did not acquire features that are found only in the Bible translations. It does not use *ol* as a definite article. It did not copy the Hebrew noun + adjective order, which is not typical of the Circum-Baltic area. It employs postpositions albeit it has copied some prepositions from Slavic (Csató 2000).

6. Type E: HIGH represents LOW

Type E implies that a message in a lower-ranking code is represented by writing in a higher-ranking code. Written records do not necessarily render the original wording of a message. A text composed in one code may be dealt with as though it were a text in another code.

Alloglottography, a term coined by Gershevitch (1979), is the technique of representing an utterance in one language by using the writing system of another language. It means writing a text in a code different from the code in which it is intended to be read, i.e. one code is used for writing a text and another code for reading it. This technique manifests a loyalty to a high-ranking code and its script regardless of the acts of reading. It is commonly used in situations of restricted literacy, when a language does not have a writing system of its own. The higher-ranking codes used for writing – prestige languages, often ritual languages or politically dominant languages of forceful states – offer cultivated formal ways of expression. Cross-culturally, alloglottography is not an unusual phenomenon. It was common in the Ancient Near East, at least partially in cuneiform writing. It was later widely used in many regions, e.g. in the Caucasus region before the spread of Christianity. Prior to the introduction of the alphabetic system, Georgian was represented by means of the Aramaic writing system. The old *man'yōgana* system represented Japanese in Chinese writing with Chinese characters used as logograms and phonetic syllable symbols (section 6.5). In medieval Europe, sermons were often written in Latin, but intended to be delivered in the vernaculars. Alloglottography requires special skills and was traditionally handled by specialised scribes mastering extempore translation techniques. Remnants of these old traditions still exist in the Middle East. A scribe in Iran may, for example, produce a document in Persian, though the customer dictates it in Azeri.

6.1. Semitic represented in Sumerian writing

The representation of Semitic languages in Sumerian writing is the first known example of alloglottography. The oldest known writing system was invented in Mesopotamia in the 3rd millennium BCE. In the proto-literate period, it was a pictographic system, a script based on pictorial representations of objects. The system developed into a cuneiform script, which was first used for Sumerian. It was based on pictograms, but it also used other devices which changed it into a script system. The scribes took advantage of the homophony of certain words that differed in meaning. For instance, they would draw the sign for 'reed' also in order to express 'to return', since the two words had the same pronunciation, *gi*. At this stage, the signs thus denoted words and not objects.

The principle of phonetic similarity was further developed. A sound script was invented. Signs standing for syllables could be added to words. Many signs could stand for both a word and a syllable, or even different syllables. To disambiguate cases open to more than one interpretation, so-called determinatives were introduced, signs that were not pronounced but marked conceptual categories of the words, indicating gods, countries, cities, vessels, birds, trees, etc. For example, the sign for 'bird' was used to mark nouns denoting birds. Determinatives served as a guide for the reader without having spoken counterparts. Functionally, they thus resembled classifiers, which are used, in Chinese and many other modern languages, to classify nouns according to their meaning. The use of word signs, syllabic signs, and determinatives is reminiscent of the way modern Japanese is written. The pictograms eventually became simplified and more abstract, many of them losing their original functions.

Sumerian was a language isolate of a peculiar grammatical structure. Its roots were mostly monosyllabic, but its verbs were conjugated in numerous forms by means of chains of prefixes. Little is known about its pronunciation. Most texts were probably written after Sumerian had ceased to be a spoken language.

Eblaite and Akkadian are old Semitic languages represented in Sumerian writing. In the ancient city of Ebla (Tell Mardikh, southwest of Aleppo in today's Syria), dating from around 2250 BCE, texts have been found that are written in Sumerian cuneiform script but obviously intended to be read in Eblaite (Civil 1984). Eblaite, which is closely related to Akkadian, is considered the oldest written Semitic language.

After the conquest of the Akkad dynasty, Akkadian, a Semitic language, supplanted Sumerian as the major language of Mesopotamia. It was spoken by Assyrians and Babylonians from the 3rd to the 1st millennium BCE on a territory stretching from the Mediterranean to the Persian Gulf. It became the first international language of diplomacy and served for centuries as the lingua franca in the Ancient Near East. It acquired a literary prestige equal to that of Sumerian.

The Sumerian cuneiform script was adopted to Akkadian in the middle of the 2nd millennium BCE. The language is documented in texts covering economy, politics, law, history, religion, scholarship, and letters. It was influenced by Sumerian in direct and intensive language contacts. The writing system was patterned on the Sumerian system. The early writers of Akkadian were probably bilingual and learned cuneiform within the Sumerian scribal tradition.

The alloglottographic nature of the Akkadian writing system is obvious. The Akkadian language was represented by the Sumerian type of writing, i.e. the system of word signs, syllabic signs, and determinatives was taken over. The texts contained numerous Sumerograms, logograms representing whole words, and phonetic symbols from the Sumerian syllabary. Most nouns were preceded by Sumerian determinatives. It is interesting to note that also noun classifiers of modern languages are often copied from other languages. It is sometimes difficult to decide whether a given sign in Akkadian writing is an unpronounced determinative or a Sumerogram intended to be pronounced.

The system was originally not well suited to represent Semitic phonology, partly owing to the syllabic values inherited from the Sumerian script. It was, however, simplified and standardised according to Akkadian needs. The original pictograms were used in a highly abstract way. The Semitic equivalents of many signs were used to represent phonetic values. Syllabic signs based on Akkadian pronunciation were added. For example, the Sumerian sign for 'king' (*lugal*) was used as a syllabic sign for *šar*, from *šarrum*, the Akkadian word for 'king'.

Most signs could still be interpreted differently depending on the context. In addition to their logographic use, many signs had a function as syllabic phonograms. Readings of this kind are marked with (B) in von Soden's introduction to the Akkadian syllabary (von Soden and Röllig 1991).

During the more than 2000-year-long history of Akkadian, many varieties of it were employed in various places and at various times. The two main dialects were Assyrian in northern Mesopotamia and Babylonian in southern Mesopotamia. The mixed methods of writing – the mixture of ideographic and phonetic writing – continued until the end of the Babylonian and Assyrian empires, though there were sometimes tendencies to spell out the words more accurately. Old Babylonian was used up to about 1590 BCE, when Sumerian was already defunct. The fact that Babylonian scribes did not have Sumerian as their native language changed the writing system. They had to indicate in more detail how the texts should be read, e.g. verbal forms, which had not been written completely in the old texts. Neo-Assyrian cuneiform was further simplified in the 10th–6th centuries BCE and remained in literary use into Parthian times (250 BCE–226 CE). Akkadian increasingly changed into a non-spoken language, just as Sumerian before it. It expired as a spoken language in the first half of the 1st millennium BCE, ousted by Aramaic, but it remained as a written language for a long time. The last Akkadian texts date from the 1st century CE.

6.2. Other codes represented in cuneiform writing

Cuneiform was used throughout the ancient Near East to write languages that lacked their own writing systems. The script was adapted for writing Hattic, Hurrian, Luvian, Hittite, Urartian, Elamite, West Semitic, etc.

Hittite texts, written in adapted Old Assyrian cuneiform, abound in Sumerograms and Akkadograms, which means that the pronunciation is frequently not clear. The script used in the Hittite scribal schools came from the late Old Babylonian schools in northern Syria, used in Nuzi, Alalakh, and Ugarit. Akkadograms are very common in the oldest Hittite texts, but later become much less frequent. It is uncertain whether they were always read out in Hittite. The numerous Sumerograms are often followed by Hittite endings or longer parts of the end of the word. Most nouns are preceded by determinatives corresponding to the old Sumerian classification. The Hittite readings of the Sumerograms are now mostly known. Exceptions include the words for 'woman' and 'daughter', 'mountain', 'gold', 'silver', and some numerals (Folke Josephson, p.c.).

Elamite, a non-Indo-European language that served as an official administrative language of the Persian Empire from the 6th to the 4th century BCE, was written in the Sumerian syllabic script, though it was not related to Sumerian or any of the Semitic and Indo-European neighbours. Ugaritic was written with an alphabet of the Semitic kind that was inspired by cuneiform techniques.

Most adaptations preserved some aspects of the Sumerian script, but the complexity of the system often led to simplified versions. The script was modified according to the requirements of the respective languages. There was a general shift from logography to spelling-based systems, which implied a reduction of alloglottographic devices.

6.3. Old Persian represented in Elamite writing

The representation of Old Persian is a continuation of earlier scribal traditions practices. Old Persian was written with a subset of simplified cuneiform characters, a semi-alphabetic syllabary and logograms for frequently occurring words. This script, which was probably never used to represent spoken Old Persian, is known from monumental inscriptions.

A multilingual inscription, attributed to the king Darius and located at Bīsitūn in the Kermānshāh province of Iran, consists of three versions of the same text, written in cuneiform script in the languages Old Persian, Elamite, a non-Indo-European language, and Babylonian, a late form of Akkadian. In his study of this inscription, Ilya Gershevitch described what he called Elamite alloglottography of Old Persian. He supposed that Darius uttered his words in Old Persian, whereas the scribes, bilingual Elamite civil servants of the Achaemenid dynasty (c. 700–330 BCE), wrote them down in Elamite, and read them back to the king, as the inscription says, in Old Persian. The Old Persian version in the inscription is thus a retranslation from Elamite.

Old Persian cuneiform is known only from monumental inscriptions. Probably very few people could write or read it. On the clay tablets of the administrative archives only Elamite is found. It is possible that the script was specially invented for Darius, even if he himself could not read it. For an edition of the inscriptions see Schmitt (1991).

An example of recognisable Elamite interference in the Old Persian text is the Elamite particle *ak*, which means 'and' or serves as a paragraph opener. Since the Old Persian for 'and' is *ca* or *uta*, 'A and B' was expressed as *A B-ca* or *A-ca B-ca*. The sequence *A B-ca C-ca with-D-ca* 'A and B and C and with D' in the Bīsitūn inscription is explained by Gershevitch as a 'retranslation' of the Elamite recording *A ak B ak C ak with-D*, which represented the Old Persian dictated utterance *A-ca B-ca C-ca with-D* (Langslow 2002: 44–45).

The written Elamite version allowed the reader to recover the original spoken Old Persian message accurately and unambiguously. Elamite was thus higher-ranking in relation to Old Persian in the sense of providing an efficient memorization technique. According to the alloglottographic method, "written communication within a huge multilingual empire became easy from the Nile to the Indus, by the simplest possible and cleverest device" (Gershevitch 1979: 139).

Semitic scripts have generally provided the basis of the writing systems used for Iranian. Aramaic forms of the Semitic alphabet have been applied to various languages. Aramaic writing, a dominant medium of written communication in the multilingual Achaemenid empire, was also used, from the 5th century BCE onwards, in an alloglottographic way for written texts intended to be read in Old Persian. Bilingual scribes of the addresser would translate the Persian message into Aramaic, and bilingual scribes of the addressee would read it out in Persian or another language. Aramaic as used in the chancelleries was the higher-ranking code in this cultural sense, though it may have been politically subordinate to the varieties spoken by the Iranian rulers and government officials.

6.4. Middle Iranian represented in Aramaic writing

Also the writing systems of later Iranian languages involve Aramaic-derived elements. For an overview of Aramaic scripts used for Iranian languages see Skjærvø (1996).

The Pahlavi script was inherited from written Imperial Aramaic as used under the Achaemenids. Pahlavi was earlier sometimes believed to be a mixture of written Imperial Aramaic and spoken Middle Iranian. It is, however, a system of writing rather than a distinct language. It is an ambiguous script with multivalent signs, but it also employs certain devices to specify phonetic values, in particular to render the comprehensive Iranian consonant inventory. Numerous copies of Aramaic words are represented as logograms, Aramaeograms, so-called *huzwārišn* 'interpretations'. For instance, the word for 'dog' is written *KLB*, Aramaic *kalba:*, but pronounced *sag*. Most of the vocabulary and the endings, however, represent spoken Middle Iranian. There is a high degree of ambiguity in this form of writing. For a review of the transliteration problems of Pahlavi see Henning (1958: 126–129). The so-called Pazend system, a reaction to these rather confusing principles, implied the replacement of non-Iranian words with Iranian equivalents through transcription into the phonetically less ambiguous Avestan alphabet.

The Avestan language was an East Iranian language used in Zoroastrian writings. Old Avestan, as reflected in the Zoroastrian sacred book Avesta, is an archaic language, developed around 1000 BCE. Young Avestan was employed to compose new texts even after it had ceased to be a spoken language, probably about 400 BCE. Avestan was a ritual language, the result of a long tradition. It remained in use as a liturgical language of the Avesta canon. The Avestan script was alphabetic. The alphabet, which comprised a large number of letters, was created in the 3rd or 4th century CE. Many of the letters were taken from the Aramaic-derived Pahlavi script. The alphabet was suitable for rendering orally recited texts in a phonetically accurate way, which was considered necessary for the correct form of the liturgy. In general, however, it is unknown to what extent the preserved Avestan texts actually mirror spoken varieties.

Middle Persian, which appeared in the 3rd century CE, may be seen as a continuation of Old Persian, though its phonology, morphology, and syntax are different. It is characterised by analytic structures, loss of genders, cases, and many verb forms (Utas 1991).

Parthian was the language of north-eastern and north-western Iran, based on Northwest Iranian dialects. The Parthian Arsacids, who succeeded the Seleucids, used it along with Persian and Greek as a state language in Parthia. Under the Arsacid dynasty, it spread over all Iran, to Armenia and to Central Asia. It was widely spoken even in the Sasanid Empire, until the 6th century CE.

The oldest known Arsacid Pahlavi documents, which date back to the 1st century BCE, are normally written alloglottographically in an Aramaic-derived alphabet supplemented by Aramaeograms, which eventually came to be understood as ideograms. Thus, the word for 'bread' would be written *LXM*, Aramaic *lahma:*, but understood as the sign for Iranian *na:n* (Nyberg 1974). Only the Iranian syntactic structure and the Iranian endings added to the Aramaeograms show that the language of the documents cannot be classified as Semitic.

The so-called Awroman documents from the 1st century CE are almost completely written in the Aramaic way. Only the use of a few participles with additions of phonetic complements suggest that the texts were intended to be read in Parthian (Nyberg 1923).

Sasanian Pahlavi was the official language of the Sasanian empire (3rd–7th centuries CE), the heir of the Parthian Arsacid empire, and probably existed until the 10th century. At the beginning of the Sasanian period, the written administrative language might still have been a variety of Aramaic, but the language in which the texts were read was Middle Persian, pronounced according to an old reading tradition. Persian elements were introduced at an increasing rate. Aramaic words represented by logograms could take on Persian endings and phonetic complements. There were practical aids for scribes, so-called *frahangs* 'word-lists', of which the most important one is a list of Aramaic logograms with their readings in Middle Persian. Book Pahlavi developed in the late Sasanian period and was in use until about 900 CE. Its script differs somewhat from the form used in the inscriptions, e.g. through ambiguity owing to coincidence of several letters.

6.5. Japanese represented in Chinese writing

The use of the complex cuneiform systems for alloglottographic representation is similar to the use of a Chinese-derived script to represent old Japanese. The Japanese *kundoku* practice mentioned above (section 3.3) is sometimes cited as an example of alloglottography (Coulmas 1996: 9). Alloglottographic representation is, however, rather characteristic of the old *man'yōgana* system. To employ Chinese characters for writing Japanese, it was necessary not only to represent complete words but also sounds. Sinograms were used as logograms, but also as phonetic characters. Their use as syllabic phonograms and phonetic complements, in particular to represent inflections, resulted in a spelling-based writing system. The phonetization process increasingly disregarded the meanings of the Chinese characters. The sound values were first applied to homonyms and then to any homophonous sequences of phonemes. This led to the rebus principle of "representing a word by means of the logogram of another which is phonetically similar or homophonous" (Coulmas 1996: 434). This practice is reminiscent of the use of *4U* instead of 'for you', *CU* instead of 'see you', etc., in modern computer jargons. The development later resulted in Japanese phonograms, whose shapes differ essentially from those of the original Chinese characters.

The old Japanese writing system is similar to the Sumerian-derived early Akkadian system. Both used logograms as syllabic phonograms and employed phonetic complements. The study of the similarities may give insights into the origins of early writing systems, i.e. into the general rules that obtain when languages borrow logographic scripts (Civil 1984: 75).

The Old Akkadian use of sound values of this kind is limited in comparison to the early Japanese use. Jun Ikeda (2007) supposes that this is partly a result of the different morphosyntactic and phonotactic structures of the languages.

Firstly, Sumerian and Akkadian have the same basic SOV word order, but Chinese is an SVO language with little morphological marking, whereas Japanese is an SOV language with extensive morphological marking.

Secondly, Sumerian and Akkadian are more similar in their phonotactic structure than Japanese and Chinese are. The fact that Japanese has much stronger phonotactic constraints than Chinese may have been an important reason for Japanese scribes to undertake extensive experiments in how to write Japanese with Chinese characters.

Furthermore, the contact situations were different. The Akkadians lived side by side with Sumerians for a long time, and their language was influenced directly by Sumerian. The early writers were probably bilingual and learned cuneiform under the direct influence of the Sumerian scribal tradition. The Japanese, however, lived far from China, and there was no massive immigration from China to Japan. Another factor was the strictness of the Akkadian scribal tradition which made it difficult to develop unconventional values for the characters. Japanese writers of the early literate period were less confined by the Chinese scribal tradition.

As far as these arguments are concerned, Tooru Hayasi (p.c.) suggests that the morphological marking of Japanese might have caused fewer problems than supposed. Morphological markers, especially case markers, are sometimes omitted in older written Japanese. For example, the nominative marker *ga*, which is very important in Modern Japanese, is omitted in the Sino-Japanese version of a famous piece by Confucius: *Tomo enpō-yori ki-taru ari* 'A friend (*tomo*) has come (*ki-*) from (*-yori*) a distant place (*enpō*)'. The sentence corresponds to Modern Japanese *Tomo-ga enpō-yori ki-ta*.

Martine Robbeets (p.c.) suggests that the omission of morphological markers was restricted to the marking of subjects and objects. In all other respects, Old Japanese was even more synthetic than contemporary Japanese. Morphological marking thus caused more problems rather than fewer problems. Marking of core arguments is not obligatory in spoken Japanese today as it was in earlier written and spoken Japanese. The obligatory marking of subjects and objects in written Japanese of today is a feature introduced with the establishment of the new normative standard written language in the beginning of the 20th century, when Japan came into contact with the West. Its introduction into standard written Japanese is usually ascribed to a desire to have a normative, regular grammar for the written language, as the European languages did.

As for the phonotactic constraints mentioned by Ikeda, Hayasi remarks that the combination of segmental phonemes in a Chinese syllable is also very restricted. What might be crucial here is not different degrees of phonotactic constraints, but differences in the kinds of constraints. Chinese words, especially Old Chinese ones, are generally monosyllabic, while Japanese words are polysyllabic.

Lastly, the contacts between speakers of Japanese and Chinese may have been much closer than hitherto argued. It is true that there is no historical evidence of massive immigration from China, but for many centuries, private-based trade between the two countries may have been much more active and influential than has been inferred from official documents.

7. A passive-active scale

The five types exemplified above stand for very different kinds of written language intertwining, some representing linguistic codes and others representing text types that involve more than one code. It is thus impossible to analyse them in terms of a unified continuum, a continuous sequence of adjacent types with gliding transitions and distinct extremes.

It seems possible, however, to arrange the types with respect to the roles of the respective higher- and lower-ranking codes. The scale suggested here goes from the most passive roles of LOW to its most active roles in its code interaction with HIGH. For the finer distinctions underlying the gradation see the discussions above.

Type E: This type is positioned at the passive end of the passive-active scale. LOW is not overtly expressed, but represented by HIGH. The type may, however, develop into stages at which LOW becomes more active, i.e. overtly expressed to a certain extent.

Type D: LOW is used to explicate texts in HIGH. This type may, however, develop into stages at which LOW becomes more active, operating in its own right, less associated with HIGH, though still under its tutor- or mentorship.

Type C: LOW operates in its own right, alternating with HIGH. This type often represents an initial stage of development of a written literary medium, when writers begin to establish themselves as authors in LOW.

Type B: LOW influences HIGH by carrying over copies to it, thus playing an active, innovative role.

Type A: This type is positioned at the active end of the scale, representing plain cases of code copying from HIGH with various degrees of adaptation in LOW.

Type Ab: This subtype is a preliminary stage that precedes the end of the scale. The copies are not quite incorporated, do not undergo normal adaption, and are thus dealt with as segregated elements, as if they would still belong to a foreign HIGH code.

Type Aa: LOW incorporates the elements copied from HIGH, conventionalising, adapting, and nativizing them. The codes representing this type do not seem to deserve characteristics such as 'intertwined', 'mixed', or 'hybrid', even if they, as English, may manifest excessive copying.

8. Conclusions

On the basis of examples from the world of written letters, the present contribution has provided a general overview over phenomena describable as 'written language intertwining'. The question has been how the phenomena are realised and how they interrelate from a contact-linguistic point of view. It appears that they mostly represent ways of writing in which a specific genre requires some kind of intertwining. They thus mostly concern texts rather than languages.

The phenomena are of dual nature, displaying elements from (at least) two different historical sources. They arise in bilingual settings as a result of marked language contact. The relative prestige of the interacting codes is an important factor. The phenomena concern the relations between higher-ranking and lower-ranking codes. The intertwining usually concerns matters of linguistic 'purity' as opposed to kinds of 'hybridity'. Writers and readers may possess very different degrees of competence in the codes involved. Lower-ranking codes may be used to secure wide accessibility of a message, e.g. of religious and political teachings. Some types have specific functions in different domains: literature, religion, administration, trade, etc. They often acquire particular stylistic functions, dictated by conventions of certain genres. A more prestigious code may serve as a kind of tutor or mentor to a less prestigious code. Efforts to keep the higher-ranking codes 'pure' are often undermined by phenomena of intertwining. Scribal traditions and their degrees of strictness are important factors. Scribal traditionalism may produce more or less 'artificial' results, e.g. alloglottography, the use of a written language different from the language of utterance.

The phenomena do not constitute a uniform class. They are of five types, whose realisation is subject to considerable variation. Since they stand for very different kinds of intertwining, it is impossible to analyse them in terms of a unified continuum. They can, however, be arranged with respect to the roles of the respective higher- and lower-ranking codes. The scale suggested here goes from the most passive roles of a lower-ranking code to its most active roles in its interaction with a higher-ranking code.

Acknowledgements

Work on this paper was carried out while the author was Fellow-in-Residence at the Swedish Collegium for Advanced Study. My most sincere thanks for valuable advice and help go to Alexandra Y. Aikhenvald, Peter Bakker, Éva Á. Csató, Bernd Heine, Folke Josephson, Andrej Malchukov, Yaron Matras, Konrad Meisig, Julian Rentzsch, Martine Robbeets, Tooru Hayasi, Bo Utas, Anna Verschik, and three anonymous referees.

References

Adams, James Noel, Mark Janse & Simon Swain (eds.). 2002. *Bilingualism in Ancient Society. Language Contact and the Written Text*. Oxford: Oxford University Press.

Aldridge, Edith. 2000. Principles of hentai kanbun word order: Evidence from the Kojiki. In Thomas E. McAuley (ed.), *Language Change in East Asia*, 207–232. Stanford: Stanford University Press.

Bakker, Peter & Marten Mous (eds.). 1994. *Mixed Languages: 15 Case Studies in Language Intertwining*. Amsterdam: Uitgave IFOTT.
Baumgarten, Jean. 2005. *Introduction to Old Yiddish Literature. Edited and translated by Jerold C. Frakes*. Oxford: Oxford University Press.
Bazin, Louis, Alessio Bombaci, Jean Deny, Tayyib Gökbilgin, Fahir İz & Helmuth Scheel (eds.). 1964. *Philologiae Turcicae Fundamenta 2* [Fundamentals of Turkic philology]. Aquis Mattiacis: Steiner.
Bechert, Heinz. 2005. *Eine regionale hochsprachliche Tradition in Südasien: Sanskrit-Literatur bei den buddhistischen Singhalesen* (Österreichische Akademie der Wissenschaften, Philosophisch-Historische Klasse, Sitzungsberichte 718; Veröffentlichungen zu den Sprachen und Kulturen Südasiens 37.) Wien: Verlag der Österreichischen Akademie der Wissenschaften.
Berberian, Haig. 1964. La litérature arméno-turque. In Louis Bazin, Alessio Bombaci, Jean Deny, Tayyib Gökbilgin, Fahir İz & Helmuth Scheel (eds.), *Philologiae Turcicae Fundamenta 2* [Fundamentals of Turkic philology], 809–819. Aquis Mattiacis: Steiner.
Bernardi Perini, Giorgio. 2001. Macaronica verba. Il divenire di una trasgressione linguistica ne seno dell'umanesimo. In Gianpaolo Urso (ed.), *Integrazione/Mescolanza/Rifiuto: Incontri di Popoli, Lingue e Culture in Europa dall'Antichità all'Umanesimo* (Centro recherche e documentazione sull'antichità classica: Monografie 22), 327–336. Roma: Fondazione Niccolò Canussio.
Birnbaum, Solomon A. 1979. *Yiddish: A Survey and a Grammar*. Toronto: University of Toronto Press.
Blondheim, David Simon. 1926a. Contribution à l'étude de la poésie judéo-française. *Revue des Études Juives* 82. 381–389.
Blondheim, David Simon. 1926b. Poésies judéo-françaises *Romania* 52. 20–22.
Böhl, Franz Marius Theodor. 1909. *Die Sprache der Amarnabriefe mit besonderer Berücksichtigung der Kanaanismen* (Leipziger Semitistische Studien 5. 2). Leipzig: J. C. Hinrich.
Bodrogligeti, András J. E. 2001. *A Grammar of Chagatay* (Languages of the World. Materials, 155). München: LINCOM Europa.
Browne, Edward Granville. 1906. *A Literary History of Persia 2*. London: T. Fisher Unwin.
Caferoğlu, Ahmed. 1964. Die aserbeidschanische Literatur. In, Louis Bazin, Alessio Bombaci, Jean Deny, Tayyib Gökbilgin, Fahir İz & Helmuth Scheel (eds.), *Philologiae Turcicae Fundamenta 2* [Fundamentals of Turkic Philology], 635–699. Aquis Mattiacis: Steiner.
Civil, Miguel. 1984. Bilingualism in logographically written languages: Sumerian in Ebla. In Luigi Cagni (ed.), *Il Bilinguismo a Ebla. Atti del Convegno Internazionale, Napoli, 19–22 aprile, 1982*, 75–97. Naples: Istituto Universitario Orientale.
Colonna, Francesco. 1904 [1499]. *Poliphili Hypnerotomachia, ubi humana omnia non nisi sōmnium esse ostendit, atque obiter plurima scitu sanequam digna*

commemorat Franciscus Columna [The strife of love in a dream]. London: Methuen.
Coulmas, Florian. 1996. *The Blackwell Encyclopedia of Writing Systems*. Oxford: Blackwell.
Csató, Éva Á. 2000. Syntactic code-copying in Karaim. In Östen Dahl & Maria Koptjevskaja-Tamm (eds.), *The Circum-Baltic Languages: Their Typology and Contacts,* 265–277. Amsterdam: John Benjamins.
Csató, Éva Á. 2011. A typological coincidence: Word order properties in Trakai Karaim biblical translations. In Bengisu Rona & Eser Erguvanlı-Taylan (eds.), *Puzzles of Language. Essays in Honour of Karl Zimmer* (Turcologica 86), 169–186. Wiesbaden: Harrassowitz.
Devereux, Robert. 1966. *Muḥākamat al-lughatain* [Judgement of the two languages] *by Mir ᶜAli Shir. Introduction, translation and notes*. Leiden: E. J. Brill.
Dixon, Robert M. W. 1997. *The Rise and Fall of Languages*. Cambridge: Cambridge University Press.
Dankoff, Robert. 1990. *Evliya Çelebi in Bitlis. The Relevant Section of the Seyahatname. Edited with Translation, Commentary and Introduction*. Leiden, New York, København, Köln: E. J. Brill.
Eckmann, János. 1966. *Chagatay Manual* (Indiana University Uralic and Altaic Series 60). Bloomington: Indiana University Press.
Edgerton, Franklin. 2004 [1953]. *Buddhist Hybrid Sanskrit Grammar and Dictionary 1–2*. Delhi: Motilal Banarsidass.
Elwert, Wilhelm Theodor. 1969. L'emploi de langues étrangères comme procédé stylistique. *Revue de Littérature Comparée* 43. 409–437.
Elwert, Wilhelm Theodor. 1972. Fremdsprachliche Einsprengel in der Dichtung. In Harald Haarmann & Michael Studemund (eds.), *Festschrift Wilhelm Giese: Beiträge zur Romanistik und Allgemeinen Sprachwissenschaft* 513–545. Hamburg: Buske.
Fewster, Penelope. 2002. Bilingualism in Roman Egypt. In James Noel Adams, Mark Janse & Simon Swain (eds.), *Bilingualism in Ancient Society. Language Contact and the Written Text*, 220–245. Oxford: Oxford University Press.
Firkavičiūtė, Karina. 2003. The musical heritage of Lithuania's Karaims. In Meira Polliack (ed.), *Karaite Judaism. A Guide to its History and Literary Sources*, 855–871. Leiden/Boston: Brill.
Forster, Leonard. 1970. *The Poet's Tongues: Multilingualism in Literature*. Cambridge: Cambridge University Press.
Fragner, Bert G. 2006. Das Persische als Hegemonialsprache in der islamischen Geschichte: Überlegungen zur Definition eines innerislamischen Kulturraums. In Lars Johanson & Christiane Bulut (eds.), *Turkic-Iranian Contact Areas. Historical and Linguistic Aspects* (Turcologica 62). 39–48. Wiesbaden: Harrassowitz.
Frellesvig, Bjarke. 2010. *A History of the Japanese Language*. Cambridge: Cambridge University Press.
Gershevitch, Ilya. 1979. The alloglottography of Old Persian. *Transactions of the Philological Society* 77. 114–190.

Gianto, Agustinus. 1990. *Word Order in the Akkadian of Byblos* (Studia Pohl 15). Roma: Editrice Pontificio Istituto Biblico.
Gorelova, Liliya M. 2002. *Manchu Grammar* (Handbook of Oriental Studies 8. Uralic and Central Asian Studies 7). Leiden: Brill.
Griffiths, Paul J. 1981. Buddhist Hybrid English: Some notes on philology and hermeneutics for buddhologists. *Journal of the International Association of Buddhist Studies* 4(2). 17–32.
Grünewald, August. 1908. *Die Lateinischen Einschiebsel in den Deutschen Gedichten von der Mitte des XI. bis gegen das Ende des XII. Jahrhunderts.* Göttingen: E. A. Huth.
Haenisch, Erich. 1961. *Mandschu-Grammatik.* Leipzig: Verlag Enzyklopädie.
Henrici, Emil. 1913. *Sprachmischung in Älterer Dichtung Deutschlands.* Berlin: Victor Fischer.
Henning, Walter B. 1958. Altiranisch. In Bertold Spuler (ed.), *Handbuch der Orientalistik 1. 4. Iranistik 1. Linguistik,* 20–130. Leiden/Köln: Brill.
von Hinüber, Oskar V. 1982. Palī as an artificial language. *Indologica Taurinensia* 10. 133–140.
von Hinüber, Oskar V. 1983. Notes on the Palī tradition in Burma (Beiträge zur Überlieferungs-geschichte des Buddhismus in Birma 1). *Nachrichten der Akademie der Wissenschaften in Göttingen, 1. Philologisch-historische Klasse 1983* 3. 65–79.
Ikeda, Jun. 2007. Early Japanese and Early Akkadian writing systems. A contrastive survey of 'Kunogenesis'. Paper presented at the conference on the Origins of Early Writing Systems, Peking University, Beijing, 6 October 2007.
Izre'el, Shlomo. 1978. The Gezer letters of the El-Amarna archive – linguistic analysis. *Israel Oriental Studies* 8. 13–90.
Izre'el, Shlomo. 1991. *Amurru Akkadian: A Linguistic Study.* Atlanta, Georgia: Scholars Press.
Izre'el, Shlomo. 2005. *Canaano-Akkadian* (Languages of the World/Materials 82). München: LINCOM Europa.
Jacobs, Neil G. 2005. *Yiddish: A Linguistic Introduction.* Cambridge: Cambridge University Press.
Jespersen, Otto. 1922. *Language. Its Nature, Development and Origin.* London: George Allen and Unwin.
Johanson, Lars. 1989. Substandard und Sprachwandel im Türkischen. In Günter Holtus & Edgar Radtke (eds.), *Sprachlicher Substandard II. Standard und Substandard in der Sprachgeschichte und in der Grammatik* (Konzepte der Sprach- und Literaturwissenschaft 44), 83–112. Tübingen: Niemeyer.
Johanson, Lars. 1993. Rūmī and the birth of Turkish poetry. *Journal of Turkology* 1. 23–37.
Johanson, Lars. 1994. Formal aspects of 'aruḍ versification. In Lars Johanson & Bo Utas (eds.), *Arabic Prosody and its Applications in Muslim Poetry,* 7–16. Uppsala: Swedish Research Institute in Istanbul.
Johanson, Lars. 2002a. Contact-induced linguistic change in a code-copying framework. In Mari C. Jones & Edith Esch (eds.), *Language Change: The*

Interplay of Internal, External and Extra-linguistic Factors (Contributions to the Sociology of Language 86), 285–313. Berlin: Mouton de Gruyter.

Johanson, Lars. 2002b. Do languages die of 'structuritis'? The role of code-copying in language endangerment. *Italian Journal of Linguistics* 14. 249–270.

Johanson, Lars & Christiane Bulut (eds.). 2006. *Turkic-Iranian Contact Areas. Historical and Linguistic Aspects* (Turcologica 62.) Wiesbaden: Harrassowitz.

Johanson, Lars & Bo Utas (eds.). 1994. *Arabic Prosody and its Applications in Muslim Poetry* (Transactions 5). Uppsala: Swedish Research Institute in Istanbul.

Katz, Dovid. 1987. *Grammar of the Yiddish Language*. London: Gerald Duckworth & Co.

Kloss, Heinz. 1952. *Die Entwicklung Neuer Germanischer Kultursprachen von 1800 bis 1950* (Schriftenreihe des Goethe-Instituts, 1). München: Pohl & Co.

Knudtzon, Jørgen Alexander. 1907–1915. *Die El-Amarna-Tafeln. Umschrift, Übersetzung und Glossar 1–2* (Vorderasiatische Bibliothek, 2. Lieferung 1–11). Leipzig: Hinrichs.

Köprülü, M. Fuad. 1964. La métrique 'arūż dans la poésie turque. In Louis Bazin, Alessio Bombaci, Jean Deny, Tayyib Gökbilgin, Fahir İz & Helmuth Scheel (eds.), *Philologiae Turcicae Fundamenta 2 [Fundamentals of Turkic philology]*, 252–266. Aquis Mattiacis: Steiner.

Kossmann, Maarten G. 1989. The case system of West-Semitized Amarna Akkadian. *Jaarbericht Ex Oriente Lux* 30. 38–60.

Kossmann, Maarten G. 1994. Amarna-Akkadian as a mixed language. In Peter Bakker & Maarten Mous (eds.), *Mixed Languages: 15 Case Studies in Language Intertwining*, 157–161. Amsterdam: Uitgave IFOTT.

Kowalski, Tadeusz. 1929. *Karaimische Texte im Dialekt von Troki*. Warszawa: L'Académie Polonaise des Sciences et des Lettres.

Langslow, David R. 2002. Approaching bilinguialism in corpus languages. In James Noel Adams, Mark Janse & Simon Swain (eds.), *Bilingualism in Ancient Society. Language Contact and the Written Word*, 23–51. Oxford: Oxford University Press.

Lazar, Moshe. 1971. Epithalames bilingues hébraïco-romans dans deux manuscrits du XVe siècle. In Irénée Cluzel & François Pirot (eds.), *Mélanges de Philologie Romane Dédiés à la Mémoire de Jean Boutière (1899–1967)*, 333–346. Liège: Editions Soledi.

Lewis, Geoffrey. 1999. *The Turkish Language Reform: A Catastrophic Success*. Oxford: Oxford University Press.

Li, Charles N. & Sandra A. Thompson. 1974. Historical change of word order: A case study in Chinese and its implications. In John M. Anderson & Charles Jones (eds.), *Historical Linguistics, Vol. A*, 199–217. Amsterdam: North-Holland Publishing Company.

Mansuroğlu, Mecdud. 1954. The rise and development of written Turkish in Anatolia. *Oriens* 7. 250–264.

Matras, Yaron & Peter Bakker (eds.). 2003. *The Mixed Language Debate: Theoretical and Empirical Advances*. Berlin: Walter de Gruyter.

Meisig, Konrad. 2008a. Buddhist Chinese. Religiolect and metalanguage. *Mitteilungen für Anthropologie und Religionsgeschichte* 19. 91–100.
Meisig, Konrad. 2008b. Review of Bechert 2005. *Internationales Asienforum* 39. 363–366.
Miller, Roy Andrew. 1967. *The Japanese Language*. Chicago, IL: University of Chicago Press.
Minegishi, Akira. 1986. *Hentai Kanbun*. Tokyo: Tôkyôdô.
Moran, William L. 1950. *A Syntactical Study of the Dialect of Byblos As Reflected in the Amarna Tablets*. Baltimore, MD: Johns Hopkins University dissertation.
Müller, Otto. 1919. *Das Lateinische Enschiebsel in der Französischen Literatur des Mittelalters*. Zürich: University of Zürich dissertation.
Musaev, Kenesbaj M. 1964. *Grammatika karaimskogo jazyka. Fonetika i morfologija* [Grammar of Karaim. Phonetics and morphology]. Moskva: Nauka.
Németh, Julius. 1953. Zur Kenntnis der Mischsprachen. Das doppelte Sprachsystem des Osmanischen. *Acta Linguistica Academiae Scientiarum Hungaricae* 3. 159–199.
Numamoto, Katsuaki. 2008. Nihon ni okeru kunten-shiryoo no tenkai: shutoshite ondoku no kanten kara [The development of kunten-data in Japan: mainly from the viewpoint of ondoku]. In Nakamura Shunsaku, Ichiki Tsuyuhiko, Tajiri Yūichirō & Maeda Tsutomu (eds.), *Kundoku-ron: higashi Ajia kanbun sekai to nihongo,* 123–150. Tokyo: Bensei shuppan.
Nyberg, Henrik Samuel. 1923. The Pahlavi documents from Avromān. *Le Monde Oriental* 17. 182–230.
Nyberg, Henrik Samuel. 1974. *A Manual of Pahlavi 2. Glossary*. Wiesbaden: Otto Harrassowitz.
Okada, Hidehiro. 1992. Mandarin, a language of the Manchus: how Altaic? In Martin Gimm, Giovanni Stary & Michael Weiers (eds.), *Historische und bibliographische Studien zur Mandschuforschung,* 165–187. Wiesbaden: Harrassowitz.
Okell, John. 1965. Nissaya Burmese – a case of adaptation to a foreign grammar and syntax. *Lingua* 15. 186–227.
Okell, John. 1967. Nissaya Burmese. *Journal of the Burma Research Society* 50. 95–123.
Olach, Zsuszanna. 2010. Numerals in Halich Karaim bible texts. Paper presented at the 15th International Conference on Turkish Linguistics, Szeged University, 20–22 August 2010.
Paccagnella, Ivano. 1979. *Le Macaronee Padovane: Tradizione e Lingua* (Medioevo e umanesimo 36). Padova: Antenore.
Paoli, Ugo Enrico. 1959. *Il Latino Maccheronico* (Bibliotechina del Saggiatore 13). Firenze: Felice Le Monnier.
Price, Glanville. 2000. French in the Channel Islands. Language in Britain and Ireland. *In* Glanville Price (ed.), *Languages in Britain and Ireland,* 187–196. Oxford: Basil Blackwell.

Pruitt, William. 1994. *Etude Linguistique de Nissaya Birmans, Traduction Commentée de Textes Bouddhiques*. Paris: Presses de l'École française d'Extrême-Orient.
Rabinovitch, Judith N. 1996. An introduction to hentai kambun (variant Chinese), a hybrid Sinico-Japanese used by the male elite in premodern Japan. *Journal of Chinese Linguistics* 24. 98–127.
de Rachewiltz, Igor. 1996. Hybrid Chinese of the Mongol period (13th-14th century). In Stephen A. Wurm, Peter Mühlhäusler & Darrell T. Tryon (eds.), *Atlas of Languages of Intercultural Communication in the Pacific, Asia, and the Americas II. 2* (Trends in Linguistics. Documentation 13), 905–906. Berlin/New York: Walter de Gruyter.
Rainey, Anson F. 1973. Reflections on the suffix conjugation in West-Semitized Amarna tablets. *Ugarit-Forschungen* 5. 235–262.
Rainey, Anson F. 1975. Morphology and the prefix tenses of West-Semitized "Amarna Tablets". *Ugarit-Forschungen* 7. 385–426.
Schendl, Herbert. 1996. Text types and code-switching in medieval and early modern English. *Vienna English Working Papers* 5. 50–62.
Schendl, Herbert. 1997. 'To London fro Kent / Sunt predia depopulantes': Code-switching and medieval English macaronic poems. *Vienna English Working Papers* 6. 52–66.
Schmitt, Rüdiger. 1991. *The Bisitun Inscriptions of Darius the Great. Old Persian Text* (Corpus Inscriptionum Iranicarum 1). London: School of Oriental and African Studies, University of London.
Shapira, Dan. 2003. The Turkic languages and literatures. In Meira Polliack (ed.), *Karaite Judaism. A Guide to its History and Literary Sources*, 657–707. Leiden/Boston: Brill.
Skjærvø, P. Oktor. 1996. Aramaic Scripts for Iranian languages. In Peter T. Daniels & William Bright (eds.), *The World's Writing Systems*, 515–535. Oxford/New York: Oxford University Press.
von Soden, Wolfram & Wolfgang Röllig. 1914. *Das Akkadische Syllabar*. Rome: Biblical Institute Press.
Stary, Giovanni. 1985. Fundamental principles of Manchu poetry. In Lin En-shean (ed.), *Proceedings of the International Conference on China Border Area Studies*, 187–221. Taipei: National Chengchi University.
Taylor, David G. K. 2002. Bilingualism and diglossia in late antique Syria and Mesopotamia. In James Noel Adams, Mark Janse & Simon Swain (eds.), *Bilingualism in Ancient Society. Language Contact and the Written Text*, 298–331. Oxford: Oxford University Press.
Utas, Bo. 1991. New Persian as an interethnic medium. In Ingvar Svanberg (ed.), *Ethnicity, Minorities and Cultural Encounters* (Uppsala Multiethnic Papers 25), 103–111. Uppsala: Centre for Multiethnic Research.
Utas, Bo. 2004. Semitic in Iranian: Written, read and spoken language. In Éva Ágnes Csató, Bo Isaksson & Carina Jahani (eds.), *Linguistic Convergence and Areal Diffusion. Case Studies from Iranian, Semitic and Turkic*, 65–78. London/New York: RoutledgeCurzon.

Wadley, Stephen A. 1991. *The Mixed-Language Verses from the Manchu Dynasty in China* (Papers on Inner Asia 16). Bloomington: Indiana University Research Institute for Inner Asian Studies.
Wadley, Stephen A. 1996. Altaic influences on Beijing dialect: the Manchu case. *Journal of the American Oriental Society* 116. 99–104.
Waley, Arhur. 1957. Chinese-Mongol hybrid songs. *Bulletin of the School of Oriental and African Studies* 20. 581–584.
Wenzel, Siegfried. 1994. *Macaronic Sermons: Bililingualism and Preaching in Late-Medieval England. (Recentiores: Later Latin Texts and Contexts)*. Ann Arbor, MI: University of Michigan Press.
Wright, Laura C. 1995. A hypothesis on the structrure of macaronic business writing. In Jacek Fisiak (ed.), *Medieval Dialectology* (Trends in Linguistic Studies & Monographs 79), 309–321. Berlin: Mouton de Gruyter.
Wright, Laura C. 1998. Mixed-language business writing: Five hundred years of codeswitching. In Ernst Håkon Jahr (ed.), *Language Change: Advances in Historical Sociolinguistics* (Trends in Linguistic Studies & Monographs 114), 99–118. Berlin: Mouton de Gruyter.
Wright, Laura C. 2001a. Models of language mixing: Code-switching versus semicommunication in medieval Latin and Middle English accounts. In Dieter Kastovsky & Arthur Mettinger (eds.), *Language Contact in the History of English,* 363–376. Frankfurt am Main: Peter Lang.
Wright, Laura C. 2001b. The role of international and national trade in the standardisation of English. In Fandino Isabel Moskowich-Spiegel, Begona Crespo Garcia, Emma Lezcano Gonzalez & Begona Simal Gonzalez (eds.), *Re-interpretations of English. Essays on Language, Linguistics and Philology 1,* 189–207. A Coruña: Universidade da Coruña.
Wright, Laura C. 2002a. Standard English and the lexicon: Why so many spellings? In Mari C. Jones & Edith Esch (eds.), *Language Change: The Interplay of Internal, External and Extra-Linguistic Factors,* 181–200. Berlin: Mouton de Gruyter.
Wright, Laura C. 2002b. Code-intermediate phenomena in medieval mixed-language business texts. *Language Sciences* 24. 471–489.
Wright, Laura C. 2005. Medieval mixed-language business texts and the rise of Standard English. In Janne Skaffari, Matti Peikola, Ruth Carroll, Risto Hiltunen & Brita Wårwik (eds.), *Opening Windows on Texts and Discourses of the Past* (Pragmatics and Beyond, New Series 134), 381–399. Amsterdam: John Benjamins.
Zograf, Irina T. 1989. *Mongol'sko-kitajskaja interferencija. Jazyk mongol'skoj kanceljarii v Kitae* [Mongolian-Chinese interference. The language of the Mongolian]. Moskva: Nauka.
Zunz, Leopold [Yom Tov Lipman Tsunts]. 1832. *Die gottesdienstlichen Vorträge der Juden.* Berlin: Asher.

Issues in the genetic classification of contact languages

April McMahon

1. The relationship between contact and classification

1.1. Two notions in opposition

A stark truth underlies the relationship between language contact and linguistic classification: strictly speaking, they are incompatible. Grouping languages into families means sorting out which languages plausibly come from a single common ancestor, and which do not; in order to do this successfully, we must isolate and prioritise those features which have existed continuously, albeit with changes in form or meaning along the way, since that single common ancestor. Language contact, on the other hand, involves the transfer of linguistic features from one language to another, to which it may or may not be related; and those borrowed features are precisely the ones we must not use in determining the genetic affiliations of the recipient language. Any confusion here can fatally undermine the enterprise of linguistic classification, as well as misleading linguists about the history of all the languages and populations involved. This might seem a particularly gloomy standpoint to begin from, and of course it is possible to spin things a little more positively – Harrison (2003: 232), for instance, asserts cheerily that "Language contact and borrowing are a normal occurrence, and make comparative linguistics interesting". But reading between the lines, we are still confronted with an opposition: linguistic borrowing, at least when it is undetected or misdiagnosed, is the enemy of successful language classification.

In this chapter, we will consider the effects of this opposition in a linguistic world where contact and its effects are increasingly (and correctly) accepted as commonplace, but where genetic classification is also more and more important. The progressive breaking down of boundaries between disciplines, and the sharing of methods (mainly but not exclusively computational) across different areas of research, means comparative linguists work increasingly with anthropologists, archaeologists, and geneticists in charting the histories of human populations (see McMahon and McMahon 2005; Forster and Renfrew 2006; McMahon and McMahon 2008; and Wichmann 2008) – but in order for this to be a successful enterprise, hypotheses about language families must be robust and testable. We shall see in sections 1.2 and 1.3 below that the effects of language contact are problematic both for traditional methods of genetic classification, and for more theoretical notions of change from generation to generation and grammar to grammar. In section 1.4, we move from the idea of contact between languages and/or speakers, to pursue the definition of 'contact language', which is generally taken to refer to pidgins, creoles and mixed languages. However, while contact and its consequences may be most salient for these languages, we shall see that there may well be problems of the same kind, even if more limited in degree, for languages where the effects of contact have been more limited. While section 1 sets out the problems that define the scope of this chapter, section 2 will consider how they have been dealt with so far. Typically, and simplifying only a little, this has involved either attempting to filter out the effects of contact so it does not interfere with the real, underlying classification; or suggesting that contact languages are exceptional and should not be dealt with in conventional models at all. Finally, section 3 will ask whether some new approaches currently under development might offer hope for future work in reconciling contact and classification.

1.2.   Contact and the Comparative Method

Campbell (1998: 108) describes the comparative method as "central to historical linguistics, the most important of the various methods and techniques we use to recover linguistic history". The method compares the characteristics of modern or attested languages to reconstruct properties of their common ancestor language, along with the changes by which this ancient, hypothesised system has turned into its various daughters. The languages to be compared in the first place are selected on the basis of regular, repeated correspondences of sound and meaning, like the initial correspondence of Ancient Greek or Sanskrit /p/ with Germanic /f/ in the words for 'five' or 'foot' used for illustration by McMahon and McMahon (2005: 7), or initial /k/ in Italian *capra*, Spanish and Portuguese *cabra*, as opposed to /š/ in French *chèvre* 'goat', or Italian, Spanish and Portuguese *caro*, compared with French *cher* 'dear' discussed by Campbell (1998: 111, in a section delightfully entitled 'The Comparative Method Up Close and Personal'). On the basis of this structured and regular variation across languages we suspect to be related, we then propose a single ancestral form (*p for the Indo-European 'five', 'foot' case, and *k for the Romance 'goat', 'dear' one), selecting the reconstructed form which will allow the most plausible series of changes into the attested forms. In both our examples, we reconstruct stops, which are retained in some daughters but change into fricatives, an extremely common example of lenition, in others.

When a change happens in the ancestor of one set of daughter languages but not in others (for instance, we find *p > /f/ in Gothic, German and English, but not in Greek or Sanskrit), this provides evidence for subgrouping within a larger family. In this case, we establish Germanic, and its own intermediate ancestor, Proto-Germanic, and distinguish the Germanic subgroup from the separate subgroup of Indo-Iranian languages which includes Sanskrit and its own present-day daughters (like Hindi-Urdu, Bengali and Gujarati). Subsequent cycles of identifying correspondences, then reconstructing ancestral forms and changes, will motivate subgroups within subgroups – North, East and West Germanic, for instance. It follows that the comparative method is closely associated with the family tree model: the idea of successive changes which progressively separate out branches and sub-branches of a family maps rather neatly onto a graphical representation with nodes, branches and split points, as in the family tree. When linguists talk about genetic classification of languages, then, they typically mean the results of the application of the comparative method, and its output in terms of typologically-reasonable reconstructed ancestral forms; sequences of plausible linguistic changes in different subgroups; and a summation of this history in a language family tree.

It is at this point that the incompatibility between contact and classification starts to become apparent: there are assumptions inherent in the application of the comparative method, and in the tree model, which sit uncomfortably with the effects of contact. This uneasy relationship is articulated, for instance, by Hall (1966: 115), who outlines two pillars of genetic classification; first, that "among languages related through having come from a common source, the process of differentiation has always been gradual"; and second, that in such cases "the relationship has always been 'pure', that is, there has been little or no introduction of structural patterns [...] from any source outside the language family concerned". Borrowing is problematic, of course, because the comparative method relies on prioritisation of changes and features which reflect common ancestry. Regular correspondences, which are the first and most important signal of relatedness, are found in cognates, which are defined as coming plausibly from a single common ancestor.

There are (at least) two difficulties here. First, this idea of linguistic purity (even leaving aside the unfortunate connotational consequence that borrowing is somehow impure or deviant) becomes more difficult to sustain as we recognise how common language contact is, and find out more and more about the limits on borrowability – or indeed the lack of such limits. There is certainly plenty of opportunity for borrowing, given that the majority of people in the world are at least bilingual, and that communications with other language groups are on the increase in the modern world; it follows therefore that "language contact is the norm, not the exception" (Thomason 2001: 12). Moreover, there is an increasing recognition that what can be borrowed depends principally on the sociolinguistic circumstances – Thomason (2003: 694) suggests that "when contact is intense enough, there appear to be no absolute linguistic barriers at all to borrowing". Given intense contact, propitious social circumstances and attitudes, and consequently considerable transfer from one language to another, it is entirely possible for the appearance of regular correspondences to arise between languages which do not in fact share a common ancestor in the genetic sense, though of course those transferred *features* would reflect a single origin in the donor rather than the recipient language.

Naturally, these pitfalls will only derail the comparative method if we do not recognise borrowings for what they are. It is straightforward to come up with 'what if' scenarios concerning apparent regularities which we might see as evidence for a spurious family resemblance, as Campbell (2003: 267) does for instance when he notes that Finnish, having borrowed liberally from Indo-European even in basic vocabulary, shows apparent correspondences between the medial consonant of *äiti* 'mother' and the initial consonant of *tytär* 'daughter' and Germanic forms like *Mutter, mother, Tochter, daughter*. As Campbell also notes, approximately 15% of the 3000 most common words in Turkish and Persian have been borrowed from Arabic, so that potentially "if Arabic, Persian, and Turkish were separated now and studied 3,000 years hence by linguists having no historical records, lists of cognates could easily be found, sound correspondences established, and an erroneous genetic relationship postulated" (Pierce 1965: 31, quoted in Campbell 2003: 271).

If contact features are misdiagnosed as indications of common ancestry, then obviously the comparative method can go awry: so, for some time Armenian was thought to be an Iranian language (still within Indo-European, but in the wrong sub-family) on the basis of shared vocabulary which turned out to be mainly loans (Ellison and Kirby 2006). Likewise, Thai has borrowed extensively from Chinese, and many of these loanwords "date back a thousand years. They are now so well assimilated that some of the identifications are controversial" (Goddard 2005: 59). Add to this the typological similarities between Thai and Chinese (which are both isolating languages with tone), and it is not surprising that the closeness of their relationship has been measured very differently at different times.

As we shall see in section 2, this potentially confusing influence of contact has often been dealt with by assuming that loans can be identified and factored out, or even by the development of methods to spot loans and remove them. However, this will apply primarily to cases where a language has a single genetic or family history, with additional influence from an unrelated or less closely related source; this is the case, for instance, for Romanian, which has borrowed extensively from Slavic languages, but can be demonstrated to be genetically Romance nonetheless. The challenge is greater in the case of genuine contact languages – those which, as Thomason (2003: 706) puts it, exhibit "contact-language genesis" as opposed to "contact-induced change". In the case of pidgins, creoles, and mixed languages, as we shall see below, there is no additional layer of borrowings which we can hope to strip away – rather, these languages owe their very existence to the mingling together of resources from more than one linguistic source, and it is challenging at best, and entirely pointless at worst, to demonstrate that one source should be prioritised over the other(s). Creoles, for instance, are spectacularly problematic here, since they inherit and adapt features from both superstrate and substrate languages (see other chapters in this volume for far more extensive discussion), but very commonly these contributors themselves come from entirely different families. How can we then say that the creole itself belongs to a single family?

To cut a classificatory knot, we might argue that the (mostly European) superstrate should be prioritised in assigning the creole to a family – this idea would have some dubious sociohistorical antecedents, if little objective linguistic validity. While this would mean that the main affinity of Haitian Creole is to French, for example, it still does not resolve key questions about the configuration of the consequent family tree: in this case, is Haitian Creole a daughter of French, or a sister, or a new branch of Romance altogether (see McMahon 1994: 269)? Matters only get worse when we consider Taylor's arguments (e.g. 1956; see Mühlhäusler 1986: 35) that genetic relationships may alter through the history of a creole, as with "languages such as Papiamento, spoken on the Dutch Antilles, which allegedly changed from a Portuguese-based to a Spanish-based creole, and Sranan of Surinam, which changed from a Portuguese creole to an English one". One can argue over the direction of change (so, Smith 1987 claims on phonological grounds that the English elements of Surinamese creoles are older than the Portuguese ones): either way, this kind of wholesale relexification is not something we would expect to find in non-creole languages; but it certainly highlights the problems of attempting to accommodate creoles in family trees. Trees do show the path of change, but the assumption is that the path is divergent, and reflects a consistent common ancestor; languages are not meant to hop out of one tree at a particular point in their history and turn up in another.

We shall return to these complex issues in section 2 below, but for the moment it is worth introducing the idea that family trees, and the assumptions inherent in their construction, might be part of the problem rather than part of the solution here. As Singh (2000: 23) suggests, "It is arguable that the linguistic family tree is only as real as the assumption that languages have stable elements that are not vulnerable to change in situations of contact. But what if this is in fact not the case?"

1.3. Contact and current theories of language change

In dealing with the difficulties contact causes for language classification, we must inevitably engage with issues of language change, and of how language change is to be defined and theorised. This, in turn, relies on what we mean by 'language' per se, since as Janda and Joseph (2003: 4) perceptively note, "The nature of an entity largely determines how it can change".

There are currently many different theories of language change, partly depending on which linguistic models they are embedded in; but at the risk of oversimplifying, they probably fall into two categories. One focuses primarily on the sociohistorical aspects of change, the concept of change in progress, and the mechanisms for the cycle from variation to change – with variation developing; one variant perhaps being extended, and acquiring social marking or significance; and this dominant variant then becoming the norm, until the whole cycle starts again. The other concept of change is more interested in the relationship between two grammars, compared as snapshots across generations. The key idea here is that change can be defined as what happens when Grammar 2 is learned on the basis of data generated by Grammar 1, but with crucial differences from Grammar 1.

We shall return to the first set of issues, around diffusion, in sections 2 and 3 below. Diffusion from one speaker to another, and hence from one linguistic system to another, is after all at the heart of contact-induced change as well as the spread of features and the transition from variation to change within a single language – though it is worth noting Thomason's (2003: 687) intriguing comment that "the spread of innovations within a speech community has traditionally been considered separately from the diffusion of features across dialect and especially language boundaries". Turning for the moment to the second concept of language change, a good recent example is Hale (2007), an advanced textbook on historical linguistics with, notably, no entry in the index for 'contact' or 'language contact'. As I shall hope to show, this very fact is relevant to our discussion.

Hale considers historical linguistics to be the search for constraints on possible changes from one generation to another. He does not propose to deal with change in speech communities, the variation-and-change end of the continuum, which he regards as belonging to another domain altogether, "the socio-political conception of language" (2007: 35–6). However, while Hale does not consider contact, he does discuss what he calls "diffusion". An obvious initial question might be why we would see change and diffusion, in Hale's terms, as distinct; and there are at least three relevant factors.

First, Hale invokes a distinction between imperfect transmission and accurate imitation: whereas change is defined as "imperfect transmission of some feature of the grammar", "[i]n the case of diffusion, an acquirer has *accurately* adopted a linguistic feature from some speaker" (2007: 36). This in itself begs a question, since the idea of accurate transfer of language material in diffusion appears not to take account of the many cases of adaptation, where the borrowed feature may alter in form as a consequence of being filtered through the borrower's own first language system (for a summary, see McMahon 1994: Chapter 8). Second, Hale suggests that children 'do' change while adults 'do' diffusion. To some extent, this assumption goes hand-in-hand with the previous point, since both follow from a difference in what is thought to be possible at different stages in the lifespan. If children can build novel computational components of their grammar, then they can be creative; but if adults can only learn new bits of linguistic material, then we expect them to be more faithful, as it were, to the input they hear.

However, Hale (2007: 47) then argues that we can effectively set aside the cases of adult change, or diffusion, on the grounds that

> there is nothing [...] which would indicate that the instances of adult change are in any way more 'valuable' for the development of a theory of language change. The restructuring – optimization – that children do would seem to be the more interesting place to look for constraints on change. The epistemological status of 'suboptimal' grammars hardly makes one want to focus the attention of a constrained theory of change in that area.

Setting aside the idea of "suboptimal" grammars for the moment, we might nonetheless suggest that even if adult changes are no *more* valuable, there is surely no necessary indication that they are *less* valuable either. Perhaps bringing 'child' and 'adult' change together would give a more complete picture? After all, we now know that adults can restructure, relearn and revise their language in ways we might not have thought possible before, for instance, Sankoff's work on lifespan changes, notably for [r] > [ʀ] in Montreal French (Sankoff and Blondeau 2007). Furthermore, while Labov (2007) does also distinguish transmission (change within a speech community) from diffusion (which involves influence from one speech community on another), and while he associates the former with children and the latter with adults, he does not categorise one as change and the other as something different. On the contrary, Labov argues that "the difference will [...] be a matter of degree, since recent studies of language change across the lifespan have shown that adults do participate in ongoing change, though more sporadically and at a much lower rate than children" (2007: 383). Moreover, Labov (2007: 382) concludes from this that "both family tree models and wave models are needed to account for the history and relatedness of language families".

In view of these ongoing debates, we must ask what we might gain by restricting our focus to just what Hale calls change and excluding diffusion. Hale argues that the two have to be distinguished because changes do not necessarily diffuse (though some do); hence, "It is clear that if we were trying to develop a set of constraints on possible change, changes which do not diffuse (because, e.g., the individual in which they are manifested does not occupy the type of sociolinguistic nexus which leads others to adopt his/her linguistic features) are every bit as relevant as those that do" (2007: 39). This, however, suggests that the two should be given equal weight, since the argument should surely cut both ways, meaning that those changes which diffuse are every bit as relevant as those which don't. Perhaps most importantly, however, Hale sees change as necessarily regular, whereas he regards diffusion as "a highly unconstrained process – i.e., that any possible 'change' could just as easily diffuse under the proper sociolinguistic conditions for diffusion" (2007: 39); consequently, "I do not [...] think that including diffusion events in the data being accounted for in our theory of 'change' will help us in our efforts to develop a constrained theory" (2007: 40).

The key point, then, seems to be that focusing only on change (in Hale's terms) might allow us to account for a heavily circumscribed set of phenomena, by excluding everything else to a self-defining periphery, a time-honoured technique for generative linguistics (and note here Hale's reference above to 'suboptimal' grammars). However, as we have seen, Labov (2007) suggests that the line between what children do, and what adults do, is porous, and the difference is one of quantity rather than quality. Furthermore, while a temporary restriction of focus might be justified on the grounds that it allows us to make progress in understanding the phenomenon we are focusing on, Hale has to concede that he is "not yet in a position to present a detailed theory of constraints on possible change –

we have not yet reached the point in the development of historical linguistics to know what such a theory would look like in any significant detail" (2007: 47). In which case, there may be no harm in bringing diffusion as well as change back into the picture, as part of a slightly different enterprise – namely, to allow us to document fully what actually happens, and perhaps what *can* happen, in the case of both internally-motivated and externally-motivated, or contact-induced, change. Part of this involves considering whether diffusion, in Hale's terms, might often lead to change, or more generally whether there is an interesting relationship between them. It might even be the case that the role children appear to play in some crucial examples of contact-driven or contact-focused change, as in the development of creoles from prior pidgins over a short interval of time, or the emergence of mixed languages within a generation or little more, could in fact bridge the gap between change and diffusion. This is important, since Hale appears to restrict change to the relationship between two grammars, the adult's and the child's, where the output of the adult's grammar provides input to the child's construction of a potentially new and distinct system. This is much more like Janda and Joseph's (2003: 13) notion of diachronic correspondence, which emerges from "juxtaposing two potentially non-adjacent times"; this might include inter-generational grammar comparison. Change, on the other hand, must be seen as "requiring adoption, over time, by all – or at least much – of a group" (2003: 13). This conception of change is necessarily social: even change which is motivated within the system of a specific language or dialect will crucially involve spread, or diffusion, from one speaker to others. We need to bear in mind that speakers, not language systems, are the agents here: "our view on the identity of the parties most responsible for linguistic change is, rather: we think speakers have something to do with it" (Janda and Joseph 2003: 10).

1.4. What is a 'contact language'?

This chapter is intended to focus on genetic classification, which we have discussed at some length already, in the specific context of contact languages. In the sections above, quite a lot has been said about language contact, but rather little about contact languages. This is a deliberate strategy, since I will argue below that the main problems for classification arise from the former rather than the latter: they may look starker and be harder to ignore when we consider contact languages, but they are just as real for any kind of contact-induced language change. This is particularly important because, in fact, contact languages are not entirely straightforward to define.

Thomason (2001: 158) notes that, when we consider 'contact language', "There is unfortunately no uniform definition of the term in the scholarly literature, but there are two main kinds of usage". The first invokes the typical usage of certain languages as lingua francas, which are found in intergroup communication; this would often apply to a pidgin or creole, which develops in part to allow communication between groups which lack any pre-existing common language, but would equally describe Latin throughout much of Europe in the Middle Ages and Renaissance, or English at many modern academic conferences. The second, and now arguably more common definition, and the one we will develop further below, has to do with the historical origins of the language in question, not primarily its pattern of usage; in Thomason's terms (2001: 158):

> [...] a contact language is any new language that arises in a contact situation. Linguistically, a contact language is identifiable by the fact that its lexicon and grammatical structures cannot all be traced back primarily to the same source language; they are therefore mixed languages in the technical historical linguistic sense: they did not arise primarily through descent with modification from a single earlier language. By definition, therefore, contact languages are not members of any language family and thus belong in no family tree – except perhaps as the ancestor of a language family [...] In other words, I am defining 'contact language' on the basis of the type(s) of historical connections to other languages.

Archetypally, Thomason's second definition involves pidgins and creoles, and bilingual mixed languages. While pidgins (and hence in a sense creoles, which develop out of pidgins) do arise as lingua francas, bilingual mixed languages obviously do not: they are products of in-group rather than out-group communication, and reflect identity of a new social group. For example, Michif, the language of the Métis of Canada, is a mixture of French noun phrases and Cree verb phrases and sentential syntax developed by bilingual speakers of both to mark the identity of their emerging ethnic group (Bakker 1997, Bakker and Mous 1994).

However, this apparently straightforward definition masks a range of persistent and variable disagreement. Mühlhäusler (1986: xi), for instance, cites Bickerton's First Law of Creole Studies, which states that "Every creolist's analysis can be directly contradicted by that creolist's own texts and citations", suggesting that definitions of pidgins, creoles and mixed languages are characteristically controversial. Thomason herself notes that bilingual mixed languages can fit into the Michif class, but can alternatively (as in the case of Ma'á or Romani) reflect a long history of borrowing from one language into another, marking the identity of a persistent rather than an emergent ethnic group. One problem, then, is that the categories of pidgin, creole and mixed language themselves are permeable and difficult to define in a way which will be agreed by all scholars: are these language types to be defined according to their origins, or the mode or speed of development, or the linguistic characteristics of the eventual system? Thomason (2001: 167) entitles a section "Pidgins and creoles are not maximally simple and not all alike", indicating part of the difficulty here. Matters get even worse when we consider Thomason's view that we also need to take into account deliberate language change, when speakers create bilingual mixed languages, for instance, to mark emerging ethnic identities, or invent a secret language explicitly to prevent access of 'outsiders' to this in-group system.

Thomason (2001: 70–71) defines contact languages in part by their location on a continuum, though she admits that the key factor in determining placement on the continuum, namely intensity of contact, "is a vague notion, but it is difficult to pin down more precisely in a way that applies to a wide range of contact situations; among the factors that contribute to greater intensity of contact are a high level of bilingualism, socioeconomic and/or political pressure on one speaker group in a two-language contact situation to shift to the other language, length of contact, and relative sizes of speaker populations" (2003: 689). Furthermore, the more intense the contact is, the less likely we are to be able to set limits on what can in principle be borrowed: "there are no absolute linguistic constraints on the kinds and degrees of linguistic interference that can occur [...] in this domain everything seems to be possible, although some things are improbable" (Thomason 2003: 695). Borrowing taken to extremes, as in the case of Ma'á, therefore leaks in terms of its effects into the category of true bilingual mixtures like Michif. It is immediately clear that this is incompatible with Hale's wish to establish clear constraints on change, especially given that (Thomason 2003: 706–07):

> The mechanisms through which contact languages arise are essentially the same as those which operate in ordinary contact-induced change – and [...] to a considerable extent in internally motivated change as well. Contact languages are therefore extreme results of quite ordinary processes. Moreover, the boundaries between contact languages and cases of heavy borrowing or extensive shift-induced interference are fuzzy [...] Because there are borderline cases, and because the same mechanisms are common to both, the differences are best characterised as ones of degree, not of kind.

So, while some languages clearly do show more effects of contact than others, and may therefore pose particular problems for genetic classification, it is unwise to assume that contact can be disregarded for any language or language group. The corollary of this is that in principle, any particular change may or may not reflect contact: to establish causation either way beyond reasonable doubt, we need to know the structure of both languages at the time of the change, and to be able to show that the change definitely happened during the period of contact. As Thomason sensibly notes, "the lesson here is that establishing contact as a cause of language change is possible under favorable circumstances but impossible under less favorable circumstances" (2003: 710). Contra Hale, then, it appears that distinguishing diffusion from change may ultimately be possible in some privileged cases at a later stage of the argument, but that we would need to know a good deal more about the theory of change first. Furthermore, it follows that contact is not relevant only for pidgins, creoles and mixed languages, but must be recognised as a major issue for language family construction and testing in the most general and global of terms.

2. Previous approaches to contact and classification

Until recently, reconciling contact with classification, given their antithetical effects, has followed two routes. First, priority may be given to aspects of language structure which are thought to be less commonly influenced by contact-induced change. Alternatively, there are attempts to remove contact languages from the group of languages to be classified.

If contact is an issue for genetic classification, then, one option is to identify the signs of contact and factor them out. If, as Kessler (2001: 5) suggests, "borrowing has been considered noise in the system", then we should expect that "loans are to be sought out and discarded before the real work can proceed". The assumption here is that there is always a real, underlying story of family affiliation, and we need to remove the loans in order to access that story. Of course, this brings along some inherent claims to the effect that some aspects of language history (and speaker history) are more important than others. It is also not clear that we have a reliable methodology for detecting loans in the first place. There is a long-standing argument in the literature about prioritising the basic vocabulary, which is thought to be less susceptible to borrowing on the grounds that every language will have words for universal human experiences in any case, but as Embleton (1986) and Kessler (2001) have demonstrated, there can still be borrowings even here, especially where contact is protracted and intense. There has been some progress on isolating sectors of basic, Swadesh-type meaning lists which change relatively slowly and appear to be resistant to borrowing, as opposed to more changeable, more borrowable meanings (see McMahon and McMahon 2005; McMahon et al. 2005; Wichmann et al. 2009), but work in this area is still in its early stages. In addition, these studies consider only lexical data, whereas we know contact can affect all levels of the grammar; we shall return in section 3 below to recent developments in phonetic and morphosyntactic comparison.

For the moment, even if we were able to sideline contact-induced changes for some languages, it is clearly not possible (or at least highly artificial) to try to do so in the case of contact languages themselves, since without a history of contact, axiomatically, these would not exist. However, as noted in section 1.4 above, it is not always possible to establish what counts as a contact language, and the emerging preferred model is to regard languages as falling on a continuum depending on the relative contribution of contact in their histories, rather than imposing a binary division between contact and non-contact languages. As suggested in the previous section, and following Thomason (2003), the mechanisms leading to normal borrowing and to the formation of contact languages are rather similar. Furthermore, there are some similarities between the mechanisms underlying contact-induced and internally-motivated change; and when we turn to causation, it is extremely challenging to demonstrate beyond reasonable doubt that contact is the sole cause of a change, or even that it did or did not play a role. It is often still assumed that the transfer of a form could relatively straightforwardly be traced from one language to another, especially where this took place across language family boundaries so that the loan would stand out like the proverbial sore thumb; but it is now becoming clear that structure may be borrowed without lexical material, native lexis being commandeered to fill a new role (Mithun 2008). Any focus on lexical comparison in such cases would see continuity; we can only hope to spot the contribution of another language if we compare different periods across levels of the grammar, and therefore note that the lexical material in question has begun to do a different job, and that the borrowing language has changed in its typological profile from one period to the next, moving closer to an adjacent or socially influential language.

Looking back in history, we must also admit that it is difficult, in the absence of plentiful written records, to determine whether a language has a pidgin, creole or mixed language history. There is a tendency to regard these contact language types as a product of the modern era, but language contact is certainly not a recent process, and there is a kind of arrogance in claiming for our own era phenomena like pidginisation, lingua francas, and new communities which might develop their own identities and require a linguistic 'badge'. There are long-standing arguments that Middle English, or Romance during the break-up of Vulgar Latin, may have been creoles. Romaine (1988) proposes 30 pan-creole features, of which Old Japanese exhibits about a third and Modern English very few; but nonetheless, the question of whether we can legitimately conclude that Old Japanese was definitely a creole, while Middle English was not, is a contentious one (McMahon 1994: 268; and see McWhorter 1998, 2000, 2005; Ansaldo, Matthews and Lim 2007; Bakker et al. 2011).

In short, there is a tendency to assume that it is easy to identify contact languages like pidgins, creoles and bilingual mixtures (and subsequently exclude them from further genealogical analysis), because these have short histories and we tend to know where they came from and under what circumstances. However, if we allow that some of the key forces in their formation may extend back beyond the recent past, we cannot necessarily assume this will always be true. It appears that these language-types do 'leak' into linguistic systems of other kinds; boundaries are fuzzy; and the kinds of changes involved often overlap (see also Trudgill 1976; McMahon 1994: Chapter 10). In that case, we should expect that it will be impossible to rule out languages and changes of a specific sort to ensure that these will not interfere with theories that are meant to hold for the general case. Perhaps there is no 'general case' to ring-fence in the first place.

Nonetheless, there have been suggestions that contact languages, or the clearest and least contentious cases of languages which show very strong signals of a contact history, cannot be accommodated in the conventional tree-based paradigm. To take just one illustrative example, there have been various attempts to reconcile the family tree with the existence of potentially disruptive pidgins and creoles. One option is to extend the tree metaphor to cover a more extensive and modern range of family types, as Taylor (1956: 413) notably does in his contention that "languages originating in a pidgin or jargon, while genetically 'orphans', may be said to have two 'foster-parents': one that provides the basic morphological and/or syntactic pattern, and another from which the fundamental vocabulary is taken". As McMahon (1994: 269) observes, this suggests a clearer and more standard division of the contribution from the substrate and superstrate languages than we tend to find in real cases; furthermore (Singh 2000: 28), much of the appeal of the family tree rests on its pictorial simplicity, and this is inevitably compromised by any attempt to introduce foster-families, step-children and orphans. There is an air of desperation in modifying the family tree to accommodate languages which simply do not fit.

On the other hand, Hall (1966: 117) argues that pidgins and creoles can be accommodated in family trees, not by changing our conception of the tree, but by taking a particular view of the development of pidgins and creoles. To be more precise, Hall argues that these contact languages are not made up of equal contributions from two (or more) sources – on the contrary, one contributing language can always be identified as first among equals. He concedes that "a language might conceivably combine elements from two or more sources so that they were perfectly evenly balanced and so that they would be, therefore, unclassifiable according to our customary assumption", but contends that "[...] in practice, such a condition of perfect balance is never found [...] In Haitian Creole, the proportion of French structure is both greater and more fundamental than that of African-type structure; and the same is true of Chinese Pidgin English, Neo-Melanesian, Sranan, Gullah, etc., in relation to English and the various substrata involved" (1966: 117). However, even if it were true that we could somehow weigh the contributions of the various languages (cf. Michaelis 2008) involved and establish which contribution was "greater and more fundamental", classifying according to that single source would necessarily mean leaving out of account those aspects of the pidgin or creole which came from other sources. Furthermore, even if Hall's comment on the lack of perfect balance was true for those languages known when he was writing, our understanding of the complexities of language mixing is now more extensive, and truly mixed languages seem to go against his argument. If we take the case of a bilingual mixture like Michif, we will be faced with the need to prioritise nouns over verbs, or the reverse, depending on whether we wish to prioritise French over Cree or vice versa. Even for the conventional picture of superstrate versus substrate contributions (which, as we have seen, is arguably idealised), it is difficult to argue convincingly that lexis should automatically outweigh structure, or the other way around. If French is essentially the lexifier language, and does not contribute much of the grammar, then classifying Haitian Creole as Romance means considering only that level of the grammar which is more and more being seen as the primary locus of borrowing. In that case, it might seem preferable to classify according to the morphosyntax, which is sometimes argued to be a more secure indicator of genetic affiliation (Longobardi and Guardiano 2009). On this basis, Sylvain (1936; quoted in Singh 2000: 27) argues that Haitian Creole is actually an Ewe language with French vocabulary (and see also Lefebvre 1998). On the other hand, pidgins may have roughly equal contributions to basic and non-basic vocabulary from two languages, but little or no morphology, as with Russenorsk, Trio-Ndyuka, and Yimas-Arafundi pidgin (Peter Bakker p.c.; and Foley 2006).

An alternative strategy is to keep the family tree model without modification, and develop a single family consisting only of pidgins and creoles (see Singh 2000: 47; Holm 1988; Rijkhoff and Bakker 1998). This proposal would run into trouble given the usual assumption that family trees in the usual comparative sense can be climbed up through reconstruction. In other words, we would expect to be able to apply the comparative method to reconstruct the original 'proto-pidgin' – and of course, it is historically impossible for all creoles to descend from the same proto-pidgin source. Even for smaller and more coherent groups of pidgins and creoles, monogenesis must often be combined with relexification, the idea that pidgin speakers arriving in a new environment (for instance through slavery) with a new superstrate language will exchange much of their vocabulary for items derived from that new superstrate. This means that pidgins and creoles reflect an extremely strong contribution from convergence rather than divergence, although it is regular divergence, descent with modification, that allows us to apply the comparative method. Even if key structural features were maintained from the original proto-pidgin despite the disruptive influence of relexification, we would not find the regular and repeated correspondences necessary to establish cognates and reconstruct changes. The influence of the (re)lexifier language also cannot be accommodated in the tree. We might retreat to work on a smaller scale, and attempt to establish family trees for relatively local groups of pidgins and creoles; but we will still face insurmountable obstacles. For instance, Goodman (1964) argued for a single origin of all French creoles, in West Africa, while Gilman (1978) proposes a Proto-Pidgin English which gives rise to both Jamaican Creole, and Cameroonian Pidgin English, and Hancock (1987) proposes a tree for English creoles (see also Schneider 1990; and Daval-Markussen and Bakker 2011). However, as Mühlhäusler (1986: 36) shows, such neat tree-based interpretations are frequently at odds with the sociohistorical evidence, which "suggests that Cameroonian Pidgin English as spoken today is not a continuation of earlier West African coastal Pidgin English, but a more recent import from Sierra Leone Krio [...] and that Krio, in turn, may be either a direct descendant of or heavily influenced by Jamaican Creole and possibly other West Indian Creole Englishes". It follows that the apparent tree is concealing a much more entangled picture, featuring various interrelationships based not only on descent but on contact. Simplification of this to fit in with the orthodoxy of the family tree risks prioritising a particular model over the complexities of actual language histories, and cannot be supported by the evidence.

In the face of these persistent difficulties, it may be best to accept that contact languages are incompatible with the family tree, as Thomason and Kaufman (1988) do when they designate pidgins, creoles and bilingual mixtures 'non-genetic' languages. Their argument is that such languages have ancestors which belonged to language families, but that pidgins and creoles developed through a process of discontinuous transmission, and therefore can no longer be classified using the conventional tree model. Here, however, we return to the problem of how and where we draw the line, an especially acute difficulty given that Thomason and Kaufman themselves extend the set of non-genetic languages to those which have undergone extensive structural borrowing. As we have already seen, intensity of borrowing is a cline, so that it is relatively straightforward to say that language X shows more signs of contact-induced change than language Y, but much harder (if indeed it is possible in principle) to motivate a binary division between X as an example of a contact language and Y as a non-contact language which is compatible with the classical family tree. Furthermore, excluding languages with strong signals of contact can have unintended detrimental effects. Romanian, for example, shows considerable effects of contact with its neighbouring Slavic languages which distance it from its relatives within Romance. However, it maintains evidence of features, such as the marking and distribution of cases in the noun phrase, which are not available in other family members, and which are therefore of great relevance for reconstruction of the common ancestor. Excluding Romanian, in other words, means accepting a much blurrier picture of Proto-Romance, and wilfully discarding data which might allow us to confirm hypothesised structures of Vulgar Latin.

Perhaps worst of all, there are emerging arguments that the biggest challenge to the comparative method is not contact languages, but long-term dialect continua and the consequent interweaving of lexical items and grammars in related languages and varieties. This is put very well by Harrison (2003: 232): "If time is one great adversary of the comparative method, prolonged socio-economic intercourse amongst small-scale (genetically related) linguistic communities is another. Language contact and borrowing are a normal occurrence, and make comparative linguistics interesting. But most instances of borrowing can be recognized as such, and factored out." Even accepting that there is an element of wishful thinking here, we can conclude that there is no chance of such 'factoring out' in situations like the one described by Grace (1981, 1985, 1990) in New Caledonia, where the languages Grand Couli and Canala clearly seem to be genetically related, but application of the comparative method conceals more than it reveals. Although the two languages have identical consonant and vowel inventories (with 24 consonants and 18 vowels), comparative reconstruction suggests a whopping 140 consonant, and 172 vowel correspondences. Something deeply irregular seems to be happening from the point of view of the comparative method, and Harrison suggests that the key is progressive contact and mixing. The New Caledonian situation "[…] appears to have been the result of a slow but relentless dissolving of lexical resources into a common pool. The effect on comparative historical method is profound too. We 'know' the languages are related, but can't demonstrate that they are by using the logic of the comparative method" (Harrison 2003: 232). More importantly, Harrison suggests that there are similar cases elsewhere, including in Arnhem Land, northern Australia – here also "the languages are grammatically quite similar, often admitting of morpheme-by-morpheme translation. The lexica look comparable. But the method doesn't work" (2003: 232; and see Heath 1978).

Dialect continua have long been recognised as a difficulty for the family tree (see the discussion in Ringe, Warnow and Taylor 2002, for instance); but their significance is only now being fully modelled. While there is a tendency to see the dialect continuum as a case of productive and continual inter-borrowing, Heggarty, Maguire and McMahon (2010) argue that continua must be distinguished very sharply from contact-induced change. Contact can take place regardless of whether the languages involved are related or not; but dialect continua necessarily involve related varieties, and represent a stage in the break-up of a proto-language or original small family. That is, the progressive distancing of daughter varieties and ultimately languages from a common ancestor may take place either through a split, archetypally involving physical separation of populations and consequent isolation by distance; or when "[a] speaker population expands (whether suddenly or more progressively) over a continuous territory, across which a degree of contact is maintained […] this leads to language divergence in a pattern of overlapping, cross-cutting waves" (Heggarty, Maguire and McMahon 2010: 3830). As this phrasing suggests, these scenarios map onto the family tree and the wave model respectively; but crucially, both represent models of language divergence, whereas contact and borrowing are essentially convergent. Again, we find a challenge to the family tree: even when we move away from contact-induced change, we will frequently find ourselves confronting mechanisms of divergence which lend themselves more to a visual representation in terms of waves or webs than in the elegant but simplistic family tree.

3. Trees, networks and computational methods

3.1. Are trees the root of the problem?

On the whole, things are not looking good for the family tree. There are three problems, only the last directly relevant to our topic of contact, but together damning for any attempt to justify the tree as the only or even the principal representation of language history. First, trees cannot sensibly deal with common, parallel changes, for instance in phonology. There are many recurring patterns across the world's languages which represent neither convergence nor divergence, but which cannot blithely be attributed to chance either, since they reflect natural and sometimes almost inevitable changes following from aspects of our biological predispositions for language. Secondly, as we saw in the previous section, divergence can involve a more tree-like series of splits, or a more wave-like, dialect continuum pattern; and indeed, the two are highly likely to interact in the history of any language family. It follows that (Heggarty, Maguire and McMahon 2010: 3842):

> [...] tree-only representations do not, indeed cannot, necessarily tell us everything significant about language histories. Indeed, by prioritising certain 'diagnostic' changes and overriding others, the tree-only approach risks misrepresenting the overall story. If our real goal is to uncover the histories of the *populations* that spoke given languages, rather than abstract schemas 'intellectually satisfying' for their binary purity, then it is served by using language data to arrive at a picture of the nature and degree of cohesion (or otherwise) of speech communities within a language family, through the story of its divergence.

Finally, returning to the central point of this chapter, some changes and some aspects of language history are genuinely convergent; and while contact-induced changes may account for a relatively small proportion of the features of some languages, there may in contact languages themselves be a much more balanced and less predictable contribution from more than one source. If, as suggested in the previous sections, we cannot hope to isolate a group of convergent languages from the general case of divergent ones, but rather face a continuum between extremes, it seems increasingly clear that the family tree in turn loses its status as the dominant or sole model of language history. What, then, are the alternatives?

3.2. Networks and computational phylogenetics

There is an understandable attraction about the family tree model: it is visually simple and uncluttered, and reflects a straightforward set of assumptions about the 'real' underlying causes and mechanisms of language change. It is, however, intrinsically connected to a single kind of history, involving relatively punctual divergence. The more inclusive we want our models to be, the less adequate the tree, and the less defensible our attempts to cling to it appear. That is not to say, of course, that there are no tree-like aspects in the histories of language families – but the degree of treeness may vary considerably from one family or one area to another. If we are to take an inclusive approach, attempting to model both sorts of divergence, convergent contact-induced change, and common parallel innovations, "what we need is a single model which could sort out for us how much of a language is tree-like and how much non-tree-like, and display the [...] driving forces, and resulting language features, differently" (McMahon and McMahon 2005: 139).

This problem is not unknown in other fields where we need to consider variation, change and their causes and origins; and most notably, solutions have been emerging for some time in biology. These involve the development of network models, which have the central aim of diagnosing and displaying similarity among systems, regardless of its source. Where such similarities are straightforwardly divergent, then a network program will display an output indistinguishable from a tree; where there are interrelationships among units, suggesting parallel innovation or contact, then a more weblike structure will emerge. For most biological populations, and as it turns out for most cases explored so far involving languages and dialects (Forster and Renfrew 2007; McMahon and McMahon 2005; McMahon et al. 2007), the truth lies somewhere in between and there will be both tree-like and non-tree-like signals. Networks, in other words, are flexible; they do not require us to abandon the insights of the family tree, and they do not rule out the possibility that tree-like divergence will be the sole or the dominant factor in the histories of some language groups; but they do not limit us to the tree model either. In these circumstances, to borrow Heggarty's memorable terms, would you rather be a tree-hugger or a networker?

Although there are various different network programs available, the one which is perhaps most intensively used at present both by linguists and by colleagues working in cognate disciplines is NeighborNet (Bryant and Moulton 2004; Huson and Bryant 2006), which is downloadable within the Splitstree package (http://www-ab.informatik.uni-tuebingen.de/software/-splitstree4). One example of a NeighborNet, for phonetic comparison of varieties of English, is shown in Figure 1. Essentially, the network is constructed on the basis of the sounds of 110 common English words, transcribed by Warren Maguire from recordings of individual native speakers, and passed through a purpose-designed computer comparison program by Paul Heggarty; details of methodology and data can be found in McMahon et al. (2007) and at http://www.languagesandpeoples.com/-MethodsPhonetics.htm.

Genetic classification of contact languages 353

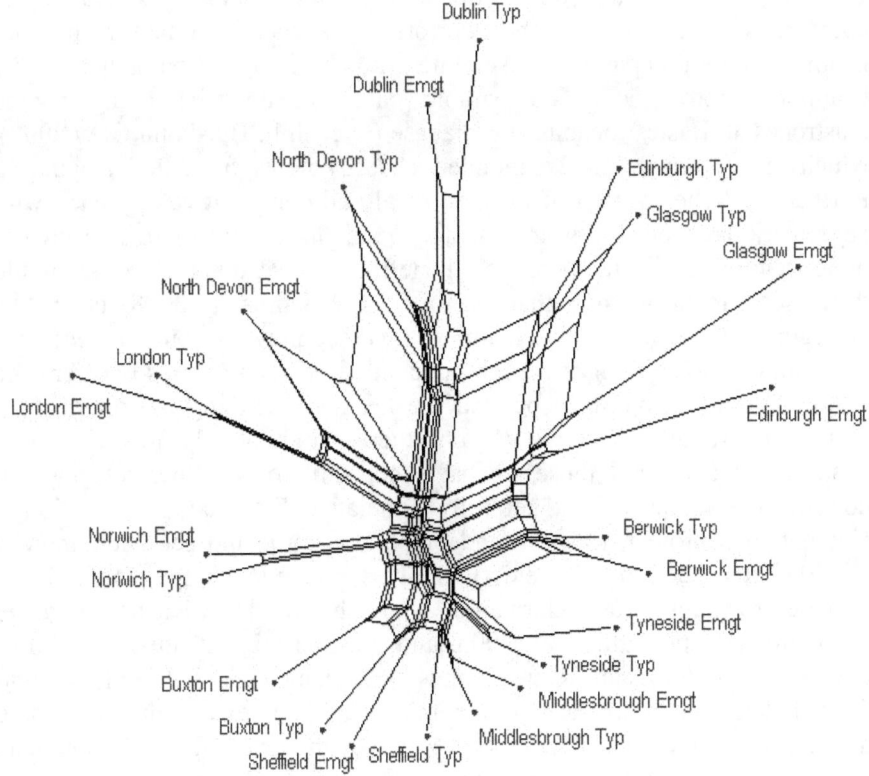

Figure 1. NeighborNet, selection of UK and Irish Typical and Emergent varieties

Even at this early stage, it is clear that network representations do have something to offer in visualising similarities, regardless of their sources. There are, however, two requirements before we can take advantage of such representations, the second specific to cases of contact, and the first more general. Initially, as we shall see in the rest of this section, we need an agreed way of measuring similarity for some linguistic feature(s), and such quantitative approaches are by no means equally far advanced in all areas of the grammar. Secondly, we need a way of figuring out which similarities reflect contact and which do not, since NeighborNet alone will not do that for us; we turn to this issue in section 3.3 below.

Until recently, the absence of comparative datasets across language families has been a fundamental difficulty in the development of quantitative, phylogenetic approaches to language: Dyen, Kruskal and Black (1992), with meaning lists for 92 Indo-European languages and varieties, is often used and cited, but is obviously restricted in scope.

Gradually, however, the construction and sharing of datasets is assuming in comparative linguistics the kind of priority it has had for some time in other historical and comparative disciplines, notably population genetics; for example, approximately comparable data can now be found in the Austronesian Basic Vocabulary Database (Greenhill, Blust and Gray 2008), which in September 2012 contained 199,224 items from 965 languages. Furthermore, the overlap of this historical and comparative approach with computational typology is increasingly recognised, and there is a greater understanding of the potential benefit that searchable, quantifiable databases can bring to both areas in what Wichmann (2008) calls "the emerging field of language dynamics" (and see now the journal *Language Dynamics and Change*). Such expanded databases also offer the opportunity of comparison beyond the lexis, introducing the option of a focus on structural features. Again, there are relatively few databases available to date, and those we have tend still to be either restricted in comparative scope, or not yet fully populated. For example, the Sound Comparisons project, (http://soundcomparisons.org; and see McMahon et al. 2007 and section 3.3 below) involves phonetic comparison only of varieties of English and Germanic; while the World Atlas of Language Structures (Haspelmath et al. 2005, and updated version http://wals.info/) covers 141 typological features and 2,650 languages, but only around 58,000 data points to date. While this is still an extremely impressive achievement, it does not represent close to the maximum 373,650 data points we would find if all languages had scores for all features; though of course the 'missing' values will reflect a mixture of truly absent data, and features which are not relevant or appropriate for a particular language or family.

More generally, there is increasing engagement with the possibilities of comparative morphosyntax, as discussed in Nerbonne (2009), who presents an overview of research using large syntactic databases, introducing a special journal issue devoted to current advances in this area. In the same volume, Longobardi and Guardiano (2009) focus not on surface typological features, but on abstract syntactic parameters derived from theoretical generative grammar, on which they base a proposal for what they call the Parametric Comparison Method, or PCM. Certainly, these abstract features depend on a particular theoretical model, which not every linguist would accept; but for those who do, the parameters offer the considerable advantage of belonging to a universal list which provides a clear basis for comparison across languages and families. As Longobardi and Guardiano note, results from PCM can also be compared with those involving lexical data; on this basis, they argue that "syntax is more conservative than the lexicon" (2009: 1695). More specifically, while "the taxonomies obtained through syntax and vocabulary closely resemble each other", it appears from PCM that "syntactic divergence from a common ancestor is slower; but also and most noticeably, that syntax continues to remain a potential good indicator of relative taxonomy among sets of distant languages whose vocabularies display too few cognates to make solid clusters identifiable" (Longobardi and Guardiano 2009: 1695). Although this analysis is still preliminary, it has considerable implications, and Longobardi and Guardiano (2009: 1679) suggest that it potentially "contributes to establishing formal grammar as a population science and historical linguistics as an important part of cognitive inquiry"; elsewhere, they refer to "parametric syntax as cognitive anthropology" (2009: 1696). Again, accessing these suggested advantages does mean accepting a certain abstract and rather universalist theoretical approach (though conversely, Longobardi and Guardiano propose that the theoretical model receives renewed support from its success in the historical domain). It must be acknowledged, though, that while we still know relatively little about the history of surface morphosyntactic features, for instance, nor about the more and less common trajectories of change in this domain, there has been work of considerable power and sophistication on change of more abstract morphosyntactic features (Roberts 2007). Whether or not diachronic generative syntax is one's model of first choice, it does offer predictions and proposals which historical and comparative linguists will increasingly have to contend with; it is easy to see future debates developing in the same direction for comparison of more abstract phonological features as opposed to closer-to-surface phonetic measures. One possible means on which to assess the relative performance of deeper as opposed to more surface-oriented comparisons in future might well be the extent to which they are able to deal with signals of contact; and as we saw in section 1.3 above, Hale's more abstract approach, which requires a perspective somewhat removed from speaker interactions and contact-induced change, might suggest there are considerable challenges in this respect for PCM and other similar approaches.

3.3. Typology, contact and common ancestry

As we have seen, finding directly comparable data in any linguistic domain is still an uphill task, and where databases are now being constructed, some are specific to particular language families or are typological rather than lending themselves necessarily to tracing language histories or affiliations. The Swadesh-type meaning list represents a positive start for lexical comparison, but its universality has been challenged and the fit of some meanings with some language families is uncertain, so that more nuanced comparisons need to be developed (see McMahon et al. 2007 for the Andean languages). In phonetics, there is an obvious universal basis, but it is not yet clear whether the optimal measures are acoustic or articulatory, and 'phonetics' is a broad term, depending on whether we interpret it as meaning very close to the surface or as relatively narrow phonology. The Sound Comparisons project, for example, is also limited by its own comparative methodology in being restricted to comparison of sounds in a list of cognates; since cognacy is a notion based on language family classification, it follows that this technique cannot be used to diagnose affiliation, and that it is also restricted in its current form to Germanic (or at best to Indo-European). For morphosyntax, the key again is finding the best set of features to compare, and ensuring that these are comparable across the widest possible range of languages; as we saw in the last section, recent developments in diachronic generative syntax offer the possibility of a universal set of parameters, but the cost is acceptance of the tenets of a particular theoretical model and its linguistic world view.

In general, we seem to be seeing a shift away from lexical and towards structural comparison. At best, this is a very positive trend, since it allows us flexibility in the features we include, and perhaps most importantly, provides an exciting opportunity to assess whether comparisons for different levels of the grammar consistently point in the same direction, or whether we should prioritise certain data as phylogenetic signals (as Longobardi and Guardiano (2009) suggested for syntax as opposed to lexis). Paradoxically, however, we seem to be making better progress for lexical comparisons in distinguishing those similarities which signal contact from those indicating common ancestry: for example, McMahon et al. (2005) have developed methods of contrasting more and less borrowable meanings, and comparing resulting trees or networks. Further development of this kind of technique might in the ideal case be expected to produce consistent visual representations which we might associate with contact or with family resemblance; McMahon et al. (2005) use this method to generalise from known histories in Indo-European to disputed ones for languages of the Andes (see also Heggarty 2007, 2008, and for an overview, McMahon 2010). Fascinatingly, Daval-Markussen and Bakker (2011) have shown on the basis of a network analysis that it is possible to isolate signals of common ancestry from those involving contact, for English-based Atlantic Creoles. The analysis can be pared back to a tree with splits coinciding with historical events; and this may equally be feasible for other regional sets of English- or French-based creoles.

The question is whether we are able to develop similar methods for distinguishing signals of contact from those of family affiliation in the case of structural features; unfortunately, the answer is not yet remotely clear. It remains very difficult to come to definitive conclusions about the source of similarities in morphosyntax, as shown by a recent (and indeed ongoing) controversy about the Papuan languages of Island Melanesia. Dunn et al. (2005) apply biological cladistic methods to a dataset of 125 binary structural features, coded for presence or absence in 15 Papuan languages and a control set of 16 Austronesian languages from the same general geographical region. The Papuan languages have no agreed cognates, which might suggest that they are not related, or that they began to diverge too long ago for lexical signals of relatedness to persist. However, Dunn et al. report that numerical scoring of their structural features across the Papuan languages produces a tree correlating very well with geography, such that each subgroup of languages corresponds to an archipelago. This analysis opens up an exciting prospect: "If grammatical structures can retain a phylogenetic signal beyond the current temporal ceiling on the reconstruction of language history, then the possibility is opened up of finding relationships between others of the world's 300 or so existing language families and isolates" (Dunn et al. 2005: 2075).

However, while engaging, this conclusion is not uncontroversial. Donohue and Musgrave (2007) take issue with the results: while they agree that structural features can and should be used in investigating linguistic history, they also contend that such features may be particularly prone to borrowing, especially in linguistic areas. This "would mean that conclusions such as those drawn by Dunn et al. are particularly prone to controversy; without establishing that a particular set of correspondences in grammatical features are *not* due to areal influence, there can be no argument about the correspondence indicating a genetic relationship" (Donohue and Musgrave 2007: 350). While the discussion is detailed, and the data complex, the locus of the disagreement is clear. The conclusion to which this leads Dunn et al. (2007: 401) mirrors our discussion of trees versus networks above:

> This leaves us with three possibilities: the relationship between the Papuan languages may be the product of ancient intra-Papuan contact, they may be the result of common ancestry, or it may be the case that both phylogeny and ancient contact have contributed to the relationships between the Papuan languages of Island Melanesia. We are unable to tease ancient contact and phylogeny apart, but we can at least begin the process.

As Dunn et al. (2007: 401) continue, "This research program is young, and there is certainly much more to be done"; work is already underway on further assessments of the relative stability of language features (see Parkvall 2008, Wichmann and Kamholtz 2008).

This seems a fitting point on which to end the chapter. A combination of quantitative approaches to language, visualisation techniques including networks, and comparison of data from different levels of the grammar, is bringing us closer to disentangling the contributions of contact and common ancestry to language patterns than we have ever been. In order to continue this progress, we need to suspend some earlier assumptions about the priorities of historical and comparative linguistics and about what constitutes the normal case, and work together to combine data, insights and approaches. Crucially, this means a rehabilitation of language contact from a peripheral concern, an exception or even a nuisance, to a crucial signal of population history which can establish historical linguistics as an equal partner in interdisciplinary research with anthropologists, archaeologists and geneticists, where population histories are seen to a great extent as histories of contact. If the normal case is for all languages, at different periods of their histories and to different extents, to be contact languages, or at least languages partially shaped by contact, there is an automatic reprioritisation. Genetic relatedness is still important and relevant, but methods for establishing it must now be developed and tested in the context of language contact. While the title of this chapter suggests that contact languages represent a special case for the dominant model of genetic classification, we have reached a rather different view, suggesting that progress in genetic classification can only be achieved by also considering contact.

References

Ansaldo, Umberto, Stephen Matthews & Lisa Lim (eds.). 2007. *Deconstructing Creole* (Typological Studies in Language 73). Amsterdam: John Benjamins.

Bakker, Peter. 1997. *A Language of Our Own: The Genesis of Michif, the Mixed Cree-French Language of the Canadian Métis*. Oxford: Oxford University Press.

Bakker, Peter, Aymeric Daval-Markussen, Mikael Parkvall & Ingo Plag. 2011. Creoles are typologically distinct from non-creoles. *Journal of Pidgin and Creole Studies* 26(1). 5–42.

Bakker, Peter & Maarten Mous (eds.). 1994. *Mixed Languages: 15 Case Studies in Language Intertwining*. Amsterdam: Uitgave IFOTT.

Bryant, David & Vincent Moulton. 2004. Neighbornet: an agglomerative algorithm for the construction of planar phylogenetic networks. *Molecular Biology and Evolution* 21. 255–265.

Campbell, Lyle. 1998. *Historical Linguistics: An Introduction*. Edinburgh: Edinburgh University Press.

Campbell, Lyle. 2003. How to show languages are related: methods for distant genetic relationship. In Brian D. Joseph & Richard D. Janda (eds.), *The Handbook of Historical Linguistics*, 262–282. Oxford: Blackwell.

Daval-Markussen, Aymeric & Peter Bakker. 2011. A phylogenetic networks approach to the classification of English-based Atlantic Creoles. *English World-Wide* 32(2). 115–146.

Donohue, Mark & Simon Musgrave. 2007. Typology and the linguistic macrohistory of Island Melanesia. *Oceanic Linguistics* 46. 348–387.

Dunn, Michael, Robert Foley, Stephen Levinson, Ger Reesink & Angela Terrill. 2007. Statistical reasoning in the evaluation of typological diversity in Island Melanesia. *Oceanic Linguistics* 46. 388–403.

Dunn, Michael, Angela Terrill, Ger Reesink, Robert A. Foley & Stephen C. Levinson. 2005. Structural phylogenetics and the reconstruction of ancient language history. *Science* 309. 2072–2025.

Dyen, Isidore, Joseph B. Kruskal & Paul Black. 1992. An Indoeuropean classification: a lexicostatistical experiment. *Transactions of the American Philosophical Society* 82(5). 1–132.

Ellison, T. Mark & Simon Kirby. 2006. Measuring language divergence by intra-lexical comparison. In Nicoletta Calzolari, Claire Cardie & Pierre Isabelle (eds.), *Proceedings of the 21st International Conference on Computational Linguistics and 44th Annual Meeting of the ACL*, 273–280. Stroudsburg, PA: The Association for Computer Linguistics.

Embleton, Sheila. 1986. *Statistics in Historical Linguistics*. Bochum: Brockmeyer.

Foley, William. 2006. Universal constraints and local conditions in pidginization: Case studies from New Guinea. *Journal of Pidgin and Creole Languages* 21. 1–44.

Forster, Peter & Colin Renfrew (eds.). 2006. *Phylogenetic Methods and the Prehistory of Languages*. Cambridge: McDonald Institute for Archaeological Research.

Gilbert, Glenn (ed.). 1987. *Pidgin and Creole Languages: Essays in Memory of John E. Reineck*. Honolulu: University of Hawaii Press.

Gilman, Charles. 1978. A comparison of Jamaican Creole and Cameroonian Pidgin English. *English Studies* 59. 57–65.

Goddard, Cliff. 2005. *The Languages of East and Southeast Asia: An Introduction*. Oxford: Oxford University Press.

Goodman, Morris. 1964. *A Comparative Study of Creole French Dialects*. Mouton: The Hague.

Grace, George. 1981. Indirect inheritance and the aberrant Melanesian languages. In Jim Hollyman & Andrew K. Pawley (eds.), *Studies in Pacific Languages and Cultures in Honour of Bruce Biggs*, 255–268. Auckland: Linguistic Society of New Zealand.

Grace, George. 1985. Oceanic subgrouping: retrospect and suspect. In Andrew K. Pawley & Lois Carrington (eds.), *Austronesian Linguistics at the 15th Pacific Science Congress,* 1–18. Canberra: Pacific Linguistics.

Grace, George. 1990. The 'aberrant' versus 'exemplary' Melanesian languages. In Philip Baldi (ed.), *Linguistic Change and Reconstruction Methodology*, 155–173. Berlin: Mouton de Gruyter.

Gray, Russell & Quentin Atkinson. 2003. Language-tree divergence times support the Anatolian theory of Indo-European origin. *Nature* 426. 435–439.

Gray, Russell & Fiona Jordan. 2000. Language trees support the express-train sequence of Austronesian expansion. *Nature* 405. 1052–1054.

Greenhill, Simon J., Robert Blust & Russell D. Gray. 2008. The Austronesian Basic Vocabulary Database: from bioinformatics to lexomics. *Evolutionary Bioinformatics* 4. 271–283.

Hale, Mark. 2007. *Historical Linguistics: Theory and Method*. Oxford: Blackwell.

Hall, Robert A., Jr. 1966. *Pidgin and Creole Languages*. Ithaca, NY: Cornell University Press.

Hancock, Ian. 1987. A preliminary classification of the anglophone Atlantic creoles with syntactic data from thirty-three representative dialects. In Glenn Gilbert (ed.), *Pidgin and Creole Languages: Essays in Memory of John E. Reineck*, 264–333. Honolulu: University of Hawaii Press.

Harrison, S. P. 2003. On the limits of the comparative method. In Brian D. Joseph & Richard D. Janda (eds.), *The Handbook of Historical Linguistics*, 213–243. Oxford: Blackwell.

Haspelmath, Martin, Matthew S. Dryer, David Gil & Bernard Comrie (eds.). 2005. *The World Atlas of Language Structures*. Oxford: Oxford University Press.

Heath, Jeffrey. 1978. *Linguistic Diffusion in Arnhem Land*. Canberra: Australian Institute of Aboriginal Studies.

Heggarty, Paul. 2007. Linguistics for archaeologists: principles, methods and the case of the Incas. *Cambridge Archaeological Journal* 17(3). 311–340.

Heggarty, Paul. 2008. Linguistics for archaeologists: A case-study in the Andes. *Cambridge Archaeological Journal* 18(1). 35–56.

Heggarty, Paul, Warren Maguire & April McMahon. 2010. Splits or waves? Trees or webs? How divergence measures and network analysis can unravel language histories. *Philosophical Transactions of the Royal Society* B 365. 3829–3843.

Hickey, Ray (ed.). 2010. *The Handbook of Language Contact*. Oxford: Blackwell.

Huson, Daniel & David Bryant. 2006. Application of phylogenetic networks in evolutionary studies. *Molecular Biology and Evolution* 23(2). 254–267.

Janda, Richard D. & Brian D. Joseph. 2003. On language, change, and language change – or, of history, linguistics, and historical linguistics. In Brian D. Joseph & Richard D. Janda (eds.), *The Handbook of Historical Linguistics*, 3–180. Oxford: Blackwell.

Joseph, Brian D. & Richard D. Janda (eds.). 2003. *The Handbook of Historical Linguistics*. Oxford: Blackwell.

Kessler, Brett. 2001. *The Significance of Word Lists*. Chicago: University of Chicago Press.

Labov, William. 2007. Transmission and diffusion. *Language* 83(2). 344–387.

Lefebvre, Claire. 1998. *Creole Genesis and the Acquisition of Grammar: The Case of Haitian Creole*. Cambridge: Cambridge University Press.

Longobardi, Giuseppe & Christina Guardiano. 2009. Evidence for syntax as a signal of historical relatedness. *Lingua* 119. 1679–1706.

McMahon, April. 1994. *Understanding Language Change*. Cambridge: Cambridge University Press.

McMahon, April. 2010. Computational models of language contact. In Ray Hickey (ed.), *The Handbook of Language Contact*, 128–150. Oxford: Blackwell.

McMahon, April (ed.). 2005. *Quantitative Methods in Language Comparison* (Special Issue of Transactions of the Philological Society, 103. 2). Oxford: Blackwell.

McMahon, April, Paul Heggarty, Robert McMahon & Natalia Slaska. 2005. Swadesh sublists and the benefits of borrowing: an Andean case study. In April McMahon (ed.), *Quantitative Methods in Language Comparison* (Special Issue of Transactions of the Philological Society, 103. 2), 147–169. Oxford: Blackwell.

McMahon, April, Paul Heggarty, Robert McMahon & Warren Maguire. 2007. The sound patterns of Englishes: representing phonetic similarity. *English Language and Linguistics* 11. 113–143.

McMahon, April & Robert McMahon. 2005. *Language Classification by Numbers*. Oxford: Oxford University Press.

McMahon, April & Robert McMahon. 2008. Genetics, historical linguistics and language variation. *Language and Linguistics Compass* 2. 264–288.

McWhorter, John H. 1998. Identifying the creole prototype: vindicating a typological class. *Language* 74. 788–818.

McWhorter, John H. 2000. Defining 'creole' as a synchronic term. In Ingrid Neumann-Holzschuh & Edgar W. Schneider (eds.), *Degrees of Restructuring in Creole Languages*, 85–124. Amsterdam: John Benjamins.

McWhorter, John H. 2005. *Defining Creole*. New York/Oxford: Oxford University Press.

Michaelis, Susanne (ed.). 2008. *Roots of Creole Structures. Weighing the Contribution of Substrates and Superstrates*. Amsterdam: John Benjamins.

Mithun, Marianne. 2008. Borrowed rhetorical constructions as starting points for grammaticalization. In Alexander Bergs & Gabriele Diewald (eds.), *Constructions and Language Change* (Trends in Linguistics. Studies and Monographs 194), 195–230. Berlin: Mouton de Gruyter.

Mühlhäusler, Peter. 1986. *Pidgin and Creole Linguistics*. Oxford: Blackwell.

Nakhleh, Luay, Don Ringe & Tandy Warnow. 2005. Perfect phylogenetic networks: a new methodology for reconstructing the evolutionary history of natural languages. *Language* 81. 381–420.

Nerbonne, John. 2009. The forests behind the trees. *Lingua* 119. 1581–1588.

Neumann-Holzschuh, Ingrid & Edgar W. Schneider (eds.). 2000. *Degrees of Restructuring in Creole Languages*. Amsterdam: John Benjamins.

Parkvall, Mikael. 2008. Which parts of language are the most stable? *Language Typology and Universals* 61. 234–250.

Pierce, Joe E. 1965. The validity of genetic linguistics. *Linguistics* 13(1). 25–33.

Rijkhoff, Jan & Dik Bakker. 1998. Language sampling. *Linguistic Typology* 2. 263–314.

Ringe, Don, Tandy Warnow & Ann Taylor. 2002. Indo-European and computational cladistics. *Transactions of the Philological Society* 100. 59–129.
Roberts, Ian. 2007. *Diachronic Syntax*. Oxford: Oxford University Press.
Sankoff, Gillian & Hélène Blondeau. 2008. Language change across the lifespan: /r/ in Montreal French. *Language* 83. 560–588.
Schneider, Edgar W. 1990. The cline of creoleness in English-oriented creoles and semi-creoles of the Caribbean. *English World-Wide* 11. 79–113.
Singh, Ishtla. 2000. *Pidgins and Creoles: An Introduction*. London: Arnold.
Smith, Norval. 1987. *The Genesis of the Creole Languages of Surinam*. Amsterdam: University of Amsterdam dissertation.
Sylvain, Suzanne. 1936. *Le Créole Haïtien: Morphologie et Syntaxe*. Port-au-Prince/Wetteren: Meester.
Taylor, Douglas R. 1956. Language contacts in the West Indies. *Word* 13. 399–414.
Thomason, Sarah Grey. 2001. *Language Contact: An Introduction*. Edinburgh: Edinburgh University Press.
Thomason, Sarah Grey. 2003. Contact as a source of language change. In Brian D. Joseph & Richard D. Janda (eds.), *The Handbook of Historical Linguistics*, 687–712. Oxford: Blackwell.
Trudgill, Peter. 1976. Creolization in reverse: reduction and simplification in the Albanian dialects of Greece. *Transactions of the Philological Society* 75. 32–50.
Wichmann, Søren. 2008. The emerging field of language dynamics. *Language and Linguistics Compass* 2(3). 442–455.
Wichmann, Søren, Eric W. Holman, Dik Bakker & Cecil H. Brown. 2009. ASJP lexical similarity as a measure of language genetic relationship. http://email.eva.mpg.de/~wichmann/-ASJPPerformance14.doc
Wichmann, Søren & David Kamholtz. 2008. A stability metric for typological features. *Language Typology and Universals* 61. 251–262.

Social factors in contact languages

Donald Winford

1. Introduction

Since the publication of Weinreich's (1953) pioneering book, the study of language contact has blossomed into a rich and diversified field of study, encompassing a wide variety of contact situations and outcomes. Weinreich saw the goals of language contact studies as being "to predict typical forms of interference from the sociolinguistic description of a bilingual community and a structural description of its languages" (1953: 86). For Weinreich, it is only "in a broad psychological and sociocultural setting that language contact can best be understood" (1953: 4). Weinreich's insight also led him to distinguish the non-structural factors that operate on both the macro (societal) level, and those that operate on the micro (individual level). For instance, on the macro level, he identified the following factors, among others (1953: 3–4):

- The size of the bilingual group and its socio-cultural homogeneity or differentiation;
- The breakdown of the community into sub-groups using one or the other language as their mother tongue;
- Demographic facts;
- Social and political relations between these subgroups.
- The prevalence of bilingual individuals with given characteristics of speech behaviour in the several sub-groups (see the micro-level factors below).
- Stereotyped attitudes toward each language ("prestige"); indigenous or immigrant status of the languages concerned.

And with regard to micro-level factors relevant to individuals, he identified the following:

- The speaker's facility of verbal expression in general and his ability to keep two languages apart.
- Relative proficiency in each language;

- Specialisation in the use of each language by topics and interlocutors;
- Manner of learning each language;
- Attitudes toward each language, and whether idiosyncratic or stereotyped.

Despite Weinreich's guidelines for the field, scholars have for the most part devoted more attention to the 'structural' aspects of language contact than to the social aspects. As a result, we now have various models of the linguistic processes that underlie and shape contact induced change, but the field still lacks a coherent framework within which to investigate the social parameters of language contact situations. This in turn means that we are still far from achieving Weinreich's vision of a unified framework that would integrate the linguistic, social, and psychological aspects of language contact. This chapter is meant to be a modest overview of the ways in which social factors come into play in situations of language contact. Its focus is primarily on the conventionalised or 'crystallised' outcomes of language contact, to which the label 'contact languages' has traditionally been applied. Thomason (1997) includes only three types in this category – pidgins, creoles and "bilingual mixed languages". However, the general consensus is that the set of contact languages includes other outcomes such as the 'indigenised' varieties of colonisers' languages, for example Indian English, as well as so-called 'converted' languages or cases of 'metatypy', for example Sri Lanka Portuguese. It is of course possible to adopt an even broader view of what constitutes the class of contact languages. An extreme position would be that every language is a contact language in some sense, since all languages have been subject to some degree of influence from at least one other external language. Most contact linguists, however, restrict their attention only to cases of significant cross-linguistic mixture that have resulted in new, conventionalised creations that have achieved autonomy. In this, they follow Thomason's (1997: 75) characterisation of a contact language as "comprised of grammatical and lexical systems that cannot all be traced back to a single parent language".

Such an approach, of course, excludes a significant number of languages that contain a high degree of mixture, including languages like English or Chamorro that have borrowed a majority of their vocabulary from other sources. It also excludes many cases of mixture that have not achieved autonomy, including for example, the L2 varieties of a host language produced by immigrants, and the various types of language mixture produced by bilinguals. Such instances of unstable, yet to be crystallised language mixture still have the potential to shed valuable light on the processes, both social and linguistic, that led to the more conventionalised outcomes. For that reason, I will refer to them where relevant. For the most part, however, the following discussion will focus on the traditionally recognised set of contact languages, and the ways in which social factors have shaped both their emergence, and where applicable, their continuing functions and statuses within their respective speech communities.

2. Social settings and language contact

Different scholars have taken very different positions on the issue of the relative importance of social as opposed to linguistic factors in shaping contact-induced change. On the one hand, Thomason and Kaufman claim that "it is the sociolinguistic history of the speakers, and not the structure of their language, that is the primary determinant of the linguistic outcome of language contact" (1988: 35). On the other hand, scholars like Müller (1875) and Jakobson (1938) argued that structural (linguistic) constraints were the primary determinants of contact-induced change. Their view is echoed, more recently, by Heine and Kuteva, who claim that "there is evidence to suggest that social variables are largely irrelevant as determinants of contact-induced change – at least of the kind studied here" (2005: 12–13). The unfortunate fact is that statements such as these are often made without any real attempt to investigate the sociolinguistic details of the contact situations in question. And it remains true, in general, that contact linguists have paid far more attention to linguistic processes and constraints than to the extra-linguistic factors that might affect their operations and results.

The evidence now available to us strongly supports the view that social factors play a significant, and in some cases a more important role than linguistic factors, in shaping the consequences of language contact. The social factors that come into play depend to a large extent on the nature of the contact situation, the communities involved, and their sociolinguistic profiles. In general, contact languages arise in two broad types of situation – those involving language maintenance, and those involving language shift, both in the context of differing degrees of bilingualism. Within such settings, as Thomason and Kaufman rightly observe, "both the direction of interference and the extent of interference are socially determined; so, to a considerable degree, are the kinds of features transferred from one language to another" (1988: 35). We will see abundant evidence of this in the way different social ecologies lead to different types of contact languages, as well as to diversity within each type of contact language.

The issue of directionality of change is directly related to the distinction Thomason and Kaufman make between situations of language maintenance, which they associate with borrowing, and situations of language shift, which they associate with mechanisms of "interference via shift" or substratum influence. In the former case, native speakers incorporate features from an external source language into their maintained native language. In the latter, speakers learning another language transfer features of their L1 into their version of the target language. While this broad distinction is a good starting point for analysis of the role of social factors in the creation of contact languages, the distinction between the two types of contact situation is by no means as clear-cut as Thomason and Kaufmann make it appear. In the first place, both situations of maintenance and shift are characterised by differences in dominance relationships between the languages in contact. Traditionally, more attention has been paid to social dominance relationships than to linguistic dominance, that is, the degree of proficiency that speakers display in each of their languages. The latter undoubtedly plays a far more crucial role than social dominance in determining the nature of contact-induced change, and is more directly related to the actuation of change, as opposed to its implementation or diffusion within the speech community. This is particularly relevant to those contact languages that arose in situations of language maintenance, whose creation has sometimes been incorrectly described because of a misunderstanding of the dominance relationships between the contributing languages. Since linguistic dominance relationships can and do differ significantly both within and across speech communities even in situations of language maintenance, they can lead to very different linguistic outcomes. The same is true in situations of shift.

The issue of the extent to which one language exerts influence on another has traditionally been explained in terms of social factors such as 'intensity of contact' and 'cultural pressure'. These relate to matters such as the demographics of the groups in contact, their socio-political relationships, their patterns of interaction, and so on. Factors like these, along with groups' attitudes to the languages in contact, and to language mixture, are particularly relevant to the conventionalisation of changes in a developing contact variety, and ultimately to the crystallisation of the variety as an autonomous language in its own right. Again, such factors vary from one contact situation to another, leading to differences in the outcomes in both maintenance and shift situations. This is not to say that we must abandon the traditional distinction between the two broad types of contact situation, but rather that we need a more comprehensive and nuanced classification of contact situations, which takes into account all of the non-linguistic factors we have outlined above, as well as others that may be relevant to specific situations. We will assume, therefore, that the broad distinction we have made between situations of language maintenance and situations of shift are crucial to explaining the outcomes of language contact.

Finally, of course, social factors also determine the synchronic status and functions of contact varieties within their respective communities. The social ecology determines whether they survive as vibrant community languages, what roles they play in the social life of the community, whether they become standardised, or are recognised as official languages, and so on. Many of the contact languages that we know to have arisen in the past have died, many more are in danger of extinction, while others flourish, and new ones appear to serve the needs of new communities. Some of these social aspects of contact languages will be included in the discussion below.

To sum up, in order to fully understand the creation and development of contact languages, we must begin with the speech community, which represents the broadest social context for language contact. In essence, the diffusion of linguistic and other cultural practices depends on social interaction within and across speech communities. Hence we need to understand both the speech economy and the social structure of the community in order to explain the outcomes of language contact. We have suggested that all contact situations share a certain set of social variables, including the types of community settings, the demographic characteristics of the groups in contact, the patterns of social interaction among them, and the ideologies that govern their linguistic choices. Other general factors that play a role include the degree of bilingualism among the individuals and groups in contact, the history and length of contact, the power relationships between the groups, and so on. The factors identified so far operate at the macro-level of social relationships, and have been investigated more extensively than the social factors that operate at the micro-level of interpersonal relationships and interaction. The latter factors are far more difficult to investigate and analyse, particularly for past contact situations which we can no longer observe, but even for contemporary cases, which require long and extensive investigation using sociolinguistic and ethnographic methods. Obviously, it is no easy task to integrate all the relevant factors into a complete and coherent picture of the social ecology of a given contact situation. In the following sections, we will try to examine the social settings of various contact situations in more detail, and show, as far as possible, how they contribute to the particular outcomes we find.

3. Bilingual mixed or 'intertwined' languages

Situations of language maintenance simply involve the preservation of an ancestral language by a speech community from generation to generation. Within these situations, however, we must distinguish those that involve relatively little bilingualism within the community, and those in which a significant part of the population is bilingual in the ancestral language, as well as another group's language. Group bilingualism of the latter type is a prerequisite for the emergence of contact languages. Such situations may include cases of stable communal bilingualism, where speakers preserve and use both languages, as well as cases of unstable bilingualism, where there is an unequal dominance relationship between the languages in contact, and speakers of one are under varying degrees of pressure to shift to the other. In general, situations of relatively stable communal bilingualism produce the kinds of contact language referred to as bilingual mixed languages, or 'intertwined' languages.

Bilingual Mixed Languages, in general, combine the lexicon of one language with the grammatical apparatus of another. From a sociolinguistic perspective, they emerge in situations of group bilingualism, and they are created to serve as in-group languages, rather than to meet a pressing need for communication. From a structural perspective, Thomason (2003: 21) describes them as languages "whose grammatical and lexical subsystems cannot all be traced back primarily to a single source language." Thomason (1997: 80) sums up the characteristics of bilingual mixed languages as follows:

- They evolve or are created in two-language contact situations.
- The setting involves widespread bilingualism on the part of at least one of the two speaker groups.
- In the resulting mixture the language material is easily separated according to the language of origin.
- There is little or no simplification in either component of the mixed language (reflecting the bilingualism of its creators).

This characterisation matches the sub-type of mixed languages that Bakker (2003) refers to as "intertwined" languages, which are my primary focus here. Bakker identifies two other subtypes of mixed languages, viz., lexically mixed languages, and "converted" languages. The former include languages like Chamorro and Maltese, which have borrowed lexicon extensively from another language, but still preserve a substantial portion of their inherited lexicon, including basic vocabulary. "Converted" languages arise under conditions of language shift, and involve processes of convergence due to imposition. They preserve the vocabulary of one language, but "copy the grammatical structure of another language" (2003: 116). They will be discussed later.

Intertwined languages differ from both of the other types in that they typically combine the lexicon of one source language, with the morphosyntactic frame of another, with the two components preserved relatively intact. Bakker refers to them as "lexicon-grammar mixed languages" (2003: 109). Among the best known of these are Media Lengua (Spanish lexicon in a Quechua frame), Ma'á (mostly Cushitic lexicon in a Bantu frame), and Angloromani (Romani lexicon in an English frame). Various other mixed languages emerged in situations in which communities of mixed ethnicity arose, for example in Indonesia, where Dutch and Chinese men formed unions with Indonesian women. Other examples include Michif (French noun phrases and prepositional phrases inserted into a Cree frame) and Mednyj or Copper Island Aleut, whose grammatical frame combines Aleut and Russian elements, while most of the vocabulary is Aleut. According to Bakker (2003), there are about 25 documented intertwined languages.

The position adopted here is that intertwined languages are the result of a process of insertional codeswitching taken to an extreme. This perspective allows for a unified account of their creation, and helps us to understand the social contexts and motivations that led to their conventionalisation. All intertwined languages manifest an across-the-board insertion of lexical (sometimes phrasal) constituents from an embedded language into a morphosyntactic frame drawn from a different matrix language. Exceptions include Mednyj Aleut and Gurindji Kriol, each of which has a "composite" grammatical frame derived from both input languages, as discussed below. In some cases, like Media Lengua, the ancestral language served as the matrix language, while in other cases such as Ma'á and Angloromani, it was the newly-acquired L2 that served this purpose. It also seems clear that the process involved was essentially the same as that found in insertional codeswitching. The only difference is the degree to which the process was applied, and then conventionalised, in intertwined languages. This view has been criticised on the grounds that the quantity of embedded lexicon is far greater in intertwined languages, and no transitory stage between the initial codeswitching behaviour and the resulting mixed language has been documented (Bakker 2003: 217). However, Mous rightly argues that "[codeswitching] may well lead to the emergence of a mixed language and in particular such a development is conceivable through conventionalization of the switches" (2003: 217). He also notes that there are in fact well documented cases of languages that represent an intermediate stage between codeswitching and language intertwining, including mixed codes used in urban settings in Africa such as Tsotsitaal and Isicamtho (South Africa), and Sheng (Kenya) (see Kießling and Mous 2004). In fact, some intertwined languages are essentially similar to these urban mixed codes both in structure, and in terms of social motivations and functions. The only differences are that intertwined languages involve two further developments not found in urban mixed codes.

Compelling evidence of the relationship between codeswitching and the emergence of an intertwined language comes from the recent creation of Gurindji Kriol, a contact language spoken by the Aboriginal Gurindji people in Northern Australia. It combines elements of the grammars of Gurindji, a Pama-Nyungan language, and Kriol, an English-lexicon creole, with a vocabulary drawn from both languages. Gurindji supplies most of the noun phrase grammar, while Kriol provides most of the VP grammar. Both languages, however, supply small parts of the grammar to the systems they do not dominate (Meakins 2008: 73). Meakins demonstrates convincingly that the language "has a close diachronic and synchronic relationship to code-switching between Gurindji and Kriol, and [that] its structure bears a strong resemblance to patterns found in this code-switching" (2012: 105).

Meakins offers the following examples to illustrate the similarities in structure between the contact language (1) and Gurindji/Kriol codeswitching (2). Note that Gurindji-derived forms are in boldface.

(1) *An   skul-**ta=ma**   jei   bin   hab-im   sport*
    And   school-LOC=TOP   3PL.SBJ   PST   have-TR   sport
    karu-walija-ngku
    child-PAUC-ERG
    'And the kids had sport at school.'
    (Meakins 2012: 112)

(2) ***kaa-rni-mpal**-said   orait   yutubala   kat-im   **ngaji-rlang-kulu**.*
    east-up-across-side   alright   2DU   cut-TR   father-DYAD-ERG
    'You two, father and son, cut it across the east (side of the cow).'
    (Codeswitching 1970s collected by Patrick McConvell; Meakins 2012: 113)

In both cases, the core VP structure including tense such as *bin* 'past' and transitive marking *-im* is derived from Kriol while the NP structure, including ergative markers *-ngku* and *-kulu* as well as locative case-marking *-ta*, is from Gurindji (Meakins 2012: 112).

According to Meakins (2008), the social context in which Gurindji Kriol emerged was shaped by contact between non-indigenous colonists and the Gurindji people, beginning in the early 1900s. White settlers established cattle stations in the Victoria River District area, including the Gurundji homelands. Battles over land led to the death of many Gurundji people, and the rest were forced to labour on Wave Hill cattle station in slave-like conditions, along with other Aboriginal groups. This situation led to the introduction of pidgin English and later Kriol as common means of communication across the groups. By the 1970s, as reported by McConvell (1988), codeswitching between Gurindji and Kriol had become the dominant language practice of Gurindji people, particularly in the town of Kalkaringi. The mixed language arose out of this situation during the 1960s to 1970s, when the Gurundji people led a historic (and successful) political struggle to regain control of their traditional lands. The emergence of the new contact language was particularly significant in view of the fact that many other Aboriginal groups in the area were giving up their ancestral languages in favour of Kriol. Meakins (2008: 70) argues that the retention of Gurindji features in the mixed language was directly linked to the lands right movement, and can be viewed as an expression of an enduring Gurindji identity. Like the political struggle, the contact language was "an act of resistance against the massive cultural incursion which accompanied colonization" (2008: 70). Though the mixed language is viewed negatively by older people as incorrect Gurindji, it has covert prestige among the young, who are the main speakers of this variety (Meakins 2012: 108).[1]

The case of Gurundji Kriol is an instructive illustration of the social motivations that promote the creation of an intertwined language. Some of these motivations apply also to the use of codeswitching in situations of stable bilingualism. In both situations, we find that extensive bilingualism in the community leads to frequent mixing of the languages, with a preference for intra-sentential or insertional codeswitching. Then patterns of codeswitching become associated with an in-group identity, and the community develops a positive attitude to mixture of the codes as a marker of the group's identity. We find evidence of this in communities such as Strasbourg where bilinguals alternate between French and Alsatian (Treffers-Daller 1999), and the Puerto Rican community of New York City, where speakers codeswitch freely between Spanish and English (Zentella 1997). Codeswitching in such situations becomes an accepted discourse strategy that is governed by social conventions. Switching between languages may mark a change in topic, interlocutors, role relationship, or situation type, or the interaction of all of these. Patterns of switching in such situations have been described as an 'unmarked choice' that is used either to express neutrality with respect to language preference, or to express social cohesiveness. This type of codeswitching reflects the "speaker's wish to symbolize the dual membership that such code switching calls up" (Myers-Scotton 1993: 119). This is what Walters (2005: 200) describes as "code switching meant to express one's ethnolinguistic identity, to bond with a listener, or to show awareness and cognizance of a particular setting, listener, or topic". Poplack (1987: 67) contrasts the situation in Ottawa-Hull, where codeswitching between English and French is not a widely accepted mode of discourse, with the preference for codeswitching among New York City Puerto Ricans, in terms of differences in attitude toward the mixed code, and goes further: "These attitudes may reflect the fact that bilingualism is seen to be emblematic of NY Puerto Rican identity [...] whereas in the Ottawa-Hull situation, knowledge of English does not appear to be associated with any emergent ethnic grouping."

Such patterns of mixture may endure for generations in a community without being conventionalised as a new contact variety. But under special circumstances, a group may embark on the creation of a more systematic pattern of mixture that eventually becomes an autonomous variety in its own right. For the Gurindji, the political struggle for their land, and the new consciousness of their traditional ethnic and cultural identity as a people was the main motivation for creating a new contact language to serve their speech community.

Conventionalisation of the mixture found in intertwined languages involves a number of developments not typical of codeswitching. These include extension of the process of lexical insertion to the point where it is complete and predictable, and crystallisation of the grammatical frame, so that it becomes fixed. These are clearly driven more by social than by linguistic processes. In the first place, there is wide agreement that the extreme degree of lexical insertion that we find in intertwined languages seems to be the result of conscious acts of "folk engineering" (Golovko 2003), or "change by deliberate decision [...] a quintessentially social factor" (Thomason 2003: 35). The ensuing conventionalisation of the mixture is reflected in the consistency with which speakers use the mixed code. With regard to Gurindji Kriol, Meakins (2012: 116) notes that "the choice of lexical items and syntactic constructions is very consistent across speakers [...]. As a result, Gurindji Kriol speakers use virtually identical constructions to express the same event." Such uniformity of usage supports the status of Gurindji Kriol "as a language independent of its sources" (2012: 117). Another crucial factor in the conventionalisation of a new contact variety is that it typically becomes a target for L1 acquisition. Meakins' observations of children up to the age of 3 in the Gurundji Kriol community revealed that they were indeed acquiring the mixed code, and that "clearly a separate linguistic entity is being identified and singled out for specific attention by children" (2012: 116). As we will see, children play a similar role in the conventionalisation of other intertwined languages and in the creation of other contact languages as well.

The social contexts that produce these "deliberate creations" differ in some ways, but also share much in common. We can identify at least three broad types of situation in which they arise. First we find cases such as Gurundji Kriol where a bilingual group creates a new language primarily to assert its separate identity. A similar case is Media Lengua, a blend of predominantly Quechua grammatical structure and Spanish-derived lexical forms that make up about 90% of the vocabulary (Muysken 1981: 52). The following examples illustrate the mixture (Spanish-derived forms in boldface):

(3) **Unu** **fabur**-ta **pidi**-nga-bu **bini**-xu-ni.
one favour-ACC ask-NOM-BEN come-PROG-1SG
'I come to ask a favour.'

(4) **No** **sabi**-ni-chu Xwan **bini**-shka-da
NEG know-1SG-NEG John come-NOM-ACC
'I don't know that John has come.'

The language came into being quite recently, apparently between 1920 and 1940, in Salcedo and other small towns or in the central Ecuador highlands. It is used as an in-group language among Indian peasants, craftsmen and construction workers, particularly among younger men who work in the nearby capital city Quito in industry and construction. Muysken explains its genesis as due to the fact that "acculturated Indians could not identify completely with either the traditional rural Quechua culture or the urban Spanish culture" (1981: 75). Hence they created Media Lengua as a means of expressing their allegiance to both the Quechua and Spanish worlds.

Bakker (2003) identifies two other broad types of social situations in which most intertwined languages have arisen. In one type, nomadic groups settle in an area where a different language is used, and create a mixed language for use as a secret or in-group language. In most such cases, the grammatical system of the new language comes from the newly-acquired local language, while most of the vocabulary comes from the ancestral language, which itself may be lost. Along with Angloromani and Ma'á, we find languages like Caló and Kayawaya (Callahuaya) in this category. Languages like Caló began as argots; while Kayawaya functioned as a spirit language, or ritual code. Other intertwined languages have been documented for nomadic groups in Afghanistan, Ireland and Scotland (Hancock 1984), India, the Middle East (Kenrick 1976–77) and elsewhere.

The case of Ma'á is representative of this group of intertwined languages. The language is spoken in several communities in the Usambara mountains of Northeastern Tanzania by groups who migrated to the region several hundred years ago. These groups refer to themselves as Ma'á, while outsiders refer to them as the Mbugu, which is also the name of the Bantu language they speak (Mous 1994). Ma'á draws its morphosyntactic frame from Mbugu, which is closely similar to Pare, a neighbouring language spoken by immigrants from the Pare mountains. Much of its lexicon comes from (mostly) Southern and Eastern Cushitic, chiefly Eastern Cushitic, but also includes words from Maasai (Nilotic) and Gorwaa (South Cushitic) and manipulated words from Pare (Mous 2003: 213).

The following examples, from Mous (2003: 212) illustrate the make-up of the language:

(5) Ma'á: *áa-té*   *mi-hatú*   *kwa*   *choká*
            3SG:PST-cut   4-trees   with   axe
     Mbugu: *áa-tema*   *mi-tí*   *kwa*   *izoka*
            3SG:PST-cut   4-trees   with   axe
            'He cut trees with an axe.'

(6) Ma'á: *w-áa-bó'i*   *koré*   *mé*
            2SG-PST-make   10.pot   how:many
     Mbugu: *w-áa-ronga*   *nyungú*   *nyi-ngáhi*
            2SG-PST-make   10.pot   how-many
            'How many pots did you make?'

There is general consensus that the Mbugu originally spoke some variety of (Southern?) Cushitic, and preserved it for a long time before shifting to Pare (or in some cases to Shambaa, the dominant language of the Usambara region). Those who call themselves Ma'á apparently resisted assimilation the longest, and created a mixed language as a sign of their resistance and their autonomy as a distinct ethnic group. The language is incomprehensible to their neighbours.

The third broad type of social situation in which intertwined languages arise is one in which men migrate to a new region and form unions with local women of a different language and ethnicity. As Bakker (2003: 139) points out, the offspring of such unions will often give themselves names that translate as 'new people', 'mixed' or 'locally-born persons'. To reflect their new identity as a distinct community, such groups often create a new mixed language, which derives its grammatical frame primarily from the mothers' language with the lexicon of the fathers' language. This general tendency has been documented for about a dozen cases. Among them are the mixed languages of Indonesia (Petjo, Javindo and Chindo), as well as Michif and Mednyj Aleut. We will briefly discuss some of these creations so as to get a sense of the social contexts in which they arose.

Michif arose during a period of sustained contact between French-speaking traders, canoe-men, guides and the like, and speakers of Plains Cree, beginning in the mid-18th century in the Hudson Bay area. The French migrants co-habited with Cree women, producing offspring who are now referred to as Métis – a French term for a person of mixed race. The morphosyntactic frame is mostly derived from Cree, which supplies the VP structure and the vast majority of the verbs, as well as various function elements such as demonstratives, postpositions, personal pronouns and question words. French supplies the NP structure, including nouns, adjectives, as well as some function items such as prepositions and negative markers. The following piece of a narrative recorded by Bakker (1997: 78) in Brandon, Manitoba illustrates the nature of the mixture. French items are in boldface.

(7) eekwaniki **lii savaaz** kii-paashamw-ak **la**
DEM.AN.PL PL Indian PST-dry-PL ART.DEM.F.SG
vyand la **vjand orjaal, la**
meat ART.DEM.F.SG meat moose ART.DEM.F.SG
vjand-di shovreu, tut kii-paashamw-ak eekwanima
meat-POSS deer all PST-dry-PL DEM.INAN.SG
eekwa kii-shikwahamw-ak **daa di pchi sæk**
then PST-mash-3PL in PART little bags
kii-ashtaaw-ak maana
PST-dry-3PL usually
'These Indians dried the meat. Moose meat, deer meat, they dried it all. And then they mashed it.They used to put it in little bags.'
(Bakker 1997: 78; spelling adjusted to Michif orthographic conventions)

The structural mixture in Michif is similar in many respects to that found in mixed languages such as Gurundji Kriol and Light Warlpiri, except that the latter two have lexicons that are more mixed, with nouns and verbs from both of their source languages (Meakins 2012: 112). These creations differ from the prototypical cases of intertwining we discussed earlier in that they have "composite" morpho-syntactic frames, similar in principle to cases of composite codeswitching (Myers-Scotton 2002). This may be attributed to the probability that these languages were created by bilinguals, probably school-age children or adolescents, who learned their mothers' language as a first language, but also had a certain degree of proficiency in their fathers' language. Differences in such proficiency may explain the differences in the extent of incorporation of structural elements from the paternal language that we find from one case to another. At the same time, the fact that the structural frame comes mainly from the mother's language would follow from its status as the language of the home and the wider community.

Michif also illustrates another characteristic of many intertwined languages, namely that once they have been transmitted to future generations, their speakers may no longer be familiar with the source languages. Most Michif speakers are not fluent in either French or Cree, and in fact most of them are elderly. The language is now in decline, having been replaced by English in most Michif communities (Bakker 1997: 74–76).

Another interesting case of bilingual language mixture is Mednyj (Copper Island) Aleut, which was once widely spoken on Copper Island, one of the two Russian-owned Commander Islands in the Aleutian Islands chain. The language is all but dead now, and like Aleut, has been replaced by Russian on these islands. The contact language is similar in some respects to Gurundji Kriol, in that its morphosyntactic frame is a blend of Russian and Aleut (primarily Attu) elements, particularly in the verbal morphology. Golovko and Vakhtin (1990: 111) summarise the mixture thus:

> [The Aleut component] comprises the majority of the vocabulary, all the derivational morphology, part of the simple sentence syntax, nominal inflexion and certain other grammatical means. The [Russian component] comprises verbal inflexion, negation, infinitive forms, part of the simple sentence syntax, and all of the compound sentence syntax.

The following examples illustrate some of the complex patterns of mixture that characterise the syntax of the language. Russian elements are in bold type.

(8) **ja segodnja** čχuuʁi-n inka-ča-l qaka-ča-anga
I today linen-PL hang-CAUS-3SG.PST dry-CAUS-INT
'Today I hung linen in order to dry it.'
(Golovko 1996: 72)

(9) iglu-ŋ **n'i** tuta-qaʁi-**it**
grandson-1SG.POSS NEG hear-DETRAN-3SG.PRS
'My grandson doesn't listen (obey).'

The language arose during the 19th century in the context of trade between Russia and the Aleutian Islands, after the Russian-American company established permanent settlements on the two previously uninhabited Commander Islands, Copper Island and Bering Island, in 1826 (Golovko and Vakhtin 1990: 98). Dozens of Aleut and creole families were brought in from the Aleutian, Kurch and Pribylof Islands, and Kamchatka. They were engaged in the processing of skins and other activities associated with the trade in seal furs. A minority of Russian employees of the company, mostly men, also settled on the islands. Unions between these men and Aleut women produced a creole population that eventually came to outnumber the Aleuts by 1897 (Golovko and Vakhtin 1990: 116). It was this creole population that created Mednyj Aleut, which eventually became an expression of their distinct identity as a mixed ethnicity group. The language apparently arose sometime between 1826 and 1900.

Further insight into the social contexts and linguistic processes involved in the creation of mixed household contact languages comes from Indonesia, where a variety of intertwined languages arose during the 18th to 19th centuries. Men of different language backgrounds and ethnicities – Dutch and Chinese – formed unions with Indonesian women of Malay, Javanese, and other ethnic and language backgrounds. These unions produced mixed ethnic groups called 'Indos' who created mixed languages such as Petjo (Malay grammar with Dutch lexicon), Javindo (Javanese grammar with Dutch lexicon) and Chindo or Peranakan Chinese (Javanese grammar with Malay lexicon). The term 'petjo' refers to "colored persons of the lower classes" (de Gruiter 1994: 153), while "Peranakan" refers to a locally-born person or a person of mixed ancestry.

Javindo, the mixed language spoken in Semarang, derives its grammar from Javanese, and the vast majority of its lexicon from Dutch. Its word order is Javanese, and it employs various structural elements from that language, including passive prefixes, a causative suffix, a subjunctive suffix, reduplication, etc. At the same time, Dutch structural elements such as post-verbal negator *niet*, passive inflection on verbs, and NP word order are also found in Javindo (de Gruiter 1994). Petjo, spoken in Batavia, draws its grammar from Malay, most likely the variety known as 'Low' or 'Bazaar' Malay, and its lexicon from Dutch. The Malay input includes word order, TMA marking, preverbal negation, and various syntactic structures such as relative clauses, yes/no interrogatives, passives, etc. Dutch input to the grammar includes negative marking, some copulas, and rare passive morphology on verbs, as well as the vast majority of prepositions, articles and conjunctions.

The social contexts in which Javindo and Petjo arose seem to be quite similar. It would appear, first, that the mothers learned Dutch as a second language, and were partly responsible for passing it on to the children. At the same time, the mother's language was the everyday language of the wider community, and was the children's first language. This would explain the greater contribution of this language to the grammar of the mixed code. Children were further exposed to Dutch outside the home and in school, though education was limited. Moreover, most children were not recognised by their fathers, and lived with their mothers in poor neighbourhoods without opportunity for a full education. Still, the nature of the Dutch input suggests more than a passing acquaintance with that language, and testifies to acts of deliberate mixture that went well beyond the bounds of lexical borrowing. It was probably young school-age children who created Javindo, Petjo and other mixed-household languages in Indonesia, as a mark of their mixed ethnicity. The languages then spread to other children – mostly boys – at school. Drawing on his own experience, de Gruiter (1994: 153) notes that all children were forced by their peers to speak Javindo at school, under penalty of being beaten up and/or excluded from games. School-age children seem to have played a role both in the creation and spread of mixed languages in various situations, including those that produced outcomes like Hawaii Creole English, Singapore colloquial English, and of course mixed household languages.

To summarise, we have seen that there is a general correlation between the social contexts in which bilingual mixed languages arose, and the type of mixture they manifest. Ex-nomadic creations generally derive their entire morphosyntactic frame from the language of their new host community, and their lexicon from the ancestral language. Mixed-household languages generally have composite morphosyntactic frames, though primarily derived from the mother's language, with lexicon and function elements from the father's language. However, not all of these languages conform to a single fixed social or linguistic profile. Media Lengua, for instance, does not entirely fit the structural profile of ex-nomadic creations since it derives its morphosyntactic frame from the ancestral language, nor does it fit the social circumstances, since the people who created it were not immigrants. Similarly, mixed-household languages differ to varying extents in both their structural and social profiles. Mednyj Aleut, for instance, stands out within this subgroup of mixed languages in the way it blends so many structural features of Russian and Aleut in its grammar, to the point where there is still debate over whether it is primarily Aleut or Russian in structure. Matras (2003) suggests that the Russian input has in fact increased over time, as a consequence of growing shift in language dominance from Aleut to Russian. This reminds us that too little attention has been paid to historical developments in contact languages over the course of time, and how changes in the social context may have influenced them.

We might also note that some mixed-household languages arise in quite different ways from those described here. For example, people have speculated that Sri Lanka Malay (discussed below) originated as a second language variety of Malay which was acquired by Tamil-speaking women from their Malay spouses (Hussainmiya 1987). Its lexical and grammatical elements are Malay, while its abstract grammatical structure is primarily Tamil in character. Its structural profile therefore departs significantly from the L-G split that we find in intertwined languages, and more closely resembles that of what Bakker calls "converted" languages. The primary reason for this appears to be the fact that mothers transmitted their L2 variety of Malay to their children as a first language. On the whole, we cannot always establish clear and consistent correspondences between the social contexts and linguistic processes involved in the creation of intertwined or other mixed languages. Different social circumstances can lead to similar processes of mixture, while different types of mixture may arise in what seem to be similar social settings. We still need to investigate the reasons for this – whether they lie in the typological relationships between the languages, the degree of bilingualism involved, speakers' attitudes to or preferences for different kinds of mixtures, or social motivations peculiar to different situations.

We can also learn a lot about the social motivations for the creation of intertwined languages from contemporary situations in which mixed codes have become symbols of identity for various other social groups throughout the world. For instance, a variety of urban vernaculars have emerged in Africa and other parts of the world, especially among younger speakers who have been socialised in the cities (see Kießling and Mous 2004). Some of these have been adopted as lingua francas, to facilitate communication among people of different language backgrounds, for example, urban-based Zulu in Pretoria and Johannesburg. Others seem to have originated as argots used by gangs, criminals, or prison populations, or by other social groups, and tend to be used primarily by younger males. Among these are Tsotsitaal, literally 'tsotsi language'[2] and Isicamtho, both of which arose in the Black urban townships of South Africa. Tsotsitaal and Isicamtho draw their grammatical frame and much of their lexicon from Afrikaans and Zulu respectively. Both employ many words from other languages, including English, Afrikaans, and Bantu, along with a liberal infusion of slang. According to Childs, "these urban varieties symbolize the high life of the city – the urban, the cool, the hip, and the sophisticated" (Childs 1997: 342). Some varieties of Tsotsitaal may have developed as vehicles of interethnic exchanges, but for the most part, both the two urban codes are not used for this purpose but rather to exclude non-group members. The rise of negative attitudes toward Afrikaans after the attempt to force everyone to learn it in 1976, has led to the increasing demise of Tsotsitaal, which has now been almost entirely replaced by Isicamtho as the language of young, Black, urban males (Childs 1997: 343). Speakers of Tsotsitaal today are primarily middle-aged or older males. Still, both vernaculars perform the same social functions for their speakers – that of unifying the group, and separating it from others.

Other mixed codes that serve similar social functions include Sheng and Engsh, used by younger males in Nairobi and other cities in Kenya (Abdulaziz and Osinde 1997). Sheng, which developed among less affluent slum dwellers, draws its morphosyntactic frame and most of its lexicon from Swahili, with copious borrowings from English and other mother tongues. Engsh emerged in the richer suburbs of Nairobi, and is based on English structure and vocabulary, but with borrowings from Swahili and other local languages. In both cases, there is a great deal of creativity and innovation in the vocabulary, with many slang terms and other new coinages, which parallel strategies of disguising English and other words in Tsotsitaal. Both mixed registers seem to have developed initially as secret codes, but "they have become more stabilized expressions of youth mixed culture and modes of speaking" (Abdulaziz and Osinde 1997: 44). Indeed, it seems that the mixed codes are slowly becoming primary languages for an emerging community of young speakers.

All of the urban mixed codes described in the literature share a number of important characteristics, both social and linguistic. Socially, they are spoken mostly by the young and almost entirely by males. They are used as markers of a distinct group identity and as a means of excluding non-group members. Abdulaziz and Osinde (1997: 49) point out that "the major factor in the formation of Sheng is the usual yearning for belonging to a group with which one identifies, a group that in most cases excludes other groups". In addition, many of these urban vernaculars originated as secret codes, associated with groups such as criminals, but also just peer-groups who sought to establish a language and identity of their own. Linguistically, these codes are characterised by a high degree of variation and innovation in the vocabulary, which can change at any time according to fashion, or the need to re-establish distinctiveness. The slang element, in particular, is always in flux. Hence these codes are not completely stable, nor have they (yet) been conventionalised as autonomous languages that can be passed on to children as first languages. As Childs (1997: 358) notes, it's doubtful where Isicamtho is sufficiently different from Zulu on a linguistic basis to constitute a separate language. The same seems to apply to the other urban mixed codes. One reason why the status of these codes remains indeterminate is because they are really cases of insertional codeswitching, which preserve the morphosyntactic frames of their matrix languages, whether Swahili, Zulu, Afrikaans, or English. Their insertion of words from the 'external' languages is quite similar to what we find in other cases of insertional codeswitching, though their sources are more variable, and the borrowing is more prolific than in most other cases. Slabbert and Myers-Scotton demonstrate convincingly that "the structures of Tsotsitaal and Isicamtho both conform to [codeswitching] as it is described and explained by the Matrix Language Frame model" (1996: 329).

Despite the trend toward more widespread use and some degree of stability, the fact is that these urban mixed codes have not yet achieved autonomy as independent systems. This is largely because their speakers do not make up separate and unified speech communities that would provide the social context for conventionalisation of the respective varieties. Childs (1997: 360) notes that the speakers of Isicamtho "constitute a large set of atomistic and even antagonistic groups". Social heterogeneity such as this is not conducive to stabilisation of a community norm. But the situation in which these mixed codes are used still offer us valuable insight into both the linguistic and social processes that led to the emergence of stable bilingual mixed languages.

4. Convergence and the creation of 'converted' languages

So far we have considered cases of relatively stable bilingualism in which communities maintain both languages relatively well, and cases where bilingualism has led to a new mixed creation, used in addition to a language of wider currency. But there are other situations that involve unstable bilingualism, in which a minority group continues to preserve its ancestral language despite tremendous pressure to shift to the socially dominant language. Many of these situations correspond to what Loveday (1996: 20) refers to as settings of "bounded" or "subordinate" bilingualism, where there is more or less restricted contact between a dominant group and a linguistic minority. This kind of contact may be brought about by migration, invasion, or military conquest, the redrawing of national boundaries or the establishment of intergroup contact for purposes of trade, marriage and so on. According to Lewis (1978), some of the factors associated with settings of this type include the following:

– geographical isolation (e.g. Gaelic speakers in the Scottish Highlands);
– urban segregation (e.g., Hispanics in the United States);

- the persistence of ethnic minority enclaves (e.g., Basques in Southern France)
- a tradition of limited cultural contact (e.g., the Pennsylvania Dutch in the US).

In situations like these, the ancestral language of the minority group often becomes subject to intense influence from the socially dominant language. In the earlier stages of contact, this influence may be restricted to substantial lexical borrowing into the minority language. Eventually, such minority groups tend to become bilingual, or to shift entirely to the host language. The greater intensity of contact during the phase of bilingualism and shift, as well as the asymmetry in power and prestige of the languages involved, promote increasing structural influence from the dominant language on the subordinate ancestral language.

Some groups, like the Greek communities in Asia Minor, manage to preserve their language and even resist any kind of overt borrowing for long periods of time. But the pressure to accommodate to the dominant community, and the ongoing language shift that ensues, can have serious consequences for the minority language, including structural interference from the majority language, language attrition, and even language death. The transfer of abstract structure in such situations involves the agency of bilinguals who have become increasingly more proficient in the socially dominant language that is the source of the structural innovations. Of course, this claim requires supporting evidence from the nature of the social setting itself. Let us therefore examine some situations that lend support to this claim.

4.1. Asia Minor Greek

Vibrant Greek communities existed for hundreds of years in Asia Minor, until the catastrophe of 1922, when most Greeks were expelled. In the Cappadocian region, Turkish had a particularly strong impact on the variety of Greek spoken there, as reflected in Dawkins' (1916) famous pronouncement that "the body has remained Greek, but the soul is Turkish". Pervasive Turkish influence could be found in all domains of the language – lexicon, phonology, morphology, and syntax. Janse (to appear) provides a comprehensive account of this influence. Thomason and Kaufman (1988) ascribe all of these changes to borrowing, in keeping with their assumption that, once a language is maintained, any changes in it must be due to this transfer type. They argue that "[i]f Turks did not shift to Greek, all of the interference must be due to borrowing" (1988: 218). This rests on their assumption that what they call "interference via shift" can only come about if a group shifts to another language, carrying over features of their original language to the new one. But this kind of language shift is not in fact a prerequisite for the transfer of structural features into an ancestral language via the mechanism of interference. It can also happen when the linguistic dominance relationship between the two languages changes – which is a consequence of ongoing language shift by speakers of the affected language. In other words, it is quite possible for bilinguals who achieve high levels of proficiency in another language to impose structure from that language onto their ancestral language. This is exactly what seems to have happened in the case of Asia Minor Greek. It seems quite probable that the changes in this contact language were introduced under the agency of bilinguals who had become Turkish-dominant (see Winford 2005 for further details). The sociolinguistic situation in Cappadocia at the time provides strong support for this scenario. Augustinos (1992) notes that Greeks and Turks often lived in the same communities and shared the same culture. Janse points out that, even before the fall of Constantinople in 1453, Turkish had replaced Greek in many Cappodocian villages. By 1922, "49 out of 81 Greek settlements in Cappadocia were Turkophone, while the remaining 32 were Grecophone" (Janse to appear: 1). Dawkins (1916) notes that seasonal migration of men to Constantinople led to their use of Turkish among themselves, while many women used Turkish in the home, so that children grew up bilingual, or speaking no Greek. The long term contact situation was clearly one of widespread bilingualism among Greeks, with continuing shift toward Turkish as their linguistically dominant language. All of these facts suggest that imposition of Turkish structure on Greek was the primary mechanism of change.

Situations like that in Asia Minor teach us that only a strict examination of the sociolinguistic contexts of language contact can illuminate the direction and mechanisms of change. There are many other situations like these, which demonstrate that bilingualism in and of itself does not necessarily lead to structural diffusion across languages. Rather, it is changes in the linguistic dominance relationships between the languages involved, which in turn is related to growing restrictions on the contexts in which the ancestral language is used. It is these aspects of the sociolinguistic history of a speech community that are crucial to determining the nature and direction of change, and the kinds of mechanism that brought it about. Of course, we are not in a position to observe the social forces that led to contact-induced changes in the historical past, so our conclusions are not based on solid empirical evidence. Fortunately, however, there are contemporary situations that reveal how changing language dominance relationships lead to structural changes in ancestral languages, and in which we can profitably observe and study how social forces play a role in such changes. Among these are the situations described for L.A. Spanish by Silva-Corvalán (1994) and for Prince Edward Island French by King (2000).

4.2. 'Converted' languages

Situations of unequal and unstable bilingualism have sometimes produced new contact languages created through massive structural imposition from a socially dominant language on an ancestral language. Such new creations carry the processes of convergence observed in languages like Asia Minor Greek to an extreme. Bakker refers to them as "converted" languages, which he defines as "languages which changed their typological outlook radically, kept their vocabulary, and used native language material in order to copy the grammatical structure of another language" (2003: 116). In other words, such creations derive all overt morphemes, lexical and grammatical, from an ancestral language, and their grammatical structure from the socially dominant language. Hence Bakker refers to them as "Form-Semantics" (FS) mixed languages. The position taken here is that such languages arise when speakers of an ancestral language gradually adopt the socially dominant language as their primary means of communication, and it becomes their linguistically dominant language. They then impose features of the newly dominant language on their ancestral language. This scenario clearly applies to Sri Lanka Portuguese, a maintained ancestral language that came under heavy influence from Tamil after its speakers became dominant in the latter language. Smith (1979a, 1979b) describes many structural characteristics that modern Sri Lanka Portuguese has adopted from Tamil (with possible reinforcement from Sinhala). These include SOV basic word order, postpositions, left-branching relative clauses without relative pronouns, tense-aspect categories, and a variety of other features. Most of these characteristics are not found in older Sri Lanka Portuguese, which was in fact a creole language that shared many of its structural traits with other Portuguese-lexicon creoles. We are fortunate in this case to have descriptions of older Sri Lanka Portuguese that demonstrate how much it has been influenced by Tamil. As a result, the language has "changed from an analytic, prepositional, and SVO language to an agglutinative, post-positional and SOV language" (Bakker 2003: 117). There seems to be little doubt, then, that the dramatic changes in Sri Lanka Portuguese were the result of imposition from the socially dominant language.

Another possible case is that of Sri Lanka Malay, which Bakker includes in his category of "converted languages". Here, however, the situation seems somewhat more complex than that of Sri Lanka Portuguese. Sri Lanka Malay, according to some, would have first emerged as a result of unions and intermarriage between Malay-speaking Indonesian men (soldiers and others) and Tamil-speaking women. The former were brought to Sri Lanka from the Indonesian and Malay peninsulas by Dutch and British colonial administrations from about the mid-17th through the 18th centuries. These men associated closely with the local Tamil-speaking 'Moor' community with whom they shared the Muslim religion (Hussainmiya 1987: 45). Contact between the groups, reinforced by frequent inter-marriage, led to the creation of a new contact language with Malay lexicon and a grammatical structure derived from Tamil, which departed radically from Malay structure. There is some controversy over the precise chronology of the contact-induced changes introduced from Tamil into this contact variety. Smith and Paauw (2006) argue that some features, such as the Tamilised TMA categories, emerged early during the "creolisation" process that gave rise to Sri Lanka Malay. On the other hand, Bakker (2003) suggests that the language later underwent a process of "conversion" similar to Sri Lanka Portuguese, in which Tamil influence was brought to bear on the earlier creole-like or second language variety of Malay. There is also disagreement about the timing of this "conversion". Smith (to appear) suggests that it took place as early as the 19th century, affecting primarily the vernacular varieties spoken in the villages. According to him, the early 20th century texts, which manifest relatively little of the massive Dravidian-influenced changes in the vernacular, reflect only an H variety that was on the decline. Bakker and others think the conversion took place in the 20th century. It is possible that both views are partially correct, but deciding this requires data on earlier Sri Lanka Malay, so as to determine whether its structure was significantly different, say, 150 years ago. Unfortunately, we lack such historical texts. But the social history of the community does provide support for the view that Sri Lanka Malay was further influenced by Tamil and Sinhala from the late 19th century on (cf. Nordhoff 2009 for an overview of the issue.) The language appears to have remained quite vibrant, though not necessarily stable, during most of the 19th century. The establishment of the Malay Ceylon Rifle Regiment by the British had provided an anchor for the community, as well as instruction in Malay. But after the regiment was disbanded in 1873, there was increasing shift toward Tamil and Sinhala. This was encouraged by increasing education of Malay children in Tamil- and Sinhala-medium schools. Tamil increasingly replaced Malay in mosques and other religious contexts, while Malay-speaking women gained access to education and became bilingual in Tamil. All of these social changes would have encouraged growing linguistic proficiency in Tamil, leading to growing imposition of the latter on the ancestral language.

In principle, the social and linguistic processes that led to the "conversion" of languages like Sri Lanka Portuguese and Sri Lanka Malay are similar to those that led to structural change in other ancestral languages such as Asia Minor Greek. This kind of scenario for the creation of a mixed language has not generally been recognised in the literature. It therefore emphasises the need for us to have adequate documentation of the social contexts of the contact, if we are to understand the true causes and mechanisms of change. Since such documentation is not always available to us, it isn't clear how many ancestral languages may have changed their typology in this way. Other possible cases include the varieties of Urdu and Kannada spoken in Kupwar, India (Gumperz and Wilson 1971), which converged primarily toward Marathi, while retaining their ancestral vocabulary. Marathi was the socially dominant language of the region where Kupwar is located, and was widely used as a lingua franca in the community. It is therefore reasonable to assume that frequent use of Marathi led to it becoming linguistically more dominant for speakers of Urdu and Kannada. This in turn would have led to structural imposition from Marathi on to the ancestral languages.

On the whole, cases of massive typological change in a community's language under imposition from a socially dominant language appear to be relatively rare. Contact languages that fit the structural profile of "Form-Semantics" mixed languages appear to arise far more commonly from group second language acquisition of a socially dominant language. However, in these cases, it is the newly acquired L2 that is transformed via structural imposition from the L1 or ancestral language. There is a wide range of such contact languages, which will be discussed in the following sections.

5. Second language acquisition and the emergence of new contact languages

The vast majority of contact languages appear to have arisen in situations where groups speaking entirely different languages come into contact for various reasons, and circumstances demand that one of the groups acquire some version of the other group's language, or some compromise between the two languages. Depending on the nature of the contact, the newly acquired L2 may manifest differing degrees and types of restructuring, of the sort associated with processes of second language acquisition. The outcomes of such restructuring include the languages referred to as pidgins, creoles, indigenised languages, and second language varieties that have been referred to variously as 'converted' languages, or cases of 'metatypy'.

5.1. Pidgin formation

Pidgins arise to facilitate communication between groups of different language backgrounds in restricted contexts such as trading, forced labour, military occupation, master-servant domestic relationships and other types of marginal contact. Because of such limitations in scope of use, pidgins are highly simplified and reduced versions of their major input language, usually the socially dominant one. Pidgins that emerged in domestic settings include Indian Butler English (Hosali 1992), Pidgin Madam and Gulf Pidgin Arabic (Bakir 2010; Avram 2010). Those that arose under military invasion or occupation include Japanese Pidgin English and Vietnamese Pidgin French, both now extinct. The two most common types of pidgin, however, are those that arose in contexts of trading and in situations involving mass migrant labour, especially on plantations and mines. Among the pidgins that served as lingua francas on plantations were Pidgin Hawaiian and Hawaii Pidgin English.

Many trade pidgins arise in situations of contact between geographically contiguous groups. Typical examples of these include indigenous American pidgins such as Chinook Pidgin (also known as Chinuk Wawa or simply Wawa 'speech'), Delaware Pidgin, and Mobilian Pidgin. These appear to have originated in pre-colonial times, as lingua francas for use among various Native American groups, but they were eventually also used for communication between Indians and Europeans. According to Drechsel (1996: 1226), they all shared a set of sociolinguistic characteristics. Their primary contexts of use included trade, hunting, and similar activities, as well as political alliances and associations. They were also used for communication across groups linked through intermarriage, and in gatherings of kinsfolk. All arose in situations of extensive linguistic diversity involving much bi- and multilingualism. They were also characterised by much use of gesture or sign language. Many of these sociolinguistic characteristics can also be found in other indigenous pidgins, such as those of Papua New Guinea (Dutton 1983; Foley 1988).

Many other trade pidgins, including Pacific Pidgin English, Chinese Pidgin English, Russenorsk, and Eskimo Pidgin, arose as a result of contact between indigenous and foreign groups. Russenorsk, for instance, was used in trade between Russian merchants and Norwegian fishermen in Northern Norway from about the end of the 18th century to the 1920s. It is somewhat different from most pidgins in that it draws almost equally from both source languages for its vocabulary, a further consequence of which is that its phonology is also a compromise between the phonologies of the source languages. Similar cases of mixed vocabulary include Chinook Pidgin and Ndyuka-Trio Pidgin, which is referred to as both Ingii 'Indian' and Mekolo 'Black'. The mixture in these cases is usually attributed to the fact that the groups in contact were of equal social status. In most other cases, it is the language of the more numerous or more powerful group that supplies the bulk of the pidgin's vocabulary.

In general, then, pidgins arise in situations involving limited contact between groups in restricted contexts of use, where neither group has either the need or the opportunity to learn the other's language fully. This accounts for the fact that pidgins are very similar in structure to early interlanguage, or what Klein and Perdue (1997) refer to as the "Basic Variety", being characterised by absence of inflectional morphology, and a grammar stripped to the bare essentials, lacking TMA systems, embedding processes, movement phenomena and other grammatical characteristics associated with more highly developed languages. In all these respects, these contact languages conform to Hymes' classic definition of pidginisation as "that complex process of sociolinguistic change comprising reduction in inner form, with convergence, in the context of restriction in use. A pidgin is the result of such a process that has achieved autonomy as a norm" (1971: 84).

Pidgins remain highly reduced in structure and marginal to their speakers' communities as long as their scope of use remains highly restricted. In most cases, when the reasons for their use end, they simply become extinct. But extension of their functions beyond the narrow contexts of trade or labour etc., has often led to their expansion into more complex languages, which can become stable community languages. For instance, Chinook Pidgin developed into a more elaborate vernacular on the Grande Ronde reservation of Northwest Oregon. This was because it continued to serve as a lingua franca for members of six Native American tribes languages from three different families. Zenk (1984: v) pointed out that the pidgin was "an important factor in the sense of identity and solidarity that many Natives of the reservation period came to feel as 'Grand Ronde Indians'".

Similarly, the history of early Pacific Pidgin English offers an excellent illustration of how changing social circumstances can affect the development and evolution of a pidgin. Thus, the earliest forms of pidgin English that were used in the whaling trade of the early 1800s started to expand when this pidgin was adopted for use in various southern Melanesian islands that were involved in the lucrative sandalwood and bêche-de-mer trades. This economic enterprise required the establishment of more or less fixed settlements, which promoted regular contact between speakers of English and Melanesian languages, as well as among the linguistically heterogeneous Melanesians themselves. Conditions therefore became ripe for the establishment of a more efficient and stable form of communication. Similar conditions emerged in the Sydney area of New South Wales, Australia, which was the most frequent port of call in the Pacific for ships engaged in trading and related activities. Here too a relatively stable pidgin emerged, which shared many features with the Melanesian pidgin varieties as a result of continuous diffusion by sailors, islanders, and other travellers. The pidgin of the Sydney area later spread to other parts of Australia, including Queensland, where it evolved into Queensland Pidgin English. Forms of Pidgin English were initially used for interaction between English speakers and Aborigines, but also became important means of communication among Aboriginal groups speaking different languages, and consequently spread throughout Australia.

When plantations were established in Queensland after 1863, labourers were recruited from various parts of Melanesia, many of whom already spoke some form of pidgin English. Thus, both Queensland Pidgin English and early Melanesian Pidgin English provided input to the plantation pidgin that emerged on the plantations in the latter half of the 19th century (Clark 1983). By the 1870s, this pidgin had evolved into a more elaborate and stable form of communication, with an expanding and more efficient grammatical apparatus. Eventually, it would develop further into the so-called 'expanded pidgins' of Melanesia, which I will designate as creoles, and discuss later.

5.2. Indigenised varieties

The colonisation of various parts of the world by European powers during the 15th to 19th centuries led to the spread of European languages and their transformation by indigenous peoples into new contact varieties. This phenomenon, of course, was not restricted to Europe, nor to this time period. It has occurred time and again throughout history, for instance in the spread of Greek and Latin throughout the Greek and Roman empires respectively, or in the spread of Arabic throughout the Muslim world. The adoption of the languages of the colonisers led to the emergence of a range of L2 varieties, diverging to varying degrees from the target language. Such divergence, as Thomason and Kaufman have pointed out, is due primarily to the effects of "imperfect" or "natural" second language acquisition by groups shifting to the socially dominant language. Such effects are brought about by imposition, which involves the use of L1 language production processes in attempting to use the L2.

The degrees of restructuring that took place depended on a variety of sociolinguistic factors, including the demographics of the colonising and colonised groups, the extent of inter-group versus intra-group interaction, the contexts in which language learning took place, and the learners' attitudes toward the new creations. What happened to the colonisers' languages in their colonial settings depended to a large extent on how they were introduced. As Gupta (1997) notes with regard to English, there were three ways in which European languages spread – by migration of Europeans; through informal or 'untutored' second language acquisition; and through instruction in schools. But each colony experienced a different mixture of these three types of transmission. For instance, the American colonies of England experienced significant immigration of English speakers, but also massive importation of African slaves. In places like Singapore, English was learned via instruction, but many people also acquired it informally, leading to a significantly different local variety. In Australia, new contact varieties of English emerged as a result of the introduction of Pacific Islanders to work on plantations in Queensland, and as a result of contact with Aboriginal languages. In short, the correlation between the ways in which European languages were introduced to the colonies and the types of outcome that resulted is by no means neat or clear cut. Still, certain general observations can be made.

In the first place, the greater the number of European settlers, the more likely it was that their varieties would survive relatively unchanged in the colonial setting. This was the case in the former English colonies in North America, Australia, and New Zealand, where the English settlers became the majority population. As Crosby (1986: 5) points out, these places are situated in the temperate zone, and were therefore ideal places for Europeans to settle in large numbers. Not surprisingly, it was in these places that the indigenous inhabitants were systematically suppressed and massacred. By contrast, the tropical regions were not conducive to Europeanisation, and slavery involving forced relocation of Africans to these areas proved most convenient. It was in these settings that creoles emerged. Even here, differences in demographics and codes of interaction led to quite different outcomes. Finally, in the colonies established in places like Ireland, India and South East Asia, there was greater reliance on indigenous populations for purposes of economic exploitation and political control. Europeans here formed small minorities, and local inhabitants, particularly those of higher social status, were provided the opportunity to learn the European language, usually in school, so they could serve European interests. But the language also spread to the wider population through untutored learning, undergoing different degrees of transformation. Such contact situations led to the emergence of 'indigenised' varieties.

'Indigenised' varieties display varying degrees of approximation to the colonisers' language, depending on the extent of influence from learners' L1s, which depends in turn on the social ecology of the contact situation. We can illustrate such differences through a comparison of the spread of English to places like Ireland and South and South East Asia.

5.2.1. Irish English

Though English was first introduced to Ireland in the 12th century, modern Irish English has its true roots in the 17th century, when British colonial settlements were established in Ulster (Northern Ireland) and eastern Ireland (Kallen 1997). Large numbers of settlers were introduced to Ulster from Scotland and Northern England, while Southern Ireland attracted smaller numbers of settlers from other parts of England, especially the south and southwest. As a result, northern varieties of Irish English show strong continuities from Scots, while Southern Irish English shows more affinities with southern and south-western English dialects. All varieties show influence from Irish (Gaelic), but that influence is more pronounced in western and other parts of Ireland where English settlers remained a small minority, and the indigenous population preserved its first language longer.

The social contexts in which Irish English emerged in many ways parallel those of indigenised varieties more generally. They all arose in settings characterised by limited interaction between native speakers of the target language and the groups learning it. Only the more affluent or elite sections of the community had full access to native target language models, including instruction in schools. Most members of the community interacted primarily among themselves rather than with native speakers, hence the contact variety itself became the primary target of learning. This reinforced the use and eventual establishment of features due to substrate influence from Irish. The patterns of contact between the locals and English speakers also played a role in the emergence of distinct varieties of Irish English. Migratory labour was an important aspect of this contact (Odlin 1997: 11). Workers from Ulster tended to go to Scotland, thus reinforcing the establishment of Ulster Scots in the north. On the other hand, southern Irish workers tended to migrate to the English settlements in eastern Ireland, or to southern England, thus reinforcing the southern English influence on varieties of Irish English in the south on their return home. Another important factor in such cases of language shift is the persistence of bilingualism within the shifting group. In the Irish case, just as in Singapore later on, the majority of those who acquired English as a second language maintained their ancestral languages as well. Odlin (1997: 4–5) suggests there were large numbers of illiterate bilinguals in 19th century Ireland, based on his analysis of the 1851 census data. It seems likely that childhood bilingualism was also common, and that bilingual children played a role in imposing Irish influence on Irish English grammar. Irish features are most pronounced in those varieties of Irish English that are spoken in areas that had or still have large numbers of bilinguals.

5.2.2. Indigenised varieties of English in Asia

The spread of English to Ireland was part of the much wider British colonial expansion in the 17th century, which also embraced the Americas and the Caribbean. By contrast, the spread of English to South and South East Asia took place during the second phase of British colonisation, after the declaration of American independence and the abolition of slavery in 1808. The colonisation of India and parts of South East Asia as well as Africa, was motivated by the desire to expand trade and political control to those areas, which supplied vast new markets and sources of raw materials. In such colonies, English was initially restricted to contexts such as administration, business, and the legal system. Eventually, however, the language spread to wider sections of the population as a result of broader contact between speakers of English and the indigenous languages, and the rise of English-medium schools. Again, however, we find very different outcomes, depending on the ways in which English spread and was used. In India, for example, a continuum of L2 varieties emerged, which depended primarily on the type and amount of education one received. Proficiency in English became associated with high social status, and elite families transmitted it to their children as a native language, along with other languages such as Hindi. But for the majority of the population, English was learned as a second language, to be used only in certain domains such as education, or as a lingua franca for interethnic communication. In most other domains of everyday life, people continued to employ their ancestral language. The varying degrees of exposure to English and the differences in its use have resulted in a continuum of L2 Englishes. Gupta (1997) points out that, in this situation, speakers do not change their variety much, but maintain the particular level of proficiency they have obtained. This means that, apart from the standard variety, there is no single established variety that has attained the status of an autonomous, conventionalised vernacular.

In Singapore, by contrast, a very different picture emerged after the colony was established in 1819. Here too, English was introduced primarily through the school system, and was acquired as a second language by speakers of various language backgrounds, including varieties of Chinese, Malay, and various Indian languages. As Platt et al. (1983: 9) note, English became widely established in the course of the early 20th century partly because it was the language of Western science and technology, and an avenue to social advancement. Members of the more prosperous Chinese and Indian groups saw the advantages of an English-medium education and a growing number of English-medium schools were established in the course of the later 19th and earlier 20th centuries. In addition, English functioned as a valuable lingua franca for use in interethnic communication, and was transmitted through natural second language acquisition. In due course, a continuum of English varieties emerged, ranging from Standard English to a basilectal variety now referred to as (Colloquial) Singapore English, and mesolectal varieties in between. Unlike the situation in India, some form of English is spoken today by most, if not all, Singaporeans, and English is in fact a native language for a significant minority. Also, while the acrolect is certainly associated with higher social status and official functions, use of the colloquial variety is by no means restricted to lower-status groups. Speakers of all social backgrounds can move along the continuum, depending on the context of use, their interlocutors, etc. Moreover, the colloquial variety has become conventionalised as a stable system in its own right. All of this makes Singapore similar in many respects to the creole continua of the Caribbean.

Platt et al. (1983: 9) suggest that Singapore English emerged among school children during the period 1930–1960 because "children were using English in natural communication situations while still in quite early stages of acquisition – some of them acquiring some competence in it before school years from elder siblings". This would explain the strong influence of local languages, especially Chinese and Malay varieties, on the new contact language. To add to this, Ansaldo (2004: 143) argues that the earliest forms of Singapore English emerged among two ethnically-mixed groups – Babas and Eurasians – who acted as go-betweens for the British in their dealings with the local population during the 19th century. The Babas were descendants of Hokkien traders and Malay women who spoke a contact variety referred to as Baba Malay. The Eurasians were descendants of mixed marriages between Asians and Europeans (primarily Portuguese), who played a role in establishing English-medium schools in Singapore. According to Ansaldo, the children of Baba and Eurasian families were the first to be exposed to education in English; hence they and their parents must have been the founder group that created and spread early forms of

Singapore English. This would suggest that the earliest substrate influence on Singapore English came from varieties of Malay, with later and more pronounced influence from Chinese varieties, as Singapore English spread. Ansaldo (2004: 144) argues that "[Singapore English] is the product of an evolution that pre-dates the arrival of the Standard English medium by at least a century". This would mean that English-medium schools contributed to the spread and development of Singapore English, but were not its original birthplace. Moreover, this scenario challenges the view that Singapore English is a restructured form of Standard English that arose in the 20th century. It seems rather to have stabilised and become conventionalised in this period as a result of its wide adoption as a lingua franca among schoolchildren of different ethnic and language backgrounds. This is reminiscent of the conventionalisation of Hawaii Creole English, as described by Roberts (1998) and Siegel (2000). As in that situation, the use of the contact variety was reinforced by its symbolic value as a marker of local identity, despite the fact that official policy opposes its use.

This brief overview omits many details relating to the community settings and patterns of interaction that played a role in these outcomes of shift. Gal's (1979) pioneering study of the shift from Hungarian to German in Oberwart, Austria, provides a model for the kind of detailed exploration that is still lacking. She appeals to various social factors – economic change, social mobility and opportunity, changing social network structures, and choices of social identity – to explain the patterns of shift in Oberwart. All of these have yet to be fully explored in studies of the emergence of the indigenised varieties. Other factors that played a role include differences in the demographic distributions of settler versus indigenous populations, which made for significant differences both within a colony, as in northern versus southern Ireland, and between colonies, as can be seen in the differences in the forms of English that emerged in India as opposed to Singapore. Differences in the nature of access to the target language (e.g. formal versus 'natural' acquisition), and in the target language itself (native as opposed to indigenous models) also made for differences in the type of outcome. Finally, Gal's emphasis on speakers' choices of social identity is particularly relevant to the conventionalisation of the indigenised varieties. The preservation of distinctive features due to substrate influence and other causes has much to do with the value of the new contact languages as symbols of group identity, whether based on ethnicity or nationality. Their conventionalisation as new languages typically follows from their association with a (new) speech community that sees itself as distinct from the target language community. In their contemporary sociolinguistic settings, this has led to an ideological conflict between their value as badges of identity and the prestigious status of the standard varieties with which they co-exist. It goes without saying that the synchronic sociolinguistic study of these situations can shed much light on the social forces that led to the emergence of these varieties in the first place. This is true of other contact languages that arose through processes of group second language acquisition, and became established as new community languages associated with new cultures.

5.3. Creole formation

Creoles make up another major sub-classification of the second language varieties of European and other languages that emerged as a result of colonial expansion and military conquest. The traditional view is that creoles all arose from pidgins (Hall 1966), but that view finds support only in certain cases of creole formation. It undoubtedly applies to Hawaiian Creole English, which is the result of the expansion of Hawaiian Pidgin English, as well as to Kriol and other creoles of Australia, which evolved out of Australian Pidgin English. Very similar developments occurred in the case of the Melanesian pidgins, which evolved into the so-called 'expanded pidgins', Tok Pisin, Bislama, and Solomon Islands Pijin. I will refer to these languages as creoles, since they share much in common with other creoles in terms of their sociohistorical background and processes of restructuring. I also extend the term to the expanded English-lexicon pidgins of West Africa, which serve as lingua francas for millions of speakers in countries like Cameroon, Ghana, and Nigeria, and are being acquired as first languages by many children. They too arose through similar processes of change, involving the types of restructuring associated with natural second language acquisition.

5.3.1. Pacific creoles

As we saw earlier, the expansion of Melanesian Pidgin can be traced back to the establishment of permanent settlements in Melanesia for purposes of cultivating sandalwood and other products for trade. Further expansion took place when the pidgin, along with Queensland Pidgin English, was employed for everyday communication on the plantations of Queensland, and later, Samoa. When the labour recruits from various parts of the Pacific took this pidgin back with them to their home territories, it became a vital medium of interethnic communication there as well. As a result, further elaboration of the pidgin's structure took place in each territory. Each pidgin continued to expand its resources through lexical borrowing, structural innovations due to imposition from native languages, as well as internal developments. Thus were born the three contemporary creoles – Tok Pisin (Papua New Guinea), Bislama (Vanuatu), and Pijin (Solomon Islands), which serve not only as lingua francas, but also as semi- or co-official languages in their respective countries, and have become first languages for many. As Singler (2008) argues, urbanisation played a significant role in the spread and expansion of these pidgins and their increasing use as a medium of communication in the multilingual urban setting. Siegel (1998, 2008) discusses their history and development in greater detail.

In Australia itself, as mentioned earlier, forms of Pidgin English appeared very soon after the arrival of English colonisers, beginning with the British occupation of the area around Port Jackson in New South Wales. Contact between Aborigines and English speakers led to the emergence of pidgin varieties that functioned as lingua francas not just between the English and Aborigines, but among the latter as well. New South Wales Pidgin became an important and widespread means of communication, and was the basis for the emergence of associated pidgins, and later creoles, in many parts of Australia (Malcolm 2008: 126). The expansion of the pastoral industry beyond New South Wales led to the spread of New South Wales Pidgin through Queensland into the Northern Territory, where it merged with other pidgin varieties to become Northern Territory Pidgin English. Colonisation led to serious social disruption among the Aborigines, particularly with the expansion of the pastoral industry. The Aborigines were systematically massacred, or succumbed to diseases such as smallpox which the settlers brought with them. They were forcibly removed from their traditional lands, and many of them were forced to labour as kitchen hands and stockmen on cattle stations under conditions very similar to those of slavery (Meakins 2008: 78). Aborigines of very different linguistic backgrounds ended up in towns, farms, or mission stations, where they adopted forms of Pidgin English as their common means of communication. According to Harris (1991: 201), Northern Territory Pidgin evolved into a creole at an Anglican Church mission established in 1908 at Roper River, which provided refuge for Aborigines faced with annihilation. A generation of children at the mission adopted the pidgin as their language, and were instrumental in restructuring it into what was then known as Roper River Creole. The name was changed to 'Kriol' in 1976 following the orthography that had been developed for the language. According to Malcolm (2008: 126), it has at least 20,000 speakers.

In the Torres Strait Islands, a different picture emerged. Here the need to exploit various products of the sea brought together Europeans, and people from Papua New Guinea and the South Sea Islands. The common language chosen in this case was the earlier Pacific Pidgin English, which was adopted by Torres Strait Islanders who worked in the marine industry. Malcolm (2008: 126) notes that, by the 1890s, the pidgin was being used by children of Torres Strait Islanders and immigrant origin on at least two islands, and the resulting creoles spread throughout the islands and along the north coast of Queensland. 'Broken' now has about 3,000 native speakers and 12,000 second language speakers (Malcolm 2008: 126).

Perhaps the best documented case of the evolution of a pidgin into a creole is that of Hawaii Creole English, which emerged out of Hawaii Pidgin English in the early twentieth century. The emergence of this contact language is highly instructive with regard to how social factors, particularly the demographic make-up of the population, can influence the course of creole creation. Hawaii Pidgin English was used on the plantations and elsewhere as the lingua franca among Hawaiians and various immigrant groups, including Portuguese, Chinese, and later, Japanese, Koreans and others. Eventually, it became a target of learning by children born to these immigrants, who were the chief architects of its expansion into the creole. Using socio-historical and sociolinguistic evidence drawn from contemporary archives and studies, Roberts (1998, 2000) demonstrated that the first generation of locally-born children, chiefly Portuguese and Chinese, were bilingual in their parents' language and Hawaii Pidgin English. They continued the process of expanding the pidgin, appealing mostly to transfer of features from their ancestral languages into the budding contact language (Siegel 2000). The second generation of immigrant children learned this expanded pidgin as their L1, and contributed further to its elaboration and stabilisation as a new contact language. Roberts' account of the social factors that led to the emergence of this creole provides a convincing rebuttal of Bickerton's (1981, 1984) view that creoles are products of first language acquisition by infants whose only input was a deficient pidgin, and who appealed to an innate language bioprogram to elaborate the grammars of creoles.

These languages demonstrate well how pidgins evolve when called upon to fulfil the functions of an everyday vernacular. From a linguistic perspective, the most significant aspect of their evolution is that it involved a high degree of substrate influence from the L1s of the speakers who acquired pidgins as L2s and later L1s, and continued to reshape their grammars in response to new communicative needs. In this respect, they match the once widely accepted description of 'creoles' as languages that result from the structural elaboration of pidgins. The social contexts and social motivations for their creation were similar in many ways, but quite different in others. For instance, they share with each other, and with other creoles, the fact that they were first adopted as media of interethnic communication, and were elaborated by speakers who drew on the resources of their L1s. In cases such as Kriol, Torres Strait Creole and Hawaii Creole, the elaboration was accomplished primarily by children of different language backgrounds, who adopted the pidgin as an in-group language. By contrast, the elaboration of Hawaii Pidgin English varieties was largely achieved by adults who needed a lingua franca for wider communication in a linguistically heterogeneous environment. The survival of these languages in all cases depended on the emergence of a stable community of speakers for whom the contact variety was not just a convenient tool, but a primary vernacular, a first language, and a badge of social identity. The same can be said of other creoles such as those that originated in the New World.

5.3.2. Atlantic creoles

By far the largest group of creoles arose in the Atlantic area, including parts of West Africa, the Caribbean and parts of the Americas, as a result of European colonisation expansion from the 15th century on. This began with the Portuguese, who established settlements on various islands off the West African coast in the 1400's, and soon began importing slaves from the mainland to cultivate crops and raise livestock. This kind of plantation economy was carried over the Atlantic to Brazil in the early 16th century, and became a model for the plantation colonies established by other European powers in the New World and elsewhere.

These plantation settings shared a number of broad socio-political, demographic, and economic characteristics, including the use of large numbers of slaves who were transplanted from their African homelands and subjected to control by a small but powerful minority of Europeans. In most cases, particularly in the Caribbean, colonisation involved the subjugation and even extermination of indigenous peoples, and the re-peopling of their lands by Europeans and Africans. But there were also significant differences in the social ecologies of different colonies, which led in turn to differences in the ways in which the colonial languages were acquired and changed. Mintz (1971: 48) outlined the three broad social conditions that shaped the emergence of creole languages in the New World:

– The demographic make-up of each colony, including population ratios between the groups, and their places of origin;

- The types and patterns of contact among the groups, which were generally determined by the codes of social interaction governing their relative statuses and relationships;

- The nature of the community settings in which the groups interacted.

This tri-partite division of the social ecology of plantation settings has become one of the classic frameworks for investigating how creole cultures and languages emerged. We are fortunate to have a great deal of information about the settlement histories of certain European colonies, which allows us to determine how these social factors affected the fate of the European languages. For a start, differences in the numbers and ratios of Europeans to Africans, and among the Africans themselves, certainly played a major role in determining the paths of creole formation. In Barbados, for instance, large numbers of indentured servants were brought to the colony, particularly from Southwest England, and the high ratio of such workers to African slaves in the first 40 years of settlement led to a contact variety, Bajan, which was in many respects modelled on Southwest English dialects. On the other hand, in Suriname, the rapid growth and increasing size of the African population, and the numerical dominance of speakers of Gbe languages in the first 70 years or so of the colony, ensured a significant Gbe influence on the grammar of the Surinamese creoles (Migge 2003). The following brief extract from an Anansi story shows how radical that influence was.

(10) a. *Unu   ben   e   leri   altijd   over   dagu nanga anansi*
       1PL   PST   IMPF learn always about dog   and   spider
   b. *Dus   den   man   ben   go   a   onti.*
       so   the.PL   man   PST go   LOC   hunt
   c. *Den   man   ben   go   onti,   go   suku   stimofo,*
       the.PL   man   PST   go   hunt   go   seek   meat/fish
   d. *den   man   e   waka,   den   man   e   waka,   te*
       the.PL   man   IMPF   walk   the.PL   man   IMPF walk   until
      ini   a   busi.
       inside the   jungle
   e. *Now   di   den   man   waka   wan   pisi,   den   man*
       now   when   the.PL   man   walk   a   piece the.PL   man
      si   tu   titei,
       see   two   rope
   f. *wan   deki   titei   nanga   wan   fatu   titei.*
       one   thick   rope   and   one   fat   rope
   a. 'We always used to learn about Dog and Spider.
   b. So they went hunting.

    c. They went hunting, looking for meat,
    d. they walked and walked until they were in the jungle.
    e. Now when they had walked for a while they saw two ropes,
    f. one thick rope and one fat rope.'

One of the important lessons from the Surinamese situation is that overall importation figures and population ratios by themselves cannot inform us reliably about the relative importance and impact of potential substrate languages. The overall figures for this colony show that far higher numbers of slaves were imported from areas other than the Slave Coast, where most Gbe speakers originated. But, as Arends (1995: 252) points out, both the timing and compactness of various African inputs have to be considered, if we are to explain the nature and degree of substrate influence on creole formation. The evidence from Suriname suggests that it was the first two or three cohorts of slaves – that is, those imported in the first 70 years – whose languages exerted most influence on the early Surinamese plantation creole.

Another important demographic factor is the rate of nativization of the population, particularly the enslaved and those of mixed race. Singler (1986) has argued that the higher and faster the rate of nativization, the closer the creole will be to the superstrate. This view gains support from colonies like Réunion and Barbados, where the slave population grew primarily through natural increase. By the mid-17th century, only some 30 years after settlement, the majority of Barbadian slaves were locally born (Rickford and Handler 1994: 237). Moreover, co-habitation between settlers and slaves in these colonies produced significant numbers of locally born persons of mixed race who were free and had closer contact with settlers and their languages. The status and linking function of such mixed race groups must have contributed to the emergence and consolidation of close second language approximations of the superstrate. By contrast, in colonies where the slave population increased through continuous large-scale importation rather than natural increase, the creoles that emerged displayed greater typological distance from the superstrates. When this was coupled with the departure of most superstrate speakers, as in Suriname, it lead to even more 'radical' creole formation, since slaves were mostly targeting contact varieties used by other slaves.

But demographic evidence is only part of the picture, and needs to be supplemented by close scrutiny of the changing situational contexts and patterns of interaction among the groups concerned. Most colonies were characterised by an initial period of settlement referred to as the *société d'habitation*, which involved small farms and homesteads in which settlers (including indentured servants and owners) lived and worked closely together. It is generally accepted that such situations allowed the earliest cohort of slaves to acquire close approximations of the colonial language. The length of time such social conditions prevailed had a direct bearing on how closely the vernacular that survived in the colony approximated the superstrate. The switch to a plantation economy, especially sugar cultivation, ushered in a totally different type of social organisation, the *société de plantation*, which brought with it significant changes in demographics and types of social interaction. In most cases, it led to not just a massive increase in the African population, but also to the demise of small farms, the withdrawal of indentured servants from the labour force, and a general reduction in contact between Africans and Europeans. This also set the stage for the emergence of creole varieties that were much further removed from their lexifier languages. Under such conditions, creoles became subject to much heavier influence from the L1s of the slaves, who were now creating a new medium of communication for use primarily among themselves, rather than with Europeans.

In addition, we cannot overlook the role played by the codes that regulated interaction between settlers and slaves. The *société d'habitation* clearly allowed far greater contact and interaction than the *société de plantation*, with its more rigid social hierarchy and laws of segregation. But there were differences in the slave codes from one colony to the next. These determined whether slaves could participate in institutions like the church, how quickly they could attain freedom, whether they could acquire property, and so on. Such differences were crucial to the linguistic outcomes in each situation. In most of the Spanish colonies, for example, the rate of manumission was generally rapid and continuous, far more so than in the French and English colonies. Freed slaves had greater privileges and opportunity for social mobility. These and other differences in the political and social milieu of the Spanish colonies may explain the paucity of Spanish-lexicon creoles in the New World, as Diaz-Campos and Clements (2008), Sessarego (to appear) and others have argued, contra McWhorter (2000). Finally, there were differences within each colony in the status and privileges afforded different categories of slaves. "Elite" slaves, including Black overseers, skilled and domestic slaves, had more freedom of movement and access to Europeans than those who laboured in the fields. In many colonies, such differences led to linguistic continua ranging from L2 varieties of the superstrate to highly divergent or 'basilectal' varieties.

To sum up, differences in the social ecologies of different colonies over time led to a continuum of outcomes both across and within colonies. At one extreme we find second language varieties such as Réunionnais and Bajan, representing closer approximations to the settler dialects. At the other extreme we find 'radical' creations such as the Surinamese creoles, whose grammars bear mark of the heavy effects of imposition from Gbe and other West African languages. Each combination of demographic, social, political and economic factors led to its own linguistic outcome. However, while we know a great deal about the ecological mix in certain colonies, a great deal remains uncertain about other colonies. Moreover, our knowledge of the micro-level of social organisation and interaction in the colonies is much more limited than our knowledge of macro-level factors such as population demographics. Arends (2001) is an attempt to address these shortcomings, but much more work still needs to be done. Hence, we are not in any position to formulate complete explanations of how social forces shaped the nature and outcomes of creole formation.

In some ways, however, what we now know about the social histories of several creoles does constitute a good basis on which we can evaluate, and in some cases refute, theories of how creoles originated. For instance, thorough examination of the socio-historical evidence has allowed us to reject earlier claims that creole genesis was the result of children targeting a deficient pidgin as the only input to their L1 acquisition process, and appealing to an innate language bioprogram to create a new creole grammar (cf. Bickerton 1981, 1984.) The evidence from Hawaii (Roberts 2000), Suriname (Arends 1995), Haiti and Martinique (Singler 1995) and elsewhere convincingly shows that creole formation was essentially a process of second language acquisition in which speakers of substrate languages, both children and adults, were the chief agents of restructuring and change.

This is what accounts for the fact that creoles manifest, to varying degrees, the effects of three types of restructuring associated with second language acquisition – processes of simplification, imposition and internally-motivated developments. The effects of simplification include absence of inflectional morphology, a preference for analytic over synthetic structures, uniform word order in basic syntactic structures, a tendency toward transparency in the form-function relationship, and other phenomena that reflect the need for ease of perception and production in the language learning process. The effects of imposition are seen in the varying extents of substrate influence, which, in extreme cases, produced radical creoles that are typologically more similar to their substrates than to their superstrates. This occurred especially when continuing importation of slaves over many decades led to successive stages of second language acquisition, in which later arrivals continued to impose features of their L1s on the evolving creole. As we have suggested, demographic factors play a crucial role in determining the degrees of substrate influence that occurred. For instance, where groups speaking the same or typologically quite similar substrate languages were in the majority, the creoles that emerged show greater evidence of their influence (Singler 1988). Siegel (1999) treats such demographic factors as part of the 'availability' constraints that determine what substrate and superstrate features find their way into the 'pool' of features that are potential input to the emerging creole. Finally, creoles manifest various types of internally motivated change at every stage of their development. The social factors that played a role in these developments have scarcely been explored.

5.4. Metatypy and 'converted' second languages

The processes of change that we observe in indigenised varieties and creoles can also be found in other contact languages that have received less attention in the literature. Among these are various Austronesian languages of Papua New Guinea, which show evidence of massive influence from indigenous Papuan languages. Ross (1996) describes two such Austronesian languages, Takia and Maisin, whose semantic and syntactic structures have been reshaped on the model of neighbouring Papuan languages, but whose lexicon, including grammatical elements, are Western Oceanic. Ross refers to this kind of restructuring as "metatypy" (a change in typology), and ascribes it to bilinguals who attempted to ease the burden of processing two languages by bringing their semantic and syntactic structures into line with each other (1996: 204). Similar shifts in typology have been described by Thurston (1987, 1994) for several Austronesian languages in Northwest New Britain (Papua New Guinea). Here too there has been a long history of contact between the indigenous languages and the Austronesian languages that were introduced by groups migrating from other parts of the Pacific. At present, only one of the indigenous languages, Anêm, still survives in Northwest New Britain, along with eight Austronesian languages. All of the latter have become markedly Papuan in their typology, sharing a common Papuan-derived grammatical and semantic structure, but preserving much of their ancestral vocabulary. As Thurston (1987: 68) points out, "in switching between languages, a speaker is mostly switching between wordlists while using the same semantic and syntactic structures". Bakker includes these restructured Austronesian languages in his category of "converted" or "Form-Semantics" mixed languages. As we saw earlier, several of these contact languages arose in situations where a group shifted to a socially dominant language, and then imposed its features on their ancestral language. In the Papua New Guinea situation, by contrast, the socio-historical evidence suggests that the Papuan influence on the Austronesian languages resulted from the fact that speakers of Papuan languages acquired the latter as second languages, transferring features of their L1s to them in the process. There was also a significant amount of transfer in the other direction, from Austronesian to Papuan languages. As the influx of Austronesian migrants increased, they merged with the indigenous inhabitants, who gradually adopted more of the newcomers' culture, including their languages. Thurston's sketch of the socio-historical context of the contact suggests that Austronesian culture became dominant in the coastal areas where they settled. He points out that "new recruits to the culture came largely from the indigenous population, who, by virtue of shared culture, became Austronesian themselves" (1987: 103). This supports the view that speakers of Papuan languages adopted Austronesian languages, imposing features of their L1s on them. A similar explanation was offered by Strong (1911: 382) for the heavy Papuan influence on Maisin, which he describes as "a Melanesian [i.e., Austronesian] language which has been modified, as is to be expected if a Melanesian language was imperfectly learned by a non-Melanesian [i.e., Papuan] speaking people". The language shift scenario is also supported by the fact that most of these Austronesian languages appear to have undergone extensive simplification and regularisation of structure. Such simplification is typical of untutored second language acquisition, particularly when the L2 varieties are used as lingua francas by groups speaking mutually unintelligible languages, as was the case in Northwest New Britain.

It seems clear, then, that indigenised varieties, creoles, and the 'converted' languages of Papua New Guinea all arise via similar processes of change, even though their social ecologies differ in many respects. The common factor they share is the fact that they arose as a result of language shift, or 'natural' second language acquisition, which set the stage for processes of imposition accompanied in many cases by simplification.

6.   Questions of status and function

It remains for us to investigate briefly the social functions that contact languages perform and the status they enjoy in their respective communities. I will confine my attention to those languages that are still in use in contemporary societies, the vast majority of which are indigenised varieties and creoles. Very few of these serve as official languages, or have been standardised. Typically, it is the standard varieties of their respective lexifier languages, or some other colonial language, that are employed in official functions in domains such as education, government, the law, literature, the mass media and so on. The standard varieties are therefore associated with high status and prestige, and are the yardstick by which the non-standard contact varieties are judged. The sociolinguistic situations in which contact varieties function are in fact similar in many respects to cases of diglossia. As in the classic cases first identified by Ferguson (1958), such situations are characterised simultaneously by socially based differences in speakers' linguistic repertoires and by functional or stylistic specialisation of the varieties employed. Moreover, this functional differentiation has a socio-cultural value, in that the standard (High, H) variety has superior status and prestige than the vernacular (Low, L) variety. These differences in social evaluation are reinforced by the fact that H is codified as a model of usage, is associated with a literary tradition and with higher learning, and must be acquired at school, as an avenue to social advancement. None of these applies to L, the creole, which is for the most part ignored and denied any role in public life.

As Tabouret-Keller (1978) points out, "diglossia has become synonymous with the inequality of the roles which each of the languages present in a complex situation could serve, and of the corresponding inequality of values which each of them represents" (p. 139; my translation). This inequality has consequences for the linguistic status of the contact varieties, as well as for the social functions they fulfil.

6.1.   Questions of status

Creoles have been particularly susceptible to negative treatment and evaluation of their status as languages. Among the exceptions are the Pacific creoles, Tok Pisin, Bislama and Solomon Islands Pijin, which enjoy more recognition and status because of the unifying function they fulfil in situations of extreme linguistic heterogeneity. In the vast majority of cases, creoles co-exist alongside their lexifier language, which functions as the official language. In such situations, as De Camp (1971: 26) pointed out, "the creole is especially unlikely to be granted status as a real language", and tends to be "inseparably associated with poverty, ignorance and lack of moral character."

Similar kinds of evaluation seem to apply to the contact varieties of English used in places like Singapore, Malaysia, Fiji, Australia, and various countries in West Africa, all of which co-exist with local standard varieties. In these situations, the contact variety is viewed as a deviant, even corrupt version of the standard, and is not accepted as an autonomous system in its own right. This is further encouraged by the fact that such situations involve a great deal of variability between standard and non-standard varieties, leading to linguistic continua in which the boundaries between the two varieties are difficult to determine. However, this conception of creole and other continua is really an artefact of the way patterns of variation have been described, particularly in quantitative sociolinguistic studies. It is true, of course, that there are correlations between linguistic variation and social stratification in these societies, with creole features being linked to speakers of lower social status, and standard features to those higher up in the social hierarchy. It is one thing to recognise this, but quite another to claim that the variation occurs within a single grammar or linguistic system. The creole continuum is, in fact, a purely sociolinguistic phenomenon similar to other continua that have arisen between quite distinct languages, for example in bilingual border communities in Europe, or in cases of diglossia such as German-speaking Switzerland or Arabic communities in the Middle East. In all of these cases, the intricate patterns of lexical, phonological and grammatical variation that have arisen are due to interaction between two quite distinct linguistic systems. However, the very fact of variability has encouraged the view that the non-standard varieties have no separate status.

Situations like these remind us that the status of a language variety is not solely, or even primarily, a linguistic question, but involves socio-political, historical, and socio-cultural considerations as well. In situations where contact varieties co-exist with unrelated official languages, for example Papiamentu in the Dutch Antilles, or Sranan Tongo in Dutch-official Suriname, their status as autonomous languages is not in question. It is interesting that such languages (unlike most creoles) tend to have names of their own. In the Francophone Caribbean, where French-lexicon creoles are side by side with French as the official language, there is also greater recognition of the autonomy of the creole vernaculars, and scholars often refer to these situations as 'bilingual'. Haitian Creole now has its own official orthography, and is being increasingly used in public communication. The French-lexicon creoles of St. Lucia and Dominica, where English is the official language, have also gained recognition as languages of national identity. However, despite this, these contact languages do not stand in a relationship of equality with the official languages.

6.2. Attitudes to contact varieties

Systematic investigation of language attitudes by Mühleisen (1993) for Trinidad and Beckford-Wassink (1999) for Jamaica reveal that social evaluation of the respective contact varieties is more complex and ambiguous than earlier assumed. While speakers agree that the standard variety is appropriate for more formal and public use, they still attach positive value to the contact variety as a badge of solidarity and identity, and as the language of intimate personal relationships. This tension between the overt evaluation of standard varieties as superior and the covert sense of pride in the contact variety is slowly being resolved – at least in some communities – in favour of more tolerant views of contact varieties and their place in their societies. This extends even to the increasing tendency for the public to view contact varieties as legitimate languages. For instance, Beckford-Wassink (1999: 66) found that 90 percent of informants in a language attitude survey regarded Jamaican Creole as a distinct language, basing their judgments primarily on lexicon and accent. The changes in attitude have been due to several factors: the growing sense of nationalism in these communities since independence; the emergence of a substantial body of scholarship that demonstrates the validity of the contact varieties as languages in their own right; the growing tendency to use the contact language in literary works; and the readiness of the powers-that-be to allow its use in contexts such as education.

6.3. Contact languages in literature and other media

As Schneider (2010: 375) points out,

> Another sign of the newly-established self-confidence that comes with new nationhood and the cultural acceptance of indigenous language forms and cultural habits is the appearance of literary productivity in a New English variety.

In the Caribbean, the use of creole in literature and other written media has expanded greatly within the last few decades. Well-known literary figures such as Vidia Naipaul and Earl Lovelace in Trinidad, Louise Bennett in Jamaica and others have exploited the resources of the creoles to evoke the distinctively Caribbean voice of their characters. Similarly, in many countries of Asia and Africa, writers such as Chinua Achebe, Wole Soyinka, Amy Tan and others "have produced highly influential and acclaimed artistic products which employ and reflect local language habits" (Schneider 2010: 375). In addition, translation of other literature such as the Bible into creole and other contact languages has contributed to the lexical and stylistic elaboration of these languages. As Mühleisen (2005) points out, literature and creative writing in creole have played an important role in the negotiation of creoles as 'legitimate' varieties, not least by contributing to the establishment of orthographic conventions. In addition, the growing acceptance of contact varieties has been reflected in the expansion of their use in the mass media and in public communication in general. For instance, in Suriname, Sranan Tongo is now used exclusively by some community radio stations, and is increasingly used in communication between the government and the people, in areas such as health, taxes, and of course politics. Sranan is also used in certain forms of popular music, such as Kawina and Kaseka (Arends and Carlin 2002: 285). There is even a creole version of the national anthem. Similarly, in the Dutch Antilles, Papiamento competes with Dutch in the written media and is used almost exclusively in radio and TV broadcasts (Kouwenberg 2006: 2107). Similar developments have taken place all over the Caribbean.

In short, speakers of these contact languages have become increasingly proud and accepting of them, though they are still far from being adopted as official languages, and are still not fully standardised. Most of them still lack official orthographies, or dictionaries and grammars, a fact that militates against their use in the domain of education.

6.4. Contact languages in education

Problems relating to educational policy are shared by many communities where contact varieties are acquired as first languages and used as everyday vernaculars. The debate over the use of the contact varieties as media of instruction dates back to the 1970s in the Caribbean, and has been repeated, for example, in Hawaii in the 1980s (Watson-Gegeo 1994), in many countries of the 'outer circle' of English such as Singapore and Hong Kong (Kachru 1997), and most recently in the US with respect to African American Vernacular English or Ebonics. Governments have become more supportive of the idea of using creole as a medium of instruction in the schools, and indeed in public education as a whole. Both in Trinidad and Jamaica, for example, educational policy calls for maintaining English as the official language, while promoting the oral use of the creole at school in the early years of primary education. Eventually, such policies may be extended to include the use of creole as both the medium of instruction, and the language in which literacy is first taught, as is happening in bilingual creole situations such as that in the Dutch Antilles. Indeed, the Jamaican government approved the establishment of the Jamaican Language Unit at the University of the West Indies, and permitted it to implement a bilingual education experiment in three public elementary schools in 2004. The four year project yielded somewhat positive results, but so far has not led to wider implementation of the bilingual policy. (See Carpenter and Devonish 2010 for an assessment of the project's achievements.)

The situation in Haiti is an instructive illustration of the disastrous consequences of a language education policy that ignores totally the linguistic reality of a society. According to Hebblethwaite (2012) Creole is natively spoken by all 10 million Haitians, while French is spoken by less than 500,000 members of the elite. French-language dominance in Haitian schools adversely impacts millions of children and it is the source of broad societal inefficiency. The effects of the current educational policy are devastating: According to recent records from the Haitian government's statistics bureau, 61% of the population over the age of 10 is illiterate; the rural rate is 80.5% and the urban rate is 47.1% (Hebblethwaite 2012: 267). Contrasting strongly with Haiti is the situation in Curacao, where the private Papiamentu primary and secondary school, Kolegio Erasmo, has operated successfully since 1987 and has proved itself to be a worthy model for the expansion of first-language education on that island (Dijkhoff and Pereira 2010: 252). The use of the students' native language has resulted in a much higher success rate than found among students educated in Dutch (Dijkhoff and Pereira 2010: 253). In 2003 the government of the Netherlands Antilles announced plans to include Papiamentu through the university level and use the Kolegio Erasmo as a pilot school.

In order for this kind of educational policy to work, language planners must address problems of status planning (code selection and the assignment of new functions to the vernaculars), corpus planning (codification and elaboration), and implementation of the new policy. Deciding which variety to codify and what orthography to use continues to pose the greatest problems. While orthographies have been proposed by linguists for varieties such as Jamaican and Belize Creole, they have not been generally accepted by the public. Resolution of the problem of the orthography will go a long way toward establishing the autonomy of the creoles. It seems to be only a matter of time before at least some contact varieties finally assert themselves as distinctive languages with their own history, and achieve the prestige and recognition they deserve.

Notes

1. Meakins also observes that a similar mixed language, Light Warlpiri, arose in an Aboriginal community close to the Gurundji. It also combines an Indigenous language (Warlpiri) with Kriol (O'Shannessy 2009).
2. Tsotsitaal is a compound made up of *tsotsi* and *taal*, which means 'language.' Glaser (2000: 50) suggests that the term 'tsotsi' was coined around 1943–1944 to refer to the style of urban youths, including gang members, but notes that many people view tsotsis as harmless adherents to fashion. Others say that the term derives from the Sotho verb *go tsotsa* 'to rob'.

References

Abdulaziz, Mohamed H. & Ken Osinde. 1997. Sheng and Engsh: development of mixed codes among the urban youth in Kenya. *International Journal of the Sociology of Language* 125. 43–63.

Ansaldo, Umberto. 2004. The evolution of Singapore English: Finding the matrix. In Lisa Lim (ed.), *Singapore English: A Grammatical Description*, 129–164. Amsterdam: John Benjamins.

Arends, Jacques. 1995. Demographic factors in the formation of Sranan. In Jacques Arends (ed.), *The Early Stages of Creolization*, 233–85. Amsterdam: John Benjamins.

Arends, Jacques. 2001. Social stratification and network relations in the formation of Sranan. In Norval Smith & Tonjes Veenstra (eds.), *Creolization and Contact*, 291–307. Amsterdam: John Benjamins.

Arends, Jacques & Carlin, Eithne B. 2002. The languages of Suriname today and tomorrow. In Eithne B. Carlin & Jacques Arends, (eds.), *Atlas of the Languages of Suriname*, 283–286. Leiden: KITLV Press.

Augustinos, Gerasimos. 1992. *The Greeks of Asia Minor: Confession, Community, and Ethnicity in the Nineteenth Century*. Kent, OH: Kent State University Press.

Avram, Andrei A. 2010. An outline of Romanian Pidgin Arabic. *Journal of Language Contact. Varia* 3. 20–38.

Bakir, Murtadha J. 2010. Notes on the verbal system of Gulf Pidgin Arabic. *Journal of Pidgin and Creole Languages* 25(2). 201–228.

Bakker, Peter. 1997. *A Language of Our Own: The Genesis of Michif, the Mixed Cree-French Language of the Canadian Métis*. New York: Oxford University Press.

Bakker, Peter. 2003. Mixed languages as autonomous systems. In Yaron Matras & Peter Bakker (eds.), *The Mixed Language Debate: Theoretical and Empirical Advances*, 107–150. Berlin/New York: Mouton de Gruyter.

Beckford-Wassink, Alicia. 1999. Historic low prestige and seeds of change: Attitudes toward Jamaican Creole. *Language in Society* 28(1). 57–92.

Bickerton, Derek. 1981. *Roots of Language*. Ann Arbor: Karoma.

Bickerton, Derek. 1984. The language bioprogram hypothesis. *Behavioral and Brain Sciences* 7. 173–88.

Carpenter, Karen & Hubert Devonish. 2010. Swimming against the tide. Jamaican Creole in education. In Bettina Migge, Isabelle Léglise & Angela Bartens (eds.), *Creoles in Education. An appraisal of Current Programs and Projects*, 167–181. Amsterdam/Philadelphia: John Benjamins.

Childs, G. Tucker. 1997. The status of Isicamtho, an Nguni-based urban variety of Soweto. In Arthur Spears & Donald Winford (eds.), *The Structure and Status of Pidgins and Creoles*, 341–370. Amsterdam: John Benjamins.

Clark, Ross. 1983. Social contexts of early South Pacific pidgins. In Ellen Woolford & William Washabaugh (eds.), *The Social Contexts of Creolization*, 10–27. Ann Arbor: Karoma.

Crosby, Alfred W. 1986. *Ecological Imperialism: The Biological Expansion of Europe, 900–1900*. Cambridge: Cambridge University Press.
Dawkins, Richard M. 1916. *Modern Greek in Asia Minor*. Cambridge: Cambridge University Press.
de Gruiter, Miel. 1994. Javindo, a contact language in pre-war Semarang. In Peter Bakker & Maarten Mous (eds.), *Mixed languages: 15 Case Studies in Language Intertwining*, 151–159. Amsterdam: Uitgave IFOTT.
Dijkhoff, Marta & Joyce Pereira. 2010. Language and education in Aruba, Bonaire and Curaçao. In Bettina Migge, Isabelle Léglise & Angela Bartens (eds.), *Creoles in Education: An Appraisal of Current Programs and Projects*, 237–272. Amsterdam: John Benjamins.
Diaz-Campos, Manuel & Clancy Clements. 2008. A creole origin for Barlovento Spanish? A linguistic and sociohistorical inquiry. *Language in Society* 37. 351–383.
Drechsel, Emanuel J. 1996. Native American contact languages of the contiguous United States. In Stephen A. Wurm, Peter Mühlhäusler & Darrell T. Tryon (eds.), *Atlas of Intercultural Communication in the Pacific, Asia and the Americas, Vol. II. 2*, 1213–1239. Berlin: Mouton de Gruyter.
Dutton, Tom. 1983. Birds of a feather: A pair of rare pidgins from the Gulf of Papua. In Ellen Woolford & William Washabaugh (eds.), *The Social Context of Creolization*, 77–105. Ann Arbor: Karoma.
Ferguson, Charles. 1958. Diglossia. *Word* 15. 325–340.
Foley, William A. 1988. Language birth: The processes of pidginization and creolization. In Frederick Newmeyer (ed.), *Linguistics: The Cambridge Survey Vol. 2*, 162–183. Cambridge: Cambridge University Press.
Gal, Susan. 1979. *Language Shift: Social Determinants of Linguistic Change in Bilingual Austria*. New York: Academic Press.
Glaser, C. 2000. *Bo-tsotsi: The Youth Gangs of Soweto, 1935–1976 (Social history of Africa)*. Portsmouth, NH: Heinemann.
Golovko, Evgeniy V. 2003. Language contact and group identity: The role of 'folk' linguistic engineering. In Yaron Matras & Peter Bakker (eds.), *The Mixed Language Debate: Theoretical and Empirical Advances*, 177–207. Berlin/New York: Mouton de Gruyter.
Golovko, Evgeniy V. & Nikolai B. Vakhtin. 1990. Aleut in contact: the CIA enigma. *Acta Linguistica Hafniensia* 22. 97–125.
Gumperz, John J. & Robert Wilson. 1971. Convergence and creolization: a case from the Indo-Aryan/Dravidian border in India. In Dell H. Hymes (ed.), *Pidginization and Creolization of Languages*, 151–67. Cambridge: Cambridge University Press.
Gupta, Anthea F. 1997. Colonisation, migration, and functions of English. In Edgar W. Schneider (ed.), *Englishes Around the World: Vol. 1, General Studies, British Isles, North America*, 47–58. Amsterdam: John Benjamins.
Hall, Robert A., Jr. 1966. *Pidgin and Creole Languages*. Ithaca, NJ: Cornell University Press.
Hancock, Ian. 1984. Shelta and Polari. In Peter Trudgill (ed.), *Language in the British Isles*, 384–403. Cambridge: Cambridge University Press.

Harris, John W. 1991. Kriol – the creation of a new language. In Suzanne Romaine (ed.), *Language in Australia,* 195–203. Cambridge: Cambridge University Press.

Hebblethwaite, Benjamin. 2012. French and underdevelopment, Haitian Creole and development: Educational language policy problems and solutions in Haiti. *Journal of Pidgin and Creole Languages* 27(2). 255–302.

Heine, Bernd & Tania Kuteva. 2005. *Language Contact and Grammatical Change.* Cambridge: Cambridge University Press.

Hosali, Priya. 1992. Syntactic peculiarities of Butler English. *South Asian Language Review* 2(2). 58–74.

Hussainmiya, Bachamiya Abdul. 1987. *Lost Cousins: The Malays of Sri Lanka.* Bangi: Institut Bahasa, Kesusasteraan dan Kebudayaan Melayu, Universiti Kebangsaan Malaysia.

Hymes, Dell. 1971. General conceptions of process: Introduction. In Dell H. Hymes (ed.), *Pidginization and Creolization of Languages*, 65–90. Cambridge: Cambridge University Press.

Jakobson, Roman. 1938. Sur la théorie des affinités phonologiques entre des langues. Actes du Quatrième Congrès Internationale de Linguistes, 48–59. Reprinted in *Selected Writings, Vol. 1*, 234–246. The Hague: Mouton.

Janse, Mark. to appear. The Cappadocian Dialect. In Christos Tzitzilis (ed.), *Modern Greek Dialects*, Thessaloniki: Institute of Modern Greek Studies (Manolis Triantafyllidis Foundation).

Kachru, Braj B. 1997. World Englishes and English-using communities. *Annual Review of Applied Linguistics* 17. 66–87.

Kallen, Jeffrey L. 1997. Irish English and World English: Lexical perspectives. In Edgar W. Schneider (ed.), *Englishes Around the World. Vol. 1. General Studies, British Isles, North America,* 139–57. Amsterdam: John Benjamins.

Kenrick, Donald. 1976–1977. Romanies in the Middle East. *Roma* 1(4). 5–8; 2(1). 30–36; 2(2). 3–39.

Kießling, Roland & Maarten Mous. 2004. Urban youth languages in Africa. *Anthropological Linguistics* 46(3). 303–341.

King, Ruth. 2000. *The Lexical Basis of Grammatical Borrowing: A Prince Edward Island Case Study.* Amsterdam: John Benjamins.

Klein, Wolfgang & Clive Perdue. 1997. The Basic Variety. Or: Couldn't natural language be much simpler? *Second Language Research* 13(4). 301–47.

Kouwenberg, Silvia. 2006. Dutch-speaking Caribbean. In Ulrich Ammon, Norbert Dittmar, Klaus J. Mattheier & Peter Trudgill (eds.), *Sociolinguistics: An International Handbook of the Science of Language and Society 3*, 2105–2114. Berlin/New York: Walter de Gruyter.

Lewis, Glyn E. 1978. Types of bilingual communities. In James E. Alatis (ed.), *International Dimensions of Bilingual Education*, 19–34. Washington, DC: Georgetown University Press.

Loveday, Leo J. 1996. *Language Contact in Japan: A Socio-linguistic History.* Oxford: Clarendon Press.

Malcolm, Ian G. 2008. Australian creoles and Aboriginal English: phonetics and phonology. In Kate Burridge & Bernd Kortmann (eds.), *Varieties of English 3: The Pacific and Australia*, 124–141. Berlin: Mouton de Gruyter.

Matras, Yaron. 2003. Mixed Languages: Re-examining the structural prototype. In Yaron Matras & Peter Bakker (eds.), *The Mixed Language Debate: Theoretical and Empirical Advances*, 151–176. Berlin/New York: Mouton de Gruyter.

McConvell, Patrick. 1988. Mix-im-up: Aboriginal codeswitching old and new. In Monica Heller (ed.), *Codeswitching: Anthropological and Sociolinguistic Perspectives*, 97–124. Berlin: Mouton de Gruyter.

McWhorter, John H. 2000. *The Missing Spanish Creoles: Recovering the Birth of Plantation Contact Languages*. Berkeley: University of California Press.

Meakins, Felicity. 2008. Land, language and identity: The socio-political origins of Gurindji Kriol. In Miriam Meyerhoff & Naomi Nagy (eds.), *Social Lives in Language*, 69–94. Amsterdam: John Benjamins.

Meakins, Felicity. 2010. Which mix – code-switching or a mixed language? – Gurindji Kriol. *Journal of Pidgin and Creole Languages* 27(1). 105–140.

Migge, Bettina. 2003. *Creole Formation as Language Contact*. Amsterdam: John Benjamins

Mintz, Sidney W. 1971. The socio-historical background to pidginization and creolization. In Dell H. Hymes (ed.), *Pidginization and Creolization of Languages*, 481–96. Cambridge: Cambridge University Press.

Mous, Maarten. 1994. Ma'á or Mbugu. In Peter Bakker & Maarten Mous (eds.), *Mixed Languages: 15 Case Studies in Language Intertwining*, 175–200. Amsterdam: Uitgave IFOTT.

Mous, Maarten. 2003. The linguistic properties of lexical manipulation and its relevance for Ma'á. In Yaron Matras & Peter Bakker (eds.), *The Mixed Language Debate: Theoretical and Empirical Advances*, 209–235. Berlin/New York: Mouton de Gruyter.

Mühleisen, Susanne. 1993. *Attitudes Towards Language Varieties in Trinidad*. Berlin: Free University Berlin MA thesis.

Mühleisen, Susanne. 2005. Introduction: creole languages in creole literatures: status and standardization. *Journal of Pidgin and Creole Languages* 20(1) (Special Issue edited by S. Mühleisen). 1–14.

Müller, Friedrich Max. 1875. *Lectures on the Science of Language, Vol. 1*. New York: Scribner, Armstrong & Co.

Muysken, Pieter. 1981. Halfway between Quechua and Spanish: The case for relexification. In Arnold Highfield & Albert Valdman (eds.), *Historicity and Variation in Creole Studies*, 52–78. Ann Arbor: Karoma.

Nordhoff, Sebastian. 2009. *A Grammar of Upcountry Sri Lanka Malay*. Amsterdam: University of Amsterdam dissertation.

Odlin, Terence. 1997. *Hiberno-English: Pidgin, creole, or neither?* (CLCS Occasional Paper 49). Dublin: Trinity College, Centre for Language and Communication Studies.

O'Shannessy, Carmel. 2009. Language variation and change in a north Australian Indigenous community. In Dennis R. Preston & James N. Stanford (eds.),

Variationist Approaches to Indigenous Minority Languages, 419–39. Amsterdam: John Benjamins.

Platt, John, Heidi Weber & Mian Lian Ho. 1983. *Singapore and Malaysia. Varieties of English Around the World. Text Series, Vol. 4*. Amsterdam: John Benjamins.

Poplack, Shana. 1987. Contrasting patterns of code switching in two communities. In Erling Wande, Jan Anward, Bengt Nordberg, Lars Steensland & Mats Thelander (eds.), *Aspects of Multilingualism: Proceedings from the Fourth Nordic Symposium on Bilingualism 1984* (Acta Universitatis Upsaliensis), 51–77. Uppsala: University of Uppsala.

Rickford, John Russell & Jerome Handler. 1994. Textual evidence on the nature of early Barbadian speech, 1675–1835. *Journal of Pidgin and Creole Languages* 9. 221–255.

Roberts, Sarah Julianne. 1998. The role of diffusion in the genesis of Hawaiian Creole. *Language* 74(1). 1–39.

Roberts, Sarah Julianne. 2000. Nativization and the genesis of Hawaiian Creole. In John H. McWhorter (ed.), *Language Change and Language Contact in Pidgins and Creoles*, 257–300. Amsterdam: John Benjamins.

Ross, Malcolm. 1996. Contact-induced change and the comparative method: Cases from Papua New Guinea. In Mark Durie & Malcolm Ross (eds.), *The Comparative Method Reviewed: Regularity and Irregularity in Language Change*, 180–217. Oxford: Oxford University Press.

Schneider, Edgar W. 2010. Developmental patterns of English: similar or different? In Andy Kirkpatrick (ed.), *The Routledge Handbook of World Englishes*, 372–384. New York: Routledge.

Sessarego, Sandro. to appear. On the non-creole bases for Afro-Bolivian Spanish. *Journal of Pidgin and Creole Languages*.

Siegel, Jeff. 1998. Substrate reinforcement and dialectal differences in Melanesian Pidgin. *Journal of Sociolinguistics* 2. 347–373.

Siegel, Jeff. 1999. Transfer constraints and substrate influence in Melanesian Pidgin. *Journal of Pidgin and Creole Languages* 14. 1–44.

Siegel, Jeff. 2000. Substrate influence in Hawai'i Creole English. *Language in Society* 29. 197–236.

Siegel, Jeff. 2008. *The Emergence of Pidgin and Creole Languages*. Oxford: Oxford University Press.

Silva-Corvalán, Carmen. 1994. *Language Contact and Change: Spanish in Los Angeles*. Oxford: Clarendon.

Singler, John. 1986. Short note. *Journal of Pidgin and Creole Languages* 1. 141–145.

Singler, John. 1988. The homogeneity of the substrate as a factor in pidgin/creole genesis. *Language* 64. 27–51.

Singler, John. 1995. The demographics of creole genesis in the Caribbean: A comparison of Martinique and Haiti. In Jacques Arends (ed.), *The Early Stages of Creolization*, 203–232. Amsterdam: John Benjamins.

Singler, John. 2008. The sociohistorical context of creole genesis. In Silvia Kouwenberg & John Singler (eds.), *The Handbook of Pidgin and Creole Studies*, 332–358. Malden, MA: Wiley-Blackwell.

Slabbert, Sarah & Carol Myers-Scotton. 1996. The structure of Tsotsitaal and Iscamtho: code switching and in-group identity in South African townships. *Linguistics* 34. 317–342.

Smith, Ian R. 1979a. Convergence in South Asia: A creole example. *Lingua* 48. 193–222.

Smith, Ian R. 1979b. Substrata versus universals in the formation of Sri Lanka Portuguese. In Peter Mühlhäusler (ed.), *Papers in Pidgin and Creole Linguistics, no. 2* (Pacific Linguistic Series A No. 57), 183–200. Canberra: Australian National University.

Smith, Ian R. to appear. Diglossia in Sri Lanka Portuguese: the role of Anglophone missionaries. *Journal of Pidgin and Creole Languages*.

Smith, Ian R. & Scott Paauw. 2006. Sri Lanka Malay: Creole or convert? In Ana Deumert & Stephanie Durrleman (eds.), *Structure and Variation in Language Contact*, 159–181. Amsterdam: John Benjamins.

Strong, W. M. 1911. The Maisin language. *Journal of the Royal Anthropological Institute* 41. 381–396.

Tabouret-Keller, Andrée. 1978. Bilinguisme et diglossie dans le domaine des créoles français. *Etudes Créoles* 1. 135–153.

Thomason, Sarah Grey. 1997. A typology of contact languages. In Arthur Spears & Donald Winford (eds.), *The Structure and Status of Pidgins and Creoles*, 71–88. Amsterdam: John Benjamins.

Thomason, Sarah Grey. 2003. Social factors and linguistic processes in the emergence of stable mixed languages. In Yaron Matras & Peter Bakker (eds.), *The Mixed Language Debate: Theoretical and Empirical Advances*, 21–39. Berlin/New York: Mouton de Gruyter.

Thomason, Sarah Grey & Terrence Kaufman. 1988. *Language Contact, Creolization and Genetic Linguistics*. Berkeley: University of California Press.

Thurston, William R. 1987. *Processes of change in the languages of Northwest New Britain* (Pacific Linguistics Series B, 99). Canberra, Australia: Department of Linguistics, Australian National University.

Thurston, William R. 1994. Renovation and innovation in the languages of Northwestern New Britain. In Tom Dutton & Darrell T. Tryon (eds.), *Language Contact and Change in the Austronesian World*, 573–609. Berlin and New York: Mouton de Gruyter.

Treffers-Daller, Jeanine. 1999. Borrowing and shift-induced interference: Contrasting patterns in French-Germanic contact in Brussels and Strasbourg. *Bilingualism: Language and Cognition* 2(1). 1–22.

Walters, Joel. 2005. *Bilingualism: The Sociopragmatic/Psycholinguistic Interface*. Mahwah, NJ and London: Lawrence Erlbaum.

Watson-Gegeo, K. 1994. Language and education in Hawai'i: Socio-political and economic implications of Hawai'i Creole English. In Marcyliena Morgan (ed.), *Language and the Social Construction of Reality in Creole Situations*, 101–120. Los Angeles: Center for Afro-American Studies Publications.

Weinreich, Uriel. 1953. *Languages in Contact: Findings and problems* (New York: Linguistic Circle of New York). The Hague: Mouton.
Winford, Donald. 2005. Contact-induced changes: Classification and processes. *Diachronica* 22(2). 373–427.
Zenk, Henry Benjamin. 1984. *Chinook Jargon and Native Cultural Persistence in the Grand Ronde Indian Community, 1856–1907: A Special Case of Creolization*. Eugene, OR: University of Oregon dissertation.
Zentella, Ana Celia. 1997. *Growing Up Bilingual: Puerto Rican Children in New York*. Oxford: Blackwell.

Subject index

adjective, 36, 41, 93, 97, 100, 107, 108, 111, 119, 120, 167, 170, 177, 210, 305, 311, 375
adolescent, 11, 231, 233, 234, 247, 249, 268, 269, 270, 375
adolescents, 229, 244
adposition, 18, 34, 36, 37, 46, 113, 122, 123, 124, 125, 170, 173, 176, 177, 188, 190, 197, 202, 204, 205, 207, 208, 216, 252, 253, 286, 290, 313, 375, 377, 384
adstrate language, 41, 67, 68, 74, 83, 85, 88, 92, 93, 127, 128, 131, 159
allochtones. *See* immigrants
alloglottography, 275, 281, 314, 318, 320, 324
aspect, 30, 40, 42, 46, 68, 94, 101, 102, 103, 104, 105, 165, 174, 197, 202, 203, 206, 209, 384, 391, 397
attitudes, 234, 253, 259, 371, 407
bilingualism, 1, 4, 5, 6, 9, 12, 168, 171, 187, 191, 194, 200, 213, 217, 218, 235, 239, 260, 273, 280, 291, 299, 301, 302, 303, 305, 315, 318, 321, 323, 336, 342, 343, 346, 347, 348, 363, 364, 368, 373, 376, 378, 381, 382, 383, 386, 392, 397, 406, 408
borrowing, 2, 10, 11, 114, 159, 166, 167, 181, 186, 187, 188, 189, 190, 192, 193, 195, 205, 206, 240, 245, 333, 335, 342, 343, 344, 345, 347, 349, 350, 357, 366, 378, 381, 382, 395
classification, 8, 11, 160, 166, 180, 273, 276, 317, 333, 335, 338, 341, 343, 344, 356, 358, 366, 395
codeswitching, 1, 10, 159, 160, 172, 173, 174, 181, 186, 187, 190, 191, 192, 193, 195, 197, 198, 199, 201, 204, 205, 206, 211, 212, 213, 214, 217, 218, 235, 238, 239, 262, 264, 273, 369, 370, 371, 372, 375, 381

comparative method, 11, 333, 334, 335, 336, 347, 349, 354, 356, 358
comparison
    lexical, 345, 350, 354, 355, 356
    structural, 345, 354, 356
complexity, 6, 15, 17, 39, 45, 79, 80, 289, 317
computational phylogenetics, 12, 351
consonant, 84, 85, 90, 210, 289, 319, 336, 349
contact, 1, 2, 3, 4, 6, 8, 10, 11, 12, 15, 19, 21, 22, 23, 26, 27, 29, 44, 49, 50, 52, 65, 66, 67, 76, 77, 78, 85, 92, 93, 100, 123, 132, 165, 174, 177, 178, 180, 188, 189, 197, 201, 205, 209, 216, 217, 232, 264, 273, 275, 277, 285, 295, 298, 313, 321, 322, 323, 324, 333, 335, 336, 337, 338, 339, 341, 343, 344, 345, 348, 350, 351, 352, 353, 355, 356, 357, 358, 364, 365, 366, 368, 371, 375, 381, 382, 383, 386, 387, 388, 389, 391, 392, 399, 400, 401
convergence, 3, 7, 88, 178, 182, 192, 217, 218, 348, 350, 369, 384, 388
converted languages, 12, 178, 385
copula, 37, 100, 107, 190, 247, 297
copying, 275, 276, 277, 278, 279, 287, 288, 294, 311, 313, 323
creole, 1, 2, 4, 5, 6, 7, 8, 9, 10, 11, 12, 15, 22, 25, 27, 29, 30, 32, 35, 36, 37, 38, 41, 42, 47, 49, 53, 65, 66, 67, 68, 69, 70, 71, 72, 73, 74, 75, 76, 77, 78, 79, 80, 82, 83, 84, 85, 86, 87, 88, 89, 90, 91, 92, 93, 94, 95, 96, 97, 98, 99, 100, 101, 102, 103, 104, 105, 106, 107, 108, 110, 112, 113, 114, 116, 117, 119, 120, 122, 123, 124, 125, 126, 127, 128, 129, 131, 132, 134, 135, 136, 137, 160, 166, 171, 174, 180, 181, 184, 185, 186, 190, 193, 205, 217,

218, 258, 262, 263, 334, 337, 341,
342, 343, 344, 345, 346, 347, 348,
356, 364, 370, 377, 384, 385, 387,
389, 390, 393, 395, 396, 397, 398,
399, 400, 401, 402, 403, 404, 405,
406, 407, 408, 409
creole continuum, 76, 77, 107, 406
creole formation, 395, 399, 400, 402
creolisation, 10, 29, 53, 69, 74, 75,
80, 81, 82, 83, 85, 90, 100, 114,
134, 178, 385
crossing, 232, 239, 242, 245, 258
cuneiform, 275, 279, 281, 282, 314,
315, 316, 317, 318, 320, 321
decreolisation, 76, 107
depidginisation, 32
derivation, 6, 46, 79
derivational, 40, 79, 91, 92, 93, 96,
97, 100, 137, 172, 174, 188, 213,
286, 376
determiner, 95, 175, 177, 206, 208,
210
diffusion, 27, 49, 77, 338, 339, 340,
341, 344, 366, 367, 383, 389
education, 80, 171, 172, 235, 275,
286, 288, 303, 378, 385, 392, 393,
404, 407, 408, 409
ethnicity, 3, 5, 9, 10, 26, 51, 67, 83,
167, 181, 184, 185, 229, 231, 232,
233, 234, 236, 242, 243, 244, 245,
247, 249, 251, 252, 255, 261, 262,
283, 342, 343, 369, 372, 374, 377,
378, 393, 394
ethnolect, 3, 8, 166, 229, 230, 231,
232, 233, 234, 236, 237, 239, 242,
243, 244, 246, 247, 248, 259, 260,
262, 263, 265
expansion, 5, 26, 29, 65, 69, 123,
388, 392, 395, 396, 397, 398, 408,
409
family tree, 9, 12, 335, 337, 338,
340, 342, 346, 347, 348, 350, 351,
352, 356
gender, 37, 40, 46, 48, 84, 94, 95,
113, 208, 231, 241, 242, 245, 248,
252, 260, 290, 305

grammaticalisation, 5, 29, 45, 80, 94,
106, 118, 180, 215
higher-ranking (code, language),
274, 275, 276, 277, 278, 279, 280,
281, 282, 292, 294, 299, 300, 301,
306, 310, 314, 318, 324
honorifics, 296
hybridity, 80, 93, 275, 277, 280, 284,
285, 323, 324
identity, 4, 5, 10, 11, 29, 81, 82, 135,
170, 171, 176, 181, 182, 183, 184,
185, 186, 216, 232, 233, 234, 235,
242, 243, 244, 246, 250, 251, 252,
258, 259, 262, 279, 341, 342, 343,
345, 371, 372, 373, 374, 377, 379,
380, 388, 394, 398, 406, 407
immigrants, 2, 3, 8, 10, 20, 21, 22,
52, 77, 171, 177, 178, 184, 229,
232, 234, 244, 246, 247, 249, 250,
251, 254, 256, 364, 374, 378, 397
imposition, 276, 369, 383, 384, 386,
390, 396, 402, 404
indefinite, 30, 38, 46, 92, 113, 114,
119, 121, 240
indigenised varieties, 364, 387, 389,
391, 392, 394, 403, 404
inflection, 6, 7, 16, 17, 32, 40, 46,
94, 101, 172, 173, 189, 201, 284,
306, 307, 310, 320, 377
inflectional, 6, 7, 39, 40, 44, 79, 91,
92, 93, 94, 97, 167, 172, 176, 188,
189, 190, 192, 206, 276, 282, 286,
388, 402
interethnic communication, 4, 20,
46, 65, 66, 78, 283, 379, 392, 393,
395, 398
interlanguages, 32, 239, 242, 249,
258, 262, 263, 264, 388
intertwined languages, 1, 12, 20,
211, 276, 277, 323, 368, 369, 370,
371, 372, 373, 374, 376, 377, 379
jargon, 8, 10, 25, 27, 28, 30, 53, 69,
70, 71, 74, 321, 346
language autonomy, 199, 200, 201,
203, 208

language maintenance, 234, 365, 366, 367, 368
language shift, 8, 10, 170, 180, 181, 182, 183, 184, 187, 194, 196, 198, 298, 365, 366, 369, 382, 383, 391, 404
lexicon, 2, 5, 7, 10, 19, 24, 26, 27, 28, 33, 34, 35, 47, 51, 52, 65, 67, 87, 96, 131, 132, 161, 165, 167, 170, 171, 172, 175, 177, 180, 182, 185, 189, 193, 194, 197, 198, 201, 207, 211, 215, 260, 276, 277, 284, 286, 288, 310, 342, 354, 368, 369, 374, 375, 377, 378, 379, 380, 382, 385, 395, 401, 403, 406, 407
lexifier language, 6, 7, 10, 15, 17, 18, 23, 24, 29, 32, 33, 34, 36, 37, 38, 39, 40, 41, 42, 45, 46, 47, 52, 53, 65, 66, 67, 72, 74, 75, 76, 79, 80, 83, 85, 86, 88, 90, 92, 93, 94, 96, 100, 101, 110, 111, 114, 118, 119, 120, 121, 122, 124, 131, 132, 180, 250, 284, 347, 348, 401, 404, 405
literature, 82, 274, 275, 278, 283, 285, 286, 291, 292, 300, 301, 302, 307, 311, 324, 404, 407
lower-ranking (code, language), 274, 276, 277, 278, 279, 280, 281, 282, 291, 292, 294, 299, 300, 301, 302, 306, 310, 314, 322, 324
metatypy, 7, 178, 364, 387, 403
mixed languages, 1, 2, 4, 5, 6, 7, 8, 9, 10, 11, 12, 47, 159, 160, 161, 162, 163, 164, 165, 166, 167, 168, 169, 170, 171, 173, 174, 175, 176, 177, 178, 179, 180, 181, 182, 183, 184, 185, 186, 187, 188, 189, 190, 191, 192, 193, 194, 195, 196, 197, 198, 199, 200, 201, 202,203, 204, 205, 206, 207, 208, 209, 210, 211, 212, 213, 214, 215, 216, 217, 232, 258, 261, 262, 263, 264, 277, 280, 299, 304, 309, 310, 334, 337, 341, 342, 343, 344, 345, 347, 364, 368,

369, 371, 373, 374, 375, 377, 378, 379, 381, 384, 386, 403, 409
monogenesis, 74, 348
morphology, 5, 6, 7, 11, 17, 18, 20, 32, 39, 40, 44, 45, 46, 79, 83, 91, 92, 94, 95, 96, 97, 108, 165, 172, 173, 174, 176, 177, 178, 183, 187, 188, 189, 190, 192, 193, 195, 202, 206, 209, 213, 216, 245, 276, 284, 286, 290, 297, 300, 319, 321, 322, 346, 347, 376, 377, 382, 388, 402
multi-ethnolect, 2, 5, 9, 11, 229, 230, 231, 232, 233, 234, 235, 236, 237, 238, 239, 240, 241, 242, 243, 244, 245, 246, 247, 248, 249, 250, 252, 256, 258, 259, 260, 262, 263, 264, 265, 266
negation, 7, 34, 40, 41, 42, 45, 105, 110, 172, 190, 375, 376, 377
network, 12, 80, 283, 352, 353, 356, 394
New Testament, 73, 279
noun, 2, 7, 16, 17, 18, 34, 36, 39, 40, 41, 46, 68, 84, 92, 94, 95, 96, 97, 112, 113, 117, 119, 121, 122, 128, 137, 163, 165, 167, 168, 170, 172, 173, 174, 175, 176, 177, 183, 185, 189, 198, 205, 206, 209, 210, 211, 213, 214, 216, 277, 284, 287, 289, 290, 305, 311, 312, 313, 315, 316, 317, 342, 347, 349, 369, 370, 375, 376
numeral, 30, 39, 95, 97, 114, 120, 121, 122, 170, 173, 188, 190, 240, 311, 317
orthography, 282, 296, 396, 406, 407, 408, 409
paralexification, 167, 170, 187, 193
phoneme, 35, 46, 85, 86, 87, 135, 208, 210, 321, 322
phonetics, 23, 83, 235, 245, 296, 297, 314, 315, 316, 319, 320, 321, 345, 352, 354, 355, 356
phonological stratification, 210, 211
phonology, 11, 35, 36, 46, 48, 83, 85, 86, 87, 89, 97, 135, 160, 187,

193, 205, 209, 210, 211, 216, 245, 247, 264, 286, 288, 289, 294, 298, 307, 316, 319, 337, 350, 355, 356, 382, 388, 406
pidgin, 1, 2, 4, 5, 6, 7, 8, 9, 10, 11, 12, 15, 16, 17, 18, 19, 20, 21, 22, 23, 24, 25, 26, 27, 28, 29, 30, 31, 32, 33, 34, 35, 36, 37, 38, 39, 40, 41, 42, 43, 44, 45, 46, 47, 48, 49, 50, 51, 52, 53, 69, 70, 72, 74, 75, 76, 80, 92, 97, 166, 174, 178, 180, 181, 185, 190, 258, 262, 263, 264, 334, 337, 341, 342, 343, 344, 345, 346, 347, 348, 364, 371, 387, 388, 389, 395, 396, 397, 398, 402
pidgincreole, 10, 29, 30, 37, 53, 69, 70
pidginisation, 8, 19, 20, 22, 35, 41, 45, 46, 47, 50, 52, 53, 76, 100, 135, 345, 388
plantation, 5, 51, 66, 67, 77, 79, 387, 389, 390, 395, 397, 398, 399, 400, 401
plural, 16, 38, 45, 68, 92, 94, 95, 97, 100, 109, 112, 120, 173, 189, 206, 277, 289, 290, 300
poems, 279, 280, 286, 299, 300, 301, 302, 303, 304
pragmatics, 43, 46, 53, 83, 91, 128, 135, 191, 216, 257, 305
preposition. *See* adposition
pronoun, 16, 36, 37, 38, 39, 40, 41, 45, 46, 94, 95, 100, 104, 109, 112, 114, 115, 116, 117, 118, 119, 125, 128, 165, 170, 173, 175, 188, 190, 193, 198, 201, 203, 206, 209, 241, 252, 253, 277, 286, 290, 312, 375, 384
prosody, 35, 46, 79, 90, 91, 235, 241, 247, 249, 257
quantifier, 120, 121, 122, 286
rap (hip-hop), 247, 252, 260
reduction, 18, 23, 24, 25, 30, 31, 33, 39, 44, 45, 47, 68, 92, 317, 388, 401

reduplication, 30, 32, 46, 95, 97, 98, 100, 135, 377
relexification, 10, 67, 75, 131, 166, 169, 183, 187, 193, 277, 337, 348
repertoire, 4, 9, 174, 186, 187, 202, 212, 244, 278
Rosetta Stone, 279
semantics, 7, 35, 53, 75, 83, 97, 100, 105, 118, 123, 133, 135, 169, 189, 209, 286, 403
serial verb, 7, 42, 105, 106, 119, 120, 122, 130
signs, 10, 253
simplification, 3, 6, 7, 20, 40, 75, 92, 173, 248, 368, 402, 404
slaves, 50, 51, 65, 66, 67, 69, 71, 72, 78, 133, 390, 398, 399, 400, 401, 402
social contexts, 9, 159, 369, 373, 375, 377, 378, 379, 386, 391, 397
social ecology, 367, 391, 399
social variables, 365, 367
substrate language, 38, 67, 68, 75, 79, 85, 86, 88, 89, 92, 93, 96, 97, 112, 127, 132, 134, 135, 184, 337, 400, 402, 403
syllable, 35, 36, 83, 84, 85, 89, 90, 91, 314, 315, 322
syntax, 5, 7, 11, 28, 46, 48, 74, 83, 94, 100, 135, 168, 169, 170, 171, 188, 189, 190, 191, 192, 201, 202, 204, 205, 206, 208, 209, 210, 216, 249, 282, 289, 291, 295, 296, 297, 298, 300, 306, 307, 310, 312, 313, 319, 320, 342, 346, 354, 355, 356, 372, 375, 376, 377, 382, 402, 403
tense, 30, 40, 42, 46, 48, 80, 94, 100, 101, 102, 103, 104, 105, 172, 174, 189, 197, 202, 203, 206, 310, 370, 384
translation, 280, 293, 295, 297, 304, 307, 308, 309, 311, 312, 313, 314, 350, 407
transmission, 4, 49, 276, 339, 340, 348, 390

typology, 9, 10, 11, 53, 80, 173, 181, 198, 210, 230, 354, 355, 386, 403
urban, 2, 10, 11, 167, 169, 185, 229, 231, 233, 244, 249, 251, 252, 255, 258, 260, 285, 291, 370, 373, 379, 381, 396, 409
urban mixed codes, 370, 380, 381
variation, 10, 24, 25, 38, 44, 46, 76, 77, 87, 89, 92, 137, 160, 170, 179, 191, 194, 196, 200, 201, 202, 206, 207, 208, 209, 215, 216, 218, 232, 262, 275, 291, 293, 306, 324, 334, 338, 339, 352, 380, 406
verb, 2, 7, 16, 17, 32, 34, 36, 39, 40, 41, 42, 45, 46, 48, 67, 90, 92, 94, 97, 100, 101, 104, 105, 106, 107, 108, 110, 119, 120, 124, 130, 163, 165, 167, 168, 169, 170, 172, 173, 174, 175, 176, 189, 193, 198, 201, 202, 204, 205, 206, 209, 211, 212, 214, 216, 246, 284, 286, 289, 290, 296, 305, 307, 315, 316, 319, 342, 347, 375, 376, 377, 409
vowel, 46, 84, 85, 86, 88, 89, 90, 91, 171, 210, 248, 287, 289, 349
word order, 17, 23, 24, 41, 46, 48, 127, 128, 168, 175, 177, 188, 209, 216, 248, 282, 293, 294, 296, 299, 306, 307, 308, 310, 312, 313, 321, 377, 384, 402
youth language, 11, 167, 249, 255, 257, 258

Languages and geography index

Aboriginal English, *see also*
 Australian Pidgin English, 163,
 176, 183, 189, 201, 202
Afghan, 234, 236
Afghanistan, 374
Africa, 11, 15, 20, 65, 66, 81, 133,
 255, 370, 379, 392, 398, 399, 407
African, 26, 68, 74, 78, 81, 83, 87,
 88, 89, 90, 96, 127, 133, 135, 256,
 265, 347, 390, 400, 401
African American Vernacular
 English, 81, 231, 239, 247, 408
Afrikaans, 74, 255, 379, 381
Afro-American, 82, 88
Afro-Bolivian Spanish, 88
Afro-Brazilian, 88
Afro-Caribbean, 245
Afro-Hispanic, 88
Afro-Portuguese Pidgin, 74
Akan, 99, 124, 130, 134
Akkadian, 2, 277, 281, 282, 315,
 316, 317, 321
Akuapem Twi, see also Twi, 127
Alalakh, 317
Alaska, 24, 49
Aleppo, 315
Aleut, 9, 163, 165, 171, 172, 183,
 186, 189, 200, 206, 369, 376, 377,
 378
Algonquian, 214
Alsatian, 20, 371
Aluku, 22
Amarna, 2
Amarna Akkadian, 276, 282
Amdo Tibetan, 164
America, 87, 390
American, 21, 24, 27, 49, 70, 74,
 231, 377, 387, 388, 390
Americas, 26, 67, 68, 392, 398
Amerindian, 24, 35, 183, 186
Amsterdam, 217, 251, 258
Anatolia, 285
Anatolian, 275, 303

Andean, 356
Andes, 356
Anêm, 403
Anglo-Norman, 304, 306
Angloromani, 22, 159, 160, 161,
 164, 165, 166, 167, 170, 171, 179,
 180, 183, 184, 185, 186, 187, 189,
 193, 194, 195, 202, 205, 206, 215,
 216, 217, 218, 369, 373
Angola, 68
Angolar Creole Portuguese, 84, 86,
 87, 88, 91, 92, 93, 98, 99, 101,
 104, 110, 121, 124, 131
Annobón Creole Portuguese, 84, 89,
 91, 136
Antwerp, 246
Arabic, 16, 26, 32, 44, 233, 234,
 238, 240, 242, 274, 276, 277, 281,
 282, 283, 284, 285, 286, 287, 288,
 289, 290, 291, 300, 302, 336, 389,
 406
Arafundi-Enga Pidgin, 45
Aragon, 303
Aramaic, 233, 279, 281, 314, 316,
 318, 319, 320
Argentina, 82
Armenia, 319
Armenian, 300, 336
Arnhem Land, 350
Aruba, 67
Asia, 65, 66, 299, 382, 392, 407
Asia Minor, 382, 383, 384, 386
Asian, 27, 95
Assamese, 39, 40, 127
Assyrian, 316, 317
Atlantic, 7, 49, 50, 66, 69, 75, 83,
 86, 88, 89, 96, 105, 106, 107, 112,
 117, 119, 122, 127, 134, 135, 356,
 398
Attu, 376
Australia, 20, 26, 27, 159, 161, 162,
 163, 168, 174, 176, 218, 350, 370,
 389, 390, 395, 396, 405

Australian, 7, 160, 184
Australian Pidgin English, 37, 48, 395
Austria, 394
Austronesia, 3
Austronesian, 7, 12, 128, 177, 184, 354, 357, 403
Avestan, 319
Azeri, 285, 302, 314
Baba Malay, 393
Babylonian, 279, 316, 317
Bahamian Creole English, 133, 134
Bahasa Gaul, 240, 257, 260
Bahasa Prokem, 240, 257
Bajan, 399, 401
Baktrian, 283
Baltic, 313
Balu, 178
Bamboo English, 27, 49
Banda, 178
Bantu, 9, 15, 35, 68, 84, 121, 134, 162, 166, 167, 183, 189, 194, 369, 374, 379
Barbados, 399, 400
Barlovento, *see also* Kabuverdianu, 92
Barranquenho, 160, 161
Basque, 17, 18, 41, 166
Batavia, 72, 377
Bazaar Malay, *see also* Vehicular Malay, Malay, 177, 377
Beijing, 298, 299
Belize, 122
Belize Creole English, 122, 133, 134, 409
Bengali, 335
Benuic, 134
Berber, 234, 263
Berbice Creole Dutch, 67, 86, 91, 129
Bering Strait, 163, 171
Bilingual Navajo, 160, 164, 167, 168, 169, 171, 179, 183, 185, 186, 189, 202, 204, 205, 215, 216
Bilkiire, 41
Bislama, 30, 97, 395, 396, 405

Bobangi, 39, 40
Bocas del Toro Creole English, 77
Bolivia, 88, 161
Bonaire, 67
Bozal Spanish, 32
Brazil, 20, 26, 65, 67, 68, 74, 81, 82, 398
Brazilian Portuguese, 134
Britain, 11, 165, 305
British, 89, 178, 245, 280, 304, 385, 391, 392, 393, 396
British English, 245
Broken, 397
Broken Oghibbeway, 41
Brussels, 20
Buddhist Chinese, 293
Buddhist Hybrid English, 293
Buddhist Hybrid Sanskrit, 292, 293, 309
Burma, 309
Burmese, 280, 309, 310, 311
California, 247
Callahuaya. *See* Kayawaya
Caló, 373
Cameroon, 395
Cameroonian Fulbe, 31
Cameroonian Pidgin English, 348
Cameroonian Pidgin French, 32
Canada, 163, 172, 342
Canala, 349
Canton, 50
Cantonese, 17, 48, 50
Cape Verdean Creole Portuguese. *See* Kabuverdianu
Cappadocia, 383
Caracas, 67
Caribbean, 67, 77, 78, 82, 89, 133, 134, 392, 393, 398, 406, 407, 408
Cartagena, 68, 71
Casamance, 71
Casamance Creole Portuguese, 68
Catalan, 166, 303
Catalonia, 303
Central Africa, 30
Central Asia, 283, 285, 290, 291, 292, 320

Central Asian, 291
Ceylon, *see also* Sri Lanka, 73, 309, 385
Chabacano, 86, 93, 98, 122, 131
Chabacano Creole Spanish, 114
Chabacano de Ternate, 119
Chaghatay, 278, 281, 283, 290, 291, 292
Chamorro, 364, 368
Chicano, 232, 247
Chicano English, 232
Chickasaw, 24, 50
China, 16, 28, 164, 283, 294, 295, 296, 297, 298, 299, 321, 322
Chindo, 161, 375, 377
Chinese, 23, 28, 38, 161, 278, 279, 280, 281, 293, 294, 295, 296, 297, 298, 299, 304, 306, 307, 308, 310, 314, 315, 320, 321, 322, 336, 369, 377, 393, 397
Chinese Pidgin English, 18, 23, 24, 34, 35, 38, 42, 43, 48, 50, 51, 347, 387
Chinese Pidgin Russian, 39
Chinook Jargon, also Chinuk Wawa, 24, 30, 33, 34, 35, 39, 44, 45, 49, 52, 387, 388
Chocó, 82
Choctaw, 16, 24, 50
Citétaal, 245, 246
Colloquial Singapore English. See Singapore English
Colombia, 67, 68, 71, 82
Congo, 68
Constantinople, 383
Copper Island Aleut, *see also* Mednyj Aleut, 9, 369
Cotabato, 93
Cree, 7, 9, 163, 172, 173, 186, 189, 198, 200, 205, 207, 210, 211, 214, 218, 277, 342, 347, 369, 375, 376
Crimea, 292
Crimean Tatar, 312
Curaçao, 67, 409
Cushitic, 9, 162, 166, 167, 183, 189, 194, 369, 374

Czech, 3
Czech Republic, 3
Danish, 72, 248, 249
Delaware Pidgin, 50, 387
Democratic Republic of the Congo. *See* Congo
Dominica, 406
Dominican Creole French, 101, 102, 103, 107, 110
Dravidian, 177, 385
Dutch, 3, 42, 66, 67, 69, 71, 72, 75, 86, 88, 93, 109, 131, 215, 234, 235, 236, 240, 241, 245, 246, 248, 251, 252, 253, 255, 257, 260, 261, 263, 369, 377, 385, 408, 409
Dutch Antilles, 337, 406, 408
Early Anatolian Turkish, 285
East Africa, 30
East Asia, 293
East Asian, 49
Eastern Ijo, *see also* Ijo, 67, 68, 91, 127
Eblaite, 315
Ebonics, 408
Ecuador, 162, 169, 373
Edo, 86, 87
Edoid, 84
Egypt, 279, 282
Egyptian, 279, 282
Elamite, 279, 281, 317, 318
Eleman Trade Language, 35
Elu, 311
Emai, 87
England, 161, 300, 304, 390, 391, 399
English, 2, 3, 9, 10, 12, 16, 17, 18, 20, 21, 27, 29, 30, 35, 37, 38, 42, 45, 48, 49, 52, 53, 66, 67, 69, 71, 75, 78, 85, 86, 88, 89, 92, 93, 94, 100, 101, 102, 106, 114, 117, 131, 132, 161, 163, 165, 166, 167, 168, 174, 176, 177, 183, 184, 185, 186, 189, 195, 200, 204, 208, 212, 214, 218, 231, 244, 245, 248, 251, 254, 255, 256, 257, 262, 274, 277, 288, 293, 304, 305, 306, 323, 335, 337,

Languages and geography index 425

342, 345, 348, 352, 354, 356, 364, 369, 370, 371, 376, 379, 380, 381, 389, 390, 391, 392, 393, 394, 396, 399, 401, 405, 406, 408
Engsh, 256, 380
Equatorial Guinea, 65
Eskimo, 17, 24, 48, 51
Eskimo Pidgin. *See* Eskimo Trade Jargon
Eskimo Trade Jargon, 38, 39, 40, 43, 48, 387
Estonia, 32
Ethiopia, 50
Ethiopian Pidgin Italian, 37
Etsako, 87
Eurasia, 291
Europe, 82, 166, 232, 233, 274, 314, 342, 389, 406
Eve. *See* Ewe
Ewe, 74, 89, 134, 347
Éwondo Populaire, 31
Fanakalo, 23, 24, 34, 35, 36, 39, 40, 51
Fante, 89, 127
Ferghana, 291
Fiji, 51, 52, 405
Fijian, 33, 41, 51, 52
Fijian Pidgin, 33, 39
Finland, 163, 170
Finnish, 163, 170, 171, 185, 189, 336
Flathead Salish, 27
Flemish, 246
Fon, 87
Français-Tirailleur, 34, 44, 51
France, 26, 254, 258, 382
French, 2, 7, 9, 16, 20, 26, 27, 28, 36, 38, 52, 66, 67, 69, 71, 72, 73, 75, 76, 78, 80, 82, 84, 86, 88, 89, 94, 100, 110, 114, 121, 131, 163, 166, 173, 186, 189, 198, 200, 205, 207, 210, 211, 214, 218, 254, 255, 256, 265, 277, 299, 301, 304, 305, 334, 337, 340, 342, 347, 348, 356, 369, 371, 375, 376, 384, 401, 406, 409

French Antilles, 82
French Canadian, 172, 183
Gã, 100
Gaelic, 381, 391
Gastarbeiterdeutsch, 22
Gaul, 257, 260
Gbe, 134, 399, 400, 402
Georgian, 314
German, 20, 22, 162, 166, 218, 236, 245, 250, 273, 274, 277, 299, 301, 335, 394, 406
Germanic, 44, 110, 305, 334, 335, 336, 354, 356
Germany, 3, 162, 217, 250
Ghana, 395
Gorwaa, 374
Göteborg, 248
Gothic, 335
Grand Couli, 349
Grand Ronde, 45, 388
Great Britain, 132, 217, 258, 353
Greek, 20, 251, 279, 280, 300, 319, 334, 335, 382, 384, 386, 389
Greenlandic, 41
Greenlandic Pidgin Eskimo, 41
Guadeloupe, 82
Guernsey, 304
Guinea Bissau, 70, 71, 93
Guinea Bissau Creole Portuguese, 66, 68, 73, 80, 85, 93, 98, 135
Guinea Bissau Kriyôl. *See* Guinea Bissau Creole Portuguese
Gujarati, 335
Gulf of Guinea, 84, 104
Gulf of Guinea Creoles, 84, 87, 91, 105, 121
Gulf Pidgin Arabic, 387
Gullah, 347
Gurindji, 9, 161, 168, 174, 175, 176, 183, 185, 186, 189, 194, 197, 198, 200, 201, 202, 206, 207, 208, 209, 212, 213, 214, 216, 218, 370, 371, 372
Gurindji Kriol, 1, 7, 9, 159, 160, 161, 164, 169, 171, 173, 174, 175, 176, 179, 183, 185, 186, 189, 192,

194, 197, 198, 199, 200, 201, 202, 205, 206, 207, 208, 209, 211, 212, 214, 216, 217, 218, 369, 370, 371, 372, 373, 375, 376
Gurundji. *See* Gurindji
Gurundji Kriol. *See* Gurindji Kriol
Guyanais, 73
Guyanas, 67
Haiti, 73, 82, 402, 409
Haitian. *See* Haitian Creole French
Haitian Creole French, 67, 73, 74, 84, 86, 88, 94, 100, 104, 105, 109, 111, 112, 114, 117, 121, 123, 124, 134, 136, 337, 347, 406, 409
Halbdeutsch, 32
Hamer, 50
Hattic, 317
Hauna Trade Language, 47
Hawaii, 27, 378, 387, 394, 397, 398, 402, 408
Hawaii Creole English, 395
Hawaiian, 28, 40, 41, 42, 48
Hawaiian Creole English, 29, 92, 378, 394, 397, 398
Hawaiian Pidgin English, 28, 29, 48, 51, 387, 395, 397
Hebrew, 3, 162, 277, 280, 282, 290, 303, 304, 311, 312, 313
Helsinki, 160, 163, 164, 170
Herat, 291
Herschel Island Eskimo Pidgin, 34, 37
Hezhou, 20
Hidatsa, 27
Hindi, 52, 300, 335, 392
Hindustani, 36, 51
Hiri Motu, 34, 39, 51
Hispanic, 87, 185
Hittite, 317
Hokkien, 393
Hong Kong, 257, 408
Hurrian, 317
Hybrid Chinese, 297
Iberoromance, 79, 90
Icelandic, 17, 18, 41
Icelandic Pidgin Basque, 36, 41

Icelandic Pidgin French, 36
Igbo, 123
Ijo, 68
Ilongo, 93
India, 39, 291, 292, 300, 309, 374, 386, 390, 392, 393, 394
Indian, 364, 373, 393
Indian Butler English, 387
Indian Ocean, 66, 84
Indic, 278, 292, 293, 309, 311
Indo-Aryan, 177
Indo-European, 69, 283, 284, 309, 317, 334, 336, 353, 356
Indo-Iranian, 335
Indonesia, 161, 257, 261, 369, 375, 377, 378
Indo-Portuguese, 74, 92, 98, 101
Indoubil, 255
Iñupiaq Eskimo, 24, 40
Iran, 314, 317, 319
Iranian, 282, 283, 284, 285, 318, 319, 320, 336
Ireland, 163, 374, 390, 391, 392, 394
Irish, 163, 353, 391
Irish English, 391
Isicamtho, 255, 258, 370, 379, 380, 381
Istanbul, 285
Italian, 3, 16, 20, 29, 245, 274, 300, 334
Italy, 303
Ivory Coast Popular French, 31
Jakarta, 257
Jamaica, 67, 68, 74, 406, 407, 408
Jamaican, 77, 79, 81, 133, 408
Jamaican Creole English, 67, 73, 76, 99, 122, 133, 348, 407, 409
Japan, 11, 27, 49, 294, 296, 321, 322
Japanese, 20, 134, 278, 279, 280, 281, 294, 295, 296, 306, 307, 308, 310, 314, 315, 320, 321, 322, 345, 397
Japanese Pidgin English, 387
Java, 178, 261
Javanese, 161, 377
Javindo, 375, 377

Jenisch, 162
Jersey, 304
Johannesburg, 255, 258, 379
Juba Arabic, 32, 39, 51
Judeo-German, 3, 162
Kabuverdianu, 66, 77, 80, 88, 92, 93, 96, 98, 99, 101, 116, 119, 120, 125, 136
Kamchatka, 377
Kanaanite, 282
Kanaksprak, 250
Kannada, 386
Karaim, 280, 311, 312, 313
Karakhanid, 291
Karluk, 291
Kashgar, 291
Kayawaya, also Callahuaya, 161, 373
Kenya, 167, 256, 370, 380
Khorasan, 302
Khorezmian, 291
Khotanese, 283
Khwarezm, 291
Khwarezmian, 283
KiKongo, 68, 87, 89, 92, 134
Kimbundu, 68, 87, 121
Kinshasa, 255
Kinubi, 30
Kipchak, 291, 311
Kirinda, 218
KiSetla Swahili Pidgin, 34, 45, 46
Kishikongo, 84
Kituba, 31, 39
Korea, 27, 49, 306
Korean, 295, 397
Koriki Hiri Trade Language, 35
Korlai Creole Portuguese, 111
Krio, 30, 79, 106, 348
Kriol, 7, 117, 161, 162, 163, 174, 175, 176, 183, 184, 185, 186, 189, 194, 197, 198, 201, 202, 203, 206, 207, 208, 209, 212, 213, 214, 216, 218, 370, 371, 395, 396, 398, 409
Kumenti, 22
Kupwar, 386
Kurdish, 233

Kwa, 100, 134
Kyakhta Pidgin Russian, 37, 40
Latin, 26, 28, 72, 273, 274, 275, 277, 281, 294, 299, 300, 301, 304, 305, 314, 342, 345, 349, 389
Latin America, 32
Lekoudesch, 162
Lesser Antillean, 73
Light Warlpiri, 1, 160, 162, 164, 165, 169, 171, 173, 174, 175, 176, 179, 181, 183, 186, 189, 192, 194, 201, 202, 203, 204, 206, 216, 217, 375, 409
Limón Creole English, 133
Lingala, 20, 31, 39, 40, 255
Lingala ya Bayankee, 255
Lingoa Geral, 20, 26, 31
Lingua Franca, 25, 26, 38, 39, 49, 50, 52, 71, 74
Lingua Geral. *See* Lingoa Geral
Lisbon, 26
Lithuanian, 312, 313
London, 244, 245, 304
London Jamaican Creole, 244
Los Angeles, 384
Louisianais, 73, 100
Low German, 166
Luvian, 317
Ma'á, 9, 160, 162, 164, 166, 167, 170, 171, 179, 183, 184, 189, 193, 194, 201, 206, 215, 216, 342, 343, 369, 373, 374
Maasai, 167, 194, 374
Macaista Creole Portuguese, 98, 99
Macao Creole Portuguese, 83
Mahallemi, 233
Maine, 20
Maisin, 4, 403
Malay, *see also* Baba Malay, Riau Indonesian, 7, 45, 83, 161, 164, 177, 178, 184, 197, 204, 205, 216, 218, 261, 377, 379, 385, 393
Malayo-Portuguese, 73, 98
Malaysia, 20, 405
Malmö, 248
Maltese, 273, 368

Manambu-Kwoma Pidgin, 47
Manchu, 278, 280, 297, 298, 304
Manchurian Russian Pidgin, 47
Mande, 134
Manding, 93
Mandinka, 68, 85, 93
Manila Bay, 74
Manitoba, 375
Mannheim, 250
Marathi, 386
Marie-Galante, 82
Marra, 184
Martinique, 71, 402
Mauritian, 73, 84, 100
Mbugu, see also Ma'á, 162, 166, 167, 183, 194, 201, 374
Media Lengua, 7, 9, 160, 162, 164, 169, 170, 171, 177, 179, 180, 183, 185, 186, 189, 193, 199, 205, 210, 211, 215, 262, 369, 373, 378
Mediterranean, 3, 16, 25, 49, 50, 71, 74, 315
Mednyj Aleut, see also Copper Island Aleut, 160, 163, 164, 171, 172, 173, 179, 183, 184, 186, 189, 192, 200, 202, 205, 206, 216, 369, 375, 376, 377, 378
Melanesia, 12, 27, 357, 389, 395
Melanesian, 29, 388, 395, 404
Melanesian Pidgin English, 37, 49, 389
Mesopotamia, 2, 281, 282, 314, 315, 316
Métis, 163, 172, 184, 186, 342, 375
Michif, 7, 9, 159, 160, 163, 164, 171, 172, 173, 174, 179, 183, 184, 186, 189, 192, 194, 195, 198, 200, 202, 205, 206, 207, 210, 211, 213, 216, 218, 277, 342, 343, 347, 369, 375, 376
Middle East, 11, 314, 374, 406
Middle Iranian, 281, 283, 319
Midlands, 132
Min, 20
Miskito, 132
Mississippi, 16
Mobilian Pidgin, 16, 24, 39, 41, 50, 52, 387
Moluccas, 74
Mon, 309
Mongolian, 164, 278, 291, 297, 298
Mongolised Chinese, 297
Montagnais-French, 214
Montana, 49
Montreal, 340
Moroccan, 3, 234, 235, 236, 246, 251, 252, 260
Moroccan Arabic, 234
Moroccan Flavoured Dutch, 234
Murks, 251, 259
Muskogee, 16
Naga Pidgin, 39
Nagamese, 31, 40, 127, 128
Nairobi, 256, 380
Navajo, 163, 167, 168, 185, 186, 189, 204, 205
Ndyuka Creole English, 67, 79, 86, 87, 106, 120
Ndyuka-Trio Pidgin, 23, 47, 388
Near East, 2, 314, 315, 317
Negerhollands, 72, 107, 108, 111, 113
Neo-Melanesian, see also Melanesian Pidgin, 347
Netherlands, 3, 217, 234, 235, 236, 251, 252, 258, 259, 261, 263, 266, 409
New Britain, 403
New Caledonia, 349
New Guinea, 2, 28, 30, 51
New South Wales, 389, 396
New Tiwi, 163
New York, 3, 231, 247, 371
New Zealand, 390
Ngarluma Pidgin, 47
Ngbandi, 37
Nheengatu, 20
Nicaragua, 53
Nicaraguan, 132
Nicaraguan Creole English, 76, 102, 104, 107, 112, 115, 117, 124, 125, 132, 133, 134

Nicaraguan Sign Language, 53
Nigeria, 395
Nigerian Pidgin English, 70, 81
Nilotic, 374
Nissaya Burmese, 309, 310
North Africa, 3
North America, 26, 35, 52
Northern Ireland, 391
Northern Territory, 396
Northern Territory Pidgin English, 396
Northwest Mandarin, 164
Norway, 249, 387
Norwegian, 48, 166, 241, 248, 249, 387
Nuzi, 317
Oberwart, 394
Oceanic, 4, 403
Oghuz, 285, 291, 292
Oghuz Turkic, 285
Old Helsinki Slang, 160, 163, 164, 170, 171, 179, 183, 185, 189, 215
Oregon, 30, 388
Ottawa-Hull, 372
Ottoman, 276, 278, 281, 283, 284, 285, 286, 287, 288, 289, 290, 311, 312
Ottoman Empire, 11
Pacific, 7, 28, 30, 37, 49, 50, 66, 69, 89, 92, 127, 186, 389, 390, 395, 397, 403, 405
Pacific Pidgin English, 387, 388
Pahlavi, 320
Palenque Creole Spanish, *see also* Palenquero, 92
Palenque de San Basilio, 67
Palenquero, 67, 88
Palestine, 282
Pali, 280, 309, 310, 311
Palmares, 67
Pama-Nyungan, 174, 370
Panama, 77
Panjabi, 245
Papa, 22
Papia Kristang Creole Portuguese, 98, 99

Papiamento. *See* Papiamentu
Papiamentu, 67, 73, 74, 76, 85, 90, 93, 98, 101, 109, 110, 112, 116, 121, 129, 131, 337, 406, 408, 409
Papua, 3, 357
Papua New Guinea, 70, 94, 387, 396, 397, 403, 404
Papua Pidgin English, 43
Papuan, 4, 12, 357, 403, 404
Para-Romani, 183
Pare, 167, 194, 374
Paris, 254
Parthia, 319
Parthian, 283, 316, 319, 320
Pennsylvania Dutch, 382
Peranakan Chinese, 377
Persia, 283
Persian, 26, 45, 275, 276, 278, 279, 281, 282, 283, 284, 285, 286, 287, 288, 289, 290, 291, 300, 302, 303, 310, 314, 317, 318, 319, 320, 336
Persian Gulf, 315
Petjo, 375, 377
Philippine, 75, 85, 86, 93
Philippine Creole Spanish, 41
Philippines, 75, 77
Philippino-Spanish Creoles, 123
Phoenician, 282
Pidgin Basque, 17
Pidgin English, 396, 397
Pidgin Fijian, 41
Pidgin Hamer, 50
Pidgin Hawaiian, 24, 39, 41, 43, 387
Pidgin Hindustani, 36
Pidgin Madam, 387
Pidgin Ngarluma, 41
Pidgin Swahili, 36
Plains Indian Sign Language, 53
Polish, 313
Polynesia, 250
Portugal, 65, 161
Portuguese, 10, 26, 28, 66, 67, 69, 70, 71, 72, 74, 81, 83, 84, 85, 87, 88, 89, 92, 95, 97, 98, 99, 100, 101, 104, 110, 116, 118, 122, 131,

160, 161, 164, 166, 262, 334, 337, 384, 393, 397, 398
Prākrit, 278, 292, 293, 309
Pretoria, 379
Prince Edward Island, 384
Principe, 84, 86, 87, 91, 95, 98, 99, 105, 111, 112, 113, 118, 126, 127, 129, 131
Principense Creole Portuguese, 84, 86, 87, 91, 95, 96, 98, 99, 105, 111, 112, 113, 118, 126, 127, 129, 131
Proto-Germanic, 335
Proto-Pidgin English, 348
Proto-Romance, 349
Provençal, 303
Provence, 303
Providence Creole English, 112, 116, 117, 122, 132, 133, 134
Puerto Rican, 231, 371
Punjabi. *See* Panjabi
Puquina, 161
Pyu, 309
Quebecois French, 94
Quechua, 7, 9, 44, 161, 162, 169, 177, 183, 185, 186, 189, 193, 211, 369, 373
Queensland, 389, 390, 395, 396, 397
Queensland Pidgin English, 389, 395
Quito, 373
Réunion, 400
Réunionnais, 100, 401
Riau Indonesian, 79
Rinkeby-Svenska, 247, 248
Rodrigues Creole French, 84
Romance, 3, 16, 25, 82, 94, 113, 162, 277, 280, 288, 303, 305, 334, 337, 345, 347, 349
Romani, 3, 161, 162, 165, 166, 167, 185, 189, 217, 248, 254, 342, 369
Romanian, 337, 349
Roper River Creole, 396
Rotwelsch, 162, 218
Russenorsk, 26, 28, 40, 47, 50, 51, 52, 347, 387
Russia, 26, 163, 377

Russian, 9, 20, 26, 36, 39, 40, 48, 163, 171, 172, 183, 186, 189, 200, 206, 291, 313, 369, 376, 377, 378, 387
Ruthenian, 313
Saami Pidgin Swedish Borgarmålet, 37
Salcedo, 373
Samarkand, 291
Samoa, 395
San Andrés, 77, 108, 115, 130
San Andrés Creole English, 77, 86, 89, 90, 91, 95, 96, 101, 102, 103, 104, 108, 109, 111, 112, 114, 115, 116, 118, 119, 120, 122, 124, 125, 126, 127, 129, 130, 131, 132, 133, 134
Sango, 29, 30, 36, 37
Sanskrit, *see also* Buddhist Hybrid Sanskrit, 278, 292, 293, 309, 311, 334, 335
Santiago, 93, 98
São Tomé, 71, 92
São Tomé Creole Portuguese, *see also* Sãotomense Creole Portuguese, 86, 98, 113
Sãotomense Creole Portuguese, 83, 84, 85, 87, 89, 104
Saramacca, 81, 86
Saramaccan, 67, 73, 86, 87, 93, 120, 129, 131
Scandinavian, 245, 248, 249, 258
Scotland, 374, 391
Scots, 391
Scottish Highlands, 381
Semarang, 377
Semitic, 276, 277, 281, 282, 284, 287, 314, 315, 316, 317, 318, 320
Senegal, 68
Sepik River, 47
Seychellois Creole French, 84, 100, 109, 126, 131
Shaba Swahili, 39
Shambaa, 374
Shelta, 163
Sheng, 256, 370, 380

Languages and geography index 431

Shibe, 298
Shoshone, 27
Siberia, 28
Sierra Leone, 30, 68, 348
Simplified Fula, 41
Singapore, 390, 392, 393, 394, 405, 408
Singapore English, 31, 378, 393
Singlish, 31
Sinhala, 3, 128, 164, 177, 178, 184, 204, 205, 216, 218, 280, 311, 384, 385
Sinhalese. *See* Sinhala
Sinitic, 17
Sino-Tibetan, 309
Siouan, 27
Slave Coast, 400
Slavic, 290, 313, 337, 349
Soghdian (also Sogdian), 283
Solomon Islands, 395, 396
Solomon Islands Pijin, 30, 395, 405
Sotho, 409
South Africa, 24, 35, 39, 51, 82, 370, 379
South African, 35
South Asia, 391, 392
South East Asia, 66, 390, 391, 392
South East Asian, 134
Spain, 161, 300, 303
Spanish, 7, 9, 20, 65, 66, 67, 69, 70, 71, 75, 77, 81, 85, 86, 87, 88, 92, 97, 98, 99, 100, 109, 110, 118, 122, 131, 132, 160, 161, 162, 166, 169, 177, 183, 186, 189, 193, 211, 300, 334, 337, 369, 371, 373, 384, 401
Sranan Creole English, 73, 85, 86, 87, 94, 106, 107, 129, 251, 337, 347, 406, 408
Sranan Tongo. *See* Sranan Creole English
Sri Lanka, 3, 7, 164, 178, 184, 205, 218, 385
Sri Lanka Creole Portuguese, 3, 41, 73, 93, 128, 164, 364, 384

Sri Lanka Malay, 3, 7, 41, 159, 160, 164, 177, 178, 179, 197, 204, 205, 206, 216, 217, 218, 379, 385
St. Lucia, 406
Steurtjestaal, 261
Stockholm, 20, 247
Straattaal, 251, 252
Strasbourg, 371
Sudanese Arabic, 32
Sumerian, 314, 315, 316, 317, 321
Suriname, 22, 67, 73, 76, 86, 89, 120, 337, 399, 400, 402, 406, 408
Surinamese, 86, 251, 252, 266, 337, 399, 402
Surkhandarya, 291
Swahili, 10, 44, 45, 255, 256, 380, 381
Sweden, 20, 247
Swedish, 20, 21, 72, 163, 166, 170, 171, 185, 189, 247, 248
Switzerland, 406
Sydney, 389
Syria, 282, 315, 317
Syriac, 280
Tagalog, 85, 122, 128
Takia, 4, 403
Tamil, 3, 128, 164, 177, 178, 184, 197, 204, 205, 216, 218, 379, 384, 385
Tanzania, 162, 166, 374
Tay Boi, 23, 26, 36, 39, 48
Taymir Pidgin Russian, 36, 39, 40
Tell el-Amarna, 282
Temne, 68
Ternate, 122, 123
Ternate Spanish Creole (Chabacano), 85, 94, 122, 126, 128
Thai, 336
Tibet, 164
Tibetan, 164
Tiwi, 163, 176
Tok Pisin, *see also* Melanesian Pidgin English, 2, 30, 34, 36, 70, 92, 94, 95, 97, 131, 395, 396, 405
Tokharian, 283

Languages and geography index

Torres Strait Creole, 398
Torres Strait Islands, 396
Trader Navaho, 23
Transoxiana, 283, 302
Trinidad, 68, 406, 407, 408
Trinidad Creole French, 73
Trio-Ndyuka, 347
Trio-Ndyuka Pidgin, 41, 51
Tsotsitaal, 255, 370, 379, 380, 381, 409
Tungusic, 298
Tunisia, 16
Tupi, 26
Türkendeutsch, 250
Turkey, 233, 289
Turki, 291
Turkic, 276, 278, 283, 285, 286, 287, 288, 289, 290, 291, 292, 300, 302, 303, 310, 311, 312, 313
Turkish, 26, 166, 215, 233, 234, 235, 236, 238, 248, 250, 251, 252, 260, 275, 276, 281, 283, 284, 285, 286, 288, 289, 290, 303, 312, 336, 382
Turkistan, 292
Turkmen, 285
Turkmenistan, 292
Turku Arabic Pidgin, 51
Turoyo, 233
Twi, 68, 89, 106, 127
Ugarit, 317
Ugaritic, 317
Ulster, 391
Ulster Scots, 391
United States, 16, 21, 26, 50, 82, 163, 172, 232, 247, 381, 382, 408
Urartian, 317
Urdu, 283, 302, 335, 386
Uto-Aztecan, 27
Utrecht, 233, 236, 259, 260
Uyghur, 291
Uzbek, 291, 292
Vanuatu, 30, 396
Vehicular Malay, *see also* Bazaar Malay, Malay, 177, 178, 197, 204, 205
Venezuela, 67
Verlan, 240, 254, 258, 265
Vietnam, 23, 26, 27, 28, 49
Vietnamese, 26
Vietnamese Pidgin French, 23, 36, 387
Virgin Islands, 72
Warlpiri, 22, 162, 168, 175, 176, 181, 183, 186, 189, 201, 202, 203, 206, 409
Warumungu, 176, 218
West Africa, 30, 82, 395, 398, 405
West African, 5, 7, 87, 106, 112, 402
West African Pidgin, 29
West Indies, 70, 408
Western Caribbean Creole Englishes, 133
Western Caribbean English, 124
White Russian, 313
Wolof, 68
Wumpurrarni, 218
Wumpurrarni English, 176
Wutun, 164
Xinjiang, 298
Yiddish, 277, 290
Yimas, 42, 45
Yimas-Alamblak, 42, 51
Yimas-Arafundi Pidgin, 24, 41, 47, 51, 347
Yoruba, 68, 81
Zamboanga, 93, 123
Zamboanga Chabacano, 99, 123
Zulu, 39, 40, 255, 379, 380

Author index

Aarsæther, F., 249
Abdulaziz, M. H., 255, 256, 380
Aboh, E. O., 6, 78, 79, 80, 164, 195, 205, 218
Abrahams, R. D., 81
Adami, N., 27
Adams, J. N., 279
Aikhenvald, A. Y., 188, 189, 324
Aldea, S., 20
Aldridge, E., 296
Alexandre, P., 31
Algeo, J. T., 27
Alkmin, T., 71
Alleyne, M. C., 68, 69, 89, 100, 129, 134
Álvarez López, L., 81, 88
Amaral, P., 160, 161
Androutsopoulos, J. K., 250, 260
Ansaldo, U., 6, 15, 69, 78, 164, 177, 178, 187, 195, 205, 217, 218, 346, 393, 394
Appel, R., 188, 251
Ardila, A., 20
Arends, J., 73, 76, 92, 93, 107, 400, 402, 408
Auer, P., 187, 190, 191, 192, 211, 212, 217, 236, 238, 250
Augustinos, G., 383
Avram, A. A., 387
Axtell, J., 27
Bailey, B. L., 76
Baissac, C., 73
Baker, P., 18, 19, 24, 25, 30, 37, 38, 39, 42, 47, 48, 49, 50, 51, 52, 65, 66, 68, 70, 78, 80, 82, 84, 100, 132
Bakir, M. J., 387
Bakker, D., 347
Bakker, P., 1, 5, 6, 7, 8, 9, 10, 11, 15, 17, 26, 27, 29, 30, 32, 35, 36, 40, 41, 53, 67, 69, 75, 79, 92, 159, 161, 163, 164, 165, 166, 172, 173, 178, 179, 180, 182, 184, 186, 187,
189, 195, 197, 198, 199, 200, 203, 206, 207, 210, 211, 212, 213, 217, 218, 273, 324, 342, 346, 347, 356, 368, 369, 373, 374, 375, 376, 379, 384, 385, 403
Baldauf, I., 72
Baptista, M., 99, 116, 125
Barrelon, P., 23
Barrena, P. N., 136
Bartens, A., 9, 10, 43, 65, 66, 67, 70, 74, 76, 77, 79, 81, 84, 86, 88, 92, 97, 100, 101, 103, 104, 106, 107, 108, 109, 111, 112, 114, 115, 116, 117, 118, 119, 120, 121, 122, 123, 124, 126, 128, 129, 131, 132, 133, 134, 135, 136, 138, 263
Bascom, W., 81
Bastide, R., 83
Baumgarten, J., 277
Baxter, A. N., 83, 99
Bechert, H., 311
Beckford-Wassink, A., 406
Bennis, H., 260
Benoist, J., 82
Bentley, W., 68
Berberian, H., 300
Berg, M. van den, 120
Bergmann, B., 20
Berlin, I., 81
Bernardi Perini, G., 300
Berry, J., 23
Bertrand-Bocandé, E., 73
Bhattacharjya, D., 127, 128
Bickerton, D., 15, 28, 39, 41, 67, 69, 75, 76, 88, 101, 107, 126, 137, 342, 397, 402
Bijvoet, E., 248
Birken-Silverman, G., 20
Birnbaum, S. A., 277
Black, P., 244, 245, 247, 353, 379, 388, 401
Blondeau, H., 340
Blondheim, D. S., 304

Blust, R., 354
Boas, F., 44, 45
Bodén, P., 248
Bodrogligeti, A. J. E., 291
Böhl, F. M. T., 282
Bold, J. D., 36
Bolland, O. N., 82
Boretzky, N., 39, 43, 161, 166, 182, 185
Borgström, M., 20
Bougerol, C., 82
Boxer, C. R., 66
Brenzinger, M., 162, 167
Bresnan, J., 39, 40, 42
Broch, I., 26
Broudy, S., 27
Brousseau, A., 86, 97
Browne, E. G., 300
Bruyn, A., 80
Bryant, D., 352
Bulut, C., 285
Burch, E., 27
Burton, R. D. E., 83
Byrne, F., 106
Caferoğlu, A., 302
Calloway, C., 27
Campbell, L., 334, 336
Cardoso, H., 92
Carlin, E. B., 408
Carlock, E., 232
Carpenter, K., 408
Carroll, S. E., 85
Casado-Fresnillo, C., 131
Cassidy, F. G., 47, 89, 129
Chambert-Loir, H., 257
Chapuis, D., 101, 102, 103, 107, 110
Charola, E., 161, 175
Chaudenson, R., 66, 69, 76, 77, 82
Chen, N., 164
Childs, G. T., 137, 379, 380, 381
Christaller, Rev. J. G., 127, 130, 134
Civil, M., 315, 321
Clark, R., 389
Clements, G. N., 83
Clements, J. C., 92, 111, 160, 161, 401

Clyne, M., 10
Cohen, R., 82
Colonna, F., 300
Corcoran, C., 106
Corne, C., 100, 109, 126
Cornips, L., 239, 252
Coulmas, F., 320
Coupland, N., 238
Courlander, H., 67, 81
Couto, H. H. do, 70, 85, 98
Cox, D., 82
Crevenant-Werner, D., 20
Croft, W., 181, 183, 195, 196, 197
Crofton, B., 161, 166
Crosbie, P., 122, 134
Crosby, A. W., 390
Crowley, T., 92, 97
Csató, É. Á., 313, 324
Cutler, C., 247
d'Ans, M.-A., 82
D'Costa, J., 76
Dalton, L., 161, 175
Danesi, M., 232
Dankoff, R., 287
Daval-Markussen, A., 348, 356
Dawkins, R. M., 382
Dawthorne, O. R., 81
De Rooij, V., 39
DeCamp, D., 76
DeGraff, M., 69, 75, 94, 105, 109, 111, 112, 114, 117, 123, 124, 180
Demuth, K., 85
Dench, A., 42, 47
Deppermann, A., 250, 251
Detges, U., 80
Devereux, R., 292
Devonish, H., 408
Diaz-Campos, M., 401
Dietze, G., 20
Dijkhoff, M., 409
Dirim, İ., 236, 250
Disbray, S., 176, 218
Dixon, R. M. W., 22, 120, 188, 190, 276
Donohue, M., 357
Doran, M., 254

Dorleijn, M., 9, 11, 229, 233, 234, 235, 236, 240, 251, 260
Drapeau, L., 173, 214
Drechsel, E. J., 16, 24, 33, 35, 41, 43, 387
Dreyfuss, G. R., 161
Dryer, M. S., 128
Ducœurjoly, S. J., 73
Dunn, M., 357
Duszak, A., 20
Dutton, T., 27, 33, 34, 35, 47, 387
Dyen, I., 353
Dyhr, S. A., 72
Eckert, P., 238, 247
Eckmann, J., 290, 291
Edgerton, F., 292
Edwards, J., 134
Ellison, T. M., 336
Elwert, W. T., 301
Embleton, S., 344
Escalante, A., 88
Eversteijn, N., 235
Faraclas, N. G., 33, 81, 94
Farquharson, J. T., 81, 92, 99, 133
Feister, L. M., 27
Fennell, B. A., 10
Ferguson, C., 405
Fernandes, M. S., 83
Ferraz, L., 83, 86, 89
Fewster, P., 279
Figueroa, E., 81
Firkavičiūtė, K., 312
Flanigan, B. O., 37
Fleischmann, U., 78
Focke, H. C., 73
Foley, R. A., 347, 387
Foley, W. A., 24, 44, 45, 47, 347, 387
Forman, M. L., 99, 123
Forster, L., 300, 302
Forster, P., 333, 352
Fortier, A., 73
Fought, C., 231
Fox, J., 28, 43
Fragner, B. G., 284
Fraurud, K., 248

Freidank, M., 251
Frellesvig, B., 294, 295, 308
Gal, S., 394
Gardani, F., 190
Gardner, H., 211
Gardner-Chloros, P., 211
Gershevitch, I., 314, 317, 318
Gianto, A., 282
Gijn, R. v., 210, 211
Gil, D., 69, 79
Gilbert, G. G., 73
Gilman, C., 44, 348
Givón, T., 15
Goddard, C., 336
Golovko, E. V., 4, 9, 163, 171, 172, 181, 184, 186, 200, 372, 376, 377
Good, J., 67, 89, 131
Goodman, J. S., 27
Goodman, M. F., 348
Goodman, M. S., 75
Goral, D., 27
Gorelova, L. M., 298
Gorenflo, L. J., 137
Gougenheim, G., 94
Gouveia, M. C., 84
Goux, A., 73
Goyette, S., 30
Goyvaerts, D., 255
Grace, G., 349
Granda, G. de, 71, 82, 87, 91
Grant, A. P., 30, 33, 45, 47, 49, 163
Gray, R. D., 354
Greenberg, J., 159
Greenhill, S. J., 354
Griffiths, P. J., 293
Gruiter, M. de, 377, 378
Grünewald, A., 301
Guardiano, C., 347, 354, 356
Güldemann, T., 106
Gumperz, J. J., 386
Günther, W., 99
Gupta, A. F., 390, 392
Haabo, V., 87
Haenisch, E., 298
Hagège, C., 69
Hagemeijer, T., 84, 91

Haiman, J., 97
Hair, P. E. H., 26
Hale, K. L., 22
Hale, M., 338, 339, 340, 341, 343, 344, 355
Hall, R. A., Jr., 19, 28, 35, 69, 74, 335, 346, 395
Haller, H., 20
Hamilton, P. J., 27
Hammarström, H., 19
Hammerly, H., 20
Hancock, I. F., 18, 22, 33, 34, 75, 77, 80, 161, 166, 348, 374
Handler, J., 400
Harris, B., 50
Harris, J. W., 396
Harrison, S. P., 47, 333, 349
Haspelmath, M., 354
Haugen, E., 188
Haviland, J., 22
Heath, J., 189, 350
Hebblethwaite, B., 409
Heggarty, P., 350, 351, 352, 356
Hein, J., 26
Heine, B., 15, 30, 33, 35, 36, 39, 43, 44, 47, 118, 324, 365
Henning, W. B., 319
Henrici, E., 301
Hensel, H., 20
Herskovits, F. S., 81
Herskovits, M. J., 81, 83
Herzog, M., 208
Hesseling, D. C., 73, 74
Hewes, G. W., 27
Hewitt, R., 244
Hinüber, O. von, 309
Holm, J., 7, 19, 24, 33, 35, 36, 39, 41, 47, 69, 70, 71, 72, 73, 74, 75, 77, 80, 85, 89, 100, 119, 122, 125, 132, 133, 134, 347
Horton, M., 27
Hosali, P., 387
Huber, M., 37, 38, 47, 49, 50, 52, 80
Hull, A., 89, 372
Hurault, J., 22
Huson, D., 352

Hussainmiya, B. A., 164, 177, 178, 204, 205, 379, 385
Huttar, G., 23
Huttar, M. L., 106, 120
Hymes, D., 388
Igla, B., 161, 166, 182, 185
Ikeda, J., 321, 322
Izre'el, S., 282
Jackson, K. D., 81, 396
Jacobs, B., 67
Jacobs, M., 45
Jacobs, N. G., 277, 290
Jahr, E. H., 26
Jakobson, R., 365
Janda, R. D., 338, 341
Janhunen, J., 164
Janse, M., 382
Jarva, V., 163, 170, 171
Jaspers, J., 246, 247
Jespersen, O., 277, 288
Johanson, L., 9, 11, 273, 275, 284, 285, 287, 303
Johnson, S. V., 33, 34
Jones, C., 161, 210
Jones, R. H., 257
Jørgensen, J. N., 249
Joseph, B. D., 338, 341
Joubert, S. M., 91
Jourdan, C., 30
Juvonen, P., 33, 34, 35
Kachru, B. B., 408
Kallen, J. L., 391
Kaltenbrunner, S., 51
Kamholtz, D., 357
Kann, H., 20
Karstadt, A., 21
Katz, D., 277
Kaufman, T., 4, 11, 33, 39, 49, 159, 162, 166, 180, 188, 189, 192, 348, 365, 382, 389
Kay, P., 36
Kaye, A. S., 34
Keesing, R. M., 7, 92
Keim, I., 238, 250
Keller, R., 79
Kenrick, D., 161, 166, 374

Kerswill, P., 245, 258
Kessler, B., 344
Khan, A., 245
Kießling, R., 11, 231, 233, 370, 379
Kihm, A., 85, 98, 135
King, R., 72, 384
Kirby, S., 336
Klein, T., 35, 85
Klein, W., 8, 22, 388
Kleine, C. d., 107, 108
Kloss, H., 302
Knudtzon, J. A., 282
Köprülü, M. F., 302
Kossmann, M. G., 282
Kotsinas, U., 20, 247, 248, 249
Kouwenberg, S., 6, 67, 75, 91, 97, 99, 109, 110, 112, 116, 129, 408
Kowallik, S., 131
Kowalski, T., 313
Kramer, J., 132
Kramp, A. A., 73
Kropp Dakubu, M. E., 100
Kruskal, J. B., 353
Kusters, W., 15, 44
Kuteva, T., 118, 365
La Charité, D., 97
Labov, W., 196, 207, 208, 232, 340
Ladhams, J., 99
Ladin, W., 20
Lafontaine, M., 82
Lalla, B., 76
Laman, K. E., 68, 134
Lang, G., 49
Langslow, D. R., 318
Laplante, A., 82
Lavandera, B., 218
Lazar, M., 303
Lee, C., 20
Lee, J., 163, 176
Lee-Smith, M. W., 164
Leezenberg, M., 233
Lefebvre, C., 75, 129, 193, 217, 347
Lefkowitz, N., 254
Léglise, I., 81
Lenz, R., 74
LePage, R. B., 89

Lewis, G., 286
Lewis, G. E., 381
Li, C. N., 299
Li, M., 17
Lim, L., 346
Lipski, J. M., 65, 75, 88, 100, 123
Longobardi, G., 347, 354, 356
Loranger, V., 129
Lorenzino, G. A., 86, 104, 110, 124, 131
Loveday, L. J., 381
Luffin, X., 30
Luís, A., 160, 161
Maddieson, I., 83
Maguire, W., 350, 351, 352
Maher, J., 190
Malcolm, I. G., 27, 48, 396, 397
Manessy, G., 33, 42
Mansuroğlu, M., 285
Marchese, L., 30
Marriott, H., 20
Marzo, S., 245, 246
Matory, J. L., 81
Matras, Y., 1, 4, 5, 7, 9, 21, 28, 29, 159, 161, 162, 165, 166, 179, 180, 181, 184, 186, 187, 188, 190, 192, 193, 194, 206, 217, 218, 273, 290, 324, 378
Matthews, S., 15, 17, 69, 346
Maurer, P., 72, 84, 85, 86, 87, 88, 91, 95, 96, 99, 105, 111, 112, 113, 118, 121, 126, 127, 129, 131, 137
Mayet, V., 16
McCann, M., 163
McConvell, P., 161, 163, 173, 174, 187, 198, 199, 211, 212, 213, 217, 218, 370, 371
McMahon, A., 9, 11, 12, 333, 334, 337, 339, 344, 346, 350, 351, 352, 354, 356
McMahon, R., 333, 334, 344, 352
McWhorter, J. H., 5, 6, 15, 28, 36, 44, 47, 65, 69, 75, 78, 79, 80, 83, 89, 91, 122, 136, 180, 190, 346, 401

Meakins, F., 4, 7, 9, 10, 159, 161, 162, 174, 175, 176, 185, 187, 189, 190, 194, 195, 197, 199, 200, 201, 206, 207, 208, 209, 210, 211, 212, 213, 214, 217, 218, 370, 371, 372, 375, 396
Meisig, K., 293, 311, 324
Meister, G., 72
Mello, H., 125
Mercier, A., 73
Mesthrie, R., 33
Métraux, A., 82
Meuwese, M., 27
Meyerhoff, M., 208
Michaelis, S., 80, 131, 347
Miestamo, M., 15
Migge, B., 81, 120, 399
Miller, R. A., 307
Minegishi, A., 295, 296
Mintz, S. W., 398
Mithun, M., 345
Moag, R., 33
Møller, J., 249
Moran, W. L., 282
Moulton, V., 352
Mous, M., 11, 159, 162, 167, 183, 184, 187, 193, 194, 201, 206, 213, 231, 233, 240, 256, 273, 342, 369, 370, 374, 379
Muawiyath, S., 161, 210
Mufwene, S., 69, 78, 180, 195, 196
Mühleisen, S., 406, 407
Mühlhäusler, P., 18, 24, 33, 34, 35, 36, 37, 39, 42, 43, 47, 48, 51, 86, 337, 342, 348
Müller, F. M., 365
Müller, O., 301
Munteanu, D., 67
Murray, E., 91, 109, 110, 112, 116
Musgrave, S., 357
Muysken, P., 15, 78, 89, 106, 118, 161, 162, 169, 181, 186, 187, 188, 190, 193, 213, 214, 373
Myers-Scotton, C., 9, 162, 163, 187, 190, 191, 192, 199, 211, 212, 217, 262, 372, 375, 381

Naro, A. J., 26, 123
Németh, J., 289
Nerbonne, J., 354
Nichols, J., 6, 198
Nichols, J. D., 41
Nicolas, P., 23
Noll, V., 68
Nordhoff, S., 6, 164, 177, 179, 385
Norman, A. M. Z., 27, 304, 306
Nortier, J., 9, 11, 229, 234, 235, 236, 240, 251, 259, 260
Numamoto, K., 306
Nunes, M. P., 82
Nyberg, H. S., 320
O'Shannessy, C., 161, 162, 175, 176, 181, 189, 199, 201, 202, 203, 204, 206, 209, 213, 409, 442
Odlin, T., 391
Oka, D., 161
Okada, H., 298
Okell, J., 309, 310
Olach, Z., 312
Oldendorp, C. G. A., 72
Ollonne, H. M. G. d', 44
Operstein, K., 26
Orléans, H. d', 28
Oshima, K., 20
Osinde, K., 255, 256, 380
Otanes, F., 128
Paauw, S., 160, 164, 177, 178, 197, 204, 205, 206, 218, 385
Paccagnella, I., 300
Palmié, S., 67, 81
Paoli, U. E., 300
Papen, R. A., 163, 210
Parkvall, M., 6, 9, 10, 15, 30, 32, 47, 69, 78, 79, 88, 132, 357
Pasch, H., 36, 37
Patrick, P. L., 80, 81, 217, 218, 370
Paunonen, H., 163, 170
Perdue, C., 8, 22, 388
Pereira, J., 409
Perl, M., 67, 73
Pierce, J. E., 336
Pinto Bull, B., 70
Plag, I., 79, 85, 190

Platt, J., 393
Pluchon, P., 82
Polomé, E., 40
Poplack, S., 208, 372
Post, M., 91, 124
Price, G., 304
Price, R., 67, 81, 82, 83
Price, S., 81
Price-Mars, J., 82
Pruitt, W., 309
Queffélec, A., 43
Quilis, A., 131
Quint, N., 116, 119, 120
Quist, P., 237, 238, 248, 249
Rabinovitch, J. N., 295, 296
Rachewiltz, I. de, 297
Rainey, A. F., 282
Ramaekers, W., 246
Rampton, B., 232, 245
Reinecke, J. E., 39, 43, 47, 48, 50, 74, 136
Reizevoort, B., 252
Rendón, J. G., 162
Renfrew, C., 333, 352
Rheeden, H. van, 261
Rickford, A. E., 81
Rickford, J. R., 81, 107, 238, 400
Rijkhoff, J., 347
Ringe, D., 350
Roberts, I., 355
Roberts, J., 24, 33, 37, 42
Roberts, S. J., 39, 40, 42, 394, 397, 402
Robertson, I. E., 68
Robinson, S., 35
Röllig, W., 316
Romaine, S., 19, 33, 44, 70, 85, 345
Rosalie, M., 131
Rosen, N., 163, 210
Ross, M., 178, 403
Rosse, I. C., 27
Rougé, J., 66, 68
Røyneland, U., 238, 241, 249
Ruane, J., 163
Russell, T., 73
Saint-Quentin, A. de, 73

Sakel, J., 188
Samarin, W. J., 19, 33
Sampson, G., 15
Sanchez, T., 109
Sankoff, G., 36, 340
Santoro, M., 123
Sasse, H. J., 167, 190
Saussure, F. de, 199
Savain, R. E., 121
Schachter, P., 128
Schaengold, C., 163, 167, 168, 169, 204
Schendl, H., 304
Schlyter, B., 20
Schmitt, R., 318
Schneider, E. W., 348, 407
Schramm, M., 85
Schuchardt, H., 25, 72, 73, 74
Schweda, N. L., 20
Schwegler, A., 67, 81, 88, 92
Sebba, M., 1, 35, 37, 38, 39, 43
Sekerina, I. A., 163, 171, 172
Sessarego, S., 401
Seuren, P. A. M., 75
Shapira, D., 312, 313
Shappeck, T., 162
Sheller, M., 82
Sherzer, J., 254
Shi, D., 18, 34, 35, 37, 42, 43, 44, 48, 49
Shilling, A. W., 134
Shnukal, A., 30
Siegel, J., 33, 34, 51, 75, 80, 92, 394, 396, 397, 403
Silva Neto, S. da, 74
Silva-Corvalán, C., 384
Simpson, J., 176, 218
Singh, I., 338, 346, 347
Singh, R., 89
Singler, J. V., 75, 396, 400, 402, 403
Síochain, S., 163
Sippola, E., 85, 94, 119, 122, 126, 128
Skjærvø, P. O., 319
Slabbert, S., 255, 381
Slomanson, P., 7, 164

Smart, H., 161, 166
Smit, M. de, 163, 170
Smith, G., 17
Smith, I. R., 128, 160, 164, 177, 178, 384, 385
Smith, N., 6, 66, 67, 68, 79, 85, 86, 87, 88, 89, 90, 91, 94, 118, 178, 186, 197, 201, 204, 205, 206, 218, 337, 385
Smith-Hefner, N., 257, 260
Soden, W. von, 316
Stary, G., 304
Stefánsson, V., 17, 24, 34, 38, 43, 44
Steinkrüger, P., 93
Stern, D., 33, 39
Stolz, T., 36, 107, 108, 111, 113
Strong, W. M., 188, 404
Suzuki, M., 125
Svendsen, B. A., 238, 241, 249
Syea, A., 100
Sylvain, S., 73, 74, 347
Tabouret-Keller, A., 405
Tadmor, U., 131
Tamis, A. M., 20
Tarallo, F., 71
Taylor, A., 350
Taylor, A. R., 38
Taylor, D. G. K., 280
Taylor, D. R., 74, 123, 337, 346
Therrien, I., 129
Thomas, H., 20, 72, 73
Thomason, S. G., 1, 2, 4, 9, 11, 39, 50, 159, 161, 162, 163, 166, 167, 171, 172, 180, 183, 184, 186, 187, 188, 189, 192, 200, 206, 218, 238, 239, 240, 336, 337, 338, 342, 343, 344, 345, 348, 364, 365, 368, 372, 382, 389
Thompson, S. A., 120, 299
Thornell, C., 33
Thurston, W. R., 403
Tinelli, H., 88
Todd, L., 19
Torgersen, E., 245
Tosco, M., 34
Treffers-Daller, J., 214, 371
Tremblay, A., 85
Trouillot, M., 81
Trudgill, P., 346
Trumelet, C., 43
Tuten, D. N., 78
Ustinova, I., 20
Utas, B., 284, 319, 324
Vakhtin, N. B., 163, 171, 172, 376, 377
Van der Voort, H., 39
Veenstra, T., 75, 93, 106
Veiga, M., 125
Velantie, F. J., 23
Versteegh, K., 69
Vitale, A. J., 34, 45, 46
Vrzić, Z., 33
Wadley, S. A., 298, 299
Waley, A., 297
Walters, J., 372
Warner-Lewis, M., 68
Warnow, T., 350
Watson-Gegeo, K., 408
Webster, G., 27
Weiner, J., 208
Weinreich, U., 189, 208, 363, 364
Wekker, H., 75
Wellens, I., 30
Welmers, W. E., 127
Wenzel, S., 300
Werner, O., 23
Werner, R., 23
West, F., 27
Whinnom, K., 74, 114, 123
Whitney, W. D., 188
Wichmann, S., 333, 344, 354, 357
Wijngaarden, A. van, 252, 258
Williams, J. P., 42, 45, 47
Wilson, P., 81
Wilson, R., 386
Wilson, W. W., 39, 41
Winford, D., 1, 4, 9, 12, 19, 32, 75, 80, 120, 127, 129, 363, 383
Wölck, W., 232
Wolfram, W., 231, 232
Wood, R. E., 76
Wright, L. C., 304, 305

Wullschlägel, H. R., 73
Wurm, S., 47, 164
Yillah, S. M., 106
Zenk, H. B., 30, 45, 388

Zentella, A. C., 371
Zograf, I. T., 297
Zunz, L., 277

www.ingramcontent.com/pod-product-compliance
Lightning Source LLC
Chambersburg PA
CBHW070257240426
43661CB00057B/2573